210235

90827

(20)

AE037115

Discard from
Hartwick College

THE JOURNAL OF INDUSTRIAL ECONOMICS

VOLUME XXXIV
1985–86

ISSN 0022–1821

BASIL BLACKWELL
OXFORD

© Basil Blackwell 1986

The material in this Journal is copyright under the Berne Convention. Apart from any fair dealing for the purposes of private study, research, criticism or review, as permitted under the Copyright Act 1965, no portion may be reproduced by any process without written permission. Inquiry should be made to the Publishers.

DONALD A. HAY (General Editor): Jesus College, University of Oxford.
STEVE W. DAVIES: University of East Anglia.
BRUCE LYONS: University of East Anglia.
LOUIS PHLIPS: Université Catholique de Louvain.
AUBREY SILBERSTON: Imperial College of Science and Technology, University of London.
GEORGE YARROW: Hertford College, University of Oxford.
LAWRENCE J. WHITE (North American Editor): New York University.
M. A. ADELMAN: Massachusetts Institute of Technology.
RICHARD E. CAVES: Harvard University.
F. MICHAEL SCHERER: Swarthmore College.
RICHARD SCHMALENSEE: Sloan School of Management, Massachusetts Institute of Technology.

Editorial Assistant: Marion Bowker.

ASSOCIATE EDITORS
BO CARLSSON: Case Western Reserve University, Cleveland.
ROGER CLARKE: University of Sheffield.
ALEXIS JACQUEMIN: Université Catholique de Louvain.
FRÉDÉRIC JENNY: E.S.S.E.C., Cergy.
H. W. DE JONG: University of Amsterdam.
JOHN KAY: Institute for Fiscal Studies, London.
COLIN P. MAYER: St Anne's College, University of Oxford.
GEOFF MEEKS: Department of Applied Economics, University of Cambridge.
DEREK MORRIS: Oriel College, University of Oxford.
WILLIAM PETERSON: Department of Applied Economics, University of Cambridge.
JOHN F. PICKERING: The University of Manchester Institute of Science and Technology.
RAY REES: University College, Cardiff.
DAVID K. STOUT: Unilever PLC.
ROGER TARLING: Department of Applied Economics, University of Cambridge.
JOHN VICKERS: Nuffield College, University of Oxford.
CHRISTIAN C. VON WEIZSÄCKER: University of Berne.
GEOFFREY WHITTINGTON: University of Bristol.

RONALD R. BRAEUTIGAM: Northwestern University.
TIMOTHY F. BRESNAHAN: Stanford University.
WILLIAM S. COMANOR: University of California.
M. THÉRÈSE FLAHERTY: Harvard University.
THEODORE KEELER: University of California, Berkeley.
R. LARNER: Charles River Associates.
ALMARIN PHILLIPS: University of Pennsylvania.
STEVEN SALOP: Georgetown Law Center, Washington, DC.
JOHN T. SCOTT: Dartmouth College.
ROBERT D. WILLIG: Princeton University.

DONALD G. MCFETRIDGE: Carleton University, Ottawa.

PETER FORSYTH: Australian National University, Canberra.
BRIAN L. JOHNS: Bureau of Industry Economics, Canberra.
L. ROY WEBB: University of Melbourne.

MASU UEKUSA: University of Tokyo.

CONTENTS

VOLUME XXXIV

Number 1, September 1985

G. K. YARROW
Shareholder Protection, Compulsory Acquisition and the Efficiency of the Takeover Process 3

ROGER FELDMAN and JAMES W. BEGUN
The Welfare Cost of Quality Changes Due to Professional Regulation 17

G. M. P. SWANN
Product Competition in Microprocessors 33

DAVID LEVY
Specifying the Dynamics of Industry Concentration 55

REINHARD ANGELMAR
Market Structure and Research Intensity in High-Technological-Opportunity Industries 69

PATRICIA L. PACEY
Cable Television in a Less Regulated Market 81

Short Articles and Notes

DAVID FLATH and CHARLES R. KNOEBER
Managerial Shareholding 93

JOHN D. CULBERTSON
Econometric Tests of the Market Structural Determinants of R & D Investment: Consistency of Absolute and Relative Firm Size Models 101

Number 2, December 1985

RICHARD E. CAVES and PETER J. WILLIAMSON
What is Product Differentiation, *Really*? 113

DAMIEN NEVEN and LOUIS PHLIPS
Discriminating Oligopolists and Common Markets 133

YVES MERTENS and VICTOR GINSBURGH
Product Differentiation and Price Discrimination in the European Community: The Case of Automobiles 151

M. L. GREENHUT, H. OHTA and JOEL SAILORS
Reverse Dumping: A Form of Spatial Price Discrimination 167

VICTOR J. TREMBLAY
Strategic Groups and the Demand for Beer 183

CHRISTOPHER C. FINDLAY
Effects of Australian International Air Transport Regulation 199

Short Articles and Notes

EDWIN MANSFIELD
How Rapidly Does New Industrial Technology Leak Out? 217

Number 3, March 1986

STANLEY S. REYNOLDS
Strategic Capital Investment in the American Aluminum Industry 225

ASHER WOLINSKY
The Nature of Competition and the Scope of Firms 247

S. J. PRAIS
Some International Comparisons of the Age of the Machine-Stock 261

FRANK A. SCOTT, JR.
Assessing USA Postal Ratemaking: An Application of Ramsey Prices 279

MARGARET E. SLADE
Exogeneity Tests of Market Boundaries Applied to Petroleum Products 291

DEVRA L. GOLBE
Safety and Profits in the Airline Industry 305

JOHN LUNN
An Empirical Analysis of Process and Product Patenting: A Simultaneous Equation Framework 319

Short Articles and Notes

GREGORY J. WERDEN and MICHAEL G. BAUMANN
A Simple Model of Imperfect Competition in Which Four Are Few But Three Are Not 331

Number 4, June 1986

DAVID R. ROSS
Learning to Dominate 337

R. W. SHAW and P. SIMPSON
The Persistence of Monopoly: An Investigation of the Effectiveness of the United Kingdom Monopolies Commission 355

JOHN R. BALDWIN and PAUL K. GORECKI
The Relationship Between Plant Scale and Product Diversity in Canadian Manufacturing Industries 373

DIRK J. FRANTZEN
The Cyclical Behaviour of Manufacturing Prices in a Small Open Economy 389

S. R. TOLOFARI, K. J. BUTTON and D. E. PITFIELD
Shipping Costs and the Controversy Over Open Registry 409

TEIN-CHEN CHOU
Concentration, Profitability and Trade in a Simultaneous Equation Analysis: The Case of Taiwan 429

Set in Monophoto Times by Advanced Filmsetters (Glasgow) Ltd
Printed and Bound in Great Britain by Whitstable Litho, Kent

210235

THE JOURNAL OF INDUSTRIAL ECONOMICS

Volume XXXIV SEPTEMBER 1985 No. 1

G. K. YARROW
Shareholder Protection, Compulsory Acquisition and the Efficiency of the Takeover Process 3

ROGER FELDMAN and JAMES W. BEGUN
The Welfare Cost of Quality Changes Due to Professional Regulation 17

G. M. P. SWANN
Product Competition in Microprocessors 33

DAVID LEVY
Specifying the Dynamics of Industry Concentration 55

REINHARD ANGELMAR
Market Structure and Research Intensity in High-Technological-Opportunity Industries 69

PATRICIA L. PACEY
Cable Television in a Less Regulated Market 81

Short Articles and Notes

DAVID FLATH and CHARLES R. KNOEBER
Managerial Shareholding 93

JOHN D. CULBERTSON
Econometric Tests of the Market Structural Determinants of R & D Investment: Consistency of Absolute and Relative Firm Size Models 101

ISSN 0022-1821
BASIL BLACKWELL OXFORD ENGLAND

© **Basil Blackwell 1985**

The material in this Journal is copyright under the Berne Convention. Apart from any fair dealing for the purposes of private study, research, criticism or review, as permitted under the Copyright Act 1965, no portion may be reproduced by any process without written permission. Inquiry should be made to the Publishers.

DONALD A. HAY (General Editor): Jesus College, University of Oxford.
STEVE W. DAVIES: University of East Anglia.
BRUCE LYONS: St John's College, Cambridge.
LOUIS PHLIPS: Université Catholique de Louvain.
AUBREY SILBERSTON: Imperial College of Science and Technology, University of London.
GEORGE YARROW: Hertford College, University of Oxford.
LAWRENCE J. WHITE (North American Editor): New York University.
M. A. ADELMAN: Massachusetts Institute of Technology.
RICHARD E. CAVES: Harvard University.
F. MICHAEL SCHERER: Swarthmore College.
RICHARD SCHMALENSEE: Sloan School of Management, Massachusetts Institute of Technology.

Editorial Assistant: Marion Bowker.

ASSOCIATE EDITORS
BO CARLSSON: Case Western Reserve University, Cleveland.
ROGER CLARKE: University of Sheffield.
ALEXIS JACQUEMIN: Université Catholique de Louvain.
FRÉDÉRIC JENNY, E.S.S.E.C., Cergy.
H. W. DE JONG: University of Amsterdam.
JOHN KAY: Institute for Fiscal Studies, London.
COLIN P. MAYER: St Anne's College, University of Oxford.
GEOFF MEEKS: Department of Applied Economics, University of Cambridge.
DEREK MORRIS: Oriel College, University of Oxford.
WILLIAM PETERSON: Department of Applied Economics, University of Cambridge.
JOHN F. PICKERING: The University of Manchester Institute of Science and Technology.
RAY REES: University College, Cardiff.
DAVID K. STOUT: Unilever PLC.
ROGER TARLING: Department of Applied Economics, University of Cambridge.
JOHN VICKERS: Nuffield College, University of Oxford.
CHRISTIAN C. VON WEIZSÄCKER: University of Berne.
GEOFFREY WHITTINGTON: University of Bristol.

RONALD R. BRAEUTIGAM: Northwestern University.
TIMOTHY F. BRESNAHAN: Stanford University.
WILLIAM S. COMANOR: University of California.
M. THÉRÈSE FLAHERTY: Harvard University.
THEODORE KEELER: University of California, Berkeley.
R. LARNER: Charles River Associates.
ALMARIN PHILLIPS: University of Pennsylvania.
STEVEN SALOP: Georgetown Law Center, Washington, DC.
JOHN T. SCOTT: Dartmouth College.
ROBERT D. WILLIG: Princeton University.

DONALD G. MCFETRIDGE: Carleton University, Ottawa.

PETER FORSYTH: Australian National University, Canberra.
BRIAN L. JOHNS: Bureau of Industry Economics, Canberra.
L. ROY WEBB: University of Melbourne.

MASU UEKUSA: University of Tokyo.

PROFESSOR H. MICHAEL MANN

With great regret we report the death on 1 March 1985 of Professor H. Michael Mann, who served as the *Journal*'s American Managing Editor from 1977 until the onset of his illness in 1984. A conscientious and dedicated editor, he worked tirelessly to promote the submission of strong manuscripts, to see that they were refereed promptly and efficiently, and to develop the *Journal*'s position as an international vehicle for research on industrial economics. He brought to the task his own longstanding interest in applied research on industrial organization and policy, which was reflected in his scholarly papers on entry barriers and their consequences and on the implementation of antitrust policy. His steadfast reliability, good judgment, and common sense will be missed by the Editorial Board.

P. W. S. ANDREWS MEMORIAL ESSAY PRIZE—£300

The PWSA Memorial Prize of £300 is awarded annually. Competitors for the prize are asked to submit an essay on a subject of their own choice within the general field of Industrial Economics and Theory of the Firm, broadly interpreted. Entry to the competition is open to anyone under 30 years of age (or over 30, if not more than eight years have elapsed since taking a first degree). The essay, written in English, and not exceeding 10,000 words in length, should be a work of original research by the candidate only, not previously published and not previously awarded any other prize.

The winning essay may, at the discretion of the Editors, be published in *The Journal of Industrial Economics.*

The closing date for entries is 31st December.

Further details are available from:

Miss B. Cox,
University House,
The University of Lancaster,
Bailrigg, Lancaster, LA1 4YX, England.

The General Editor,
Journal of Industrial Economics,
The Institute of Economics and Statistics,
The University of Oxford,
St Cross Building, Manor Road,
Oxford, OX1 3UL, England.

The North American Editor,
Journal of Industrial Economics,
Graduate School of Business Administration,
New York University, 90 Trinity Place,
New York 10006, USA.

THE JOURNAL OF INDUSTRIAL ECONOMICS 0022-1821 $2.00
Volume XXXIV September 1985 No. 1

SHAREHOLDER PROTECTION, COMPULSORY ACQUISITION AND THE EFFICIENCY OF THE TAKEOVER PROCESS*

G. K. YARROW

This paper examines public good problems connected with takeovers. Two broad categories of exclusion device—oppression of minority interests and compulsory acquisition of shares—are evaluated. It is argued that inability to control the level of oppression with any precision renders the first method unsatisfactory from the policy viewpoint, but that strong protection of minorities coupled with compulsory acquisition rights for the acquiror can straightforwardly generate an efficient solution to the public good problems. It is shown that, in the U.K., company law and the City Code on Takeovers and Mergers combine to produce an approximation to this efficient solution.

I. INTRODUCTION

THE THREAT of an involuntary takeover provides an important sanction against managements which are performing poorly in the eyes of the capital market and, since the work of Marris [1964], this incentive mechanism has come to play a prominent role in the economic analysis of company behaviour. The usual argument is that, as the market value of a particular company falls relative to the level that it is generally believed could be obtained by other managers following different policies, the firm becomes increasingly vulnerable to a takeover by a raider attracted by the prospect of the capital gains that would ensue following managerial changes. In turn, the threat to the incumbent managers acts as a deterrent to behaviour which runs counter to shareholders' interests. The effectiveness of the workings of the takeover mechanism is therefore of some importance for the efficient utilisation and allocation of resources.

Potential obstacles to the smooth functioning of the takeover process have, however, been recognised for quite some time. As long ago as 1926 the Greene Committee on Company Law Reform identified cases where a takeover had been inhibited by the actions of small minorities of shareholders. Much more recently Grossman and Hart [1980] have formalised some of the earlier points in a way that clearly highlights one of the major difficulties: that free-riding strategies on the part of shareholders in firms with dispersed share ownership can prevent successful bids. The argument is that shareholders of the target company, believing their own actions have a trivially small effect on

* I am grateful to Donald Hay and the referees for a number of helpful comments on the first draft of this paper.

the probability of success of a particular bid, will have an incentive to decline the offer if they expect others to accept, since in this way they can participate in the post-raid improvement in performance of the firm. That is, they are content to let the raider bear the costs associated with managerial changes while they, as minority shareholders in the post-raid victim, costlessly enjoy part of the benefits in the form of an increase in the price of their shares. If all owners expect the bid to succeed then it will in fact fail. Hence, there can be no equilibrium in which expectations are realised and takeovers occur.

This is just another way of saying that improved company performance has important public good characteristics: the "good" is provided jointly to all shareholders; no one can be excluded without buying them out; and if each expects that the good will be provided anyway they will have no incentive to sell their shares on terms that would allow a raider to make a positive profit once the transactions costs of the bid are taken into account.

What is needed in these circumstances is a method of excluding existing shareholders of the target from the gains generated by the takeover and of channelling these returns to the raider, thus restoring the incentives necessary to encourage the latter to incur the expenses associated with actions to change managerial policy. In practice a range of such methods may be available, and the present paper is devoted to an analysis of the implications for the takeover process of two, broad categories of exclusion device: namely, oppression of minority interests and compulsory acquisition of shares.

Grossman and Hart have suggested that the level of permissible oppression of minority shareholders (or, in their own terminology, the level of dilution of minority rights) can be used, *via* the articles or memoranda of association of companies, as a control variable to yield that degree of exclusion which optimally solves the public good problem associated with takeovers. It will be argued below, however, that sole reliance upon this mechanism is likely to produce unsatisfactory results because (a) it will usually be extremely difficult to control the level of oppression at all precisely (section II), and (b) it will tend to provide incentives for undesirable, partial takeovers when, *ex post*, the protection afforded to minority holders turns out to be weak (section III).

Section IV of the paper therefore examines an alternative approach to the problem: the granting of rights to controlling interests to compulsorily acquire minority shareholdings. The procedure is shown to produce a simple and elegant solution of the free rider problem. Given, however, that company law in Britain offers opportunities for quite extensive oppression, the problem of partial takeovers remains. Section V shows how this residual difficulty has been tackled *via* rules in the City Code on Takeovers and Mergers which have been developed to extend the protection accorded to minorities at the time of a takeover bid. It will be argued that the Code, taken together with the compulsory acquisition provisions of the 1948 Companies Act, provides a regulatory environment which allows the takeover mechanism to function in a way closely approximating that traditionally assumed in the theory of the firm. That is, in the U.K. at least, "solutions" of the relevant public good problems are already embodied in the existing legal and regulatory frameworks.

II. OPPRESSION OF MINORITY INTERESTS

By oppression we here mean any action or course of actions, whether legal or illegal, which reduces the wealth of minority shareholders to the benefit of a controlling interest. Thus the parent company of a partially owned subsidiary which rigged transactions between the two firms in a way that transferred profit to the former from the latter would be said to be acting oppressively. By definition, minority shareholders will not be protected against such actions by either a takeover to oust the present management or by the possibility of obtaining a majority vote against the managers in a shareholders' meeting. Their only remedy, therefore, lies in recourse to the legal or regulatory systems, and the payoffs to the majority from oppression will depend crucially upon the strength of protection offered to the minority in company law and company constitutions.

It is easy to see how opportunities for oppression following a takeover will weaken the incentives towards free-riding strategies on the part of the acquiree's shareholders. For, if the raid is expected to succeed, each investor will anticipate that refusal of the offer will lead to a minority shareholding, the value of which will be vulnerable to the post-raid, wealth-transferring actions of the acquiror. It follows that, in circumstances where free-riding strategies would otherwise render successful takeovers impossible, reduction of minority rights—either through provisions in the articles or memoranda of association, or through the more general provisions of company law—could be used as an instrument to restore the incentive effects of the takeover threat.

Unfortunately, apart from the fact that the relevant rules and laws will also typically be concerned with other, possibly competing, objectives, there are reasons for doubting the effectiveness of this approach. Since oppression of minority interests can occur in a wide variety of ways, its level will tend to be extremely difficult to control in a precise fashion. To comprehensively limit the actions of controlling directors would require either a highly detailed company constitution or a closely specified body of company law, both relatively free of enforcement problems. If shareholdings are dispersed, however, enforcement of minority rights would itself tend to be subject to free-riding strategies.

Consider, for example, the following situation. A controlling interest in the firm reduces the price of shares, of which there are n outstanding, to a level x below the maximum. Any shareholder can bring an action which, if successful, will enforce value-maximising policies. On the other hand, if the action fails, current policies are unaltered. The costs of the action are assumed to be $a_1 (a_2)$ to the shareholder and $nb_1 (nb_2)$ to the company if it succeeds (fails), where

$b_1 > b_2 > 0$ and $a_2 > a_1 > 0$. Because information about the true state of nature is imperfect, actions will sometimes fail when the minority is being oppressed. Assume, therefore, that the probability of success is $f(x)$ where $f(.)$ is a non-decreasing function taking values less than unity. If shareholder i owns a fraction $s(i)$ of the company's equity, his expected net benefits from litigation are

$$(1) \qquad EB(s(i)) = ns(i)\{[x-b_1]f(x)-b_2[1-f(x)]\} \\ -a_1 f(x)-a_2[1-f(x)]$$

If shareholders are risk neutral and take the actions of the controlling interest as given, there will be litigation only if, for some i, $EB(s(i)) > 0$. Hence, the maximum level of oppression per share, say w/n, is that value of x which solves the equation $EB(s(m)) = 0$, where $s(m) = \max\{s(i)\}$. It can be seen that potential oppression will, in these circumstances, depend upon the size of the largest minority shareholding—a variable that will be very hard to predict at the legislative stage. Moreover, if shareholdings are highly dispersed, so that $s(i)$ is trivially small for all i, investors will never find it profitable to litigate and oppression would then be unrestricted. Similar conclusions will also follow from more sophisticated treatments of the litigation decision. The relationship between the holder of the largest minority stake and the controlling interest is one characterised by bilateral power, and, in an attempt to secure a more favourable outcome, the former may threaten litigation (which will inflict costs on the latter) even when the expression given by (1) is non-positive. The size of the holding will, of course, continue to affect the outcome since it is a parameter of the "game" which strongly affects the payoffs of one of the players. Note, however, that uncertainties about the type of game-theoretic equilibrium which will be relevant in the post-takeover litigation problem will add to the difficulties of using oppression as policy instrument.

Although the actual returns from litigation may not take the precise form assumed above there is little doubt that finite costs and uncertain payoffs will, in practice, be an important feature of the enforcement process. In an analysis of shareholders' appraisal rights in the U.S. it has been pointed out that anyone who

> "files the dissenter's claim will certainly encounter delay in payment ... may encounter substantial litigation costs and ... may make a procedural gaff that will cost him his option." (Manning [1962].)

In the U.K. the odds against a successful and rewarding minority action are stacked even higher. In the case of derivative or class actions the litigating shareholder may be awarded costs if the action succeeds, but this does not affect the conclusions. Thus, although a_1 may be zero in equation (1), it is apparent that w remains a function of $s(m)$ and still tends to infinity as the latter variable tends to zero.

Further complexities are introduced by the fact that shares can be traded and that the largest minority shareholding can vary in size during the period following the offer. It is tempting to argue that one investor could acquire each of the other minority holdings so as to be able to appropriate the full, collective benefits from a successful action. But, since all minority shareholders tend to benefit from successful actions, this possibility will be undermined by free-riding strategies exactly analogous to those facing a takeover raider. Thus, anyone expecting higher share prices as a result of diminished oppression following litigation would not sell to the intending litigant at a price which would allow the latter any profit on the transaction. In this case, though, there is no obvious exclusion device available to the litigant which would overcome or mitigate the free-rider problem. His/her best hope lies in the possibility that holdings of shares might be built up secretly, so that the planned actions were not anticipated by other members of the minority. The resulting outcome will, therefore, necessarily be highly uncertain.

Finally, it can be noted that the scope for oppressive behaviour will be influenced by the precise nature of the trading links between the two companies. Where there is a naturally large volume of transactions between the parent and the subsidiary, as would be the case if one were a major producer of a commodity used as an input by the other, it will tend to be more difficult for shareholders to detect any given level of profit shifting (achieved *via* manipulation of transfer prices) and subsequently to establish in the courts that oppressive conduct has occurred.

As a result of variations in the size distributions of shareholdings, the nature of the activities of individual firms and the uncertainties surrounding litigation, it can be seen that, for any given framework of company law and any set of company constitutions, the opportunities for oppression may vary considerably from case to case depending upon the precise circumstances at the time of the firms involved in the takeover. This would be a relatively unimportant conclusion if there were no social costs associated with high potential levels of oppression since protection of minorities could then be relaxed to levels at which the probability of free-riding strategies occurring in a particular case becomes negligibly small. But, as will be shown in section III, high potential returns from oppression could encourage (costly) partial takeover bids aimed at creating new minorities. Randomness in the target variable does, therefore, tend to limit the effectiveness of this method of restoring incentives in the takeover process.

III. PARTIAL TAKEOVER BIDS

Partial takeover bids are problematic when minorities are weakly protected because of the existence of incentives for raiders to acquire only a controlling fraction of the target's equity and to subsequently derive returns from oppression. There are two cases to analyse, depending upon whether the bid is conditional or unconditional, and they will be considered in turn. In what follows it is assumed that market prices reflect *all* of the anticipated future returns from holding shares. That is, demand curves for the income streams are taken to be horizontal in the formal analysis.

Suppose first that a raider offers to purchase a fraction $g > 0.5$ of the target's outstanding shares at a price p/n per share, conditional upon receipt of the requisite number of acceptances. Let z be the fraction of the target's equity actually offered for sale at that price. If $z > g$ the raider is assumed to purchase a fraction g/z of each holding offered for sale. The bid is successful when $z \geqslant g$ and in that event the raider will be assumed to pursue policies which reduce the price of minority shares below their maximum level (v/n) by an amount w/n per share. At the same time the acquiring firm is taken to gain an equivalent amount from the oppression, so that what happens is a simple transfer of w/n per minority share to the raider. If $z < g$, however, the offer is assumed to lapse. Letting q/n be the market price of equity in the absence of a takeover, the returns to a shareholder owning a fraction $s(i)$ of the equity of the target are as follows:

	$z < g$	$z \geqslant g$
from accepting the offer:	$s(i)q$	$s(i)\{gp/z+\{v-w\}\{1-g/z\}\}$
from rejecting the offer:	$s(i)q$	$s(i)\{v-w\}$

When $p > v-w$ it can be seen that, provided only that shareholders believe that there is some chance of the raid succeeding, it will be better to sell. Only if a particular shareholder believed that his own decision would have a material effect upon the likelihood of success would there be any incentive to refuse. In effect, shareholders can be stampeded into acceptance by the threat of being left as part of a heavily oppressed minority—a phenomenon sometimes known as the "whiplash" effect.

The return to the raider from a successful takeover is $g\{v-p\}+\{1-g\}w-c$, where c is the transactions cost of the bid. Since $p > v-w$ the return is a decreasing function of g, and hence it is optimal for the acquiror to offer to purchase just over 50% of the target's shares. For simplicity, g will be taken to be equal to 0.5 in what follows. The condition for a profitable raid then becomes

$$(2) \qquad p < v+w-2c$$

Combining this with $p > v-w$, we have that a profitable raid will take place iff $w > c$. Note that the condition is independent of the pre-raid market value and that good performance is therefore no defence against takeover: raids are attractive because of the returns from oppression. We are thus left with a situation in which (a) raids will never take place, whatever the behaviour of the incumbent management, if $w < c$, and (b) all companies, including profit maximisers, will be completely vulnerable to takeover if $w > c$. It need hardly be said that this is not a very satisfactory incentive system!

When the offer to purchase shares is made unconditionally the payoffs to the target's shareholders are as before, excepting that the return from accepting the offer in the event that the bid fails becomes $s(i)p$ rather than $s(i)q$. Hence, if $p > q$, there will be an incentive to accept the offer if the bid is expected to fail. Indeed, when $p > \max\{q, v-w\}$ shareholders will always find it advantageous to accept the offer no matter what beliefs they hold about its likelihood of success.

In the unconditional bid case there are further complications in that equilibria exist in which raids are successful and $q > p > v-w$. If everyone expects the bid to succeed they will accept the offer since, although the price is below the previous market level, it is greater than what the shares will be worth after the takeover. Note, though, that if the bid is expected to fail, all shareholders will refuse the offer (since $p < q$) and it will indeed fail. Thus there are multiple equilibria. In what follows it will be assumed that it is the latter equilibrium which is relevant. One justification for this is that if we start out with a disequilibrium situation where there are two groups of shareholders who believe respectively that the bid will succeed and that the bid will fail, shares in the immediate post-announcement period will be worth less to the former than the latter. Since shares can be traded it is to be expected that the latter group will purchase equity from the others, so that holdings will be built up by investors who will refuse the offer. It therefore appears more likely that the equilibrium which is established will be that in which such bids fail.

From the condition for profitable raids (inequality (2)), it can be seen that the target's managers can prevent a raid by setting q such that

$$\max\{q, v-w\} > v+w-2c \tag{3}$$

If $w < c$, inequality (3) is always satisfied and, whatever the policies adopted by the target management, there will be no successful bids. Again we find that the lack of a sufficiently strong exclusion device leads to an incentives failure. When $w > 2c$, however, the inequality will only hold if

$$q > v+w-2c \tag{4}$$

But (4) can never be satisfied if $w > 2c$ since v is the maximum market value of the firm's equity. Hence, once again, value maximisation is an ineffective defence against predators attracted by the possibility of gains from the oppression of minority interests: an outcome that is clearly undesirable from the social viewpoint as resources are being absorbed by a process which is producing no social gains.

With unconditional bids there remains, though, the possibility that the incentives to good performance generated by the takeover threat might be effective provided that $c < w < 2c$. Indeed, if $w = 2c$, only profit maximising firms will survive. If oppression could be controlled precisely this would offer the possibility of an attractive incentive mechanism, but the arguments of section II suggest that such an outcome would be impossible to achieve.

At this point a number of policy options suggest themselves. For example, it might be decided to

(i) ban all partial bids, or
(ii) ban all conditional partial bids and attempt to limit oppression to levels which allow the incentive mechanism to work, or
(iii) separate, by some means, the decisions to accept the offer for an individual holding and to approve the bid.

These alternatives will be discussed in section V, but at this point we can simply note that none of them is entirely satisfactory, either as a result of the problems of controlling oppression or because of conflicts with other policy objectives. It would therefore be desirable if some alternative means could be found whereby takeovers aimed at increasing the market values of targets were allowed to proceed, preferably in a way that did not conflict with policies concerned with the protection of minorities. As will now be shown this objective can, in fact, be straightforwardly achieved by the introduction of compulsory acquisition rights.

IV. COMPULSORY ACQUISITION OF SHARES

Compulsory acquisition rights allow an acquiror to purchase minority holdings in a company, usually on the same terms as were accepted by the majority, once acceptances have been received which account for some prescribed fraction, say h, of the target's equity. To explore the impact of this type of legislation suppose that (a) the raider makes an offer for all the target's shares at price p/n conditional upon acceptances in respect of at least $100h\%$ of the equity; (b) if the desired percentage is reached the remainder of the shares can be compulsorily acquired on the same terms (that is, at price p/n); and (c) if the desired percentage is not attained the bid is allowed to lapse.

Then the expected return to shareholder i, if he initially rejects the offer, is $ns(i)\{yp+[1-y]q\}$, where y is his assessment of the probability of a successful takeover contingent upon this rejection. Letting $y+dy$ be the anticipated probability of success if i accepts the offer, where dy is assumed to be positive but very small as a result of the dispersion of shareholdings, the return from this second course of action is $s(i)\{[y+dy]p+[1-y-dy]q\}$. The investor will therefore find it profitable to sell iff

$$(5) \qquad \{p-q\}dy > 0$$

Provided that shareholders believe that their own decisions do have some effect on the likelihood of success, *by no matter how small an amount*, fully anticipated takeovers will occur when the bid price exceeds the market price in the absence of takeovers. It follows that profitable raids will be possible when $v-q-c > 0$. Hence the management of a potential target will be safe only if $q > v-c$, and compulsory acquisition rules can be viewed as validating the traditional approach to the takeover constraint on managerial discretion (see Hay and Morris [1979], Singh [1975] and Yarrow [1976]).

In practice the incentive to sell may well be reinforced by the possibility of oppression if the raid succeeds. Suppose shareholder i declines the offer but the raid succeeds. Then the acquiror would only want to compulsorily acquire the remaining shares if $p < v-w$. Thus the return to the shareholder in this event would be $\min\{p, v-w\}$. Given uncertainty about the level of w this would greatly strengthen the pressure to sell. Note also that the incentive to sell will be strengthened when refusal of a subsequently successful offer leads to a deferred payment with a lower present value than that associated with initial acceptance. For example, time discounting would lower the value of a cash payment which was delayed by refusal.

It is crucial for the above argument that shareholders of the acquiree do not believe that a failure of the offer will lead to a further, successful bid at a higher price, say p^*/n. For if they did, the return from rejection, $ns(i)\{yp+[1-y]p^*\}$, would be greater than the return from acceptance, $ns(i)\{[y+dy]p+[1-y-dy]p^*\}$. The raider could, in principle, prevent this outcome by binding itself to the initial price unless some rival bidder enters the market. Supposing that some fraction f of c is a sunk cost, so that a revised offer would entail a further expenditure of $(1-f)c$, no rival would find it profitable to enter the contest if its own total transactions cost exceeded $(1-f)c$. By committing resources to the takeover and restricting its post-bid actions a raider can use its first-mover advantages to limit competition, since if entry occurs it will be willing to bid an amount up to $v-(1-f)c$, at which price the entrant will make a loss. More realistically perhaps, it can also be argued that shareholders will not be certain that another bid will be forthcoming if they refuse the offer. Even though it may appear profitable for the raider to make an improved offer in any particular case, reputation effects may dominate in a way that makes non-revision the optimal policy (cf. Kreps and Wilson [1982]).

The potential benefits of compulsory acquisition have been recognised by policy makers in the U.K. for some time. In 1926 the Greene Committee on Company Law Reform noted that, where an acquiror wished to purchase all the equity of a target, takeovers were sometimes being frustrated by a small minority of shareholders who did not accept the offer "either from a desire to extract better terms than their fellow shareholders or from a lack of real interest in the matter" (see Davies [1976]). Partly in response to these problems the 1948 Companies Act included a section (no. 209(1)) allowing acquirors to compulsorily purchase the shares of a dissenting minority. The general rule is that, if the acquiror receives acceptances from the holders of not less than 90% by value of the shares to which the offer relates, the offeror is entitled to compulsorily acquire the remaining shares on the same terms as were accepted by the majority (see Walmsley [1982] and Weinberg [1981]).

It can also be noted that similar, "freezeout" provisions exist in U.S. corporation law, although their use is considerably more restricted and costly than in Britain (see Brudney and Chirelstein [1978]).

Section 209(1) clearly represents an attenuation of shareholders' rights in the interests of improved efficiency of the takeover process. The result does not, however, rely upon an attempt to specify some maximum permissible level of oppression of the minority. Instead the limitation of minority rights is allowed to be determined *ex post* by the decisions of the overwhelming majority of the shareholders, and case to case flexibility is thus built in to the solution.

If the opportunities for post-raid oppression are small the acquiror will, of course, find it optimal to exercise the compulsory purchase option. In view of the weak position of minority shareholders in U.K. company law, however, it could be argued that section 209(1) is superfluous. Thus, it was in general perfectly feasible for acquirors to gain control of targets before the introduction of the legislation. The principal motivation for the section appears to lie rather in a desire to make the complete absorption of a subsidiary company administratively more convenient. Indeed, section 209(2) of the 1948 Companies Act *strengthens* the position of small minorities by conferring an opposite right: where at least 90% of the equity has been acquired the residual shareholders can compel the acquiror to purchase their shares on the same terms as were accepted by the majority. Nevertheless, whatever the motivations for the original legislation, its existence does allow the simultaneous achievement of well protected minorities and a properly functioning acquisitions market.

Finally, it should be stressed that, in the model presented above, the only costs of the compulsory acquisition provisions are those associated with the enforcement process. More generally, though, the valuations placed upon blocks of securities by investors will tend to exceed their market values. Compulsory acquisition could then lead to situations where an investor is compelled to sell a holding for a consideration which is less than his/her subjective valuation of that holding. Apart from the direct distributional effects, this implication of the legislation will have negative consequences for the demand for securities and will therefore tend to raise the cost of capital. Indeed the 90% acceptance requirement contained in section 209(1) can be interpreted as reflecting an implicit judgement about the trade-off between these other costs of coercion and the benefits of compulsory acquisition detailed earlier.

V. THE CITY CODE ON TAKEOVERS AND MERGERS

It has been shown in the previous section that compulsory acquisition rights can solve the free rider problem in the presence of strong protection of minority interests. It remains the case, however, that in many situations, given the relatively weak position of minorities under present U.K. company law, there will be opportunities for sizeable returns from oppression and that, in the absence of further regulation, there would be incentives for firms to attempt socially undesirable partial takeover bids. In response to this problem the City Code on Takeovers and Mergers—developed by City of London organisations involved in the takeover process as a form of self-regulation—has sought to provide additional protection for shareholders against the threat of being forced unwillingly into new minorities. Thus General Principles 7 and 8 (all numbers quoted in this section referring to the 1976 version of the code) state respectively that:

RIGHTS OF CONTROL

> Rights of control must be exercised in good faith and the oppression of a minority is wholly unacceptable.

EQUALITY OF TREATMENT

> All shareholders of the same class of an offeree company shall be treated similarly by an offeror.

The detailed regulations embodying these principles are set out in several of the rules of the Code which are designed to provide explicit guidelines to be followed during the course of a bid.

In the early stages of the development of the Code the problem was tackled by strong discouragement of partial bids by the Panel which oversees its operation. The view was taken that, when effective control of the company was an issue, shareholders should have an opportunity to use all their shares to oppose the change or to get the proffered price for all their shares if they did not like what was happening. With a full bid it is for each shareholder to decide whether he wishes to remain in a minority whereas in the case of a partial bid he/she is very unlikely to have that choice.

Attitudes have now changed, however, and it is recognised that there may well be circumstances (for example, financial constraints on the acquiror) where partial bids might be justified. In moving in this direction the panel also seems to have been influenced by the more lenient treatment accorded to such bids in other countries such as the U.S. Nevertheless, safeguards for shareholders facing partial takeover bids are built in to the Code at several points, and in this context the most relevant rules are numbers 21, 23 and 26. Rule 21 includes the following provisions:

> No offer, which, if accepted in full, would result in the offeror having voting control of the offeree company, shall be made unless it is a condition of such offer that the offer will not become or be declared unconditional as to acceptances unless the offeror has acquired or agreed to acquire (either pursuant to the offer or by shares acquired or agreed

> to be acquired before or during the offer) by the close of the offer shares carrying over 50 % of the votes attributable to the equity share capital.
>
> No offer for equity share capital may be declared unconditional as to acceptances unless, in addition to complying with the foregoing, the offeror has acquired the right to exercise over 50 % of the voting rights of offeree company.

Offers which are unconditional at the outset are therefore disallowed by the rule, eliminating the possibility of the unfavourable (for the offeree's shareholders) equilibria, discussed in section III, which are associated with this type of bid. Nor is it possible for a raider to build up a majority stake by piecemeal purchases, since rule 34 requires anyone who has acquired shares carrying 30 % or more of the voting rights of a company to extend an offer to other shareholders with voting rights at a price not less than the highest price paid by the offeror for that class of share within the previous twelve months.

Rule 23 goes on to strengthen the position of the offeree's shareholders by stipulating that:

> After an offer has become or is declared unconditional as to acceptances, the offer must remain open for acceptance for not less than 14 days after the date on which it would have otherwise expired, except in the event that the offer becomes or is declared unconditional as to acceptances on or by an expiry date and the offeror has given at least 14 days' notice in writing to the shareholders of the offeree company that the offer will not be open for acceptances beyond that date.

Thus if shareholders know that they will have a period in which they can accept after the offer has been declared unconditional, they can, if they are opposed to the bid, simply ignore the offer without facing the threat of being left with a larger minority holding. Thus bids which value the firm at less than its previous price will fail.

The rule is designed to protect the reluctant acceptor, but unfortunately the second part opens the door to the whiplash effect discussed earlier. The ability of an offeror to deny shareholders the extra period is known as a shut-off, and undoes much of the protection intended by the rule. Johnston [1980, p. 250] implies that the primary rationale for permitting shut-offs is that many bids may involve the option of an underwritten cash alternative, and that the costs of underwriting may increase rapidly with the duration of the offer period. The costs of underwriting are, however, an option that will have a zero net present value in a competitive capital market and the argument clearly lacks substance. Although a number of restrictions are placed on shut-offs—designed to prevent them being used as a tactic to force responses from shareholders—the possibility of abuse remains and the case for their retention appears to be weak.

The impact of shut-off threats is attenuated in the case of partial bids by virtue of provisions contained in rule 27:

> The Panel's consent is required for any partial offer.
>
> In the case of an offer which would result in the offeror holding shares carrying over 50% but less than 100% of the voting rights of a company, such consent will not normally be granted if an offer for the whole of the equity share capital of the offeree company has already been announced, or if the offeror or persons acting in concert with it have acquired, selectively or in significant numbers, shares in the offeree company during the 12 months preceding the application for consent. Any such offer must be conditional upon approval of the offer by shareholders in respect of over 50% of the voting rights not held by the offeror or persons acting in concert with it.

Hence, the specific approval of the Panel is required for a partial takeover bid and it is unlikely in practice that a significantly coercive bid would be allowed. Moreover the approval of the bid referred to in the rule is regarded as being separate from acceptance of the offer. Approval is therefore normally signified by an entry in a designated box on the acceptance form:

> "Approval must be specific and separate. It was envisaged that a shareholder might disapprove of the bid but complete the acceptance form in case it went through." (Johnston [1980, p. 254]).

Hence, in cases where individuals face incentives to accept an offer which would leave them worse off than before, separation of the two decisions will imply that the bids will be unsuccessful.

The effect of the provisions of the Code is thus to effectively rule out bids which value shares at less than their previous market levels, even where minorities are weakly protected ($w > c$). Successful bids will therefore again have to satisfy the condition that $p > q$ and takeovers will occur when the potential capital gain from improved performance ($v-q$) exceeds the transactions cost of the change (c). Combining the compulsory acquisition provisions of the 1948 Companies Act with the rules of the City Code, then, we have the result that, whatever the prospects for oppression, the condition for successful raids is simply $q < v-c$. In circumstances where the capital gain $v-q$ can be regarded as a social gain (reflecting, say, increased efficiency rather than greater market power), the result is a socially efficient solution to these particular public good problems.

VI. CONCLUSIONS

It has been shown that U.K. company law and the City Code on Mergers and Takeovers combine to produce an approximately efficient solution to public good problems connected with takeovers. Compulsory acquisition rights provide the necessary exclusion device when opportunities for oppressive behaviour towards minorities is limited, while the rules of the Code prevent the occurrence of undesirable partial bids in cases where minority shareholders are likely to be only weakly protected by their legal rights. Thus, the incentives towards efficient management resulting from the existence of the takeover threat will not be impaired by free riding strategies, and there is no conflict between policy measures designed to strengthen the position of minorities and to preserve the effectiveness of the takeover mechanism.

This is not to say the current regulatory framework cannot be improved, but its weaknesses lie rather in the lack of protection afforded to the shareholders of the acquiror rather than to the shareholders of the acquiree. For example, approval of the former's shareholders for a bid is not required, and only if the takeover involves an increase in the company's authorised capital will there be any legal requirement that the matter be referred to a shareholders' meeting. In view of evidence which suggests that, on average, the returns from takeover to acquirors' shareholders have been negative (see Firth [1979], [1980]), there does appear to be a case for requiring greater shareholder involvement in acquisition decisions when the latter involve a major expansion of the company.

G. K. YARROW,
Hertford College,
Oxford.

ACCEPTED NOVEMBER 1984

REFERENCES

BRUDNEY, V. and CHIRELSTEIN, M. A., 1978, 'A Restatement of Corporate Freezeouts', *Yale Law Journal*, 87, 7 (June), pp. 1354–76.

DAVIES, P. L., 1976, *The Regulation of Takeovers and Mergers* (Sweet and Maxwell, London).

FIRTH, M., 1979, 'The Profitability of Takeovers and Mergers', *Economic Journal*, LXXXIX (June), pp. 316–28.

FIRTH, M., 1980, 'Takeovers, Shareholder Returns and the Theory of the Firm', *Quarterly Journal of Economics*, XCIV, 2 (March), pp. 235–60.

GROSSMAN, S. J. and HART, O. D., 1980, 'Takeover Bids, the Free-Rider Problem and the Theory of the Corporation', *Bell Journal of Economics*, 11, 1 (Spring), pp. 42–64.

HAY, D. A. and MORRIS, D. J., 1979, *Industrial Economics: Theory and Evidence* (Oxford University Press).

JOHNSTON, A., 1980, *The City Take-over Code* (Oxford University Press).

KREPS, D. M. and WILSON, R., 1982, 'Reputation and Imperfect Information', *Journal of Economic Theory*, 27, 2 (August), pp. 253–79.

MANNING, B., 1962, 'The Shareholder's Appraisal Remedy', *Yale Law Journal*, 72, 2 (December), pp. 223–65.

MARRIS, R., 1964, *The Economic Theory of Managerial Capitalism* (Macmillan, London).

SINGH, A., 1975, 'Takeovers, Economic Natural Selection and the Theory of the Firm', *Economic Journal*, LXXXV (September), pp. 497–515.

WALMSLEY, K. (ed.), 1982, *Butterworths Company Law Handbook* (Butterworths, London).

WEINBERG, M. A. and BLANK, M. V., 1981, *Weinberg and Blank on Take-Overs and Mergers* (Sweet and Maxwell, London).

YARROW, G. K., 1976, 'On the Predictions of Managerial Theories of the Firm', *Journal of Industrial Economics*, XXIV, 4 (June), pp. 267–79.

THE JOURNAL OF INDUSTRIAL ECONOMICS 0022-1821 $2.00
Volume XXXIV September 1985 No. 1

THE WELFARE COST OF QUALITY CHANGES DUE TO PROFESSIONAL REGULATION*

ROGER FELDMAN AND JAMES W. BEGUN

We present a method for measuring the welfare cost of legislated restrictions on the activities of professionals in markets where consumers can substitute between brands of different quality. In the market for vision examinations by optometrists, quality changes due to three selected professional regulations result in economic profits for producers of some $140 million, and positive changes in quality due to the regulations are not valued by consumers at their marginal cost. A small annual welfare loss of about $8 million results from these professional regulations. When quantity effects are also included, the welfare loss increases to $16 million.

As is the case for other regulated markets, researchers have devoted much attention recently to the effects of legal restrictions in markets for professional services (see Cox *et al.* [1982], Leffler [1978], Rottenberg [1980] and Shepard [1978]). These restrictions, often largely promulgated by the professions themselves, include advertising bans, educational requirements and other barriers to entry, and restrictions on permissible employment settings.

Measuring the cost of monopoly or legislated restrictions is a standard tool of welfare economics (see Deyak and Smith [1976] and Harberger [1954]). However, the conventional method is not well suited to measuring costs which arise when consumers substitute between brands of different quality, or between different-quality providers of the same general professional service. In this paper, we first discuss a method for measuring the welfare cost of quality changes due to regulation. We then apply the method to vision examinations given by optometrists in markets governed to varying degrees by three different professional regulations.

I. THEORY OF WELFARE COST WHEN QUALITY CHANGES

Suppose consumers purchase a "vision care index" q which consists of one vision examination with varying quality. Let a consumer with income y have a utility function $U = U(x, q)$ where x is all other goods consumed. Setting the price of x equal to one dollar and maximizing U subject to $y = p(q)+x$, we have the usual solution that $U_q/U_x = p'(q)$.

Define expenditure functions $\theta = \theta(q; U, y)$ representing the consumer's

* This project was supported by Grant No. HS-03085 from the National Center for Health Services Research. We would like to thank Sherwin Rosen, Michael Grossman, and an anonymous reviewer for helpful advice.

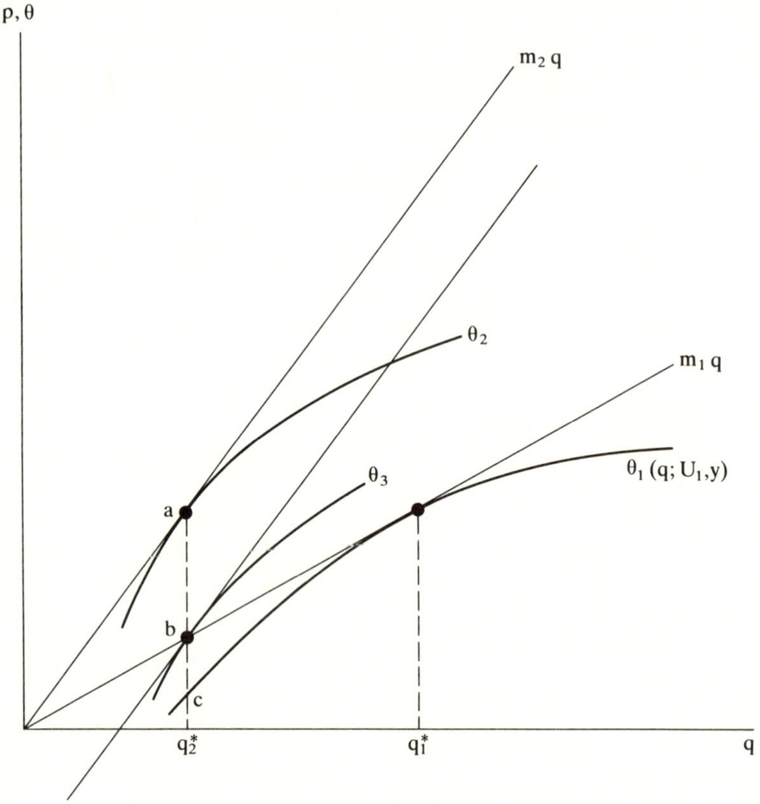

FIGURE 1
The Effect of Regulation on the Consumer's Choice of Optimal Product Quality.

willingness to pay for alternative qualities of vision care, given utility and income. Then $U = U(y-\theta, q)$ can be differentiated to obtain $\theta_q = U_q/U_x > 0$, the slope of an indifference curve between q and the price of q. By further differentiation, $\theta_{qu} = (U_x U_{qx} - U_q U_{xx})/U_x^3$.[1] The numerator of this expression determines the sign of the income effect for good q in standard theory. If $(U_x U_{qx} - U_q U_{xx}) = 0$, the family of expenditure functions is parallel, as shown in Figure 1.

The comparative statics of this model are ambiguous, due to the nonlinear budget constraint; therefore, for simplicity assume that $p(q) = mq$, where m is a shift parameter that varies across markets. With this simplification, also shown in Figure 1, optimal q clearly falls from q_1^* to q_2^* when m increases.

How do differences in m arise? Rosen [1974] has shown that $p(q)$ is determined, in the long run, by supply conditions. Competitive supply

[1] This expression is found (but with a typographical error) in Rosen [1974, p. 39].

implies that each quality is produced at minimum average cost by firms of optimal size. The social marginal cost of producing a higher quality good is thus m_1. Differences in m could arise, then, if factor prices differ among separate competitive markets. Differences in m could also be caused by local taxes on quality or monopolistic restrictions which raise the price of quality above its marginal cost.

In the latter case, the value of the restriction to the producer per unit of the good is given by distance *ab* in Figure 1.[2] If the consumer were compensated with *ab* income at the higher price of quality, he/she would willingly buy q_2^* and enjoy U_3. But $U_3 < U_1$, that is, the income transfer of *ab*, is accompanied by a pure welfare cost whose monetary measure is *bc*.

In terms of derivatives, assuming there are no income effects, θ_q is the inverse of an income-compensated demand curve, and the situation is shown in Figure 2. Welfare cost is measured in the standard way by triangle *def*.[3]

Rosen [1974] has suggested a method by which market observations on price and quality can be used to estimate the demand curve for quality required to measure *def*. He suggests estimating the $p(q)$ function from data on price and quality. Denote the estimated function by $\hat{p}(q)$. Partial derivatives evaluated at the amounts of quality actually bought, $\partial\hat{p}/\partial(q)$, represent payments necessary to upgrade quality by a small amount, that is, the marginal prices of quality. Estimation of marginal prices plays the same role here as do direct observations on price in the standard theory.

In principle, data are available on exogenous variables y_1 and y_2 which influence consumers' and producers' choices of quality. These include income, age and insurance (for consumers), and factor prices or technological differences for producers. Thus, we have a set of simultaneous equations.

$$q = d(\partial\hat{p}/\partial q, y_1) \qquad \text{(demand)}$$

$$q = s(\partial\hat{p}/\partial q, y_2) \qquad \text{(supply)}$$

which can be estimated by appropriate regression techniques.

Unfortunately, Rosen's method has been extremely difficult to implement empirically. All the observations are envisioned as coming from a single national market. There are no truly exogenous shifters with which to identify the demand curve, so the job of identification depends on the appropriate functional form of $\hat{p}(q)$. The function must have sufficient curvatures to generate different slopes at different levels of quality corresponding to

[2] We thank an anonymous referee for noting that *ab* will overstate the unit value of regulations to the firm if the firm bears positive enforcement costs.

[3] We thank Sherwin Rosen for pointing out that, if there was an income effect, the demand curve would not be identified because the compensated demand curve through f would not pass through d—there would be two compensated demand curves, corresponding to two levels of utility, through f and d. But in this problem, income effects are likely to be small and can be ignored. This is because x accounts for most of the budget. If $p(q)$ were not linear, the marginal supply curves corresponding to m_1 and m_2 would not be linear, but the argument is otherwise unaffected.

marginal prices actually faced by consumers and producers at those qualities. A linear function, for example, is unacceptable because it forces $\partial \hat{p}/\partial q$ to be constant. In practice, selection of an appropriately sensitive functional form may simply overburden the data.

However, if the good is traded in separate local or regional markets, then the price function will be shifted by variables which affect price and differ between markets. As shown in Figure 2, these shift variables identify the demand curve. Markets for services such as vision care are local; therefore, they offer an opportunity to implement Rosen's method and measure the welfare cost of quality changes.

II. THE DEMAND FOR QUALITY OF VISION EXAMINATIONS

We have discussed the market for vision care in more detail elsewhere [1981] and [1978]. Optometrists occupy one segment of the market, performing vision examinations and dispensing eyeglasses and contact lenses. Begun and Lippincott [1980] call optometry a "profession in process", as it has not yet achieved the status of professions like dentistry or medicine. Professional organization of optometrists is highly variable among the states, with the percentage of practitioners belonging to state affiliates of the American Optometric Association varying from 45 percent to 100 percent (Begun [1981]).

The professional segment of optometry has sought a variety of goals which require the approval of state political systems. The goals concern such matters as educational standards for licensure, the moral character of licensees, the employment settings in which practitioners can locate, and the definition of their work domain. Success in achieving these goals is highly variable among states. The degree of *professional regulation*, therefore, is an exogenous variable which differs among states.

Economists broadly agree that occupations acquire and operate the regulatory process for their own benefit (see Horowitz [1980] and Stigler [1971]). A review of the health occupations literature by Frech [1974] concludes that licensing of health occupation has restricted entry, reduced productivity and competition, and interfered with geographic mobility. More recently, we have shown [1978] and [1980] that vision examinations are more expensive in states where price advertising of optometrists' and opticians' services is banned, holding quality of service constant. Our hypothesis for the present study is that price advertising bans and other professional regulations shift the estimated $\hat{p}(q)$ function between states, identifying the demand curve for quality.

In this paper, we concentrate on professional regulations which ban price advertising, restrict the commercial employment of optometrists, and require continuing education for licensing of optometrists. The first two regulations have been central to the profession's attempt to shed its "commercial" image.

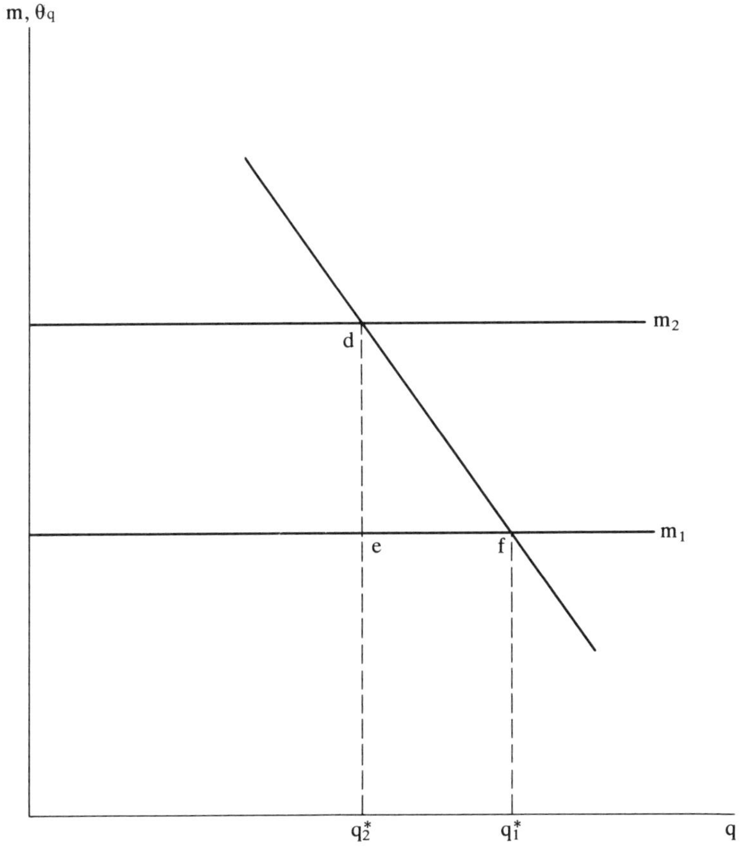

FIGURE 2
The Welfare Cost of Quality Changes.

They are more generally important because they reflect and reinforce the largely noncompetitive structure of the U.S. health services delivery system. Continuing education requirements for licensure have been used to justify the status of optometry as a profession; they also have proven to be a useful device for promoting optometry's boundary expansion into diagnostic and therapeutic drug use, fields typically reserved for physicians.

Regulations are coded by dummy variables which take the value of one if the regulation was present in 1976 and zero if it was not. Formally, the *ADVERTISING BAN* variable equals one if all price advertising by optometrists and opticians was banned by state law or licensing board regulation. These bans apply to both eyeglasses and vision examinations. *EMPLOYMENT BAN* is defined by state laws prohibiting the employment of optometrists by non-professional corporations or the location of practices in commercial settings, such as department stores. *CONTINUING EDUCATION REQUIREMENTS*, which

TABLE I
DESCRIPTION OF VARIABLES*

Label	Definition	Mean	Standard Deviation
PRICE	Charge for complete examination of presbyopic patient in dollars	24.353	7.200
LENGTH	Length of presbyopic examination in minutes	33.335	9.939
PROCEDURES	Technical procedures performed during examination, 1–8 scale	4.328	1.558
ADVERTISING BAN	Optometrist and optician price advertising banned; 1 = yes	0.308	0.462
EMPLOYMENT BAN	Corporate employment or mercantile location of optometrist restricted; 1 = yes	0.638	0.481
CONTINUING EDUCATION REQUIREMENT	Continuing education required for optometrist relicensure; 1 = yes	0.846	0.361
WHITE %	Optometrist's estimate of percent of patients who are white	83.585	19.861
MEDICAID	Optometrist's estimate of percent of income from Medicaid	7.328	12.156
THIRD PARTY %	Optometrist's estimate of percent of income from other third party payers	9.320	12.705
INSURANCE	State mean of sample optometrists' estimate of percent of income from all third party payers	11.317	13.533
INCOME	Optometrist's estimate of income status of majority of patients; 3 = over $15,000, 2 = $10,000–$15,000, 1 = under $10,000	1.954	0.545
PCTOLD	Percent of state population over 65 years old	9.731	2.503
PCTWHITE	Percent of state population white	86.726	14.024
STINCOME	State per-household income, in $1,000s	12.312	1.638
EXAMINATIONS PER CAPITA	(Sample optometrists' reported annual volume of examinations* Number of optometrists in state) ÷ state population	0.169	0.049

* Number of observations for individual optometrist data is 1,182; for state data is 51.

ranged from 4 to 25 hours per year for relicensure, assumed a value of one in all states which required any continuing education for licensure. Means and standard deviations of the regulatory variables and all other variables used in the analyses below are reported in Table I.

Data for this study were collected by Begun [1981]. A 10 percent systematic sample (N = 2,238) of all optometrists in the U.S. was selected in late 1976, and 1,195 usable responses were received from a questionnaire survey. Price is measured by the individual optometrist's charge for a complete visual examination of a presbyopic patient (presbyopia is a deterioration in focusing ability usually associated with aging). Quality is measured by self-reported examination length in minutes (LENGTH) and the number of procedures, on a 1–8 scale, performed during the examination (PROCEDURES). Examination length and procedures are both "input" or "process" measures of quality, and therefore they may not be correlated with vision examination "outcomes". That is, longer, more complex examinations may or may not lead to more accurate lens prescriptions or better visual health. We justify the use of these process measures on the basis of the unavailability of outcome measures, the likelihood that consumers of medical services use various dimensions of input and process to evaluate the quality of provider services (see Sloan and Lorant [1976]), and the possibility that some inputs may be desired by consumers *per se*. A common complaint about doctors, for example, is that they do not spend enough time with patients. Personal consultation and even handholding may be key attributes of their service. In addition, earlier studies of medical services have revealed significant positive relationships between visit length and visit price (Feldman [1979] and Reinhardt [1975, p. 156]). Clearly, however, similar studies to this one should be conducted using outcome measures of quality (for example, Bond *et al.* [1980]).[4]

A linear interactive price function is general enough to allow restrictions to affect the price of quality:

$$\hat{p} = \sum_{i=1}^{m} \alpha_i q_i + \sum_{k=1}^{n} \beta_k R_k + \sum_{i=1}^{m} \sum_{k=1}^{n} \delta_{ik} q_i R_k,$$

where the q_i are quality variables and R_k are professional regulations.[5] This equation is an accurate representation of Figure 2, because it shows that the price of q_i is constant within a state and is shifted up by regulations $\left(\text{if } \sum_{k=1}^{n} \delta_{ik} R_k > 0\right)$.

An ordinary least squares regression estimate of this equation is shown in Table II.[6] A key result of Table II is that professional regulations *reduce* the

[4] Another issue surrounding the use of length as a measure of quality is the fact that individuals will value longer examinations differently depending on their time costs. We have no suitable measures of individual time costs in these data.

[5] We also considered the effects of factor costs (annual rent per room of office space, annual wage of office attendants) and the nominal price level (1975 state consumer price index) on the price of an optometric visit. Each additional variable plus its interactions with examination length and procedures was individually added to the price equation shown in Table II. Joint F-statistics for the added groups of variables were 0.727, 1.544, and 1.896, respectively. None of the added groups of variables were statistically significant at $\alpha = 0.05$ ($F \approx 2.60$). Therefore, they were omitted from further consideration.

[6] For OLS to yield unbiased estimates of the parameters in the price function, the quality of services supplied must be independent of the marginal price of quality. Goldman and Grossman [1978], in their study of physicians' services, assume that quality is related to predetermined physician characteristics. They admit that some dimensions of quality are endogenous, but to estimate an instrumental variable for each endogenous dimension would inordinately "tax" the data. (Most of this discussion can be found in two preliminary drafts of Goldman and Grossman's 1978 article.) In the present paper, we assume that the marginal cost of quality is constant. Shifts in the demand function for quality trace out the relation between price and

TABLE II
LINEAR INTERACTIVE PRICE EQUATION

Variable	*Including* PROCEDURES *Interactions* Coefficient (T-Value)	*Excluding* PROCEDURES *Interactions* Coefficient (T-Value)
PRICE = *Dependent Variable*		
LENGTH	0.306	0.324
	(5.33)	(6.11)
PROCEDURES	1.393	1.031
	(3.80)	(8.39)
ADVERTISING BAN	2.571	1.945
	(1.63)	(1.38)
EMPLOYMENT BAN	3.287	3.622
	(2.21)	(2.69)
CONTINUING EDUCATION	6.091	5.036
REQUIREMENT	(3.06)	(2.76)
LENGTH · ADVERTISING BAN	0.0350	0.0247
	(0.80)	(0.61)
LENGTH · EMPLOYMENT BAN	−0.0669	−0.0799
	(2.06)	(2.04)
LENGTH · CONTINUING	−0.0368	−0.0602
EDUCATION REQUIREMENT	(0.63)	(1.12)
PROCEDURES · ADVERTISING BAN	−0.222	—
	(0.77)	—
PROCEDURES · EMPLOYMENT BAN	0.134	—
	(0.50)	—
PROCEDURES · CONTINUING	−0.446	—
EDUCATION REQUIREMENT	(1.20)	—
CONSTANT	4.243	5.104
$\bar{R}^2$	0.285	0.285
d.f. REGRESSION, RESIDUAL	11,1170	8,1173
MEAN SQUARE ERROR	37.09	37.05

quality along a perfectly elastic supply curve. In general, since this need not be true, OLS estimates of the price function will be biased.

Since we could not rule out the existence of simultaneous equations bias, we tried some 2SLS estimates of the price equation. Goldman and Grossman's warning that this will "tax" the data is immediately relevant: with eight endogenous explanatory variables (LENGTH, PROCEDURES, and six interaction terms) and only four excluded exogenous variables (WHITE %, THIRD PARTY %, MEDICAID %, and INCOME), the equation is clearly under-identified. Therefore, we drastically simplified the set of endogenous variables to three: LENGTH, PROCEDURES, and LENGTH · EMPLOYMENT BAN (the most significant interaction term). A 2SLS estimate of this equation is:

$$\underset{(t\,=\,1.83)}{PRICE = 0.785\ LENGTH} + \underset{(2.61)}{5.333\ PROCEDURES} - \underset{(1.77)}{1.49\ LENGTH \cdot EMPLOYMENT\ BAN}$$

$$+ \underset{(3.81)}{4.267\ ADVERTISING\ BAN} + \underset{(1.77)}{4.96\ EMPLOYMENT\ BAN}$$

$$+ \underset{(0.537)}{0.724\ CONTINUING\ EDUCATION\ REQUIREMENT} - 2.635.$$

This is not plausible, because it suggests that the marginal price of length is negative in restrictive states. The single interaction term is forced here to "reveal" too much information about the price-quality surface. We conclude that the 2SLS approach is theoretically valid but difficult to implement.

marginal prices of both length and procedures. For optometrists who practice in states without regulations, all R variables are set equal to zero; $\partial\hat{p}/\partial$ *LENGTH* $= 0.306$ and $\partial\hat{p}/\partial$ *PROCEDURES* $= 1.393$. In states with regulations (all $R=1$), $\partial\hat{p}/\partial$ *LENGTH* $= 0.306+0.0350-0.0669-0.0368 = 0.2373$ and $\partial\hat{p}/\partial$ *PROCEDURES* $= 1.393-0.222+0.134-0.446 = 0.859$. Therefore, extra quality is less expensive in states with regulations. We show below that the difference in the marginal price of length is statistically significant while the difference in the marginal price of procedures is not.

We interpret these results in the following way. Under pure competition, at a given level of quality, marginal price and marginal cost will be equal. Since professional regulations are a departure from the norm of pure competition, we infer that vision examination length is priced below marginal cost in regulated states. Survival of producers in these states is possible because regulations raise the price of vision examinations. The reduced price of length may be due to "quality" or "amenity" competition. Professional and legal sanctions largely prevent price competition; quality competition is much harder to detect and is used to attract customers. A similar interpretation is that producers in regulated states find price competition to be a less profitable strategy than "quality" competition. An analogy can be drawn to pre-deregulation airline competition in the U.S. on such dimensions as scheduling convenience, food quality, and storage space, rather than price.

To continue the welfare loss calculation, marginal prices of length and procedures computed from Table II are used to estimate linear demand curves for length and procedures shown in columns one and two of Table III.

TABLE III
DEMAND EQUATIONS FOR EYE EXAMINATION LENGTH AND PROCEDURES

Independent Variables	*Dependent Variable*			
	LENGTH	*PROCEDURES*	*LENGTH**	*PROCEDURES**
	Coefficient (T-Value)	*Coefficient (T-Value)*	*Coefficient (T-Value)*	*Coefficient (T-Value)*
$\partial\hat{p}/\partial$ *LENGTH* (*PRICE OF LENGTH*)	−17.383 (2.80)	−4.022 (4.18)	−18.830 (3.13)	−4.394 (4.71)
$\partial\hat{p}/\partial$ *PROCEDURES* (*PRICE OF PROCEDURES*)	−2.752 (1.75)	−0.659 (2.43)	— —	— —
WHITE %	0.0761 (4.39)	0.00826 (3.07)	0.0739 (4.29)	0.00771 (2.89)
THIRD PARTY %	0.0371 (1.61)	0.0119 (3.33)	0.0375 (1.63)	0.0200 (3.36)
MEDICAID %	0.0166 (0.59)	0.00999 (2.28)	0.0178 (0.63)	0.0103 (2.35)
INCOME	0.718 (1.26)	0.304 (3.43)	0.777 (1.37)	0.319 (3.61)
CONSTANT	31.964	4.481	29.515	3.900

* Based on price equation that excludes *PROCEDURES* interactions.

The regressions use Zellner's [1962] procedure for estimating seemingly unrelated regressions.[7] Table III shows that own-price elasticities of demand are negative, as predicted by economic theory. Evaluated at the mean, the elasticity of demand for length is -0.120 and for procedures is -0.157. The cross-price coefficients indicate that length and procedures are complementary goods. Other variables in the demand functions are individual optometrists' reports of the percent of their patients who are white (*WHITE* %), the percentage of practice income derived from Medicaid (*MEDICAID* %) and other third party payers (*THIRD PARTY* %), and an estimate of their patients' income category (*INCOME*). The *WHITE* % variable is included in the demand equations because it is positively related to the frequency of vision examinations and eyeglass purchases (Benham and Benham [1975] and Coate [1974]); we find that it increases the demand for quality, too. Enabling variables (represented by insurance and income) also increase the demand for quality; that is, better-insured and higher income consumers demand longer, more complex visits. The effects are statistically significant for procedures but not for length. Thus high income, well-insured consumers may be willing to pay for increased exam complexity, but may be less interested in buying long exams.

The price equation was also estimated under the constraint that interactions between *PROCEDURES* and professional regulations are jointly equal to zero, because the addition of these interactions to a basic group consisting of *LENGTH*, *PROCEDURES*, and regulations resulted in a reduction of the residual sum of squares of the price equation that was insignificant at conventional confidence levels ($F = 1.1455$). This is equivalent to finding that difference in the marginal price of procedures between regulated and unregulated states is not statistically significant. Interactions between *LENGTH* and regulations were significant ($F = 2.35$ has probability of 0.07 at 3 and 1173 degrees of freedom), and, therefore, were not dropped. The estimated price equation excluding *PROCEDURES* interactions is shown in the second column of Table II.

The marginal price of length in the constrained price equation is lower in states with regulations (0.2086) than in states without regulations (0.324). These values were used to estimate demand curves for length and procedures shown in the third and fourth columns of Table III.[8] We see that the coefficients and t-values are similar to those obtained using marginal prices from the unconstrained price equation.

III. MEASURING THE WELFARE COST OF QUALITY CHANGES IN OPTOMETRY

We use Table III's estimates to measure the welfare cost of professional regulations in optometry. Harberger [1964] has given a general formula for

[7] The demand functions for length and procedures may be affected by the same random factors, causing correlation between the disturbances in the equations. OLS estimates of the regression coefficients are inefficient in this case (Kmenta [1971, pp. 517–29]).

[8] Our assumption that *PROCEDURES* does not interact with professional regulations implies that the marginal price of procedures is constant. Therefore, $\partial p/\partial$ *PROCEDURES* is omitted from these regressions.

the welfare cost of taxes or subsidies in interrelated markets: welfare cost equals $-1/2\sum_{ij}\sum T_i T_j S_{ij}$, where i and j are indices of the goods, T_i is the tax on good i, and S_{ij} is the income-compensated substitution effect. Subsidies, in this formula, are defined as negative taxes.

We have the following values for S_{ij} (let 1 = length and 2 = procedures):

$$S_{11} = -17.383$$
$$S_{22} = -0.659$$
$$S_{12} = -2.752 \text{ or } -4.022$$ [9]

The subsidies on the prices of length and procedures due to regulations were taken from Table II:

$$-T_1 = (\text{ADVERTISING BAN}^* \ 0.0350) + (\text{EMPLOYMENT BAN}^* \ -0.0669) + (\text{CONTINUING EDUCATION REQUIREMENT}^* \ -0.0368)$$

$$-T_2 = (\text{ADVERTISING BAN}^* \ -0.222) + (\text{EMPLOYMENT BAN}^* \ 0.134) + (\text{CONTINUING EDUCATION REQUIREMENT}^* \ -0.446).$$

These values were inserted into Harberger's formula and two calculations of welfare cost were made—one for each empirical value of S_{12}. The average welfare cost per examination in states with one or more regulations was $0.26 or $0.21, depending on which estimate of S_{12} was used. We multiplied the welfare cost per visit times the number of vision examinations in each regulated state, to get total dollar values for welfare cost. Using the estimate of $0.26 per visit, we calculated that the total national welfare cost was $8,018,687 in 1976.

Our next calculation is an estimate of the economic profit for optometrics due to the regulations. This is easily done by multiplying the extra price per examination resulting from regulations (from Table II) times the annual number of examinations in regulated states. Results indicate that regulations raise the price of an examination by $4.11, on the average, in the 46 states with at least one regulation. The total annual value to optometrists is $139,530,000.

For comparison, we repeated these calculations using the price equation from Table II that excludes PROCEDURES interactions. The welfare loss of $3,685,965 was smaller than previously obtained, but the annual economic profit for optometrics, $142,359,000, was still quite large.

Our data are not ideal for measuring the welfare cost of *quantity* changes caused by professional regulations. The data were obtained from a survey of individual optometrists, who provided estimates of their weekly and annual examination volumes. In a competitive market,[10] each producer takes the

[9] Economic theory predicts that $S_{ij} = S_{ji}$ but, in practice, empirical estimates differ. We calculate a welfare cost for both estimates.

[10] Some evidence that local vision care markets are competitive is found in Begun's 1976 (Begun [1981]) survey, where responding optometrists indicated a median number of seven other optometrists in the market area, as well as three opticians and five ophthalmologists.

price of a given-quality good as constant and maximizes utility or profit. The optimal volume of services determined in this manner lies neither on the individual consumer's demand curve nor on the market demand curve. Therefore, disaggregated data from individual producers are not ideal for analyzing the welfare cost of quantity changes. They are suited, however, for the welfare analysis of quality changes because the average quality of examinations produced by an optometrist equals the average quality consumed by his/her patients.[11] This enables the estimation of demand curves for quality, and welfare analysis can be done, using those demand curves.

However, data from individual producers can be used to estimate the market demand curve for quantity if they are aggregated up to the market level. We aggregated the data by state and estimated a demand curve for quantity. The following results are tentative, since states may not be relevant markets for eye examinations.

Dependent variables in the state market demand equations are *LENGTH*, *PROCEDURES*, and *EXAMINATIONS PER CAPITA*. Exogenous variables are the percent of state population in 1970 over 65 years old (*PCTOLD*), the percent of state population in 1974 that was white (*PCTWHITE*), the state per-household income in 1974 (*STINCOME*), and the percent of state optometrists' revenue derived from all third-party payers in 1976 (*INSURANCE*). These variables are not identical to those used in Table III, due to the availability of different state and local data; thus, the state and local demand analyses are not directly comparable.

Endogenous explanatory variables are the state average price of an optometric exam for presbyopia in 1976 (*PRICE*) and the "shadow price" of quality (*QUALPRICE*). The latter variable represents the marginal change in expenditures necessary for a consumer to upgrade the quality of his/her examinations by one unit when the quantity of examinations may exceed one.[12] Instrumental variables were estimated for *PRICE* and *QUALPRICE*; to improve the efficiency of these estimates, the set of instruments included the percent of state population unionized, the percent male, and the percent living in urban areas. All variables were also weighted by the square root of the state sample size, to correct for heteroscedasticity.

Two stage least squares estimates of the state-level demand equations are shown in Table IV. The quantity of eye examinations demanded *per capita* falls as price increases (although the t-value of 1.35 is not statistically significant), with an elasticity at the mean of -0.53. Likewise, the relation between

[11] If the optometrist produces examinations of uniform quality, then this statement applies to all his/her examinations, as well as to the average examination. For example, if the optometrist produces only 30-minute examinations, then all his/her patients consume this quality. Thirty minutes, therefore, is one point on each consumer's demand curve for quality. For some arguments to support the one-quality assumption, see Feldman [1976].

[12] See Goldman and Grossman [1978] for a more complete discussion of the shadow price of quality. Computationally, *QUALPRICE* = *EXAMINATIONS PER CAPITA* · *PRICE OF LENGTH*. The price of length is computed from the price equation in Table II that excludes *PROCEDURES* interactions.

TABLE IV
STATE DEMAND EQUATIONS FOR EYE EXAMINATION LENGTH, PROCEDURES, AND QUANTITY PER CAPITA

Independent Variables	*Dependent Variable*		
	LENGTH	PROCEDURES	EXAMINATIONS PER CAPITA
	Coefficient (T-Value)	*Coefficient (T-Value)*	*Coefficient (T-Value)*
PRICE (*endogenous*)	0.515	0.0394	−0.00374
	(3.31)	(1.64)	(1.35)
QUALPRICE* (*endogenous*)	−40.733	−20.616	−0.173
	(0.81)	(2.67)	(0.19)
PCTOLD	0.325	0.0491	0.000492
	(2.45)	(2.40)	(0.21)
PCTWHITE	0.127	0.0163	0.00227
	(3.25)	(2.70)	(3.26)
STINCOME	0.567	0.184	0.00690
	(2.07)	(4.34)	(1.41)
INSURANCE	−0.0113	−0.00313	0.00322
	(0.19)	(0.34)	(0.30)
CONSTANT	4.44	−0.0275	−0.0883

* Based on price equation that excludes PROCEDURES interactions.

LENGTH and QUALPRICE has the expected sign but it is not statistically significant. Our calculated price elasticity of −0.53 is similar to the −0.52 which Coate [1974] argues is the most plausible of several estimates from similar data. The elasticity is larger than most of the reported elasticities for hospital and physician services, as vision examinations are a more discretionary good.

Exogenous variables generally have the same effects on aggregate and local demand for quality. That is, consumers in high-income states with mainly white populations buy relatively long visits with many procedures (the same results that were found in Table III). PCTWHITE is also an important determinant of examinations *per capita*. Age is positively correlated with length and procedures but not significantly with examinations *per capita*.

We next use the results of Table IV and Harberger's formula to do a welfare-loss calculation. Let length = 1, procedures = 2, and quantity = 3; then $S_{11} = -40.733$, $S_{33} = -0.00374$, $S_{13} = 0.515$, and $S_{31} = -0.173$. Note that we have two choices for the cross-price effect—S_{13}, which is statistically significant, suggests that length and quantity are substitutes, whereas S_{31}, which is not statistically significant, suggests that they are complements. Note also that terms involving procedures do not enter into the welfare loss calculations, because we use the price equation that excludes procedures interactions; that is, we use the second column of Table II in which restrictions do not affect the marginal price of procedures.

Results suggest that the total annual welfare loss in 1976 was $15,968, 080 if length and quantity are substitutes and $6,047,730 under the assumption of complementarity. Generally speaking, these are *larger* than our previous estimates of $3.7 to $8.0 million. This is because restrictions raise the price of a visit, thus lowering quantity and causing a welfare loss *in addition to* losses in the quality dimensions of the product.

The loss is greater when quality and quantity are assumed to be substitutes. This occurs because restrictions *reduce* the price of quality in our analysis. Thus consumers substitute away from quantity toward quality. Since they are already consuming "too little" quantity, there is an additional welfare loss caused by the substitution effect. When quantity and quality are complements, the reverse occurs—consumers tend to buy more quantity when the price of quality falls. This partially compensates for the monopolistic restriction in the market for quantity.

IV. SUMMARY

In this paper we have measured the welfare cost of selected quality changes caused by professional regulations in optometry. A significant innovation of our work was the estimation of demand equations for vision examination length and procedures. We followed Rosen's method by estimating price as a function of quality and regulations and using computed marginal prices in demand functions for quality.

We discovered that professional regulations reduce the marginal prices of quality. Therefore, it is likely that deregulation[13] of the industry will raise marginal prices of quality and reduce the quality of vision examinations. Professional spokespersons may point to lower quality as evidence that deregulation leads to shoddy optometric practice. But we strongly suggest that such claims (if they are made) be disregarded. The extra quality engendered by regulations is not valued by consumers at its marginal cost. We found that the welfare cost for excess examination length and procedures was about $8 million annually. In addition, it appears that professional regulations, by raising the price of eye examinations, cause quantity demanded to fall below its competitive level. If this is the case, the $8 million welfare loss understates the total welfare cost of professional regulations in optometry.

We argue that reduced prices of length and procedures in regulated states are due to quality competition. The profession limits entry, mobility, and competition; consequently, the market is restricted and prices rise. Professional and legal sanctions prevent would-be price cutters from expanding

[13] Bans on advertising the price and availability of prescription eyeglasses, contact lenses and eye examinations have been invalidated by a unanimous decision of the Federal Trade Commission [1978] and by various court judgements, particularly *Virginia Board of Pharmacy v. Virginia Citizens Consumer Council, Inc.*, 422 U.S. 748 (1976) and *Bates v. State Bar of Arizona*, 433 U.S. 350 (1977).

their share of the market. But, cutting the price of quality is harder to detect and prevent; therefore, quality competition is used to attract customers in a monopolized profession. This explanation is consistent with high examination prices and low quality prices in the optometric profession.

ACCEPTED SEPTEMBER 1984

ROGER FELDMAN,
Center for Health Services Research and
Department of Economics,
University of Minnesota,
Minneapolis, MN 55455,
USA.

JAMES W. BEGUN,
Department of Health Administration,
Medical College of Virginia,
Virginia Commonwealth University,
Richmond, VA 23298,
USA.

REFERENCES

BEGUN, J. W., 1981, *Professionalism and the Public Interest: Price and Quality in Optometry* (The MIT Press, Cambridge, Mass.).

BEGUN, J. W. and FELDMAN, R., 1981, *A Social and Economic Analysis of Professional Regulation in Optometry* (National Center for Health Services Research, USA), DHHS Publ. No. (PHS) 81–3295.

BEGUN, J. W. and LIPPINCOTT, R. C., 1980, 'The Politics of Professional Control: The Case of Optometry', in J. ROTH, ed., *Research in the Sociology of Health Care*, Vol. I (JAI Press, Greenwich, Conn.).

BENHAM, L. and BENHAM, A., 1975, 'Regulating Through the Professions: A Perspective on Information Control', *Journal of Law and Economics*, 18, 2 (October), pp. 421–47.

BOND, R. S., KWOKA, J. E. JR., PHELAN, J. J. and WHITTEN, I. T., 1980, *Staff Report on Effects of Restrictions on Advertising and Commercial Practice in the Professions: The Case of Optometry* (U.S. Federal Trade Commission, Washington, D.C.).

COATE, D., 1974, *Studies in the Economics of the Profession of Optometry*, unpublished Ph.D. Dissertation, City University of New York.

COATE, D., 1974, 'The Market for Optometric Services in the United States', Working Paper No. 122, National Bureau of Economic Research, New York.

COX, S. R., DESERPA, A. C. and CANBY, W. C. JR., 1982, 'Consumer Information and the Pricing of Legal Services', *Journal of Industrial Economics*, 30, 3 (March), pp. 305–18.

DEYAK, T. A. and SMITH, V. K., 1976, 'The Economic Value of Statute Reform: The Case of Liberalized Abortion', *Journal of Political Economy*, 84, 1 (February), pp. 83–100.

FELDMAN, R., 1976, *The Supply and Demand for Physicians' Hospital and Office Visits*, unpublished Ph.D. Dissertation, University of Rochester.

FELDMAN, R., 1979, 'Price and Quality Differences in the Physicians' Services Market', *Southern Economic Journal*, 45, 3 (January), pp. 885–91.

FELDMAN, R. and BEGUN, J. W., 1978, 'The Effects of Advertising Restrictions: Lessons from Optometry', *Journal of Human Resources*, 13 (Supplement), pp. 248–62.

FELDMAN, R. and BEGUN, J. W., 1980, 'Does Advertising of Prices Reduce the Mean and Variance of Prices?', *Economic Inquiry*, 18, 3 (July), pp. 487–92.

FRECH, H. E., 1974, 'Occupational Licensure and Health Care Productivity: The Issues and the Literature', in J. RAFFERTY, ed., *Health Manpower and Productivity: The Literature and Required Future Research* (Lexington Books, Lexington, Mass.).

FTC News Summary, June 2, 1978, 2, No. 22 (U.S. Federal Trade Commission, Washington, D.C.).

GOLDMAN, F. and GROSSMAN, M., 1978, 'The Demand for Pediatric Care: An Hedonic Approach', *Journal of Political Economy*, 86, 2, Part 1 (April), pp. 259–80.

HARBERGER, A. C., 1954, 'Monopoly and Resource Allocation', *American Economic Review*, 44, 2 (May), pp. 77–87.

HARBERGER, A. C., 1964, 'The Measurement of Waste', *American Economic Review*, 54, 3 (May), pp. 58–76.

HOROWITZ, I., 1980, 'The Economic Foundations of Self-Regulation in the Professions', in R. D. BLAIR and S. RUBIN, eds., *Regulating the Professions* (D. C. Heath, Lexington, Mass.).

KMENTA, J., 1971, *Elements of Econometrics* (Macmillan, New York).

LEFFLER, K. B., 1978, 'Physician Licensure: Competition and Monopoly in American Medicine', *Journal of Law and Economics*, 21, 1 (April), pp. 165–86.

REINHARDT, U. E., 1975, *Physician Productivity and the Demand for Medical Manpower* (Ballinger, Cambridge, Mass.).

ROSEN, S., 1974, 'Hedonic Prices and Implicit Markets: Product Differentiation in Pure Competition', *Journal of Political Economy*, 82, 1 (January/February), pp. 34–55.

ROTTENBERG, S., ed., 1980, *Occupational Licensure and Regulation* (American Enterprise Institute for Public Policy Research, Washington, D.C.).

SHEPARD, L., 1978, 'Licensing Restrictions and the Cost of Dental Care', *Journal of Law and Economics*, 21, 1 (April), pp. 187–201.

SLOAN, F. A. and LORANT, J. M., 1976, 'The Allocation of Physicians' Services: Evidence on Length-of-Visit', *Quarterly Review of Economics and Business*, 16, 3 (Autumn), pp. 85–103.

STIGLER, G. J., 1971, 'The Theory of Economic Regulation', *Bell Journal of Economics and Management Science*, 2, 1 (Spring), pp. 3–21.

ZELLNER, A., 1962, 'An Efficient Method of Estimating Seemingly Unrelated Regression Equations and Tests for Aggregation Bias', *Journal of the American Statistical Association*, 57, 298 (June), pp. 348–68.

THE JOURNAL OF INDUSTRIAL ECONOMICS 0022-1821 $2.00
Volume XXXIV September 1985 No. 1

PRODUCT COMPETITION IN MICROPROCESSORS*

G. M. P. SWANN

This paper assesses the empirical usefulness of some recent developments in the theory of spatial and product competition, drawing on the history of product competition in microprocessors over the period 1971–81. In particular, a role is found for agglomeration economies in explaining the observed clustering of designs.

INTRODUCTION

THERE HAVE been some striking recent developments in the theory of spatial and product competition, but relatively few empirical studies—see, however, Shaw [1982(a) and (b)]. This paper is an attempt to assess the empirical usefulness of these developments drawing on the history of product competition in microprocessors over the period 1971–81. In particular, our interest centres on attempts to introduce a role for what have been called "agglomeration" economies:[1] that is, mutual external economies accruing to two or more producers selling similar products. In a recent survey, Graitson [1982] suggested that this particular development would provide theoretical models of special empirical relevance, and the evidence presented here, though by no means conclusive, tends to support that view.

The paper is in five parts. Section I gives a brief review of some of the relevant developments in spatial and product competition theory. Section II gives a brief account of how the wide variety of microprocessors will be classified for the purposes of this study. Section III describes the history of developments in microprocessors over the period 1971 to 1981, and section IV assesses the theoretical developments in the light of this evidence. Finally, section V summarises the main points of the paper.

I. SPATIAL AND PRODUCT COMPETITION THEORY

Here we shall briefly review some of the main developments in the theory, outline their predictions for the nature of spatial and product competition, and stress the key assumptions on which these predictions depend.[2]

* Much of the work in this paper was done when the author was at the International Centre for Economics and Related Disciplines at the London School of Economics; financial support from I.C.E.R.D. is gratefully acknowledged. I am indebted to the referee, Meghnad Desai, David Burningham, Tony Horsley, Bob Keyfitz, John Race, Richard Shaw, Tony Shorrocks, and participants in seminars at Brunel and St Andrews for most helpful comments, but they are not responsible for remaining errors.

[1] The term was used by Weber [1929] in his seminal work on industrial location.

[2] This section draws heavily on Keyfitz [1981].

Following the work of Abbott [1955], Gorman [1956], Lancaster [1971], and others, it has been common to think of differentiated products being located at different points in "characteristics" or product space, and for consumer preferences and producer costs to be defined over these characteristics. It is not surprising, therefore, that many economists have thought that models suitable for analysis of geographical location may also be suitable for the analysis of product "location".

The celebrated analysis by Hotelling [1929] refers to a simple duopoly model of pure spatial competition along a linear market. In this model, consumers have inelastic demand but buy from the nearest seller: they are assumed to have no doubt about which is the nearest seller. Sellers are able to relocate freely, and they assume that their rival will not react to any such relocation. Hotelling demonstrated that the model would have a single equilibrium where the two sellers were back to back in the middle of their market. Some writers conjectured that clustering of this sort might prove to be a pervasive equilibrium property of more general spatial models, but subsequent work suggests that the famous result is sensitive to the particular assumptions made.

Extensions to Hotelling's original analysis have been made in several directions. Here we consider the effects of the following features: (a) a greater number of competing firms; (b) location on a plane rather than a line; (c) relaxing the assumption of inelastic demand; (d) introducing seller relocation costs; (e) consumer inability to distinguish between very similar goods; (f) non-zero conjectural variations; and finally (g) "agglomeration" economies, or mutual economies accruing to sellers who locate close to each other.

(a) Lerner and Singer [1937], Eaton and Lipsey [1975], Shaked [1975] and Graitson [1982], *inter alia*, have looked at the question of increasing the number of competing firms. Lerner and Singer showed that when a third firm entered the same linear market, it would locate itself next to the two existing firms so as to sandwich one of them in the middle. This, however, would not be a stable position as the sandwiched firm would be starved of its market share, and would leapfrog into the largest open segment of the market. This process of leapfrogging would continue indefinitely: there is no Nash equilibrium with three firms in a linear market. With four or five firms, there are unique equilibria with clustering; with six or more firms, the equilibria are not unique, but still involve some clustering.

(b) The extension of Hotelling's analysis to location in two dimensional space has proven to be rather difficult. Here, any equilibrium must be robust not only to movements up and down a line, but also to diagonal movements. Indeed, Eaton and Lipsey [1975] and Shaked [1975] found that in many cases equilibrium does not exist or is not unique. Nevertheless, Eaton and Lipsey did find that there was a tendency for clusters to emerge; this occurs especially when firms have open spaces on one side of them, so that there is no loss from moving towards the cluster.

(c) Lerner and Singer [1937] relaxed Hotelling's assumption of inelastic demand, by introducing a reservation price. The outcome now depends on the length of the line and transport costs. The maximum length of each seller's market depends on the size of transport costs in relation to the reservation price. If the line is long enough, both sellers can act as independent monopolists, but if not central clustering will occur.

(d) Hay [1976] extended the analysis to the case where relocation is costly, and firms take a long term view of location. At the planning stage, firms must take into account the probable location decisions of subsequent entrants. Faced with a decision of where to locate on a line between two other firms, the entrant recognises that if it locates beside an existing firm it will leave an attractive wide open space for a subsequent entrant. Hay's model leads to a dispersion of firms.

Hay's paper is important for two reasons: the introduction of relocation costs, and the long term or entry-deterring view of location. Other things being equal, the existence of relocation costs will encourage the firm to locate so as to minimise the risk of enforced relocation. In Hay's paper, competitive entry could force an established firm to relocate, so the firm locates to deter entry, but, as we see below, this is not the only context in which relocation costs may be important.

(e) Devletoglou [1965] examined the question of consumer inability to distinguish between similar products. If a consumer finds himself almost equidistant from the two nearest sellers, his custom might in practice alternate between them in a random way. If the two sellers are located back to back, then all consumers will find there is little to choose between the sellers. If, on the other hand, the two sellers are located well apart, only a relatively small number of consumers will find the two sellers equally satisfactory. Devletoglou argued therefore that a desire to minimise sales uncertainty would encourage sellers to locate apart. This will be especially relevant if there are high relocation costs.

(f) Smithies [1941], and more recently Gannon [1973], Eaton [1972], and others, have examined the matter of non-zero conjectural variations. Smithies suggested that the prospect of rival reaction would prevent a seller moving towards a cluster, but Eaton found that the outcome depends on the length of the market. If the market is short enough, the clustering can survive, but in a wide open market firms locate apart. Gannon found that the outcome with non-zero conjectural variations depends on the elasticity of demand: for given conjectures, clustering can still survive so long as demand is sufficiently inelastic. Nevertheless, when relocation costs are high, firms may be sufficiently keen to avoid the risk of enforced relocation that they locate to minimise the risk of rival reaction.

As Keyfitz [1981] points out, these results—and those mentioned in (c) above—illustrate an essential feature of the Hotelling model. In Hotelling's analysis, the sellers do not perceive any cost in moving toward the cluster.

(g) The final extension is the introduction of agglomeration economies—or mutual economies of adjacent location. Various writers have made reference to them—for example, Nelson [1958], Stahl and Varaiya [1978], Webber [1972]—but, as Graitson [1982] has suggested, there is room for further integration of such agglomeration economies into the models of location discussed above.

In the context of geographical location, these agglomeration economies are of three sorts: (1) the shared infrastructure available to firms locating close to each other—transport, communications, and ease of supply; (2) the informational externality about the density of demand or the technical feasibility of production which accrues to the prospective entrant who sees an established firm trading profitably at a particular location—see Stahl and Varaiya [1978]; (3) the reduction of consumer search costs, beneficial for total market demand—a striking example of this is to be found in the clustering of antique shops.

How do such agglomeration economies operate for location in product space? Particular examples that are found in microprocessors will be discussed in section V; in general it is fairly easy to find examples similar to (1) and (2) above, but examples comparable to (3) are harder to envisage.

(1) "Infrastructure": these are really standardisation economies. A trivial example is that the firm making non-standard sizes of paper may find that the product does not sell because it does not fit into standard envelopes, ring binders, or photocopiers.

(2) Informational externality: one firm's success in producing and selling a particular design demonstrates to the potential entrant the feasibility of production and the strength of demand.

These agglomeration economies are clearly an incentive for clustering. The existence of informational externalities implies that from one point of view location in a cluster is less risky—contrast this with the arguments above. The existence of high relocation costs would again encourage the firm to locate so as to minimise the risk of enforced relocation, but from this point of view that risk is reduced by locating in a cluster.[3] We might conjecture that especially for location in product space, firms locate sufficiently closely (in some dimensions) to benefit from these economies, but differentiate the product in other ways (other dimensions).

To sum up: four main points emerge from this very brief review. Firstly, extending the Hotelling analysis to more sellers and higher dimension spaces introduces difficulties with the uniqueness and sometimes the existence of equilibrium. Nevertheless, the tendency to cluster does not necessarily disappear. Secondly, Hotelling's clustering result does seem to be sensitive to some of the assumptions he makes. In particular, the tendency to cluster can

[3] As Webber [1972, p. 155] puts it, "...the location decisions of uncertain firms are more conservative than those made by certain firms".

TABLE I
CLASSIFICATION OF MICROPROCESSORS

(1) *Bit size:*
4, 8, 12, 16, or 32 bit data bus;
there are also devices with an 8 bit external data bus and 16 bit internal data bus (8/16), and devices with a 16 bit external data bus and a 32 bit internal data bus (16/32).

(2) *Level of integration:*

CPU:	processing logic alone
CPU + RAM:	processing logic plus read and write memory (RAM)
MC − ROM:	processing logic, RAM, and Input/Output circuitry
MC:	a single-chip microcomputer with processing logic, RAM, I/O, and program memory (ROM)
MC + A/D:	an extended single-chip microcomputer with analog to digital circuitry.

(3) *Generation:*

A (first):	the simplest devices in the category
B (second):	improved devices
C (third):	the most advanced devices within the category.

break down when allowance is made for elastic demand, relocation costs, sales uncertainty arising from the consumer's inability to distinguish between close sellers, and non-zero conjectural variations. Thirdly, the existence of agglomeration economies can provide an additional incentive to cluster, not present in Hotelling's analysis. Finally, relocation costs are seen to play a central role in the analysis. If relocation costs are high, firms will locate so as to reduce the risk of enforced relocation. If, for example, rival reaction is seen as the greatest risk, firms locate apart, but if doubts about market demand or technical feasibility are paramount, then firms will cluster.

II. MEASURING THE MICROPROCESSOR

The first microprocessor was introduced in 1971, but because of the very rapid technical change that has taken place, the products that appeared at the end of 1981 give a quite different level of performance. Nevertheless, it is not perhaps too misleading to think of these recent designs as "no more than" much higher quality versions of the earlier devices.

A glance at a comprehensive microprocessor data book—for example, Osborne and Kane [1981]—makes it clear that a large amount of information may be needed fully to describe these devices. Even the more modest data books—for example Bursky [1978]—list at least twenty relevant characteristics. For the purposes of this paper it is essential to concentrate on a small number of parameters, or otherwise it will be difficult to chart and follow product developments.[4] In the end, the classification in Table I has been

[4] Many dimensional cluster analysis could be used, but it is far from clear what would be the appropriate relative weights for discrepancies in different directions.

adopted. It may be rather rough and ready, but it corresponds quite closely to classifications used in the trade press. It is reasonably satisfactory for describing developments up to the end of 1981, but it would not do for some of the more recent developments.

The "bit size" refers to the size of the data bus; this is an indication of the processing power of the device. The "level of integration" describes the number of computer features incorporated into the one device. The term, "generation", is an essentially subjective[5] measure of the status of the device within its "bit size"/"level of integration" category.

Within any category there may be considerable difference between products. For example, within the "8/16 bit, processor logic only" category come four products: the Intel 8088, the Texas Instruments 9980, the Motorola 6809, and the Zilog Z800. While most technical writers would agree that these are similar products, they are certainly not identical, and not really minimally differentiated[6]—see Whitworth [1979] [1980] and *Electronics* [19th May 1981, p. 62]. Nevertheless, the classification is probably the most useful three-way classification available, and as mentioned before it is widely used.[7]

III. DEVELOPMENTS IN MICROPROCESSORS, 1971–81

Over this period, some twenty-two firms have produced and sold their own microprocessors. These are not, however, the only microprocessors that are sold. In microelectronics, there is a widespread practice of producing "second source" products: these are (almost) identical copies of another manufacturer's design. The production of these copies may or may not be authorised by the original designer.

Table II lists the main microprocessor producers who between them account for the greater part of the world market.[8] Six firms have made at least five products of their own design, while a further sixteen have produced one or two designs of their own. Some of these firms have also produced a significant number of second source products, while a further sixteen have produced one or more second source products, but no designs of their own. Between 1971 and 1981, 203 separate products have been introduced, of which 69 are original designs, while 134 are second source products;[9] in short, almost two thirds are second source products.

The production of second source products is a clear case of clustering; it is,

[5] I am grateful to Richard Kaczynski for helpful discussions on the relative merits of various microprocessors.

[6] Such a classification may, therefore, bias the results towards clustering.

[7] Another method of measuring the microprocessor is the benchmark test—see Penney [1977].

[8] The data sources are American and British, and will to some extent understate the contribution of Japanese companies, especially in the last few years.

[9] The precise number depends on the definition adopted: here, extensive families of similar designs have been reduced to a few key members.

TABLE II
MICROPROCESSORS PRODUCED BY PRINCIPAL MANUFACTURERS
1971–81

	Manufacturer	Own Design Products	Second Source Products
A	Intel	12	0
B	National Semiconductor	9	7
C	Texas Instruments	9	1
D	Motorola	7	5
E	Rockwell	5	2
F	Zilog	5	0
G	AMI	2	12
H	NEC	2	9
I	Fairchild	2	8
J	Mostek	2	3
K	Toshiba	2	1
L	General Instruments	2	0
M	Fujitsu	1	7
N	Hitachi	1	7
O	Signetics	1	7
P	Intersil	1	5
Q	Bell Labs.	1	0
R	Data General	1	0
S	Electronic Arrays	1	0
T	Hewlett Packard	1	0
U	MOS	1	0
V	RCA	1	0
—	AMD	0	12
—	Siemens	0	8
—	Harris	0	7
—	Mitsubishi	0	7
—	SGS-ATES	0	6
—	ITT	0	4
—	AEG Telefunken	0	3
—	Matra-Harris	0	2
—	Philips	0	2
—	Plessey	0	2
—	Sharp	0	2
—	Marconi	0	1
—	Mitel	0	1
—	NCR	0	1
—	Sescosem	0	1
—	Thomson CSF	0	1
	Total	69	134

Sources: Bursky [1978], *Electronics* [1971–82], *Microprocessors and Microsystems* [1979–82], Osborne and Kane [1981], Webbink [1977].

however, a rather special case, as some particularly important agglomeration economies operate here that do not apply to own design products. For this reason, we discuss the development of own design and second source products separately.

The history of own design product developments is described in Table III. For each year the table presents the cumulative picture at the end of the year, where all components introduced to that date are left in the sample.[10] The components are labelled A to V according to the manufacturer, as in Table II; the capital letters represent new designs introduced during that year, while the lower case letters represent products introduced before that year.

The early developments (1971–74) were almost entirely in the "CPU only" category. The earliest microprocessors were "first generation" four and eight bit designs, but twelve bit and some sixteen bit designs appeared soon after. By the end of 1974, the most striking cluster is in the second generation 8 bit, CPU only category, where 5 of the 13 devices are located. The only product outside the CPU only category is the Texas Instruments TMS 1000, a four bit single chip microcomputer.

From 1975 to 1977 there are further additions to the eight bit CPU only category, and a few further developments in the second generation sixteen bit category, but the most important development is the emergence of components with higher levels of integration than CPU only. Of particular importance are the four and eight bit single chip microcomputer categories.

In 1978 and 1979 many new designs are clustered in the eight bit microcomputer category (second and third generation), but perhaps the most important development is the appearance of the third generation sixteen bit CPU, as well as the eight/sixteen bit category. One outlier which still stands alone at the end of 1981, is a sixteen bit single chip microcomputer (Texas Instruments TMS 9940).

Finally, in 1980 and 1981, the most interesting developments are in the third generation sixteen bit, CPU only category, and the sixteen/thirty-two and thirty-two bit categories.

How much evidence of clustering is there? Inspection of Table III certainly suggests that products are not randomly scattered in product space. The cumulative picture at the end of 1981 can be described by a "μ" shape: all but three of the sixty-nine designs fall within the "CPU only" category, the eight bit categories, and the four bit single-chip microcomputer category (with or without analog to digital features).

The initial impression is that clustering is quite important, although we do not attempt a formal test here.[11] Indeed, the drift towards the bottom right-hand corner in the table—a result of technical progress—makes for a wider dispersion of products than would otherwise be observed.

Nevertheless, it could be argued that "clustering" is observed simply because the product locations that remain empty represent impossible or

[10] It has often been difficult to establish the dates at which manufacturers stop active marketing of an old design, and even then the product will still be sold to serve replacement demand.

[11] An appropriate test is described in Swann [1986]; the results there suggest a very strong clustering tendency.

TABLE III
PRODUCT LOCATION HISTORY

1971/72

	CPU	*CPU+RAM*	*MC−ROM*	*MC*	*MC+A/D*
4A	A	.	.	.	.
4B	.	.	.	.	.
4C	.	.	.	.	.
8A	A	.	.	.	.
8B	.	.	.	.	.
8C	.	.	.	.	.
12A	.	.	.	.	.
8/16	.	.	.	.	.
16A	.	.	.	.	.
16B	.	.	.	.	.
16C	.	.	.	.	.
16/32	.	.	.	.	.
32A	.	.	.	.	.

1973

	CPU	*CPU+RAM*	*MC−ROM*	*MC*	*MC+A/D*
4A	a	.	.	C	.
4B	E	.	.	.	.
4C	.	.	.	.	.
8A	a	.	.	.	.
8B	A	.	.	.	.
8C	.	.	.	.	.
12A	K	.	.	.	.
8/16	.	.	.	.	.
16A	.	.	.	.	.
16B	.	.	.	.	.
16C	.	.	.	.	.
16/32	.	.	.	.	.
32A	.	.	.	.	.

1974

	CPU	*CPU+RAM*	*MC−ROM*	*MC*	*MC+A/D*
4A	a	.	.	c	.
4B	eA	.	.	.	.
4C	.	.	.	.	.
8A	a	.	.	.	.
8B	aDEOV	.	.	.	.
8C	.	.	.	.	.
12A	k	.	.	.	.
8/16	.	.	.	.	.
16A	BL	.	.	.	.
16B	.	.	.	.	.
16C	.	.	.	.	.
16/32	.	.	.	.	.
32A	.	.	.	.	.

TABLE III—*continued*

1975

	CPU	*CPU+RAM*	*MC−ROM*	*MC*	*MC+A/D*
4A	a	.	.	c	.
4B	ea	.	.	E	.
4C	.	.	.	.	.
8A	a	.	.	.	.
8B	adeovBU	.	I	.	.
8C	.	.	.	.	.
12A	kP	.	.	.	.
8/16	.	.	.	.	.
16A	bl	.	.	.	.
16B	.	.	.	.	.
16C	.	.	.	.	.
16/32	.	.	.	.	.
32A	.	.	.	.	.

1976

	CPU	*CPU+RAM*	*MC−ROM*	*MC*	*MC+A/D*
4A	a	.	.	c	.
4B	ea	.	.	eB	.
4C	.	.	.	.	.
8A	a	.	.	.	.
8B	adeovbu	S	iA	AEL	.
8C	F	.	.	.	.
12A	kp	.	.	.	.
8/16	.	.	.	.	.
16A	bl	.	.	.	.
16B	C	.	.	.	.
16C	.	.	.	.	.
16/32	.	.	.	.	.
32A	.	.	.	.	.

1977

	CPU	*CPU+RAM*	*MC−ROM*	*MC*	*MC+A/D*
4A	a	.	.	c	.
4B	ea	.	.	ebGH	.
4C	.	.	.	.	.
8A	a	.	.	.	.
8B	adeovbu	sD	ia	aelJ	.
8C	fA	.	.	.	.
12A	kp	.	.	.	.
8/16	C	.	.	.	.
16A	bl	.	.	.	.
16B	cIR	.	.	.	.
16C	.	.	.	.	.
16/32	.	.	.	.	.
32A	.	.	.	.	.

TABLE III—*continued*

1978

	CPU	*CPU+RAM*	*MC−ROM*	*MC*	*MC+A/D*
4A	a	.	.	c	.
4B	ea	.	.	ebgh	.
4C	.	.	.	.	.
8A	a	.	.	.	.
8B	adeovbu	sd	ia	aeljA	A
8C	fa	.	.	J	.
12A	kp	.	.	.	.
8/16	cAC	.	.	.	.
16A	blB	.	.	.	.
16B	cir	.	.	C	.
16C	A	.	.	.	.
16/32	.	.	.	.	.
32A	.	.	.	.	.

1979

	CPU	*CPU+RAM*	*MC−ROM*	*MC*	*MC+A/D*
4A	a	.	.	c	.
4B	ea	.	.	ebgh	.
4C	.	.	.	.	.
8A	a	.	.	.	.
8B	adeovbu	sd	ia	aeljaD	a
8C	fa	.	D	jDFH	.
12A	kp	.	.	.	.
8/16	cacD	.	.	.	.
16A	blb	.	.	.	.
16B	cir	.	.	c	.
16C	aF	.	.	.	.
16/32	.	.	.	.	.
32A	.	.	.	.	.

1980

	CPU	*CPU+RAM*	*MC−ROM*	*MC*	*MC+A/D*
4A	a	.	.	c	.
4B	ea	.	.	ebgh	.
4C	.	.	.	.	.
8A	a	.	.	.	.
8B	adeovbu	sd	ia	aeljadB	a
8C	faB	.	dB	jdfhB	.
12A	kp	.	.	.	.
8/16	cacd	.	.	.	.
16A	blb	.	.	.	.
16B	cir	.	.	c	.
16C	afFK	.	.	.	.
16/32	D	.	.	.	.
32A	.	.	.	.	.

TABLE III—*continued*

	1981				
	CPU	*CPU+RAM*	*MC−ROM*	*MC*	*MC+A/D*
4A	a	.	.	c	.
4B	ea	.	.	ebgh	.
4C	.	.	.	.	CG
8A	a	.	.	.	.
8B	adeovbu	sd	ia	aeljadb	a
8C	fab	.	db	jdfhbCN	.
12A	kp	.	.	.	.
8/16	cacdF	.	.	.	.
16A	blb	.	.	.	.
16B	cir	.	C	c	.
16C	affkEM	C	.	.	.
16/32	dB	.	.	.	.
32A	AQT	.	.	.	.

Sources: See Table II.

unsuitable products, or alternatively products for which there would be little demand. Unfortunately, we do not have the evidence with which to endorse or refute this view. The sales data we have are for much broader categories than those used here. Moreover, we have no data on sales for the sparsely populated categories, and obviously there are no sales for the empty categories. Besides, there are undoubtedly problems of interpretation: sales data cannot express potential demand for non-existent products.

While there are obvious dangers in interpreting any non-uniformity in dispersion as "clustering", our view on balance is that the observed pattern should be interpreted in this way. All the categories in Table III represent possible and suitable products in the sense that they could be made (given a sufficiently advanced technology) and sold.

As the overall picture was a little inconclusive, it is worth looking more closely at the product strategies of individual firms. Does a particular firm tend to move towards its rival (a symptom of clustering)? Alternatively, does it tend to move away into less densely populated categories? According to Table II, the six main producers of own designed microprocessors are Intel (A), National Semiconductor (B), Texas Instruments (C), Motorola (D), Rockwell (E) and Zilog (F). Table IV describes the sequence of locations for these six companies.

Intel are the acknowledged market leader, not only in the sense of being first to locate in many of the categories that have subsequently become important clusters, but also in the sense of attracting the greatest number of second source copies—see below. Throughout the period, their strategy has been one of steadily improving the product, whether in terms of higher bit sizes, higher levels of integration, or a higher "generation" product.

In terms of the crude categories used in this paper, Motorola, Zilog and

TABLE IV
PRODUCT LOCATION SEQUENCES FOR 6
MAJOR MICROPROCESSOR MANUFACTURERS

Intel (A)

	CPU	*CPU+RAM*	*MC−ROM*	*MC*	*MC+A/D*
4A	71	.	.	.	.
4B	74	.	.	.	.
4C	.	.	.	.	.
8A	71	.	.	.	.
8B	73	.	76	76, 78	78
8C	77	.	.	.	.
12A	.	.	.	.	.
8/16	78	.	.	.	.
16A	.	.	.	.	.
16B	.	.	.	.	.
16C	78	.	.	.	.
16/32	.	.	.	.	.
32A	81	.	.	.	.

National Semiconductor (B)

	CPU	*CPU+RAM*	*MC−ROM*	*MC*	*MC+A/D*
4A	.	.	.	.	.
4B	.	.	.	76	.
4C	.	.	.	.	.
8A	.	.	.	.	.
8B	75	.	.	80	.
8C	80	.	80	80	.
12A	.	.	.	.	.
8/16	.	.	.	.	.
16A	74, 78	.	.	.	.
16B	.	.	.	.	.
16C	.	.	.	.	.
16/32	81	.	.	.	.
32A	.	.	.	.	.

Texas Instruments (C)

	CPU	*CPU+RAM*	*MC−ROM*	*MC*	*MC+A/D*
4A	.	.	.	73	.
4B	.	.	.	.	.
4C	.	.	.	.	81
8A	.	.	.	.	.
8B	.	.	.	.	.
8C	.	.	.	81	.
12A	.	.	.	.	.
8/16	77, 78	.	.	.	.
16A	.	.	.	.	.
16B	76	.	81	78	.
16C	.	81	.	.	.
16/32	.	.	.	.	.
32A	.	.	.	.	.

TABLE IV—*continued*

Motorola (D)					
	CPU	*CPU+RAM*	*MC−ROM*	*MC*	*MC+A/D*
4A	.	.	.	.	.
4B	.	.	.	.	.
4C	.	.	.	.	.
8A	.	.	.	.	.
8B	74	77	.	79	.
8C	.	.	79	79	.
12A	.	.	.	.	.
8/16	79	.	.	.	.
16A	.	.	.	.	.
16B	.	.	.	.	.
16C	.	.	.	.	.
16/32	80	.	.	.	.
32A	.	.	.	.	.

Rockwell (E)					
	CPU	*CPU+RAM*	*MC−ROM*	*MC*	*MC+A/D*
4A	.	.	.	.	.
4B	73	.	.	75	.
4C	.	.	.	.	.
8A	.	.	.	.	.
8B	74	.	.	76	.
8C	.	.	.	.	.
12A	.	.	.	.	.
8/16	.	.	.	.	.
16A	.	.	.	.	.
16B	.	.	.	.	.
16C	81	.	.	.	.
16/32	.	.	.	.	.
32A	.	.	.	.	.

Zilog (F)					
	CPU	*CPU+RAM*	*MC−ROM*	*MC*	*MC+A/D*
4A	.	.	.	.	.
4B	.	.	.	.	.
4C	.	.	.	.	.
8A	.	.	.	.	.
8B	.	.	.	.	.
8C	76	.	.	79	.
12A	.	.	.	.	.
8/16	81	.	.	.	.
16A	.	.	.	.	.
16B	.	.	.	.	.
16C	79, 80	.	.	.	.
16/32	.	.	.	.	.
32A	.	.	.	.	.

Sources: See Table II.

Rockwell can be said to have followed Intel's lead,[12] and the same is true of most other producers, except for National Semiconductor and Texas Instruments.

National Semiconductor's product profile fits into the "μ" shape mentioned above, but the sequence they follow is a little unusual. They have located in (mostly) the same categories as Intel, but the sequence has been sufficiently different that they cannot really be called a follower.

Texas Instruments' product strategy has been the most unusual. Unlike National Semiconductor, and unlike the other main manufacturers, their product profile does not fit into the "μ" shape. Moreover, it could not be said that they follow the product leader, Intel. Indeed, Texas Instruments' strategy seems to have been to locate as far away from Intel as possible.

It remains finally to say something about the production of second source microprocessors. Table V presents the most important second source activity. Of the 134 second source products introduced over the period, 115 are copies of products originally designed by five companies: Intel, Motorola, Texas Instruments, Zilog, and Mostek. The table shows which manufacturers have produced second source versions of which products. The categories used are broader than those in Tables III and IV: "mp" refers to CPU only and CPU plus RAM, while "mc" refers to MC less ROM, MC and MC plus A/D.

Two points should be made. First, the designs of Intel and Motorola have attracted the greatest number of second sources: 62 and 29 products respectively. Zilog (11 products), Texas (7 products) and Mostek (6 products) are less important.

Secondly, within any product category, a second source is unlikely to copy the products of more than one original manufacturer. There are four exceptions to this—AMD, AMI, NEC, SGS-ATES—but there is a special reason in each case.[13] It is not unusual, however, to find a second source copying the eight bit designs of one manufacturer and the sixteen bit designs of another.

IV. IMPLICATIONS FOR PRODUCT COMPETITION THEORY

In this section, we attempt to draw out the implications of the history of developments in microprocessors for the empirical value of product competition theory.

First, let us examine the strategy of second source production. This is a clear case of clustering, albeit a rather special one. Any model predicting the absence of clustering cannot therefore be fully appropriate for the analysis of all aspects of product competition in microprocessors. Is this an indication that the extensions discussed in section I which predict dispersion are irrelevant here? We shall argue that they are by no means irrelevant, but rather

[12] While they have undoubtedly made some important innovations of their own.
[13] These are discussed in Swann [1986].

TABLE V
SECOND SOURCE PRODUCTS

Second Source	Intel				Motorola				Texas			Zilog			Mostek	Total
	8mp	*8mc*	*8/16*	*16*	*8mp*	*8mc*	*8/16*	*16*	*8/16*	*16mp*	*16mc*	*8mp*	*8mc*	*16*	*8mc*	
AMD	2	4	1	1	.	.	.	.	.	.	.	1	1	1	.	11
AMI	.	.	.	.	2	3	1	.	2	1	1	.	.	.	.	10
NEC	2	4	1	1	.	.	.	.	.	.	.	1	.	.	.	9
Fairchild	.	.	.	.	2	3	1	.	.	.	.	.	.	.	2	8
Mitsubishi	2	4	1	1	.	.	.	.	.	.	.	.	.	.	.	8
Siemens	2	4	1	1	.	.	.	.	.	.	.	.	.	.	.	8
Fujitsu	.	4	1	1	1	.	.	.	.	.	.	.	.	.	.	7
Hitachi	.	.	.	.	2	3	1	1	.	.	.	.	.	.	.	7
Harris	.	4	1	1	.	.	.	.	.	.	.	.	.	.	.	6
Signetics	1	4	.	.	.	.	.	1	.	.	.	.	.	.	.	6
National	1	4	.	.	.	.	.	.	.	.	.	.	.	.	.	5
SGS-ATES	.	.	.	.	.	.	.	.	.	.	.	1	1	1	2	5
Intersil	.	4	.	.	.	.	.	.	.	.	.	.	.	.	.	4
ITT	.	.	.	.	.	.	.	.	1	1	1	.	.	.	.	3
Matra-Harris	.	.	1	1	.	.	.	.	.	.	.	.	.	.	.	2
Mostek	.	.	.	.	.	.	.	1	.	.	.	1	.	.	.	2
Motorola	.	.	.	.	.	.	.	.	.	.	.	.	.	.	2	2
Philips	1	.	.	.	.	.	.	1	.	.	.	.	.	.	.	2
Sharp	.	.	.	.	.	.	.	.	.	.	.	1	1	.	.	2
Marconi	.	.	.	.	1	.	.	.	.	.	.	.	.	.	.	1
Mitel	.	.	.	.	1	.	.	.	.	.	.	.	.	.	.	1
NCR	.	.	.	.	.	.	.	1	.	.	.	.	.	.	.	1
Plessey	.	.	.	.	1	.	.	.	.	.	.	.	.	.	.	1
Sescosem	.	.	.	.	1	.	.	.	.	.	.	.	.	.	.	1
Texas	1	.	.	.	.	.	.	.	.	.	.	.	.	.	.	1
Thomson-CSF	.	.	.	.	1	.	.	.	.	.	.	.	.	.	.	1
Toshiba	.	.	.	.	.	.	.	.	.	.	.	.	.	1	.	1
Total	12	36	7	7	12	9	3	5	3	2	2	5	3	3	6	115

Sources: As Table II, plus Sciberras [1977] and Wilson, Ashton and Egan [1980].

that they are incomplete if they do not take account of agglomeration economies.

The demand for microprocessors is certainly not inelastic to product characteristics. Likewise, relocation costs are not negligible, although the costs involved in copying another device are much less than the costs involved in designing a new product. Even so, it is interesting to observe that second sources rarely copy the products of more than one manufacturer in a particular category. Consumers are usually unable to find any important differences between the second source product and the original product. There is no brand loyalty to the second source, and so the sales of the second source product may be volatile.

The nature of conjectural variations is a little uncertain, essentially because microprocessor manufacturers have a somewhat ambivalent attitude to those who produce second source copies of their products. Some manufacturers have strongly discouraged any second source production, resorting to law suits if necessary. Others actively encourage a small number of authorised second sources, and tolerate some unauthorised second sources. The reason is that while the second source product will inevitably compete with the original product, and often at a lower price, the existence of a second source has been seen to convey some benefits to the original producer.[14]

The importance of agglomeration economies for the second source is quite evident. Firstly, he can economise on the otherwise substantial design and development costs. Secondly, he has much lower technical uncertainty as the original producer has already shown that the product is technically feasible. Thirdly, part of his market uncertainty is reduced as the success of the original product demonstrates the strong demand for the product. For these two reasons, second source production is seen to be relatively free of risks. Finally, there are the substantial externalities that accrue from producing a standard product: for example, the existence of support devices, development systems and software produced by the original manufacturer, or indeed another second source.

Next we consider the implications of the observed pattern of product competition in own design microprocessors. While there was some doubt about whether the observed pattern represented clustering, we saw that many firms had a strong tendency to follow the leader. Not only did they locate in the same categories as the leader, but their products were introduced in the same sequence as the leader's. It seems fairly reasonable to interpret this as a tendency to cluster. Nevertheless, this tendency was not observed for all firms. For one firm, National Semiconductor, the locations were more or less the same as the leader, but the sequence was not, while for another, Texas Instruments, neither the locations nor the sequence coincide.

[14] On this see: Osborne and Kane [1981]—the chapter on the 8080; Wilson, Ashton and Egan [1980, Chapter 4]; *Electronics* [15 May, 1975, p. 74 and 15 March, 1979, p. 56].

The observed clustering has the same implications as before for the theory discussed in section I. Once again, we would not argue that this makes the extensions which predict dispersion irrelevant, but rather that there are sufficient agglomeration economies to ensure clustering. The demand is clearly not inelastic, and relocation costs are much higher for the design of a new product than for the copying of a new product.[15] There is an element of brand loyalty here, so that even if the products of two manufacturers are similar, the repeat buyer will not switch from one product to another in a random fashion. For this reason, the argument that clustering promotes sales uncertainty is somewhat less relevant. On the other hand, the prospect of rival reaction seems more likely. The incidental benefits that arise from having a second source do not apply when the producer has a close rival producing a similar but differentiated product.

Agglomeration economies remain important, although some of the special economies that applied to the second source product do not apply here. The agglomeration economies are essentially of two types: "infrastructure" and informational externalities. There are "infrastructure" advantages to producing a conventional product because, for example, some general purpose support devices can be used by any microprocessor conforming to certain design conventions, and memory components are widely available for a four, eight or sixteen bit bus, but not so easily for unconventional sizes. In a few cases, firms have designed their products so that they can run software originally intended for other devices, a considerable "infrastructure" economy. Barron and Curnow [1979, Chapter 5] discuss other examples.

The informational externalities were mentioned before in the context of second source production, and they are also important here. The greater initial success of the eight bit microprocessors (especially the 8080 and 6800) than the sixteen bit designs led some entrant firms to revise their estimates of the relative sizes of the eight bit and sixteen bit markets. Moreover, some would argue (for example, Barron and Curnow [1979, pp. 69–70]) that the true importance of the microprocessor as an innovation was not simply producing a miniature computer—which was by no means a new idea—but rather in demonstrating that small computers could be used for all sorts of applications never before thought of. In this sense, the success of the early products conveyed an informational externality to prospective entrants.

For a product subject to such rapid technical change, moreover, there are informational externalities about technical feasibility of production. Perhaps the most important is what engineers in the industry call "coming down the learning curve together". Those who make the same product as other producers are in a position to exchange technical information. It might be thought that such information would be a jealously guarded secret, and in principle it might be. In practice, however, there has been a high degree of

[15] There is an additional relocation cost: firms who discontinue a line will lose the goodwill of existing users who require replacements.

cross-fertilisation, chiefly as a result of the close geographical location of many of the main U.S. manufacturers, and the high staff mobility. It is evident from some of the law suits that have attempted to stop such cross-fertilisation that it is information from firms making similar products that is especially valuable.[16] Given that cross-fertilisation is a fact of life in the industry, it is least risky for the manufacturer to locate in a position (both geographically and in product space) where he can benefit.[17]

The predominant tendency for firms to cluster can then be explained in at least two ways:

(1) firms are risk averse and find the risks of clustering less serious than the risks of isolation;

(2) they are not particularly risk averse and are encouraged to cluster by the forces at work in the unmodified Hotelling model.

In view of the arguments above, we incline towards the first explanation.

What, though, of the two firms who have not shown this tendency to cluster? A variety of explanations might be offered, for example:

(1) they are risk averse but they perceive the risks of clustering to be greater than the risks of isolation (so they conform to some of the extensions to the Hotelling model mentioned in section I);

(2) they are not particularly risk averse, and although they consider that the risks of isolation may exceed the risks of clustering, they realise that demand is elastic with regard to characteristics, and find the potential rewards to radical innovation decisive.

The first explanation has its virtues, but we incline to the second interpretation. Both these firms, but especially Texas Instruments, have a reputation for competitive or even aggressive pricing—see Sciberras [1977, Chapter 5]. A risk averse firm would surely prefer to avoid such intense price competition. Moreover, Texas Instruments have produced only one second source product; as we saw, the second source strategy is particularly suitable for the risk averse firm.

V. SUMMARY AND CONCLUSION

In this paper we have attempted to assess the empirical usefulness of certain aspects of spatial and product competition theory by drawing on the history of product competition in microprocessors over the period 1971 to 1981. The original model of Hotelling predicted that firms would cluster together, but when allowance is made for elastic demand, seller relocation costs, competitive entry or rival reaction, the model does not necessarily predict clustering.

[16] For examples, see *Electronics*, [13 November, 1975, p. 38, and 25 December, 1975, p. 37].

[17] This might be by formal technology exchange pact or by more informal arrangements—see Webbink [1977, Chapter 4B], and Braun and MacDonald [1978, Chapter 9, especially p. 129 ff.].

On the other hand, the introduction of "agglomeration" economies (or mutual economies accruing to firms that locate close to each other) can provide an added incentive for clustering. The history of developments in microprocessors over the period shows two types of clustering: first, the practice of second source production (or copying established designs); and second, a marked, though not uniform tendency for producers to cluster in their own designs. We argue that these findings do not make models which predict product dispersion irrelevant; rather we argue that such models are incomplete for the analysis of product competition in this industry if they do not give a role to agglomeration economies.

G. M. P. SWANN
ACCEPTED JULY 1984
Centre for European Industrial Studies,
University of Bath,
Claverton Down,
Bath BA2 7AY

REFERENCES

ABBOTT, L., 1955, *Quality and Competition* (Columbia University Press, New York).
BARRON, I. and CURNOW, R., 1979, *The Future with Microelectronics* (Frances Pinter, London).
BRAUN, E. and MACDONALD, S., 1978, *Revolution in Miniature: The History and Impact of Semiconductor Electronics* (Cambridge University Press, Cambridge).
BURSKY, D., 1978, *Microprocessor Data Manual* (Hayden, Rochelle Park, New Jersey).
DEVLETOGLOU, N. E., 1965, 'A Dissenting View of Duopoly and Spatial Competition', *Economica*, XXXII, 2 (May), pp. 140–60.
EATON, B. C., 1972, 'Spatial Competition Revisited', *Canadian Journal of Economics*, V, 2 (May), pp. 268–77.
EATON, B. C. and LIPSEY, R. G., 1975, 'The Principle of Minimum Differentiation Reconsidered: Some New Developments in the Theory of Spatial Competition', *Review of Economic Studies*, XLII, 1 (January), pp. 27–49.
Electronics, Selected Issues, XLIV–LV (1971–82).
GANNON, C. A., 1973, 'Central Concentration in Simple Spatial Duopoly: Some Behavioural and Functional Conditions', *Journal of Regional Science*, XIII, 3 (December), pp. 357–75.
GORMAN, W. M., 1956, 'A Possible Procedure for Analysing Quality Differentials in the Egg Market', *Iowa Agricultural Experiment Station*, Journal Paper J-3129 (November). Reprinted in *Review of Economic Studies*, XLVII (1980), 5 (October), pp. 843–56.
GRAITSON, D., 1982, 'Spatial Competition a la Hotelling: A Selective Survey', *Journal of Industrial Economics*, XXXI, 1/2 (September/December), pp. 13–25.
HAY, D., 1976, 'Sequential Entry and Entry Deterring Strategies in Spatial Competition', *Oxford Economic Papers*, XXVIII, 2 (July), pp. 240–57.
HOTELLING, H., 1929, 'Stability in Competition', *Economic Journal*, XXXIX, 1 (March), pp. 41–57.
KEYFITZ, R., 1981, 'A Selective Survey of Spatial Economic Theory', unpublished Paper, *London School of Economics*.
LANCASTER, K. J., 1971, *Consumer Demand: A New Approach* (Columbia University Press, New York).

LERNER, A. and SINGER, H., 1937, 'Some Notes on Duopoly and Spatial Competition', *Journal of Political Economy*, XLV, 2 (April), pp. 145–86.

Microprocessors and Microsystems, Selected Issues, III–VI (1979–82).

NELSON, R. L., 1958, *The Selection of Retail Locations* (F. W. Dodge, New York).

OSBORNE, A. and KANE, G., 1981, *4 and 8 bit Microprocessor Handbook* and *16 Bit Microprocessor Handbook* (Osborne/McGraw Hill, Berkeley, California).

PENNEY, B. K., 1977, 'The Implications of Microprocessor Architecture on Speed, Programming and Memory Size', *Proceedings of the Institution of Electronic and Radio Engineers Conference (no. 36): Computer Systems and Technology* (Institution of Electronic and Radio Engineers).

SCIBERRAS, E., 1977, *Multinational Electronics Companies* (JAI Press, Greenwich, Connecticut).

SHAKED, A., 1975, 'Non-Existence of Equilibrium for the Two-Dimensional Three Firms Location Problem', *Review of Economic Studies*, XLII, 1 (January), pp. 51–56.

SHAW, R. W., 1982(a), 'Product Proliferation in Characteristics Space: The U.K. Fertiliser Industry', *Journal of Industrial Economics*, XXXI, 1/2 (September/ December), pp. 69–91.

SHAW, R. W., 1982(b), 'Product Strategy and Size of Firm in the U.K. Fertiliser Market', *Managerial and Decision Economics*, III, 4 (December), pp. 233–43.

SMITHIES, A., 1941, 'Optimum Location in Spatial Competition', *Journal of Political Economy*, XLIX, 3 (June), pp. 423–39.

STAHL, K. and VARAIYA, P., 1978, 'Economics of Information: Examples in Location and Land-Use Theory', *Regional Science and Urban Economics*, VIII, 1 (February), pp. 43–56.

SWANN, G. M. P., forthcoming 1986, *Quality Innovation: An Economic Analysis of Rapid Improvements in Microelectronic Components* (Francis Pinter Publishers, London).

WEBBER, M. J., 1972, *Impact of Uncertainty on Location* (MIT Press, Cambridge, Mass.).

WEBBINK, D. W., 1977, *The Semiconductor Industry: A Survey of Structure, Conduct and Performance* (U.S. Federal Trade Commission Staff Report, Government Printing Office, Washington D.C.).

WEBER, A., 1929, *Theory of the Location of Industry*, translated by C. J. Friedrich (University of Chicago Press, Chicago).

WHITWORTH, I., 1979, 'Review of Microprocessor Architecture', *Microprocessors and Microsystems*, III, 1 (January/February), pp. 21–28.

WHITWORTH, I., 1980, 'Developments in 16 Bit Microprocessors', *Microprocessors and Microsystems*, IV, 1 (January/February), pp. 17–22.

WILSON, R. W., ASHTON, P. K. and EGAN, T. P., 1980, *Innovation, Competition and Government Policy in the Semiconductor Industry* (Lexington Books, D. C. Heath, Lexington, Mass.).

THE JOURNAL OF INDUSTRIAL ECONOMICS 0022-1821 $2.00
Volume XXXIV September 1985 No. 1

SPECIFYING THE DYNAMICS OF INDUSTRY CONCENTRATION*

DAVID LEVY

Previous studies generally explain changes in concentration by its initial determinants or by changes in its determinants. Little attention is paid to the dynamic structure of the model. This study provides a framework to sort out adjustment effects in a systematic manner. The empirical model distinguishes long-term from short-term effects and estimates the rate of adjustment when concentration deviates from its long-term equilibrium level.

I. INTRODUCTION

CONSIDERABLE attention has focused on industry concentration as a key element of market structure. While earlier empirical studies examined determinants of the level of industry concentration, a more recent literature focuses on changes in concentration.[1] These more recent papers typically explain intertemporal *changes* in concentration by the past *levels* of industry growth, concentration, advertising intensity and minimum efficient plant size. However, the dynamic relationship between changes in concentration and the levels of the independent variables has not been explicitly specified.

Caves and Porter [1980] have argued that explaining changes in concentration by past levels of market structure variables is tantamount to assuming that the sampled industries are in the process of adjusting to a disequilibrium situation. As an alternative, they adopt a "long-term equilibrium" approach, whereby changes in concentration are explained by lagged changes in the relevant market conditions. They find that this approach "as a whole was unsuccessful, exhibiting low levels of significance and a lack of robustness when the cross-section regressions were shifted to different time periods" [p. 14].

While Caves and Porter allow for adjustments to occur with a lag, they still assume that all adjustments take place during the period in which changes in concentration are measured. They do not directly test the assumption of complete adjustment even though it may not hold. Indeed, adjustment may be quite slow if oligopolists adopt pricing strategies which lead to gradual adjustment over time (see, for example, Gaskins [1971]) or if markets adjust

* I would like to thank the Research Council of Rutgers for their financial support and the Research Program in Competition and Business Policy, U.C.L.A., directed by J. Fred Weston, for generously providing data. I would also like to thank P. Asch, K. Chung, D. Golbe, J. Scheraga, an anonymous referee and the editors for comments on previous drafts of this paper. The author alone is responsible for any remaining errors.

[1] For a recent review of these studies, see Curry and George [1983].

slowly due to higher costs of rapid adjustment (see, for example, Lucas [1967]). Failure to account for incomplete adjustments may explain the poor performance of Caves and Porter's model.[2]

The purpose of this paper is to develop and test a model of concentration which addresses the issue of incomplete adjustments of industry concentration. The empirical model distinguishes long-term from short-term effects and estimates the rate of adjustment when concentration deviates from its long-term equilibrium level. In developing the model tested in this paper, the dynamic structure inherent in previous analyses is made explicit.

A long-run equilibrium model is presented in section II, the arguments for a gradual adjustment process are examined in section III, the model incorporating gradual adjustment is developed in section IV and empirical results are reported in section V. A summary and conclusions are found in the final section.

II. A LONG-RUN EQUILIBRIUM MODEL OF CONCENTRATION

Before examining the dynamics of concentration, it is useful to present a model explaining the long-run level of concentration across industries. In empirical studies, concentration is generally explained by scale economies and entry barrier determinants.[3] According to scale economy explanations, the level of concentration depends on such variables as production economies, capital economies and advertising economies. Explanatory variables suggested by entry barrier explanations are production economies, capital requirements, product differentiation and market growth (which affects ease of entry).

In the absence of any dynamic adjustments, the effects of these determinants might be estimated by the following equation:

$$C4_i^L = \beta_0 + \beta_1 MES_i + \beta_2 CAPR_i + \beta_3 ADV_i + \beta_4 MGR_i + \varepsilon_i \tag{1}$$

where $C4^L$ is the long-run level of four-firm industry concentration, MES is minimum efficient plant size relative to market size, $CAPR$ is the value of

[2] The bias will depend on the correlation between changes in determinants of concentration and the adjustment effect. Failure to distinguish adjustment effects may cause an overestimate or underestimate of the coefficients depending on whether these effects reinforce or counteract the effect of changes in the determinants of long-run concentration. A tendency for adjustment effects to counteract changes in market structure may explain the "unsuccessful" attempt by Caves and Porter to explain changes in market structure.

[3] Industry concentration has also been explained by stochastic growth processes, countervailing market power and mergers (see, for example, Ornstein *et al.* [1973]). Of these rationales, only stochastic growth is given explicit attention in the empirical literature. According to this rationale, concentration is positively related to market growth, the degree of product differentiation and the variability of demand. (See also Scherer [1980, pp. 145–50].) Proxies for the first two of these factors are included in our equations. Preliminary investigation of a variable measuring the variability of demand (measured as the variability of sales around a time trend) did not yield statistically significant results or substantively affect the results reported in equations below.

fixed assets of MES plants, *ADV* is advertising intensity and *MGR* is market growth, all for industry *i*.[4] *MES* is a measure of production scale economies, *CAPR* is a measure of capital requirements and economies of scale in raising capital and *ADV* is a measure of product differentiation. It is expected that $\partial C4^L/\partial MES$, $\partial C4^L/\partial CAPR$ and $\partial C4^L/\partial ADV$ are positive according to both the scale economy and entry barrier explanations, the ability to distinguish between the explanations being limited by theoretical difficulties (see, for example, Baumol and Willig [1981]) and measurement problems (see, for example, Curry and George [1983, pp. 217–27]). Entry barrier explanations also suggest that $\partial C4^L/\partial MGR$ is negative reflecting the ability of entrants to take advantage of scale economies, but the sign of $\partial C4^L/\partial MGR$ might be positive if large firms in the industry are able to more quickly expand in reaction to anticipated demand growth.[5]

Equation (1) may be estimated in intertemporal form by differencing each variable, yielding:

$$(2) \qquad \Delta C4_i^L = \beta'_0 + \beta'_1 \Delta MES_i + \beta'_2 \Delta CAPR_i + \beta'_3 \Delta ADV_i + \beta'_4 \Delta MGR_i + \eta_i$$

where, for example, $\Delta C4_i^L$ equals $C4_{i,t}^L$ minus $C4_{i,t-1}^L$ and $\eta_{i,t}$ equals $\varepsilon_{i,t}$ minus $\varepsilon_{i,t-1}$. If equation (1) is well specified so that the coefficients are invariant to the choice of time period and ε is not autocorrelated, then the coefficients in the difference form equation have the same interpretation as the corresponding coefficients of the variables in the levels form equation.

The specifications in equations (1) and (2) both assume long-run equilibrium in the sense that all adjustments to unexpected changes in market conditions have taken place. In level forms, the long-run level of concentration is assumed to have completely adjusted to any unexpected change, be it far in the past or recent. In difference form, the equilibrium assumption translates into complete adjustment of industry concentration during the time period examined. Caves and Porter [1980] lag the independent variables, so that, for example, ΔMES_i is $MES_{i,t-1}$ minus $MES_{i,t-2}$. Then the independent variables are assumed to affect concentration with a lag, but the entire effect is still assumed to take place during the interval in which intertemporal changes in concentration are examined. Neither this formulation nor those of equations (1) or (2) allow for adjustments of concentration prior to or after the period in which concentration is measured.

[4] Another variable that has been included in many studies is the number of firms in the industry. This variable was not included here to avoid a near tautological relationship between that variable (in conjunction with *MES*) and concentration.

[5] Note that in this long-run model, the market growth variable represents anticipated market growth as distinct from (short-run) unanticipated market growth (see Lucas [1967]). Even when market growth is anticipated, there may be different rates of expansion by larger firms than by smaller firms or entrants because of different costs of acquiring managerial and other types of capital.

It should be mentioned that anticipated and unanticipated demand growth are difficult to empirically disentangle. For an attempt to distinguish anticipated and unanticipated market growth, see Caves and Bradburd [1982].

III. CAUSES OF INCOMPLETE ADJUSTMENT

Adjustments in concentration to changing market conditions may be quite slow due to costs of adjustment for firms within the industry and for potential entrants. This is true in a competitive environment where firms take market prices as given or in an oligopolistic environment where established firms may adopt a policy calling for gradual adjustment in prices.

Brozen [1970], [1971] argues that above-average concentration is a disequilibrium phenomenon which is eliminated by competition. He claims that high levels of concentration are found when a firm or group of firms expand to take advantage of an unanticipated change in demand or a new technology. Over time, industry concentration falls as smaller firms expand and new firms enter the industry.[6] Thus, a high initial level of concentration is expected to be a temporary state which is followed by a decline in its level as firms adjust.

Within an oligopolistic or monopolistic industry, gradual adjustments may result from the dynamic pricing policy adopted by a firm or a group of firms with short-run market power. Gaskins [1971] presents a model of the dominant firm whose pricing policy affects the rate of entry of firms into the industry. The optimal strategy for the dominant firm may be to set price above or below the entry deterring price (that is, limit price) and let its market share adjust over time. When the price is set above (below) the limit price, the dominant firm's market share will initially be above (below) its long-run level and firms will enter (exit) the industry. The dominant firm's market share and, hence, industry concentration will continue to decline (increase) until the market price equals the limit price. Long-run equilibrium will then obtain. A model by Kamien and Schwartz [1971] implies similar results for colluding firms facing uncertain entry.

IV. THE EMPIRICAL MODEL

The analyses by Brozen and Gaskins both suggest that concentration will change over time when initial concentration deviates from its expected long-run equilibrium level. A dynamic model is presented here which allows incomplete adjustment to deviations of concentration from its expected long-run equilibrium value. The manner in which expected long-run concentration is specified in this model is crucial and receives special attention.

To allow for incomplete adjustments in the concentration variable, a partial adjustment model is adopted. The model is the same as the partial adjustment model used in studies of money demand and investment behavior

[6] This argument presumes slow market adjustment. Costs of adjustment have been examined by Penrose [1959], Lucas [1967] and Prescott and Visscher [1980], who all conclude that the period of adjustment depends on how rapidly the costs of obtaining capital (including information about employees, technology and market conditions) rise with the rate of acquisition.

except that the equation is estimated cross-sectionally (across industries) rather than using time series data.[7] Formally,

$$(3) \qquad C4_{i,t} - C4_{i,t-1} = \lambda(C4^*_{i,t} - C4_{i,t-1})$$

$C4_{i,t}$ is the actual level of concentration in period t and $C4^*_{i,t}$ is the long-run level of concentration in period t expected by entrants and by established firms in period $t-1$, all for industry i. The coefficient, λ, represents the rate of adjustment to deviations of the initial level of concentration from its long-run equilibrium level. According to arguments by Brozen and Gaskins, concentration will partially adjust when its expected long-run future level differs from its initial level implying a positive value of λ. For stability, λ must be greater than zero and less than one.

Since expectations are not observable, the variable $C4^*$ must be replaced by a proxy. Equation (1) above is modified for that purpose. Several formulations which differ in the way they treat *expectations* of long-run concentration in period t by firms in period $t-1$ are proposed.

One formulation simply assumes that firms in period $t-1$ expect equilibrium concentration in period t to be determined by the level of determinants of concentration in period $t-1$. The equation for long-run concentration, equation (1), is then lagged one period and substituted for $C4^*$ into equations (3) to obtain:

$$(4) \qquad \Delta C4_{i,t} = \alpha_0 + \alpha_1 C4_{i,t-1} + \alpha_2 MES_{i,t-1} + \alpha_3 CAPR_{i,t-1} + \alpha_4 ADV_{i,t-1} + \alpha_5 MGR_{i,t-1} + \varepsilon_{i,t}$$

The coefficient of $C4_{t-1}$, α_1, estimates the adjustment rate, λ, in equation (3).[8] The coefficients of the other variables represent their short-run effect, which equals λ times their long-run effect (their β coefficient in equation (1)). This specification is similar to that adopted in previous studies explaining changes in concentration by variables measured in level form. However, the dynamic adjustment model is not explicitly stated in those studies and adjustment effects are not distinguished from long-run effects.

A limitation of the specification of long-run concentration in equation (4) is that it implies firms consistently neglect and are unaffected by changes in long-run equilibrium concentration occurring between period $t-1$ and period t. For firms to take into account changes in the long-run level of industry concentration between period $t-1$ and period t, the long-run concentration equation can be expanded to allow for the effect of changes in its determinants. Adding difference form variables to equation (1) provides for

[7] A similar adjustment mechanism was suggested by Martin [1979] in a simultaneous equation model of market structure and performance. He then adopted the first of the expectation models suggested below.

[8] In some studies of changes in concentration, $C4_{t-1}$ is included as an explanatory variable to control for a spurious correlation problem arising out of the boundedness of the dependent variable. In this study, special precautions described below are taken to avoid this problem.

the effects of changes in the determinants of long-run concentration between period $t-1$ and period t. Thus:

$$C4^*_{i,t} = \beta'_0 + \beta'_1 MES_{i,t-1} + \beta'_2 CAPR_{i,t-1} + \beta'_3 ADV_{i,t-1} + \beta'_4 MGR_{i,t-1} + \beta'_5 \Delta MES_i + \beta'_6 \Delta CAPR_i + \beta'_7 \Delta ADV_i + \beta'_8 \Delta MGR_i + \varepsilon_{i,t} \tag{5}$$

Equation (5) is substituted into equation (3) to obtain:

$$\Delta C4_i = \alpha'_0 + \alpha'_1 C4_{t-1} + \alpha'_2 MES_{i,t-1} + \alpha'_3 CAPR_{i,t-1} + \alpha'_4 ADV_{i,t-1} + \alpha'_5 MGR_{i,t} + \alpha'_6 \Delta MES_i + \alpha'_7 \Delta CAPR_i + \alpha'_8 \Delta ADV_i + \alpha'_9 \Delta MGR_i + \varepsilon_{i,t} \tag{6}$$

where

$$\alpha'_0 = \lambda\beta'_0,$$
$$\alpha'_1 = -\lambda < 0,$$
$$\alpha'_2 = \lambda\beta'_1 > 0,$$
$$\alpha'_3 = \lambda\beta'_2 > 0,$$
$$\alpha'_4 = \lambda\beta'_3 > 0,$$
$$\alpha'_5 = \lambda\beta'_4 \gtrless 0,$$
$$\alpha'_6 = \lambda\beta'_5 > 0,$$
$$\alpha'_7 = \lambda\beta'_6 > 0,$$
$$\alpha'_8 = \lambda\beta'_7 > 0,$$

and

$$\alpha'_9 = \lambda\beta'_8 \gtrless 0.$$

This equation is more general than equation (4) since it allows for the effect of expected changes in long-run concentration during the period in which firms are considering entry or expansion. To determine whether actual changes in determinants of concentration between periods $t-1$ and t significantly affect the expected value of long-run concentration in period $t-1$, statistical tests of the joint hypothesis, $\beta'_5 = \beta'_6 = \beta'_7 = \beta'_8 = 0$, may be conducted.

A special case which is nested in equation (5) is the case where firms in period $t-1$, on average, correctly anticipate and fully react to the values of the explanatory variables in period t.[9] In terms of equation (5), changes in the determinants of concentration will then have the same effects on expected

[9] This case is similar to the implications of the rational expectations hypothesis as proposed by Muth [1961].

long-run concentration as the corresponding initial levels of the determinants (have on the level of long-run concentration) and thus $\beta'_1 = \beta'_5$, $\beta'_2 = \beta'_6$, $\beta'_3 = \beta'_7$ and $\beta'_4 = \beta'_8$. Since $\beta' x_{t-1} + \beta' \Delta x = \beta' x_t$ for any determinant x with effect β' in equation (5), equation (5) can be rewritten as equation (1). Substituting equation (1) into equation (3) implies the following:

$$(7) \qquad \Delta C4_{i,t} = \alpha_0 + \alpha_1 C4_{i,t-1} + \alpha_2 MES_{i,t} + \alpha_3 CAPR_{i,t} + \alpha_4 ADV_{i,t} + \alpha_5 MGR_{i,t} + \varepsilon_{i,t}$$

where the expected determinants of long-run concentration are their actual levels in period t. The coefficient α_1 represents the adjustment rate and the coefficients of the other variables represent their β coefficient in equation (1) times λ. Since equation (7) is nested in equation (6), the assumption that firms correctly anticipate and fully react to changes in the determinants of concentration can be tested by determining whether $\beta'_1 = \beta'_5$, $\beta'_2 = \beta'_6$, $\beta'_3 = \beta'_7$ and $\beta'_4 = \beta'_8$ in equation (6).[10]

One further assumption investigated below is that the rate of adjustment and the effects of *MES*, *ADV*, *CAPR* and *MGR* on long-run equilibrium are independent of the initial level of concentration. To the extent that the effectiveness of entry barriers depends on collusion and, thus, a certain degree of industry concentration (see, for example, Caves and Porter [1977]), the rate of adjustment and the effect of *MES*, *CAPR* and *ADV* on expected long-run concentration is expected to be less in concentrated industries.[11]

V. THE EMPIRICAL RESULTS

For estimation purposes, data were obtained at the four-digit level for the years 1963 and 1972. Observations were eliminated from the sample due to changes in industry definition between 1963 and 1972 and due to the lack of

[10] While assuming that the effects of changes in the determinants of concentration on long-run concentration have the same long-run effect as the levels of the determinants (that is, restricting $\beta'_1 = \beta'_5, \beta'_2 = \beta'_6, \beta'_3 = \beta'_7, \beta'_4 = \beta'_8$ in equation (6)), it is possible to allow for less than complete adjustment of these effects between period t and period $t-1$. Partial adjustment to changes in concentration may be assumed by restricting $\beta'_1 = \delta\beta'_5, \ldots, \beta'_4 = \delta\beta'_8$, where $0 \leqslant \delta \leqslant 1$.

Statistical tests of this assumption were conducted on equation (7). The value of δ was not significantly different from one, thus failing to imply incomplete adjustment to changes in the determinants. Consequently, the incomplete adjustment model is not reported here.

[11] Attempts were also made to distinguish whether consumer goods industries have different effects from producer good industries. It has been argued that consumer good industries are more conducive to product differentiation than are producer good industries, suggesting differential effects of advertising and other determinants across industries. Industries are classified as consumer good industries if the ratio of total consumer sales to total consumer and producer sales is greater than 0.5. Sales to consumers and producers was obtained from *Input–Output* data.

The computed F-statistics for stability over consumer and producer good industries are 3.66 (6,185), 2.25 (10,177) and 1.33 (6,185) for equations (4), (6) and (7), respectively. None of these are significant at the 0.05 level. For this reason and because an advertising variable was included in the estimation equations to control for product differentiation, these equations are not reported here.

advertising data corresponding to some four-digit industries.[12] Eliminating industries from the sample which change industry definition (for example, due to rapid technological change) may cause sample selection bias, but does act to reduce measurement error problems from poorly specified industries. The final sample contained 197 industries.

The estimation equations examine changes in concentration between 1963 and 1972. Because the concentration measure is bounded between zero and one and thus the magnitude of possible changes in concentration is reduced as these bounds are approached, a negative correlation between changes in concentration and the level of correlation may be induced (see, for example, Curry and George [1983, p. 224]). To reduce the potential bias, a nonlinear transformation of the dependent variable (suggested by Wright [1978]) which converts the change in concentration variable into proportional terms is used.[13] Discussion of how each of the variables are measured can be found in the Appendix.

Equations (4), (6) and (7) above were estimated. Since each of these equations is nonlinear with respect to λ and the β coefficients, nonlinear estimation techniques were employed to distinguish adjustment effects from expected long-run determinants of concentration (see, for example, Kmenta [1971, pp. 442–48]). The coefficients of *MES*, *CAPR*, *ADV* and *MGR* are reported as their long-term effects, that is, their β coefficients, in the tables below.[14]

The specifications of equations (4) and (6) are reported as equations 1 and 2 in Table I. Except for the lagged levels *ADV* variable, the coefficients are of the expected sign, but not all significant. The coefficients of the lagged levels and difference form *MES* variables are positive and significantly different from zero at the 0.01 level in both equations. The coefficient of the levels and difference form *MGR* variable is negative in both equations and is significant at the 0.10 level in equation 1. The coefficient on $C4_{t-1}$, that is, the

[12] In 1972, some SIC codes changed without significant changes in the industry itself. Also, some industries were aggregated or disaggregated in 1967 and 1972. These industries were matched up or aggregated. If there were other changes in the industry definition the industry was excluded from the sample.

Since data were also available for the year 1967, equations were also estimated for changes in concentration over the subperiods 1963 to 1967 and 1967 to 1972. Upon failing to reject the null hypothesis of intertemporal stability, these subperiods were pooled. The results were consistent with those reported below, with the adjustment rate approximately half that for the 1963–72 period equations, as expected.

[13] It should be noted that the transformation of the dependent variable affects the interpretation of the coefficients in the estimation equation. However, the equations were also estimated using a nontransformed dependent variable and the significance of the coefficients was not noticeably affected. Similar results were also obtained by Wright [1978]. These results are not surprising considering that very few of the industries in the sample have four-firm concentration ratios near zero or one.

[14] The magnitude of the β coefficients (after transforming the original coefficients) and the sum of squared residuals for equations estimated using ordinary least squares were identical to those for equations estimated using nonlinear techniques. However, the nonlinear estimation technique, unlike ordinary least squares, provides estimates of the standard errors of the coefficients.

In Tables I and II, the estimated coefficients and their standard errors were obtained using nonlinear estimation, while the F-statistics and R^2 were obtained using ordinary least squares.

TABLE I
ESTIMATES OF CONCENTRATION EQUATION DEPENDENT VARIABLE = $C4_{1972} - C4_{1963}$

Eqn.	*Intercept*	$C4_{t-1}$	MES_{t-1}	$CAPR_{t-1}$ × 10−6	ADV_{t-1}	MGR_{t-1}	ΔMES	$\Delta CAPR$ × 10−6	ΔADV	ΔMGR	*DF*	R^2	F-*stat*	*MSE*
1	0.26 (2.81) ‡	0.30 (3.03) ‡	0.0019 (2.00) †	1.20 (0.54)	−0.86 (−0.63)	−0.45 (−1.48) *					191	0.073	3.00 ‡	0.042
2	0.24 (2.31) ‡	0.33 (3.48) ‡	0.0047 (3.84) ‡	2.70 (0.84)	−0.0089 (−0.01)	−0.34 (−1.23)	0.012 (2.78) ‡	0.60 (0.17)	0.30 (0.12)	−0.12 (−0.88)	187	0.18	4.50 ‡	0.038
						Low Concentration Industries								
3	0.20 (1.08)	0.90 (3.22) ‡	0.0040 (2.58) ‡	3.20 (0.85)	−0.18 (−0.26)	−0.11 (−0.07)					112	0.29	2.16 *	0.055
4	0.19 (1.01)	1.00 (4.11) ‡	0.0063 (4.56) ‡	4.20 (0.73)	0.79 (0.88)	0.018 (0.12)	0.015 (3.33) ‡	−1.21 (−0.10)	1.033 (0.74)	−0.052 (−0.77)	108	0.36	6.86 ‡	0.043
						High Concentration Industries								
5	0.30 (3.38) ‡	0.15 (1.38) *	0.0018 (1.25)	8.5 (0.31)	−2.61 (−0.82)	−1.42 (−1.29) *					73	0.22	4.14 ‡	0.013
6	0.28 (3.10) ‡	0.12 (1.20)	0.0055 (1.29) *	−0.96 (−0.18)	−1.94 (−0.50)	−1.76 (−1.10)	0.013 (1.11)	0.92 (0.57)	−0.77 (−0.14)	−0.27 (−0.69)	69	0.37	4.49 ‡	0.011

t-statistics in parentheses.
* Indicates statistically significant at the 0.10 level (one-tailed tests).
† Indicates statistically significant at the 0.05 level.
‡ Indicates statistically significant at the 0.01 level.

adjustment rate, is about 0.30 in both equations and is statistically significant at the 0.01 level. A statistical test was conducted to determine the appropriateness of including the difference form variables in equation 1, that is, the joint hypothesis $\beta'_5 = \beta'_6 = \beta'_7 = \beta'_8 = 0$. The computed F-statistic was 5.97 (4,187), which is statistically significant at the 0.01 level, thus rejecting the null hypothesis that changes in determinants of concentration between period $t-1$ and period t have no independent effects.

Given the joint significance of the difference form variables, equation (6) was re-estimated with the coefficients of the lagged levels form and difference form variables restricted to be the same, that is, equation (7) above. A statistical test of the joint hypothesis $\beta'_1 = \beta'_5$, $\beta'_2 = \beta'_6$, $\beta'_3 = \beta'_7$ and $\beta'_4 = \beta'_8$ was conducted. The computed F-statistic is 2.39 (4,187), which is not statistically significant at the 0.05 level. Thus, the restriction imposed in equation (7) that the effects of changes in determinants of long-run concentration are the same as the effect of their initial level could not be rejected. This equation performs better in terms of the mean square error than equation 1 in Table I with lagged level variables.

The estimation equation with the lagged levels and difference form coefficients restricted to be the same is reported as equation 1 in Table II. The results are broadly consistent with those above. The adjustment rate was slightly higher at 0.43 and still statistically significant at the 0.01 level. The effect of *MES* is positive and statistically significant at the 0.01 level. The effect of *MGR* is negative and statistically significant at the 0.10 level.

As suggested above, separate equations were estimated for high and low concentration industries and tests of stability were conducted. The hypothesis of homogeneity over high and low concentration industries was rejected at the 0.01 level for equation 1 in Table I and at the 0.05 level for equation 1 in Table II.[15] Consequently, separate equations are reported in the tables for high and low concentration industries.

Equations (4) and (6) from the previous section above are reported for high and low concentration industries as equations 3–6 in Table I and equation (7) above is reported as equations 2 and 3 in Table II. The most notable distinction between high and low concentration industries in these equations is that the speed of adjustment is quicker in low than in high concentration industries. This suggests that entry barriers may be more effective in inhibiting market adjustment for more highly concentrated industries. How-

[15] Industries were classified as high concentrated industries if their four-firm concentration level was greater than 0.45. This level was chosen because it approximates the critical level of the four-firm concentration level found in earlier studies (see Scherer [1980, p. 280]) and it is very close to the mean four-firm concentration of our sample, which is 0.42.

The computed F-statistic for stability over high and low concentration industries is 1.66 (6, 185), 5.52 (10,177) and 6.22 (6,185) for equations (4), (6) and (7), respectively. The F-statistic for equation (6) is significant at the 0.01 level and the F-statistics for equation (7) is significant at the 0.05 level.

Tests for heteroskedasticity were conducted using the Goldfeld–Quandt test. The null hypothesis of homoskedasticity could not be rejected at the 0.05 level for any of these equations.

TABLE II
CONCENTRATION EQUATION WITH RESTRICTED COEFFICIENTS DEPENDENT VARIABLE = $C4_{1972} - C4_{1963}$

Eqn.	*Intercept*	$C4_{t-1}$	MES_t	$CAPR_t$ $\times 10-6$	ADV_t	MGR_t	*DF*	R^2	F-*stat*	*MSE*
1	0.22 (3.23) ‡	0.43 (4.71) ‡	0.0036 (4.44) ‡	1.00 (1.04)	−0.091 (−0.07)	−0.17 (−1.53) *	191	0.13	5.47 ‡	0.0398
				Low Concentration Industries						
2	0.34 (3.10) ‡	1.38 (5.91) ‡	0.0062 (6.31) ‡	2.10 (1.41) *	0.56 (0.89)	−0.056 (−1.17)	112	0.29	9.18 ‡	0.0463
				High Concentration Industries						
3	0.15 (1.90) †	0.22 (2.01) †	0.0035 (2.09) †	−1.10 (−0.85)	1.21 (0.54)	−0.30 (−1.23)	73	0.17	2.93 †	0.0141

t-statistics in parentheses.
* Indicates statistically significant at the 0.01 level (one-tailed tests).
† Indicates statistically significant at the 0.05 level.
‡ Indicates statistically significant at the 0.01 level.

ever, the initial level of *MES*, *CAPR* and *ADV* do not appear to have a stronger effect in high than in low concentrated industries, as might be expected according to entry barrier theories.

VI. CONCLUSION

Previous studies generally explain changes in concentration as a function of either adjustments to initial market structure or as a function of (lagged or contemporaneous) changes in market structure. Little attention has been paid to the dynamic structure of the model. It was argued here that both the initial level and contemporaneous changes in the determinants of concentration may be important. A model was developed which provides for long-run determinants of concentration and adjustments to deviations from long-run equilibrium. A variety of specifications of the long-run level of concentration were specified and estimated.

The results obtained here are consistent over a variety of specifications. In all cases, the adjustment effect is of the expected sign and strongly significant. It was found that the minimum efficient plant size variable has positive and statistically significant effects. The effect of *CAPR* and *ADV* are generally weak. The effect of demand growth is generally negative and sometimes significant. The scale economy variables do not have stronger effects in more concentrated industries as might be expected when entry barriers are effective, but concentrated industries display slower adjustment to above average concentration.

These results are broadly consistent with those obtained in earlier studies. In previous studies, the effect of initial concentration on changes in concentration have been found to be negative (even after correcting for measurement bias) and the effect of initial minimum efficient size is positive in studies where it is included (see Curry and George [1983]). While some studies have found a positive and significant effect of advertising on changes in concentration (see, for example, Marcus [1969] or Mueller and Rogers [1980]), Asch [1979] and Jenny and Weber [1978] found the relationship to be statistically weak.

Results obtained in this study suggest that earlier studies may be subject to specification bias from their failure to incorporate contemporary changes in the long-run determinants of concentration. Statistical tests conducted in this study indicate that the assumption that difference form variables have no effect can be statistically rejected. This study also provides evidence in favor of the hypothesis that changes in long-run concentration are on average correctly anticipated over the ten year period examined.

This study provides a framework to sort out adjustment effects in a systematic manner. There is still substantial variation yet to be explained. This study did not endeavor to obtain evidence on behavioral determinants of concentration other than those considered in earlier studies. Other determinants of concentration might be considered for inclusion in the model, such as the role of technological innovation (see, for example, Nelson and Winter [1978]). Further research is also warranted in devising better measures of scale economies and entry barriers and in distinguishing entry barrier effects from pure scale economy effects.

DAVID LEVY,
Department of Economics,
Faculty of Arts and Sciences,
Rutgers, The State University of New Jersey,
New Brunswick, NJ 08903,
USA.

ACCEPTED JUNE 1984

APPENDIX

MEASUREMENT OF VARIABLES

$C4$ = four-firm concentration ratio.
MES = average plant size among the largest plants producing 50% of industry sales/total industry sales.
$CAPR$ = $MES \times$ Gross Book Value of Fixed Assets/Industry sales.
ADV = advertising outlays/sales.
MGR = (present period sales–previous period sales)/previous period sales.

The entry barrier variables are measured as in the Comanor and Wilson study [1967] except that four digit rather than three digit level industry data is used here (see also Scherer [1980]). The data for all variables except ADV were obtained from the Census of Manufactures reports and the ADV variable was obtained at the four digit level from the Bureau of Economic Analysis *Input-Output Reports.*

The difference form variables were created by simply calculating the absolute value of the change in the variable from its initial level to its final level. An exception was the difference form concentration variable which was corrected for measurement problems (see footnote 7). Following Wright [1978], changes in concentration were calculated as:

$$\Delta C4/[(50-|50-C4_t|)^{1/2}(50-|50-C4_{t-1}|)^{1/2}]$$

REFERENCES

ASCH, PETER, 1979, 'The Role of Advertising in Changing Concentration, 1963–1972', *Southern Economic Journal*, 46, 1 (July), pp. 288–97.

BAIN, JOE S., 1956, *Barriers to New Competition* (Harvard University Press, Cambridge).

BAUMOL, W. J. and WILLIG, R. D., 1981, 'Fixed Costs, Sunk Costs, Entry Barriers and Sustainability of Monopoly', *Quarterly Journal of Economics*, 95 (August), pp. 405–31.

BROZEN, YALE, 1970, 'The Antitrust Task Force Deconcentration Recommendation', *Journal of Law and Economics*, 13, 1 (October), pp. 279–92.

BROZEN, YALE, 1971, 'Concentration and Structural and Market Disequilibria', *Antitrust Bulletin*, 6 (Summer), pp. 241–48.

BROZEN, YALE, 1974, 'Entry Barriers: Advertising and Product Differentiation', in Goldschmidt, Mann and Weston, *Industrial Concentration: The New Learning* (Little, Brown and Company, Boston), pp. 115–36.

CAVES, RICHARD and BRADBURD, RALPH, 1982, 'A Closer Look at the Effect of Market Growth on Industries' Profits', *Review of Economics and Statistics*, 64 (November), pp. 635–45.

CAVES, RICHARD E. and PORTER, MICHAEL E., 1977, 'From Entry Barriers to Mobility Barriers', *Quarterly Journal of Economics*, 91 (May), pp. 241–61.

CAVES, RICHARD E., 1980, 'The Dynamics of Changing Seller Competition', *Journal of Industrial Economics*, XXIX, 1 (September), pp. 1–15.

COMANOR, WILLIAM S. and WILSON, THOMAS A., 1967, 'Advertising, Market Structure and Performance', *Review of Economics and Statistics*, 49 (November 1967), pp. 423–40.

CURRY, B. and GEORGE, K. D., 1983, 'Industrial Concentration: A Survey', *Journal of Industrial Economics*', XXXI, 3 (March), pp. 203–55.

GASKINS, DARIUS, 1971, 'Dynamic Limit Pricing. Optimal Pricing Under Threat of Entry', *Journal of Economic Theory*, 3 (September), pp. 306–22.

JENNY, FREDERIC and WEBER, ANDRE-PAUL, 1978, 'The Determinants of Concentration Trends in the French Manufacturing Sector', *Journal of Industrial Economics*, XXVI, 3 (March), pp. 193–207.

KAMIEN, MORTON and SCHWARTZ, NANCY, 1971, 'Limit Pricing and Uncertain Entry', *Econometrica*, 39 (May), pp. 441–54.

KMENTA, JAN, 1971, *Elements of Econometrics* (Macmillan Co., New York).

LUCAS, ROBERT E., JR., 1967, 'Adjustment Costs and the Theory of Supply', *Journal of Political Economy*, 75 (August), pp. 321–34.

MADDALA, G. S., 1977, *Econometrics* (McGraw-Hill, New York).

MANN, H. MICHAEL, 1977, 'A Note on Barriers to Entry and Long-Run Profitability', *Antitrust Bulletin*, 14 (Summer), pp. 845–49.

MARCUS, MATITYAHU, 1969, 'Advertising and Changes in Concentration', *Southern Economic Journal*, 38 (October), pp. 117–21.

MARTIN, STEPHEN, 1979, 'Advertising, Concentration and Profitability: The Simultaneity Problem', *Bell Journal of Economics*, X, 2 (Autumn), pp. 639–47.

MUELLER, WILLARD F. and ROGERS, RICHARD T., 1980, 'The Role of Advertising in Changing Concentration of Industries', *Review of Economics and Statistics*, LXII, 1 (February), pp. 89–96.

MUTH, J. F., 1961, 'Rational Expectations and the Theory of Price Movements', *Econometrica*, 36 (October), pp. 315–35.

NELSON, RALPH and WINTER, SIDNEY, 1978, 'Forces Generating and Limiting Concentration Under Schumpeterian Competition', *Bell Journal of Economics*, IX, 2 (Autumn), pp. 524–49.

ORNSTEIN, S. I., WESTON, J. F., INTRILLIGATOR, M. D. and SHRIEVES, R. E., 1973, 'The Determinants of Market Structure', *Southern Economic Journal*, LXXXIX, 4 (April), pp. 612–25.

ORNSTEIN, S. I. and LUSTGARTEN, S., 1978, 'Advertising Intensity and Industrial Concentration' in D. G. Tuerck, *Issues in Advertising* (American Enterprise Institute, Washington D.C.), pp. 217–52.

PENROSE, EDITH T., 1959, *The Theory of the Growth of the Firm* (Basil Blackwell, Oxford).

PRESCOTT, EDWARD C. and VISSCHER, MICHAEL, 1980, 'Organization Capital', *Journal of Political Economy*, 88 (June), pp. 446–61.

SCHERER, FREDERICK M., 1980, *Industrial Market Structure and Economic Performance* (Rand McNally, Chicago).

WRIGHT, NEIL R., 1978, 'Product Differentiation, Concentration and Changes in Concentration', *Review of Economics and Statistics*, LX, 4 (November), pp. 628–31.

THE JOURNAL OF INDUSTRIAL ECONOMICS 0022-1821 $2.00
Volume XXXIV September 1985 No. 1

MARKET STRUCTURE AND RESEARCH INTENSITY IN HIGH-TECHNOLOGICAL-OPPORTUNITY INDUSTRIES*

REINHARD ANGELMAR

Where the cost and uncertainty of R & D are high and conditions favor speedy imitation by competitors, concentration has a statistically significant and substantial positive impact on research intensity. But its impact is clearly negative when R & D cost and uncertainty are low, and where high barriers to imitation exist.

A sample of 160 business unit observations for 1978 was drawn from the PIMS Data Base. All the sample business units' industries recently experienced major technological changes. Research intensity was measured by non-government-financed R & D expenditures as a percentage of sales.

INTRODUCTION

How important is market structure for research investments when opportunities for technical advance are high in comparison to situations with low technological opportunity? This has been a major research question in studies concerned with the interactions between market structure, R & D, and technological opportunity (Globerman [1973]; Scherer [1967]; Shrieves [1978]). The results of these studies have been interpreted as showing that market concentration, while having a favorable impact on research investments in low-technological-opportunity situations, is less favorable in high-technological-opportunity environments. In fact, its impact there might even be negative (Scherer [1980]).

While its objective is not to question this comparative judgment, the present study does aim at providing a more differentiated view of the role of market structure in high-technological-opportunity environments. Under what conditions might high concentration be essential for heavy research investments, even in a technologically fertile environment? What are the characteristics of industries where high concentration may, in fact, slow down the exploitation of technological opportunities?

Before presenting hypotheses regarding conditions that might interact with concentration, past empirical studies will be reviewed. Subsequently, the data and variables and, finally, the results for this study will be presented.

* The author wishes to thank the Strategic Planning Institute for granting access to the PIMS Data Base.

PAST STUDIES

Evidence for the proposition that concentration may lead to reduced R & D investment in high-technological-opportunity environments basically comes from three studies. Scherer [1967] assigned 56 industry groups to one of four technology classes thought to differ in scientific and technological opportunity. In the chemical class, which he considered a high-technological-opportunity environment, the correlation between scientists and engineers per 1,000 employees, and concentration was negative. However, only five observations were involved, and the t-coefficient for concentration was only marginally significant ($t = -1.24$). Globerman [1973] using Scherer's classification scheme, assigned 9 Canadian manufacturing industries to the high-technological-opportunity class. The t-coefficient for concentration in the regression of R & D personnel per 1,000 employees was significantly negative ($t = -3.62$). Finally, Shrieves [1978] assigned firms to one of four classes depending on the characteristics of the products involved. In the "specialized durable equipment" group ($n = 129$), which included many firms operating in high-technological-opportunity environments, concentration had a negative, but not statistically significant coefficient ($t = -0.88$) in the regression of R & D employees.

Because their objective was to compare high with low-technological-opportunity industries, none of these three studies attempted to specify under what conditions the role of concentration might vary in high-technological-opportunity environments.

HYPOTHESES

Why should concentration reduce research investment in high-technological-opportunity environments? Scherer [1980] recently provided a cogent interpretation of past studies in terms of a model developed earlier by him [1967].

According to this model, the level of research investment depends essentially on the speed with which firms decide to bring an innovation to the market. Higher speed will generally increase revenues but also costs. Firms will choose the speed and, therefore, the level of research investment, that will maximize profits.

When the technological environment is barren, the cost of research, for any speed, will frequently exceed the benefits of innovation, especially in atomistic markets, where the innovator has to share the total profit potential with many rivals. Under these circumstances, an increase in concentration, by improving the benefits the innovator can hope to keep, may trigger research investment. But when the technological environment is fertile, the cost of developing new products decreases such that research investment now becomes profitable even in atomistic industries. Here, high concentration is not needed and may even reduce the level of research investment by diminishing the importance of speed in new product introduction.

The average picture of innovation in high-technological-opportunity industries may aggregate a number of disparate situations. In certain contexts, the cost and uncertainty of research may be too high, and/or the benefits too low to stimulate research investment in the absence of high concentration.

On the cost side, not all opportunities provided by scientific and technological progress can be exploited with research budgets affordable by firms of all sizes. Some projects require investments approaching one hundred million dollars or more (Wise [1966]). The length of time needed to bring an innovation to the market may also vary widely between industries because of technological or regulatory constraints independent of market structure. The resulting lengthening of the payback time, and the increase in uncertainty, may be sustainable only by members of concentrated industries.

Regarding the benefits, the speed with which imitation takes place is a major determinant of the benefits from innovation. A high speed of imitation may reduce benefits below profitable levels in all but highly concentrated industries. Key factors affecting the speed of imitation are (1) patents, trade secrets, or similar devices, (2) the frequency with which the purchasers buy the product, and (3) the possibilities for inducing brand loyalty in buyers.

Patents, trade secrets, and similar methods for preventing competitors from gaining access to the technical knowhow underlying an innovation, are important devices for retarding competitive imitation and, therefore, for maintaining high levels of profitability (Scherer [1980]).

Shrieves [1978] suggested purchase frequency as a determinant of the speed of imitation. The firm which is first on the market with a significant new product may precipitate replacement of obsolete equipment. When buyers purchase infrequently, imitators will find it difficult to achieve significant penetration in the short term, and may have to wait until a significant replacement sales volume develops. But when the purchase frequency is high, imitators may rapidly obtain a significant share of repeat purchase, without having incurred the expenses involved in developing the market. Shrieves's [1978] hypothesis concerning the role of purchase frequency fits with his own empirical results as well as those obtained by Comanor [1967]. In both studies, concentration had a favorable impact on research employment for non-durables, i.e., high purchase frequency products, and was non-significant or slightly negative for durable products. However, since purchase frequency was confounded with many other factors in these studies, many alternative interpretations are possible. Thus, Comanor [1967] interpreted his own findings in terms of product "differentiability", and while Shrieves thought his results demonstrated the role of the speed of imitation, Scherer [1980, p. 436] only saw the effect of differential technological opportunities in both Comanor's and Shrieves's studies.

A third major strategy for blunting the impact of competitive imitation consists in the attempt to create brand loyalty. A number of techniques may be used to render supplier switching difficult for the customer, including tying the customer to an operating pattern, committing him to an inventory of parts and supplies, and training his employees such that supplier switching would involve substantial retraining (Weigand [1980]).

The preceding considerations lead to the following expectations regarding empirical findings: (1) factors related to low R & D cost and uncertainty, and those which create barriers to imitation increase incentives for research investment and, therefore, should have a positive impact on research intensity; (2) because these factors increase incentives for research, high concentration is not needed and may even lead to reduced spending. In other words, concentration is expected to have a negative impact on research intensity when R & D cost and uncertainty are low, and when conditions creating barriers to imitation are present. In the opposite case, concentration should increase research intensity.

SAMPLE AND VARIABLES

The hypotheses were studied at the business unit level using data drawn from the PIMS data base of the Strategic Planning Institute. The PIMS Data Basc consists of annual business unit level data supplied by the over 200 member companies of the institute. A business unit as defined by PIMS is a unit of the firm selling a distinct set of products to an identifiable set of customers in competition with a well-defined set of competitors (Strategic Planning Institute [1978]). Member companies provide annual income statements and

TABLE I
SAMPLE CHARACTERISTICS

	Percent of Sample
(1) *By Type of Business*	
consumer durable products	9
consumer non-durable products	7
capital goods	23
raw or semi-finished materials	9
components for finished products	33
supplies for consumer products	19
Total	100
(2) *By Location of Served Market*	
entire United States	44
all of Canada	2
United States and Canada	24
regional within the U.S.A. or Canada	12
United Kingdom	4
Common Market	4
Regional within Europe	3
Other	7
	100

balance sheets, as well as information about market structure, technology, and competitive strategy for each business unit.

A sample of 160 business units providing data for 1978 and fulfilling the following criteria was selected: (1) new product development occurred in the business; (2) the business was involved in production (service and distribution businesses were excluded); (3) the data on the business unit were complete with respect to the variables used here; and (4) the business unit indicated that there had been major technological changes in the products offered by the business or its major competitors, or in methods of production, during the last 8 years. When in doubt about whether a technological change was "major", businesses are instructed to indicate that no changes have taken place. Criterion (4) is used here as a measure of high technological opportunity. The average R & D investment for the selected business units was 2.91 percent of sales, compared to 1.73 for businesses satisfying the first three criteria but indicating no major technological changes. The difference is significant at the 1 percent level, thus indicating that the sample businesses indeed enjoyed superior technological opportunities.

Approximately one third of the sample businesses produced components for finished products, and 22% produced capital goods. For reasons of confidentiality, most respondents chose not to indicate their SIC code. The vast majority of the businesses operated in North America (see Table I for information on the sample).

The dependent variable for this study is the privately financed R & D investment as a percent of current revenues. This refers to all non-government-financed expenses (material, labor, etc.) incurred to improve existing products or to develop new products, and all expenses for improving the efficiency of the manufacturing process. All R & D expenses are specific to the business and exclude charges for "basic" research performed by a corporate facility.

The SIC 4-digit four-firm concentration ratio, the served-market four-firm concentration ratio, and the business unit's served-market share (Rosenberg [1976]) were the measures of market structure employed. Given the business unit level of analysis, SIC market boundaries are probably too broad, and served-market data are more appropriate. The SIC concentration ratio was used mainly for the purpose of comparing this data set with previous studies, all of which used SIC-derived concentration ratios.

The typical time lag between the beginning of development effort for a new product and market introduction was used as a measure of the uncertainty of R & D. This assumes that the typical length of new product development reflects the impact of technological and regulatory constraints, as well as that of market structure. Because market structure will be explicitly present in the regression equation, the resulting coefficient for development time will reflect primarily the influence of non-market structure factors.

One question asked for each unit is whether it benefits to a significant degree from patents, trade secrets, or other proprietary methods of production or operation. The answer to this question was used to indicate the possibility of protecting itself against imitation in this industry.[1] Purchase frequency is measured through a series of categories. Finally, one question asks how important installation, repair, customer education, and other product-related services are to end users. This was employed as an indicator of the ease with which users can switch suppliers. The more important these product-related services, the more difficult it should be for a competitor to break into an established relationship.

Table II summarizes the definitions of the basic variables used in this study and shows their means and standard deviations. R & D intensity, the dependent variable, was first regressed against the basic independent variables. Subsequently, interaction terms between concentration and the other relevant variables were introduced in order to see whether the impact of concentration varies with R & D uncertainty and speed of imitation.

RESULTS

The regression results are presented in Table III. Before discussing the results for the other basic variables and the interaction terms, the results for the SIC and the served-market concentration ratios, and for market share will be considered.

The negative, yet non-significant coefficient for the SIC concentration ratio in Equation (1.1), is similar to what past studies have found for high-technological-opportunity industries (Globerman [1973]; Scherer [1967]; Shrieves [1978]).

Equation (1.2) introduces the square of the SIC concentration ratio. With significance levels of 6% (SIC concentration) and 3% (squared SIC concentration) respectively, some support for a nonlinear relationship between SIC concentration and research intensity is found. The maximum predicted research intensity is reached at a SIC concentration level of 44 percent, slightly below the 50 to 55 percent level suggested by Scherer's [1967] study. Despite the differences in dependent variables (R & D expenditures vs. employment), level of aggregation (business unit vs. firm or industry), and period of reference (1978 versus 1960 for Scherer and 1965 for Shrieves) compared to past studies, the results are remarkably similar.

The coefficient for served-market concentration in Equation (1.3) is not significant. This parallels the SIC concentration ratio results (Equation (1.1)). In contrast to Equation (1.2), Equation (1.4) shows no evidence for a nonlinear relationship between served-market concentration and R & D intensity. This difference may be due to the narrower definition of the competitive

[1] Although proprietary technology and R & D are likely to be linked in a two-way relationship over time, the time lags involved make the interpretation of the coefficient fairly unproblematic. Here, interest centres on the impact of current proprietary technology on current R & D intensity. In order to study the reverse impact of R & D intensity on proprietary technology one would have to relate past R & D intensity to current proprietary technology.

TABLE II
DEFINITIONS, MEANS, AND STANDARD DEVIATIONS OF BASIC VARIABLES ($n = 160$)

Variable	*Definition*	*Mean*	*S.D.*
$R\&D \times 100/S$	Privately-financed R & D as a percent of sales	2.91	3.13
$C(SIC)$	4-digit SIC four-firm concentration ratio	55.48	22.55
$C(SM)$	Four-firm concentration ratio for business unit's served market	76.17	19.36
MS	Business unit's served market share (percent)	25.99	19.49
DEV	= 1 if typical product development time is equal to or less than five years; = 0 otherwise	0.94	—
$PROP$	= 1 if business unit benefits to a significant degree from patents, trade secrets, or other proprietary methods of production or operation; = 0 otherwise	0.35	—
$1/6MO–1/YR$	= 1 if end users purchase the product between once/6 months and once/year; = 0 otherwise	0.11	—
$1/YR–1/5\ YRS$	= 1 if end users purchase the product between 1/year and 1/5 years; = 0 otherwise	0.22	—
$> 1/5\ YRS$	= 1 end users purchase the product less than 1/5 years; = 0 otherwise	0.06	—
$SERV$	= 1 if installation, repair, customer education and other product-related services provided to end users are of great importance; = 0 otherwise	0.47	—

arena that is implicit in the concept of a served market. Competitors in a highly concentrated served market could still be vulnerable to entry by competitors active in the same industry yet in other served markets. Whether high served-market concentration indeed reduces competitive threats, and by the same token incentives for innovation, will then depend on other factors such as protection via proprietary technology or the possibility of "locking in" customers.[2]

The introduction of the market share measure in the linear (Equation (1.5)) and the non-linear model (Equation (1.6)) has no significant effect on the concentration coefficients. Market share itself lacks statistical significance in both equations.

Considering the results of equations (1.3) through (1.5) it appears as though served-market concentration has no effect on research intensity.

Turning now to the other variables, length of product development time shall be considered first. The coefficient for this variable comes nowhere near statistical significance, except in Equation (1.7) where a term accounting for the interaction between development time and concentration is present

[2] This explanation of the results would be invalidated by a high correlation between the SIC and the served-market concentration ratio. In fact, the two variables are only modestly correlated: $r = 0.29$.

TABLE III
REGRESSION RESULTS: DEPENDENT VARIABLE: R & D × 100/S (n = 160)

	Equations										
	(1.1)	(1.2)	(1.3)	(1.4)	(1.5)	(1.6)	(1.7)	(1.8)	(1.9)	(2.0)	(2.1)
Constant	2.54	0.976	1.318	−1.064	1.080	−0.900	−3.725	−0.404	1.276	−0.244	−1.993
C(SIC)	−0.01189	0.06566[c]									
	(−1.12)	(1.55)									
$C(SIC)^2$		−0.0007421[b]									
		(−1.89)									
C(SM)			0.00919	0.08532	0.01704	0.08026	0.7689[c]	0.02702[b]	0.00970	0.03159[b]	0.04977[a]
			(0.71)	(1.12)	(1.08)	(1.05)	(1.55)	(1.85)	(0.74)	(1.94)	(2.86)
$C(SM)^2$				−0.0005559		−0.0004735					
				(−1.01)		(−0.84)					
MS					−0.1377	−0.01091					
					(−0.89)	(−0.69)					
DEV	−0.150	−0.281	−0.202	−0.158	−0.227	−0.184	5.193[c]	0.238	−0.201	−0.327	0.1147
	(−0.15)	(−0.28)	(−0.20)	(−0.16)	(−0.22)	(−0.18)	(1.31)	(0.23)	(−0.20)	(−0.33)	(0.11)
PROP	1.627[a]	1.609[a]	1.469[a]	1.460[a]	1.525[a]	1.506[a]	1.584[a]	7.506[a]	1.469[a]	1.569[a]	7.651[a]
	(3.19)	(3.18)	(2.80)	(2.78)	(2.88)	(2.84)	(2.99)	(3.08)	(2.79)	(3.02)	(3.18)
1/6MO–1/YR	1.583[b]	1.785[a]	1.608[b]	1.622[b]	1.643[b]	1.648[b]	1.646[a]	1.466[a]	1.609[b]	1.694[a]	1.552[a]
	(2.12)	(2.39)	(2.15)	(2.17)	(2.19)	(2.20)	(2.21)	(1.99)	(2.15)	(2.29)	(2.13)
1/YR–1/5YR	0.4918	0.4858	0.4553	0.3915	0.4447	0.3926	0.5138	0.358	0.4509	0.4524	0.3543
	(0.80)	(0.80)	(0.74)	(0.63)	(0.72)	(0.63)	(0.83)	(0.59)	(0.73)	(0.74)	(0.59)
> 1/5 YRS	−0.638	−0.763	−0.724	−0.921	−0.838	−0.983	−0.686	−0.828	2.639	−0.725	−0.8302
	(−0.61)	(0.75)	(−0.70)	(−0.88)	(−0.81)	(−0.93)	(−0.67)	(−0.82)	(0.40)	(0.71)	(−0.83)
SERV	0.7079[c]	0.7909[c]	0.6647[c]	0.6704[c]	0.6781[c]	0.6802[c]	0.6153[c]	0.8067[b]	0.6695[c]	5.070[a]	5.254[a]
	(1.42)	(1.59)	(1.32)	(1.33)	(1.34)	(1.34)	(1.41)	(1.61)	(1.32)	(2.51)	(2.65)
DEV × *C(SM)*							−0.07284[c]				
							(−1.41)				
PROP × *C(SM)*								−0.07554[a]			−0.07609[a]
								(−2.53)			(−2.59)
> 1/5 YRS × *C(SM)*									−0.0442		
									(0.38)		
SERV × *C(SM)*										−0.05715[b]	−0.05768[a]
										(−2.25)	(−2.32)
R^2	0.12	0.14	0.11	0.12	0.12	0.12	0.13	0.15	0.12	0.14	0.18
F	2.92[a]	3.04[a]	2.80[a]	2.58[a]	2.54[a]	2.34[b]	2.71[a]	3.34[a]	2.54[a]	3.15[a]	3.65[a]
d.f.	7/152	8/151	7/152	8/151	8/151	9/150	8/151	8/151	8/151	8/151	9/150

Figures in parentheses are *t*-statistics.
Levels of significance: [a] = 1 %; [b] = 5 %; [c] = 10 %.

($t = 1.31$, $p = 0.10$). On the whole, it would seem that business units with a short development time spend a similar annual percentage of revenues for R & D as those where development time is long. This means, however, that the total cost and risk of completing an R & D project is lower in the former type of business than in the latter. Concentration should, therefore, be less necessary where development time is short. The significant negative coefficient for the interaction between development time and concentration (Equation (1.7), $t = -1.41$, $p = 0.08$) bears out this expectation. While a 10 percent increase in concentration adds 0.77 percentage points for a business with long product development, it adds only 0.04 percentage points (0.77 − 0.73) to research spending where product development time is short.

The coefficient for the dummy variable indicating that a business can prevent imitation of its products by competitors is significantly positive in all equations. The corresponding interaction term is also highly significant in equation (1.8) ($t = -2.53$, $p = 0.01$). For businesses without proprietary products, a 10 percent increase in concentration adds 0.27 percentage points to research spending, whereas the same increase in concentration reduces research spending by 0.49 percentage points (0.27 − 0.76) for the other type of business.

Following Shrieves [1978], it was expected that research intensity should be highest for low purchase frequency businesses and lowest when purchase frequency is high. The results suggest a nonlinear relationship, with very low and high frequency products spending least, and products purchased in intervals of between once every six months and once every year spending most on R & D relative to sales. The following reasons may explain the failure to observe the expected pattern of findings. First, Shrieves's argument was based on the assumption that innovators in low-purchase frequency markets benefit from precipitated replacement purchases. However, incumbent firms may well attempt to prevent this behavior, for example by announcing the imminent availability of their own models with superior features. A second reason for the results may be that purchase frequency is related to other factors affecting innovation incentives such as the speed of market penetration. Low purchase frequency products may penetrate markets more slowly than other types of products. In conclusion, because low purchase frequency products, contrary to initial expectations, offer no superior research incentives, concentration also should not interact with it. In fact, the interaction term in equation (1.9) lacks statistical significance ($t = -0.38$, $p = 0.35$).

Finally, the coefficient for the dummy variable indicating the possibility of creating barriers to supplier switching through the provision of various types of product-related services is positive and statistically significant in all equations. Its interaction with concentration, as expected, is negative and significant ($t = -2.25$, $p = 0.01$). A 10 percent increase adds 0.32 percentage points to research spending when no barriers to supplier-switching exist, but reduces research spending by 0.25 percentage points (0.32 − 0.57) otherwise.

In Equation (2.1), the interaction terms for proprietary technology, and services are introduced simultaneously.[3] The non-interaction term for concentration, therefore, refers to businesses which are characterized by the absence of protection against product imitation, and of barriers against supplier switching.[4] For these businesses, a 10 percent increase in concentration increases research spending by 0.50 percentage points. But for businesses with the opposite characteristics (i.e., enjoying proprietary products and barriers to supplier switching), a 10 percent increase in concentration reduces research spending by 0.84 percentage points (0.50 − (0.76 + 0.58)).[5] Considering the average research spending in this sample is 2.91 percent, concentration appears to be not only statistically but also practically significant.

CONCLUSION

In keeping with past findings, this study confirms that concentration, measured in broadly defined industries, has a negligible, possibly slightly negative, average impact on research investment in industries facing a fertile technological environment. But when concentration is measured within more appropriately defined industry boundaries and when the R & D cost and uncertainty and the speed of imitation are taken into account, this average picture resolves into sharply differentiated situations. On one extreme are industries with low cost and uncertainty of R & D and strong barriers against imitation. Here, sufficient incentives for innovation exist even in the absence of high concentration. When concentration does exist, it tends to reduce significantly the level of research investment. High concentration appears to be detrimental to the vigorous exploitation of technological opportunities under these circumstances. At the other extreme are industries with high cost and uncertainty of R & D, and no barriers to imitation. Here, an increase in concentration is accompanied by a significant increase in research investment. In these industries, existing technological opportunities may not be exploited as long as industry structure remains atomistic. Here, high concentration appears to be essential to provide adequate incentives for innovation.

REINHARD ANGELMAR,
INSEAD,
European Institute of Business Administration,
Boulevard de Constance,
77305 Fontainebleau Cedex,
France.

ACCEPTED APRIL 1984

[3] Introduction of the interaction term for product development time, although conceptually desirable, was not possible, as there would have been only one observation in one of the cells.

[4] 56 business units were in this situation. This group was composed of the following types of businesses: consumer durables = 18 %; consumer non-durables = 11 %; capital goods = 14 %; raw- or semi-finished materials = 9 %; components for finished products = 29 %; supplies for consumable products = 20 %.

[5] 27 business units were in this group which was composed of the following types of businesses: consumer durables = 4 %; capital goods = 33 %; raw- or semi-finished materials = 7 %; components for finished products = 44 %; supplies for consumable products = 11 %.

REFERENCES

COMANOR, W. S., 1967, 'Market Structure, Product Differentiation, and Industrial Research', *Quarterly Journal of Economics*, 81 (November), pp. 639–57.

GLOBERMAN, S., 1973, 'Market Structure and R & D in Canadian Manufacturing Industries', *Quarterly Review of Economics and Business*, 13 (Summer), pp. 59–67.

ROSENBERG, J. B., 1976, 'Research and Market Share: A Reappraisal of the Schumpeter Hypothesis', *Journal of Industrial Economics*, 25 (December), pp. 101–12.

SCHERER, F. M., 1967, 'Market Structure and the Employment of Scientists and Engineers', *American Economic Review*, 57 (June), pp. 524–31.

SCHERER, F. M., 1967, 'Research and Development Resource Allocation under Rivalry', *Quarterly Journal of Economics*, 81 (August), pp. 359–94.

SCHERER, F. M., 1980, *Industrial Market Structure and Economic Performance*, 2nd Ed. (Rand McNally, Chicago, 1980).

SHRIEVES, R. E., 1978, 'Market Structure and Innovation: A New Perspective', *Journal of Industrial Economics*, 26 (June), pp. 329–47.

Strategic Planning Institute, 1978, *Data Manual* (Cambridge).

WEIGAND, R. E., 1980, 'Buying in to Market Control', *Harvard Business Review*, (November–December), pp. 141–49.

WISE, T. A., 1966, 'IBM's $5,000,000 Gamble', *Fortune Magazine*, (September).

THE JOURNAL OF INDUSTRIAL ECONOMICS 0022–1821 $2.00
Volume XXXIV September 1985 No. 1

CABLE TELEVISION IN A LESS REGULATED MARKET

PATRICIA L. PACEY*

With many regulations and limitations on U.S. cable television being lifted, new opportunities for consumers and cable suppliers are available. Using a logistic function I estimate a model for the demand for basic cable television services. My model differs from earlier cable penetration analyses primarily because of the inclusion of pay television characteristics. The results suggest that reception quality has improved over time and the earlier disadvantages of UHF stations have diminished. As expected, the addition of pay television has enhanced the desirability of cable. Also, the elasticity of the basic subscription fee differs between urban and rural systems.

I. INTRODUCTION

CABLE TELEVISION was originally developed in the United States to aid the transmission of over-the-air television in order to serve those who could not receive local broadcast signals (i.e., rural areas or areas with terrain obstacles). In its inception, the community antenna television system, or CATV, transmitted local signals into these areas to improve television reception. Local television stations and networks had resisted further inroads by cable operators as they feared the availability of other distant signals would divert viewers away from them. The initial Federal Communication Commission (FCC) rules, in accommodating this concern, limited cable growth outside rural markets. Then, in the early 1970s, the FCC allowed the importation of some distant signals in an effort to stimulate cable growth.[1]

The most noteworthy study on assessing the effects of the new FCC rules was undertaken by Park [1972].[2] Park, employing a nonlinear model of cable penetration, found that the proposed new FCC rules (*circa* 1970) would help stimulate cable growth but that more relaxation of these rules was probably necessary to attract customers living in urban areas to cable.

* The author would like to thank Les Taylor, Keith Maskus, and Ulrich Kohli for assistance at the early stages of this project. Also, I especially appreciate the improvements suggested by an anonymous referee. The former National Telecommunications and Information Agency made some of the needed data available.

[1] The FCC, in recognizing the potential consumer benefits of cable, attempted to increase the availability of cable without harming over-the-air broadcast signals.

[2] All of the earlier studies were undertaken during highly restrictive FCC policies toward cable TV. The first significant contribution in the area of cable television demand was forwarded by Comanor and Mitchell [1971]. Others that have added to the understanding of cable TV are Park [1972], Noll–Peck–McGowan [1973], and the Johns Hopkins study [1976]. In all of these studies, the dependent variable is the ratio of the number of cable subscribers to the number of homes passed by the cable TV company (or some slight modification of this).

Since the Park study, a combination of favorable judicial decisions and a general trend toward deregulation has inspired significant growth in the cable industry. Cable is now expanding into the more populous urban areas, and it is developing more attractive programming. As a result, a fairly wide range of choices is being offered in an increasing number of markets. The variety of options now available to the cable subscriber range from news and sports to religion and programs designed for special groups (e.g., foreign language, children, etc.).

Using a modified Park model, this paper investigates how the cable industry has fared since the relaxation of the FCC rules in the early and then again in the late 1970s. My model differs from Park's in that it includes both urban and rural cable systems, pay television characteristics, the availability of superstations and the recognition of terrain obstacles. The model in this paper is designed to examine the changes in broadcast signals and to evaluate how the more flexible FCC rules have affected cable penetration rates.

The theoretical considerations are discussed and modeled in section II, while section III describes the data and develops the estimating equation. The empirical results are reviewed in section IV, and section V has my concluding remarks.

II. THEORETICAL ASPECTS OF THE DEMAND FOR CABLE TV SERVICES

Basic cable television services refers to that group of services offered by a cable television system at a fixed monthly price. Such services include, *inter alia*, retransmitted local or distant broadcast television signals and also cable and local origination networks, where the marginal price of any one of these services individually is zero.

For the purpose of modelling the demand for basic cable service, several characteristics must be considered. First, a household must have the opportunity to purchase the service. Although a cable system may serve a particular community, it is not necessarily true that all households located there have access to the service. Thus, demand analysis must be restricted to that group of households passed by the cable.

Second, once given access to the system, an individual household must decide whether or not to subscribe to basic service. The choice will depend on the individual household's demographic characteristics and on the price, quantity, and quality of service offered by the system.

Third, once the household has decided to subscribe to basic service, it then may have the opportunity to subscribe to a pay service. Generally, a household cannot subscribe to a pay service without purchasing basic service first.[3] Hence, pay services enter the demand function for basic service as an

[3] In some major cities, households can subscribe to over-the-air pay services provided by STV (Subscription Television) stations or MDS (Multipoint Distribution Service) stations. These media outlets are for the most part located in areas without cable. Hence, the household deciding on cable services rarely has STV or MDS as an available option. Moreover, the prices charged for these services are generally at least double those of pay cable services.

additional programming option. Since pay cable services require the payment of an additional subscription fee and not all cable systems offer pay services, these programming options must be treated differently than the basic services included in the fixed monthly fee to gain cable access.

The utility function for the ith household is given by the LaGrangian function below:[4]

$$(1) \qquad L = U(\theta_i q_{ij}, x_i) - \lambda(\theta_i r_{ij} q_{ij} + p x_i - y_i)$$

where

θ_i = dichotomous variable where $\theta_i = 1$ if the ith household chooses to obtain basic cable TV; $\theta_i = 0$ if not;
q_{ij} = vector of basic and pay TV options facing i^{th} household in system j;
x_i = composite good of all other private goods and services;
p = price of composite good x;
r_{ij} = vector of prices of basic and pay TV options for i^{th} household in system j;
y_i = income of the ith household.

Assuming $\theta_i = 1$ and maximizing equation (1) I find the usual Marshallian demand functions. From this, the inverse demand function for cable TV is obtained and the net benefits to a household for each option can be determined by the expression

$$(2) \qquad w_{ijk}(r_{ij}, p, y_i) - r_{ijk}$$

Here w_{ijk} is the willingness to pay (from the inverse demand function) by household i in system j for the kth option, where k is the index of the service options. A consumer will subscribe only if there is a configuration of services (one of which must be basic) such that the summation of consumer surplus is positive; I will subsequently refer to this summation as S_i. Thus, the condition for $\theta_i = 1$ is $S_i > 0$.[5]

The penetration rate, the proportion of houses passed by cable TV that subscribe to cable TV, is obtained by aggregating over the household demand functions. Let N_{HP} denote the number of households passed by cable and N_S the number of basic cable TV subscribers. Thus, the number of subscribers is given by

$$(3) \qquad N_S = \sum_{i=1}^{N_{HP}} \theta_i$$

[4] The specification, $r_{ij}q_{ij}$, assumes the vector of basic and pay TV options and their respective prices are independent. Also, it is assumed that the unavailability of pay TV and the decision not to subscribe to any pay TV channels can be treated for purposes here as the same decision.

[5] More precisely, household i will subscribe if there is any combination that yields a positive consumer surplus. That is, household i may get a negative consumer surplus from pay services but if $S > 0$ for basic, it subscribes. Another possibility is that the consumer surplus from pay services outweighs the negative consumer surplus household i derives from basic service such that $S > 0$ and it subscribes.

Given N_{HP}, the number of cable subscribers, N_S, will be determined by the probability that the typical household's consumer surplus is greater than zero.[6] Hence,

$$(4) \qquad N_S/N_{HP} = P(S_i > 0) = f(p, y, r)$$

III. DESCRIPTION OF THE DATA AND MODEL

Since penetration is the ratio of subscribers of basic services to homes passed by cable, its value must fall between zero and one. The empirical evidence of earlier studies suggests that the appropriate functional form for the model is a logistic specification[7]

$$PR = 1/(1+e^{-f})$$

where

PR = the penetration rate defined as the ratio of subscribers to homes passed by the cable system,

f = a linear function of the independent variables describing cable system, environmental characteristics and subscriber demographics.

By rearranging the logistic formulation and taking the natural logarithm of both sides, the resulting equation becomes

$$(5) \qquad \ln(PR/1-PR) = f$$

With the addition of an error term, the parameters of the function f can be obtained from a least squares regression. The independent variables defining f are classified in three categories: cable system characteristics, demographic information, and what has been termed in the literature as the comparative service variables. The definition and source of each variable are discussed and identified in Table I.

The inclusion and specification of the cable system's age assumes that the length of time it takes households to learn about cable does not vary across systems and that all the systems are in short-run equilibrium so that the number of homes passed by cable is fixed. System age, measured as the number of months in operation, typically has been specified as a logarithmic function of the inverse of age and its coefficient is expected to be negative.[8]

As noted above, the early stages of cable television development were highly regulated and limited primarily to rural areas where network programming was not available. In addition, the initial monthly subscription fee was typically very low and, since little or no television viewing was available

[6] This assumes the distribution of incomes, tastes, etc. within each cable system to be similar.

[7] For example, see Park [1972] and Comanor and Mitchell [1971].

[8] Observation of cable systems over time indicates that despite different cable market characteristics, growth trends are similar. For further support of this specification, see Comanor and Mitchell [1971], and Noll, Peck, and McGowan [1973].

without cable in these rural areas, one would not expect the cable subscription fee to be a significant factor in determining cable demand. Yet my sample considers both urban and rural areas in a more relaxed regulatory environment. This suggests that the price specification should include two variables: (1) the basic subscription fee,[9] and (2) the product of the subscription fee and a dichotomous variable distinguishing urban systems from rural systems. Basic subscription price is specified in logarithmic form and its coefficient is expected to be negative or insignificant while the second price variable (given urban systems are identified as = 1) should be negative.

Superstations enter the model as a dichotomous variable, where the value of 1 is used when a cable system carries any one (or all) of the superstations, and a value of 0 is assigned to systems without superstation availability.[10]

Geographic obstacles such as mountains, tall buildings, etc., will reduce reception quality. The value of 1 identifies these terrain difficulties; 0 is the value assigned to cable systems without these obstacles. One expects, *ceteris paribus*, the average penetration rate to be higher, for systems incurring terrain problems, i.e., a positive coefficient.

The Johns Hopkins study [1976], hypothesized that an increase in local origination would reduce the demand for basic cable services. Hence, the logarithm of the number of local origination channels plus one has been incorporated into my model.

Pay cable is introduced into the model in two ways: first with a dummy variable indicating the availability of pay TV, and second with a multiplicative dummy variable incorporating the average price of pay and the pay dummy.[11] The value of the dichotomous variable for pay TV availability is 1 if one or more pay channels are available; and 0 otherwise. It is expected to have a positive impact on subscription to basic service. This conditional variable incorporating the price of pay TV is defined as the product of the dummy variable and the log of the average price of pay channels on the system. As with the other price variable, one expects a negative sign on this variable, but a larger price elasticity than basic cable since a higher price for this service may make basic cable subscription less attractive.

Mean household income for the county or counties in which each cable system operates is the demographic variable which also enters in logarithms. A preferred variable would have been the log of mean household income for *homes passed* by the cable system, but since, the data are unavailable, the

[9] Installation charges would normally be considered in the modeling of the demand for cable services. However, this fee is often reduced or waived as part of the marketing efforts of cable operators to generate new subscriptions. The discriminating buyer of cable services thus can normally avoid the payment of these fees and their inclusion in the model would be misleading.

[10] Superstations are standard broadcast stations, the signals of which are picked up by video common carriers (microwave and satellite) and retransmitted to cable systems all over the United States. For four systems in the sample, one of these three superstations was available as a local signal.

[11] Average price of pay TV for each system is used since a relatively small number of systems have two or more pay channels and very little variation in their prices.

more general data were utilized. Thus, the inclusion of this variable may well lead to lower penetration estimates since cable operation will generally provide access to higher income areas first.

The variables described in earlier studies as comparative service variables are generally considered to be most important in explaining penetration rates

TABLE I
VARIABLES IN THE EQUATION

Variable	*Definition*	*Source*
PEN	Natural log of ratio of subscribers of basic service to homes passed by cable system.	Federal Communications Commission [FCC], Form 325, Schedule 1.
Y	Natural log of the mean income per household for 1979.	U.S. Department of Commerce, Bureau of Economic Analysis, Survey of Current Business.
BASIC	Natural log of the monthly fee for basic cable TV service.	*1980–81 Television Factbook Services Volume* [*TVFSE*], or *Broadcast Cable Yearbook 1981* [*BCY*].
URBAN	Natural log of the monthly fee for basic cable TV service times a dichotomous variable identifying urban cable systems as = 1 and rural cable systems = 0.	1980 Bureau of Census.
PAY	Natural log of the average monthly fee for pay TV times the dichotomous variable for the availability of pay TV.	*Pay TV Census*, Volume 1, December 1980.
AGE	Natural log of the inverse of the age of the cable system in months.	FCC, Form 325, Schedule I or *TVFSE*.
NET	Natural log of the primary network comparative service variable.	*Television Factbook Stations Volume* [*TVFST*], and *Television Digest's 1980–81 Cable and Station Coverage Atlas* [*TDCSCA*].
DUP	Natural log of the duplicate network comparative service variable.	FCC, Form 325, Schedule II, *TVFST* and *TDCSCA*.
IND	Natural log of the independent network comparative service variable.	FCC, Form 325, Schedule II, *TVFST*, and *TDCSCA*.
ED	Natural log of the educational network comparative service variable.	FCC, Form 325, Schedule II, *TVFST*, and *TDCSCA*.
ORIG	Natural log of the number of current origination channels plus 1.	FCC, Form 325, Schedule II.
T	Dichotomous variable where $T = 1$ if physical obstacles obstruct reception quality; = 0 if otherwise.	*TDCSCA* and Topographical maps.
SUPER	Dichotomous variable where $SS = 1$ if one or more superstations are available on the cable system; = 0 if not.	FCC, Form 325, Schedule II.
DPAY	Dichotomous variable where $DPAY = 1$ if pay TV is available; 0 if not.	*Pay TV Census*, Volume 1, December 1980.

in the cable industry. The comparative service variables are defined as the ratio of service on cable to service over-the-air by the type of broadcast (i.e., primary network, duplicate, independent, or educational station). In previous studies service was simply measured as the number of stations (cable or over-the-air) in the area. Park found substantial differences in the quality of the reception of over-the-air services and that these differences depended on the distance of the station from its transmitter as well as on the type of station signal (VHF or UHF).[12] Park accounted for these differences in over-the-air signals by reformulating the comparative service variable to include δ, a parameter to estimate the distance discount factor, and γ, a parameter estimating the relative value of UHF to VHF stations.[13]

The signs for all of the comparative service variables are expected to be positive, since, as the availability of selected types of cable stations increase relative to their over-the-air counterpart, cable penetration should also increase.

Thus, the estimating equation is specified below:[14]

$$(6) \quad PEN = \beta_0 + \beta_1 Y + \beta_2 BASIC + \beta_3 URBAN + \beta_4 PAY + \beta_5 AGE + \beta_6 NET + \beta_7 DUP + \beta_8 IND + \beta_9 ED + \beta_{10} ORIG + \beta_{11} T + \beta_{12} SUPER + \beta_{13} DPAY + \varepsilon.$$

[12] To calculate a value for over-the-air services, it was necessary to estimate the "d" value for each station, d being defined as the ratio of distance of the cable system from the broadcast station's transmitter to the distance of the station's B contour from its transmitter. The geographic coordinates of the station transmitter and the coordinates of the main post office of the city in which the cable system was located were obtained and run in a special statistical program that will compute the distance values for the numerator of "d". These coordinates were obtained from *TVFST* or *BCY*, and from the *Rand McNally International Atlas*, respectively. Again, data from *TVFST* and *BCY* was utilized to find the radius (average) of each broadcast station's B contour.

At its inception UHF stations were considered inferior because many households had older television sets that could not receive UHF signals; the reception quality was lacking; and the tuner required special attention and was inconvenient.

[13] For example, a Park specification for the comparative service variable for primary network stations can be expressed as

$$NET = \frac{1+W}{1+\gamma\sum_u (1-d^\delta)^{1/\delta} + \sum_v (1-d^\delta)^{1/\delta}}$$

where

W = the number of primary network stations carried on cable,
d = the ratio of the distance between the cable system and the station transmitter to the distance between the station's B contour and its transmitter,
u = set of UHF stations with primary network stations carried over-the-air,
v = set of VHF stations with primary network stations carried over-the-air,
γ, δ = parameters to be estimated.

[14] A random sample of 480 systems from the *1980–81 Television Factbook, Services Volume* (*TVFSE*), was eventually reduced to 241 systems, due to problems with non-availability and/or inconsistency of some aspects of the data. However, tests comparing the characteristics of the large and paired sample showed no bias, indicating that the smaller sample has the same characteristics of the larger initial sample.

TABLE II
CABLE PENETRATION

Variable	$\hat{\beta}$	*Standard Error of* $\hat{\beta}$	*t-statistic*	*Elasticity**
Y	0.649	0.311	2.08	0.079
BASIC	0.148	0.346	0.43	0.063
URBAN	−0.415	0.103	−4.03	−0.208
PAY	−1.632	0.659	−2.48	−1.566
AGE	−0.680	0.109	−6.26	−0.025
NET	0.500	0.173	2.89	0.205
DUP	0.296	0.101	2.91	0.125
IND	−0.200	0.151	−1.32	−0.106
ED	−0.368	0.185	−1.99	−0.198
ORIG	−0.083	0.110	−0.76	−0.042
T	0.430	0.186	2.31	0.519
SUPER	0.301	0.152	1.98	0.548
DPAY	3.080	1.479	2.08	0.914
CONSTANT	−4.464	1.278	−3.49	

R-squared = 0.49
n = 241
* Evaluated at the mean, for the probability of penetration.

IV. THE EMPIRICAL RESULTS

Table II presents the empirical results of OLS regressions on the cross-section of 241 cable systems in 1980.[15]

For the most part, the empirical results are as expected. In general, the model suggests that cable systems carrying primary and duplicate network programming relative to over-the-air will have higher penetration rates. Also, basic and pay cable specifications for price and the aggregate income variables corresponds to *a priori* expectations.

Of significant interest is the implication of the empirical results that $\delta = 1.3$ and $\gamma = 0.92$ as compared to Park's [1972] values of 1.6 and 0.73, respectively. Since values of 1.0 indicate no distortion, these results indicate that UHF stations may still have a small disadvantage relative to VHF stations and that reception quality still declines with distance though at a considerably slower rate than it had in the past. This slower rate of decline is probably due to the improved technology of home reception equipment.

Since the dependent variable in the estimating equation (7) is not the penetration rate, *PR*, but rather is the logarithm of $PR/(1-PR)$, the estimated parameters cannot be interpreted in the usual manner.[16]

[15] The referee raised the possibility of feedback onto the price of pay TV from basic cable penetration. To test for this, an instrumental variable was created for the price of pay TV using characteristics of pay television and other exogenous variables. The results using this instrumental variable are similar to the equation reported, thus, suggesting that there is not a problem of simultaneity. In addition, Goldfeld-Quandt tests were run to check for heteroskedasticity. None was found.

[16] The method for finding the appropriate calculations is available from the author upon request.

Interestingly, the price of basic cable TV service for rural systems is statistically insignificant while urban cable systems are sensitive to price changes. The findings here suggest that, on average, a 10 percent price increase (decrease) will have no statistically significant effect on the penetration rate of rural systems but should decrease (increase) the penetration rate of urban cable systems by 1.5 percentage points.

Moreover, the coefficient for the pay TV price variable (*PAY*) is of the correct sign and statistically significant. The results indicate that the demand for basic cable is quite elastic with respect to the price of pay TV with an elasticity of −1.57. Thus, its coefficient indicates that a 10 percent increase in the price of pay TV will reduce the demand for cable services by 11.0 percentage points, i.e., from an average penetration rate of 70 percent to 59 percent. It is not surprising, then, that the rate of basic cable TV penetration is quite sensitive to the availability of pay TV and its price.

The estimated coefficient for the comparative variable for primary network service, *NET*, of 0.500 indicates an elasticity of 0.205. Since an additional network signal provided by cable will cause, on average, a 24 percent increase in *NET*, basic penetration will increase by approximately 4.9 percent or an increase of 3.4 percentage points. The increase in basic penetration due to the addition of another duplicate station, *DUP*, is somewhat smaller, approximately 2.1 percentage points.

The age parameter, *AGE*, estimates the coefficient to be −0.680, indicating that the cable system approaches maturity very quickly.

The coefficient for income per household, *Y*, 0.649, is of the expected sign and size and indicates that a 1 percent increase in income (per household) would result in approximately one-tenth of a percent increase in cable penetration. Given that cable operators had entered rural markets that did not have access to the primary networks and/or into the high income, high density urban markets, this result is not unreasonable.

The three dummy variables recognizing terrain obstacles (*T*); the availability of pay TV (*DPAY*); and the availability of a superstation (*SUPER*), all proved to be significant and of the expected sign. Thus, the average level of cable penetration is higher by 0.519 when terrain obstacles exist, by 0.914 when pay TV is available and by 0.548 when superstations are available.

Unfortunately, the comparative service variable for independent stations is statistically insignificant. This result is unexpected, as one would expect an increase in the number of independent stations carried on cable relative to over-the-air to have a positive effect on cable penetration. Three probable explanations for this perverse sign can be offered. First, stations that are not technically defined as superstations but have expansive broadcast signals are included in the independent services category. Results would likely be improved if these stations had been classified separately or as superstations. Second, the comparative service specification does not account for differences in the attractiveness of the imported signal and these signals are not likely to be of similar value. Third, a closer inspection of the data indicates that a large number of the independent stations are situated on/or very near the *B* contour (not surprising, given the earlier FCC regulations). This means the value of the comparative service variable for the independents in this system will reduce to one and, hence, in a large number of observations will cluster at one point—perhaps obscuring the true relationship.

Finally, local origination and the comparative service variable for educational service have unexpected signs. However, the local origination variable is statistically insignificant, and the inconclusiveness here may be due, in part, to the inability of the data to account for differences in the attractiveness of the signal. The negative and statistically significant coefficient on educational service suggests that an increase in these educational offerings on cable relative to over-the-air will have an adverse effect on cable penetration rates. Further investigation is needed to determine the validity of this particular result.

V. CONCLUSIONS

Park's findings in his 1972 study were that cable operators were not likely to displace over-the-air broadcast signals and that the FCC permission to transmit some distant signals would help to increase cable penetration rates in the cities. Park also called for even more relaxation of the FCC rules and additional programming by cable operators so as to have the flexibility and opportunity necessary to attract new customers.

An important finding here is that the UHF handicap has declined and that there is now little difference between UHF and VHF broadcast signals. Also, my model confirms Park's expectations of rapid maturation of cable systems.[17] Not surprisingly, this study indicates that urban cable subscribers are likely to be responsive to the basic subscription fee and that pay television options are quite elastic.

PATRICIA L. PACEY,
College of Business and Administration,
University of Colorado,
Boulder, Colorado 80309,
USA.

ACCEPTED MARCH 1985

[17] More specifically, the model does not indicate which came first—new subscribers or new programming—but rather that additional programming options will have a positive impact on cable penetration rates.

REFERENCES

BESEN, C. M. and CRANDALL, R. W., 1981, 'The Deregulation of Cable Television', *Law and Contemporary Problems* 44 (1) (Winter), pp. 130–50.

BESEN, C. M., MITCHELL, B. M., NOLL, R. G., OWEN, B. M., PARK, R. E. and

ROSSE, J. N., 1977, 'Economic Policy Research on Cable Television: Assessing the Costs and Benefits of Cable Deregulation', from *Deregulation of Cable TV*, edited by MacAvoy (American Enterprise Institute, Washington, DC), pp. 45–87.

Broadcast Cable/Yearbook 1981, Broadcasting Publications Inc.: Washington, DC, 1981.

Charles Rivers Associates, Inc., 1973, 'Analysis of the Demand for Cable Television', CRA Report No. 178–2 (Cambridge, Massachusetts), pp. 1–101.

COMANOR, W. S. and MITCHELL, B. M., 1971, 'Cable Television and the Impact of Regulation', *Bell Journal of Economics and Manpower Science* (Spring), pp. 154–212.

Federal Communication Commission, FCC Form 325 Schedules I and II.

LYALL, K., DUNCAN, R. and DEKAY, C. F., 1976, Johns Hopkins Cable Project: 'Estimation of an Urban Cable Demand Model and Its Implications for Regulations for Major Markets', Center for Metropolitan Planning and Research (Johns Hopkins University, Baltimore, Maryland), pp. 1–80, appendices.

MCGOWAN, J. J. and PECK, M. J., 1970, 'Estimating Consumer's Valuation of Additional Television Programming from CATV: Data', mimeographed manuscript.

NOLL, R. G., PECK, M. J. and MCGOWAN, J. J., 1973, *Economic Aspects of Television Regulation* (The Brookings Institute, Washington, D.C.).

PARK, R. E., 1972, 'Prospects for Cable in the 100 Largest Television Markets', *Bell Journal of Economics* (Spring), pp. 130–50.

PARK, R. E., 1979, 'Audience Diversion Due to Cable Television: A Statistical Analysis of New Data' (The Rand Corporation), R-2403-FCC, (April), pp. 1–59.

Paul Kagan Associates, 1981, *The Pay TV Census*, Volume I (Carmel, CA).

Rand McNally and Company, 1980, *The New International Atlas* (Rand McNally, Chicago), pp. 15–232.

TAYLOR, L. D., 1980, *Telecommunications Demand: A Survey and Critique* (Ballinger, Cambridge, Massachusetts).

Television Digest, 1980, *Cable and Station Coverage Atlas, 1980–81* (Television Digest Inc.: Washington, DC).

Television Digest, 1981, *Television Factbook, Services Volume* (Television Digest Inc.: Washington, DC), 50.

Television Digest, 1981, *Television Factbook, Stations Volume* (Television Digest Inc.: Washington, DC), 50.

U.S. Department of Commerce, Bureau of Economic Analysis, Survey of Current Business.

Wharton Economic Forecasting Associates Study by SCHINK and THANAWALA, 1978, 'The Impacts of Cable TV on Local Station Audience', (March), pp. 1–102.

THE JOURNAL OF INDUSTRIAL ECONOMICS 0022-1821 $2.00
Volume XXXIV September 1985 No. 1

MANAGERIAL SHAREHOLDING

DAVID FLATH AND CHARLES R. KNOEBER

The extent of a manager's shareholdings in his employing firm is modelled as part (along with the extent of reliance on incentive contracting) of an "optimal contract" between the manager and other shareholders. Implications are that manager shareholding will be less in firms with greater variance of shareholder income and in non-cash businesses. Empirical evidence supports these implications as well as the contention that where manager shareholding is less, there is more reliance on incentive contracting. Consequently, there may be no difference in managerial behavior where manager shareholding is great and where it is small.

THE COINCIDENCE of interests between the manager of a firm and the (other) shareholders is often asserted to vary with the extent of manager-held shares. For example, managers who do not hold shares in their employing firms are said to face a low penalty for using the firms to provide themselves with security, emoluments, an easy life, and so on.[1] However, this overlooks the fact that manager shareholding is not the only mechanism which ties a manager's interest to that of the other shareholders. An alternative is incentive contracting whereby the manager's salary is made to depend upon a shareholder estimator of his performance. Variation in manager shareholding may be offset by greater or less reliance on incentive contracting. Thus, there is no necessary relation between the extent of manager shareholding and managerial behaviour.[2]

The extent of manager shareholding and the extent of incentive contracting can be viewed as parts of a contract between the manager and shareholders of a corporation. Each strengthens the manager's incentive to please the other shareholders but also increases the manager's risk-bearing costs—for which he must be compensated. Specifically, increased manager shareholding impedes diversification of the manager's personal stock portfolio, and increased reliance on incentive contracting allows shareholders' errors in the measurement of the manager's performance to more greatly affect his salary. The optimal contract will be gauged so that the gains from improving manager performance by either method are just offset by the costs.

It is our intention to show that the "optimal contract" model of the firm

[1] For a statement of this argument, see Monsen and Downs [1965].

[2] The obvious corollary is that there is no necessary relation between the extent of manager shareholding and measures of firm performance. This may partially explain the inconclusive and sometimes contradictory empirical results of those who have attempted to test the effect of "managerial control" on measures of firm performance. See, for example, Kania and McKean [1976] and Palmer [1973], [1975], Boudreaux [1975], McEachern [1976].

has refutable implications regarding the extent of manager shareholding—that it is less in firms with greater annual variance of shareholder income and in non-cash businesses—and to validate the implications with some data. In the process we also hope to demonstrate empirical support for the view that where manager shareholding is less, incentive contracting is relied upon to a greater extent than would otherwise be so. The paper is divided into two sections, one detailing the manager's contract with shareholders and the other developing hypotheses and presenting and interpreting empirical evidence. A brief conclusion follows.

I. THE MANAGER'S CONTRACT WITH SHAREHOLDERS[3]

Let the manager's pecuniary salary be described by the function

(1) $$W = \psi_1 - \psi_2 \hat{a},$$

where ψ_1 and ψ_2 are parameters, and $\hat{a}$ is the shareholders' unbiased, normally distributed estimator of nonstochastic "a", the manager's consumption of perquisites (measured as the dollar reduction in residual earnings of the firm). "Perquisites" is to be given the broadest possible interpretation. It includes slackened or ineffective effort as well as job-related amenities.

Let the residual earnings of the firm be represented as

(2) $$y = \phi - W - a,$$

where ϕ is an exogenous, normally distributed random variable, the firm's annual earnings gross of managerial compensation. Further, let α represent the manager's fractional claim on residual earnings. Shareholders other than the manager are presumed to hold fully diversified portfolios.

The value of the firm's stock is

(3) $$V = \frac{E(y)}{E(R)},$$

where R is the rate of return on the firm's stock and $E(\cdot)$ is the expected value operator. Let R_p denote the rate of return on the market portfolio of securities. Assume that ψ_1, ψ_2, and α have no influence upon cov RR_p; then these affect the value of the firm only by altering the expected level of the residual $E(y)$, and not the rate at which this expected stream is discounted $E(R)$.[4]

[3] Jensen and Meckling [1976] suggested a framework similar to this one.

[4] This is because holders of fully diversified portfolios will bid the price of the firm's stock to a level such that

$$E(R) = R_f + \frac{E(R_p) - R_f}{\sigma_{R_p}} \cdot \frac{\operatorname{cov} RR_p}{\sigma_{R_p}}$$

where R_f is the rate of return on the riskless security and $\frac{E(R_p) - R_f}{\sigma_{R_p}}$ is the "market price of risk". Note use of the assumption that ϕ, and hence R, is distributed normally. See, for example, Fama and Miller [1972, p. 292].

Now arrangements made by the shareholders with the firm's manager ideally will have the object of maximizing annual expected residual earnings subject to the constraint that the manager receive compensation with expected utility to him equal to that of his most attractive competing offer, $\bar{U}$:

$$\text{(4)} \qquad \text{Max } E(y) = E(\phi) - (\psi_1 - \psi_2 a) - a$$
$$\text{with respect to } \alpha, \psi_1, \psi_2$$
$$\text{subject to } E(U(\,\cdot\,)) = \bar{U}$$

Shareholders would like the manager to consume only those perquisites worth more to him than their cost (equal to one dollar). By choosing α and ψ_2 the shareholders impose a "price" for perquisites upon the manager.[5] This "price" is $\alpha(1-\psi_2)+\psi_2$. The last term represents the expected penalty imposed by the incentive contract for consumption of a perquisite. The first term represents the expected loss to the manager as shareholder for the consumption of a perquisite.[6] The shareholders would like to move this price toward one by raising α and/or ψ_2. However, doing so reduces the manager's expected utility. Raising α increases manager risk-bearing by impeding the diversification of his portfolio. Raising ψ_2 increases manager risk-bearing by increasing the variance of his pecuniary salary. To compensate for this drop in expected utility, the manager must be paid a larger expected pecuniary wage—ψ_1 must be raised. Because of this, shareholders incur a cost from raising the "price" of perquisites. The solution to (4), then, entails setting α

[5] Derivation of this "price" of perquisites proceeds as follows. The manager's income has the form

$$Z = \alpha(\phi - W - a) + W + h(a)$$

where $h(a)$ is the manager's valuation of perquisites which is assumed to be concave ($\partial h/\partial a > 0$, $\partial^2 h/\partial a^2 < 0$). Note that, by assumption in the text, ϕ and W are distributed normally and the other variables are not stochastic. Thus the manager's income is distributed normally and has mean and variance respectively

$$E(Z) = (1-\alpha)(\psi_1 - \psi_2 E(\hat{a})) + h(a) - \alpha a + \alpha E(\phi)$$

and

$$\sigma_Z^2 = (1-\alpha)^2 \psi_2^2 \sigma_{\hat{a}}^2 + \alpha^2 \sigma_\phi^2$$

Since the manager's consumption of perquisites, a, affects only the mean of his income and not its variance, the amount of perquisites consumed solves the equation

$$\frac{\partial E(Z)}{\partial a} = -(1-\alpha)\psi_2 - \alpha + \frac{\partial h}{\partial a} = 0$$

or

$$\frac{\partial h}{\partial a} = \alpha(1-\psi_2) + \psi_2$$

That is, marginal value of perquisites equals the "price" of perquisites.

[6] Notice that the agency problem persists even if the manager "owns" the firm in the sense of possessing more than fifty percent of the shares. For example, if ψ_2 is zero, a manager owning fifty-one percent of the shares pays a "price" of fifty-one cents when he consumes a perquisite which costs one dollar to the shareholders as a group. This is different in degree but not in kind from the case of a manager owning only forty-nine percent of the firm's shares.

and ψ_2 at levels such that the marginal net gain from raising either is zero.[7] Obviously, the levels at which α and ψ_2 are set depend upon the associated risk-bearing costs to the manager[8] and will vary across managers and across firms.[9]

Because manager shareholding and incentive contracting are each ways of improving manager performance, the more onerous is one to the manager, the greater would seem to be the reliance upon the other. In general, however, this result depends upon specific characteristics of the manager's distaste for risk-bearing. For example, it may be that a reduction in the accuracy with which shareholders estimate manager performance makes incentive contracting more distasteful to the manager, but that the induced response in his contract entails movement to a point on his (mean/variance) utility surface where manager shareholding becomes more distasteful, with the end result being less of both incentive contracting *and* manager shareholding. Thus in general where less manager shareholding is observed, one cannot necessarily presume that there is greater reliance upon incentive contracting than would otherwise be so, though intuitively this seems to be the likely case. In the following section we provide some empirical evidence that affirms this intuition.

II. EMPIRICAL EVIDENCE

A. *Incentive contracting and manager shareholding in 1930s retail firms*

Although data on manager shareholding and on incentive contracting are usually difficult to obtain, a study of retailing firms performed about forty years ago (Baker, [1938]) does contain such data. For 37 department stores and chain stores, Baker reported "percentage of stock owned by management near the end of 1934" determined by an SEC survey. Also, from data reported by Baker, it was possible to calculate the annual coefficient of variation (C.V.) in real salary of the three top executives in each company 1928–36. Finally, from data contained on the CRSP tapes, it was possible to calculate

[7] A similar result is derived by Marcus [1982, p. 376], using a framework like ours but considering a contract which includes only ψ_1 and α.

[8] Murthy [1977] provides evidence consistent with this argument. He suggests that firms with a dominant single product will have residual earnings less closely related to manager performance (more influenced by exogenous factors) than firms with a mix of products [pp. 36–8]. If residual earnings are used to estimate manager performance, then, the associated manager risk-bearing costs will be greater for those firms with a dominant product. The implication of our argument is that manager compensation will be less directly associated with firm residual earnings for dominant product firms than for those with a product mix. Murthy finds this to be true [pp. 88, 92–93, 98–99].

[9] Ignoring tax considerations, if shareholders adopt as their estimator of manager consumption of perquisites $\hat{a}$ the stock price of the firm, then manager shareholding and incentive contracting would be perfect substitutes, only their combined extent being fully determinant. This indeterminancy is not present in the actual case in which capital gains are taxed at a lower rate than ordinary income. That is, an incentive contract will not have any component based upon the stock price alone for the incentive effects of that component could be duplicated with a tax saving through manager shareholding.

TABLE I
SPEARMAN RANK CORRELATION COEFFICIENTS

Variables	*Annual Variance of Shareholder Income, 1926–34*	*Percent Voting Stock Owned by Management Near the End of 1934*
Percent of voting stock owned by management near the end of 1934	−0.418	
Annual C.V. in real compensation of three highest paid executives 1928–36	0.426	−0.459

Note: All correlation coefficients are significant at the 1 % level.

(for 32 firms) the annual variance of shareholder income for the period 1926–34. Shareholder income is defined as the change in the total market value of a firm's shares between the beginning and end of the year plus the total dollar value of dividends paid during the year.[10] With an executive's salary, W, as described in (1), variance of W is $\psi_2^2\sigma_{\tilde{a}}^2$. With $\sigma_{\tilde{a}}^2$ the same for all firms, differences across firms in reliance on incentive contracting (different ψ_2) will be reflected as differences in C.V. in executive salaries. We assume that $\sigma_{\tilde{a}}^2$ is the same for all firms and so interpret the C.V. in executive salary as a measure of reliance on incentive contracting.[11] Notice that if $\sigma_{\tilde{a}}^2$ is not the same across firms, it is likely smaller where greater reliance is placed on incentive contracting. Here more monitoring will likely be performed which reduces $\sigma_{\tilde{a}}^2$. If this is the case, using C.V. in executive salary as a measure of reliance on incentive contracting creates a bias against finding an inverse relation between extent of manager shareholding and reliance on incentive contracting.

For firms with greater annual variance of shareholder income, the risk-bearing costs associated with the manager holding any specific fraction of the stock ought to be greater, so that one expects less manager shareholding in such firms. These data are entirely consistent with this reasoning, the Spearman rank correlation between "percent voting stock owned by management" and the "variance of shareholder income" being significantly negative (see Table I).

[10] A list of firms along with figures for "percent of voting stock owned by management near the end of 1934", "annual C.V. in real compensation of three highest paid executives, 1928–36" and "annual variance of shareholder income, 1926–34" is available from the authors upon request.

[11] Within the logic of the model, the standard deviation (S.D.) in executive compensation would have been preferable to coefficient of variation but could not be inferred from the Baker data. The C.V. and S.D. will be most correlated by rank if the 1928–36 means in executive compensation do not vary by company. There is some evidence of a tendency for 1928–36 mean compensation of the three highest paid executives to have been higher in the larger retail firms, measured by asset size (Baker, [1938, exhibit 45, p. 99]). This would imply that the C.V. overstates the relative size of the S.D. for smaller firms, understates it for the larger firms, and would seem to strengthen our conclusion of more reliance upon incentive contracting in firms having large annual variance of shareholder income.

A further hypothesis is that in those firms for which the cost of manager shareholding is greater, the reliance on incentive contracting will be greater. These data also fail to refute this, for the Spearman rank correlation between "C.V. in executive salary" and "variance of shareholder income" is significantly positive (again see Table I). Our interpretation of this is that the firms with more variable shareholder income tended to rely more upon incentive contracting. Nor is this all. The even greater negative Spearman rank correlation between "percent voting stock owned by management" and "C.V. in executive salary" (Table I once more) at least suggests that the influences on these variables other than the variability of shareholder income, further exaggerated their tendency to move in opposite directions—that is, that manager shareholding and incentive contracting were substitutes, a higher cost of one inducing greater reliance on the other. This suggests that the usual conclusion of significantly greater substitution of manager goals for the owners' goal by managers with small shareholdings may be premature. Increased reliance on incentive contracting likely has accompanied, if not precipitated, reduced manager shareholding.

B. *Tax evasion and manager shareholding*

Another example of substitutability between manager shareholding and incentive contracting may be found in cash businesses such as fast food outlets and taverns. The cost of incentive contracting will be larger in such businesses than in others because of the greater sacrifice in tax evasion opportunities if an accurate shareholder estimator of manager performance is to be maintained. That is, tax evasion requires not reporting or "hiding" sales from tax collectors and that is less difficult for cash sales than for credit, as records of credit sales must be kept to ensure payment. However, unrecorded cash sales not only make tax collection difficult, they also make it difficult to estimate manager performance. Consequently, incentive contracting will be more costly and relied upon less as a result. Now if there exists substitutability between incentive contracting and manager shareholding we would expect cash businesses to a greater extent than others to be "owner-operated" and this indeed seems to be the case.[12,13]

[12] There is an additional reason why manager shareholding is likely larger in cash businesses. Since these businesses afford greater opportunity for skimming profits by the manager, the agency problem is more severe. As a consequence, the "price" for perquisites will be set higher, very likely by both requiring more manager shareholding, α, and by imposing a larger penalty in the incentive contract, ψ_2. For this point we are indebted to the referee.

[13] A similar argument can be made to explain the preponderance of owner-operated franchise outlets relative to company owned outlets in certain markets. Where estimating manager performance is more difficult, owner-operated franchises will be more prevalent. Caves and Murphy [1976] suggest this as a reason for the relatively high proportion of owner-operated franchises in auto sales, business aids (accounting, credit, and general business services), and soft-drink bottlers [p. 582].

CONCLUSION

The extent of a manager's shareholdings in his employing firm is modelled here as part (along with the extent of reliance on incentive contracting) of an "optimal contract" between the manager and other shareholders. Increased manager shareholding improves manager performance but at a cost to other shareholders since the manager must be compensated for his additional risk-bearing costs. Implications are that manager shareholding will be less in firms with greater variance of shareholder income, and in non-cash businesses. These implications are found to have empirical support. In addition, empirical evidence supports the contention that where manager shareholding is less, there is more reliance on incentive contracting. Consequently, there may be no difference in managerial behavior where manager shareholding is great and where it is small. Managers may have similar incentives in both situations.

DAVID FLATH AND CHARLES R. KNOEBER,
Department of Economics and Business,
North Carolina State University,
P.O. Box 8110,
Raleigh, NC 27695,
USA.

ACCEPTED JULY 1984

REFERENCES

BAKER, JOHN CALHOUN, 1938, *Executive Salaries and Bonus Plans* (McGraw-Hill, New York).

BOUDREAUX, KENNETH J., 1975, 'The Profit Variability Effects of the Managerial Enterprise: Comment', *Economic Inquiry*, 13 (March), pp. 124–26.

CAVES, RICHARD E. and MURPHY, WILLIAM F., II, 1976, 'Franchising: Firms, Markets and Intangible Assets', *Southern Economic Journal*, 42 (April), pp. 572–86.

FAMA, EUGENE F. and MILLER, MERTON H., 1972, *The Theory of Finance* (Holt, Rinehart and Winston, New York).

JENSEN, MICHAEL C. and MECKLING, WILLIAM H., 1976, 'Theory of the Firm: Managerial Behavior, Agency Costs and Ownership Structure', *Journal of Financial Economics*, 3 (October), pp. 305–60.

KANIA, JOHN J. and MCKEAN, JOHN R., 1976, 'Ownership, Control, and the Contemporary Corporation: A General Behavioral Analysis', *Kyklos*, 29, Fasc. 2, pp. 272–91.

MARCUS, ALAN J., 1982, 'Risk Sharing and the Theory of the Firm', *Bell Journal of Economics*, 13 (Autumn), pp. 369–78.

MCEACHERN, WILLIAM A., 1976, 'Corporate Control and Risk', *Economic Inquiry*, 14 (June), pp. 270–78.

MONSEN, R. JOSEPH, JR. and DOWNS, ANTHONY, 1965, 'A Theory of Large Managerial Firms', *The Journal of Political Economy*, 73 (June), pp. 221–36.

MURTHY, K. R. SRINIVASA, 1977, *Corporate Strategy and Top Executive Compensation* (Division of Research, Harvard Business School, Boston).

PALMER, JOHN, 1973, 'The Profit Variability Effects of the Managerial Enterprise', *Economic Inquiry*, 11 (June), pp. 228–31.

PALMER, JOHN, 1975, 'A Further Analysis of Profit Variability and Managerialism', *Economic Inquiry*, 13 (March), pp. 127–30.

THE JOURNAL OF INDUSTRIAL ECONOMICS 0022-1821 $2.00
Volume XXXIV September 1985 No. 1

ECONOMETRIC TESTS OF THE MARKET STRUCTURAL DETERMINANTS OF R & D INVESTMENT: CONSISTENCY OF ABSOLUTE AND RELATIVE FIRM SIZE MODELS*

JOHN D. CULBERTSON

This paper examines how the estimated coefficients in firm-level tests of the market structure—R & D hypothesis can be used to determine the effect of market restructuring on expected industry R & D. A theoretical taxonomy is illustrated with a simple single equation econometric model, and this example illustrates that even if the coefficients on the market power variables are significantly positive, market restructuring to reduce market concentration may increase expected industry R & D.

OUR STOCK of hypotheses about the determinants of privately financed research and development (R & D) contains two logically independent classes—those that address the influence of the firm's absolute size and those that address the structure of the market in which the firm operates. Normative conclusions reached from tests of these hypotheses accordingly may prescribe the optimal firm size for performance of research in two different and potentially conflicting senses. The former hypotheses lead us to search out an optimal *absolute* size. The latter point to an optimal level of concentration in the market, and thus a preferred firm size *relative to* the market. But firm size, market size, and market share are linked by an identity. Given that we test our hypotheses about absolute and relative size independently—often using firm-level data for the one, industry-level data for the other—we have no assurance that the implied optima are consistent, either in general or in any particular market. In this note, we examine this consistency problem in the context of an econometric model of the determinants of research and development expenditures.

The prevailing theory of the determinants of R & D includes independent hypotheses pointing toward both market structure and prevailing firm size as important influences. (See Scherer [1980, chapter 15] for a detailed discussion of these hypotheses.) For example, market structure may affect R & D performance by determining the firm's prospect for appropriating cash flows imputable to its innovative effort. If the arm's-length financing of investments in R & D is subject to failures in the capital market, then market structure affects the firm's capacity to undertake R & D through the amplitude of its cash

* I am indebted to Richard Caves, the late H. Michael Mann, Willard F. Mueller, Richard Schmalensee, and an anonymous referee for helpful comments.

flow. Absolute firm size may affect R & D performance through scale economies (or diseconomies) in the research process itself. Or firm size may be collinear with diversification, which is hypothesized by Nelson [1959] to promote the firm's R & D spending.

These and other hypotheses have been tested, in various combinations, on data sets in which both firms and industries serve as units of observation. The policy conclusions flowing from these tests pose the problem that concerns us in this note. If a test at the firm level implies that enlarged firm sizes improve R & D performance, does that logically imply that higher concentration levels (to accommodate larger firms) are desirable? Conversely, if industry-level tests confirm the Schumpeterian hypothesis that high concentration favors R & D performance, can we conclude that the increased firm sizes that result when concentration is increased will themselves improve R & D performance? Neither inference is possible. Structural relationships at the firm level require supplemental analysis before their implications for public policy become unambiguous. Conversely, statistical tests at the industry level are not sufficient for addressing the firm-level hypotheses.

The regressors used in these econometric models can usefully be divided into two groups, for purposes of our analysis. The first comprises regressors that are a function of the sizes of one or more firms classified to an industry. Included here are direct measures of absolute firm size and some of the market-power variables: firm market share, four-firm concentration, or the Herfindahl Index. Those variables independent of absolute or relative firm size—barriers to entry, firm diversification, and control variables—form the second set.[1] The second set of variables will be combined with the constant term, and the analysis focuses on disentangling the absolute and relative aspects of firm size measured in the first set of variables. Accordingly, the term "market power variables" will refer only to those that are dependent on the number and size distribution of firms.

I. FIRM SIZE, MARKET POWER, AND NUMBERS EFFECTS

The consistency problem between absolute and relative size arises from the simple definitional identity that the sum of firm sizes in an industry equals a constant industry size. Since there is no theoretical expectation that changes in the size distribution of firms are accommodated by a changed industry size, firm size cannot change *ceteris paribus*. Changing the size of one firm in an industry necessarily induces changes in the sizes or numbers of other firms.

[1] Technological opportunity is an important control variable in market structure—R & D models, and is included here in the constant term on the assumption that technological opportunity is an immutable industry characteristic determined by the exogenous rate of change or susceptibility to change of the scientific base of knowledge underlying the applied industrial technology. If technological opportunity is itself determined by economic factors—firm size, market power, or advertising intensity—the model should be broadened to include a technological—opportunity-effect.

Moreover, these changes in the firm size distribution lead to changes in some or all of the market power variables, depending on which firm sizes were changed and the choice of variables measuring market power.

Conversely, changes in a market-power variable typically induce accommodating changes in other market power variables, and in the number and sizes of firms. These changes are determined by the choice of relative-size measures, and the definitional identities among them. For example, if the firm-level econometric model measures market power by the Herfindahl Index and firm market share, changes in market share and the Herfindahl Index are interdependent. These constraints cannot be formalized, but depend on the particular choice of market power variables.

The change in expected industry R & D due to a change in market structure is easily calculated by substituting into the firm-level model the values for firms' structural variables, subject to all constraints, and then directly comparing the sums of expected firms' R & D. If the number of firms is expected to change concomitantly with changes in other (e.g., market power) variables, then *the firm level effects of these other variables must be multiplied by the changed number of firms.* While this calculation is simple, it does not illuminate the process whereby changes in market structure lead to changes in expected industry R & D. We can decompose the changes in expected industry R & D into three distinct parts, and this analysis illustrates clearly the complicated way in which changes in market structure change expected industry R & D.

Decomposition of changes in expected industry R & D: numbers-effect

The first factor in the decomposition of the change in expected industry R & D is the effect due solely to the change in the number of firms in the industry, the numbers-effect. The numbers-effect has been pervasively ignored in interpreting studies of R & D. The estimated coefficients in a firm-level model on the size-unrelated variables and the constant term determine a constant c. The value for c can be interpreted as the point estimate of firm R & D for a small firm in a competitive industry. Thus, c should be non-negative. This variable is independent of the size distribution of firms. If an industry initially is composed of m_0 firms and an increase in firm sizes and market power is accompanied by a reduction in firm numbers to m_1, there will be a numbers-effect reduction in expected industry R & D of $c(m_1 - m_0)$. Even if all of the estimated coefficients for the market-power and firm-size variables are positive supporting the Schumpeterian–Galbraithian hypothesis, industry R & D may decline with increasing firm size and market power if the numbers-effect is sufficiently strong. Since c is the point estimate of firm R & D for a small firm in a competitive industry, for a given reduction in the number of firms the numbers-effect will be larger the greater are technological opportunities in the industry.

Decomposition of changes in expected industry R & D: firm-size and market power effect

The Schumpeterian–Galbraithian firm-size hypothesis is that firm R & D is a positive, strictly-convex function of firm size. The second factor explaining changes in expected industry R & D, the size-effect, is that contribution to the change in expected industry R & D due solely to the changes in the firm-size variables. As is well known, if the firm-size relationship is strictly convex, increasing the sizes of larger firms at the expense of smaller firms increases expected industry R & D.

The change in expected industry R & D due solely to the change in size-related market power variables, the market-power-effect, is the most complicated of the three effects because of the complex interrelationships among the market power variables. Changes in the size-related market power variables are affected by changes in the firm size distribution, and must be consistent with the definitional constraints among the market power variables. Since the extent and nature of the interrelationships among market power variables depends on the specific variables involved, no general theorems exist on the size of the market-power-effect. For example, market share and four-firm concentration are the market power variables most frequently used in firm R & D studies. Here, changes in the market shares of firms have an indeterminate effect on four-firm concentration without additional information on their initial and final market shares, and the market shares of each of the leading four firms.

The market-power-effect may be negative, neutral, or positive even if the data are consistent with the Schumpeterian–Galbraithian hypothesis. To illustrate, suppose that market power is measured by market share and the four-firm concentration ratio, and the estimated coefficients on each are positive. If firms' market shares change without changing four-firm concentration or the number of firms, the market-power-effect will be zero (of course there will still, in general, be a size-effect). If firms' market shares change and there is a reduction in the number of firms while four-firm concentration remains unchanged, the market-power-effect is negative because the loss of each firm reduces expected industry R & D by an amount equal to the product of four-firm concentration and its estimated coefficient.[2] Finally, if four-firm concentration increases without a reduction in the number of firms, the market-power-effect is positive. However, if the increase in market concentration is effected through mergers, the market-power-effect may be positive or negative.

[2] Recall that the numbers-effect is the product of the change in firm numbers with the sum of the size-independent regressors; this calculation excludes size-dependent market power variables. One part of the market-power-effect is the effect of changing firm numbers on size-dependent market power variables.

II. DECOMPOSITION OF CHANGES IN EXPECTED INDUSTRY R & D: AN ILLUSTRATION

The relative contributions of the size-effect, market-power-effect, and numbers-effect in determining the change in expected industry R & D induced by changing market structure is illustrated below. Culbertson and Mueller's [1980] single-equation model has three market power variables: weighted four-firm concentration ($CR4$), weighted relative-firm market share ($RFMS$),[3] and weighted industry advertising intensity. Four-firm concentration and relative-firm market share are size-dependent market power variables, while industry advertising intensity is independent of the firm size distribution. Firm size (L) is measured by the natural logarithm of firm assets. Technological opportunity class and percent nonfood control variables are also included in the model, but are independent of the firm size distribution. Equation (1) presents the point estimates and t-statistics from Culbertson and Mueller's regression model.[4]

$$\text{(1)} \qquad R\,\&\,D\ Expenditures = \underset{}{12.22} + \underset{(2.03)^{*}}{0.13\,CR4} - \underset{(-1.97)^{+}}{0.0011\,(CR4)^2}$$

$$R^2 = 0.73 \qquad + \underset{(2.06)^{*}}{0.027\,RFMS} - \underset{(4.81)^{**}}{7.97\,L} + \underset{(5.40)^{**}}{1.03\,(L)^2}$$

Significance levels: **1 percent; *5 percent; $^{+}$10 percent

The constant term is the sum of the estimated intercept and the estimated coefficients on the control and the size-independent market power variables in the model. For purposes of illustration, it is assumed that all firms are specialized in one food industry with advertising intensity of 2.7%, which advertising intensity is the simple average for all firms in Culbertson and Mueller's [1980] 1967 sample.

In Culbertson and Mueller's model, the coefficients on the size-dependent regressors all are significant at the 10 percent level or better. The quadratic function in four-firm concentration has a maximum at $CR4 = 60$. The relationship between firm size and expected firm R & D has a point of inflection at a firm-asset size of about \$130 million (1967 dollars).[5]

The relative contributions of the firm-size, market-power, and numbers-effects to the change in expected industry R & D resulting from a change in

[3] Relative-firm market share is the ratio of market share and the four-firm concentration ratio, thus the size of the firm relative to the leading four firms. For a discussion of the rationale for using relative-firm share see Marion *et al.* [1979]. While Culbertson and Mueller [1980] use relative-firm market share instead of market share, the present analysis does not depend on that substitution.

[4] Equation (2), p. 8, of Culbertson and Mueller [1980].

[5] The test of the Galbraithian hypothesis is whether the estimated firm-size function is positive and convex (Scherer [1965]). The estimated function (1) is also negative below an asset size of \$47.94 million. However, where the function is negative, which relationship is not hypothesized, it has nearly a zero slope over the range of the sample data. The smallest firm in the sample is approximately \$20 million, and the estimated function has a slope of -0.188 at that firm size.

TABLE I
INITIAL AND FINAL INDUSTRY

	Four-firm concentration	*Relative firm market share*	*Firm assets (millions)*
I	57%	25%	$130
II	29	25	65

market structure is illustrated above with the two industry structures given in Table I. The industry consists initially of seven firms each with assets of $130 million. Assuming that firms' assets are equal to their sales and that all firms are specialized, industry sales equals $910 million, four-firm concentration equals 57, and relative-firm market share equals 25. This industry configuration was chosen so that the firm size and market power variables would be near the upper end of the range where the estimated relationship is consistent with the Schumpeterian–Galbraithian hypothesis. Then, market restructuring to reduce firm size and market concentration occurs over the range of firm sizes and market power where expected firm R & D increases with market power and increases at an increasing rate with firm size.

The less concentrated industry structure is constructed by halving firm sizes and doubling the number of firms in the industry. Firms now have assets of 65 million, four-firm concentration is 29, and relative firm market share is unchanged at 25.

Table II presents total expected industry R & D for the two industry structures and the size-effect, numbers-effect, and market-power-effect explaining this change.

The total change in expected industry R & D between industry structures I and II is $10.50 million. (As an aid to the discussion that follows, it should be remembered that equation (1) provides *firm-level* coefficients.) The numbers-effect equals $85.54 million, which is the increase in the number of firms

TABLE II
DETERMINANTS OF THE CHANGE IN EXPECTED INDUSTRY R & D

(1) *Total expected industry R & D*				
Industrial structure I			$16.38	
Industrial structure II			5.88	
(2)		*Difference*		−$10.50
(3) *Numbers-effect*			$85.54	
Size-effect			−113.77	
Market-power-effect			17.64	
Due to RFMS		$4.76		
Due to CR4		12.88		
(4)		*Sum of three effects**		−$10.59

* Line (4) differs from line (2) due to rounding

multiplied by the constant term. The market-power-effect, the sign of which could not be predicted *a priori*, is also positive. The market-power-effect of \$17.64 million is the sum of that due to relative-firm market share, \$4.76 million, and that due to four-firm concentration, \$12.88 million. Since the value of relative-firm market share does not change with the alteration in industry structure, its contribution to the market-power-effect is the product of the effect of relative-firm market share on firms' expected R & D (\$0.68 million) and the increase in firm numbers. While expected firm R & D decreases with decreasing market concentration, this function is concave so the reduction in individual firms' R & D attributable to market concentration, from \$3.84 million to \$2.84 million, is more than offset by the addition of 7 firms. The firm-size-effect, which has the theoretically expected negative sign, is calculated by substituting the firm-size values from Table I into the last two terms in equation (1), and then summing the resulting value by the appropriate number of firms.

This example illustrates the hazard with inferring the effect of market restructuring on industry R & D from the signs on the estimated coefficients on firm-size and market-power variables in firm-level models. In this example, the decline in expected industry R & D effected through a reduction in firm sizes and market power is due entirely to the firm-size effect. Even though relative firm market share and market concentration have positive effects at the firm level over the range of market restructuring, the contribution of the market power variables to expected industry R & D is positive when market concentration declines.

III. CONCLUSION

Econometric studies of the relationship between market structure and firms' R & D investments can be used to determine the effect of market structure changes on expected industry R & D. However, this calculation is significantly more complicated than is generally recognized and requires that the distinct market-power, firm-size, and numbers-effects, together with the interrelationships among these effects, be considered explicitly. Even if expected firm R & D increases with market power and increases more than proportionately with firm size, expected industry R & D may decline with increasing firm size and market power. The extent to which expected industry R & D will be enhanced by modifying market structure depends on the strength of the relationship between market structure and firm R & D, technological opportunities in the industry, and the particular restructuring under consideration.

JOHN D. CULBERTSON,
Department of Economics,
Case Western Reserve University,
Cleveland, Ohio 44106,
USA.

ACCEPTED JULY 1984

REFERENCES

CULBERTSON, JOHN D. and MUELLER, WILLARD F., 1980, 'The Influence of Market Structure on Technological Performance in the Food Manufacturing Industries', *Working Paper 47* N.C. Project 117 (University of Wisconsin–Madison).

GALBRAITH, JOHN KENNETH, 1956, *American Capitalism* (revised edition) (Houghton Mifflin, Boston).

IMEL, B., BEHR, M. R. and HELMBERGER, P., 1972, *Market Structure and Performance* (Lexington Books, Lexington).

MARION, B., MUELLER, W. F., COTTERILL, R., GEITHMAN, F. and SCHMELZER, J., 1979, *The Food Retailing Industry: Market Structure, Profits, and Prices* (Praeger, New York).

NELSON, RICHARD R., 1959, 'The Simple Economics of Basic Science Research', *Journal of Political Economy*, 67, 3 (June), pp. 297–306.

SCHERER, F. M., 1965, 'Firm Size, Market Structure, Opportunity, and the Output of Patented Inventions', *American Economic Review*, 55, 5 (December), pp. 1097–1125.

SCHERER, F. M., 1980, *Industrial Market Structure and Economic Performance* (second edition) (Houghton Mifflin, Boston).

SCHUMPETER, JOSEPH A., 1950, *Capitalism, Socialism and Democracy* (third edition) (Harper & Row, New York).

We are very grateful to the following, in addition to our Associate Editors, for acting as referees over the past year:

Yakov Amihud,
New York University
James Anderson,
Boston College
Richard Arnould,
University of Illinois
Robert Bacon,
Lincoln College,
University of Oxford
Martin Beckmann,
Brown University
Charles Berry,
Princeton University
Ernst Berndt,
Massachusetts Institute of Technology
R. Bruce Billings,
University of Arizona
George Bittlingmayer,
Federal Trade Commission
Ralph Bradburd,
Williams College
Michael Bradley,
University of Michigan
Timothy Brennan,
U.S. Department of Justice
M. Chalkley,
University of Southampton
Nina Cornell,
Cornell, Pelcovits & Brenner
Robert Crandall,
Brookings Institution
Robert Dansby,
American Telephone Telegraph
David DeNoon,
New York University
Arthur DeVany,
University of Houston
Donald Dewees,
University of Toronto
Donald Dewey,
Columbia University
V. A. Dickson,
University of New Brunswick
Huw Dixon,
Birkbeck College,
University of London
Marie-Paule Donsimoni,
CRIDE, Louvain
Paul Downing,
Florida State University
Thomas Duchesneau,
University of Maine
Curtis Eaton,
University of Toronto
B. Espen Eckbo,
University of British Columbia
Kenneth Elzinga,
University of Virginia
Louis Esposito,
University of Massachusetts
Julian Franks,
London Graduate School of
Business Studies
Ann Friedlaender,
Massachusetts Institute of Technology
James Friedman,
Virginia Polytechnic Institute
Paul Geroski,
University of Southampton
Pankaj Ghemawat,
Harvard University
Richard Gilbert,
University of California, Berkeley
Devra Golbe,
Rutgers University
Peter Goodwin,
Transport Studies Unit,
University of Oxford
Paul Gorecki,
Economic Council of Canada
Henry Grabowski,
Duke University
William Greene,
New York University
Douglas Greer,
San Jose State University
James Griffin,
University of Houston
Jeffrey Harris,
Massachusetts Institute of Technology
Robert Hawkins,
Rensselaer Polytechnic Institute
George Hay,
University of Cornell
William Hseao,
Harvard University
Norman Ireland,
University of Warwick
Michael Jensen,
University of Rochester

Paul Joskow,
U.S. Department of Justice
Barbara Katz,
New York University
Michael Keenan,
New York University
John Kwoka,
George Washington University
D. J. Lecraw,
University of Western Ontario
David Levy,
Rutgers University
Bruce Lyons,
St John's College,
University of Cambridge
Robert McGuckin,
U.S. Department of Justice
David McNichol,
U.S. Department of Justice
Alan Marcus,
Boston University
Robert Masson,
Cornell University
G. Frank Mathewson,
University of Toronto
John Menge,
Dartmouth College
John Meyer,
Harvard University
Michael Morrisey,
American Hospital Association
William Myslinski,
Economists, Inc.
Julianne Nelson,
New York University,
Richard Nelson,
Yale University
Roger Noll,
Stanford University
George Norman,
University of Leicester
William Nye,
U.S. Department of Justice
E. H. Oksanen,
McMaster University
Janusz Ordover,
New York University
Stanley Ornstein,
UCLA
Bruce Owen,
Economists, Inc.
John Panzar,
Northwestern University
Merton Peck,
Yale University
Martin Perry,
Bell Communications Research
Bruce Petersen,
Northwestern University
Russell Pittman,
U.S. Department of Justice
Irving Plotkin,
Arthur D. Little, Inc.
Charles Plott,
California Institute of Technology
Anne Preston,
Wellesley College
Lee Preston,
University of Maryland
Thomas Pugel,
New York University
Ruth Raubitschek,
New York University
David Ravenscraft,
Federal Trade Commission
Stephen Rhoads,
Federal Reserve System
Marc Roberts,
Harvard University
Jeffrey Rohlfs,
Shooshan & Jackson
Sherwin Rosen,
University of Chicago
T. W. Ross,
Carleton University
Michael Rothschild,
University of California, San Diego
Richard Ruback,
Massachusetts Institute of Technology
Michael Salinger,
Columbia University
Garth Saloner,
Massachusetts Institute of Technology
David Sappington,
Bell Communications Research
Andrew Schotter,
New York University
Richard Shaw,
Paisley College
David Sheffman,
Federal Trade Commission
Roger Sherman,
University of Virginia
John Siegfried,
Vanderbilt University

Marilyn Simon,
U.S. Department of Justice
Margaret Slade,
IRES, Louvain
Frank Sloan,
Vanderbilt University
George Sorter,
New York University
Thomas Spavins,
Federal Communications
Pablo Spiller,
Hoover Institute
T. Stoker,
Massachusetts Institute of Technology
Michael Stutzer,
Federal Reserve Bank of Minneapolis
Lester Taylor,
University of Arizona
David Teece,
University of California, Berkeley
Jacques Thisse,
CORE, Louvain
L. G. Thomas,
Columbia University
Alastair Ulph,
University of Southampton
T. S. Ward,
Department of Applied Economics, University of Cambridge
Mike Waterson,
University of Newcastle
Peggy Weir,
University of Oregon
Leonard Weiss,
University of Wisconsin
Louis Wells,
Harvard University
Gregory Werden,
U.S. Department of Justice
Stephen Wildman,
Economists, Inc.
Oliver Williamson,
Yale University
R. Winter,
University of Toronto

THE JOURNAL OF INDUSTRIAL ECONOMICS

Published first in October 1952, the *Journal* has a very wide international circulation, and has established itself as the leading journal in the field of industrial economics. It was founded to promote the analysis of modern industry, particularly the behaviour of firms, and the functioning of markets. More specifically it seeks to bring the tools of modern economic analysis to bear on the analysis of real problems of industrial economies.

Contributions are welcomed covering all the major areas of industrial economics. One such area is the relationship between market structure and market behaviour in the areas of pricing, product differentiation, advertising and the dissemination of information and R & D. Another area focuses more directly on the firm, its objectives, finance, investment and growth. A third area comprises the background environment within which industrial firms operate: the changing structure of industry, public policy on monopoly and restrictive trade practices, regulation, fiscal and monetary policies as they affect firms, and underlying changes in productivity and international competitiveness.

The *Journal* has a tradition of publishing a blend of theory and evidence. Theoretical discussion is welcomed provided that the more abstract theory includes sufficient introduction and other explanation to convey the significance of the material to the general reader who wants to decide whether to follow the analysis through. Empirical analysis, and especially econometric analysis, should include an explanation of the data sources used, of the methods applied and of the underlying theoretical basis of the study. The *Journal* has a particular tradition of case studies of firms and industries, which the Editors would wish to continue. However contributors of such studies are asked to remember that a study will be of interest to the international readership of the *Journal* only if it makes a particular contribution to the methodology of such studies, or if the empirical results are exceptionally interesting.

Alongside articles of more normal length, the Editors are ready to publish shorter notes, especially where these give interim results of important research studies, or where they report significant new empirical results. Books are not reviewed, although books received will be listed, sometimes with a short note: but substantial review articles will be considered.

Information for Contributors

Submissions (*three* copies are required) should be in typescript, double-spaced, and should conform to the style of the *Journal*. Detailed Information for Contributors is available from the General Editor. The submission should include an Abstract, not exceeding 100 words.

Typescripts from North America should be sent to the North American Editor, Journal of Industrial Economics, Graduate School of Economics and Business Administration, New York University, 100 Trinity Place, New York, NY 10006, USA.

Typescripts from *all* other countries should be sent to the General Editor, Journal of Industrial Economics, Institute of Economics and Statistics, University of Oxford, St Cross Building, Manor Road, Oxford OX1 3UL, UK.

Information for Subscribers

The *Journal* is published four times a year, in September, December, March and June, by Basil Blackwell Ltd., 108 Cowley Road, Oxford OX4 1JF, UK Prices are as follows:

	UK	Overseas	USA
Institutions	£29.00	£36.50	$65.75
Individuals	£16.25	£20.35	$35.00
Single issue prices for:			
Institutions	£7.20	£8.80	$17.70
Individuals	£5.20	£6.40	$12.00

CONTRIBUTORS TO THIS ISSUE

G. K. YARROW: Hertford College, University of Oxford, UK, and Editor of this *Journal.*
ROGER FELDMAN: Center for Health Services Research and Department of Economics, University of Minnesota, USA.
JAMES W. BEGUN: Department of Health Administration, Medical College of Virginia, Virginia Commonwealth University, USA.
G. M. P. SWANN: Centre for European Industrial Studies, University of Bath, UK.
DAVID LEVY: Department of Economics, Faculty of Arts and Sciences, Rutgers, The State University of New Jersey, USA.
REINHARD ANGELMAR: INSEAD, European Institute of Business Administration, Fontainebleau, France.
PATRICIA L. PACEY: College of Business Administration, University of Colorado, USA.
DAVID FLATH: Department of Economics and Business, North Carolina State University, USA.
CHARLES R. KNOEBER: Department of Economics and Business, North Carolina State University, USA.
JOHN D. CULBERTSON: Department of Economics, Case-Western Reserve University, USA.

RECEIVED
OCT 28 1985
Hartwick College Library

US Mailing: Second class postage paid at New York. Postmaster: Send address corrections to: Journal of Industrial Economics, c/o Expediters of the Printed Word Ltd., 515 Madison Avenue, New York, NY 10022 (US Mailing Agent).

Photocopying: Permission is granted by the publisher for those institutions registered with the Copyright Clearance Center to authorize internal photocopying of any article in this journal for a fee of $2.00 per copy per article. Payment should be made direct to the Copyright Clearance Center, 21 Congress Street, Salem, Massachusetts 10970, USA. Individuals, or institutions not registered with the CCC, must obtain permission to photocopy either from the CCC or from Basil Blackwell Ltd., when the same fees will apply.

Reprints of Back Volumes: Volumes 1–28 of the *Journal* are available (in complete volumes only) from the Kraus Reprint Corporation, Route 100, Millwood, New York 10546, USA. More recent back issues are available from the publisher at the current single issue price.

Microfilm: An agreement for the supply of microfilm copies from Volume 1 onwards has been made with University Microfilms International, Department PR, 30–32 Mortimer Street, London W1N 7RA, England, or 300 North Zeeb Road, Ann Arbor, Michigan 48106, USA.

Advertising: For details contact the Advertisement Manager, Bill Drake. Telephone (0869) 38477, or write c/o the publisher.

Set in Monophoto Times by Advanced Filmsetters (Glasgow) Ltd
Printed and Bound in Great Britain by Whitstable Litho, Kent

THE JOURNAL OF INDUSTRIAL ECONOMICS

Volume XXXIV DECEMBER 1985 No. 2

RICHARD E. CAVES and PETER J. WILLIAMSON
What is Product Differentiation, *Really*? 113
DAMIEN NEVEN and LOUIS PHLIPS
Discriminating Oligopolists and Common Markets 133
YVES MERTENS and VICTOR GINSBURGH
Product Differentiation and Price Discrimination in the European Community: The Case of Automobiles 151
M. L. GREENHUT, H. OHTA and JOEL SAILORS
Reverse Dumping: A Form of Spatial Price Discrimination 167
VICTOR J. TREMBLAY
Strategic Groups and the Demand for Beer 183
CHRISTOPHER C. FINDLAY
Effects of Australian International Air Transport Regulation 199

Short Articles and Notes
EDWIN MANSFIELD
How Rapidly Does New Industrial Technology Leak Out? 217

ISSN 0022-1821
BASIL BLACKWELL OXFORD ENGLAND

© Basil Blackwell 1985

The material in this Journal is copyright under the Berne Convention. Apart from any fair dealing for the purposes of private study, research, criticism or review, as permitted under the Copyright Act 1965, no portion may be reproduced by any process without written permission. Inquiry should be made to the Publishers.

DONALD A. HAY (General Editor): Jesus College, University of Oxford.
STEVE W. DAVIES: University of East Anglia.
BRUCE LYONS: St John's College, Cambridge.
LOUIS PHLIPS: Université Catholique de Louvain.
AUBREY SILBERSTON: Imperial College of Science and Technology, University of London.
GEORGE YARROW: Hertford College, University of Oxford.
LAWRENCE J. WHITE (North American Editor): New York University.
M. A. ADELMAN: Massachusetts Institute of Technology.
RICHARD E. CAVES: Harvard University.
F. MICHAEL SCHERER: Swarthmore College.
RICHARD SCHMALENSEE: Sloan School of Management, Massachusetts Institute of Technology.

Editorial Assistant: Marion Bowker.

ASSOCIATE EDITORS
BO CARLSSON: Case Western Reserve University, Cleveland.
ROGER CLARKE: University of Sheffield.
ALEXIS JACQUEMIN: Université Catholique de Louvain.
FRÉDÉRIC JENNY, E.S.S.E.C., Cergy.
H. W. DE JONG: University of Amsterdam.
JOHN KAY: Institute for Fiscal Studies, London.
COLIN P. MAYER: St Anne's College, University of Oxford.
GEOFF MEEKS: Department of Applied Economics, University of Cambridge.
DEREK MORRIS: Oriel College, University of Oxford.
WILLIAM PETERSON: Department of Applied Economics, University of Cambridge.
JOHN F. PICKERING: The University of Manchester Institute of Science and Technology.
RAY REES: University College, Cardiff.
DAVID K. STOUT: Unilever PLC.
ROGER TARLING: Department of Applied Economics, University of Cambridge.
JOHN VICKERS: Nuffield College, University of Oxford.
CHRISTIAN C. VON WEIZSÄCKER: University of Berne.
GEOFFREY WHITTINGTON: University of Bristol.

RONALD R. BRAEUTIGAM: Northwestern University.
TIMOTHY F. BRESNAHAN: Stanford University.
WILLIAM S. COMANOR: University of California.
M. THÉRÈSE FLAHERTY: Harvard University.
THEODORE KEELER: University of California, Berkeley.
R. LARNER: Charles River Associates.
ALMARIN PHILLIPS: University of Pennsylvania.
STEVEN SALOP: Georgetown Law Center, Washington, DC.
JOHN T. SCOTT: Dartmouth College.
ROBERT D. WILLIG: Princeton University.

DONALD G. MCFETRIDGE: Carleton University, Ottawa.

PETER FORSYTH: Australian National University, Canberra.
BRIAN L. JOHNS: Bureau of Industry Economics, Canberra.
L. ROY WEBB: University of Melbourne.

MASU UEKUSA: University of Tokyo.

THE JOURNAL OF INDUSTRIAL ECONOMICS 0022–1821 $2.00
Volume XXXIV December 1985 No. 2

WHAT IS PRODUCT DIFFERENTIATION, *REALLY*?

RICHARD E. CAVES AND PETER J. WILLIAMSON

Empirical research on industrial organization has failed to identify the empirical bases of product differentiation (that is, each seller facing an individual downward-sloping demand curve). Two sets of conditions are theoretically sufficient: one resting on complex attribute structures coupled with fixed costs, the other on costs of information to guide buyers' choices among brands. Factor analysis of observable decision variables and market patterns appears to reveal and confirm these underlying causes. The estimated factors perform successfully to test hypotheses about the effects of product differentiation on the mutual sensitivity of prices of Australian domestic manufactures and competing imports.

PRODUCT DIFFERENTIATION is a well-defined theoretical concept resting on two conditions. First, buyers must recognize that goods ("brands") belonging to a product class are close substitutes for one another but face only relatively poor substitutes with goods outside the class. At the same time, these brands must be sufficiently imperfect substitutes that each seller perceives his brand to face a downward-sloping demand curve. Research on industrial organization often refers to differentiated products, yet the empirical correlates of structural differentiation have received little attention. Our inability to control for differences among industries in their structural bases for differentiation has arguably been the source of important shortcomings of inter-industry research in industrial organization.[1] In the standard terminology of industrial organization, product differentiation colors both the structure and the conduct observed in a market. The structural condition is the imperfect substitution between competing brands. The conduct encompasses those actions taken by producers to induce, exploit, or otherwise respond to this structural feature.

We first identify the conditions that are theoretically sufficient to give rise to Chamberlinian downward-sloping demand curves facing individual sellers. Then we employ factor analysis to ascertain whether these fundamental bases can be imputed from the observable attributes of products and buyers' methods of selecting among them. Upon reaching an affirmative conclusion, we show that price adjustments in a cross-section of industries respond to the

[1] Simon [1970, pp. 289–99] and Peterson [1980] have pointed to the inadequacies. Comanor and Wilson [1974, p. 139] stated: "Ideally, we should specify equations relating advertising directly to the exogenous factors determining the differentiability of the product. Unfortunately, measures of product differentiability . . . are impossible to obtain."

factors in the manner predicted from the theoretical bases for differentiation, as a test of this device for measuring differentiation.

I. THEORETICAL CONDITIONS FOR PRODUCT DIFFERENTIATION

At least two models seem to provide conditions sufficient to link downward-sloping demand curves for individual producers to underlying characteristics of demand and technology. One—the product-attribute model—rests on the intrinsic complexity of the generic product, coupled with fixed costs of producing each variety. Assume that the nominal product offered in the market-place combines numerous primary Arrow–Debreu attributes, and that buyers' preferences defined in terms of these primary attributes are diverse. If every possible combination of primary attributes could be produced at constant long-run average costs and offered at competitive prices, the number of attribute bundles produced would be large enough for each buyer to enjoy a customized variety.[2] This output set is not attainable, however, if fixed costs or scale economies are present in the production of each distinct bundle. In that case only some of the many possible bundles are actually produced. The typical buyer finds no attribute bundle that matches exactly the one he would choose under the idealized conditions just defined. Relative prices determine the bundle actually chosen from among those offered. Although each buyer may make discrete switches between brands as relative prices change, buyers generally differ in their reservation prices for a given configuration. Therefore, downward-sloping demand curves are likely to result when the preferences of individual buyers are aggregated. We conjecture that the assurance of downward-sloping demand curves (that is, imperfect substitution between competing brands) becomes stronger the more numerous are the product's primary attributes and the more diverse the buyers' tastes.

These conditions underlie models of differentiation that were advanced by Spence [1976], Lancaster [1979], and others. They share the property of confronting individual sellers with downward-sloping demand curves, and differ mainly in whether or not they employ a spatial approach to the characteristics embodied in the competing brands, and thus whether a given product has distinguishable near and distant neighbors or is symmetrically substitutable for all products in the class.[3]

The other theoretical model linking downward-sloping demand curves to

[2] Rosen [1974] developed a model with these properties: in the absence of scale economies, there is no constraint on the number of sellers of any given configuration of the product. Rosen did investigate the implications of locational and comparative-advantage factors that make some configurations "easier" to produce than others.

[3] For an excellent discussion see Archibald, Eaton, and Lipsey [1983]. These models yield important normative results, concerning the appropriateness of the set of varieties actually produced, that are not central to the concerns of this paper.

ambient structural conditions comes from the literature on consumer information and transactions costs. Although the formal side of this literature has emphasized optimal price search by the buyer (Wilde [1980]), it also appears to generate a satisfactory model of product differentiation. Although Nelson's [1970], [1974] distinction between search and experience goods has received much attention, a more useful and general starting point is Porter's [1976] description of the structure of information flows utilized by buyers and provided by interested sellers of the product (as well as by other participants in the information market). The buyer, constrained by information costs and bounded rationality in choosing the best brand, invests in various types of information up to the point where the expected marginal benefits from a better choice among brands become equal to the marginal information costs (both money and time). Various types of information are available to the buyer—advertisements, advice from friends, his own experience (subject to depreciation), data collected by personal search (physical inspection of products, advice of salespersons), and technical information from independent sources (advisors, testing agencies).

These types of information differ in their perceived accuracy and cost, including subjective utility or disutility associated with gathering and absorbing each type. The buyer generally faces a trade-off between the accuracy of information and its cost: advertisements and the advice of friends are cheap but biased or simply inaccurate; technical information and the findings of personal search are more accurate but costly. If we assume that the marginal value of each information source declines with the quantity of information acquired, it follows that the buyer generally selects not one but a portfolio of information sources.[4]

The equilibrium portfolio of information of course depends on the supply or price of information as well as the demand for it. Some but not all types of information on competing product brands are controlled by their makers, who provide information and jointly adjust their prices and product qualities in the pursuit of maximum expected profits. Telser [1964] stressed that it may be efficient for the seller to provide information rather than for the buyer to commission it from independent sources. However, because of buyers' imperfect access to "objective" information to verify the seller's claims, there is scope for puffery and opportunistic adjustment of product price and quality as well (Schmalensee [1978]; Klein and Leffler [1981]).[5] Sellers

[4] Empirical implications of this model for the seller's outlays on information directed to the buyer were confirmed by Caves [1983].

[5] Shapiro [1983] showed that if sellers acquire reputational assets for product quality with consumers who can interchange their information about product quality costlessly, although with a lag, then the firms possessing goodwill assets reputations for quality products will not face downward-sloping demand curves. This proof highlights the assumption that the positive costs to buyers of acquiring information importantly include the costs of interchanging it with other buyers.

indulge in opportunism even though buyers expect it and discount the accuracy of seller supplied information.[6]

This information equilibrium is sufficient to imply a downward-sloping demand curve for the individual brand. Each buyer's information set is incomplete, and generally no two buyers hold identical information sets. Therefore, even if all buyers had identical preferences about the relevant primary attributes of the class of products, they would still express heterogeneous preferences among brands at any given set of prices because of differing information sets. And a change in the price of one brand, the others held constant, would induce some but not all buyers to switch. Hence, another sufficient basis for downward-sloping demand curves lies in costly information governing choice among brands and the resulting equilibrium of information flows and producers' price-quality offers.[7] Unlike the product-attribute model, this informational basis for differentiation has not been developed extensively as a theoretical market model. A suggestive approach was provided by Satterthwaite [1979], who explored a market equilibrium in which consumers can inform themselves only through the advice of friends and associates ("reputation"). His model ascribes the expected properties to demand curves faced by individual firms and also delivers some distinctive comparative-statics results: an increase in the number of sellers causes equilibrium industry price to rise.

The product-attribute and information models are both theoretically sufficient to generate the structural attribute of product differentiation (downward-sloping demand curves for individual brands). They are not mutually exclusive—a product class might both possess complex attributes and confront potential buyers with a substantial information problem. However, they are logically independent and need not be collinear empirically.[8] Finally, they probably do not exhaust the distinctive theoretical bases for differentiation. Other foundations can be identified, such as a "fashionable" good marked by positive correlations among buyers' preferences defined over attributes of a generic good (Robinson [1961]; Monsen and Downs [1971]). Nonetheless, we assert the hypothesis that the product-attribute and information models have empirical counterparts and account for many of the empirical market conditions that correspond to Chamberlinian product differentiation.

To test this hypothesis, we proceed as follows. We first devise a way to represent the differentiation properties of goods empirically and relate them

[6] The resulting information equilibrium is better conceived not as a static equilibrium but as a repeating stationary one. Information is subject to a decay rate because sellers turn over, and the information and product specifications that they offer can be changed periodically.

[7] Breit and Elzinga [1974] found some anticipations of this model in the literature of institutional economics.

[8] Perloff and Salop [1985] showed the relationship between preferences over attribute differences and information costs as bases for market equilibrium with product differentiation.

to these two prototype models. Then we show that the empirical indicators serve to flag market behavior that agrees with predictions of the product-attribute and information models.

II. MATCHING THEORY AND DATA

How can we test this hypothesis? Indeed, how should we meter the structural underpinnings of differentiation in real-life industries when we test theoretical models that require controlling for them? Previous researchers have settled for *force majeure*, judgmentally sorting products into discrete classes (search vs. experience goods, convenience vs. nonconvenience goods) suited to their concerns and testing for differences between the resulting samples. Although this approach has supported valuable conclusions, one hopes for something better.

The theoretically appropriate measure for the extent of product differentiation in a market is the degree of substitutability in demand between the "representative" pair of product varieties. Were that substitution elasticity observable in the typical industrial market, we could test the preceding models of differentiation by relating the representative substitution elasticities in various markets to structural variables indicating the complexity of the product's attributes and the structure of information flows to buyers. We could also use the substitution elasticities to test hypotheses about the effects of structural differentiation. However, given the manifest scarcity of data on relative prices and market shares of competing differentiated products and the paucity of such estimates in the literature, we assume that they are practicably unavailable.

We can, however, obtain indirect measures of various traits of the product in the form of buyers' usage patterns or methods of selecting it, and sellers' decision variables set in response to these things—each plausibly reflecting in some degree the prevalence in a market of product-attribute and informational bases for differentiation. (Specific examples include the degree to which product units are tailored to the user's needs, the durability of the class of goods, the services provided to the buyer jointly with the good itself, the producer's expenditures on advertising or other direct promotion, and the research and development outlays aimed at creating new or improved varieties.) In most cases, however, there is not a straightforward, unique pairing between the observed traits and the underlying attribute and information bases. Each feature generally reflects both hypothesized bases of differentiation in some proportion. Furthermore, the features are overlapping and inter-related in their reflection of underlying structural differentiation. As a result they defy any simple effort to combine them or utilize them jointly, either to test the hypothesized models of differentiation or to indicate differences among markets' degrees of differentiation.

In attempting to capture the structure lying behind these assorted indicators, we look to the technique of factor analysis. The essence of the factor analysis approach to the detection and diagnosis of product differentiation is perhaps best illustrated by an analogy. Consider a relatively simple product such as a packing container. Suppose that we have available several measurements of each container offered by various potential suppliers: the wall thickness, impermeability, and density of the construction materials employed, along with the height and surface area of each container. As the buyer we are relatively uninterested in the density of the material or surface area of the container as dimensions in their own right. What basically differentiates the various types or brands are their relative durability and the volumes they are capable of holding. Our task in measuring the differentiation of these products is therefore to derive some indicator of these underlying characteristics.

One approach to this problem is to examine the correlation between the various parameters we observe. It is probable, for example, that wall thickness, density, and impermeability, will be highly correlated among products on the market. We may be able to summarize these measures statistically into a single underlying dimension that is important in differentiating products from the buyer's point of view, that is, durability. Similarly, height, surface area, and like measurements might be summarized into a single dimension roughly equivalent to capacity. Each type (brand) would then have a numerical index which indicated its position on the spectrum of these new dimensions. In somewhat simplified terms, this is exactly what factor analysis attempts.

The technique of factor analysis

We need not embark on a substantive discussion of the mathematical underpinnings of factor analysis. Excellent surveys are available in Rummel [1970], Press [1972], and Harman [1976]. Because the technique has been used only rarely by researchers on industrial organization (compare Meyer [1967], Shrieves [1978]), however, we provide a brief review of the basic methodology.

The key aim of factor analysis is to utilize the correlations within a set of observed variables to produce an estimate of a number of unobservable "factors" that are assumed to be generating observations on these variables. This objective is achieved by estimating the following model:

$$Z_{ij} = a_{i1}f_{1j} + a_{i2}f_{2j} + \ldots + a_{im}f_{mj} + e_{ij}$$

where Z_{ij} are observations of each variable Z_i, f_{kj} $(k = 1 \ldots m)$ may be regarded as the new, theoretical variables (factors), the a_{ik} are the "factor loadings", and the e_{ij} are error (random) terms, respectively.

The model is therefore analogous to a standard multiple regression model except that the independent variables are unobserved. Unlike multiple regression, however, it must be structured such that there are more dependent variables than there are unobserved explanatory factors, and it is the correlations between the pairs of dependent variables that allow the smaller number of unobserved "regressors" (factors) to be estimated. Various methods are available to undertake this analysis. In our empirical application we employed the canonical factor technique because of its desirable mathematical properties.[9]

In addition to the basic data, the researcher is required to specify the maximum number of underlying factors which are of interest.[10] A number of useful statistics can then be computed, specifically the *communality* for each variable, the *factor loading* and the *magnitude* of each factor.

The communality of a variable is the fraction of its total variance that is due to the estimated factors; the remainder is assumed to be due to the random factor (e_{ij} above). Each factor loading (a_{ik}) represents the correlation of a given variable i with any individual factor k. Finally, the square of the factor loading thus measures the proportion of the observed variance in any single variable accounted for by the factor k. The magnitude of any factor measures the total variance among all variables accounted for (or explained by) that underlying factor as a percentage of the variance explained by all factors (total communality). It is thus equal to the sum of the squares of the loadings associated with that factor (Schlaifer [1981, chap. 18]).

Conceptually, computation of these values provides a complete analysis. More often than not, however, the canonical factors in raw form cannot be usefully interpreted from an economic point of view until they are "rotated" to produce "derived factors". This problem, and the role of rotation as a solution, can be illustrated with our simple example of the packing container.

Suppose we were to graph the set of appropriately scaled observations on the containers available in the market. If each variable were represented as a vector we might expect to find two "clusters": one formed by the variables such as material density, impermeability, wall thickness, and the other by the measures of height and surface area. These clusters are denoted by "A" and "B" respectively in Figure 1(a). Because the canonical technique maximizes the total variance explained by each successive, orthogonal factor, it will choose an axis such as X_1 to represent the first factor, resulting in strong positive weights for both sets of variables. The second factor would then be chosen as the axis X_2 with positive loadings on those variables in cluster "A" and negative on those in cluster "B". The resulting factors would therefore lack a meaningful economic interpretation.

Suppose, however, that we were to rotate the axes by applying a linear transformation to the factors such that the number of factors with high

[9] These include the invariance of the final results to the scale of the raw data and the orthogonality of the estimated factors [Rummel, 1970, chap. 5].

[10] Although this choice must be made *a priori*, statistical tests can be applied *ex post* to determine the number of significant factors.

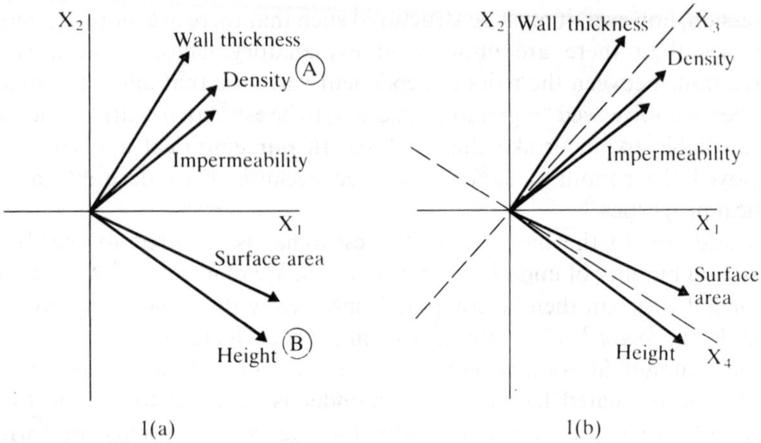

Figure 1
"Rotation" Illustrated by Attributes of Containers

loadings on each variable was minimized and each factor tended to be dominated by a different subset of variables. The basic correlations would remain invariant to such a transformation, yet the axes would be repositioned so as to align with the clustering of the data. The resulting "derived" factors would then be of the form X_3 and X_4 (Figure 1(b)). The economic interpretation is then much clearer: the factor X_3 represents "durability" with strong positive loadings on material density, wall thickness and impermeability; the factor X_4 essentially measures "capacity".

We employ the so-called "Quartimax" criterion for selecting the optimal rotation (the details of which are available in Harman [1976, chap. 13]). This tends to produce loadings such that a subset of factors dominate the explanation of each observed variable (Schlaifer [1981, chap. 16]). The rotation yields a second set of derived values for the factor loadings. From these new loadings we can then compute the final "factor scores". To determine the factor scores for each case (such as a product or industry in cross-section data), we simply compute the weighted sum of the observations on each variable for that case, where the weights are the relevant factor loadings.

An application

We are concerned with the usefulness of this methodology for investigating product differentiation in the sorts of industrial cross-sections commonly used in quantitative research on industrial organization. Therefore, we used a set of variables that are available for a number of United States manufacturing industries or Australian industries matched to them. This data base was developed for an investigation of competitive processes in Australian industry, and in the section that follows the usefulness of the derived factors will be tested on the relationship between prices of Australian manufactures and of competing imports.

The variables were selected from those available on the general guidance of the product-attribute and information models of differentiation reviewed above. They pertain to various years in the early and mid 1970s. They are:

INFPUR Proportion of product lines within the industry for which the final buyer generally purchases with a frequency of one year or less often;
NOTMAJ Proportion of product lines that do not represent a major purchase for the buyer (less than $100 for households, judgmentally determined for non-household buyers);
FRQSER Proportion of product lines requiring a "moderate to high" degree of sales or technical service;
MKFOCUS Proportion of product lines for which marketing activities focus on advisers to the final user rather than the buyer;
TORDER Proportion of product lines manufactured to the customer's order specifications;
MEDIA Media advertising expenses expressed as a fraction of total sales;
OSALEX Total selling and sales-administration expenses less media advertising, expressed as a fraction of total sales;
CFRD Research and development outlays financed from company funds expressed as a fraction of total sales.

The preceding variables were all taken from data sources for the United States (details are provided in the data appendix); we assume that they would differ little had they been compiled for another major industrial country. In addition, we employed the variable *ACFRD*, which is identical to *CFRD* except for applying to the corresponding industries in Australia.[11]

We proceeded to apply factor analysis to these data, employing the canonical correlation technique. The results were then rotated using the Quartimax criterion. The factors were constrained to a maximum of five. The estimated factor loadings, factor magnitudes, and variable communalities are presented in Table I. The statistics on the communality for each variable indicate that a high proportion of the total variation in each variable was explained by the estimated factors, with a maximum of 0.94 correlation for *NOTMAJ* and an average of over 0.7.

Before evaluating the results in Table 1, we should indicate what *a priori* expectations flow from our models of differentiation. Although factor analysis does not permit formal tests of our hypotheses about the bases of differen-

[11] Australian Bureau of Statistics [1981]. Because Australia is predominantly an importer of technology from the rest of the world, *ACFRD* measures the scope for adapting international technology to the specific conditions of a national market; it therefore does not duplicate the function of *CFRD*.

TABLE I
FACTOR ANALYSIS RESULTS

Variable	Factor Loadings 1	2	3	4	5	Communality
TORDER	−0.860[a]	−0.111	−0.266	0.000	0.257	0.89
MKFOCUS	0.177	−0.133	0.044	0.810[a]	0.031	0.71
FRQSER	−0.279	0.192	0.023	0.071	0.819[a]	0.79
INFPUR	−0.302[a]	0.364[a]	0.175	0.418[a]	0.122	0.44
NOTMAJ	0.882[a]	−0.226	0.221	0.158	−0.181	0.94
CFRD	−0.110	0.671[a]	0.202	0.109	0.246	0.58
ACFRD	0.036	0.929[a]	−0.021	−0.212	0.010	0.91
MEDIA	0.371	−0.042	0.609[a]	0.086	0.073	0.52
OSALEX	0.116	0.214	0.885[a]	0.054	−0.030	0.85
Fraction of Total Communality Explained	0.285	0.243	0.203	0.140	0.129	
Cumulative Communality Explained	0.285	0.528	0.731	0.871	1.000	

[a] Major loadings.
[b] Factor "magnitude".

tiation, it can serve to confirm or falsify our models in the looser sense that expected patterns are or are not strongly evident. Although no variable corresponds exclusively to one model, we hypothesize that some—TORDER, FRQSER, CFRD, ACFRD—mainly reflect the complexity of the product's attributes or the degree to which attributes are adapted to individual buyers' needs. Others primarily indicate the buyer's cost of obtaining information or his benefits (or their lack) from obtaining "objective" information—INFPUR, NOTMAJ, MKFOCUS, MEDIA.[12] Some variables respond strongly to both bases of differentiation; OSALEX bespeaks complex attributes that must be explained to the buyer, but also an extensive demand by the buyer for brand-specific information. We expect the leading factors to indicate this complementarity among variables having relatively strong associations with the one or the other basis for differentiation. Our expectations will be falsified if this complementarity fails to appear. However, since each model of differentiation surely has identifiable subcases, we also expect the secondary factors will show some heterogeneity among the groups of variables strongly associated with each model.

In Table I the dominant factor, which we denote hereafter DIF1, not sur-

[12] The buyer of infrequently purchased goods suffers from holding a stock of information that is much depreciated since his previous purchase. The buyer making minor purchases suffers from high unit costs of obtaining relevant information relative to the benefits. Media advertising (compare OSALEX) exploits the buyer's inability to employ information from sources not controlled by the seller, or their cost or irrelevance. Information structures of product markets are discussed in Caves [1983].

prisingly reflects the degree of user specificity: the basic split between major purchases made to order (low values) and more standardized mass-produced products (high values). It is strongly positively correlated with *NOTMAJ* and strongly negatively with *TORDER*, *FRQSER* and *INFPUR*. This measure of basic product homogeneity accounted for some 28.5 percent of the total common variance observed in the data.

The second factor (*DIF2*) may be regarded as the scope for differentiation based on attribute mix and durability inherent in a group of potentially substitutable products. Because it is, by construction, uncorrelated with the first factor, it indicates that both user-specific and mass-produced goods may differ significantly in attribute complexity and hence in their potential for product differentiation on this basis. Both *CFRD* and *ACFRD* are strongly positively correlated with this factor, as is *INFPUR*. At the same time, minor purchases evidently have less scope for differentiation on attribute complexity (*NOTMAJ* appears with negative sign).

DIF3 flags the scope for marketing the product by promotional outlays pitched directly to consumers as a characteristic determining the level of differentiation. The level of media advertising, for example, does not appear as a significant *independent* indicator of the extent of product differentiation. However, a key factor is the suitability of a product for marketing through promotional outlays directed to potential consumers, reflecting in turn the equilibrium of information flows utilized to guide choices among brands. This factor, which explained a further 20 percent of the total communality, was strongly positively correlated with both *MEDIA* and *OSALEX*.[13]

The fourth factor (*DIF4*), meanwhile, distinguishes the scope for differentiation by means of the distribution channel (which may be the locus for providing information, creating image, or various forms of so-called "push" marketing), as an independent force. It is strongly and positively related both to *MKFOCUS* and *INFPUR*, and explains a further 14 percent of total communality.

Finally, *DIF5*, of somewhat less importance, is the scope for differentiation based on after-sales service and technical support. This factor is, of course, heavily dominated by *FRQSER*.

How closely are these patterns aligned to the theoretical models of structural differentiation, set forth above? A direct evaluation must be judgmental, in the nature of the factor-analysis methodology. Nonetheless, the correspondence seems clear. *DIF1*, *DIF2*, and *DIF5* pick up the essential features of the product-attribute model: the continuum running from customized to homogeneous goods (*DIF1*); the complexity and innovation potential inherent in the product's attribute structure (*DIF2*); and the further element of

[13] The mixture of manufacturers' sales promotion outlays addressed to the ultimate buyer differs considerably among products, and yet this result suggests that media and other outlays have commensurate effects for differentiating the product to the final buyer. It indicates the mismeasurement involved in treating media advertising outlays alone as an indicator of product differentiation.

attribute complexity reflected by the joint consumption of services supplied by the good's maker (DIF5). Likewise, DIF3 and DIF4 represent the underpinnings of information-based differentiation, indicating respectively the extent of information flowing directly from manufacturer to ultimate customer and information passing to and through distribution channels and other intermediaries.[14]

Although we cannot test these associations between the factors and the theoretical models directly, we can test them indirectly. Suppose economic theory tells us that some partial relationship takes the form

$$Y = a_0 X + a_1 f_1 X + a_2 f_2 X \ldots + u$$

where the signs of the a_i ($i \geqslant 1$) are predicted *via* the theoretical models of differentiation and their associations with the empirically estimated factors f_i. A significant and correctly signed a_i then serves to confirm jointly the interpretation of the factor and the hypothesis about its influence.

III. TESTING PREDICTED INFLUENCE OF FACTORS

We performed this test as part of an investigation of the mutual sensitivity of the prices of domestic manufactures and competing manufactured imports for 36 Australian markets, observed annually over the period from 1968–69 to 1977–78 (Williamson [1984]). Cross-section and time-series observations were pooled in the estimation of the model, because we sought to capture the effects of both long-run structural differences among markets and short-run adjustment processes over time. We estimated the model as a system of simultaneous equations with the following endogenous variables: the price of imported manufactures; importers' share of domestic disappearance; and the price of competing domestically produced goods, decomposed into its identity-related components of materials costs, wages, and nonwage value added (gross mark-up). Changes in some parameters of the organizational structures of domestic producers were also investigated, although outside the simultaneous model.

The factors indicating aspects of product differentiation were put to use throughout the model. However, because the model is too complex for a full presentation here, we focus on the import-price equation and summarize the roles played by the factors in the other simultaneous equations.[15] Most investigators of import competition have assumed that importers may be treated as pure competitors confronting their domestic rivals with a passive excess-supply function. Our approach instead allows for the possibility that

[14] Because the variables were selected on the theoretical guidance of the product-attribute and information models of differentiation, we can make no claim that the analysis rejects the existence of still other substantial models of the bases of differentiation. Such models might call for quite different empirical indicators.

[15] Williamson [1984] contains details of the model and its theoretical foundations. The sources and construction of variables used are summarized below in the data appendix.

competition among importers is imperfect. Some industries may be concentrated at the worldwide level outside Australia, so that an oligopoly game between foreign and domestic sellers takes place in the Australian market. Even in the more typical sector with moderate to low concentration at the world level, the markets served by the world's exporters may be segmented, especially in the short run, by goodwill assets and sunk investments in local distribution systems, paving the way for oligopolistic behavior in each segment. Finally, even if foreign producers behave as atomistic competitors in supplying imports to Australia, barriers to entry into the distribution sector may limit their access to final Australian buyers and make possible noncompetitive behavior among import merchants or distributors.[16]

The formal model underlying our estimating equation for import prices assumes that importers may recognize their interdependence with domestic sellers and other importers. The importer maximizes the present value of his expected profits through the instrument of a target long-run market share, but he also manipulates his price to adapt to the effect of short-run disturbances in a way that supports long-run maximization. Thus, product differentiation and other structural features of markets affect the importer's plans through his pattern of response to short-run disturbances as well as the size of his long-run target share.

Importers are assumed to adjust their prices to changes in their domestic competitors' prices and in the components of their own delivered costs. These components include capacity levels and costs of production overseas, along with Australia's tariffs and effective exchange rate. Higher levels of domestic concentration meanwhile may encourage imperfectly competitive import suppliers to act in concert with local oligopolistic pricing so as to share in above-average price-cost margins rather than pricing independently so as to impair the rents accruing to the players as a whole. Product differentiation enters among the elements that affect the reaction of importers' prices to changes in their domestic rivals' prices. The first of the factors appearing in Table I (DIF1) captures the contrast between customized (negative) and standardized (positive) goods. Importers of standardized goods are least able to maintain a price differential from domestic substitutes or delay in following a change in their domestic competitors' price. Hence, we expect the importers' price to be related positively not only to the domestic price (PD) but also to its interaction with the first factor (PD*DIF1).[17] The second factor positively reflects the attribute complexity and novelty of goods, which

[16] A few theoretical papers such as Lyons [1981] have investigated the behavior of noncompetitive foreign suppliers. Empirical investigations of imperfect competition among importers have emphasized their short-run responses to temporary disturbances—for example, Norman [1975] and Murfin and Cowling [1981].

[17] DIF3, DIF4, and DIF5 were tried; they had weaker theoretical rationales and in fact did not appear to influence the responsiveness of import prices systematically. We also note that the factors performed better than the raw traits of buyer and seller behavior which were observed directly, in terms of both sign consistency and statistical significance.

TABLE II
DETERMINANTS OF PRICES OF COMPETING IMPORTS, 36 AUSTRALIAN MANUFACTURING INDUSTRIES, 1968–69 TO 1977–78

Variable	*Two-stage Least Squares*			*Ordinary Least Squares*		
	Coefficient	*Standard Error*	*t-statistic*	*Coefficient*	*Standard Error*	*t-statistic*
CONSTANT	47.19	14.88	3.17	66.52	14.96	4.45
TARIFF*CU	0.98	0.49	2.01	0.61	0.50	1.22
EXCHRT*CU	−0.30	0.14	−2.14	−0.33	0.15	2.26
PD	0.51	0.08	6.22	0.33	0.07	4.47
PD*CN4	0.17	0.10	1.73	0.10	0.10	0.97
PD*DIF1	0.39	0.21	1.86	0.28	0.22	1.27
PD*DIF2	−0.64	0.22	−2.91	−0.53	0.23	2.32
PD*FCN4	0.13	0.05	2.45	0.11	0.06	2.04
FORWGE	0.12	0.04	2.79	0.19	0.04	4.48
FORGWTH	−8.46	2.69	−3.14	−7.50	2.78	2.70
FORGWTH*NTPRT	6.23	2.44	2.55	5.37	2.53	2.12
Adjusted R^2		0.442			0.403	

should insulate importers' and domestic producers' prices from each other. Accordingly, a negative coefficient is expected for PD*DIF2. Other variables that affect the response of the importers' price to domestic price changes are the concentration of the domestic producers (CN4) and of the importers themselves (FCN4). Import prices might be expected to track domestic prices more closely when the domestic producers are concentrated, and concentration of the foreign producers is necessary to generate the capacity to recognize interdependence with the domestic rivals.[18]

We examine the statistical results for these variables in Table II, then briefly report on other hypotheses that fill out the model. The table contains the two-stage least squares regression equation, estimated with the domestic price endogenous in the system, and for comparison an estimate of the model by ordinary least squares. In the TSLS equation PD wields its expected positive and significant influence on importers' prices. Its interactions with DIF1 and DIF2 take the expected signs and are significant at the 5 percent level. Thus, the factors perform in the theoretically predicted manner.

The coefficients of the interactions of PD with CN4 and FCN4 are positive and significant as expected. The remaining variables, whose coefficients are all significant and correctly signed, require only brief description here. An increase in Australia's nominal tariff (TARIFF) should prompt importers to raise their delivered price, especially when capacity utilization (CU) is high for

[18] We could not calculate a weighted-average concentration ratio over producers in the countries that chiefly supply Australia's imports. Instead, FCN4 is a dummy set equal to one if the producer concentration ratio for the most important overseas supplier country lies in the top quartile of that nation's industries.

their domestic rivals. A decrease in the effective exchange rate for the Australian dollar (EXCHRT) should have the same effect. Importers' prices should increase with an imports-weighted index of wages in the countries producing the imports (FORWGE). The dependent variable should decrease with the capacity of foreign producers (FORGWTH, the average rate of increase of output in the corresponding industry class of the region principally supplying Australia's imports), although this effect is mitigated when the Australian industry enjoys substantial natural protection from transportation costs (NTPRT).

The factors describing product differentiation also appear in the equations determining the domestic producer's gross mark-up and the importers' market share. The gross mark-up increases with the price of imports, but that sensitivity is dampened by two interactions with the differentiation factors. The first of these is with the *product* of DIF1 and DIF3. That is, Australian producers respond less sensitively to importers' prices if they are producing goods that are homogeneous but heavily advertised. The second is the *product* of DIF2 and DIF4. That is, Australian producers match changes in importers' prices less promptly or fully if they produce goods with complex attributes and promote them to the distribution channels and to independent advisors or specifiers consulted by final buyers. These interactions of factors show how the structural properties of goods and the investments of domestic producers in goodwill assets may combine to insulate Australian manufacturers from import competition. The first of these two interactions also significantly reduces the sensitivity of the importers' market share to the ratio of the price of domestic goods to that of competing imports.

In conclusion, we cannot reject the hypothesis that the factors computed in the preceding section capture essential features of product differentiation, and serve effectively to test hypotheses about the economic effects of product differentiation. Of course, this is only a beginning. Other data sets than the one available to us may contain more comprehensive statistical manifestations of product differentiation. Other applications of the method are needed to assure the robustness of the approach.[19] But with these qualifications noted, it does seem possible to improve greatly on past treatments of product differentiation in statistical investigations of industrial organization.

IV. SUMMARY AND CONCLUSIONS

Empirical research in industrial organization has suffered from failing to identify the empirical bases for product differentiation—defined theoretically by the presence of downward-sloping Chamberlinian demand curves facing

[19] Caves [1981] employed principal components to establish that intraindustry trade increases with the structural heterogeneity of goods and decreases with informational differentiation through media advertising and related sales promotion.

individual competitors. We find two sets of conditions that are theoretically sufficient to produce this market pattern. One rests on the complexity of the product's attribute structure and the presence of a fixed cost of assembling any given combination of attributes. The other stems from the costliness to buyers of information to guide their choice among competing brands. We applied factor analysis to variables that measure various decision outcomes and market patterns that should result from differentiation and concluded that the estimated factors do indeed correspond to these theoretical models of differentiation. That conclusion itself is judgmental, but it can be pursued statistically by using the factors to test hypotheses about the effects of structural and behavioral product differentiation on the mutual sensitivity of the prices of imports and domestic production in a sample of Australian manufacturing industries. Employed in that fashion, the factors (interacted with other appropriate variables) obtained significant coefficients consistent with the structural and behavioral interpretations that we had tentatively assigned to them.

Thus, we conclude overall that the two models of the structural bases of product differentiation which appear in the literature do have observable empirical counterparts, and that factor analysis seems to permit the testing of hypotheses about differentiation's effects in a more satisfying way than heretofore. Our findings also hold some broader implications for research in industrial organization, which has sometimes blurred the distinction between differentiation as structure and the behavior that it elicits. Product differentiation has structural bases in the technology of production and consumption and in the information costs that condition buyers' choices among competing products. Those structural bases in turn influence the behavior of market participants and the equilibrium settings of market variables. The distinction between the structural foundation of differentiation and the behavior that it supports has been recognized in some lines of empirical research.[20] However, it was missed by many debaters over the product-differentiation barrier to entry, who settled for the (behavioral) advertising–sales ratio as a proxy without conditioning it on structural variables: the buyer's poor access to relevant information sources other than advertising; the producer's lack of an alternative market strategy that does not entail heavy advertising; and economies of scale or experience in advertising itself.[21] Properly interpreted, a product-differentiation barrier to entry has at its heart information-based

[20] Comanor [1967] and Shrieves [1978] showed that structural differentiation influenced the behavioral relationship between seller concentration and R & D spending, and Wilson [1977] provided some evidence that the research activities of industries subject to information-based differentiation are inefficiently oriented toward the production of knowledge that is proprietary and not licensible. Caves and Porter [1978] showed that structural differentiation tends to increase the stability of market shares while nonprice rivalry in markets with informational differentiation destabilizes them.

[21] Scitovsky [1950] anticipated most of this argument. Schmalensee [1983] recently clarified some of the issues.

differentiation coupled with scale economies in sales promotion. Perhaps the operational approach to structural differentiation suggested in this paper can help to clarify such lines of empirical research where the distinction between structural differentiation and its behavioral consequences is critical.

ACCEPTED MARCH 1985

RICHARD E. CAVES,
Department of Economics,
Littauer Center,
Harvard University,
Cambridge,
Massachusetts 02138,
USA.

PETER J. WILLIAMSON,
London Business School,
Sussex Place,
Regent's Park,
London NW1 4SA

DATA APPENDIX

The sample used in this study consisted of 36 Australian manufacturing industries defined at the four-digit level of the Australian Standard Industrial Classification (ASIC). They correspond in aggregation roughly to the three-digit level of the US standard industrial classification, and they can be matched fairly well to aggregations of US four-digit industries. The sample consists of those Australian industries that could be matched well and for which all other data were available. They are (with ASIC code): 2112, fresh and frozen poultry; 2161, bread; 2162, cakes and pastries; 2191, soft drinks, cordials, and syrups; 2194, wine and brandy; 2411, hosiery; 2425, underwear, nightwear and shifts; 2431, rubber footwear; 2432, leather footwear; 2511, sawn timber; 2512, resawn and dressed timber; 2512, furniture (ex. sheet metal); 2522, mattresses; 2613, solid fibreboard containers; 2623, printing trade supplies; 2713, synthetic resins and synthetic rubber; 2722, paints; 2724, pesticides and agricultural chemicals; 2727, inks; 2931, alloying of nonferrous metals; 3131, cutlery and hand tools; 3132, springs and wire products; 3322, refrigerators, household appliances; 3335, space heating, air conditioning equipment; 3337, dies, saw blades, and machine tools; 3338, food processing machinery; 3421, rubber tires, tubes, belts, hose and sheets; 3422, rubber products, n.e.c.; 3443, brooms and brushes.

The factor analysis of product differentiation employed data for US industries matched to their Australian counterparts that were taken from Bailey [1975] and Federal Trade Commission [1982] as well as Australian Bureau of Statistics [1981] (see text). We assumed that (for countries as similar in income *per capita* and culture as the United States and Australia) measured structural attributes underlying product differentiation could appropriately represent markets in either country. R & D figures from both countries were used because the evidence suggests that research and development in Australia principally performs the function of adapting overseas products to Australian conditions, whereas US R & D is oriented more toward pure innovation. Bailey's [1975] industries are rather aggregated, although (fortunately) less so in producer goods where the bases of differentiation are otherwise difficult to observe systematically.

A number of the Australian variables were obtained in machine-readable form from the Australian Bureau of Statistics (ABS), Bureau of Industry Economics, and Industries Assistance Commission (IAC). These were consolidated and matched to the United States data through the PICA Data Base, Harvard Business School. Of those variables appearing in Table II, the dependent variable is an annual index of import prices for each year with base year 1968–69, prepared by the IAC, which similarly supplies an annual index of the prices of domestic output (*PD*) for each year based on 1968–69. *TARIFF* is the rate of nominal assistance computed by the IAC using value-of-production weights, and *EXCHRT* (from the IAC) is an index of bilateral exchange rates weighted by the percentage of imports coming from each trading partner, averaged from quarterly data for each year of the sample period. *CU* is the complement of the percentage of respondents in each manufacturing-industry group reporting that orders are limiting their ability to expand production (Australian Chambers of Manufacturers Association-Bank of New South Wales Survey, distributed in the last two weeks of each quarter, averaged over the year). *CN4* is the proportion of total industry value-added accounted for by the four largest enterprise groups in 1972–73 (ABS, *Industry Concentration Statistics, Manufacturing Census 1972–73* (1975)).

FCN4 is a dummy variable taking the value 1 when seller concentration in the major region supplying imports of products competing with each domestic industry was in the upper quartile of measured concentration indices for that region. The following import supply categories were used: the EEC, the US, Japan, ASEAN, and other Asia. The largest supplying region was identified on the basis of trade data for the commodity groups corresponding to each industry in ABS, *Statistical Yearbook*, 1973–74. Data on the concentration within the countries comprising the relevant region was obtained from R. Linda, *Methodology of Concentration Analysis Applied to the Study of Industries and Markets* (Brussels: Commission of the European Communities, 1976); OECD, Committee of Experts on Restrictive Trade Practices, *Concentration and Competition Policy* (Paris: OECD, 1979); and US Bureau of the Census, *1972 Census of Manufactures*, Special Report Series, *Concentration Ratios in Manufacturing*, MC72(SR)-2 (Washington: Government Printing Office, 1975). *FORWGE* is an index of wage costs in each country of import supply, weighted by the proportion of total competing imports accounted for by that country source. It was computed from an import-weighted series compiled by the IAC (see IAC, *Annual Report*, 1979–80). *FORGWTH* is a measure of the growth of output of the corresponding industry class in each major import supplying region averaged over the period from 1968–69 to 1977–78. The regions used include: the EEC, US, Japan, ASEAN, and other Asia (data from the United Nations, *Yearbook of Industrial Statistics*, 1980).

NTPRT is a dummy variable set equal to 1 when the industry is defined by the IAC as being subject to substantial natural protection (for example, by transportation costs), 0 otherwise (17 percent of our industry sample was so classified).

The remainder of the model of price determination and shares in Australian manufacturing markets was reported in Williamson [1984], including the definitions and sources of variables used in other equations but not the one reported in Table II.

REFERENCES

Archibald, G. C., Eaton, B. C. and Lipsey, R. G., 1983, 'Address Models of Value Theory', Institute for Economic Research, Queen's University, Discussion Paper No. 495.

AUSTRALIAN BUREAU OF STATISTICS, 1981, *Research and Experimental Development: Business Enterprises, Australia, 1978–79*, Catalogue No. 8104.0. Australian Bureau of Statistics, Canberra.

BAILEY, E. L., 1975, *Marketing Cost Ratios of US Manufacturers*, Conference Board Report No. 662. Conference Board, New York.

BREIT, W. and ELZINGA, K. G., 1974, 'Product Differentiation and Institutionalism', *Journal of Economic Issues*, 8 (December), pp. 813–826.

CAVES, R. E., 1981, 'Intraindustry Trade and Market Structure in the Industrial Countries', *Oxford Economic Papers*, 33 (July), pp. 203–223.

CAVES, RICHARD E., 1983, 'Information Structures of Product Markets', Discussion Paper No. 1002, Harvard University.

CAVES, R. E. and PORTER, M. E., 1978, 'Market Structure, Oligopoly, and Stability of Market Shares', *Journal of Industrial Economics*, 26 (June), pp. 289–313.

COMANOR, W. S., 1967, 'Market Structure, Product Differentiation, and Industrial Research', *Quarterly Journal of Economics*, 81 (November), pp. 639–657.

COMANOR, W. S. and WILSON, T. A., 1974, *Advertising and Market Power* (Harvard University Press, Cambridge).

FEDERAL TRADE COMMISSION, BUREAU OF ECONOMICS, 1982, *Statistical Report: Annual Line of Business Report, 1976*. Federal Trade Commission, Washington.

HARMAN, H. H., 1976, *Modern Factor Analysis* (3rd ed.; University of Chicago Press, Chicago).

KLEIN, B. and LEFFLER, K. B., 1981, 'The Role of Market Forces in Assuring Contractual Performance', *Journal of Political Economy*, 89 (August), pp. 615–641.

LANCASTER, K., 1979, *Variety, Equity and Efficiency: Product Variety in an Industrial Society* (Columbia University Press, New York).

LYONS, B., 1981, 'Industrial Behaviour, the Technology of Demand, and the Pattern of International Trade between Identical Countries', *Recherches Economiques de Louvain*, 47 (September), pp. 243–258.

MEYER, J. R., 1967, 'An Experiment in the Measurement of Business Motivation', *Review of Economics and Statistics*, 49 (August), pp. 304–318.

MONSEN, R. J. and DOWNS, A., 1971, 'Public Goods and Private Status', *The Public Interest*, No. 23 (Spring), pp. 64–76.

MURFIN, A. and COWLING, K., 1981, 'Price Formation and Import Penetration in UK Manufacturing Industry', *Recherches Economiques de Louvain*, 47 (September), pp. 307–334.

NELSON, P., 1974, 'Advertising as Information', *Journal of Political Economy*, 82 (July/August), pp. 729–754.

NELSON, P., 1970, 'Information and Consumer Behavior', *Journal of Political Economy*, 78 (March/April), pp. 311–329.

NORMAN, N. R., 1975, 'On the Relationship Between Prices of Home-Produced and Foreign Commodities', *Oxford Economic Papers*, 27 (November), pp. 427–439.

PERLOFF, J. M. and SALOP, S. C., 1985, 'Equilibrium with Product Differentiation', *Review of Economic Studies*, 52 (January), pp. 107–120.

PETERSON, R. D., 1980, 'Product Differentiation, Implicit Theorizing, and the Methodology of Industrial Organization', *Nebraska Journal of Economics and Business*, 19 (Spring), pp. 22–36.

PORTER, M. E., 1976a, 'Interbrand Choice, Media Mix and Market Performance', *American Economic Review*, 66 (May), pp. 398–406.

PORTER, M. E., 1976b, *Interbrand Choice, Strategy, and Bilateral Market Power* (Harvard University Press, Cambridge).

PRESS, S. J., 1972, *Applied Multivariate Analysis* (Holt, Rinehart, and Winston, New York).

ROBINSON, D. S., 1961, 'The Economics of Fashion Demand', *Quarterly Journal of Economics*, 75 (August), pp. 376–398.

ROSEN, S., 1974, 'Hedonic Prices and Implicit Markets: Product Differentiation in Pure Competition', *Journal of Political Economy*, 82 (January/February), pp. 34–55.

RUMMEL, R. J., 1970, *Applied Factor Analysis* (Northwestern University Press, Evanston).

SATTERTHWAITE, M. A., 1979, "Consumer Information, Equilibrium Industry Price, and the Number of Sellers', *Bell Journal of Economics*, 10 (Autumn), pp. 483–502.

SCHLAIFER, R. O., 1976, *User's Guide to the AQD Collection* (8th ed.; Harvard Business School Case No. 9-0173-095. Harvard Business School, Boston).

SCHMALENSEE, R., 1983, 'Advertising and Entry Deterrence: An Exploratory Model', *Journal of Political Economy*, 91 (August), pp. 636–653.

SCHMALENSEE, R., 1978, 'A Model of Advertising and Product Quality', *Journal of Political Economy*, 86 (June), pp. 485–503.

SCITOVSKY, T., 1950, 'Ignorance as a Source of Oligopoly Power', *American Economic Review*, 40 (May), pp. 48–53.

SHAPIRO, C., 1983, 'Premiums for High Quality Products as Returns to Reputations', *Quarterly Journal of Economics*, 98 (November), pp. 659–679.

SHRIEVES, R. E., 1978, 'Market Structure and Innovation: A New Perspective', *Journal of Industrial Economics*, 26 (June), pp. 329–347.

SIMON, J. L., 1970, *Issues in the Economics of Advertising* (University of Illinois Press, Urbana, IL).

SPENCE, M., 1976, 'Product Selection, Fixed Costs and Monopolistic Competition', *Review of Economic Studies*, 42 (June), pp. 217–235.

TELSER, L. G., 1964, 'Advertising and Competition', *Journal of Political Economy*, 72 (December), pp. 537–562.

WILDE, L. L., 1980, 'The Economics of Consumer Information Acquisition', *Journal of Business*, 53 (July), pp. S143–189.

WILLIAMSON, P. J., 1984, 'Import Penetration in Imperfectly Competitive Markets: A Study of Firm and Industry Behaviour under Import Threat', PhD dissertation, Harvard University.

WILSON, R. W., 1977, 'The Effect of Technological Environment and Product Rivalry on R & D Effort and Licensing of Inventions', *Review of Economics and Statistics*, 59 (November), pp. 171–178.

THE JOURNAL OF INDUSTRIAL ECONOMICS 0022–1821 $2.00
Volume XXXIV December 1985 No. 2

DISCRIMINATING OLIGOPOLISTS AND COMMON MARKETS

DAMIEN NEVEN AND LOUIS PHLIPS*

We analyse the properties of a Cournot–Nash equilibrium which arises when two monopolies, operating each in a separate market, become a duopoly in a common market with two sub-markets (the formerly separated markets) and are allowed to price discriminate across sub-markets. This equilibrium implies "intra-industry" trade (or "cross-hauling") of identical commodities and freight absorption (which is an increasing function of the slope of the marginal cost schedule). It also leads to price differences such as those observed in the European car market.

INTRODUCTION

POPULAR wisdom tends to associate common markets with a unique price, presumably with reference to the "competitive mechanism" which is supposed to drive prices down to a unique level when markets which were separated are brought together. Admittedly, some price dispersion is considered normal at the retail level, given differences in transaction costs, tax laws and what not. But when price differences persist over time, or even increase, inside common industrial (wholesale) markets—where oligopolists have the power to set prices—then suspicion arises.

Belgian consumers find it hard to understand why a big Belgian producer of, say, photographic material[1] sells his films cheaper in Italy than in Belgium. And considerable discussion arose in the UK around the fact that British cars are cheaper in Belgium than at home.[2] Explanations offered tend to incriminate restrictive trade practices or invoke high costs of UK producers. The latter argument is not convincing, since cars "sold in the UK are expensive, regardless of the country in which they are manufactured" (Ashworth, Kay and Sharpe [1982]). On the other hand, restrictive practices may, and to some extent do, explain the observed price differences. There is, however, a third explanation which remained largely unnoticed and whose theoretical underpinning is examined in this paper.

* Nuffield College (Oxford) and CORE (Louvain-la-Neuve). We are grateful to Victor Ginsburgh and an anonymous reference for constructive comments and we benefitted from seminar discussions at the Industrial Economics Study Group meeting in the London Business School, the Gorman workshop and the University of Southampton.

[1] Empirical evidence on the prices of photographic material can be found in Phlips [1962, chapter VII].

[2] See Ashworth, Kay and Sharpe [1982].

Our point is simply that, whenever demand has a different price elasticity in different markets, oligopolists will tend to price discriminate exactly in the same way as "the discriminating monopolist" would. Strangely enough, price discrimination has been associated with monopoly, and with monopoly only in the standard literature. Notable exceptions[3] where discriminating *oligopolists* are discussed, are the papers by Greenhut and Greenhut [1975], who consider a spatial oligopolistic market, by Spulber [1979], who discusses existence of a non-cooperative equilibrium, and by Mertens and Ginsburgh [this issue] who study prices of specific car makes in the EEC. In addition, Brander and Spencer [1984] mention this problem, stressing the role of import taxes. (See also Brander and Krugman [1983].)

To the extent that arbitrage is not operative because of natural barriers (such as transport costs or the value of time) or artificial barriers (such as exclusive dealing arrangements or taxes), a non-cooperative equilibrium of the Cournot–Nash type may imply discriminatory price differences. It is compatible with producers restricting the freedom of their dealers to export to other markets and helps to understand why they do so. And it does add a better theoretical explanation of why significant price differences between markets can persist (or increase) without collusion among producers located in different markets and without cost differences among them.

References to this type of equilibrium may also lead to new insights when compared with an approach in which exporters are assumed to be price makers in their home country and price takers in their export markets[4] (often called "world" markets on the assumption that competitors are few at home and many in the outside world). First, there seems to be no reason why, in a particular industry with a given technology, export markets should be systematically less oligopolistic than the domestic markets (we will therefore have the same number of competitors in each market considered, whether home or foreign). Second, our Cournot equilibrium explains the otherwise puzzling and often observed fact that trade takes place for identical commodities, leading to what has become known as "intra-industry trade" in the theory of international trade[5] or "cross-hauling" in spatial economics.

A first section sets up a general model and derives the Cournot–Nash equilibrium which arises when two monopolies, operating each in a separate market, become a duopoly in a common market with two sub-markets (the formerly separated markets). In ensuing sections, the respective role of demand and cost conditions is further examined, using a more specific model, which is spelled out in section II. Section III examines the properties of the equilibrium when each firm operates without transportation costs. Section IV introduces costs of transportation. This is the case of bulky products, for which discrimination operates through freight absorption.

[3] In addition, of course, to the second author's book on price discrimination.
[4] See Huveneers [1981].
[5] See the survey by Tharakan [1981].

Finally, we wonder, in section V, whether the discrimination outcome is socially desirable. We examine the welfare implications of discrimination in duopoly, restricting ourselves to the simplest case of constant marginal cost. By so doing, we extend somewhat Schmalensee's analysis [1981].

The illustrative model used is kept as simple as possible: aggregate demands in the two markets are linear, cost differences are ruled out and the cost of production is quadratic. The lack of generality is more than compensated, in our opinion, by economic relevance and clarity of exposition. Needless to say, our results apply to regional sub-markets inside a country as well as to national markets inside a common market such as the EEC, as long as some natural barrier continues to separate sub-markets (as is implied in their definition).

I. DISCRIMINATING OLIGOPOLY AND INTRA-INDUSTRY TRADE

Let there be two sub-markets ($j = 1, 2$) with different aggregate demands:

$$P_1 = P_1(q_1)$$
$$P_2 = P_2(q_2)$$

in which P_j, q_j stand, respectively, for the price and the total quantity sold in the jth market.

There is a firm located in each sub-market. Each firm can sell its output in both markets. No transportation cost is incurred for local sales but a transportation cost t is supported for each unit of output shipped to the foreign market. Henceforth, each firm ($i = 1, 2$) will be denoted by the market in which it operates.

We provide both firms with a production cost function (C_i):

$$C_i = C_i(Q_i) \tag{1}$$

in which Q_i stands for the total quantity produced by firm i.

This situation gives rise to a two-person game, with players $i = 1, 2$. We assume that each firm decides on the level of its sales. Local sales and shipments are decided upon at the same time. Consequently, each firm's ($i = 1, 2$) strategy can be described as a couple $q_{.i} = (q_{1i}, q_{2i})$ and the payoff functions are given by the following profit functions:

$$\pi_1 = q_{11}P_1(q_1) + q_{21}(P_2(q_2) - t) - C_1(q_{11} + q_{21})$$
$$\pi_2 = q_{12}(P_1(q_1) - t) + q_{22}P_2(q_2) - C_2(q_{11} + q_{21})$$

A Cournot–Nash equilibrium point in this game, is a pair of strategies $(q^*_{.1}, q^*_{.2})$ such that $q^*_{.1}$ is a best reply strategy to $q^*_{.2}$ and vice-versa, that is $(q^*_{.1}, q^*_{.2})$ is such that:

$$\pi_1(q_{.1}^*, q_{.2}^*) \geqslant \pi_1(q_{.1}, q_{.2}^*) \quad \text{for all } q_{.1}$$

$$\pi_2(q_{.1}^*, q_{.2}^*) \geqslant \pi_2(q_{.1}^*, q_{.2}) \quad \text{for all } q_{.2}$$

Let us assume that each payoff function is concave in its decision variables. The unique Cournot–Nash equilibrium in this game is then given by the solution to these following sets of first order conditions:

$$(1.1) \qquad q_{11}P_1'(q_1)+P_1(q_1)-C_1'(q_{.1}) = 0$$

$$(1.2) \qquad -t+P_2(q_2)+q_{21}P_2'(q_2)-C_1'(q_{.1}) = 0$$

$$(1.3) \qquad -t+P_1(q_1)+q_{12}P_1'(q_1)-C_2'(q_{.2}) = 0$$

$$(1.4) \qquad q_{22}P_2'(q_2)+P_2(q_2)-C_2'(q_{.2}) = 0$$

If both firms face the same cost function, in the absence of transportation cost ($t = 0$), it is clear, by inspection of (1.1)–(1.4), that the equilibrium is symmetric; we have $q_{11}^* = q_{12}^*$, $q_{21}^* = q_{22}^*$. It follows that the production sold at home by a local firm is equal to the quantity exported by its foreign competitor. This means that the total quantity sold in any market is produced by the local and foreign firms in equal shares. It follows that whenever both markets are served, some cross-hauling occurs. The same commodity is being shipped in both directions. It is worth noticing, though, that there is a net trade, since imports of a sub-market are generally not equal to its exports (except if both sub-markets have the same demand, which is a trivial case in this context).

The trade might also appear in only one direction or might not take place at all. If trade is unilateral, one market is not served at all; nothing is being sold in the sub-market in which the exporting firm is located. If there is no trade, nothing is produced either. Next, if some positive transportation cost is incurred, the equilibrium is not symmetric anymore. According to (1.1)–(1.4), the firm's optimal policy consists of equalising "net" marginal revenues (after subtracting the transport cost) between markets. As an example, for firm 1, its marginal revenue from market 1 is $q_{11}P_1'(q_1)+P_1(q_1)=C_1'(q_{.1})$, whereas its net marginal revenue from market 2 is $P_2(q_2)-t+q_{21}P_2'(q_2)=C_1'(q_{.1})$. It should be noticed that this marginal revenue is a firm's marginal revenue, as opposed to the usual "market" marginal revenue. The marginal revenue earned by a firm from one market is contingent on the quantity sold by the other firm. The firm's marginal revenue which is relevant to the equilibrium is thus a function of the quantity produced by the other firm and differs from the usual marginal revenue curve (which typically, would be faced by a monopolist). With $t > 0$, unilateral trade might occur, even when both markets are served. For some high transportation costs, both markets might also be isolated, being served by local producers only. The conditions under which these possibilities will arise are made precise in the next section, in which demand and cost conditions are further specified.

II. AN ILLUSTRATIVE MODEL

Assume that both markets have linear aggregate demands:

$$P_1 = A - Bq_1$$
$$P_2 = C - Bq_2$$

We provide each firm with a quadratic cost function:

$$K + \lambda/2Q_i^2$$

The payoff functions are then written:

(2) $$\pi_1 = q_{11}(A - Bq_1) + q_{21}((C - Dq_2) - t) - K - \lambda/2(q_{11} + q_{21})^2$$

(3) $$\pi_2 = q_{12}((A - Bq_1) - t) + q_{22}(C - Dq_2) - K - \lambda/2(q_{12} + q_{22})^2$$

The first order conditions for the maximisation of these payoffs, are the following:

$$\begin{bmatrix} (-2B-\lambda) & -B & -\lambda & 0 \\ -\lambda & 0 & (-2D-\lambda) & -D \\ -B & (-2B-\lambda) & 0 & -\lambda \\ 0 & -\lambda & -D & (-2D-\lambda) \end{bmatrix} \begin{bmatrix} q_{11} \\ q_{12} \\ q_{21} \\ q_{22} \end{bmatrix} = \begin{bmatrix} -A \\ t-C \\ t-A \\ -C \end{bmatrix}$$

The solution to this system of simultaneous equations can be written:

(4) $$q_{11}^* = 1/S[\lambda^2(C - A - 3t)(B + D) + \lambda D(B(C - 9t) - A(3D + 4B)) - 3BD^2(A + t)]$$

(5) $$q_{12}^* = 1/S[\lambda^2(C - A + 3t)(B + D) + \lambda D(B(C + 12t) + 3Dt - A(3D + 4B)) - 3BD^2(A - 2t)]$$

(6) $$q_{21}^* = 1/S[\lambda^2(A - C + 3t)(B + D) + \lambda B(D(A + 12t) + 3Bt - C(3B + 4D)) - 3B^2D(C - 2t)]$$

(7) $$q_{22}^* = 1/S[\lambda^2(A - C - 3t)(B + D) + \lambda B(D(A - 9t) - C(3B + 4D)) - 3B^2D(C + t)]$$

in which $S \equiv 3[4\lambda(B^2D + D^2B) - \lambda^2(B + D)^2 - 3B^2D^2]$.

It is easy to check that the Hessians, for π_1 and π_2 respectively, are both negative definite if $\lambda > 0$. If, on the other hand $\lambda < 0$, the second order conditions will be satisfied, provided $|\lambda| < 2B_2$, $|\lambda| < 2D$, $|\lambda| < 2BD/(B+D)$, which are usual stability conditions, for each market taken individually and for the common market. Provided these conditions are satisfied, the solution given above is the simultaneous global maximum for each firm's optimisation problem. It follows that (4)–(7) gives the unique Nash equilibrium in this game.

III. COURNOT MODEL WITHOUT TRANSPORTATION COSTS

Assume first that $K = \lambda = t = 0$. This assumption enables us to emphasise the role of the demand elasticities in examining the properties of the Nash equilibrium derived above. Now (4)–(7) can be rewritten as:

(8) $$q_{11} = q_{12} = A/3B$$

(9) $$q_{21} = q_{22} = C/3D$$

As suggested above, cross-hauling takes place at the equilibrium. Both firms penetrate each other's market and the equilibrium is symmetric. Each sub-market is thus shared equally between the two firms.

It is well known that, if a monopolist were to serve these two sub-markets alone, he would produce (and sell) the same quantity (here $q = q_1 + q_2 = (AD+BC)/(2BD)$ whether he discriminates or not, since production is determined by the same marginal revenue (equalised at zero level). But a discriminating policy would be more profitable. This result carries over in our duopoly case in the sense that total production $q = 2(AD+BC)/3BD$ is the same whether the two firms act as monopolists in each separate sub-market, as discriminating non-cooperating duopolists on both sub-markets, or as non-cooperating duopolists selling at the same unique price in both sub-markets. Yet, duopoly is "better" than monopoly, since the total quantity sold by the two firms is larger than the quantity sold by a monopolist serving the two markets, and the duopolists make less profit.

With a monopolist in each sub-market, prices are $P_1 = A/2$ and $P_2 = C/2$. In the common market with discriminating oligopolists, the non-cooperative Cournot–Nash equilibrium implies a drop in prices. Substituting (8)–(9) into the demand curves, we find the equilibrium prices to be $P_1 = A/3$ and $P_2 = C/3$. The sub-market with the highest intercept has the highest price. Besides, the price ratio $P_1/P_2 = A/C$ is the same in the monopoly and the duopoly cases.

All in all, the non-cooperative behaviour only restricts the level of prices (and, therefore, the level of profits) and improves the level of total production, but does not affect the price ratio as compared with the monopoly behaviour. We know that a discriminating monopolist is able to equate marginal revenues of both sub-markets to zero. Furthermore, we know that the marginal revenue curve in each sub-market has a slope equal to 1/2 of the slope of the demand curve. Therefore, if the price ratio is not affected, while sales are increased, it must be that in duopoly the sub-market marginal revenues, evaluated at the Cournot equilibrium point, are not equated to each other, as opposed to the individual firm's marginal revenues. Taking the monopolist equalisation of marginal revenues as a benchmark for discrimination, it can be said that competition does hamper an effective discrimination strategy. In duopoly, the discrimination is less effective than in monopoly. Indeed, computing the sub-markets marginal revenues at the duopoly

Cournot equilibrium shows that both marginal revenues are negative and will only be equal if $A = C(MR_1 = -A/3, MR_2 = -C/3)$.

Intuition and/or a moment of reflexion could have led to these results. They can be extended to the less obvious case where each duopolist has the (same) increasing marginal cost of production. Setting $t = 0$ in (4)–(7), the equilibrium quantities reduce to:

$$q_{11} = q_{12} = \frac{A(3D+\lambda)-\lambda C}{3(3BD+\lambda(B+D))} \tag{10}$$

$$q_{21} = q_{22} = \frac{C(3B+\lambda)-\lambda A}{3(3BD+\lambda(B+D))} \tag{11}$$

As before, the equilibrium is symmetric and involves a foreign penetration in both markets.

Again, it is well known (Robinson [1933, p. 192] and Schmalensee [1981]) that if the demand curves are straight lines, discriminating monopoly output is equal to simple monopoly output, whether marginal cost is rising, falling or constant, provided both sub-markets are served under simple monopoly. We find the same to be true when discriminating duopoly is compared to simple duopoly output (i.e. duopoly output without discrimination, when both firms serve both sub-markets). For a monopoly serving both sub-markets, $q = (AD+BC)/(2BD+\lambda(B+D))$, with or without price discrimination. For a duopoly serving both sub-markets, $q = 2(AD+BC)/(3BD+\lambda(B+D))$, with and without price discrimination.

As mentioned above, in the absence of production costs, opening the markets will unambiguously increase sales in both sub-markets. Previously isolated monopolists become duopolists in a common market and output increases. With production costs, the tendency to increased output is lessened with increasing marginal costs and enhanced with decreasing marginal costs. As usual, the duopolists have an interest to discriminate.

Tables I and II provide a numerical example that facilitates the comparison between the different outcomes. We consider five different situations; isolated monopolists, a monopolist in the common market, with and without discrimination, and duopolists operating in the common market, with and without price discrimination. Table I is concerned with equilibrium quantities

TABLE I
TOTAL SALES ($A = 4, C = 6, B = D = \lambda = 1$)

	Sub-market 1	*Sub-market 2*	*Total*
Two Monopolies	1.33	2.0	3.33
Discriminating Monopoly	0.75	1.75	2.5
Discriminating Duopoly	1.33	2.66	4.0
Non-discriminating Monopoly	0.25	2.25	2.5
Non-discriminating Duopoly	1.0	3.0	4.0

TABLE II
PRICES ($A = 4, C = 6, B = D = \lambda = 1$)

	Sub-market 1	*Sub-market 2*
Two Monopolies	2.66	4.0
Discriminating Monopoly	3.25	4.25
Discriminating Duopoly	2.66	3.33
Non-discriminating Monopoly	3.75	
Non-discriminating Duopoly	3.0	

and Table II with equilibrium prices. We suppose $A = 4$, $C = 6$, $B = D = \lambda = 1$. The numbers are chosen in such a way that both sub-markets are served under both regimes. The situation in which one market is not served under non-discriminatory pricing is discussed in section V. From these tables (see also equations (4)–(7)), it is clear that creating a common market increases sales, in both sub-markets. However, if the firms are obliged to sell at the same price in the two sub-markets, total sales will be spread less evenly over the two markets. A less even distribution of sales is also the result of non-discriminatory pricing by a monopolist. Hence, both in monopoly and duopoly, the discrimination strategy consists of transferring output from the sub-market with a low elasticity to the highly elastic market.

As before, one may wonder whether the discrimination is as "effective" in the duopoly case as it is in the monopoly situation. A first answer to this question can be found by comparing the ratios of the market prices in the duopoly and in the monopoly cases.

We find that these ratios generally differ. Only if the two sub-markets have an identical slope and if this common slope is equal to twice the slope of the marginal cost curve ($B = D = -2\lambda$), will the two ratios be equal. It follows that with increasing marginal costs, this situation never occurs. As these ratios usually differ as well as the outputs in each sub-market, it could well be that discrimination in duopoly might turn out to be as effective as in monopoly. Working out the sub-markets marginal revenues, it appears, though, that at the duopoly equilibrium, those marginal revenues are again not equated to each other, except if $A = C$. Of course, the monopolist succeeds in equating these marginal revenues. The conclusion previously derived also holds with increasing marginal costs: competition between firms does hamper an effective discrimination.

IV. COURNOT MODEL WITH TRANSPORTATION COSTS

Throughout this section, we will explicitly include transportation costs in the analysis. Hence, we allow the discrimination to operate through freight absorption. In order to single out the role of transportation costs, let us assume for the time being that the marginal cost of production is constant (zero without loss of generality). Setting $\lambda = 0$ in the system (4)–(7), we derive the following equilibrium quantities:

$$(12) \qquad q_{11} = \frac{(A+t)}{3B}$$

$$(13) \qquad q_{12} = \frac{(A-2t)}{3B}$$

$$(14) \qquad q_{21} = \frac{(C-2t)}{3D}$$

$$(15) \qquad q_{22} = \frac{(C+t)}{3D}$$

As suggested earlier, a main difference appears from inspection of (12)–(15). The equilibrium is not symmetric. Quite unsurprisingly, existence of transportation costs induces local producers to increase their sales at home and to reduce their shipment abroad. Hence, some cross-hauling takes place, but to a lesser extent than before, and the volume of trade decreases as the transportation cost increases. It is worth mentioning the conditions in which unilateral trade could occur. For $C/2 < t < A/2$, firm 1 exports to the second market, while the second firm chooses not to ship any of its production to the first market. Obviously, if $A/2 < t < C/2$, the direction of trade would be reversed. Equations (12)–(15) can be rewritten as:

$$(16) \qquad q_{11} = \overline{q_{11}} + \frac{t}{3B}$$

$$(17) \qquad q_{12} = \overline{q_{12}} - \frac{2t}{3B}$$

$$(18) \qquad q_{21} = \overline{q_{21}} - \frac{2t}{3D}$$

$$(19) \qquad q_{22} = \overline{q_{22}} + \frac{t}{3D}$$

and

$$(20) \qquad q_{.1} = \overline{q_{.1}} - \frac{t(2B-D)}{3BD}$$

$$(21) \qquad q_{.2} = \overline{q_{.2}} - \frac{t(2D-B)}{3BD}$$

in which $^{-}$ denotes optimal quantities without transportation costs. From (17)–(18), it appears that shipments in one direction will be equal to shipments in the other only if the sub-market demands have the same slope.

Hence, apart from its impact on the volume of trade, transportation cost tends to alter the pattern of trade. A larger volume will be transported to the more inelastic market. This is also to say that the firm producing in the sub-market with the highest elasticity will have a competitive advantage. It is easy to check that (for $A = C$), the firm located in the sub-market with the shallowest demand will make more profit than the other. From (20)–(21), it also follows that the total sales of one firm can actually increase after the introduction of transportation costs (or equivalently, an import tax): if $2B < D$, the first firm will experience an increase in total sales (conversely, if $2D < B$, the second firm increases its total sales). If sales drop, the reduction will always be less pronounced for the firm facing a shallow demand at home.

Altogether, the introduction of transportation costs implies a significant departure from the symmetric equilibrium. Differences in elasticities play a major role in re-distributing profit and sales between duopolists. This is so because the firm's location matters in this case: the firm in an elastic market has a competitive advantage. Nevertheless, at the sub-market level, this uneven distribution of sales leads to a symmetric outcome, as can be seen by looking at equilibrium prices:

$$(22) \qquad P_1 = A/3 + t/3 = \overline{P_1} + t/3$$

$$P_2 = C/3 + t/3 = \overline{P_2} + t/3$$

Equations (22) provide a nice answer to the popular objection according to which arbitrage will displace demand curves in the two countries until both curves are equal. Since t is the cost of transportation to an independent importer, he can benefit from arbitrage only as long as the price difference is larger that $P_1 - P_2 = t$ or $A/3 + t/3 - C/3 - t/3 = t$, or as long as the difference between the intercepts is larger than $A - C = 3t$. Arbitrage, however massive, will not eliminate differences in demand which are such that $A - C < 3t$.

The reader might think that this little calculation is incorrect and that what counts is the difference between P_1 and $\overline{P_2}$, or $A/3 + t/3 - C/3 = t$ if $P_2 < P_1$. Then the maximum difference in intercepts would only be $A - C = 6t/3 = 2t$. This is wrong, however, since the importer located in country 1 who goes to country 2 (crosses the Channel) to pick up the goods will not be charged $\overline{P_2}$ but $\overline{P_2} + t/3$. Only delivered prices exist: $\overline{P_2}$ exists only in the economist's imagination in an oligopolistic world in which transportation costs matter. And the same is true for $\overline{P_1}$, so that it would be even more incorrect to think that arbitrage will bring the maximum difference between A and C down to t. All one can say is that arbitrage (or equivalently the removal of artificial trade barriers at the distribution level) puts an upper limit to the differences in demand that can subsist in a common market. If demands were different in the separate markets, arbitrage would *not* make these equal.

In both markets, the price is thus inflated by one third of the unit transportation cost, compared to the situation without transportation costs. Again it is well known that a monopolist located in the first market would set his price (sales) such that:

$$(23) \qquad P_1 = \overline{P_1}$$
$$P_2 = \overline{P_2} + t/2$$

In other words, a monopolist would absorb one half of the freight. In our duopoly problem everything happens as if, at the equilibrium, two thirds of the freight were absorbed in both directions. In both markets, one third of the transportation cost is passed on to the consumers, whether they purchase local production or not. Moreover, as the transportation cost increases, the price difference between the two markets gets smaller. In other words, high transportation costs lead to a more uniform pricing whereas, under monopoly, the price difference tends to increase.

Finally, let us evaluate the discrimination in both the monopoly and duopoly situations. At the equilibrium, the monopolist does not equate the marginal revenues to each other: $MR_1 = 0$, $MR_2 = t$. From these equalities, one could say that the discrimination strategy of the monopolist consists in equating marginal revenues net of transportation costs to each other. In the duopoly situation, the sub-market marginal revenues can be written:

$$MR_1 = -A/3 + 2t/3, \; MR_2 = -C/3 + 2t/3$$

As before, the marginal revenues will be equal only if $A = C$. Moreover, as t increases, the difference between the two marginal revenues is kept constant. The magnitude of the transportation cost, thus, does not affect the effectiveness of the discrimination, in absolute terms. Altogether, the discrimination arising out of duopoly will differ, as before, from the discrimination set out by a monopolist.

Let us allow λ to vary and examine the impact of production costs on the foregoing analysis. The equilibrium quantities (4)–(7) are rewritten in a more convenient way:

$$(24) \qquad q_{11} = \overline{q_{11}} + \frac{t}{(BD+\lambda(B+D))}\left[\lambda + \frac{BD^2}{(3BD+\lambda(B+D))}\right]$$

$$(25) \qquad q_{12} = \overline{q_{12}} - \frac{t}{(BD+\lambda(B+D))}\left[\lambda + D\frac{(2BD+\lambda(B+D))}{(3BD+\lambda(B+D))}\right]$$

$$(26) \qquad q_{21} = \overline{q_{21}} - \frac{t}{(BD+\lambda(B+D))}\left[\lambda + B\frac{(2BD+\lambda(B+D))}{(3BD+\lambda(B+D))}\right]$$

$$(27) \qquad q_{22} = \overline{q_{22}} + \frac{t}{(BD+\lambda(B+D))}\left[\lambda + \frac{B^2D}{(3BD+\lambda(B+D))}\right]$$

Next, provided trade takes place in both directions ($q_{12} > 0, q_{21} > 0$), the resulting prices can also be rewritten as;

$$(28) \qquad P_1 = \overline{P_1} + t\frac{BD}{(3BD+\lambda(B+D))}$$

$$(29) \qquad P_2 = \overline{P_2} + t\frac{BD}{(3BD+\lambda(B+D))}$$

As before, we observe that, for any given production condition, if the transportation cost increases, quantities sold by local producers in their home market increase, whereas exports decline (in both directions). The drop in imports overweights the increase in local sales in both markets. Hence both prices go up. It is noticeable, though, that both prices increase by the same fraction of the transportation cost (consequently, total sales decline more in the most elastic market). As before, the two prices become more similar if the transportation cost increases. This is also to say that the freight absorption is the same for each sub-market. Nevertheless, the freight absorption varies with the marginal cost: from (28)–(29), we can observe that as λ increases, the freight absorption tends to increase.[6]

We should bear in mind, though, that these equations are only valid if there is some cross-hauling. This is to say that the freight absorption will never reach unity.

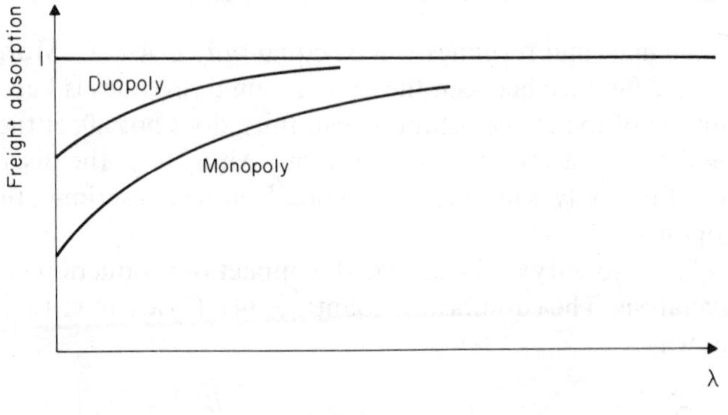

The same tendency can be observed in the monopoly case, but the extent of freight absorption will always be higher in duopoly.

By the same token, the prices in both markets will be closer to the equilibrium prices without transportation costs, when λ increases, as long as trade takes place in both directions. In other words, the gap between the total production sold (in each market) respectively with and without transpor-

[6] If λ is negative, the freight absorption will tend to decrease (the function describing the freight absorption continues downwards to the left). For $|\lambda| = 2BD/(B+D)$, which is the minimum value of λ for which the market is stable, the freight absorption will be zero. (This can be checked by inserting this value of $|\lambda|$ in (28)–(29).)

tation costs, gets smaller as the marginal production cost increases. The transportation cost becomes negligible in comparison to the production cost and the market outcome converges to the equilibrium without transportation costs.

The foregoing discussion suggests that when the production cost increases, the maximum transportation cost compatible with market penetration also increases. One can check that this is, indeed, the case. What matters is not the absolute value of the transportation cost but its value relative to the production outlays.

All in all, the interaction of transportation and production costs is such that, on the one hand, transportation cost tends to fade out price differentials resulting from differences in elasticities. On the other hand, an increased production cost tends to enhance those price differentials.

V. SOME WELFARE IMPLICATIONS

Assuming out income effects and neglecting distribution effects, we use the standard Marshallian welfare indicator (W), the sum of profits and consumers' surplus. The consumer surplus (CS) from each market (j) can be easily derived:

$$CS_1 = \frac{B}{2} q_1^2,$$

$$CS_2 = \frac{D}{2} q_2^2$$

Any output increase therefore leads to an improvement in consumer welfare. That is why we could say above that more output is "better".

Schmalensee [1981] has shown that allowing a monopolist to discriminate would lead to a net welfare loss, when demand curves are linear, marginal cost is constant and provided both markets are served under simple monopoly. This result can be easily reproduced in our model: we find

$$W_m - W'_m = \frac{(A-C)^2}{8(B+D)}$$

in which $'$ refers to a discrimination outcome. Unsurprisingly, the welfare loss is larger, the larger is the difference in elasticities between the two sub-markets. This is so because large elasticities differences lead to a wider discrepancy between the discrimination and the non-discrimination outcomes.

We obtain a similar result in the duopoly case. The welfare loss is, then, given by:

$$W_d - W'_d = \frac{(A-C)^2}{18(B+D)}$$

Hence, allowing duopolists to discriminate between sub-markets leads to a net welfare loss. It is noticeable, though, that the welfare loss implied by the discrimination is smaller, in absolute terms, in the duopoly situation than in the monopoly case.

In addition, one can compare the total welfare under monopoly and duopoly. First, total welfare in duopoly is always higher than total welfare in monopoly under both regimes. Moreover, the discrimination monopoly outcome is equivalent to the equilibrium reached with two separate monopolies (one in each market). Hence, if a common market is created, the two local monopolists become duopolists in the new entity and total welfare increases, whether the (newly formed) duopolists are allowed to discriminate or not. If both markets are served under both regimes, total welfare increases more if discriminatory practices can be restricted. Besides, if discrimination takes place, the consumers' surplus and total welfare increase in each market, taken individually. This is not necessarily the case if a uniform price is enforced. Creating a common market is, therefore, always socially desirable for the new entity as a whole and socially desirable for each sub-market taken individually if discrimination is allowed.

The message from this last observation is clear: allowing discriminatory practices tends to allocate more evenly between sub-markets the welfare improvement brought about by the creation of a common market. (In more practical policy terms, allowing firms to discriminate inside the EEC could be a simple device to avoid troublesome cash compensation payments.)

Second, it appears that a discriminating duopoly generally yields a higher total welfare than a non-discriminating monopoly. (This is always true if both sub-markets have the same slope ($B = D$).) This is also to say that the increase in welfare brought about by an increased number of firms (more intense competition) tends to overweight the decrease in welfare that is induced if these additional firms can discriminate.

At this point, we would like to add an essential caveat: all the welfare results discussed above are valid only under the restrictive assumption that both markets are served in the absence of price discrimination. This assumption is embodied in the specification of the model, with only two firms and two markets and one firm in each market.

In real world situations, price discrimination typically serves to open new markets, and thus to increase sales, which can potentially improve total welfare. To illustrate this, let us consider the simplest situation in which market 1 is not served under simple duopoly. Without transportation cost and under constant marginal production cost, the discriminating duopoly equilibrium is also the equilibrium reached with two separate duopolies (a duopoly in each sub-market). It can, thus, be said that each duopolist takes his output decision for each sub-market independently of the other sub-market (in this discriminating duopoly equilibrium). When discrimination is allowed, the duopolists will serve the first sub-market without altering their decision about the second sub-market, so that total welfare unambiguously increases in the common market. Even more, the welfare improvement in the first market does not imply any welfare deterioration in the second market: the first market is better off and the second market is not affected.

All in all, it appears that discriminatory price strategies lead to a more even welfare allocation between markets and can also imply a net welfare improvement when both markets are not served under simple duopoly.

VI. CONCLUSIONS

We constructed the simplest possible model capable of describing the price and sales policy of oligopolists operating in several markets: two monopolies, operating each in a separate market, become a duopoly in a common market and are allowed to price discriminate across sub-markets. The Cournot–Nash equilibrium was compared with the monopoly outcome under constant and increasing marginal costs and with and without transport costs.

This Cournot–Nash equilibrium was shown to have a number of interesting properties.

(1) "Intra-industry" trade or "cross-hauling" is a property of the equilibrium.
(2) The opening of the markets is always welfare improving for the new entity as a whole.
(3) Price discrimination is the most profitable policy to pursue.
(4) The effectiveness of price discrimination is restricted, however, by the competition among duopolists.
(5) Increases in the slope of the marginal cost of production curve lead to a smoothing of the (discriminatory) delivered prices over space. (This result is similar to the results obtained by Phlips and Richard [1984] with respect to price smoothing over time when inventory accumulation is allowed for.)
(6) Having more firms is always better, whether they are discriminating or not.
(7) Creating a common market is socially desirable for each sub-market taken individually, if price discrimination is allowed.

Throughout the paper, the firms' strategic variable is supposed to be their output, equal to their sales. This Cournot type of situation is thought to capture the essence of the automobile market. Although car makers obviously make price decisions about differentiated products, we agree with the remark by Friedman [1983, p. 47–48] that automobile manufacturers must plan production far in advance and face very high costs of holding inventories, so that they will make sure to match sales to production by letting prices adjust to market conditions. One might as well, therefore, suppose a homogeneous good, one single price (for our two firms) in each market, and firms using output (sales) as their strategic variable.

Let us notice in addition, that our Cournot equilibrium can be reinterpreted in the light of the results recently put forward by Kreps and Scheinkman [1983], at least when the marginal cost is constant. In a duopoly model with linear demand and constant marginal cost, Kreps and Scheinkman show that the Cournot outcome is also a perfect equilibrium in a two stage game in which the firms choose their capacity in the first stage and compete in prices in the second stage. This result can be carried forward in our duopoly game with two sub-markets. This is so because, with constant marginal cost, the discrimination equilibrium is also the outcome obtained with two separate duopolies (a duopoly in each sub-market). Or, put another way, each duopolist takes his output decision for each sub-market independently of the other sub-market. It follows that the Cournot equilibrium can be thought of as a pair of equilibria, one for each market. In turn, each of these equilibria can be thought of as a perfect equilibrium in a two-stage game in which firms commit themselves by selecting a capacity in the first stage and subsequently compete in prices.

The Bertrand–Nash type of approach, in a one-stage game, with price strategies, would be more appropriate for oligopolists selling differentiated products or storable goods, such as photographic material. Indeed, storability, product differentiation (leading to demand inertia) or a combination of both[7] turn the Bertrand model into a realistic one. However, allowing for storage strategies requires a dynamic approach. Similarly, the issue of product selection is tied to the pricing policy in a model with differentiated products. Neither storability, nor product differentiation could, therefore, be coped with satisfactorily in the present framework.

DAMIEN NEVEN AND LOUIS PHLIPS,
CORE,
Université Catholique de Louvain,
34 Voie du Roman Pays,
B-1348 Louvain-la-Neuve,
Belgium.

ACCEPTED MAY 1985

REFERENCES

ASHWORTH, M. H., KAY, J. A. and SHARPE, T. A. E., 1982, *Differentials between Car Prices in the United Kingdom and Belgium* (The Institute for Fiscal Studies, London).

BRANDER, J. A. and KRUGMAN, P. R., 1983, 'A Reciprocal Dumping Model of International Trade', *Journal of International Economics*, 15, pp. 313–323.

BRANDER, J. A. and SPENCER, B., 1984, 'Tariff Protection and Imperfect Competition', in H. Kierzkowski (ed.), *Monopolistic Competition and International Trade*, Chap. 12 (Oxford University Press).

[7] Such a dynamic model combining demand inertia and storability is constructed in Phlips and Richard [1984].

FRIEDMAN, J. W., 1983, *Oligopoly Theory* (Cambridge University Press).

GREENHUT, J. and GREENHUT, M. L., 1975, 'Spatial Price Discrimination, Competition and Location Effects', *Economica*, 42, pp. 401–419.

HUVENEERS, C., 1981, 'Price Formation and the Scope for Oligopoly Conduct in a Small Open Economy', *Recherches Economiques de Louvain*, 47, pp. 209–242.

KREPS, O. and SCHEINKMAN, A., 1983, 'Cournot Pre-commitment and Bertrand Competition yields Cournot Outcome', *Bell Journal of Economics*, 14(2), pp. 326–338.

MERTENS, Y. and GINSBURGH, V., 1985, 'Product Differentiation and Price Discrimination in the European Community. The Case of Automobiles', *The Journal of Industrial Economics*, this issue.

PHLIPS, L., 1962, *De l'intégration des marchés* (Nauwelaerts, Leuven).

PHLIPS, L., 1983, *The Economics of Price Discrimination* (Cambridge University Press).

PHLIPS, L. and RICHARD, J.-F., 1984, 'A Dynamic Oligopoly Model with Demand Inertia and Inventories', CORE Discussion Paper.

ROBINSON, J., 1933, *The Economics of Imperfect Competition* (Macmillan, London).

SCHMALENSEE, R., 1981, 'Output and Welfare Implications of Monopolistic Third Degree Price Discrimination', *American Economic Review*, 71, pp. 242–247.

SPULBER, D. F., 1979, 'Non-cooperative Equilibrium with Price Discriminating Firms', *Economic Letters*, 4, pp. 221–227.

THARAKAN, P. K. M., 1981, 'The Economics of Intra-industry Trade: A Survey', *Recherches Economiques de Louvain*, 47, pp. 259–290.

THE JOURNAL OF INDUSTRIAL ECONOMICS 0022–1821 $2.00
Volume XXXIV December 1985 No. 2

PRODUCT DIFFERENTIATION AND PRICE DISCRIMINATION IN THE EUROPEAN COMMUNITY THE CASE OF AUTOMOBILES

YVES MERTENS AND VICTOR GINSBURGH*

The paper is concerned with the determinants of prices of European and Japanese cars in five EEC countries. The basic idea is that under perfect competition, prices should reflect production costs, and hence depend on the technical characteristics of the commodities. Differences between list prices and prices explained by these characteristics result from market imperfections or product differences not accounted for by measurable characteristics. Estimation results show that there is both discrimination and differentiation; but to a very large extent, price differentials across countries are due to discriminating practices.

I. INTRODUCTION

THE PAPER is concerned with the determinants of prices of European and Japanese cars in five European countries: Belgium, France, Germany, Italy and the United Kingdom.

The basic idea is that, under perfect competition, prices should reflect production costs and hence depend on the technical characteristics of the commodities. Differences between list prices and prices explained by these characteristics result from market imperfections (like oligopoly power, or discrimination) or product differentiation not accounted for by measurable characteristics.

As will be clear from the results, there is both discrimination and differentiation; but to a very large extent price differentials across countries are due to discriminating practices.

The results thus strongly support the observation made by National Consumer Unions (and by the European Bureau of these Unions) that European car producers are discriminant oligopolists. In 1983, the European Commission decided to react against these practices by elaborating a set of regulations enforcing the application of Art. 85 of the Treaty in matters concerning the distribution and sale of automobiles.[1]

* We are grateful to A. Farber, J. Mercenier, J. Waelbroeck and to an anonymous referee for comments on a previous version. We also acknowledge very stimulating discussions with L. Phlips. Similar ideas, though seen from a more theoretical viewpoint, can be found in Neven and Phlips [1985].

[1] See the *Journal Officiel* no. C165, June 24, 1983.

The paper is organized as follows.

In Section II, we introduce the simple microeconomic framework leading to an econometric model which can be estimated. Section III develops the data base used and briefly describes the main characteristics of the five markets analyzed. Section IV discusses the empirical findings, while we draw conclusions and suggest extensions in Section V.

II. THE MODEL. THEORY AND ESTIMATION PROCEDURE

We consider the following model. There are two countries (markets) a and b, and one national producer i $(i = 1,2)$ located in each country but selling his output in both; these enjoy enough protection so that buyers cannot purchase the commodity in one place and sell it in the other. Let the (inverse) demand functions be $p_i^k = f_i^k(q_1^k, q_2^k)$; p_i^k represents the price charged by producer i in country k, while q_i^k are his sales $(i = 1,2;\ k = a,b)$; if $C_i(q_i^a + q_i^b)$ is the cost function of producer i, his profits are given by

$$(2.1)\qquad B_i(\cdot) = q_i^a f_i^a(q_1^a, q_2^a) + q_i^b f_i^b(q_1^b, q_2^b) - C_i(q_i^a + q_i^b),\ i = 1,2$$

We assume that each producer i maximizes his profits by setting his sales q_i^a, q_i^b, given $q_j^a, q_j^b (i \neq j)$. An equilibrium solution $\bar{q}_1^a, \bar{q}_1^b, \bar{q}_2^a, \bar{q}_2^b$ is such that

$$(2.2a)\qquad B_1(\bar{q}_1^a, \bar{q}_1^b, \bar{q}_2^a, \bar{q}_2^b) \geqslant B_1(q_1^a, q_1^b, \bar{q}_2^a, \bar{q}_2^b)$$

$$(2.2b)\qquad B_2(\bar{q}_1^a, \bar{q}_1^b, \bar{q}_2^a, \bar{q}_2^b) \geqslant B_2(\bar{q}_1^a, \bar{q}_1^b, q_2^a, q_2^b)$$

and can, if it exists, be obtained by solving the following four equations system:

$$(2.3a)\qquad f_1^a(q_1^a, q_2^a) + q_1^a \frac{\partial f_1^a(q_1^a, q_2^a)}{\partial q_1^a} = C_1'(q_1^a + q_1^b)$$

$$(2.3b)\qquad f_1^b(q_1^b, q_2^b) + q_1^b \frac{\partial f_1^b(q_1^b, q_2^b)}{\partial q_1^b} = C_1'(q_1^a + q_1^b)$$

$$(2.3c)\qquad f_2^a(q_1^a, q_2^a) + q_2^a \frac{\partial f_2^a(q_1^a, q_2^a)}{\partial q_2^a} = C_2'(q_2^a + q_2^b)$$

$$(2.3d)\qquad f_2^b(q_1^b, q_2^b) + q_2^b \frac{\partial f_2^b(q_1^b, q_2^b)}{\partial q_2^b} = C_2'(q_2^a + q_2^b)$$

where $C_i'(\cdot)$ represents the marginal cost of producer i.

Two polar cases can be distinguished. The first corresponds to the *discriminating monopolist* situation, in which it is assumed that

$$(2.4)\qquad \frac{\partial f_i^a}{\partial q_j^a} = \frac{\partial f_i^b}{\partial q_j^b} = 0 \qquad i,j = 1,2;\ i \neq j$$

so that the demand functions reduce to $p_i^k = f_i^k(q_i^k)$, $i = 1,2$, $k = a,b$. Though there are two sellers, the commodities they sell are so different that the result is the same as if they were two discriminating monopolists; in that case, conditions (2.3) boil down to

$$(2.5a) \quad f_i^a(q_i^a) + q_i^a \frac{\partial f_i^a(q_i^a)}{\partial q_i^a} = C_i'(q_i^a + q_i^b) \qquad i = 1,2$$

$$(2.5b) \quad f_i^b(q_i^b) + q_i^b \frac{\partial f_i^b(q_i^b)}{\partial q_i^b} = C_i'(q_i^a + q_i^b) \qquad i = 1,2$$

and each seller makes his decision without taking into account the decision of the other. In this first setting, the two producers will end up charging different prices for two *completely differentiated products*. However, since (2.5a)–(2.5b) can also be written

$$p_i^a\left(1 - \frac{1}{e_i^a}\right) = C_i'; \ p_i^b\left(1 - \frac{1}{e_i^b}\right) = C_i', \qquad i = 1,2$$

where

$$e_i^a = -\frac{\partial q_i^a}{\partial f_i^a}\frac{f_i^a}{q_i^a}; \ e_i^b = -\frac{\partial q_i^b}{\partial f_i^b}\frac{f_i^b}{q_i^b}, \qquad i = 1,2$$

are the price elasticities in countries a and b, there will be no price discrimination if price elasticities are equal.

The second polar case is similar to the usual *Cournot duopoly* solution in which

$$(2.6) \quad f_1^k(\cdot) = f_2^k(\cdot) = f^k(q_1^k + q_2^k) \qquad k = a, b$$

entailing evidently

$$(2.7) \quad \frac{\partial f_1^k}{\partial q_2^k} = \frac{\partial f_2^k}{\partial q_1^k} = \frac{\partial f^k}{\partial q_1^k} = \frac{\partial f^k}{\partial q_2^k}$$

Then, the equilibrium, if it exists, will satisfy

$$(2.8a) \quad f^a(q^a) + q_i^a \frac{\partial f^a(q^a)}{\partial q^a} = C_i'(q^a) \qquad i = 1,2$$

$$(2.8b) \quad f^b(q^b) + q_i^b \frac{\partial f^b(q^b)}{\partial q^b} = C_i'(q^b) \qquad i = 1,2$$

where $q^a = q_1^a + q_2^a$ and $q^b = q_1^b + q_2^b$. The two producers sell an *undifferentiated commodity* at the same price, but the prices on the two markets need not be the same. They will however be equal if the two price elasticities e^a and e^b are equal.

In all other cases, we will have

$$(2.9) \quad \frac{\partial f_i^k}{\partial q_i^k} \neq \frac{\partial f_i^k}{\partial q_j^k} \neq 0 \qquad i,j = 1,2; \ i \neq j; \ k = a, b$$

and anything between the discriminating monopolist with complete product differentiation and duopoly with undifferentiated commodities can happen.

We thus end up with four cases:

(1) discriminating monopolists with complete differentiation; then the four prices p_i^k $(i = 1, 2; k = a, b)$ will be different;

(2) equal price elasticities in the two countries, with complete differentiation; here $p_i^a = p_i^b$ $(i = 1, 2)$, but $p_1^k \neq p_2^k$ $(k = a, b)$;

(3) Cournot duopoly with undifferentiated commodities; here $p_1^k = p_2^k$ $(k = a, b)$, but $p_i^a \neq p_i^b$ $(i = 1, 2)$;

(4) Cournot duopoly with equal price elasticities in the two countries; in this case, all prices will be equal, that is, $p_i^k = p$ $(i = 1, 2; k = a, b)$.

This categorization allows encompassing all these cases by the following general model which we assume, for simplicity, to be linear:

$$(2.10) \qquad p_i^k = \pi + \pi_i + \pi^k + \pi_i^k$$

Cases (1), (2), (3) and (4) respectively correspond to the model with (1) $\pi_i = \pi_k = 0$; (2) $\pi^k = \pi_i^k = 0$; (3) $\pi_i = \pi_i^k = 0$; (4) $\pi_i = \pi^k = \pi_i^k = 0$. But (2.10) also shows the possibility of the intermediate situation $p_i^k = \pi + \pi_i + \pi^k$, from which the interaction terms π_i^k are absent, and which seems less "intricate" than (2.10); we will come back to this case later on.

In turn, (2.10) suggests the possibility of setting up an econometric model which would enable us to test which is the prevailing case. Indeed, denoting by p_{ij}^k an observation j on a price charged by producer i selling in country k, (2.10) can be written

$$(2.11) \qquad p_{ij}^k = \pi + \pi_i + \pi^k + \pi_i^k + \text{other effects} + \varepsilon_j$$

where the π's are parameters to be estimated and ε_j is a random error endowed with the usual statistical properties; in "other effects" we include price variations which are neither due to discrimination, nor to producer differentiation.

These observations could either consist of time series of aggregate price indexes (with a common basis) or a cross-section of brands and/or makes at one point in time (or a combination of both). We chose to work with the second type of data, which makes it necessary to convert brands and makes to a common yardstick, in such a way that the variety of cars sold on a market is reduced to as many commodities as there are countries (or producers) exporting to that country, including the domestic producer himself, if any. This then means that all the brands and makes produced in country i are sold at the same price in country k; all the technical characteristics which explain the difference in prices between say a Mini and a Rolls-Royce are absorbed by the "other effects", and both will be sold in France at the same price $\pi + \pi_i + \pi^k + \pi_i^k$.

To achieve this, we have made use of the technique known as "hedonic price regression" developed by Griliches [1961], [1971] and used since by many authors, including Kravis *et al.* [1971], [1975] in their comparison of international purchasing powers, Cowling and Cubbin [1971] to study competition, Friedlander *et al.* [1983] to estimate hedonic cost functions.

The basic assumption of hedonic price regressions is that the price of a brand j, p_j, is a function of its observable m technical characteristics X_{jl} $(l = 1,\ldots,m)$, so that we can write

$$p_j = f(X_{j1}, X_{j2}, \ldots, X_{jm})$$

The marginal contribution of X_{jl}, $\partial f(\cdot)/\partial X_{jl}$, can be interpreted as the contribution of characteristic l to the price p_j; in other words, it is the "price" of one unit of the lth characteristic. Clearly, technical characteristics are used here as proxies for characteristics that consumers actually value but which are difficult or sometimes impossible to measure: comfort, performance, style, reliability, etc.

In most studies, the form of $f(\cdot)$ is

$$\log p_j = \beta_0 + \beta_1 X_{j1} + \beta_2 X_{j2} + \ldots + \beta_m X_{jm} + \varepsilon_j \tag{2.12}$$

where ε_j is an error term. The superiority of this form is that it makes the computation of indexes particularly easy, as will be shown later on.

Let us then write (2.11) as

$$\log p_j = \pi + \sum_{l=2}^{q} \pi_l z_l + \sum_{l=2}^{q} \pi^l y_l + \sum_{l}\sum_{l'} \pi_l^{l'} z_l y_{l'} + \sum_{l=1}^{m} \beta_l X_{jl} + \varepsilon_j \tag{2.13}$$

where the z_l's and y_l's are suitably defined dummy variables so that

$$\log p_{ij}^k = \pi + \pi_i + \pi^k + \pi_i^k + \sum_l \beta_l X_{jl}^k + \varepsilon_j \tag{2.14}$$

Now (2.14) is directly comparable to (2.11), and allows for the possibility of testing the market structure. Indeed, *ceteris paribus*,

(1) $\pi_i = \pi^k = 0$ all i, k corresponds to discriminating "monopolists" with complete differentiation;
(2) $\pi^k = \pi_i^k = 0$ all i, k corresponds to equal price elasticities in all countries, with complete product differentiation;
(3) $\pi_i = \pi_i^k = 0$ all i, k corresponds to oligopolistic markets with undifferentiated commodities;
(4) $\pi_i = \pi^k = \pi_i^k = 0$ all i, k corresponds to oligopolistic markets with equal price elasticities in all countries;
(5) $\pi_i^k = 0$ all i, k is an intermediate situation with some discrimination (different π^k's) and some differentiation (different π_i's); more specifically, if for instance the π_i's are small compared to the π^k's, one may conclude that discrimination is large, while commodities sold by various producers (countries) are not too much differentiated; the opposite would hold for π_i's large and π^k's small.

That the logarithmic form makes the computation of price indexes easy, can be seen by the following argument. Assume we wish to compare prices in

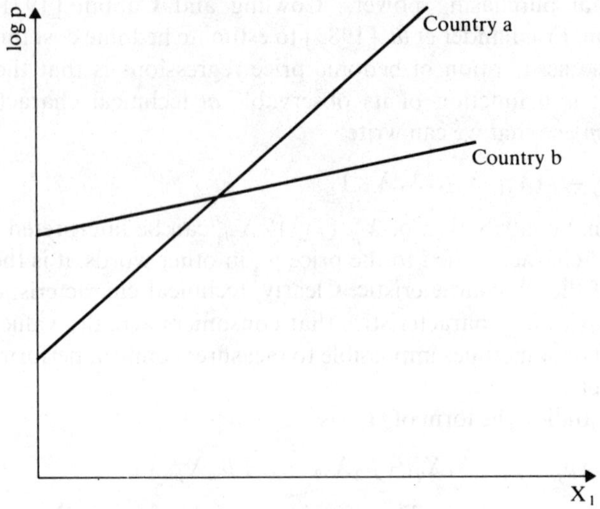

Figure 1

q countries $k = 1,\ldots,q$, for which we have observations on the same makes $j = 1,\ldots,n$. We then set up a regression

$$\text{(2.15)} \qquad \log p_j^k = \pi + \sum_{l=2}^{q} \pi^l y_l + \sum_{l=1}^{m} \beta_l X_{jl}^k + \varepsilon_j$$

where the y_l's are dummy variables taking the value 1 if the observation belongs to country k, and 0 otherwise; country 1 serves as standard of reference; then, it is easy to check that $\exp \hat{\pi}^k = \hat{p}_j^k / \hat{p}_j^1$ is the price index for country k, with respect to country 1; $\hat{p}_j^k = \hat{\pi} + \Sigma \hat{\pi}^l y_l + \Sigma \hat{\beta}_l X_{jl}$ where the $\hat{\pi}$'s and $\hat{\beta}$'s are estimates of the parameters. Note that for this to hold, the β_l's must be the same for all countries. If this were not the case, we could end up with situations like the one pictured in Figure 1, showing that commodities for which characteristic 1, say, is low, are more expensive in country b than in a, while the opposite holds for commodities endowed with high amounts of characteristic 1.

All our estimations are based on producer prices, but, if taxes are *ad valorem*, it is straightforward to compute price indexes which include taxes. Indeed, let $\bar{p}^k = (1+\tau^k)p^k$ where p^k is the price charged by a monopolist on market k and τ^k is the *ad valorem* tax rate. Since the dependent variable in our regressions is expressed in logarithms, we have $\log \bar{p}_{ij}^k = \log(1+\tau^k)p_{ij}^k = \log(1+\tau^k) + \log p_{ij}^k$ and the effect of regressing $\log \bar{p}_{ij}^k$ on the various variables instead of $\log p_{ij}^k$ will only change the π_k's which will be equal to $\bar{\pi}^k = \pi^k + \log(1+\tau^k)$.

III. THE DATA SET

Our study is concerned with five countries belonging to the European Community: Belgium, France, Germany, Italy and the United Kingdom. These countries represent a large spectrum on several accounts: the dimension of the market (annual sales vary between 350,000 in Belgium and 2,330,000 in Germany); the market share of domestic producers (0% in Belgium, over 70% in France and Germany); the penetration of Japanese cars (0.1% in Italy, 24.6% in Belgium); the rates of taxation (13% in Germany, over 33% in France). Table I reproduces these basic data.

As is well known, various local regulations make it difficult, if not impossible for private consumers to directly import cars from foreign countries; the most obvious case is of course the fact that British cars are right hand driven contrarily to all other countries; but there are less well known regulations, like yellow headlights in France, etc.

The sample used in our regressions has been set up as follows: for each of the 5 countries we have chosen 100 brands/makes, with as much overlap over countries as possible. But it proved impossible to find more than 25 common brands/makes which represent substantial sales in each country, for reasons which are evidently due to the relatively small degree of market interpenetration.

Each country sample tries to roughly reflect the share of cars using fuel, the degree of penetration by Japanese makes, the share of domestic producers vs imports.

We have collected prices posted between August 15 and September 15, 1983, as well as technical characteristics for 100 brands/makes in each of the five countries studied. Prices have been expressed in the common European currency, using average exchange rates during the period considered. For obvious reasons, prices are based on dealers' (producers') lists and do not take into account possible discounts, which may, in some cases (UK especially) be important, and would somewhat alter the results, though

TABLE I
CHARACTERISTICS OF THE VARIOUS MARKETS

	Belgium	*France*	*Germany*	*Italy*	*United Kingdom*
Size of the market (1000 cars sold in 1981)	350	1840	2330	1740	1480
Share of domestic producers (in %)	0	>70	>70	>60	>45
Share of Japanese cars (in %)	24.6	3.1	10.3	0.1[a]	11.9
Tax on value added (rate in %)	25–33[b]	33.33	13	20–38[b]	15[c]

Notes: [a] An agreement reached between Italy and Japan limits Japanese imports to 2000 cars per year.
[b] Rates vary according to the size of the car.
[c] The 15% are paid on the following value: $\frac{5}{6}$ of the mill price + special tax of 10%.

probably not the conclusions. Prices do not include taxes either.[2] Technical characteristics have been carefully collected in various professional journals in each country.[3] They include for each of the 100 brands/makes: length (in m), width (in m), fuel or gas engine (0, 1 variable), power (in Kw), weight (in Kgs), number of doors, engine capacity (in 1000 cc), maximal speed (in Km/H).

IV. EMPIRICAL FINDINGS

The first regressions were run in order to find a common set of technical characteristics which would explain a substantial part of (the log of) prices. The results are given in Table II.

As can be checked, the same set of explanatory variables accounts for at least 78% of the variance (as much as 90% for Germany) in each case. We decided to keep this set unchanged for the rest of our regressions.

Since prices of characteristics looked fairly close to each other, we ran an analysis of covariance in which we checked:

(a) that all countries had similar prices for these characteristics, (that is equal slopes) but that the intercepts were different. The computed value for F is 0.65, which is much lower than tabulated values with 16 and 475 d.f., at the 1 and the 5% significance level. We cannot reject the hypothesis of equal slopes;

(b) that all countries had similar prices, *and* intercepts. The computed value

TABLE II
HEDONIC REGRESSIONS BY COUNTRY

	Belgium	*France*	*Germany*	*Italy*	*United Kingdom*
Intercept	6.1295	6.3971	6.3553	6.1667	6.9929
	(0.2937)	(0.2149)	(0.1855)	(0.1927)	(0.2328)
Length	0.3410	0.3232	0.3545	0.4010	0.2886
	(0.0777)	(0.0582)	(0.0482)	(0.0534)	(0.0615)
Power/Weight	10.6772	9.7605	8.3997	12.2269	7.3119
	(2.3029)	(1.3941)	(1.3042)	(1.2579)	(1.5921)
Diesel	0.2470	0.2024	0.1636	0.2217	0.1320
	(0.0742)	(0.0510)	(0.0470)	(0.0537)	(0.0689)
E. Capacity	0.2519	0.2665	0.2923	0.1905	0.3617
	(0.0697)	(0.0509)	(0.0363)	(0.0509)	(0.0556)
R^2	0.787	0.867	0.907	0.882	0.839
$\bar{R}^2$	0.778	0.862	0.903	0.877	0.833
F	88.0	155.3	231.4	177.9	124.2
n	100	100	100	100	100

[2] Since taxes are almost proportional to posted prices in each country, including these does not change relative prices too much.

[3] These journals are *Le Moniteur de l'Automobile* (Belgium), *L'Auto-Journal* (France), *Auto Zeitung* (Germany), *Gente Motori* (Italy) and *Autocar* (United Kingdom).

for F is 79.85, which is much higher than tabulated values at both significance levels. We thus strongly reject the hypothesis of equal intercepts.

We hence consider the following regression, with equal slopes, but different intercepts, where F, G, I and UK are dummy variables for France, Germany, Italy and the United Kingdom; Belgium operates as reference country:

$$\log p = \underset{(0.0994)}{6.1988} + \underset{(0.0215)}{0.1592F} + \underset{(0.0217)}{0.2046G} + \underset{(0.0215)}{0.2752I} + \underset{(0.0216)}{0.3641UK}$$

$$+ \underset{(0.0261)}{0.3033}\, Length + \underset{(0.6772)}{9.8208}\, Power/Weight + \underset{(0.0255)}{0.1989}\, Diesel$$

$$+ \underset{(0.0227)}{0.2703}\, E.\ Capacity$$

$$R^2 = 0.872;\ \bar{R}^2 = 0.870;\ F = 417.6;\ n = 500.$$

This regression allows us to compute price indexes for each country. The calculation is essentially based on the various intercept terms, as explained earlier; since these are significantly different across countries, we can conclude that the price indexes will also be; and, indeed, as can be seen from Table III, price levels are quite different. Remember that prices do not include taxes. To check whether their inclusion would affect the results, we did our computations again, with prices including taxes. The slopes are only very slightly changed, since in some cases (Belgium and Italy), tax rates get higher for large cars; but as large cars do not represent a large market share, only a few such brands are included in the sample, and hence slopes are only very marginally affected. Intercepts clearly have to shift, since tax rates are not the same across countries. As can be seen from Table III, this does change the ranking (Germany becomes second cheapest) but does not change either the range, or the values of the index for the other countries.

TABLE III
PRICE INDEXES BEFORE AND AFTER INCLUSION OF TAXES

Country	*Index*	
	Before Taxes	*After Taxes*
Belgium	100	100
France	117	125
Germany	123	111
Italy	132	129
United Kingdom	144	144

The results significantly point in the direction of very serious price discrimination.

We next examine the question of product differentiation. It is clear that a large part of product differentiation, if not the largest, is due to differences in

TABLE IV
HEDONIC PRICE REGRESSIONS BY COUNTRY, INCLUDING THE "IMAGE" OF DOMESTIC PROCEDURES

	Belgium[a]	*France*	*Germany*	*Italy*	*United Kingdom*
Intercept	—	6.3848	6.4095	6.0804	6.9208
		(0.2133)	(0.1874)	(0.1876)	(0.2442)
Length	—	0.3238	0.3392	0.4232	0.2461
		(0.0577)	(0.0489)	(0.0518)	(0.0641)
Power/Weight	—	9.4918	7.8985	11.1376	7.5602
		(1.3932)	(1.3343)	(1.2632)	(1.5125)
Diesel	—	0.1927	0.1407	0.1969	0.1375
		(0.0510)	(0.0489)	(0.0522)	(0.0692)
E. Capacity	—	0.2684	0.2993	0.2072	0.3439
		(0.0505)	(0.0364)	(0.0492)	(0.0585)
Domestic Producer	—	0.0474	0.0473	0.0892	0.0326
		(0.0297)	(0.0305)	(0.0300)	(0.0333)
R^2	—	0.871	0.909	0.892	0.841
$\bar{R}^2$	—	0.864	0.904	0.887	0.833
F	—	126.7	188.4	155.9	99.5
n	—	100	100	100	100

[a] No domestic producer.

technical characteristics. These differences are of course removed by the hedonic regression technique. What we are interested in here, is whether there is more than just technical differentiation.

The first thing we did was to verify whether domestic producers had some advantage or power over importers; this simply required introducing a dummy variable equal to 1 if the car is produced in the country, and zero otherwise. The results, given in Table IV, are identical to those of Table II, except for the inclusion of the domestic producer dummy, which is significantly different from zero in the case of Italy only (at the usual 5% level): *ceteris paribus*, an Italian car seems to be about 9% more expensive than an imported car in Italy. In other countries a domestic car is only 3 to 5% more expensive, but the difference is insignificant at the 5% probability level. This suggests that the hedonic regressions carried out in each country are adequate and that domestic and imported cars do not have very different "images". Note, however, that the sign of the various coefficients points in the direction of at least some power associated with domestic brands on their own markets. We will come back to this point later on.

Since we know from our analysis on discrimination that this effect is clearly present, we directly turned to estimate the model (2.15) which includes both discrimination and differentiation effects, and their interactions.[4] Table V gives the resulting analysis of (co)variance.

All effects, including interactions between discrimination and differentiation effects (the π_i^k's of model (2.15)) are significant. However, as is evident

[4] In what follows, we consider all producers in a specific country as one single producer. A finer analysis should include more makes per producer to increase the sample size and introduce producer effects instead of country of origin effects.

TABLE V
ANALYSIS OF COVARIANCE FOR MODEL (2.15)

	Sum of Squares	*Degrees of Freedom*	*Mean Square*	*F Stat.*	*Significance of F*
Total[a]	76.450	499	—	—	—
Due to Techn. Charac.	57.769	4	14.442	833.6	0.00001
Due to Discrimination	7.411	4	1.853	106.9	0.00001
Due to Differentiation	2.393	5	0.479	27.6	0.00001
Due to Interactions	0.787	19	0.041	2.4	0.00091
Residual	8.090	467	0.017	—	—

[a] Centred around the mean.

from Table V, discrimination (the π^k's) exerts a much larger influence on prices than differentiation (the π_i's) whereas the effect of interactions (the π_i^k's), though significant, is fairly small compared to the rest. Since anyway the π_i^k's make the model somewhat less easy to interpret, we decided to drop all interaction terms from our study. The resulting model is given in Table VI, columns (1)–(2).[5] As can be seen, the discrimination effect remains large, and

TABLE VI
DISCRIMINATION AND DIFFERENTIATION

	Coeffic. (1)	*St. Dev.* (2)	*Coeffic.* (3)	*St. Dev.* (4)
Intercept	6.0967	(0.0955)	6.1314	(0.0960)
Length	0.3585	(0.0252)	0.3538	(0.0251)
Power/Weight	9.2955	(0.6265)	9.0055	(0.6343)
Diesel	0.1596	(0.0237)	0.1492	(0.0239)
E. Capacity	0.2608	(0.0221)	0.2678	(0.0222)
Domestic Dummy (Goodwill)	—	—	0.0380	(0.0155)
Discrimination Dummies				
Belgium	—	—	—	—
France	0.1406	(0.0199)	0.1260	(0.0207)
Germany	0.1587	(0.0210)	0.1337	(0.0224)
Italy	0.2568	(0.0204)	0.2479	(0.0207)
United Kingdom	0.3564	(0.0210)	0.3497	(0.0211)
Differentiation Dummies				
Belgium	—	—	—	—
France	0.0582	(0.0233)	0.0450	(0.0238)
Germany	0.1027	(0.0244)	0.0938	(0.0226)
Italy	0.0675	(0.0261)	0.0493	(0.0270)
United Kingdom	0.0672	(0.0289)	0.0388	(0.0310)
All Others	−0.2371	(0.0341)	−0.2408	(0.0339)
R^2	0.899		0.900	
$\bar{R}^2$	0.896		0.897	
F	331.9		311.9	
n	500		500	

[5] The two regressions appearing in Table VI should be interpreted as follows: for a car sold in Belgium (discrimination effect) and imported from Japan (differentiation effect), the adjusted price is given by

$$\log \hat{p}_{ij}^k = \hat{\pi} + \sum_l \hat{\beta}_l X_{jl}^k$$

The reference is thus Belgium for the first effect and Japan for the second, and the differences given by the $\hat{\pi}_i$ and $\hat{\pi}^k$ coefficients are with respect to Belgium and Japan.

TABLE VII
DISCRIMINATION EFFECTS

	Regressions	
	Without Diff. Effect	*With Diff. Effect*
Intercept	6.1988	6.0967
Belgium	—	—
France	0.1592	0.1406
Germany	0.2046	0.1587
Italy	0.2752	0.2568
United Kingdom	0.3641	0.3564

is of the same order of magnitude as in the regression which ignores differentiation (see Table VII); hence, price differences due to discrimination are comparable to those of Table III.

Price disparities due to product differentiation are much smaller, with the exception of cars originating from the group of "other countries" which sell some 20% cheaper than Japanese cars, while German cars are 10% more expensive than Japanese. But concentrating on European cars, differences are small across origins, and small when compared to the consequences of discrimination. Table VIII illustrates this fact.

Table IX constructs price indexes obtained from the main regression. Each index gives the value of a car sold in country k, constructed in country i; the base is 100 for a Japanese car sold in Belgium. The differences get very large in some cases, when both effects are cumulated: a German car sold in the United Kingdom is exactly twice as expensive (index 158) as a Soviet car (other countries) sold in Belgium (index 79), both cars being endowed with similar technical characteristics, included in the hedonic regression.

In the hedonic regressions described in Table IV, we included, among the various technical characteristics, a dummy variable assumed to represent the

TABLE VIII
EFFECTS OF DISCRIMINATION AND DIFFERENTIATION ON PRICE INDEXES

	Effects of	
	Discrimination	*Differentiation*
Belgium	100	—
France	115	106
Germany	117	111
Italy	129	107
United Kingdom	143	107
Japan	—	100
Other Countries	—	79

TABLE IX
PRICE INDEXES BY ORIGIN (DIFFERENTIATION) AND DESTINATION (DISCRIMINATION)

	Destination				
Origin	*Belgium*	*France*	*Germany*	*Italy*	*United Kingdom*
Belgium	—	—	—	—	—
France	106	122	124	137	151
Germany	111	128	130	143	158
Italy	107	123	125	138	153
United Kingdom	107	123	125	138	153
Japan	100	115	117	129	143
Others	79	91	92	102	113

goodwill associated with a producer selling on his home market. As we pointed out, the effect was not very significant. Including the variable among the characteristics in equation (2.15) is, on the contrary, significant at the 5% probability level (Table VI, col. (3)–(4)). A domestically produced car can charge a price which is some 4% higher, *ceteris paribus*. This decreases somewhat all the discrimination and differentiation effects (especially the British differentiation coefficient).

We have so far considered product differentiation as associated to the country of origin exclusively. Evidently enough, brand names (like Renault, Fiat, Mercedes and British Leyland) can also be carriers of goodwill. This can be tested by introducing into the hedonic regression as many dummies as there are brands and/or makes. But since in some cases a brand or make only appears once or twice in our sample, we have resorted to analyzing the residuals of the various hedonic regressions run for every country, which are given in Table II: if a residual is positive, the characteristics do not explain "enough" of the price, and the corresponding car is assumed to enjoy some positive goodwill; the inverse holds for negative residuals. In Table X we distinguish between two situations depending on whether the make is sold on the market in which it is produced, or abroad.

To measure the association of brands and the sign of residuals, we ran three χ^2 statistics; the results of the tests are given in Table XI. In all three cases the differences are significant; in other words, the association between brands and the sign of the residuals is positive. Without going into too many details about Table X, it is useful to point out that some brands which sell both nationally and internationally practice the same type of discrimination ("high" prices for Alfa Romeo, Audi, Austin, BMW, Lancia, Mercedes, Porsche, Renault; "low" prices in the case of Ford). On the other hand, Citroen, Talbot and Fiat sell cheaper on export markets, contrarily to Volkswagen and Opel who practice "lower" prices in Germany than on other markets. Most of the brands produced in Japan and other countries are

TABLE X
RESIDUALS OF HEDONIC EQUATIONS

		Domestic Markets			*Export Markets*		
		No. of	*Residuals*		*No. of*	*Residuals*	
	Origin	*Cases*	*< 0*	*> 0*	*Cases*	*< 0*	*> 0*
Alfa Romeo	I	6	2	4	5	2	3
Audi	G	8	2	6	9	0	9
Austin	UK	8	3	5	7	1	6
Autobianchi	I	3	1	2	—	—	—
BMW	G	9	0	9	8	1	7
Citroen	F	13	4	9	21	13	8
Datsun	J	—	—	—	12	11	1
Fiat	I	21	11	10	27	21	6
Ferrari	I	1	0	1	—	—	—
Ford	G-UK[a]	27	15	12	20	11	9
Giannini	I	2	1	1	—	—	—
Honda	J	—	—	—	9	7	2
Hyundai	J	—	—	—	2	2	0
Jaguar	UK	1	1	0	4	2	2
Lada	Other	—	—	—	8	8	0
Lancia	I	7	0	7	4	1	3
Mazda	J	—	—	—	11	8	3
Mercedes	G	9	2	7	8	0	8
Mitsubishi	J	—	—	—	7	3	4
Opel	G	14	11	3	24	13	11
Peugeot	F	10	7	3	17	8	9
Porsche	G	2	0	2	2	0	2
Reliant	UK	1	0	1	—	—	—
Renault	F	20	7	13	27	10	17
Rover	UK	2	1	1	5	3	2
Saab	Other	—	—	—	4	3	1
Seat	Other	—	—	—	1	1	0
Skoda	Other	—	—	—	3	3	0
Subaru	J	—	—	—	1	1	0
Suzuki	J	—	—	—	1	0	1
Talbot	F	13	6	7	7	5	2
Toyota	J	—	—	—	12	6	6
Triumph	UK	1	1	0	2	2	0
Vauxhall	UK	6	3	3	—	—	—
Volkswagen	G	16	10	6	26	10	16
Volvo	Other	—	—	—	6	3	3

[a] UK origin in the UK; G in all other countries.

"cheap" cars, with the exception of Mitsubishi and Toyota. Even Saab sells cheap for the bundle of characteristics it is endowed with!

V. CONCLUSIONS

Using samples of 100 brands/makes sold in five European countries (Belgium, France, Germany, Italy and the United Kingdom) we have shown that there

TABLE XI
ASSOCIATION OF BRANDS AND RESIDUALS OF THE HEDONIC REGRESSIONS

	χ^2 *Value*	*Degrees of Freedom*	*Significance Level*
On Domestic Markets	37.3	23	0.05
On Export Markets	74.6	31	0.001
On all Markets[a]	93.4	51	0.001

[a] The χ^2 statistic is computed only for those brands which exist both on domestic and export markets.

exist (in some cases large) differences in prices across countries, which are mainly due to producer discrimination, and to some extent to product differentiation. The same "bundle of characteristics" sells for twice as much in the United Kingdom as in Belgium!

We have also tried to isolate discrimination and differentiation, showing that the former explained more than the latter of the price differentials. It is worthwhile to go back to the results displayed in Table III (or in Table VIII) which gives the effects of discrimination on the price level of a car in the five European countries. It is tempting to conclude that the ranking corresponds to the degree of competition and concentration on the markets: competition and low concentration is at its best in Belgium, where there exist no domestic producers, and where Japan has its highest penetration rate (with some 25 % of the market); on the other side of the spectrum, and despite the fact that domestic producers share only one half of the market, we find the United Kingdom; this can probably be partly explained by the protection enjoyed, and by right hand drive, which isolates the country from "non official" imports. Between Belgium and the United Kingdom there are France, Germany and Italy, in that order if we ignore taxes, or Germany, France and Italy if taxes are included. These three countries have similar market sizes, and shares of domestic producers are close to each other (60 to 70 %); France and especially Italy have succeeded in avoiding massive imports of Japanese cars; Germany, on the other hand, has domestic producers who seem to enjoy more goodwill than others and can afford to sell "expensive" cars; German importers seem to benefit from and use this shelter by also charging higher prices.

Clearly a careful study of the various price elasticities in these countries would help in interpreting the results, as would a deeper analysis of product differentiation. The paper does not examine whether price differentials originate in deliberate international producer discrimination policies, or whether this situation is the consequence of collusion among local dealers.

An analysis of the practices of non-EEC producers is also needed. Indeed there is little doubt that the European Commission will eventually succeed in harmonizing prices; however, suppressing discrimination will decrease profits and worsen the situation of the already ailing European car industry.

Y. MERTENS AND V. GINSBURGH,
CEME,
Université Libre de Bruxelles,
C.P. 139,
Avenue F.-D. Roosevelt 50,
B-1050 Brussels,
Belgium.

ACCEPTED OCTOBER 1984

REFERENCES

COWLING, K. and CUBBIN, J., 1971, 'Price, Quality and Advertising Competition. An Econometric Investigation of the UK Car Market', *Economica*, pp. 378–394.

FRIEDLANDER, A., WINSTON, C. and WANG, K., 1983, 'Costs, Technology and Productivity in the US Automobile Industry', *The Bell Journal of Economics*, 14, pp. 1–20.

GRILICHES, Z., 1961, 'Hedonic Price Indexes for Automobiles: An Econometric Analysis of Quality Change', reprinted in Griliches (1971), pp. 55–87.

GRILICHES, Z., editor, 1971, *Price Indexes and Quality Change* (Harvard University Press).

KRAVIS, I. and LIPSEY, R., 1971, International Price Comparisons by Regression Methods', in Griliches (1971), pp. 150–179.

KRAVIS, I., KENNESSEY, Z., HESTON, A. and SUMMERS, R., 1975, *A System of International Comparisons of Gross Product and Purchasing Power* (The Johns Hopkins University Press).

NEVEN, D. and PHLIPS, L., 1985, 'Discriminating Oligopolists and Common Markets', *The Journal of Industrial Economics*, this issue.

of spatial monopoly. The cost-of-production factors, in particular the existence of scale economies, are shown to be a common determinant of dumping. Section III then extends classical dumping theory to different frontiers beyond those of costless and costly distance. The demand factors, such as consumer thresholds, are shown to be another important determinant of the local consumer welfare as the monopolist firm practices discriminatory pricing. Section IV next relaxes the simplifying assumption of section III. Section V concludes the paper.

I. SOME ESTABLISHED PRINCIPLES OF SPATIAL PRICE THEORY

As demonstrated by Greenhut and Ohta [1972], [1975], the spatial monopolist's discriminatory marginal revenue (DMR), net of freight costs, tends to be greater than the nondiscriminatory simple marginal revenue (SMR) when homogeneous buyers are distributed uniformly along a transport route. To briefly review the vital relationship of $DMR > SMR$, consider the local demand density function of the form f:

$$(1) \qquad q_D = f(p_D), \qquad D \geqslant 0,$$

where p_D stands for the price charged to consumers located D distance units from the firm, and q_D is the corresponding demand density at market point D. This equation can be transformed to the firm's net revenue function, i.e., net of freight costs, in obtaining:

$$(1)' \qquad m_D = f^{-1}(q_D) - tD$$

where t stands for a positive freight rate and m_D the mill price (or net revenue derivable from sales at market point D).

The SMR is the marginal curve to the aggregate demand

$$Q \equiv \int_0^{D_0} f(m+tD)\,dD, \qquad D_0 = (f^{-1}(0)-m)/t;$$

it derives from (1) in terms of a unique mill price, $m_D = m$, parametrically given to all market points D. Thus, given t, the aggregate demand is seen to be a unique function of mill price m: $Q = F(m)$. The related marginal revenue is correspondingly derived as $SMR = F^{-1} + (dF^{-1}/dQ)Q$. In contrast to this, the DMR is the horizontal aggregate of the marginal curves to (1)′ for all relevant D's. It can then easily be shown that an algebraic form of f, defined below, yields the result $DMR > SMR$ [1975, Chapter 4].[1]

$$(2) \qquad p_D = a - bq_D^{\alpha}, \qquad a, b, \alpha > 0$$

Since the profit maximizing calculus under the alternative pricing tech-

[1] The form of the demand represented by equation (2) belongs to the class of demands which are "relatively less convex" (Ohta [1980], [1981]). The "positive" output effects of spatial price discrimination does not, however, require or depend on this limited class of basic demands. The same $DMR > SMR$ result can be derivable also from the opposite class of basic demands, namely those which are "relatively more convex" (Ohta [1984, mimeo]).

niques equating these alternative MR's with the common marginal cost curve, the critical relation $DMR > SMR$ establishes an equilibrium output which is necessarily greater under discriminatory pricing than it is under f.o.b. pricing (that is, the invariable mill price system). This result obtains regardless of the form of the production cost function. Moreover, the conclusion remains basically invariant under conditions of spatial competition.

Contrary results conformable to Pigou–Robinson's findings (that is, $SMR \equiv DMR$) have been set forth by Beckmann [1976]. But they apply strictly to his assumptions of linear demand *and* fixed market spaces for each competing seller regardless of the pricing policy followed. The classical Pigou–Robinson and the Beckmann spatial results thus do not relate readily to situations in which the firm's market radius varies with its price. In particular, any pricing policy which yields higher profit induces greater entry, in the process generating smaller individual market areas in the zero profit equilibrium. Somewhat asymmetric results, accordingly, follow in that *in the long run* the individual firm's output is smaller, but the industry output is greater under spatially discriminatory prices than under nondiscriminatory f.o.b. mill pricing (Holahan [1975]).

Discriminatory pricing over distance signifies that a veritably limitless number of delivered price schedules apply over economic landscapes, each relating to the demand and competitive conditions that prevail at the different market points (Greenhut and Greenhut [1975], [1977], Greenhut [1981] and Phlips [1976]). Typically, mill prices were proposed to be higher for nearby customers and lower for distant buyers than those projected if the firm priced nondiscriminatorily rather than discriminatorily. This expectation signified greater benefits for nearby customers when the seller prices f.o.b. mill than when the seller discriminated spatially in his prices.

An important caveat applies to the last proposition which could easily be overlooked. Unlike the *general* proposition covering the output effect of spatial price discrimination, the demand curve must be of a well-defined form and the marginal cost of production must either be constant or increasing in order for spatial price discrimination to favor the distant (foreign) buyers. The constraint on marginal cost differs sharply from that of Mrs. Robinson in her finding that *home-country buyers may even benefit* from dumping, that is, when marginal production costs slope monotonically downward with output [1933]. Moreover, the correspondence between that particular Robinson result and one derivable from spatial price theory will later be seen to stem from a sharply contrasting assumption involving costly distance.

II. CORRESPONDENCES BETWEEN CLASSICAL DUMPING THEORY AND SPATIAL PRICE THEORY

Let us use Figure 1 to identify what happens to local prices and the firm's output when a spatial monopolist changes the firm's price policy from the

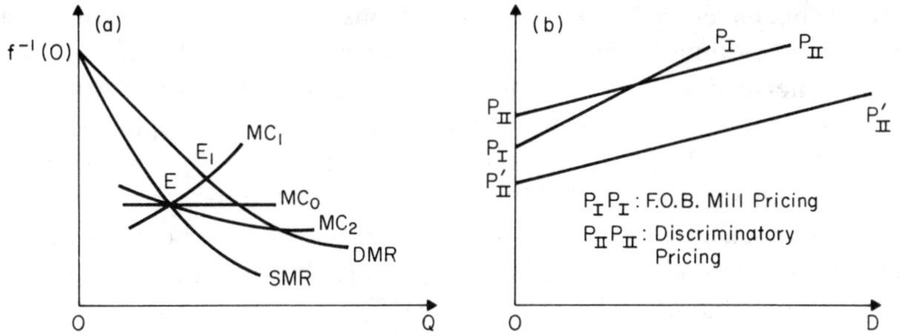

Figure 1
Alternative Cost Conditions and Spatial Price Schedules

nondiscriminatory f.o.b. mill form (referred to as Policy I) to the discriminatory form (Policy II). Figure 1(a) provides the marginal revenue curves, *DMR* and *SMR*, of the spatial monopolist and three alternative marginal cost curves: MC_0, MC_1 and MC_2. The initial nondiscriminatory price equilibrium at E shifts to either E_0, E_1 or E_2 when the firm changes its price policy to the discriminatory one; thus discriminatory output is unambiguously greater than simple monopoly output *regardless of how MC changes with output*. It is noteworthy that the increase in output is greater the smaller is the increase in (or the greater the decrease in) *MC*. Moreover, the equilibrium *MC* under discriminatory pricing is higher (lower) than the nondiscriminatory counterpart *MC* if and only if the *MC* slopes upward (downward).

It is important to recognize that the comparisons just noted are based on the common departure point E which itself may be given arbitrarily along *SMR*. Related to this point is a unique optimal f.o.b. mill price, which in turn determines a unique delivered price schedule under Policy I. (See the $P_I P_I$ schedule in Figure 1(b), where the horizontal scale measures the distance D while the vertical axis provides the delivered price.) Unlike the unique f.o.b. spatial price schedule $P_I P_I$ in Figure 1(b), the discriminatory price schedule $P_{II} P_{II}$ applicable to Policy II cannot be uniquely given because it depends on the alternative *MC* equilibria associated with E_0, E_1 and E_2.

Under the basic demand given by equation (2) *and* constant *MC*, it has been further established that $P_{II} > P_I$ at the zero distance cost point, while $P_{II} P_{II}$ is flatter than $P_I P_I$. Manifestly, the discriminatory price schedule is higher under increasing *MC*. We have established the following proposition:

Proposition 1. Given the demand equation (2), a price policy change from f.o.b. to discriminatory pricing generates a welfare loss for the home country (more proximate) customers, which loss is greater under increasing marginal costs than constant marginal costs.

Does Proposition 1 support the conventional notion that dumping *always* takes place at the expense of the home-country (nearby) customers? Our answer is no, *under equation* (2) *demands*. Consider in this regard the effect of a downward-sloping marginal cost curve, such as MC_2 of Figure 1(a). Note that the intersection of MC_2 with DMR involves a much lower equilibrium MC value and thus a much greater output than that applicable to the horizontal MC_0. It is therefore possible that the $P_{II}P_{II}$ schedule shifts downward all the way to the $P'_{II}P'_{II}$ schedule of Figure 1(b). This significantly lower schedule, to repeat, reflects the sharply lower equilibrium MC value applicable under discriminatory pricing, thereby establishing Proposition 2 predicated on the basic demand (2):

Proposition 2. Given the demand equation (2), *it is possible for all customers to benefit from spatial price discrimination (compared to f.o.b. mill pricing) when substantial economies of scale prevail.*

A case example of Proposition 2 exists when $\alpha = 1$ and the MC under the simple f.o.b. monopoly pricing is greater than $a/4$ while the equilibrium MC under the discriminating monopoly approaches zero. Our Proposition 2 is particularly remarkable in the Robinsonian sense since even home-country (nearby) customers would benefit from the discriminatory price system. This kind of pricing creates greater industry-wide output thereby benefiting all customers in the economy, *ceteris paribus*. The delivered price schedule $P'_{II}P'_{II}$ is simply lower than the f.o.b. P_IP_I schedule throughout the space involved. This special "spatial price theory" case converts Professor Robinson's two country example of advantaged home country buyers to the more general situation which includes a full set of market points.

In summary to this point in the paper: Mrs. Robinson's "spaceless" theory of dumping has been generalized to include impacts of price discrimination on buyers who are distributed uniformly along a transport route. At the same instance, the theory of dumping has been altered to include the theory of spatial price discrimination under conditions where even nearer buyers benefit somewhat because of the resulting lower prices in the home market. Symmetric conclusions to those of Mrs. Robinson were obtained by assuming alternative marginal cost conditions. However, the concept of dumping requires further generalizing, as in the section that follows. We will observe there the case where the home-country (nearby) customers benefit directly *and* completely from the discrimination, *regardless of the shape of the marginal cost curve*. In the strict confines of spatial microeconomics alone, this case is similar to the situation where distant buyers are charged a phantom freight, that is, where a phantom freight is *in effect* added to the actual freight costs involved.

III. EXTENDING THE CLASSICAL THEORY OF DUMPING TO DIFFERENT FRONTIERS

Demand curves not included in the specification of (2), such as demand curves lacking finite price intercept values, can be said to be empirically irrelevant to the space economy. Irrelevance applies because the firm's market area becomes infinite if positive demand still obtains at the distant points where delivered prices are unimaginably high. Of course, a finite price intercept can be imposed on demand curves of types other than (2), which constraint would simply involve the concept of consumer thresholds as proposed by Devletoglou [1971]. The *a priori* basis for rejecting other demand functions would thus be eliminated, and need therefore arises to evaluate these demands in the context of the international–interregional dumping of goods.

Consider the *specific* demand curve:

$$(3) \qquad q = \alpha/p^2, \qquad \beta \geqslant p \geqslant 0$$
$$\qquad = 0, \qquad p > \beta$$

where the demand elasticity is assumed, for the time being, to be equal to 2.

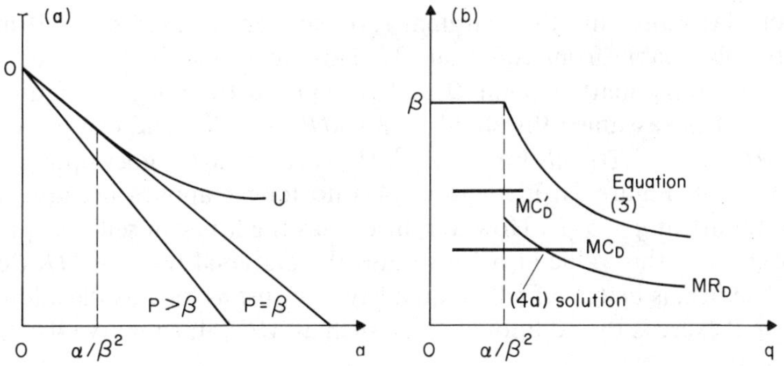

Figure 2
Preference Structure and Consumer Thresholds

The preference structure underlying our specification, as depicted in Figure 2, relates to a buyer who is assumed to consume only other goods 0 when the price of q exceeds the threshold β, panel (a). This panel utilizes a budget line $p = \beta$ which is merged with an indifference curve U over $q \leqslant \alpha/\beta^2$. The budget line $p > \beta$ indicates that demand for q vanishes completely at prices exceeding β, even if the demands at prices yielding positive q's happen to be of constant elasticity, as illustrated by Figure 2(b).

To develop the requisite background principles further, let us evaluate the implications of the price intercept of the (otherwise) hyperbolic demand curve given by (3). Towards this end, recall that third degree discriminatory pricing involves profit maximization in *each* and all of the relevant separate (spatially separated) markets. Thus for any given market point D we must have:

$$(4) \qquad MR_D \geqslant MC_D, \qquad D_{0II} \geqslant D \geqslant 0$$

where MR_D stands for the marginal revenue obtained on sales to a market point D distance units from the firm, MC_D provides the marginal production cost MC plus marginal cost of transporting the good to market point D, and the distance D_{0II} designates the boundary limit to the seller's market area under discriminatory price policy II.[2] To better appreciate the meaning of (4) assume a constant marginal production cost k, and also an invariable freight rate t. Condition (4) combined with (3) may then be decomposed advantageously into two parts, an equality and inequality, as specified by:[3,4]

$$\text{(4a)} \qquad \tfrac{1}{2}\sqrt{\alpha/q} = k+tD, \qquad \text{for } q > \alpha/\beta^2$$
$$\therefore q^* = \alpha/4(k+tD)^2, \qquad D^* \geqslant D \geqslant 0, \qquad D^* = (\beta/2-k)/t,$$

$$\text{(4b)} \qquad \beta > k+tD, \qquad \text{for } q \leqslant \alpha/\beta^2$$
$$\therefore q^* = \alpha/\beta^2, \qquad D_{0II} \geqslant D \geqslant D^*, \qquad D_{0II} = (\beta-k)/t,$$

where q^* stands for optimal sales quantity to market point D. The left-hand-side of (4a) represents the marginal revenue from market point D and is directly obtainable from equation (3). This same marginal revenue curve applies to every market point D and is depicted by MR_D in Figure 2(b). Because of the assumed threshold β, this MR_D is valid, and can be equated with MC_D $(=k+tD)$ *only* for $q>\alpha/\beta^2$. However, as MC_D goes up with D to, say, MC_D' in Figure 2(b), equation (4a) no longer applies because of the discontinuity at $q=\alpha/\beta^2$. However, insofar as the firm can sell this quantity at the price β, this value also constitutes the marginal revenue MR_D of the firm. The firm is better off selling quantity α/β^2 just as long as the additional revenue β exceeds the additional costs, such as MC_D'. Inequality (4b) depicts such relations.

Substituting (4a) and (4b) into (3) provides the spatial discriminatory price schedule in terms of the distance variable D. This substitution establishes:

$$\text{(5)} \qquad P_{II} = 2k+2tD, \qquad D^* \geqslant D \geqslant 0$$
$$= \beta, \qquad D_{0II} \geqslant D \geqslant D^*$$

which yields Proposition 3 for the case of homogeneous consumers distributed uniformly over.

[2] Recognize with respect to (4) that the conventional $MR=MC$ condition is neither a necessary nor sufficient condition for profit maximization. The first order condition is not sufficient unless combined with the second in yielding maximum profits. It is not necessary since in cases such as the one represented by (3), $MR=MC$ is not an attainable condition, for example, when MC is as high as MC_D' in Figure 2(b) above. The maximum quantity which still yields an $MR>MC$ is the profit-maximizing quantity in this event. Quantities exceeding this particular solution involve $MR<MC$, and thus provide nonprofit-maximizing positions.

[3] The D^* is the critical distance that makes the firm's marginal costs MC_D barely equal to the maximum marginal revenue MR_D under (4a), that is, $MR_D^* = \beta/2$.

[4] The D_{0II} is the distance limit that makes MC_D as high as the threshold price level β. Clearly, no sales can willingly be made beyond this market point.

Proposition 3. Given demand of the form (3), the spatial monopolist will practice reverse dumping in the form of (5) unless legally or otherwise restricted, in effect creating phantom freight charges for distant consumers.

Following Hoover [1937] and Smithies [1941], the implications of (5) would be rejected on grounds of potential resale by nearer buyers to more distant ones. The constrained optimal solution for P_{II} could, in turn, be derived according to the method proposed by Greenhut and Ohta [1975, Chapter 5]. Dewey [1955], on the grounds of monopolistic power over buyers, and Olson [1972], on the grounds of extra cost of repackaging, accepted the possibility (feasibility) of phantom freight extras being added to delivered prices in demand situations characterized by equation (3). And though such pricing is tantamount to applying phantom freight charges which would most likely be illegal in the United States *if* the practice was coterminous with a systematically followed base point price schedule, there is accumulated evidence that sporadic forms of this type of pricing is practiced in the USA (Greenhut, Greenhut and Li [1980]), much more generally in W. Germany and Japan (Greenhut [1981]), and apparently elsewhere in Europe as well (Phlips [1976]). Notwithstanding the *a priori* arguments of Hoover and Smithies, the basis for evaluating the various implications of equation (3) is therefore provided. It follows that the discriminatory spatial price practice resulting from equation (3) demands must be compared with the f.o.b. price schedule that would exist under that particular type of demand function. Let us accordingly determine next the f.o.b. price structure that would stem from equation (3) demands.

Let m stand for the f.o.b. mill price. Then via (3) the quantity demanded at distance D is specifiable as:

$$(3)' \qquad q = \alpha/p^2 = \alpha/(m+tD)^2, \qquad D_{0I} \geqslant D \geqslant 0$$

where D_{0I} refers to the limit distance under f.o.b. mill pricing, that is, $D_{0I} = (\beta - m)/t$. The aggregate demand Q over an assumed line market, where $q(p)$ is uniformly distributed, is then:

$$(6) \qquad Q = 2\int_0^{D_{0I}} \alpha/(m+tD)^2\, dD = 2\alpha(\beta-m)/tm\beta, \qquad D_{0I} = (\beta-m)/t$$

For any given mill price m, profit is defined by:

$$(7) \qquad \pi = (m-k)Q = 2\alpha(\beta-m)(m-k)/tm\beta$$

Differentiating (7) with respect to m and setting the result equal to zero provides the unique profit-maximizing mill price; that is:

(8) $$d\pi/dm = 2\alpha[(k-m)+(\beta-m)]tm\beta - 2\alpha t\beta(\beta-m)(m-k)/(tm\beta)^2 = 0$$
$$m = \sqrt{k\beta}$$

The optimal spatial price schedule under f.o.b. mill pricing is therefore:

(9) $$P_I = \sqrt{k\beta} + tD, \qquad (\beta - \sqrt{k\beta})/t \geqslant D \geqslant 0$$

The essential feature of this equation may be stated in the form of Proposition 4 below.

Proposition 4. Given the demand (3)′, the profit maximizing f.o.b. mill price m is higher (lower) the higher (lower) is the price ceiling β vis-à-vis the marginal cost.

Now the discriminatory and f.o.b. pricing techniques stemming from equation (3) demands can be compared by evaluating equations (5) and (9). For $D = 0$, $P_{II} \lesseqgtr P_I$, depending on whether $\beta \lesseqgtr 4k$. That is to say, if the price ceiling β is greater than $4k$, or more generally when consumer thresholds are relatively high, the prices charged to nearby customers are lower under discriminatory pricing than they are under f.o.b. mill pricing, and *vice versa.*

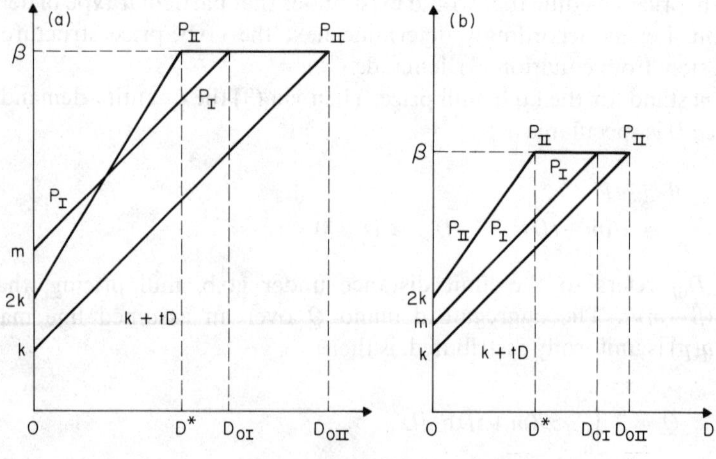

Figure 3
Consumer Threshold Levels and Spatial Price Schedules

Figure 3(a) depicts the two alternative spatial price schedules for $\beta > 4k$. These prices may be compared with those shown in Figure 3(b) for $\beta < 4k$. Note that the welfare implications for the nearby-distant sets of buyers are simply reversed as different levels of β are assumed. In particular, panel (a) of

Figure 3 indicates that a relatively high β combined with discriminatory pricing benefits buyers located proximate to the seller's plant while in panel (b) a relatively low β can be seen to benefit the same nearby buyers if f.o.b. mill pricing is practiced. A reversing of effects therefore applies to panels (a) and (b), given high and low β's respectively.

A caveat is in order at this point because in addition to benefiting nearby buyers, discriminatory prices can also provide advantages to *very distant* buyers (that is, those located between D_{0I} *and* D_{0II}); it does this since the latter groups of buyers would have been unable to purchase the good at all under the profit-maximizing f.o.b. mill price schedule but can purchase some of it at prices equal to or slightly below β, in the process creating a consumers' surplus.

Additional observations are warranted. The entire price schedule P_I can be recognized to shift upward (downward) in (9) as β is parametrically changed upward (downward). On the other hand, the price schedule P_{II} of (5) remains basically invariant to changes in β as only the size of the firm's market area can be altered.

To summarize briefly to this point: Diverse forms of dumping are possible under selected demands, such as those represented by homogeneous, constant demand elasticity conditions. (1) If the level of consumer thresholds (sensitivity for the commodity) is relatively high compared with marginal cost, the form of dumping which benefits nearby customers (and some very distant buyers) is most profitable for the seller, *ceteris paribus.* (2) If the threshold price is relatively low, dumping *in favor of nearby buyers* nevertheless results in a *loss to them,* in fact to *all* of the nearby consumers who could have been supplied under f.o.b. mill pricing. (For example, compare the two alternative delivered price schedules in Figure 3(b) over the market domain OD_{0II}.) (3) Regardless of the threshold price, the very distant consumers who would not purchase any units under f.o.b. mill pricing will benefit from discriminatory prices, as this price system alone enables them to purchase some positive quantity of the good. It follows that when dumping is viewed in the perspective of spatial price theory, more complicated asymmetric results obtain than those which derive from the classical view of prices.

It warrants special mention that dumping in favor of home (nearby) customers involves more complicated relationships than is evident by the typical protectionist argument one bears. This does not necessarily mean that predatory international dumping fails to exist. Rather, it simply suggests that profit-maximizing firms may price variously over space, and *home country advocates can frequently find examples of whatever they wish to claim is improper in the importing of goods from foreign countries.*

A related point is this: what appears to be *improper* may *not* be attributable to the predatory motives typically ascribed to the foreign seller. Rather, it can be that so-called discriminatory dumping in favor of distant buyers is strictly the result of profit maximizing pricing which, under different demand conditions, would have generated the opposite forms of pricing. Before laws are passed establishing "reference prices" which implicitly condemn foreign sellers, economists should probe deeply behind all facets of spatial pricing and the particular industry under examination. Indeed, not only have we previously noted the prevalence of discriminatory prices uncovered in the United States, W. Germany, and Japan, but diverse forms thereof reflecting heterogeneous demand and competitive conditions over the firms' market areas have been identified (Greenhut and Greenhut [1975], [1977]).

IV. A GENERALIZATION

Consider a demand curve defined generally as:

$$(10) \qquad q = \alpha/p^x, \qquad \beta \geqslant p \geqslant 0, \qquad x > 1$$
$$= 0, \text{ elsewhere—as previously specified.}$$

The spatial price schedule under discriminatory pricing (Policy II) would then be provided by:

$$(11) \qquad p_{II} = [x/(x-1)]\,(k+tD), \qquad (x-1)\beta/xt - k/t \geqslant D \geqslant 0$$
$$= \beta, \qquad (\beta-k)/t \geqslant D > (x-1)\beta/xt - k/t$$

The spatial price schedule under mill pricing (Policy I) can, in turn, be shown as:

$$(12) \qquad P_I = m^* + tD, \qquad (\beta - m)/t \geqslant D \geqslant 0,$$

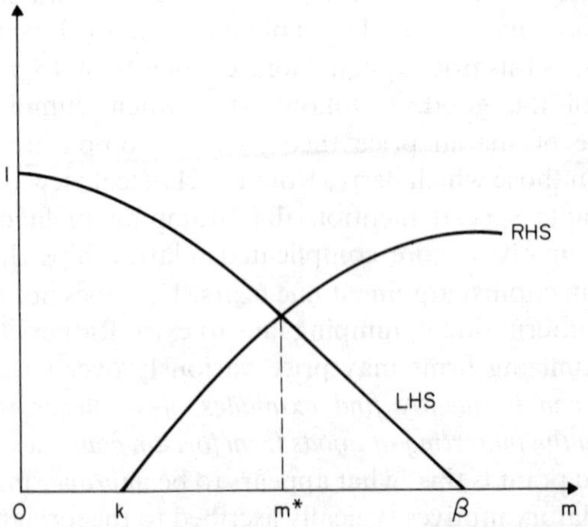

Figure 4
Marginal Cost, Threshold Levels and Equilibrium Mill Price

where m^* is the solution for m of the following equation:

$$(13) \qquad m^x - (2-x)\beta^{x-1}m - k(x-1)\beta^{x-1} = 0, \qquad x > 1$$

Existence of a solution falling between k and β is guaranteed since the present equation can be rearranged as:

$$(13)' \qquad 1-(m/\beta)^{x-1} = (1-k/m)(x-1)$$

In fact, the graphs of the LHS and RHS of this equation are unambiguously specifiable, with m^* determined at the intersection of the two curves in Figure 4. It can, furthermore, readily be seen that the equilibrium mill price m^* will be higher or lower depending on whether β (or k) is higher or lower. In contrast, via (11) we recognize that the delivered price is invariant under discriminatory pricing, being independent of β. The same general relations as those given in section III that were illustrated by Figure 3 therefore apply.

V. CONCLUSION

Many industrialists and advocates of "home country" products contend that the international dumping of goods is not only prevalent but an undesirable practice for two reasons: (1) it damages the home country by reducing the welfare of residents of the country; and (2) the industries in the nation which imports dumped goods can be damaged irreparably by the loss of domestic buyers. Of course, this second argument ignores the gains from comparative advantage. Moreover, the present paper has shown that the first argument is unacceptable since free trade would allow domestic (local) firms to maximize profits *market by market* and thereby to generate lower product prices under certain well-defined demand and cost conditions. *Quite significantly, this argument does not depend on (nor require) Mrs. Robinson's specification of decreasing marginal costs.*

Perhaps most importantly, we have shown that the international dumping of goods is simply a special case of intra-country spatial price discrimination, just as Phlips [1980] has shown that intertemporal price theory is a special case of spatial price discrimination theory. More inclusively, international sales of f.o.b. mill pricing firms should also be analyzed under the framework of spatial price theory. We further propose that spatial price theory and empirical realities generate sharper views of differential pricing (dumping) besides alternative forms of it than those provided by the classical spaceless theory of industrial and international prices. Ignoring the controversial case where price differences are related to costs, the theory of spatial pricing can explain dumping and reverse dumping in international trade under the simplest of conditions, namely one requiring only that buyers are spatially separated from a seller. Most vitally, insights into the dumping and reverse dumping process do not require the very restrictive, special assumptions that comprise the classical theory of price discrimination, such as the monopoly and non-identical demands assumptions. It follows that the most general exposition of price discrimination in international trade is the one based on the theory of spatial pricing.

M. L. GREENHUT,
Department of Economics,
Texas A & M University,
College Station, Texas 77843,
USA.

ACCEPTED JUNE 1985

H. OHTA,
SIPEB,
Aoyama Gakuin University,
Tokyo,
Japan.

J. SAILORS,
Department of Economics,
The University of Houston,
Houston, Texas 77004,
USA.

REFERENCES

BECKMANN, J., 1976, 'Spatial Price Policies Revisited', *Bell Journal of Economics*, 7 (Autumn), pp. 619–630.

BRANDER, J. and KRUGMAN, P., 1983, 'A "Reciprocal Dumping" Model of International Trade', *Journal of International Economics*, 15, pp. 313–321.

DEVLETOGLOU, N. E., 1971, *Consumer Behavior* (Harper and Row, London).

DEWEY, D., 1955, 'A Reappraisal of F.O.B. Pricing and Freight Absorption', *Southern Economic Journal*, 22 (July), pp. 48–54.

DORWARD, N., 1982, 'Recent Developments in the Analysis of Spatial Competition and Their Implications for Industrial Economics', *The Journal of Industrial Economics*, 31 (September–December), pp. 133–151.

GREENHUT, J. and GREENHUT, M. L., 1975, 'Spatial Price Discrimination, Competition and Locational Effects', *Economica*, 42, 4 (November), pp. 401–419.

GREENHUT, J. and GREENHUT, M. L., 1977, 'Nonlinearity of Delivered Price Schedules and Predatory Pricing', *Econometrica*, 45, 8 (November), pp. 1871–1875.

GREENHUT, J., GREENHUT, M. L. and LI, S., 1980, 'Spatial Pricing Patterns in the United States', *Quarterly Journal of Economics*, 94, 2 (March), pp. 329–350.

GREENHUT, M. L. and OHTA, H., 1972, 'Monopoly Output Under Alternative Spatial Pricing Techniques', *American Economic Review*, 62, 4 (September), pp. 705–713.

GREENHUT, M. L. and OHTA, H., 1975, *Theory of Spatial Pricing and Market Areas* (Duke University Press, Durham, NC).

GREENHUT, M. L., 1981, 'Spatial Pricing in U.S.A., West Germany and Japan', *Economica*, 48 (February), pp. 79–86.

HIRSHLEIFER, J., 1976, *Price Theory and Applications* (Prentice-Hall, Englewood Cliffs, NC).

HOLAHAN, W. L., 1975, 'The Welfare Effects of Spatial Price Discrimination', *American Economic Review*, 65, 3 (June), pp. 498–503.

HOOVER, E. M., 1937, 'Spatial Price Discrimination', *Review of Economic Studies*, 4 (June), pp. 182–191.

NORMAN, G., 1981, 'Spatial Competition and Spatial Price Discrimination', *Review of Economic Studies*, 48, 1 (January), pp. 97–111.

NORMAN, G., 1981, 'Uniform Pricing as an Optimal Spatial Pricing Policy', *Economica*, 48, 1 (February), pp. 87–91.

OHTA, H., 1980, 'Spatial Competition, Concentration and Welfare', *Regional Science and Urban Economics*, 10, 1 (February), pp. 3–16.

OHTA, H., 1981, 'The Price Effects of Spatial Competition', *Review of Economic Studies*, 48, 2 (April), pp. 317–325.

OHTA, H., 1984, 'The Output Effects of Spatial Price Discrimination Revisited' (mimeo).

OLSON, J. E., 1972, 'Price Discrimination by Regulated Motor Carriers', *American Economic Review*, 62, 3 (June), pp. 395–402.

PHLIPS, L., 1976, 'Spatial Pricing and Competition', in *Studies in Competition*, Approximation of Legislation Series (Commission of the European Communities, Brussels).

PHLIPS, L., 1980, 'Intertemporal Price Discrimination and Sticky Prices', *Quarterly Journal of Economics*, 3 (May), pp. 525–542.

ROBINSON, J., 1933, *The Economics of Imperfect Competition* (Macmillan, London).

SMITHIES, A., 1941, 'Monopolistic Price Policy in a Spatial Market', *Econometrica*, 9, 1 (January), pp. 63–73.

THE JOURNAL OF INDUSTRIAL ECONOMICS 0022-1821 $2.00
Volume XXXIV December 1985 No. 2

STRATEGIC GROUPS AND THE DEMAND FOR BEER*

VICTOR J. TREMBLAY

Caves and Porter [1977] developed a theory of strategic groups to explain why national and regional producers behave differently in most consumer-goods industries. One implication of this theory is that the structure of demand and cost conditions differ between groups. This article tests for the presence of demand asymmetries between national and regional strategic groups by estimating a firm demand function for U.S. beer producers. The results suggest that these demand differences do exist. The impact of firm advertising differs between national and regional producers, and there is greater rivalry among competitors inside than outside strategic groups.

I. INTRODUCTION

WITHIN MOST consumer-goods industries groups of firms behave differently. Frequently within the same industry a group of firms offering nationally advertised name brand products coexists with a group of producers offering unadvertised or little advertised regionally marketed products. Caves and Porter [1977] developed the theory of strategic groups to explain the sources and consequences of the long-run existence of such groups within industries. Their research is important because it showed that industry performance is better explained when the structure and conduct of strategic groups are understood. One of the implications of this theory is that the presence of strategic groups indicates that the structure of demand and cost conditions would differ between groups. However, to date the presence of strategic group demand or cost asymmetries has not been tested.

The purpose of this paper is to test for the presence of demand asymmetries between strategic groups in the U.S. brewing industry.[1] The brewing industry is selected because of its close resemblance to the typical consumer-goods industry and because of data availability. From 1950 to 1980 there were four national beer producers each of whom marketed heavily advertised national brands and a group of regional brewers who typically marketed popular priced and regionally advertised brands. Thus, the emphasis of this research is to determine if advertising has had a different impact upon firm demand for the two strategic groups in brewing.

* The author is grateful to William Hallagan, Frederick Inaba, D. Stanton Smith, Carol Horton Tremblay, Lawrence White, and an anonymous referee for their helpful comments on earlier drafts. The author is responsible for remaining errors.

[1] A discussion of strategic group cost asymmetries goes beyond the scope of this paper. See Tremblay [1984] for a discussion of these cost asymmetries in brewing.

This article proceeds as follows. In section II the theory of strategic groups, the classification of strategic groups in brewing, and the potential strategic group demand asymmetries in brewing are discussed. In section III the data are described and the empirical model is developed. The empirical results are presented in section IV, and a conclusion of this analysis is found in section V.

II. STRATEGIC GROUPS AND THE DEMAND FOR BEER

Strategic group theory

The theory of strategic groups was developed by Caves and Porter to explain the presence of long-run heterogeneity among firms within the same industry and to improve the structure-conduct-performance paradigm.[2] In their research a strategic group consists of firms within an industry which follow similar long-run strategies.[3] At the poles an industry may contain one group if all firms within the industry are homogeneous or as many groups as there are firms if each firm follows a significantly unique strategy. For most consumer-goods industries, however, a delineation of national and regional producers is common. In the words of Caves and Porter,

> A typical pattern in consumer-goods industries is the presence of a small group of producers of a full line of nationally branded goods and a large group of producers of unadvertised goods, regionally branded goods, and producers of private labels.[4]

They argued that the presence of more than one strategic group is likely to persist if mobility barriers, barriers to entry specific to a particular group, are present. The level of mobility barriers within an industry may vary between groups, making entry more difficult into one group than another. For example, in the market for bleach the high sunk cost of entry and the high risk associated with a national advertising campaign may make it more difficult to compete nationally with Clorox (a national brand) than to enter at a regional level. Profitability may differ between groups, but mobility barriers can keep less profitable rivals out of the most successful group and enable more than one group to survive even in the long-run.[5]

This theory indicates that, since the mixture of firm strategic activities differs between groups, the structure of their demand and cost functions would be different even though they belong to the same industry. For

[2] Others papers important to the development of the theory of strategic groups include: Newman [1978], Porter [1979], and Hallagan and Joerding [1983].

[3] A strategic group is not simply a more narrow definition of an industry. The industry remains while firms are allowed to be heterogeneous in their behavior by offering a different product line or vertically integrating to a different degree, for example.

[4] Caves and Porter [1977, p. 251].

[5] Hallagan and Joerding [1983] showed that even if mobility barriers are zero but advertising spillover effects (a firm's demand is increased by its rivals' advertising) or consumer brand loyalty are present, then multiple strategic groups can coexist in the long-run.

example, national producers may receive a greater net benefit from their advertising effort because they are able to advertise nationally or are able to buy advertising at a lower cost than regional producers. Furthermore, because of the strategic similarities within groups and differences across groups, rival behavior may affect firm demand differently for firms inside and outside the rival's own strategic group. For instance, a dollar increase in one national producer's advertising effort may affect the demand function of a national rival differently than the demand function of a regional competitor.

The theory of strategic groups has proven important because industry performance can be better analyzed when the structure and conduct of strategic groups are understood. Recent empirical evidence supports the view that more than one strategic group can persist in the long-run, and has shown that industry performance frequently deteriorates as an industry becomes more homogeneous (has fewer strategic groups). Newman [1978] found that chemical industry performance deteriorated as the number of strategic groups declined, and Porter [1979] and Oster [1982] found empirical support for the presence of multiple strategic groups within many industries.

Strategic groups in brewing

Beer producers are classified into national and regional strategic groups between 1950 and 1980.[6] There are two reasons for this delineation. First, Anheuser-Busch, Miller, Schlitz, and Pabst remained national producers during this entire period. The national group experienced no entry or exit. However, the number of regional producers have declined rapidly since World War II; in 1950 there were 382 regional beer producers while in 1980 there were only 32. This suggests the possibility of significant mobility barriers into the national group. Second, the brewing industry closely resembles Caves and Porter's description of a typical consumer-goods industry. National producers have generally marketed a heavily, nationally advertised premium priced brand, and regionals have primarily marketed popular priced or regionally advertised brands. National producers have consistently outadvertised regional producers. Table I indicates that the average advertising expenditures per barrel were generally greater for national producers between 1950 and 1977.[7] In their study of the brewing industry, Ackoff and Emshoff [1975a] found that television advertising is a more powerful marketing tool than radio, newspaper, or billboard advertising. Mueller and Rogers [1980] found large scale advertisers have a marketing advantage over other firms in consumer-goods industries. This suggests that

[6] This delineation is only accurate from 1950 to 1980. Beginning in the mid-1970s Schlitz and Pabst became weaker national producers; so much weaker that in 1982 Stroh, a strong regional brewer, bought Schlitz, and Pabst retreated to its strongest regional markets. In the early 1980s Heileman became a national producer by selling a patchwork set of regional brands across the nation.

[7] A barrel contains thirty-one gallons of beer.

TABLE I
AVERAGE NATIONAL AND REGIONAL GROUP ADVERTISING EXPENDITURES PER BARREL: 1972 DOLLARS*

Year	*Nationals' Advertising Per Barrel*	*Regionals' Advertising Per Barrel*	*Year*	*Nationals' Advertising Per Barrel*	*Regionals' Advertising Per Barrel*
1950	0.57	0.41	*1965*	1.73	1.33
1951	0.61	0.45	*1966*	1.61	1.38
1952	0.58	0.48	*1967*	1.53	1.32
1953	0.83	0.54	*1968*	1.34	0.98
1954	1.76	1.11	*1969*	1.16	0.80
1955	1.32	0.88	*1970*	1.19	1.08
1956	1.99	1.44	*1971*	1.27	1.06
1957	1.96	1.33	*1972*	1.15	0.93
1958	1.64	1.46	*1973*	0.82	0.86
1959	1.47	1.56	*1974*	0.67	0.69
1960	1.75	1.44	*1975*	0.72	0.51
1961	1.66	1.43	*1976*	0.67	0.49
1962	1.69	1.39	*1977*	1.30	0.84
1963	1.84	1.38			
1964	2.02	1.20			

* For a description of the sample of firms used in this table, see the Appendix.
Source: *Advertising Age*.

national beer producers, who are large scale television advertisers, may have had a marketing advantage over regional beer producers. Therefore, firm demand conditions are likely to be different between these two groups.[8]

The presence of national and regional strategic groups in brewing leads to two interesting hypotheses. First, firm advertising may have a larger positive impact upon demand if the firm is a national producer. Second, advertising from a rival inside a firm's own strategic group is expected to have a greater adverse effect upon the firm's demand, because of their strategic similarities, than advertising from a rival outside the firm's group.

[8] One might question this taxonomy of groups since firm behavior within each group has not been perfectly homogeneous. For example, in 1964 Carling, a regional producer, and in 1972 Schlitz began using a new batch brewing process in order to cut costs; however, both companies found this strategy to be unsuccessful since, according to some beer experts, product quality was reduced (*Advertising Age* [1981, p. 64]). In addition, at various times since 1958 Pabst followed a regional strategy by selling its national premium Blue Ribbon brand at popular prices, and Coors, a regional producer, was as successful as national producers in the 1960s and early 1970s. Finally, Heileman, another regional producer, has been unusually successful since 1964 in gaining market share and brands through merger, a strategy followed by no other brewers during this period. It may have been these exceptions which motivated the work of Hatten and Schendel [1977] who used a Chow test to classify beer producers into six groups. Nevertheless, the reason for maintaining the national-regional strategic group taxonomy here is that these exceptions are predominately atypical and temporary in nature. Both Carling and Schlitz discontinued using the batch process within five years of its introduction. Since the middle 1970s Pabst has attempted to regain a national premium image for its Blue Ribbon brand, and Coors has been much less successful. Therefore, because firms should be classified into strategic groups if they follow similar long-run strategies, the national-regional delineation is appropriate.

Demand for beer

The demand function of the representative national and regional producer is being modeled since data are available only at the firm level.[9] In addition, it is important to recognize that product differentiation may have an important impact upon the demand for beer. A hedonic technique is used to control for product differentiation.[10] In this technique the quantity of "effective output", a quality adjusted output measure, is defined as a function of the quantity of physical output and hedonic quality or attribute descriptors.

The presence of strategic groups and product differentiation imply that firm i's inverse demand function can be written as follows.

$$(1) \qquad P_i = P_i(\Psi_R, \Psi_N, \Psi_I, \Psi_O, \underline{X}), \text{ and } \Psi = \Psi(q, Z)$$

where:

i = a subscript for each firm;
R = a firm subscript when firm i is a regional producer;
N = a firm subscript when firm i is a national producer;
I = a subscript for rivals which are inside firm i's strategic group;
O = a subscript for rivals which are outside firm i's strategic group;
P = the price of beer;
Ψ = the quantity of effective output;
q = the quantity of physical output;
Z = an attribute or product differentiation control variable;
$\underline{X}$ = a vector of nonstrategic demand determining variables.

This specification implies that if firm i is a national producer, then Ψ_N equals the firm's effective output, Ψ_R equals zero, Ψ_I equals the effective output of the firm's national rivals, and Ψ_O equals the effective output of the firm's regional rivals. This model is in keeping with the strategic group literature which hypothesizes that the impact of q and Z would differ for national and regional producers and would differ for rivals inside and outside the firm's own strategic group.[11] The impact of nonstrategic variables, which will be discussed shortly, are assumed to be the same for all firms.

III. DATA AND EMPIRICAL MODEL

The variables and data

This study uses a pooled data set consisting of annual market and firm data from three national producers, Anheuser-Busch, Schlitz, and Pabst, and

[9] Hicks' Composite Commodity Theorem (Green [1976, p. 111]) justifies this procedure if the relative prices of a firm's brands remain in fixed proportion.

[10] See Spady and Friedlaender [1978] for a description and an application of this technique.

[11] One might argue that the impact of strategic variables for outside (inside) strategic group rivals would be different if the outside (inside) rivals are national rather than regional competitors, but there was no empirical support for this argument.

nineteen regional producers for the period 1950–1977. Since some firms exited the industry before 1977, the final sample includes only 316 observations. Data sources and a description of the method of collection can be found in the Appendix.

A difficult task is to accurately describe effective output. It is unobservable but a function of q and Z; therefore, measures of q and Z will be used as proxy variables for Ψ. Physical output is measured as the firm's annual barrel production. Since the typical product being modeled here is a light domestic Pilsner beer, it is maintained that the only characteristic which distinguishes one firm's product from another's is the image created by the firm for its representative brand.[12] The main factors which can influence image are the quality and intensity of a firm's advertising effort and consumers' product quality perceptions. However, because of data limitations, image is assumed to be captured by advertising intensity alone.

Current advertising messages or the quantity of advertising, rather than advertising expenditures, influence image. Following Schmalensee [1972] an advertising message is defined as an advertisement of a given length of time communicated (seen, heard, or read by television viewers, radio listeners, or magazine readers respectively) to a particular set of observers. It is derived by dividing a firm's total advertising expenditure by a price index for advertising to a thousand media observers as described in the Appendix. Advertising messages are preferred since the amount of advertising expenditures may not correctly measure advertising levels for the time series data if the price of advertising changes over time. For example, a doubling of the price of advertising, for a given level of advertising expenditure, reduces advertising messages by one half.[13]

Typically, a characteristic is measured as the quantity of that characteristic per unit of physical output.[14] However, image created through advertising is similar to a public good. Advertising messages can be received by many consumers simultaneously. The image characteristic should therefore be defined as the firm's total advertising messages, not messages per unit of output. The

[12] There is little real difference between brands of U.S. beer. The light Pilsner beer produced by most U.S. beer producers is nearly homogeneous. On the production side, an identical technology and similar inputs are used to brew domestic malt beverages. On the demand side, only perceived differentiation appears to be relevant to the consumer. The results of numerous studies indicate that consumers cannot generally distinguish real quality differences whether they exist or not. For example, Allison and Uhl [1964] conducted blind taste tests on various brands of beer and found that beer drinkers could not distinguish one brand from another and could not identify their favorite brands. In addition Ackoff and Emshoff [1975b] conducted blind taste tests using the same brand of beer. They placed four different labels on the same product and presented them to their subjects as four different brands. They found that "All of the subjects believed that the brands were different and that they could tell the difference between them. Most (of the 250 subjects) felt that at least one of the four brands was not fit for human consumption" (Ackoff and Emshoff [1975b, p. 12]).

[13] One might criticise this approach since it ignores the investment nature of advertising discussed by Demsetz [1979]. That is, image may be influenced by both present and past advertising messages. However, Grabowski [1977–78] found that the effect of advertising depreciates to zero after one year in the brewing industry.

[14] See Leffler [1982].

representative image of a firm's products is defined as its total advertising messages per brand. This controls for the fact that a firm, with a given number of advertising messages, could introduce a new generic brand which would "water down" this representative image.

To accurately measure q and Z for firm i's rivals, each variable is aggregated separately over the dominant rivals inside and outside firm i's strategic group. Dominant inside group members are defined as *all three* national rivals for a national producer and the largest three regional rivals for a regional producer. Dominant outside group members are defined as all regional rivals for a national producer and *all four* national rivals for a regional producer.[15]

There are a number of non-strategic variables which may have an important impact upon firm demand. These include income, defined as real *per capita* income, and population, defined as the twenty to forty-four year old population since the majority of beer drinkers are in this age group.[16] In addition, it is assumed that a consumer's decision to buy firm i's beer is dependent upon a small class of commodities. One might argue that this class should include spirits and wine as well as firm i's rivals' beer. Nevertheless, spirits and wine are ignored since previous studies indicate that they are not significant substitutes for beer.[17] Thus, the only commodities assumed to be a close substitute for firm i's beer are U.S. rival and imported beer. The impact of imported beer is modeled by physical output alone since advertising expenditures are small and unavailable. Finally, price is defined as revenue per thousand barrels of beer; however, six of the twenty-two firms sampled were conglomerate with unobservable beer revenues over part of this period.[18] Thus, a conglomerate dummy variable is added to the demand function to control for this measurement error.

Final specification

The empirical model of firm i's inverse demand function in period t is written as:

$$(2) \qquad P_{it} = b_0 + b_1 Rq_{it} + b_2 Nq_{it} + b_3 Iq_{it} + b_4 Oq_{it} + b_5 RA_{it} + b_6 NA_{it} + b_7 IA_{it} + b_8 OA_{it} + b_9 M_t + b_{10} POP_t + b_{11} y_t + b_{12} N_i + b_{13} CO_{it} + e_{it}$$

[15] Data are available on q and Z for all four national producers and all regional producers.

[16] According to *Brewers Almanac* [1980, p. 82] persons aged 21 to 44 accounted for approximately 68 % of the U.S. beer consumption.

[17] Horowitz and Horowitz [1965] found wine and spirits to have no significant effect upon the demand for beer. Johnson and Oksanen [1977] and Clements and Johnson [1983] found that wine had no significant impact while spirits had a small but positive impact upon the demand for beer.

[18] These firms were retained in the sample because non-beer revenues typically accounted for less than ten percent of total revenue and in order to increase the sample size.

where:

P = revenue per thousand barrels;
Rq = the quantity of physical output when firm i is a regional producer, zero otherwise;
Nq = the quantity of physical output when firm i is a national producer, zero otherwise;
Iq = the quantity of physical output of the three dominant rivals inside firm i's own strategic group;
Oq = the quantity of physical output of all dominant rivals outside firm i's own strategic group;
RA = the number of advertising messages per brand when firm i is a regional producer, zero otherwise;
NA = the number of advertising messages per brand when firm i is a national producer, zero otherwise;
IA = the number of advertising messages per brand of the three dominant rivals inside firm i's own strategic group;
OA = the number of advertising messages per brand of all dominant rivals outside firm i's own strategic group;
M = the quantity of imported beer;
POP = the population of twenty to forty-four year olds;
y = *per capita* income;
N = a national dummy variable which equals one if firm i is a national producer and zero otherwise;
CO = a conglomerate dummy variable;
e = the disturbance term.

This specification assumes that q and Z are separable in the effective output function and that demand can be approximated by a linear function.[19] In addition this specification allows strategic variable slope parameters to differ for national and regional producers (b_1, b_2, b_5, and b_6) and for firm i's inside and outside strategic group competitors (b_3, b_4, b_7, and b_8). A national producer dummy variable is added to the demand function in order to capture any additional demand asymmetries which may exist between national and regional producers.

Before turning to the empirical results, an economic interpretation of the parameters is warranted. First, b_1 through b_4 and b_9 should each be negative since brewers are not price takers.[20] Since an increase in the advertising of a firm's product, relative to that of its competitors, should increase its demand,

[19] Since there is no *a priori* reason for functional form selection, a linear specification was chosen. Results from alternative functional forms are discussed in section IV. The five firm concentration ratio rose from 23% to 74% between 1950 and 1978, and one might think that the elasticity of demand decreased as concentration rose. However, Lynk [1984] did not find this to be the case. No other time or group asymmetries were detected.

[20] Both Greer [1981] and Ornstein [1981] argue that U.S. brewers have market power.

b_5 and b_6 should be positive and greater than b_7 and b_8. Demand should increase with the drinking age population; therefore, b_{10} should be positive.

Although previous analyses of the impact of income upon the demand for beer has been extensive, results have been conflicting. Hogarty and Elzinga [1973] and Clements and Johnson [1983] found beer to be a normal good. Johnson and Oksanen [1977] and McGuinness [1980] discovered income to have a neutral effect upon the demand for beer. Finally, Niskanen [1962] and Lynk [1984] found beer to be an inferior good. Therefore, the expected sign of b_{11} is unknown *a priori.*

This specification allows one to test for the presence of demand asymmetries which might generate strategic groups in the U.S. brewing industry. The hypothesis that national and regional demand asymmetries exist would be rejected if the following joint linear restriction is found to be valid.[21]

$$(3) \qquad b_1 = b_2;\ b_3 = b_4;\ b_5 = b_6;\ b_7 = b_8;\ b_{12} = 0$$

For example, the research of Ackoff and Emshoff and Mueller and Rogers suggests that nationals may be better able, because of their size advantage and ability to use national television advertising, to create a premium image. This implies that b_6 wiould be greater than b_5. In addition, the theory of strategic groups suggests that greater rivalry exists inside groups than between them; therefore, b_7 would be less than b_8.

IV. EMPIRICAL RESULTS

The nature of the data used in this study creates a number of estimation problems. Since brewing companies had market power between 1950 and 1977, firm output is endogenous. In addition, advertising messages are assumed to be predetermined at the beginning of each year; however, advertising expenditures were measured with error.[22] Consequently, an instrumental variable technique is used to handle these problems.[23] The data set used in this study is pooled, and, given the time series component of the data set, serial correlation might be a problem. An autocorrelation correction

[21] Acceptance of this hypothesis does not preclude the possibility that strategic groups were generated by differences in cost conditions. Tremblay [1984] found evidence that cost asymmetries between national and regional producers exist.

[22] This measurement problem is discussed in the Appendix.

[23] If these endogeneity and measurement error problems are ignored, least squares parameter estimates would be biased and inconsistent. The following variables were used as instruments: brewing workers' hourly wage rate, weighted average price of materials used in brewing, weighted average price of advertising, interest rate on ten year Treasury bonds, firm assets, the number of brands offered by the firm's inside group rivals, the number of brands offered by the firm's outside group rivals, a merger dummy variable which equals one when the firm merged with another firm, the industry five firm concentration ratio, the number of barrels produced by the industry, total industry advertising expenditures, a time trend, and all exogenous variables in the demand function. This procedure assumes that physical output and advertising messages are correlated with all predetermined variables from the firm's demand function, cost function, and important industry structure and conduct variables.

TABLE II
DEMAND FUNCTION PARAMETER ESTIMATES

Variable	*Parameter*	*Parameter Estimates*	*t-ratios*
Intercept	b_0	−14493	−5.914[a]
Rq	b_1	−2.8511	−5.144[a]
Nq	b_2	−0.4034	−4.416[a]
Iq	b_3	−2.0106	−7.715[a]
Oq	b_4	−1.4715	−3.640[a]
RA	b_5	1.3829	0.706
NA	b_6	3.0608	2.093[b]
IA	b_7	−0.0039	−1.627[c]
OA	b_8	0.5219	4.017[a]
M	b_9	−8.4071	−6.060[a]
POP	b_{10}	3.5257	7.410[a]
y	b_{11}	−4.7738	−2.144[b]
N	b_{12}	795.12	0.093
CO	b_{13}	3703.5	2.987[a]

Adjusted $R^2 = 0.8907$
[a] significant at the one percent level
[b] significant at the five percent level
[c] significant at the ten percent level

is made with a different correction for each strategic group.[24] Large brewers seem to face less variation in demand than smaller brewers; therefore, heteroscedasticity might also be a problem. Heteroscedasticity is detected using a Goldfeld and Quandt [1965] test, and it is eliminated by using weighted least squares.[25]

The estimated parameters, their *t*-ratios and the R^2 of the regression are presented in Table II. This model yields expected signs for all parameters, a high degree of significance, and a high R^2. All output parameters, b_1, b_2, b_3,

[24] This process was considered since an autoregressive process of sufficiently large degree can approximate any stationary stochastic process (Harvey [1981, p. 203]). A technique described by Judge *et al.* [1980, p. 190] was used to test for a fourth order autocorrelation process. This technique requires that the ρ's are tested for significance using the following regression.

$$e_t = \rho_1 e_{t-1} + \rho_2 e_{t-2} + \rho_3 e_{t-3} + \rho_4 e_{t-4} + u$$

where e equals the predicted residuals from regression equation (2), t equals the time period, and u equals the error term. A separate regression was run on residuals for national (N) and regional (R) producers since the error structure is probably different for these two groups. The error structure for both groups followed a second order autoregressive process with ρ estimates equaling:

$$\rho_{1N} = 0.43139,$$
$$\rho_{2N} = 0.253514,$$
$$\rho_{1R} = 0.968676, \text{ and}$$
$$\rho_{2R} = -0.061819.$$

This error structure is stationary for both groups since $\rho_{1i} + \rho_{2i} < 1$ and $-1 < \rho_{2i} < 1 \, \forall i = N$ and R.

[25] The weight equaled the square root of assets.

and b_4, have a significant negative impact upon demand, implying that neither national nor regional producers are price takers.

Advertising has an important influence on the demand for an individual firm's product. Advertising by both national and regional producers has a positive impact upon demand; however, this effect is not significantly different from zero for regional producers. The greater impact of a national firm's advertising may have been due to marketing advantages for large scale advertisers. The impact of dominant rivals' advertising upon a firm's demand is found to be negative and significant for rivals inside the firm's strategic group while positive and significant for outside strategic group rivals. The advertising of rivals from within a firm's own strategic group decreases firm demand while outside group rivals' advertising increases firm demand. Advertising rivalry is more detrimental to a firm's demand within groups as predicted by the strategic group literature. The positive sign for b_8 may seem disturbing since it suggests that advertising from outside a firm's own strategic group has spillover effects.[26] However, similar advertising spillover effects were observed in the cigarette industry.[27] Furthermore, these spillover effects are relatively small, since b_8 is less than b_6 and b_5. This indicates that if a firm increases its advertising effort, its market share would rise and its rivals' market share would fall even though b_8 is positive.

It was hypothesized that two strategic groups have been present in the U.S. brewing industry between 1950 and 1977. Using an F-test, the validity of restriction (3) from section III is rejected at the 0.0001 level of significance. This implies that demand asymmetries between national and regional producers did exist. Important differences between groups appear to be that nationals are better able to generate a premium image than regionals, $b_6 > b_5$, and that advertising and production rivalry are more rigorous from inside the firm's own strategic group, $b_7 < b_8$ and $b_3 < b_4$.

The impact of market variables is as expected. Imports have a significant negative impact and population has a significant positive impact upon demand. There has been some debate over whether or not beer is a normal good. Results found here imply that beer is an inferior good; consumers drink more beer in recessions and less in boom periods.[28] This is consistent with the results found by Niskanen and Lynk. In addition, the national dummy variable parameter is not significantly different from zero. This suggests that the model adequately captures the main demand differences between groups. As expected, the conglomerate dummy variable does control for non-beer revenues.

[26] One might suspect a specification error generated this spillover effect. Sensitivity results described at the end of this section suggest that it is unlikely that the functional form is incorrect. The absence of Miller, a large advertiser in the 1970s and 1980s, may have biased the results, but Miller's advertising data were included in rivals' advertising levels.

[27] See Hallagan and Joerding [1983, p. 198].

[28] This of course may not be true for particular brands. In recessions consumers may drink more popular priced and less premium priced beer.

One might be curious to know how sensitive these results are to various functional forms. As a result, three alternative specifications were analysed: a log linear, a semi-log linear, and a linear system of separate demand functions for national and regional producers.[29] Results from each supported the hypothesis that strategic group demand asymmetries have existed in the U.S. brewing industry between 1950 and 1977. The only significant sign reversals occurred on the *Oq* parameter in the semi-log specification and on the *Iq* parameter in the regional demand function from the system of equations.

V. CONCLUSIONS

Several interesting results have emerged from this study. First, significant differences in the demand for nationals' and regionals' beer do seem to exist. Second, nationals appear to have a marketing advantage over regionals, perhaps because they are large scale advertisers. Third, advertising and production rivalry from inside, relative to outside, a firm's strategic group can have a more detrimental effect upon the firm's demand. Finally, beer is found to be an inferior good.

These results support Caves and Porter's theory of strategic groups. The impact of strategic variables between national and regional producers and between rivals inside and outside a firm's own strategic group are different. In addition, these results at least partially explain the decline in numbers of regional producers between 1950 and 1977. Regionals have a marketing disadvantage since each dollar spent on advertising by a regional producer is less effective, relative to that spent by a national producer, in increasing demand. The high risk of a new national advertising campaign and the high sunk cost needed to go national may have been great enough to keep regionals out of the successful national strategic group.

Because of data limitations, these results can only be interpreted as preliminary. In order to better understand the nature of strategic groups in brewing one would need to estimate demand functions by brand and total cost functions by strategic group. However, these results are theoretically appealing in spite of these limitations.

VICTOR J. TREMBLAY,
Department of Economics,
Kansas State University,
Manhattan, KS 66506,
USA.

ACCEPTED MARCH 1985

[29] In the log specifications only variables which took non-zero values were transformed into logs. In the model with separate demand functions, a three stage least stage technique was used with corresponding market variable parameters constrained to be equal.

APPENDIX

THE SAMPLE, MEASUREMENT OF VARIABLES, AND SOURCES OF DATA

The number of firms available for this study was limited by the data availability for the output and advertising variables. *Advertising Age*, the source of these variables, only published brewery data when the firm's yearly output exceeded one million barrels of beer. A truncated sample exists when knowledge of variables is only available when output exceeds a certain level. If the usual least squares technique was used on such a sample, parameter estimates would have been biased. A number of relatively small breweries were contacted to see if the sample could be enlarged and made more representative. Two of these breweries agreed to provide data under the condition that their identities and data remain confidential.

It was maintained that the addition of these two smaller regionals eliminated the truncation problem. Brewers can be classified into groups of national, regional, and boutique brewers. Boutique brewers are not considered a part of the U.S. brewing industry since they offer expensive specialty products which compete mainly with imported brands. Thus, the breweries of interest to this study include national and regional producers. With the addition of two small regionals, the sample becomes quite representative of the relevant U.S. brewers from 1950–1977.

The final sample included annual data from twenty-two brewing companies: three out of the four national producers, seventeen large regional producers, and the two additional small regional brewers. Because some firms exited the industry before 1977 and data for each variable were not available for each year, the final sample included only 316 observations of pooled data. Information in Table I was produced from a sample which included all four national producers, all regional producers with an annual output level greater than one million barrels, and the two small regional breweries described above. This sample contained thirty-three firms and 620 observations. Data sources are listed below.

All input and output prices were put in real terms by deflating them by the wholesale price index and the consumer price index respectively, taken from the *U.S. Bureau of Labor Statistics*. Physical output was measured in thousands of barrels of beer sold per year. These data were taken from *Advertising Age*. The quantity of imports was measured in thousands of barrels and taken from *Brewers Almanac*. The price of a firm's representative product was defined as the firm's revenue per thousand barrels of beer. Revenue (minus beer excise taxes) data were taken from *Moody's Industrial Manual* and *Moody's OTC Industrial Manual*.

A measure of advertising messages was developed in the following way. Firm advertising expenditures were taken from *Advertising Age*. They included firm expenditures on television, radio, and printed material; however, radio advertising expenditures were not available for 1950 through 1956 and newspaper advertising expenditures were not available for 1971. Advertising messages were obtained by dividing advertising expenditures by a price index for advertising. This variable was measured in thousands.

A separate advertising price index was developed for each strategic group. It was defined as the weighted average price of the six major media (national and spot television, national and spot radio, magazines, and newspapers) used to advertise beer. The weights were defined as the average fraction spent on each media by each group over the entire time period data were available. The price of advertising to a thousand media observers for each of the six media was taken from Schmalensee [1972] for 1950–1966 and Sterling and Haight [1978] for 1966–1977. Firm advertising expenditures by media were available from *Leading National*

Advertisers for 1957–1973, 1975, and 1977. In order to obtain the number of advertising messages per brand, the total number of brands sold by a firm was collected from *Moody's Industrial Manual*, *Moody's OTC Industrial Manual*, and various firm reports.

Population was measured as the total U.S. population of twenty to forty-four year olds and income was measured as *per capita* income. Both variables were measured in thousands and taken from the *U.S. Bureau of the Census.*

The prices of inputs used in the production of beer were also collected. The price of labor was measured as the average hourly wage for laborers in brewing as published by *Brewers Almanac*. The price of capital was measured as the yield, in percent, on ten year Treasury bonds, taken from *Moody's Bond Survey.*

The price of materials was defined as the weighted average price of the major materials used in brewing. Material prices and quantities were only available at the industry level; therefore, to develop this index it was necessary to assume all firms were material price takers and used the same proportion of inputs. Only materials which contributed at least 0.1 pounds per barrel of beer were considered. They included: corn, rice, sugar, barley, malting barley, and hops. Weights were defined as the proportion of pounds per barrel of each material to total pounds per barrel of the six materials considered. The input prices were taken from *Commodity Yearbook* and *Agricultural Statistics*, and quantities per barrel were taken from *Brewers Almanac.* Since firms were assumed to be input price takers and to use the same proportion of each material, the materials price index was constant across firms.

A number of industry variables were used in this study. They included the five firm concentration ratio taken from Ornstein [1981] and Greer [1971], the number of firms, industry output measured in thousands of barrels, and industry advertising expenditures measured in thousands of dollars, all of which were taken from *Brewers Almanac.*

REFERENCES

Ackoff, R. and Emshoff, J., 1975a, 'Advertising Research at Anheuser-Busch, Inc. (1963–68)', *Sloan Management Review*, 16, 2 (Winter), pp. 1–15.

Ackoff, R. and Emshoff, J., 1975b, 'Advertising Research at Anheuser-Busch, Inc. (1963–68)', *Sloan Management Review*, 16, 3 (Spring), pp. 1–15.

Advertising Age, 1978, 'Brewers Tap Package Goods Expertise', (January 23), p. 3.

Advertising Age, 1981, 'What Went Wrong?' (Parts I and II), (April 13 and April 20), p. 61 and p. 49.

Agricultural Statistics, 1980, U.S. Department of Agriculture.

Allison, R. and Uhl, K., 1964, 'Influence of Beer Identification on Taste Perception', *Journal of Marketing Research*, 1, 3 (August), pp. 36–39.

Brewers Almanac, various years, Washington, D.C., United States Brewers Association.

Business Week, 1980, 'Schlitz Brew of Old and New', (May 12), p. 31.

Caves, R. and Porter, M., 1977, 'From Entry Barriers to Mobility Barriers: Conjectural Decisions and Contrived Deterrence to New Competition', *Quarterly Journal of Economics*, 91, 2 (May), pp. 241–261.

Clements, K. and Johnson, L., 1983, 'The Demand for Beer, Wine, and Spirits: A Systemwide Analysis', *Journal of Business*, 56, 3 (July), pp. 273–304.

Commodity Yearbook, various years, Commodity Research Bureau, Inc., New York.

Demsetz, H., 1979, 'Accounting for Advertising as a Barrier to Entry', *Journal of Business*, 52, 3 (July), pp. 345–360.

Dielman, T., 1983, 'Pooled Cross-Section and Time Series Data: A Survey of Current Statistical Methodology', *The American Statistician*, 37, 2 (May), pp. 111–112.

ELZINGA, K., 1973, 'The Restructuring of the U.S. Brewing Industry', *Industrial Organization Review*, 1, 2, pp. 101–114.

ELZINGA, K., 1982, 'The Beer Industry', in W. ADAMS (Ed.) *The Structure of American Industry* (The MacMillan Co., sixth edition), pp. 189–215.

Forbes, 1963, 'Counterattack', (July 15), p. 22.

Fortune, 1972, 'While the Big Brewers Quaff, The Little Ones Thirst', (November), pp. 103–107.

GOLDFELD, S. and QUANDT, R., 1965, 'Some Tests for Homoscedasticity', *Journal of the American Statistical Association*, 60, 310 (June), pp. 539–547.

GRABOWSKI, H., 1977–78, 'The Effects of Advertising on Intraindustry Shifts in Demand', *Explorations in Economic Research*, 4, 5 (Winter–Spring), pp. 675–701.

GREEN, H. A. J., 1976, *Consumer Theory* (Academic Press, New York).

GREER, D., 1971, 'Product Differentiation and Concentration in the Brewing Industry', *Journal of Industrial Economics*, 19, 3 (July), pp. 201–219.

GREER, D., 1980, *Industrial Organization and Public Policy* (Macmillan Publishing Co., Inc., New York).

GREER, D., 1981, 'The Causes of Concentration in the U.S. Brewing Industry', *Quarterly Review of Economics and Business*, 21, 4 (Winter), pp. 87–106.

HALLAGAN, W. and JOERDING, W., 1983, 'Polymorphic Equilibrium in Advertising', *Bell Journal of Economics*, 14, 1 (Spring), pp. 191–201.

HARVEY, A., 1981, *The Econometric Analysis of Time Series* (Halsted Press, New York).

HATTEN, K. and SCHENDEL, D., 1977, 'Heterogeneity Within an Industry: Firm Conduct in the U.S. Brewing Industry, 1952–1971', *Journal of Industrial Economics*, 26, 2 (December) pp. 97–113.

HOGARTY, T. and ELZINGA, K., 1972, 'The Demand for Beer', *Review of Economics and Statistics*, 54, 2 (May), pp. 195–198.

HOROWITZ, I. and HOROWITZ, A., 1965, 'Firms in a Declining Market: The Brewing Case', *Journal of Industrial Economics*, 13, 2 (March), pp. 129–153.

JOHNSON, J. and OKSANEN, E., 1974, 'Socio-Economic Determinants of the Consumption of Alcoholic Beverages', *Applied Economics*, 6, 4 (December), pp. 293–301.

JOHNSON, J. and OKSANEN, E., 1977, 'Estimation of Demand for Alcoholic Beverages in Canada from Pooled Time Series and Cross Sections', *Review of Economics and Statistics*, 59, 1 (February), pp. 113–118.

JUDGE, G., GRIFFITHS, W., HILL, R. and LEE, T., 1980, *The Theory and Practice of Econometrics* (John Wiley and Sons, New York).

KEITHAHN, C., 1978, 'The Brewing Industry', Staff Report of the Bureau of Economics, Washington, U.S. Federal Trade Commission, (December).

KELTON, C. and KELTON, D., 1982, 'Advertising and Intraindustry Brand Shifts in the U.S. Brewing Industry', *Journal of Industrial Economics*, 30, 3 (March), pp. 293–303.

LEFFLER, K., 1982, 'Ambiguous Changes in Product Quality', *American Economic Review*, 72, 5 (December), pp. 956–967.

LELAND, H., 1977, 'Quality Choice and Competition', *American Economic Review*, 67, 2 (March), pp. 127–137.

LYNK, W., 1984, 'Interpreting Rising Concentration: The Case of Beer', *Journal of Business*, 57, 1 (January), pp. 43–55.

MCCONNELL, J., 1968, 'The Price-Quality Relationship in an Experimental Setting', *Journal of Marketing Research*, 5, 3 (August), pp. 300–304.

MCGUINNESS, T., 1980, 'An Econometric Analysis of Total Demand for Alcoholic Beverages in the U.K., 1956–1975', *Journal of Industrial Economics*, 29, 1 (September), pp. 85–109.

Moody's Bond Survey, various years, Moody's Investors Service, New York.

Moody's Industrial Manual, various years, Moody's Investors Service, New York.
Moody's OTC Industrial Manual, various years, Moody's Investors Service, New York.
MUELLER, W., 1978, Testimony in Hearings, Mergers, and Industrial Concentration, U.S. Senate Committee on the Judiciary, Subcommittee on Antitrust and Monopoly, 95th Congress, 2nd Session (May 12).
MUELLER, W. and ROGERS, R., 1980, 'The Role of Advertising in Changing Concentration of Manufacturing Industries', *Review of Economics and Statistics*, 62, 1 (February), pp. 89–96.
National Advertising Investments, various years, Leading National Advertisers, Inc., New York.
NELSON, P., 1974, 'Advertising As Information', *Journal of Political Economy*, 82, 4 (July/August), pp. 729–754.
NEWMAN, H., 1978, 'Strategic Groups and the Structure-Performance Relationship', *Review of Economics and Statistics*, 60, 3 (August), pp. 417–427.
NISKANEN, W., 1962, 'The Demand for Alcoholic Beverages: An Experiment in Econometric Method', The Rand Corporation, Mimeo., Santa Monica.
ORNSTEIN, S., 1981, 'Antitrust Policy and Market Forces as Determinants of Industry Structure: Case Histories in Beer and Distilled Spirits', *Antitrust Bulletin*, 26, 2 (Summer), pp. 281–313.
OSTER, S., 1982, 'Intraindustry Structure and the Ease of Strategic Change', *Review of Economics and Statistics*, 64, 3 (August), pp. 376–383.
PORTER, M., 1979, 'The Structure Within Industries and Companies' Performance', *Review of Economics and Statistics*, 61, 2 (May), pp. 214–227.
SCHMALENSEE, R., 1972, *The Economics of Advertising* (North-Holland Publishing Co., Inc., New York).
SPADY, R. and FRIEDLAENDER, A., 1978, 'Hedonic Cost Functions for the Regulated Trucking Industry', *Bell Journal of Economics*, 9, 1 (Spring), pp. 159–179.
STERLING, C. and HAIGHT, T., 1978, *The Mass Media* (Praeger Publishers, New York).
TREMBLAY, V., 1984, 'Costs, Economies of Scale, and Strategic Groups in the U.S. Brewing Industry', Kansas State University Working Paper (December).
U.S. Bureau of the Census, 1980, Washington, Government Printing Office.
U.S. Department of Labor, 1980, Bureau of Labor Statistics.
Wall Street Journal, 1983, 'New Little Breweries Cause Some Ferment in the Beer Business', (March 15), p. 1.

THE JOURNAL OF INDUSTRIAL ECONOMICS 0022–1821 $2.00
Volume XXXIV December 1985 No. 2

EFFECTS OF AUSTRALIAN INTERNATIONAL AIR TRANSPORT REGULATION*

CHRISTOPHER C. FINDLAY

International civil aviation is subject to regulation by governments. A model of civil aviation demand and supply in competitive markets is presented. Four different approaches to regulation are then identified. These all involve attempts to control entry and flight frequency, but with different motivations and different degrees of effectiveness. These regulatory practices are then imposed on the market model. Predictions are derived and checked against observed results of Australian regulation. These are used to generate upper and lower bound estimates of the welfare cost of Australian regulation.

I. INTRODUCTION

INTERNATIONAL civil aviation is characterised by persistent and pervasive regulation. The aim of this paper is to choose one from a number of models of the regulatory process in Australia and to estimate the significance of the burden imposed on consumers.

The method is to present a basic model which captures the significant characteristics of an air transport system and then to depict pricing and capacity rules which represent different regulatory systems. The depiction suggests tests for deciding which system corresponds to the actual regulatory policy. The model of regulation chosen is then used to estimate its welfare cost.

The sovereignty of a country over its air space has become a convention in international relations. Countries have enforced this power and, subsequently, international air services can only be provided by the agreement of countries at both ends of a route. The mechanism is a series of bilateral agreements in which countries agree to exchange access rights. The agreements also determine which airlines can operate on routes between the parties, how much capacity those airlines can offer and how fares will be set. This system is characterised below as control of capacity, fares and entry. Variants of this basic policy operate in all countries. Also the basic policy, until recently, corresponded to Australian policy. Towards the end of 1981, there was a major change in Australian policy when control of money fares

* An earlier version of this paper was presented at the 10th EARIE Conference in Bergen. Work on the paper was supported by the ASEAN-Australia Joint Research Project. Thanks are due to Prue Phillips for programming assistance, and to an anonymous referee for helpful comments. All errors are due to the author.

was relaxed while control of entry and capacity was maintained.[1] The effects of this policy change are estimated below. The change made legitimate a practice already common in other countries, and thus the Australian experience has wide relevance.

II. MODELS OF REGULATION

II.1 *Air transport model*

The model[2] of an air transport system is depicted in Figure 1. The curves resemble the standard relationships from the theory of the firm but they are given a different interpretation. The curves are the sum of costs incurred by the firm and costs of travel incurred by passengers.

For simplicity, it is assumed that the costs of providing air transport on the route and over the time period to which the model refers are related only to the total capacity on the route and not the actual number of passenger trips. Also it is assumed that the capacity of each flight is fixed. Therefore, the firm's costs depend only on the number of flights offered (F) and not the number of passengers (T). Cost per flight is assumed to be constant. The average cost

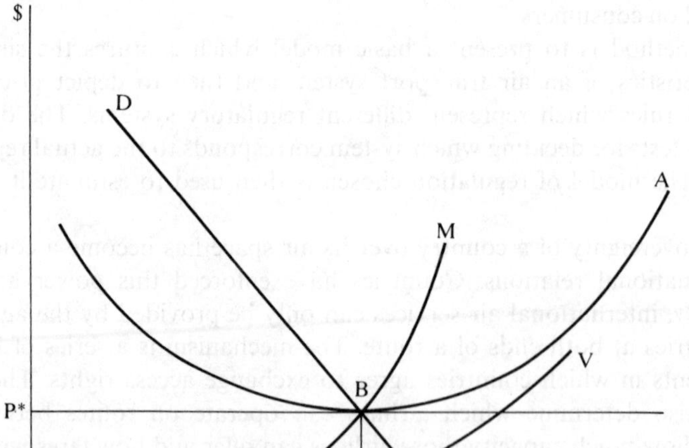

Figure 1

[1] See Findlay [1983a] for more detail of Australian regulation and the policy changes.
[2] This model is formally presented and Figure 1 derived in Findlay [1983b].

curve (A) is drawn for a given number of flights. Average cost includes the average costs of capacity but also costs incurred by passengers which are described below. Each point on the long run average cost curve (LA) corresponds to a different level of capacity.

Passengers pay a money fare but also they face costs due to delay or inconvenience. These costs occur because demand for a flight at a particular time is stochastic. As a result there is a chance the flight will be full. Failure to obtain a seat at the ideal departure time generates delay or inconvenience by having to wait or to change plans. The probability of delay rises with the load factor.

The V (average variable cost) curve measures the cost of stochastic delay per passenger. It is the product of the probability of having to wait and the cost of the wait. V rises as T increases for a given frequency because the load factor increases.

The M (marginal) cost curve is the marginal cost associated with the A curve. It is equal to the sum of V plus the effect on total cost of an extra passenger. In this model, the marginal effect on total cost is the addition to delay faced by all other passengers.[3]

An increase in capacity, or flight frequency, shifts the set of curves to the right. In the conditions described here the minimum point of the A will be at the same unit cost and therefore the LA curve is horizontal.[4]

Demand is assumed to be a function of the full cost of travel, that is, the sum of the money fare and the cost of delay. A demand schedule (D) is also depicted in Figure 1.

The optimal solution is point B where the demand curve cuts the long run average cost curve. At B, the cost of delay is QC and the money fare is BC. The money fare is interpreted as an optimal congestion toll, since it is equal to the congestion imposed on other passengers by the marginal traveller.[5] This toll ensures that available capacity is efficiently utilised. Optimal frequency minimises the average (full) cost of travel. Profits at the optimum will be zero,[6] and the optimal solution can be provided by competition.[7]

[3] Let C be total cost, d be the unit cost of delay and k be the constant cost per flight; then

$$C = kF + Td$$
$$A = kF/T + d$$
$$M = d + Td_T, \qquad d_T > 0$$
$$V = d$$

[4] The LA curve is found by minimising $R = kF + Td$ by choosing F for a given T. The solution is to choose F so that $k = -Td_F$. The envelope curve is then $LA = d - Fd_F$. Its marginal curve is $LM = d + Td_T$. The difference $(LA - LM) = -(Fd_F + Td_T)$ is zero when delay is a function of only the load factor, as assumed here. The relevance of this special case is justified in Findlay [1982].

[5] The difference between the M curve and the V curve is Td_T. See footnote 3.

[6] Total cost of capacity is kF and total revenue will be $T^2 d_T$; then, since $k = -Td_F$, profit at the optimum is $T(Td_T + Fd_F)$ which is zero. This is a standard result; see Mohring [1976, Chapter 3].

[7] See Findlay [1983b] for more discussion of the process of competition and see De Vany and Saving [1983] for this result in an equivalent model.

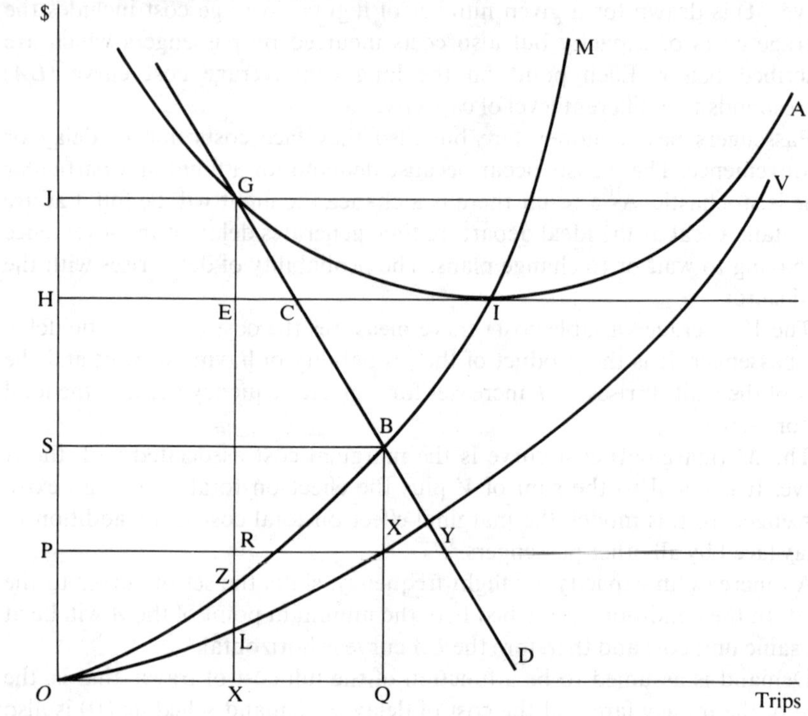

Figure 2

II.2 *Models of regulation*

Regulatory policy has been to control entry, capacity and fares. There are various combinations of fares and frequencies which could be adopted under regulation and these are depicted in Figure 2.

There are various levels of long run average cost depicted in Figure 2. The *LA* curve corresponding to the lowest costs available is the horizontal line at *P*. Higher levels like *H* or *J* might be observed because regulation protects an inherently high cost carrier or it permits inefficiency to develop. Point *Y* will be the competitive solution in the absence of regulation; *P* is the minimum full cost of travel per passenger.

There are four models of regulation to consider. Before identifying these models, it is helpful to specify the airlines operating in the industry. First, there is the flag carrier of the home country (in this application, Qantas). Second, there is the flag carrier from the country at the other end of a route (for example, British Airways, on the Europe–Australia (Kangaroo) route). Attention is restricted to the case of two flag carriers which have a very large share of traffic on the route. There could also be other airlines from third countries serving both destinations. This is unavoidable given the connections between routes and the bargaining power of countries located in strategic positions on long routes. This feature of air transport is stressed in one of the regulatory models presented below. There could also be other airlines based in a number of countries which are potential competitors on the route but which are excluded by the regulatory system.

(i) *Break-even regulation.* It is assumed, initially, that there are two flag carriers from different countries operating on a route and that these airlines have similar costs. The aim of regulators in both countries is to permit each flag carrier to break-even. The constraint is that the full cost of travel to consumers should be minimised. If the long run average cost of the protected carrier corresponds to OJ, then given the demand curve D, the regulatory solution will be point G.

The rationale for this model is discussed in Findlay [1985]. Briefly, its origin is the monopoly power countries have over access to their air space. They have incentives to exercise that power to extract rents from foreigners, as in the optimal tariff case in international trade. Other countries will always retaliate to this action and the result will be a negotiated solution, which we now observe, with "flag carriers" breaking-even, on average. Of course, there would be a gain from leaving point G and moving to Y, perhaps by contracting out provision of air transport services to least-cost carriers operating under the bilateral agreement. An argument against this change has been, implicitly, that there are monitoring costs involved and that having a national flag carrier, which continues to break-even, provides valuable information for the negotiations. The break-even constraint could be due to some perception of the costs of financing a subsidy.

The mechanics of regulation should be made explicit. Only total frequency need be controlled to reach a point like G. Attempted control of frequency, and thereby capacity, is a feature of the international regulatory system. Reasons why this control may not be effective are examined below and those reasons suggest an alternative model of regulation. Also frequency control can permit capacity to be offered by airlines from third countries. If third country airlines have relatively low costs, they can earn profits if the regulatory solution is at point G.

The model could be complicated by assuming the flag carriers have significantly different costs or the regulators have motivations other than achieving a break-even solution. A case of the latter variation is examined below. The assumption of unequal costs would mean the regulators negotiate a compromise solution, but this would not significantly alter the analysis or results below. The assumption of similar costs of operation by the flag carriers is retained in discussion of the other models of regulation.

(ii) *Mark-up model.* In this model the protected carriers may or may not have higher costs than potential competitors but they act jointly to extract profits from the route, and this strategy is sanctioned by regulation. Let the relevant *LA* curve correspond to *OH* and the observed full fare be *OJ*. Profit will be earned by minimising the full cost of travel but charging a mark-up on that full cost. The mark-up is equal to *HJ* in Figure 2. In the extreme case, profits (the box *JGEH*) may be maximised. The rationale for this model is that the regulators have always been pressured by, or, since the introduction of regulation, captured by rent-seeking factor owners.

(iii) *Excess capacity model.* This model is a variant on the first. The problem is that regulators find it difficult in international negotiations to effectively restrict capacity. The incentive for entry is present because, under the break-even model, some low cost carriers can earn profits at the regulated money fare. The ability to gain access arises from bargaining power in international relations. For example, countries located along a long route can use the need for technical stops, and their air space sovereignty, to bargain for access to traffic on the longer route. A case study of this bargaining on the Kangaroo route through South-East Asia is reported in Findlay [1983a]. The aim of the regulators in this model is to allow the targets of the policy to break-even. Since frequency is excessive, the regulators must set a higher money fare to earn zero profits.

This case can also be illustrated in Figure 2. Suppose the *LA* curve of the target airlines corresponds to the horizontal line at *H*. Then suppose the actual frequency corresponds to the *A* curve in the figure. In order for the target airlines to break-even, the regulators will have to set a money fare equal to *GL*. Therefore the regulators set a money fare in response to the observed frequency and, in this model, it is assumed that the fare set can be enforced. The regulated fare exceeds the optimal toll, which is always the difference between the *M* and *V* curves and is equal to *LZ*. The full cost of travel is not minimised under this regulatory policy, but the target airlines will earn zero profits.

The outcome in the excess capacity model can be contrasted with the effects of US domestic regulation (see, for example, Douglas and Miller [1974]). That policy can be characterised as control of fares without control of capacity. In Figure 2, if the money fare were set equal to *GL*, frequency would increase until the *A* curve was tangential to the demand curve. Profits would be zero, only low cost operators would survive but consumers would bear a cost because of the price control. In the excess capacity model, there is some expansion of capacity but not necessarily to the same extent as predicted in models of US domestic regulation.

(iv) *Discounting model.* There will always be competitive pressure on the regulatory solution in the excess capacity model. This pressure will be to shift to the profit maximising position for the minimum cost carriers, given the capacity available. This point is where the *M* curve cuts the demand curve at point *B*. The money fare would then be *BX* which is also the optimal toll,

TABLE I
MODELS OF REGULATION

Model	*Flag Carrier Profits*	*Full Cost Level*
Break-even	Zero	Minimised
Excess capacity	Zero	Not minimised
Discounting	Negative	Not minimised
Mark-up	Positive	Minimised

given the demand curve and existing capacity. Discounting occurs, not directly because some airlines have lower costs but because regulated fares exceed the level that generates efficient use of existing capacity. In this case, capacity is excessive but regulators cannot enforce a money fare, as they were assumed to do in the excess capacity model.

Point *B* is the extreme solution in the discounting model. It is reached by airlines offering lower money fares than the regulated level. This practice was strictly illegal in Australia before the recent policy change, but the regulations proved difficult to enforce. To the extent they were effective, the solution will lie on the demand curve to the left of point *B*.

At the solution of the discounting model, the target airlines will earn losses, presuming their *LA* curves are at level *OH*. Also the full cost of travel to consumers will not be minimised.

There are two distinguishing features of these four models. They are (i) the level of flag carrier profits and (ii) the level of the full cost. In the break-even and excess capacity models, profits are zero. Profits are positive in the mark-up model and negative in the discounting model. The full cost of travel is minimised in the mark-up and break-even models but not in the excess capacity or discounting models. These relationships are summarised in Table I. Data on these variables can be used to distinguish which model is relevant.

It seems reasonable to immediately exclude the mark-up model in the current application. Profits of the target airline of Australian regulation (Qantas) have not been at super-normal levels.[8] It is possible that other factor owners have earned rents and that these have been reflected in Qantas' costs. There is evidence that pilots have earned rents (see Findlay [1984]). This rent seeking activity is more likely to reflect exploitation by various groups of factor owners of the regulatory environment than the deliberate operations of the system to make transfers to those groups. It must be admitted, however, that these models are difficult to distinguish. The next section contains data that can be used to distinguish the other three models.

[8] Using data from Qantas annual reports, the geometric average rate of return on funds employed was estimated in the range 3–6 percent over the decade to 1983–84. This is lower than the estimated return on a representative portfolio of shares on the stock market of 9.5 percent over the same period. This rate was estimated using data in Swan [1983]. Use of the market portfolio for a target rate of return implies a systematic risk (beta) coefficient of unity.

TABLE II

CURRENT FARES AND LOADS AND FULL-FARE MINIMISING LOADS, 1981

Route	*Average Aircraft Size* (1)	*Actual Load Factor* (2)	*Actual Money Fare* $A (3)	*Actual Cost of Delay* $A (4)	*Actual Full Fare* $A (5)	*Passenger Revenue Per Flight* $A (6)	*Predicted Load Factor* (7)	*Predicted Optimal Toll* $A (8)	*Predicted Cost of Delay* $A (9)	*Predicted Full Fare* $A (10)
PNG	124	0.65	294	40	334	23,520	0.70	271	57	.328
Fiji	234	0.71	220	28	248	36,520	0.74	210	36	246
New Caledonia	429	0.67	155	11	166	44,640	0.77	136	21	157
New Zealand	262	0.70	188	23	211	34,592	0.74	178	31	209
Hong Kong	390	0.65	508	10	518	128,524	0.83	397	43	440
Singapore	421	0.69	420	12	432	122,640	0.83	352	38	390
Thailand	376	0.73	550	18	568	150,150	0.84	477	49	526
India	408	0.64	557	9	566	144,263	0.84	423	44	467
Indonesia	377	0.55	338	6	344	70,642	0.80	236	31	267
Malaysia	295	0.55	438	8	446	70,956	0.79	304	41	345
Philippines	307	0.63	455	12	467	87,815	0.81	355	45	400
Japan	306	0.63	723	13	736	140,262	0.83	551	59	610

III. RESULTS

III.1 *Fares, loads and delay*

The models of the previous section applied to a single route. On long journeys a number of sectors will be involved and each sector is a single route in terms of the model. The appropriate pricing rule for long journeys is the sum of the sector fares. The regulatory system could be tested by examining any number of sectors around the world, but attention here is restricted to first-stops out of Australia. There are two reasons. The first is that the data required are readily available for these sectors. Second, all these sectors have in common the influence of the Australian regulators.

Data for 1981 on the dozen routes used in this analysis are reported in Table II. Aircraft size in column (1) varies between routes but on each route it is assumed to be fixed when policy changes. Load factors in column (2) in 1981 lay in the range 55 to 73 percent. The money fare in column (3) is a weighted average of one-way fares by various ticket types out of Sydney filed under the Australian regulatory system, where the weights are based on a 1980 survey of passengers on international flights.

The cost of delay is based on estimates by Douglas and Miller [1974] of the probability of delay in a scheduled air transport service. The probability of delay depends on the load factor and on the capacity of the flight. The cost of inconvenience is assumed throughout to be $200. This figure is the upper limit to the compensation for being bumped-off a Qantas flight when the passenger agrees that the carrier has no further liability. The cost of delay in column (4) is $200 times the probability of not obtaining a seat. At 1981 loads, the cost of delay was very low. The full fare in column (5) is the sum of the money fare and the cost of delay. Revenue in column (6) is the product of the average money fare in column (3) and the number of passengers per flight.

There is a potential inconsistency in these data. The fares in column (3) are based on filed fares. Actual fares charged would be much lower because of the discounting that was occurring at the time. Discounting will increase passenger traffic and tend to raise load factors. Therefore revenue per flight will be an overstatement of actual revenue per flight because the calculation is based on observed traffic but also on fares higher than those actually paid. In the analysis reported below, the revenue estimate is interpreted as the regulators' target revenue per flight but, because passenger loads reflect the influence of discounting, the revenue estimate in column (6) will also exceed this target.

Consider, first, a choice between the break-even and excess capacity models. According to Table I, these models are distinguished by whether or not the full cost of travel is minimised. The problem is then whether the full cost estimates in column (5) of Table II represent the minimum levels given current capacity.

The estimation procedure can be illustrated in Figure 2. Suppose the

TABLE III
CURRENT FARES AND LOADS AND LEVELS UNDER FARE DEREGULATION, 1981

Route	Average Aircraft Size (1)	Actual Load Factor (2)	Actual Money Fare $A (3)	Actual Cost of Delay $A (4)	Actual Full Fare $A (5)	Full Fare Outlay Per Flight $A (6)	Predicted Load Factor (7)	Predicted Optimal Toll $A (8)	Predicted Cost of Delay $A (9)	Predicted Full Fare $A (10)
PNG	124	0.65	294	40	334	26,718	0.70	255	55	305
Fiji	234	0.71	220	28	248	41,140	0.74	202	35	237
New Caledonia	429	0.67	155	11	166	47,871	0.76	126	20	146
New Zealand	262	0.70	188	23	211	38,899	0.74	171	30	201
Hong Kong	390	0.65	508	10	518	131,192	0.83	367	41	408
Singapore	421	0.69	420	12	432	126,288	0.82	328	37	365
Thailand	376	0.73	550	18	568	155,055	0.83	448	47	495
India	408	0.64	557	9	566	146,749	0.83	391	42	433
Indonesia	377	0.55	338	6	344	71,997	0.79	213	29	242
Malaysia	295	0.55	438	8	446	72,372	0.79	274	39	313
Philippines	307	0.63	455	12	467	90,328	0.80	326	42	368
Japan	306	0.63	723	13	736	143,002	0.83	509	56	565

break-even model is operating and the observed full fare is *OJ*. Actual capacity must then correspond to point *G* on the *LA* curve horizontal at level *OJ*. The observed money fare (not shown) will be the optimal toll.

Suppose the excess capacity model is operating. The observed full fare is *OJ* but suppose actual capacity is excessive and corresponds to the *A* curve drawn in Figure 2. The actual money fare is *GL* and revenue is the product of *GL* and the number of passengers carried (*OX*). The full fare is not minimised. The minimum level, given the costs of the target airline, is *OH*, not the actual level of *OJ*. Therefore, the method of choosing between these models is to estimate the minimum fare level like *OH* and compare it to the observed level, *OJ*.

A method of estimating *OH* is suggested by the observation that when *LA* is horizontal, the optimal load factor is constant on a route whatever the level of total capacity. Therefore *OH* can be estimated by considering a single flight rather than total capacity. The constraint is imposed that revenue per flight is the same as the observed levels, since profits are zero in both models.

The next step is to consider a range of load factors, each of which, given aircraft capacity on the route, implies a particular probability of delay, therefore a congestion toll and consequently a particular revenue per flight. The load factor finally chosen generates the target revenue per flight. The full fare implied by this load factor (congestion toll plus delay cost) is then compared to the observed full fare. In terms of Figure 2, this procedure is equivalent to starting at a point near the origin on the *M* curve, moving along that curve, while calculating the money fare as the difference between the *M* and *V* curves until the appropriate revenue is raised (in this case, at point *I*).

The results are shown in columns (7)–(10) of Table II. In all cases, the full fare can be reduced by raising the load factor and charging a lower fare, while raising the same revenue. The money fare is also an optimal congestion toll. The cost of delay increases, because of the higher load factor, but not sufficiently to offset the fall in the money fare. The average decrease in the full fare is 11 percent with a range from 2 to 23 percent.

These results indicate that the full cost of travel was not minimised under the 1981 regulatory system. The results do not support the break-even model but are consistent with the excess capacity model. They are also consistent with the discounting model. In theory, the excess capacity and discounting models are distinguishable by the level of profits of the target airline (see Table I). In practice, the profitability data are not sufficiently precise to distinguish them. Anecdotal evidence, however, supports the discounting model. Discounting money fares has been a persistent problem facing Australian regulators and eventually led to the abandonment of attempts to control fares. The regulations were found to be restricting Qantas' marketing strategies rather than protecting the airline.[9]

[9] See Findlay [1983a] for discussion of market pressure and regulatory responses.

TABLE IV

CURRENT FARES AND LOADS AND FARES UNDER DEREGULATION OF FARES AND CAPACITY, 1981

Route	Average Aircraft Size (1)	Actual Load Factor (2)	Actual Money Fare $A (3)	Actual Cost of Delay $A (4)	Actual Full Fare $A (5)	Passenger Revenue Per Flight $A (6)	Least-Cost Operator $A (7)	Predicted Load Factor (8)	Predicted Optimal Toll $A (9)	Predicted Cost of Delay $A (10)	Predicted Full Fare $A (11)
PNG	124	0.65	294	40	334	23,520	16,464	0.67	198	47	245
Fiji	234	0.71	220	28	248	36,520	25,564	0.72	152	30	182
New Caledonia	429	0.67	155	11	166	44,640	31,248	0.74	98	17	115
New Zealand	262	0.70	188	23	211	34,592	24,214	0.72	129	26	155
Hong Kong	390	0.65	508	10	518	128,524	89,967	0.81	285	35	320
Singapore	421	0.69	420	12	432	122,640	85,848	0.81	252	31	283
Thailand	376	0.73	550	18	568	150,150	105,105	0.82	342	40	382
India	408	0.64	557	9	566	144,263	100,984	0.82	303	35	338
Indonesia	377	0.55	338	6	344	70,642	49,449	0.77	170	26	196
Malaysia	295	0.55	438	8	446	70,956	49,669	0.77	219	34	253
Philippines	307	0.63	455	12	467	87,815	61,471	0.78	256	36	292
Japan	306	0.63	723	13	736	140,262	98,183	0.81	395	48	443

IV. DEREGULATION

This section reports estimates of the effects of deregulation of money fares and of both fares and capacity. Estimation requires a choice of model of the current regime. Results of the previous section are consistent with both the excess capacity model and the discounting model. Both are employed in the calculations below. Since the full fare actually paid by consumers is higher in the excess capacity model than the discounting model, the former tends to generate upper-bound estimates.

IV.1 *Deregulation of money fares*

Australian policy has recently changed to relax control of money fares. In Figure 2, if capacity is held constant at the level corresponding to frequency of the *A* curve, but control of fares is removed, then the full price will fall to *OS* at point *B* on the demand curve. The full fare *OS* can be estimated by assuming that the full price demand curve has unitary elasticity between points *G* and *B*. Then the full fare outlay, that is the product of the full fare and the number of passenger trips, must be constant at points *G* and *B*.

At point *G* in Figure 2, full fare outlay is *OJGX*, and at point *B* it is *OSBQ*. Therefore the characteristics of the point *B* solution can be found by holding frequency constant, calculating the optimal toll for various passenger levels, increasing the number of passengers from the current level until the full fare outlay based on optimal utilisation of observed capacity is equal to the full fare outlay such as *OJGX*. In terms of Figure 2, this is equivalent to moving along the *M* curve from point *Z* to point *B*. The calculations were actually performed at the level of a single flight since frequency is the same at *G* and *B*.

The results are reported in Table III. The first five columns are the same as Table II. Column (6) contains the estimate of the full fare outlay per flight, which is held constant as policy changes, and the last four columns contain the estimates of loads and fares when fare control is relaxed. In all cases, as predicted from Figure 2, the money fare is lower, the cost of delay higher but the full fare lower. The fall in the full fare ranges from 5 percent to 30 percent with an average of 17 percent. This policy will generate unambiguous gains for consumers. However, compared to successful operation of the excess capacity model, the target airlines of the regulatory policy will earn losses. Not all carriers need earn losses since some may have lower costs, a point pursued in the next section.

IV.2 *Deregulation of fares and capacity*

Consumers will gain more by deregulation of capacity as well as fares. The reason is that the current system protects carriers whose costs are higher than those of least-cost operators. The full fare under deregulation can be

TABLE V

CHANGE IN FULL FARES AND CONSUMER COST,[a] 1981

Route	Current Full Fare (1)	Deregulation of Fares (2)	Deregulation of Fares and Capacity (3)	Annual Full Fare Outlay ($m)	Consumer Cost Factor (1)–(3)	Annual[b] Consumer Cost ($m) (1)–(3)	Consumer Cost Factor (2)–(3)	Annual[b] Consumer Cost ($m) (2)–(3)
PNG	334	305 (0.087)	245 (0.267)	16.966	0.310	5.260	0.219	3.716
Fiji	248	237 (0.004)	182 (0.266)	20.982	0.309	6.483	0.264	5.539
New Caledonia	166	146 (0.121)	115 (0.307)	2.537	0.367	0.931	0.239	0.606
New Zealand	211	201 (0.047)	155 (0.265)	155.910	0.308	35.700	0.260	30.137
Hong Kong	518	408 (0.212)	320 (0.382)	56.281	0.482	27.127	0.243	13.676
Singapore	432	365 (0.155)	283 (0.345)	132.220	0.423	55.929	0.255	33.716
Thailand	568	495 (0.129)	382 (0.328)	37.368	0.397	14.835	0.259	9.678
India	566	433 (0.235)	338 (0.403)	18.197	0.516	9.390	0.248	4.513
Indonesia	344	242 (0.297)	196 (0.430)	37.511	0.563	21.119	0.211	7.915
Malaysia	446	313 (0.298)	253 (0.433)	19.034	0.567	10.792	0.213	4.054
Philippines	467	368 (0.212)	292 (0.375)	21.589	0.470	10.147	0.231	4.987
Japan	736	565 (0.232)	443 (0.398)	39.612	0.508	20.123	0.243	9.626

[a] Numbers in brackets are the price falls as a proportion of the current full fare.

[b] The welfare cost (W) is $W = \ln(1+t)C$ where t is the tax rate due to regulation and C is total full fare outlay. The "consumer cost factor" is $\ln(1+t)$.

estimated by replacing current cost per flight by a figure for the least-cost per flight that would be attained under competition and free entry, and then applying the previous technique for estimating the optimal load factor and money fare.

An estimate of the cost decrease as a result of deregulation can be obtained from the results of Findlay and Forsyth [1984]. They estimate a cost frontier for civil aviation services. Their results indicate that other carriers could provide Qantas' services at approximately 70 percent of Qantas' costs.

In Table IV, the least-cost per flight is estimated as 70 percent of current revenue per flight in column (6), which is assumed to be the target cost level of the regulators, and which is reflected in the regulated fares. The least-cost estimate is reported in column (7). The first six columns of Table IV are the same as Table II, and the loads that minimise the full cost of travel and the corresponding fares and costs of delay at the competitive cost per flight are reported in the last four columns.

The results are, first, that load factors are higher under deregulation than those observed in 1981. This result is consistent with previous results that regulation appears to have generated excess capacity and loads that were too low. Loads under deregulation are lower than loads estimated to reflect optimal utilisation of 1981 capacity, given a revenue target, which were reported in column (7) of Table II (compare column (7) of Table III). This is because the benefits of lower costs per flight are being consumed, in part, by a higher service quality.

A second result is that the money fares are all lower but the costs of delay are greater (at least 12 percent of the money fare). Finally, all the full fares are lower by between 27 and 43 percent and an average of 35 percent.[10]

IV.3 *Welfare effects*

The loss of consumer surplus due to regulatory policy can be illustrated in Figure 2. The loss is equal to the area *JGYP* under the error model and *SBYP* under the discounting model. These areas will be upper and lower bounds respectively to the true loss. Figures for the total annual burden on consumers (for one-way trips out of Australia) are reported in Table V. The first three columns of that table summarize the changes in full fares, and the consumer

[10] The sensitivity of the results to changes in the value of the cost of delay was checked by lowering and raising the estimate of the cost of delay. If the cost is lowered to $100, load factors are even higher under deregulation than in 1981 and full fares fall by between 34 and 48 percent compared to 1981 levels. If the cost of delay is raised to $300, load factors fall under deregulation compared to 1981 on three routes with the smallest aircraft sizes (PNG, Fiji and New Zealand), where the probability of delay is greater at a given load, and rise on all other routes. Full fares fall by between 20 and 40 percent. In summary, as the cost of delay rises, the scale of decrease in full fares declines and the increase in load factors is smaller or negative in the move to deregulation of fares and capacity.

burdens are shown in the last few columns, both in absolute terms and as a proportion of the full fare outlay.[11]

These consumer burdens are clearly substantial. The upper bound estimates range from 30 to 57 percent of total consumer full fare outlays. The lower bound loss ranges from 21 to 26 percent.

The consumer loss is made up of a (rectangular) subsidy component and a (triangular) deadweight loss. For example, under the error model, the subsidy is *JGRP* and the triangular loss is *GYR*. Part of the subsidy component will be a transfer. It will be earned as profits by low cost airlines. The balance will be absorbed by higher costs, in the case of other carriers. Part of these higher costs could be rents earned by factors other than capital, in which case this component will also be a transfer. The balance will be a deadweight cost. The deadweight cost will be greater to the extent that rents are offset by rent-seeking activity (see Posner [1975]).

The transfers and deadweight costs could also be divided according to the nationality of the airlines and the passengers. For example, in 1981 Qantas' share of the Australian market was 42 percent, so Qantas would account for that proportion of the subsidy component. Australian consumers accounted for 57 percent of total (short term) movements and hence bore that share of the total consumer burden.[12]

V. CONCLUSION

The data collected here support a model of regulation in which the regulators had in mind a target airline (Qantas) which they were obliged to ensure earned a non-negative profit. They would not expose Qantas to competition because it was a relatively high cost airline. Also there were seen to be institutional constraints to "open skies", which related to fears of exploitation by other countries. This environment led to a series of bilateral agreements on air transport between countries. In that context, the flag carrier was seen to have some value to the country but the airline also had to be commercially viable.

Given these institutional constraints the regulators attempted to control capacity in order to protect their target airline. They had difficulty in doing so and capacity controls were supplemented by controls of money fares. Not only did regulators have difficulty in controlling capacity, they also had difficulty suppressing market pressure, which was toward lower money fares. The actual outcome was excess capacity and fares that were too low from the

[11] The demand curve is assumed to have unitary elasticity. An expression for the consumer loss is then $W = \ln(1+t)C$ where C is the total full fare outlay and t is the effective tax rate due to regulation.

[12] These data are from Department of Transport, Air Transport Statistics, International Air Transport, 1981, and Australian Bureau of Statistics, Overseas Arrivals and Departures, 1981 (Cat. No. 3404.0).

regulators' point of view. More recently the regulators have abandoned attempts to control money fares.

What were the effects of these policies? Some factor owners in the civil aviation industry may earn rents under the current arrangements. Pressure from such groups may not have been the original reason for the introduction of regulation but their presence would be a barrier to its removal. These rents can be traced to the protection which the current system offers firms in the industry. The flag carrier Qantas does not appear to have earned profits in recent years.

The policies imposed a substantial burden on consumers. It was estimated that deregulation of fares without relaxation of capacity control created substantial gains for consumers. If control of capacity were also relaxed, the gain to consumers would still be significant. The estimated additional gain is between 21 and 26 percent of total consumer outlays. This estimate is based on a comparison of the results of flexible money fares and the result of free competition. Fares under free competition were calculated using estimates of the costs of least-cost airlines providing Qantas' services.

CHRISTOPHER C. FINDLAY,
Economics Department,
University of Adelaide,
GPO Box 498 Adelaide,
Australia.

ACCEPTED FEBRUARY 1985

REFERENCES

De Vany, A. and Saving, T. R., 1983, 'The Economics of Quality', *Journal of Political Economy*, 91, pp. 979–1000.

Douglas, G. W. and Miller, III, J. C., 1974, *Economic Regulation of Domestic Air Transport: Theory and Policy* (The Brookings Institution, Washington DC).

Findlay, C. C., 1982, 'The Optimality of Competitive Air Transport Markets: A Review of Aspects of the ICAP Report', *Economic Record*, 58 (June), pp. 141–151.

Findlay, C. C., 1983a, 'Australian International Civil Aviation Policy and the ASEAN-Australia Dispute', *ASEAN-Australia Economic Papers, No. 1*, ASEAN-Australia Joint Research Project, Kuala Lumpur and Canberra.

Findlay, C. C., 1983b, 'Optimal Air Fares and Flight Frequency and Market Results', *Journal of Transport Economics and Policy*, Vol. 17, pp. 49–66.

Findlay, C. C., 1984, 'Occupational Regulation in a Regulated Industry: The Case of Airline Pilots', in R. P. Albon and G. J. Lindsay (eds.), *Occupational Regulation and the Public Interest*, CIS Readings 5, Sydney.

Findlay, C. C., 1985, 'The Persistence and Pervasiveness of the Regulation of International Trade in Civil Aviation Services', *Singapore Economic Review* (forthcoming).

Findlay, C. C. and Forsyth, P. J., 1984, 'Competitiveness in Internationally Traded Services: The Case of Air Transport', ASEAN-Australia Joint Research Project, Working Paper No. 10, Canberra.

MOHRING, H., 1976, *Transportation Economics* (Ballinger, Cambridge, Mass.).
POSNER, R., 1975, 'The Social Costs of Monopoly and Regulation', *Journal of Political Economy*, 33 (August), pp. 807–827.
SWAN, P., 1983, 'The Marginal Cost of Base-Load Power: An Application to Alcoa's Portland Smelter', *Economic Record*, 59 (December), pp. 332–344.

THE JOURNAL OF INDUSTRIAL ECONOMICS 0022–1821 $2.00
Volume XXXIV December 1985 No. 2

HOW RAPIDLY DOES NEW INDUSTRIAL TECHNOLOGY LEAK OUT?*

EDWIN MANSFIELD

There have been no systematic empirical studies of the speed at which various kinds of technological information leak out to rival firms. To help fill this gap, data were obtained from 100 American firms. According to the results, information concerning development decisions is generally in the hands of rivals within about 12 to 18 months, on the average, and information concerning the detailed nature and operation of a new product or process generally leaks out within about a year. These results have important implications both for incentives for innovation and for public policies aimed at stemming the outflow of technology.

I. INTRODUCTION

TO UNDERSTAND the process of industrial innovation and how rapidly innovations are imitated, it is obvious that economists should study the nature and extent of the information that firms have about their rivals' technology and R & D programs. Yet there have been no systematic empirical studies of the speed at which various kinds of technological information leak out to rival firms. In this paper, I summarize briefly the results of an investigation of this sort based on data obtained from 100 American firms. These results are some of the first that are available concerning this important topic.

II. LEAKAGE OF INFORMATION CONCERNING DEVELOPMENT DECISIONS

How quickly is a firm's decision to develop a major new product or process known to its rivals? To obtain information on this score, a random sample of 100 firms was chosen from a list of firms in thirteen major manufacturing industries (chemicals, pharmaceuticals, petroleum, primary metals, electrical equipment, machinery, transportation equipment, instruments, stone, clay, and glass, fabricated metal products, food, rubber, and paper).[1] Each firm's chief executive officer was asked to provide an estimate of the average length

* The research on which this paper is based was supported by a grant from the National Science Foundation, which, of course, is not responsible for the views expressed here. I am indebted to the very large number of firms that provided the basic data without which this study could not have been carried out. Also, thanks go to Lawrence J. White of New York University for useful suggestions in revising the manuscript.

[1] This sample was chosen at random from a list of all firms in these industries spending over $1 million (or 1 percent of sales, if sales were at least $35 million) on R & D in 1981.

TABLE I

PERCENTAGE DISTRIBUTION OF FIRMS, BY AVERAGE NUMBER OF MONTHS BEFORE THE FIRM'S DECISION TO DEVELOP A MAJOR NEW PRODUCT OR PROCESS IS REPORTED TO BE KNOWN TO ITS RIVALS, 10 INDUSTRIES, UNITED STATES

Industry	Products (Average Number of Months)					Processes (Average Number of Months)				
	Less than 6	*6 to 12*	*12 to 18*	*18 and more*	*Total*[a]	*Less than 6*	*6 to 12*	*12 to 18*	*18 and more*	*Total*[a]
	(Percentage of Firms)									
Chemicals	10	20	40	30	100	0	11	11	78	100
Pharmaceuticals	29	14	14	43	100	0	0	33	67	100
Petroleum	0	44	44	11	100	10	40	10	40	100
Primary Metals	40	20	20	20	100	20	60	20	0	100
Electrical Equipment	22	33	33	11	100	0	43	0	57	100
Machinery	0	43	21	36	100	0	25	25	50	100
Transportation Equipment	25	25	25	25	100	0	33	33	33	100
Instruments	18	27	36	18	100	20	20	20	40	100
Stone, Clay, and Glass	20	0	20	60	100	0	0	20	80	100
Other[b]	33	17	25	25	100	20	30	20	30	100
Average	20	24	28	28		7	26	19	48	

Source: see section II.
[a] Because of rounding errors, figures sometimes do not sum to total.
[b] Fabricated products, food, rubber, and paper are included in the "other" category.

of time before such information is in the hands of at least some of its rivals. Of course, it is not easy to pinpoint exactly when the decision is made to develop a product or process, because for each product or process there generally is a series of such decisions, not one. Thus, we asked each firm to base its estimate on the first such decision it made concerning a particular product or process. For obvious reasons, this should result in a conservative estimate of the speed at which such information leaks out.

According to the firms in our sample, information concerning development decisions of this sort is generally in the hands of at least some of their rivals within about 12 to 18 months, on the average, after the decision is made (Table I).[2] For about one-fifth of the firms, information leaks out within 6 months, on the average, in the case of new product development. (In chemicals and glass, leakage of this sort occurs somewhat more slowly than in other industries.) Although firms ordinarily cannot tell precisely when such information is in the hands of their rivals, the firms in our sample seemed to feel that the averages they presented were accurate enough for present purposes. Nonetheless, it is obvious that the data in Table I (as well as Table II) are rough approximations.

Because new processes can be developed with less communication and interaction with other firms than can new products, process development decisions tend to leak out more slowly than product development decisions in practically all industries.[3] However, the difference, on the average (measured by the median), is less than 6 months. Thus, for both processes and products, the odds are better than 50-50 that a development decision will leak out in less than 18 months. If it takes about three years or more before a major new product or process is developed and commercialized (which is fairly typical in many industries), this means that there is a better-than-even chance that the decision will leak out before the innovation project is half completed.

III. LEAKAGE OF INFORMATION CONCERNING A NEW PRODUCT OR PROCESS

Although rival firms are interested in a firm's development decisions, they generally are even more interested in the detailed nature and operation of the new product or process developed by the firm. That is, they would like to know how it functions and is made. According to the firms in our sample, this information is in the hands of at least some of their rivals within about a year,

[2] Although there are 13 industries, four (fabricated metal products, food, rubber, and paper) are lumped together as "other" in Table I because the sample contains relatively few firms in each of these industries. There was little or no problem of nonresponse. Only one firm provided no information. Besides the firms in the sample, other firms were contacted to obtain related types of information and to test the questionnaire. Practically all of the data were obtained through mail questionnaires and correspondence.

[3] For further discussion of the differences between products and processes in the ease of imitation, see Mansfield, Rapoport, Romeo, Villani, Wagner, and Husic [1977].

TABLE II

PERCENTAGE DISTRIBUTION OF FIRMS, BY AVERAGE NUMBER OF MONTHS (AFTER DEVELOPMENT) BEFORE THE NATURE AND OPERATION OF A NEW PRODUCT OR PROCESS ARE REPORTED TO BE KNOWN TO THE FIRM'S RIVALS, 10 INDUSTRIES, UNITED STATES.

Industry	Products (Average Number of Months)					Processes (Average Number of Months)				
	Less than 6	*6 to 12*	*12 to 18*	*18 and more*	*Total*[a]	*Less than 6*	*6 to 12*	*12 to 18*	*18 and more*	*Total*[a]
	(Percentage of Firms)									
Chemicals	18	36	9	36	100	0	0	10	90	100
Pharmaceuticals	57	14	29	0	100	0	33	0	67	100
Petroleum	22	33	22	22	100	10	50	10	30	100
Primary Metals	40	20	0	40	100	40	40	0	20	100
Electrical Equipment	38	50	12	0	100	14	14	57	14	100
Machinery	31	31	31	8	100	10	20	30	40	100
Transportation Equipment	25	50	0	25	100	0	67	0	33	100
Instruments	50	38	12	0	100	33	33	33	0	100
Stone, Clay, and Glass	40	60	0	0	100	0	20	20	60	100
Other[b]	31	15	15	38	100	27	0	36	36	100
Average	35	35	13	17		13	28	20	39	

Source: see section II.
[a] See note a, Table I.
[b] See note b, Table I.

on the average, after a new product is developed (Table II).[4] Indeed, for over one-third of the firms, it is in their hands within 6 months. For processes, this information leaks out more slowly, for reasons cited above. But even in this case, it generally leaks out in less than about 15 months. The major exception is chemical processes which frequently can be kept secret for a number of years.

There are many channels through which this information spreads. In some industries there is considerable movement of personnel from one firm to another, and there are informal communications networks among engineers and scientists working at various firms, as well as professional meetings at which information is exchanged. In other industries, input suppliers and customers are important channels (since they pass on a great deal of relevant information), patent applications are scrutinized very carefully, and reverse engineering is carried out. In still other industries, the diffusion process is accelerated by the fact that firms do not go to great lengths to keep such information secret, partly because they believe that it would be futile in any event. Thus, the intelligence-gathering process varies considerably from industry to industry (and from case to case).[5] In view of this diversity, it is remarkable that, with the exception of processes in a few industries like chemicals, there seems to be so little difference among industries in the rate of diffusion of such information. In practically all industries in Table II, the median time lag for products is between 6 and 12 months, and the median for processes (other than chemicals and drugs) is 6 to 18 months.

Of course, the fact that information of this sort leaks out relatively quickly does not mean that imitation will occur equally fast. It often takes considerable time to invent around patents (if they exist), to develop prototypes, to alter or build plant and equipment, and to engage in the manufacturing and marketing start-up activities required to introduce an imitative product or process. (The factors determining the cost and length of time taken by these activities are taken up in Mansfield, Schwartz, and Wagner [1981].) Nonetheless, the basic information concerning the nature and operation of the innovation, even if it is not sufficient in many cases to permit the immediate introduction of an imitative product or process, is of great importance to the innovator's rivals. And if it is true (as Table II indicates) that information of this sort is very likely to find its way into the hands of rivals within a year or two, this has obvious and important implications for both the incentives for innovation and for public policies aimed at stemming the outflow of technology to other countries.

[4] As in the case of Table I, the data in Table II should be viewed as rough approximations. See section II.

[5] For some relevant discussion concerning the electronics industry, see Rogers [1982]. Based on interviews I carried out with a sample of European and Canadian firms, there is a widespread feeling that information of this sort spreads more rapidly in the United States than in Europe, but the evidence is fragmentary.

IV. IMPLICATIONS AND CONCLUSIONS

Specifically, the above findings seem to have at least three major implications. First, they help to explain why industrial innovations so often are imitated relatively soon after first introduction. Mansfield, Schwartz, and Wagner [1981] found that about 60 percent of the patented innovations in their sample were imitated within four years. Given that development decisions and new technology leak out so quickly (and that it is so often possible to invent around patents), it is easy to understand why this was the case. Moreover, these results provide new insight into the problems involved in providing proper incentives for innovation in a free-enterprise economy. The fact that information concerning new industrial technology spreads so rapidly helps to explain why many firms have great difficulty in appropriating much of the social benefits from their innovations.[6]

Second, the results suggest that differences in the rate of diffusion of technological information do not play a major role in explaining inter-industry differences in the ease with which innovations can be imitated. The interindustry differences in Table II seem too small to be of major importance in this regard.[7] In a previous paper,[8] we estimated the average cost of imitation in a variety of industries, studied the determinants of this cost, and showed that this cost was directly related to an industry's concentration level. Although one might suppose that there are considerable differences in the rate of diffusion of technological information, and that these differences are responsible for substantial differences in imitation costs (and thus for differences in concentration levels), this does not seem to be the case.

Third, turning to issues of public policy, the results help to indicate the magnitude of the difficulties faced by recent (and not so recent) attempts by the US government to prevent the outflow to other countries of new American technology. As is well known, the United States has tried in a variety of ways to stem the flow of defense-related industrial technology to various Communist countries.[9] Also, both government agencies and firms (like IBM) have been concerned about improper leaks of industrial technology

[6] Of course, it should be stressed once again that Tables I and II reflect firms' perceptions of how quickly technological information leaks out to their rivals, and that these perceptions undoubtedly contain errors. However, the fact that Tables I and II are so consistent with the data in Mansfield, Schwartz, and Wagner (1981) suggests that these tables, while only rough approximations, provide a reasonably adequate general picture. Moreover, for many important purposes, the firms' perceptions are what matter most. For example, firms' perceptions of how rapidly their new technology will leak out to their rivals determines how much of the social benefits of a prospective innovation they believe they can appropriate, and thus whether or not they are willing to develop and introduce such an innovation.

[7] Also, there is no direct relationship between an industry's average four-firm concentration ratio and its median in Table II. However, evidence of this sort is obviously very crude.

[8] See Mansfield, Schwartz, and Wagner [1981].

[9] For example, see 'Technology Transfer: A Policy Nightmare', *Business Week*, April 4, 1983. Also, Stobaugh and Wells [1984] and US Department of Commerce [1983] contain relevant material.

to foreign firms. If the leakages typically are as quick and as great as our results seem to indicate, such efforts clearly face enormous problems.[10]

EDWIN MANSFIELD,
Department of Economics,
University of Pennsylvania,
Philadelphia,
Pennsylvania 19104,
USA.

ACCEPTED APRIL 1985

REFERENCES

MANSFIELD, E., SCHWARTZ, M. and WAGNER, S., 1981, 'Imitation Costs and Patents: An Empirical Study', *Economic Journal*, 91 (December), pp. 907–918.

MANSFIELD, E., ROMEO, A., SCHWARTZ, M., TEECE, D., WAGNER, S. and BRACH, P., 1982, *Technology Transfer, Productivity, and Economic Policy* (W. W. Norton, New York).

MANSFIELD, E., RAPOPORT, J., ROMEO, A., VILLANI, E., WAGNER, S. and HUSIC, F., 1977, *The Production and Application of New Industrial Technology* (W. W. Norton, New York).

ROGERS, E., 1982, 'Information Exchange and Technological Information', in D. Sahal (ed.), *The Transfer and Utilization of Technical Knowledge* (Lexington Books, Lexington).

STOBAUGH, R. and WELLS, L. (eds.), 1984, *Technology Crossing Borders* (Harvard Business School, Boston).

US DEPARTMENT OF COMMERCE, 1983, *An Assessment of US Competitiveness in High Technology Industries* (Government Printing Office, Washington, DC).

[10] In this connection, it is worth noting that the technologies transferred by US-based multinational firms to their overseas subsidiaries seem to leak out to non-US firms more slowly than is indicated by Table II. See Mansfield, Romeo, Schwartz, Teece, Wagner, and Brach [1982], pp. 38–40. Where possible, these firms may tend to avoid transferring overseas those technologies that are likely to leak out relatively quickly. (There is evidence that these firms are more hesitant to send overseas their process technology than their product technology, because they feel that the diffusion of process technology, once it goes abroad, is harder to control. See *ibid.*, p. 54.) Also, holding other factors constant, one would expect that American technology would leak out more rapidly, on the average, to US firms than to non-US firms.

ANNOUNCEMENTS

The Fourth Annual Meeting of the Association of Managerial Economists (AME) will be held in New Orleans, Louisiana, December 28–30, 1986.

Three sessions of contributed papers will be featured in conjunction with the Allied Social Science Association meetings. Theoretical, empirical and policy studies across a broad spectrum of topics are invited. Areas of interest include advertising, competitive strategy, diversification, financial decisions, forecasting, innovation, managerial labor markets, market for corporate control, and pricing. Studies of topics on the role of government in the market economy (antitrust, regulation and public enterprise) are also encouraged.

Both members and nonmembers are invited to submit papers and/or make program suggestions to the Program Chairman, Professor Mark Hirschey, Graduate School of Business Administration, University of Colorado, Denver CO 80202 (303/623-4436). *Submission Deadline: June 15, 1986.*

The Thirteenth Annual Conference of EARIE, the European Association for Research in Industrial Economics, will be held on 24th to 26th August 1986 at the German Institute of Economic Research (DIW) in Berlin, W. Germany.

Sessions include the economics of industry and firm organization, industrial and competition policy, industrial organization and international trade, industry studies, regulation of industries and firms, industrial organization theory, technological and organizational change and industry structure, public enterprise economics, innovation, technical change and public policy as well as other areas of current research interest in industrial economics.

Those interested in presenting a paper should send a one page abstract and three copies of the complete paper by *April 1, 1986* to Jürgen Müller, c/o DIW, Koenigin-Luise-Str. 5, 1000 Berlin 33 (*Tel.* 49-30-82991 328 or 829910), for a review by the programme committee.

THE JOURNAL OF INDUSTRIAL ECONOMICS

Published first in October 1952, the *Journal* has a very wide international circulation, and has established itself as the leading journal in the field of industrial economics. It was founded to promote the analysis of modern industry, particularly the behaviour of firms, and the functioning of markets. More specifically it seeks to bring the tools of modern economic analysis to bear on the analysis of real problems of industrial economies.

Contributions are welcomed covering all the major areas of industrial economics. One such area is the relationship between market structure and market behaviour in the areas of pricing, product differentiation, advertising and the dissemination of information and R & D. Another area focuses more directly on the firm, its objectives, finance, investment and growth. A third area comprises the background environment within which industrial firms operate: the changing structure of industry, public policy on monopoly and restrictive trade practices, regulation, fiscal and monetary policies as they affect firms, and underlying changes in productivity and international competitiveness.

The *Journal* has a tradition of publishing a blend of theory and evidence. Theoretical discussion is welcomed provided that the more abstract theory includes sufficient introduction and other explanation to convey the significance of the material to the general reader who wants to decide whether to follow the analysis through. Empirical analysis, and especially econometric analysis, should include an explanation of the data sources used, of the methods applied and of the underlying theoretical basis of the study. The *Journal* has a particular tradition of case studies of firms and industries, which the Editors would wish to continue. However contributors of such studies are asked to remember that a study will be of interest to the international readership of the *Journal* only if it makes a particular contribution to the methodology of such studies, or if the empirical results are exceptionally interesting.

Alongside articles of more normal length, the Editors are ready to publish shorter notes, especially where these give interim results of important research studies, or where they report significant new empirical results. Books are not reviewed, although books received will be listed, sometimes with a short note: but substantial review articles will be considered.

Information for Contributors

Submissions (*three* copies are required) should be in typescript, double-spaced, and should conform to the style of the *Journal*. Detailed Information for Contributors is available from the General Editor. The submission should include an Abstract, not exceeding 100 words.

Typescripts from North America should be sent to the North American Editor, Journal of Industrial Economics, Graduate School of Economics and Business Administration, New York University, 100 Trinity Place, New York, NY 10006, USA.

Typescripts from *all* other countries should be sent to the General Editor, Journal of Industrial Economics, Institute of Economics and Statistics, University of Oxford, St Cross Building, Manor Road, Oxford OX1 3UL, UK.

Information for Subscribers

The *Journal* is published four times a year, in September, December, March and June, by Basil Blackwell Ltd., 108 Cowley Road, Oxford OX4 1JF, UK. Prices are as follows:

	UK	Overseas	USA
Institutions	£29.00	£36.50	$65.75
Individuals	£16.25	£20.35	$35.00
Single issue prices for:			
Institutions	£7.20	£8.80	$17.70
Individuals	£5.20	£6.40	$12.00

CONTRIBUTORS TO THIS ISSUE

RICHARD E. CAVES: Littauer Center, Harvard University, Massachusetts, USA and Editor of this *Journal*.
PETER J. WILLIAMSON: London Business School, London, UK.
DAMIEN NEVEN: CORE, Université Catholique de Louvain, Louvain-la-Neuve, Belgium.
LOUIS PHLIPS: CORE, Université Catholique de Louvain, Louvain-la-Neuve, Belgium. and Editor of this *Journal*.
YVES MERTENS: CEME, Université Libre de Bruxelles, Brussels, Belgium.
VICTOR GINSBURGH: CEME, Université Libre de Bruxelles, Brussels, Belgium.
M. L. GREENHUT: Texas A & M University, Texas, USA.
H. OHTA: SIPEB, Aoyama Gakuin University, Tokyo, Japan.
J. SAILORS: University of Houston, Houston, Texas, USA.
VICTOR J. TREMBLAY: Kansas State University, Manhattan, USA.
CHRISTOPHER C. FINDLAY: University of Adelaide, Adelaide, Australia.
EDWIN MANSFIELD: University of Pennsylvania, Philadelphia, Pennsylvania, USA.

JAN 30
Hartwick College Library

US Mailing: Second class postage paid at New York. Postmaster: Send address corrections to: Journal of Industrial Economics, c/o Expediters of the Printed Word Ltd., 515 Madison Avenue, New York, NY 10022 (US Mailing Agent).

Photocopying: Permission is granted by the publisher for those institutions registered with the Copyright Clearance Center to authorize internal photocopying of any article in this journal for a fee of $2.00 per copy per article. Payment should be made direct to the Copyright Clearance Center, 21 Congress Street, Salem, Massachusetts 10970, USA. Individuals, or institutions not registered with the CCC, must obtain permission to photocopy either from the CCC or from Basil Blackwell Ltd., when the same fees will apply.

Reprints of Back Volumes: Volumes 1–28 of the *Journal* are available (in complete volumes only) from the Kraus Reprint Corporation, Route 100, Millwood, New York 10546, USA. More recent back issues are available from the publisher at the current single issue price.

Microfilm: An agreement for the supply of microfilm copies from Volume 1 onwards has been made with University Microfilms International, Department PR, 30–32 Mortimer Street, London W1N 7RA, England, or 300 North Zeeb Road, Ann Arbor, Michigan 48106, USA.

Advertising: For details contact the Advertisement Manager, Bill Drake. Telephone (0869) 38477, or write c/o the publisher.

Set in Monophoto Times by Advanced Filmsetters (Glasgow) Ltd
Printed and Bound in Great Britain by Whitstable Litho, Kent

THE JOURNAL OF INDUSTRIAL ECONOMICS

Volume XXXIV MARCH 1986 No. 3

STANLEY S. REYNOLDS
Strategic Capital Investment in the American Aluminum Industry 225

ASHER WOLINSKY
The Nature of Competition and the Scope of Firms 247

S. J. PRAIS
Some International Comparisons of the Age of the Machine-Stock 261

FRANK A. SCOTT, JR.
Assessing USA Postal Ratemaking: An Application of Ramsey Prices 279

MARGARET E. SLADE
Exogeneity Tests of Market Boundaries Applied to Petroleum Products 291

DEVRA L. GOLBE
Safety and Profits in the Airline Industry 305

JOHN LUNN
An Empirical Analysis of Process and Product Patenting: A Simultaneous Equation Framework 319

Short Articles and Notes

GREGORY J. WERDEN and MICHAEL G. BAUMANN
A Simple Model of Imperfect Competition in Which Four Are Few But Three Are Not 331

ISSN 0022-1821
BASIL BLACKWELL OXFORD ENGLAND

© Basil Blackwell 1986

The material in this Journal is copyright under the Berne Convention. Apart from any fair dealing for the purposes of private study, research, criticism or review, as permitted under the Copyright Act 1965, no portion may be reproduced by any process without written permission. Inquiry should be made to the Publishers.

DONALD A. HAY (General Editor): Jesus College, University of Oxford.
STEVE W. DAVIES: University of East Anglia.
BRUCE LYONS: St John's College, Cambridge.
LOUIS PHLIPS: Université Catholique de Louvain.
AUBREY SILBERSTON: Imperial College of Science and Technology, University of London.
GEORGE YARROW: Hertford College, University of Oxford.
LAWRENCE J. WHITE (North American Editor): New York University.
M. A. ADELMAN: Massachusetts Institute of Technology.
RICHARD E. CAVES: Harvard University.
F. MICHAEL SCHERER: Swarthmore College.
RICHARD SCHMALENSEE: Sloan School of Management, Massachusetts Institute of Technology.

Editorial Assistant: Marion Bowker.

ASSOCIATE EDITORS
BO CARLSSON: Case Western Reserve University, Cleveland.
ROGER CLARKE: University of Sheffield.
ALEXIS JACQUEMIN: Université Catholique de Louvain.
FRÉDÉRIC JENNY, E.S.S.E.C., Cergy.
H. W. DE JONG: University of Amsterdam.
JOHN KAY: Institute for Fiscal Studies, London.
COLIN P. MAYER: St Anne's College, University of Oxford.
GEOFF MEEKS: Department of Applied Economics, University of Cambridge.
DEREK MORRIS: Oriel College, University of Oxford.
WILLIAM PETERSON: Department of Applied Economics, University of Cambridge.
JOHN F. PICKERING: The University of Manchester Institute of Science and Technology.
RAY REES: University College, Cardiff.
DAVID K. STOUT: Unilever PLC.
ROGER TARLING: Department of Applied Economics, University of Cambridge.
JOHN VICKERS: Nuffield College, University of Oxford.
CHRISTIAN C. VON WEIZSÄCKER: University of Berne.
GEOFFREY WHITTINGTON: University of Bristol.

RONALD R. BRAEUTIGAM: Northwestern University.
TIMOTHY F. BRESNAHAN: Stanford University.
WILLIAM S. COMANOR: University of California.
M. THÉRÈSE FLAHERTY: Harvard University.
THEODORE KEELER: University of California, Berkeley.
R. LARNER: Charles River Associates.
ALMARIN PHILLIPS: University of Pennsylvania.
STEVEN SALOP: Georgetown Law Center, Washington, DC.
JOHN T. SCOTT: Dartmouth College.
ROBERT D. WILLIG: Princeton University.

DONALD G. MCFETRIDGE: Carleton University, Ottawa.

PETER FORSYTH: Australian National University, Canberra.
BRIAN L. JOHNS: Bureau of Industry Economics, Canberra.
L. ROY WEBB: University of Melbourne.

MASU UEKUSA: University of Tokyo.

THE JOURNAL OF INDUSTRIAL ECONOMICS 0022-1821 $2.00
Volume XXXIV March 1986 No. 3

STRATEGIC CAPITAL INVESTMENT IN THE AMERICAN ALUMINUM INDUSTRY*

STANLEY S. REYNOLDS

A dynamic game model of production and capital investment choice is formulated and used to explain the behavior of leading firms in the post-war American aluminum industry. A dominant firm equilibrium simulation is found to predict behavior of leading firms better than a Nash equilibrium. The model performs well in its prediction of average real prices in the post-war period. The model explains some, but not all, of the observed excess production capacity that arises. The remedy following Alcoa's monopolization conviction in 1945 is examined. Industry simulations involving a more competitive post-war market structure predict a small welfare gain.

I. INTRODUCTION

ONE OF the 'stylized facts' of industrial organization is the tendency of oligopolistic markets to exhibit excess capacity. Both Wallace [1937, pp. 205–206] and Bain [1956, pp. 189–190] hypothesized such a relationship in early studies of oligopolistically structured manufacturing industries. Several explanations for this stylized fact have been suggested.[1] One explanation is based on the strategic incentives for capital investment by an existing firm (or, group) that faces potential entry. For example, Spence [1977] argues that a group of existing firms will deter entry by investing in excess capacity (with a fixed proportions technology) or excess capital (with a variable proportions technology). This investment strategy has the advantage of deterring potential entrants while simultaneously permitting the established firms to restrict output and charge supra-competitive prices.[2]

Another strand of the literature has emphasized the influence of strategic

* This paper is a revised version of a chapter from my Ph.D. thesis. The paper has benefited from helpful comments by Rus Janis, several of my colleagues at Arizona and my advisor, Ron Braeutigam. Two anonymous referees also provided very helpful suggestions. Herold Kruschina provided competent research assistance. Any remaining errors are the responsibility of the author.

[1] Esposito and Esposito [1974] have found empirical support for the hypothesis that oligopolistic market structures contribute to excess capacity. Scherer [1980, pp. 370–371] provides a good discussion of the incentives for capital investment in oligopolistic markets.

[2] Wenders [1971] made a similar argument in an earlier paper. More recent analyses by Dixit [1980] and Spulber [1981] have questioned this argument. They claim that there is no incentive for such investment in excess capacity since the incumbent firm would not choose to carry out its threat of utilizing its excess capacity when actually confronted with a viable entrant. Reynolds [1985] shows that incentives for investment in excess capital do exist with a variable proportions technology. Overinvestment in production capital lowers the incumbent's marginal costs and makes the incumbent a more effective competitor in the post-entry 'game'.

interaction among existing firms on the incentives for capital investment. In an early analysis of the aluminum industry, Wallace [1937] suggests that oligopolistic rivalry could lead to a rapid rate of investment when one or more firms see an opportunity to gain market share. He characterizes such a situation as one of overinvestment and underutilization of capacity, relative to 'ideal' investment. Brander and Spencer [1983] provide a theoretical rationale for strategic overinvestment by noncooperative duopolists when the production technology is characterized by variable proportions.[3] If firms are able to commit to a fixed amount of capital prior to choosing their outputs in a Cournot–Nash game, then each firm has an incentive to invest in more than the cost-minimizing amount of capital. This incentive exists because an increase in capital lowers a firm's marginal cost of output and improves the outcome for the firm in the Cournot–Nash output game.

A dynamic game model of output and capital investment choice is used in this paper to explore the influence of strategic interaction among existing firms on the incentives for investment. The model is confronted with data from the American aluminum industry for 1950 through 1970. The following questions are addressed. First, can the evolution of the capital stocks of major firms in the industry over time be explained well by a dynamic game model of value-maximizing firms? Second, is strategic investment in excess capacity a quantitatively important explanation for observed excess capacity in the industry? Third, what is the appropriate equilibrium concept for the analysis? We compare the results for noncooperative Nash and dominant firm equilibria. Finally, would the creation of a fourth major domestic producer in the aluminum industry after World War II have had a significant welfare-improving effect?

One approach to obtain answers to these questions would be econometric estimation. However, there are some serious problems with the use of an econometric approach, which are discussed below. Instead, we opt for a simulation approach. Equilibria for the model are computed based on previous empirical estimates of demand and cost parameters and on reasonable choices of free parameters. A series of nonstochastic equilibrium simulations is the basis for our answers to the questions posed above.

The main results are as follows. A dominant firm equilibrium is found to predict the evolution of capital stocks better than a Nash equilibrium. Even so, the dominant firm equilibrium still tends to underpredict Alcoa's average market share. The "best-fit" dominant firm simulation does a good job of predicting average output prices, yielding an average real price prediction within 10 percent of the actual average real price. The amount of excess capacity arising from strategic investment was 2 percent or less in all cases examined. It may be necessary to introduce additional factors to explain fully

[3] Brander and Spencer's model is formulated in terms of investment in R&D. However, as they point out, their model may easily be interpreted in terms of investment in capital.

the average observed excess capacity of approximately 9 percent.[4] The model predicts that the creation of a fourth major aluminum producer in the industry following World War II would have resulted in a small welfare improvement.

The equilibrium simulations predict excess capacity as a result of strategic investment. This is consistent with observed excess capacity in the aluminum industry. Other factors need to be introduced in order to explain why actual excess capacity exceeds predicted excess capacity in the simulations. One important factor is measurement error in the excess capacity data, which is discussed below. A second factor may have been overly optimistic expectations by firms about future demand levels. A third factor may have been demand uncertainty, with firms holding excess capacity to guard against fluctuations in demand. Explicit introduction of demand uncertainty into the model presents some technical difficulties and is not considered in the simulations.[5]

The model of capital investment that is used in the analysis is formulated and discussed in section II. This section includes a discussion of alternative equilibrium concepts for the model. A brief description of the structure, conduct and performance of the American aluminum industry during the post war period appears in section III. The parameters of the model are specified in section IV. The main results are presented in section V. Concluding comments appear in section VI.

II. A MODEL OF OLIGOPOLISTIC CAPITAL INVESTMENT

Each firm $i = 1,\ldots,m$ has decision variables x_{it} and z_{it} representing its (homogeneous) output and capital investment in period t, respectively. The capital stock held by firm i in t, k_{it}, evolves according to the following equation.

[4] One way to interpret the approach taken in this paper is as a test of how well a (deterministic) noncooperative equilibrium model explains observed behavior in the aluminum industry. The model explains the evolution of capital stocks and prices fairly well. Its performance is less satisfactory in terms of explaining observed excess capacity. Clearly there are alternative models one might wish to consider. For example, a stochastic demand and supply model, as in De Vany and Frey [1982], may provide a better explanation of observed excess capacity and production variability. However, such models provide neither a fully closed solution for output price nor an explanation of the intraindustry distribution of capacity. Others have argued that the behavior of the leading firms was collusive rather than noncooperative and that part of the collusive strategy involved holding excess capacity. However, the noncooperative equilibrium simulations all predict average prices above the observed average price. It seems unlikely that a collusive model would yield better predictions than a noncooperative model.

[5] The technical difficulties arise because of the second order Taylor series approximation procedure used in this paper. In the certainty case, value functions are derived based on a series of local quadratic approximations of variable cost functions. With demand uncertainty it is necessary to derive expected value functions. If the linear-quadratic structure of the model is to be retained, the quadratic approximations of variable cost functions must be globally accurate in order to derive expected value functions. Given the nature of the aluminum production technology, quadratic approximations will not be globally accurate.

$$k_{i,t+1} = (1-\delta)k_{it} + z_{it} \tag{1}$$

The depreciation rate per period is δ. Each firm is assumed to have access to the same variable proportions technology for production of its output. A firm's variable cost of production in any period is given by C, where C depends on its output and its capital stock in that period. The single period cost of investment is I, where I is permitted to depend on the firm's current period capital stock as well as on the quantity of investment.

$$I(z_{it}, k_{it}) = qz_{it} + \tfrac{1}{2}d(z_{it} - \delta k_{it})^2 \qquad q > 0, d > 0 \tag{2}$$

There is a constant unit cost of acquisition of capital equal to q. In addition there is an internal adjustment cost term that is proportional to the square of net investment. These adjustment costs would arise from costs of installing or removing equipment and/or increasing unit costs of acquiring financial capital for expansion (see Mussa [1977]). The market price of output is assumed to be determined by the inverse demand function, $P\left(t, \sum_{j=1}^{m} x_{jt}\right)$. The time dependence of inverse demand allows for demand growth and variability over time.

The objective function for firm i, J^i, is defined as follows:

$$J^i = \sum_{t=1}^{T} \left(\frac{1}{1+r}\right)^{t-1} \left[x_{it} P\left(t, \sum_{j=1}^{m} x_{jt}\right) - C(x_{it}, k_{it}) - I(z_{it}, k_{it})\right] + \left(\frac{1}{1+r}\right)^{T} qk_{i,T+1} \tag{3}$$

Each firm is assumed to discount its future profits at the per-period rate r. The final term on the RHS of (3) is the salvage value of capital. The salvage value of capital at the end of the planning horizon, T, is assumed to be equal to the cost of acquisition of an equivalent amount of capital. The objective of firm i is to choose its output and investment sequence for periods one through T to maximize (3) given k_{i0} and z_{i0}, subject to (1).

Attention will be restricted to two equilibrium types: noncooperative Nash and dominant-firm (i.e. dominant-player). In a noncooperative Nash equilibrium, each firm adopts a strategy for output and investment choice that is a value-maximizing response to the strategies chosen by its rivals. In a dominant-firm equilibrium, the dominant firm announces its output and investment decisions at the beginning of each period. Non-dominant firms then respond by optimally selecting their output and investment levels for the period. The dominant firm takes these reactions into account in its decision-making, acting as a kind of dynamic Stackelberg-leader (see Simaan and Cruz [1973]).

There are three different solution concepts that might be utilized for each of the two equilibrium types described above. These concepts are the open-loop, closed-loop and feedback solutions. Using the open-loop concept, each firm announces its decisions for all periods at the start of the game, given the initial capital stocks (in a dominant-firm equilibrium, the dominant firm takes the reaction of its rivals to its path into account). Under the closed-loop concept, each firm adopts a decision rule in which its decisions depend on the date and the state (the vector of capital stocks) in the previous period (in a dominant-firm equilibrium, the decision rules of non-dominant firms also depend on the current actions of the dominant firm). The feedback solution is obtained via a game-theoretic variant of the dynamic programming method. Each firm determines its optimal decisions given its current information and given the expectation that all firms continue to make optimal decisions in subsequent periods (in a dominant-firm equilibrium, the current information of non-dominant firms includes the current period decisions of the dominant firm).

The feedback solution concept is adopted in this paper. The feedback and closed-loop solutions are identical for a Nash equilibrium but may differ in a dominant-firm equilibrium (see Simaan and Cruz [1973]). In a dominant-firm equilibrium, the closed-loop solution suffers from time-inconsistency (see Kydland [1977]). The open-loop solution also has drawbacks. In an open-loop solution firms fail to consider how their decisions affect the state variables and, through this effect, have an impact on later decisions of their rivals.[6] In contrast, these effects are considered in a feedback solution. Specifically, firms consider how a marginal cost reduction due to an increase in their capital stock would affect subsequent decisions by their rivals. The equilibrium capital stock sequences will be compared to the sequences that minimize the discounted present value of costs for each firm. The necessary conditions for cost-minimization are provided in Appendix 1.

III. THE AMERICAN ALUMINUM INDUSTRY IN THE POST-WAR ERA

Structure

The American aluminum industry was transformed from a monopoly into a triopoly following World War II. This transformation was accomplished by the sale of special war-time aluminum production facilities to Reynolds Metals and Kaiser Aluminum following Alcoa's conviction as a monopolist by a US federal court in 1945 (Scherer [1980, p. 533]). Reynolds and Kaiser were vertically integrated since they obtained alumina production facilities (upstream) and fabricating plants (downstream) as well as aluminum production facilities (Peck [1961, pp. 12–13]). A time series of primary aluminum production capacity for the three leading US firms and for the industry for 1950 to 1970 is provided in Table I. In spite of the appearance and growth of smaller aluminum producers beginning in the 1950s, over one-half of the

[6] Because of this, an open-loop Nash equilibrium may fail to satisfy the subgame perfection property. The open-loop solution for a dominant-firm equilibrium also suffers from time-inconsistency (see Kydland [1977]).

TABLE I
CAPACITY AND UTILIZATION DATA FOR THE ALUMINUM INDUSTRY
(CAPACITY DATA IN THOUSANDS OF SHORT TONS PER YEAR)

Year	*(1) Alcoa Capacity*	*(2) Reynolds Capacity*	*(3) Kaiser Capacity*	*(4) Capacity of Competitive Fringe Firms*	*(5) Industry Capacity*	*(6) Industry Utilization*
1950	369.75	238.50	143.00	0.00	751.25	—
1951	371.25	259.50	170.00	0.00	800.75	104.5%
1952	484.25	353.25	318.20	0.00	1155.70	81.2
1953	548.00	359.50	428.20	0.00	1335.70	93.7
1954	570.50	414.50	428.20	0.00	1413.20	103.3
1955	706.50	440.00	428.20	60.00	1634.70	95.8
1956	792.50	488.50	434.50	60.00	1775.50	94.6
1957	792.50	488.50	500.75	60.00	1841.75	89.6
1958	798.25	601.00	537.00	258.00	2194.25	71.3
1959	798.25	701.00	609.50	294.00	2402.75	81.3
1960	853.25	701.00	609.50	305.00	2468.75	81.6
1961	853.25	701.00	609.50	320.00	2483.75	76.6
1962	853.25	701.00	609.50	325.00	2488.75	85.1
1963	853.25	701.00	609.50	347.00	2510.75	92.1
1964	858.10	725.00	609.50	366.00	2599.10	98.2
1965	950.00	724.50	650.00	433.28	2758.28	99.9
1966	1050.00	815.00	640.00	630.28	3165.28	93.8
1967	1150.00	815.00	670.00	686.00	3321.00	98.4
1968	1150.00	855.00	670.00	901.00	3686.00	88.3
1969	1325.00	935.00	710.00	914.30	3884.30	97.6
1970	1325.00	945.00	710.00	1235.00	4215.00	94.3

Data Sources:

(1)–(5), Various issues of *Minerals Yearbook* (US Dept. of Commerce) and the *Aluminum Statistical Review*, 1972 (The Aluminum Association).

(6), Domestic primary production (taken from *Aluminum Statistical Review*, 1972) divided by industry capacity.

expansion in industry capacity from 1950 to 1970 was due to internal expansion of the three leaders.[7]

Conduct

In this paper we focus on the investment and pricing behavior of the three

[7] Economies of scale in aluminum production may have been one factor that limited the extent of entry in the post-war American market. The minimum optimal scale (MOS) for aluminum reduction (production of refined aluminum from alumina) had been estimated at 50–60 thousand tons of capacity per year (Mason [1972, pp. 143, 147]). However, the MOS for upstream operations such as alumina production, bauxite mining and electricity generation is significantly higher than the MOS for reduction alone (see Peck [1961, p. 169]). Since vertical integration seemed to be a prerequisite for being a low-cost competitor, a new entrant would have to be vertically integrated and enter at a fairly large scale in order to achieve costs as low as the industry leaders. The three leading firms all appeared to produce at levels exceeding the MOS for aluminum production.

Primary aluminum producers also face competition from secondary aluminum producers. Secondary production is a very good (almost perfect) substitute for primary aluminum in most applications. The interaction of primary and secondary producers has been analyzed in Gaskins [1974] and Swan [1980].

leading firms: Alcoa, Kaiser and Reynolds. The 1970 cut-off date was chosen for two reasons. First, continued expansion and entry by smaller firms after 1970 made the industry more competitive and less oligopolistic. Second, there were changes in aluminum production technology and large energy price increases in the early 1970s after a long period of stable technological and cost conditions in the industry (see Mork [1982]). Peck [1961, pp. 144–165] describes the capacity investment behavior of primary aluminum producers. He characterizes the interaction among the leading firms as a rivalry that led to an 'investment race' in the post-1954 period. Peck suggests that this rivalry may contribute to the development of excess capacity later on.

Peck [1961, pp. 35–62] also provides an interesting account of pricing behavior in the post-war period. He argues that pricing behavior can be explained by an oligopoly model in which different sellers have different preferred prices. The seller with the lowest preferred price sets the market price and its rivals follow. Peck suggests that Alcoa's behavior as a price leader throughout most of the post-war period is consistent with this theory.[8] Mason [1972] evaluates the explanatory power of several models of oligopolistic output choice in explaining the behavior of primary aluminum producers. The model that performs best has the three leading firms behaving as Cournot oligopolists and the remaining competitive fringe firms behaving as price-takers. The approach taken in this paper provides a new way to evaluate behavioral assumptions about aluminum producers. The pricing and investment behavior of firms is described as an equilibrium solution of a dynamic game.

Performance

There are two dimensions of industry performance that are of particular interest for the purposes of this study. The first of these is the relationship between the price of aluminum and its average (or marginal) cost of production. A comparison of price and unit cost will give us some indication of whether or not the condition for long run allocative efficiency is satisfied (or approximately satisfied). A report by Charles River Associates [1971] provides a time series of estimates of the long run average cost (*LRAC*) of aluminum production.[9] The estimates for *LRAC* are listed in Appendix 4 for

[8] In a recent theoretical paper, Friedman [1984] generates pricing behavior of this kind as an outcome of a noncooperative Nash equilibrium. It is not clear whether Peck viewed pricing behavior in the aluminum industry as noncooperative or as a form of imperfect collusion.

[9] Their estimates are based on a United Nations study of aluminum production costs in 1966. A breakdown of unit production costs into amounts contributed by different inputs is available in the UN study. Price indices for these inputs were used to calculate *LRAC* for these years. These estimates of *LRAC* assume a 1966 production technology, constant capacity utilization and production levels above the MOS. The estimates were adjusted for productivity growth. Real *LRAC* was relatively stable over the 1950–1970 period. There were no major changes in aluminum production technology. Increases in labor productivity were, to some extent, offset by increases in real wage rates.

1951–1969. In the late 1950s and early 1960s, aluminum prices are 30 to 40 percent above *LRAC*. During the remainder of the sample period, prices are 12 to 20 percent above *LRAC*.

The second aspect of performance that is of interest is the rate of utilization of capacity. Since World War II, the industry has gone through several episodes of over-expansion of capacity followed by low utilization rates. Capacity utilization rates for the industry for the years 1951–1970 are listed in Table II. The average utilization rate over this period was 91.9 percent. Utilization rates above 100 percent are possible because some firms (notably Alcoa) had high-cost stand-by capacity that was not included in reported capacity figures. In fact, the measured utilization rates in Table I understate true utilization since production accrues throughout the calendar year and capacity is measured only at year-end.[10] During the middle years of this period the industry experienced substantial excess capacity.

IV. CALIBRATION OF THE MODEL

The information in section III plus information from several empirical studies are used to specify the parameters of the model formulated in section II. The basic approach taken here is to specify precisely as many of the parameters as possible, leaving a small number of unspecified (free) parameters. Equilibria are then computed for various combinations of the free parameters. We seek the combination of free parameters that yields the equilibrium capacity and price paths that are 'closest' to the actual paths.[11] The approach outlined above is utilized instead of direct econometric estimation of the model parameters because of a serious difficulty associated with econometric estimation in this context. Econometric estimation methods for dynamic game models have been developed only for games having a linear-quadratic structure (see Chow [1981]). If the objective function is a quadratic form, then the variable cost function is quadratic in output and capital and short run marginal cost is linear in output, given the capital stock. In the aluminum industry, the short run marginal cost function is highly non-linear (or, even 'L-shaped') because the elasticity of substitution between capital and other inputs is quite low. Because of the extreme non-linearity in the marginal cost function, an econometric approach utilizing a linear-quadratic structure is not likely to be fruitful.

Mason's [1972] estimates of the demand for aluminum in the post-war

[10] Published capacity figures have been defined as, '. . . the capacity of the physical equipment in place which is deemed competitive in normal times.' (Simone [1962, p. 104].) This suggests a definition of capacity which exceeds economic capacity (output at minimum of short run average cost).

[11] A similar approach is taken in Kydland and Prescott [1982]. In their model, as in ours, a non-quadratic objective function poses severe difficulties for direct econometric estimation of the dynamic model.

period seem best suited for the purposes of this study. Mason estimates the parameters of a linear long run demand function of the following form.

(4) $$X_t = \alpha_0 + \alpha_1 P_t + \alpha_2 Y_t$$

where X_t equals total aluminum sales in year t, P_t is the average real price of aluminum in t, and Y_t is an index of durable manufacturing output in t. The mean price elasticity and income elasticity for this equation are 0.889 and 1.67, respectively. The demand coefficients estimated by Mason are listed in Table II. Total sales are defined by

(5) $$X_t = SEC_t + NI_t + FRG_t + \sum_{j=1}^{m} x_{jt}$$

where SEC_t is secondary output in t, NI_t is net imports in t and FRG_t is competitive fringe output in t. Total sales take account of shipments to the federal stockpile (see Appendix 4). Using (4) and (5) the inverse demand function may now be written as

(6) $$P\left(t, \sum_{j=1}^{m} x_{jt}\right) = \theta_t - b \sum_{j=1}^{m} x_{jt}$$

$$= (SEC_t + NI_t + FRG_t - \alpha_0 - \alpha_2 Y_t)/\alpha_1 + (1/\alpha_1) \sum_{j=1}^{m} x_{jt}$$

The leading producers are assumed to treat secondary output, net imports, and competitive fringe output as exogenously determined variables. In this analysis the (admittedly extreme) assumption that firms have perfect foresight over future values of the demand intercept θ_t is adopted.

The rate of depreciation of capital, δ, is assumed to be 4 percent, based on Peck's [1961, p. 144] description of the durability of aluminum reduction capacity. The interest rate, r, is taken to be 10 percent. This figure was used in Gaskins [1974] and Swan [1980].

The remaining cost and production parameters are derived indirectly based on information about production costs or are left as free parameters in the model. The production technology of aluminum reduction is generally characterized as involving fixed proportions (e.g., see Peck [1961, pp. 85–91]). This would certainly seem to be true of technology at the level of the individual production unit (the pot line). However, in a detailed study of short run aluminum production costs aggregated to the (multi-plant) firm level, Simone [1962] finds smooth marginal costs and u-shaped average costs. This pattern of production costs emerges because each firm's plants have a variety of capacity vintages and because more recent capacity vintages embody minor technological improvements.

A firm's aggregate variable cost function is derived from a 2-factor CES production function,

(7) $$x_{it} = (a_0 + a_1 L_{it}^{(\sigma-1)/\sigma} + a_2 k_{it}^{(\sigma-1)/\sigma})^{\sigma/(\sigma-1)}$$

where L_{it} is the composite variable input ('labor') for firm i in year t and σ is the elasticity of input substitution. It would appear that all three firms maintained output levels above the minimum optimal scale so that $a_0 = 0$. It is assumed that L_{it} and k_{it} are measured in units such that $a_1 = a_2 = 0.5$. This implies that input quantities are of the same order of magnitude as output quantities.

Let w be the price of the variable input. The variable cost function may be derived from (7).

$$C(x_{it}, k_{it}) = w(2x_{it}^{(\sigma-1)/\sigma} - k_{it}^{(\sigma-1)\sigma})^{\sigma/(\sigma-1)} \tag{8}$$

Let RC be the implicit rental cost of capital. From Appendix 4 average real $LRAC$ for 1951 to 1969 was 167.89. Simone [1962, ch. 6] estimated that fixed costs were approximately 40 percent of total costs at 100 percent of (measured) capacity utilization. In Appendix 2 we show how w and RC may be defined as a fraction of $LRAC$, where the fraction in each case depends on the value of σ. The elasticity of substitution, σ, is one free parameter in the analysis. The two σ-values that are used are listed in Table II.

It is also necessary to specify the adjustment cost parameter. Let ρ be the increase in unit investment cost for a one year increase in investment sufficient to increase a firm's capital stock by 5 percent. There does not appear to be any direct econometric evidence on the magnitude of capital adjustment costs. So, ρ is left as a second free parameter in the analysis. However, potential values of ρ are restricted so that capital adjustment costs are a relatively small part of overall capital expenditures (see Table II). Appendix 2 explains how the capital acquisition cost, q, and the adjustment cost, d, are determined given a value for ρ.

We are interested in the evolution of capital stocks and output in the industry over the period, 1951–1970. The planning horizon is extended beyond 20 years to $T = 30$ in order to reduce any end-period effects that might arise in the model if $T = 20$. The demand intercept, θ_t, is set to θ_{20} for $t > 20$.

Kydland [1975], [1977] has devised a dynamic programming algorithm for computing feedback equilibria (Nash and dominant-firm) when a player's objective is a quadratic function of the state vector and the state equations are linear. Computational details are provided in Appendix 3. In order to make this model consistent with Kydland's framework, the state vector y_t is defined to include the firms' decision variables in period t as well as their capital stocks in t. The functional form for a player's single period objective is consistent with a quadratic form in y_t except for the form of the variable cost function, (8). A method for computing approximate feedback equilibria is devised here in order to accommodate non-linearities in short run marginal costs. The method devised is a game theoretic variant of a solution technique suggested by Chow [1975, pp. 284–285] for single player, discrete-time control problems with a non-quadratic objective. First, a tentative path of outputs and capital stocks for all players is selected. Second order Taylor series approximations of the variable cost function in (8) are computed around this tentative path for each player in each period. Kydland's algorithm for computing a feedback equilibrium is then applied to the quadratic profit functions. The resulting 'equilibrium' sequence of state vectors is used as a basis for a new set of Taylor series approximations of the variable cost functions. These approximations are then utilized to compute a second sequence of 'equilibrium' state vectors. This iterative process is repeated until successive sequences of state vectors converge.[12]

V. EQUILIBRIUM SIMULATIONS

This section is devoted to describing and discussing the results of predictions of aluminum industry behavior using the model developed in sections II and IV. The same tentative path of output and capital was used as a basis for computation of equilibria in all cases. Capital and output for a firm are initially set equal to the firm's actual capacity for that period. Approximate equilibria were initially computed for six combinations of the free parameters for each equilibrium type. The iterative process for computing approximate equilibria was judged to converge if each element of the sequence of state vectors was within 0.01 percent of the corresponding element from the previous iteration. Convergence was achieved in 5 to 7 iterations for all cases.

A summary of the results is provided in Table II. Actual data appear in the first row. The cases for the simulation runs are identified by three characters. An N in the first position indicates a Nash equilibrium while a D indicates a dominant-firm equilibrium. The number in the second position indicates the number of leading firms in the simulation. The number in the third position indicates the particular combination of free parameters that was used. The six combinations that were used are identified in Table II. Six statistics are provided for the cases: average real output price, the exponential trend growth rate per year for real price, real price variability (the estimated standard deviation of real price around the trend real price), Alcoa's average market share, average industry capacity utilization and average strategic excess capacity for the leading firms. Strategic excess capacity for a firm in a period is the percentage by which the firm's actual capacity exceeds its cost-minimizing capacity in that period.

The average real price predictions for the 3-firm runs range from 8.1 to 16.8 percent above the actual average real price over the sample period. In the model, the three leading firms failed to expand their output and capacity as much as their real-world counterparts did. The high predicted prices in the model may be due in part to the fact that the leading firms take the output decisions of competitive fringe firms as given in the model, rather than

[12] Several FORTRAN computer programs were written to perform the equilibrium computations. These programs are available from the author upon request.

TABLE II
SUMMARY OF RESULTS

Cases	(1) Average Real Price $	(2) Price Trend Growth Rate %	(3) Price Variability	(4) Alcoa's Average Market Share %	(5) Average Industry Capacity Utilization %	(6) Average Strategic Excess Capacity
Actual	205.50	−0.76	0.119	42.2	91.1	—
N31	222.44	0.75	0.169	37.4	99.7	1.77%
N32	233.44	1.04	0.173	38.8	101.2	1.08
N33	238.37	1.18	0.177	39.3	101.7	0.97
N34	222.63	0.76	0.182	37.4	99.8	0.89
N35	234.18	1.06	0.190	38.8	100.6	0.59
N36	239.38	1.21	0.188	39.3	100.9	0.39
D31	223.61	0.74	0.169	39.0	100.1	1.38
D32	235.44	1.09	0.175	40.5	101.5	0.78
D33	240.31	1.23	0.177	40.7	102.0	0.58
D34	222.35	0.72	0.180	38.8	99.8	0.89
D35	234.92	1.08	0.185	39.8	100.7	0.49
D36	240.18	1.23	0.186	40.1	101.0	0.39
D34 ($\eta = 1.2$)	217.92	0.36	0.146	36.1	100.3	0.80
D34 ($\eta = 1.5$)	216.03	0.15	0.123	35.9	100.5	0.68
D34 ($r = 0.05$)	214.10	0.57	0.183	37.1	97.8	1.03
D34 ($r = 0.15$)	226.95	0.80	0.181	36.3	101.0	0.64
D34 ($T = 31$)	222.20	0.70	0.174	38.8	99.8	0.90
N44	209.80	0.36	0.184	—	99.6	1.09
D44	213.50	0.39	0.180	—	100.0	0.60

Parameter values: $r = 0.1$; $\delta = 0.04$; $\alpha_0 = 616.46 \times 10^3$; $\alpha_1 = -108.04 \times 10^4$; $\alpha_2 = 235.10 \times 10^2$; $a_0 = 0.0$; $a_1 = 0.5$; $a_2 = 0.5$.
Free parameter combinations:
(1) $\rho = 0.01$; $\sigma = 1/8$
(2) $\rho = 0.03$; $\sigma = 1/8$
(3) $\rho = 0.05$; $\sigma = 1/8$
(4) $\rho = 0.01$; $\sigma = 1/16$
(5) $\rho = 0.03$; $\sigma = 1/16$
(6) $\rho = 0.05$; $\sigma = 1/16$.

expecting the fringe firms to react to their output (and hence price) decisions. Note that higher adjustment costs lead to higher predicted prices. An increase in the adjustment cost parameter causes each firm to reduce its capital investments, leading to restricted output and higher prices.

A time-series graph of actual prices and predicted prices for case D34 (the best of the 3-firm runs in terms of average price prediction) is provided in Figure 1. There is a small upward trend over time in predicted prices compared to a small negative trend in actual prices. Note also that predicted price variability over time is greater than actual price variability. The major aluminum producers appear to have placed more emphasis on real price

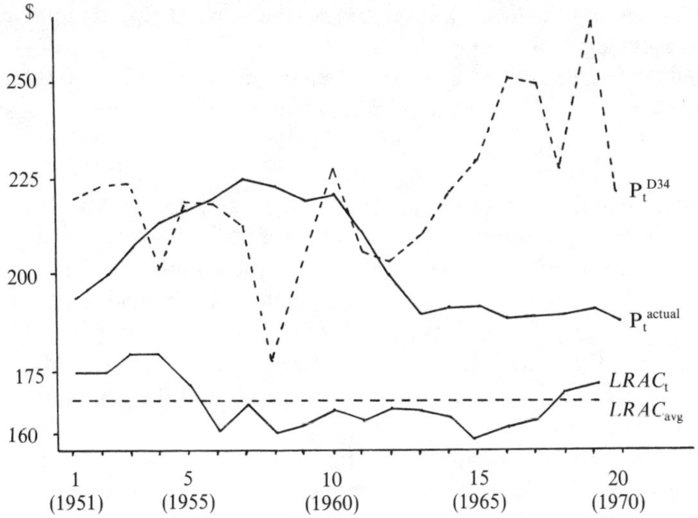

FIGURE 1
Price and *LRAC* Time Series

stability over time than our model would predict (at least, given the specification of aluminum demand). This difference in actual and predicted price stability is coupled with a difference in actual and predicted capacity utilization variability. In the model, variations in demand over time are accommodated more by price changes than by utilization changes whereas the actual data suggests more of a utilization response than a price response. As an extreme example, consider 1958, a year in which aluminum demand for the three leading firms dropped significantly. In case D34, the model predicts a large real price decline, down 18 percent from 1957, and a small reduction in utilization, to 96.7 percent. In reality, the real price of aluminum fell less than 2 percent, while industry utilization dropped to 71.3 percent.

There was positive strategic excess capacity on average for each case reported. Something analogous to the effect reported by Brander and Spencer appears to motivate firms to expand their capital investment beyond the cost-minimizing levels. However, this effect is rather small—less than 2 percent in all cases. The magnitude of strategic excess capacity is not sufficient to explain the 91.1 percent observed utilization rate in the industry. (However, recall from section III that observed utilization understates true utilization.) Strategic excess capacity is low in the model because the elasticity of substitution values are low. Note that the cases reported in Table II with lower σ-values have lower strategic excess capacity. Average capacity utilization under cost minimization, the sum of columns (5) and (6) in Table II, is greater than 100 percent in all cases. With positive adjustment costs, a cost-minimizing firm's investments would tend to lag behind demand increases, leaving the firm (on average) on the upward-sloping portion of its short run average cost curve.

It is also of some interest to see how well the model predicts relative market shares (of capacity) for the three leading firms over time. In this regard, the dominant-firm equilibrium is superior to the Nash equilibrium predictions. For each combination of free parameters, the Nash equilibrium predicts a more rapid equalization of market shares than the corresponding dominant-firm equilibrium. However, Alcoa maintained a slightly larger market share on average throughout this period than even the dominant-firm equilibrium would predict. It may have been the case that Kaiser and Reynolds were subject to liquidity constraints more binding than those implied by adjustment costs in the model. If this was true, their investment rate would have been limited and Alcoa could have invested to 'fill in the gap' and maintain a high market share.

The dominant-firm model performs better than the Nash equilibrium model because the dominant-firm model yields better predictions of real output prices and of the distribution of capacity among leading firms. Both models yield fairly low predicted levels of strategic excess capacity. Dominant-firm equilibrium case D34 is judged to provide the best fit to the data in terms of the catagories listed in Table II.

After the initial simulations of Nash and dominant-firm equilibria were run, several tests were performed to evaluate the sensitivity of the parameter specifications. Case D34 was used as benchmark for these sensitivity tests. The results are reported in Table II. The first two runs consider the effect of an increase in demand elasticity η (the initial value used was $\eta = 0.889$). This can also be interpreted as an illustration of the net effect of an increase in the price elasticity of supply from the competitive fringe, net import and stockpile sources. Recall that these supply elasticities were initially set equal to zero. These elasticity changes yield improved price predictions, both in terms of the price level and its variability. However, the average price prediction does not change drastically. An increase in the demand elasticity to 1.5 lowers average predicted price by about 3 percent. Two additional sensitivity tests consider the effects of changes in the discount rate. A decrease (increase) in the discount rate yields increased (decreased) capital investment and lower (higher) predicted prices, as one would expect. Again, the effects are not large. Cutting the discount rate from 10 to 5 percent lowers average predicted price by less than 4 percent. As a final test, the time horizon T was increased from 30 to 31 periods. The effects of this change were small.

The equilibrium simulation approach can be used to shed some light on an antitrust issue of historical interest. Adams [1951] criticized the public policy decisions following Alcoa's monopolization conviction for failing to create a sufficiently competitive market structure. Adams argued that, in addition to the creation of Kaiser and Reynolds, the court should have ordered Alcoa to divest some of its assets in order to create one or more additional independent primary aluminum producers. Adam's argument is evaluated here by predicting the behavior of firms in the aluminum industry, given a more competitive initial market structure, and comparing these results to the 3-firm simulation results.

Two different changes in initial market structure were considered. In the first instance (case N44) it is assumed that Alcoa is split into two equal-sized firms. This change is approximated by dividing total industry capacity in 1951 among four equal sized firms. In the second instance (case D44) it is assumed that Alcoa remained intact but that the 1951 assets of Kaiser and Reynolds are evenly split among three firms. The results of these changes are compared to the dominant-firm equilibrium of case D34, with $\rho = 0.01$ and $\sigma = 1/16$. For the first policy change, it is assumed that the outcome is described by a Nash equilibrium, since there is no longer a dominant firm in terms of market share. For the second policy change, it is assumed that Alcoa continues to act as a dominant firm.

The results appear in Table II. Predicted average prices fall relative to case D34. For the 4-firm Nash equilibrium (case N44) predicted average real price is 5.5 percent lower than it is for the 3-firm dominant firm equilibrium (case D34). The predicted effects of the policy changes on capacity utilization are quite small in both cases. The predicted effects of these two policy changes may also be evaluated using a consumer plus producer surplus measure of social welfare. The welfare measure W_τ is defined below

$$W_\tau = \sum_{t=1}^{\tau}\left(\frac{1}{1+r}\right)^{t-1}\left[\int_0^{\sum_{i=1}^{m} x_{it}} P(t,s)\,ds - \sum_{i=1}^{m}\left(C(x_{it},k_{it}) + I(z_{it},k_{it})\right)\right] + \left(\frac{1}{1+r}\right)^{\tau}\sum_{i=1}^{m} qk_{i,\tau+1} \tag{9}$$

The social discount rate is assumed to be equal to the private discount rate, $r = 0.10$. The social salvage value of capital is assumed to equal the private salvage value. The value of this welfare measure over 20 years, W_{20}, for the two 4-firm cases was compared to W_{20} for the 3-firm case, D34. This welfare measure increased by 1.0 percent for case N44 and increased by 1.5 percent for case D44.

The model developed in this paper predicts that the addition of a fourth major competitor in the American aluminum industry after World War II would have resulted in lower prices and an increase in social welfare for the 1951 to 1970 period. This result holds whether the fourth firm was created through divestiture of Alcoa's assets or through a split of War Asset Administration facilities among three new firms. However, the magnitude of predicted welfare improvement is small in both cases. In view of these results (and with the benefit of hindsight) Adams' criticism of the Alcoa remedy appears to have little validity. It should be noted that the welfare results reported above are subject to several qualifications. Only two will be mentioned here. First, the pattern of entry and competitive fringe expansion is assumed to remain unchanged with appearance of a fourth major producer. Second, since the model overpredicts capacity utilization, an increase in competition might have had utilization increasing benefits that are not captured by the model.

VI. CONCLUSION

Dynamic noncooperative Nash equilibrium and dominant firm models were compared in terms of their ability to predict investment, output prices, and capacity utilization in the post-war American aluminum industry. Both models do a good job in terms of average price prediction. The dominant-firm model was judged to be superior to the Nash equilibrium model because it yielded more accurate predictions of relative market shares. Both models predicted less excess capacity and more price variability than was actually observed in the industry. The effect of creating a fourth major producer after World War II was considered using equilibrium simulations. The results indicate that this hypothetical policy change would have had a small positive effect on industry performance.

Based on the results of this analysis two extensions of the model can be suggested that might improve the explanatory power of the model for homogeneous product manufacturing industries. It would be useful to extend the analysis to include competitive fringe firms and potential entrants explicitly as decision makers. Judd and Peterson [1984] provide a recent dynamic game-theoretic analysis along these lines. Introducing uncertainty about future demand levels may help explain the periodic emergence of substantial excess capacity.

STANLEY S. REYNOLDS,
College of Business and Public Administration,
Department of Economics,
University of Arizona,
Tucson, Arizona 85721,
USA

ACCEPTED JUNE 1985

APPENDIX 1

Cost Minimization

The necessary conditions for the cost-minimizing capital sequence, given $\{x_{it}\}_{t=1}^{T}$, are as follows:

$$\text{(A-1)} \quad 0 = \left(\frac{1}{1+r}\right)^{t-1} [C_k(x_{it}, k_{it}) - q(1-\delta) - d(k_{i,t+1} - k_{it})] + \left(\frac{1}{1+r}\right)^{t-2} [q + d(k_{it} - k_{i,t-1})], \qquad t = 2, \ldots, T$$

$$\text{(A-2)} \qquad 0 = \left(\frac{1}{1+r}\right)^{T-1} [q + d(k_{i,T+1} - k_{iT})] - \left(\frac{1}{1+r}\right)^{T} q$$

Note that if the variable cost function is a quadratic form then (A-1) and (A-2) is a finite system of linear difference equations. Such a system may be easily solved by moving recursively backwards from the final period.

Equation (A-1) may be used to approximate the implicit rental cost of capital in the model. Suppose each firm's capital stock grows at the rate g in each period and also satisfies (A-1). Then equation (A-1) may be rewritten as,

$$\text{(A-3)} \qquad 0 = C_k(x_{it}, k_{it}) - q(1-\delta) - dgk_{it} + (1+r)(q + dgk_{i,t-1})$$

The implicit rental cost of capital, RC, may be rewritten as,

$$\text{(A-4)} \qquad RC = -C_k(x_{it}, k_{it}) = q(r+\delta) + dg(r-g)k_{i,t-1},$$

if $k_{it} = (1+g)k_{i,t-1}$. The implicit rental cost depends on the level of capital if g is non-zero because of capital adjustment costs.

APPENDIX 2

Derivation of Factor Prices

Let x^0 be economic capacity, given capital stock k. Then,

$$RC \cdot k = 0.4(RCk + C(x^0, k))$$

or,

$$\text{(A-5)} \qquad RC \cdot k = 2C(x^0, k)/3$$

Given the input prices w and RC and the production function (7) it is easy to show that,

$$\text{(A-6)} \qquad x^0 = k\left[\frac{1}{2}(RC/w)^{\sigma-1} + \frac{1}{2}\right]^{\sigma/(\sigma-1)}$$

Substituting (A-6) into (A-5) and solving for RC we have,

$$\text{(A-7)} \qquad RC = w(2/3)^{1/(1-\sigma)}$$

$LRAC$ is equal to average fixed cost plus average variable cost at x^0.

$$\text{(A-8)} \qquad LRAC = (RC \cdot k + C(x^0, k))/x^0$$

Substituting (A-7) into (A-8) allows us to solve for w as a function of $LRAC$.

$$\text{(A-9)} \qquad w = ((1.25)^{\sigma/(\sigma-1)}/2.5(2/3)^{1/(1-\sigma)})LRAC$$

$$\text{(A-10)} \qquad RC = ((1.25)^{\sigma/(\sigma-1)}/2.5)LRAC$$

Recall that ρ specifies the increase in unit investment cost for a one year increase in investment sufficient to raise a firm's capital stock by 5 percent. The parameter ρ satisfies the following equation:

$$\text{(A-11)} \qquad (1+\rho)q = [qk_{it} + d(0.05k_{it})^2/2]/k_{it}$$

The parameters q and d are determined simultaneously by (A-4) and (A-11) given values for RC, r, δ, g, ρ and the capital stock. An average capital figure is used, where average capital is proportional to average capacity (658,962 short tons per year) according to (A-6). The growth parameter g is set to 7.09 percent, the average yearly growth rate of capacity for the three firms over the sample period.

APPENDIX 3

Feedback Equilibrium Computation

Define the state vector y_t as $y_t' = (x_{1t}, z_{1t}, k_{1t}, \ldots, x_{mt}, z_{mt}, k_{mt})$, where the prime symbol denotes a vector transpose. Let n_t be the vector of decision variables in period t, $n_t' = (x_{1t}, z_{1t}, \ldots, x_{mt}, z_{mt})$. The system of state equation (1) may now be rewritten as,

$$\text{(A-12)} \qquad y_t = Ay_{t-1} + Bn_t$$

where the coefficient matrices A and B are defined to be conformable with (1).

In a feedback Nash equilibrium, each firm i chooses its decision variables x_{it} and z_{it} to maximize the objective

$$\text{(A-13)} \qquad F_{it}(y_t) = p_{it}'y_t + \tfrac{1}{2}y_t'Q_{it}y_t + V_{i,t+1}(y_t)/(1+r)$$

subject to equation (A-12). The coefficient vector p_{it} and matrix Q_{it} are defined below. The value function $V_{i,t+1}(y_t)$ is a quadratic form in y_t and is derived using the backward recursion method of dynamic programming (see Kydland [1975]). In a Nash equilibrium, each firm's choice of decision variables in a period maximizes its objective given its rivals' decisions in that period.

In a dominant firm equilibrium, the dominant firm moves first in each period. The non-dominant firms choose their decisions in each period after observing the choices of the dominant firm in that period. A non-dominant firm i chooses its decisions in t to maximize F_{it} subject to (A-12), the decisions of the dominant firm in t and the expected decisions of non-dominant rivals in t. A dominant firm j chooses its decisions in t to maximize F_{jt} subject to (A-12) and to the necessary conditions that specify its rivals' decisions in t as functions of its own decisions in t. Kydland [1977] provides a detailed derivation of equilibrium decision rules. The p_{it} vector and Q_{it} matrix are defined below.

$$p_{it}' = (0, 0, 0, \ldots, \theta_t - C_x - x_{it}C_{xx} - k_{it}C_{xk}, -q, -C_k - x_{it}C_{xk} - k_{it}C_{kk}, \ldots, 0, 0, 0)$$

$$Q_{it} = \begin{bmatrix} 0 & 0 & 0 & \cdots & -b & 0 & 0 & & 0 & 0 & 0 \\ 0 & 0 & 0 & \cdots & 0 & 0 & 0 & & 0 & 0 & 0 \\ 0 & 0 & 0 & \cdots & 0 & 0 & 0 & & 0 & 0 & 0 \\ \vdots & & & & \vdots & & & & & & \\ -b & 0 & 0 & \cdots & -(2b + C_{xx}) & 0 & -C_{xk} & \cdots & -b & 0 & 0 \\ 0 & 0 & 0 & \cdots & 0 & -d & \delta d & \cdots & 0 & 0 & 0 \\ 0 & 0 & 0 & \cdots & -C_{xk} & \delta d & -(d\delta^2 + C_{kk}) & \cdots & 0 & 0 & 0 \\ \vdots & & & & & & & & & & \\ 0 & 0 & 0 & \cdots & -b & 0 & 0 & \cdots & 0 & 0 & 0 \\ 0 & 0 & 0 & \cdots & 0 & 0 & 0 & \cdots & 0 & 0 & 0 \\ 0 & 0 & 0 & \cdots & 0 & 0 & 0 & \cdots & 0 & 0 & 0 \end{bmatrix}$$

APPENDIX 4
SELECTED TIME SERIES DATA FOR THE ALUMINUM INDUSTRY

Year	(1) Secondary Output	(2) Net Imports	(3) Estimated Competitive Fringe Output	(4) Shipments to Strategic Stockpile	(5) Index of Durable Manufacturing	(6) Price Index (1926 = 100)	(7) Average Nominal Price ($/ton)	(8) Average Real Price (7)/(6) × 100	(9) Nominal LRAC ($/ton)	(10) Real LRAC (9)/(6) × 100
1951	292.608	148.420	0.0	111.0	128	193.4	380.00	196.5	339.40	175.49
1952	304.522	139.470	0.0	−18.0	136	193.7	388.00	200.3	339.40	175.22
1953	368.566	344.760	0.0	384.0	153	199.8	418.60	209.5	364.40	182.38
1954	292.041	196.103	0.0	1168.0	137	201.5	435.60	216.2	368.60	182.93
1955	335.994	203.385	57.480	344.0	155	215.0	473.40	220.2	364.40	169.49
1956	339.768	196.277	56.760	41.0	159	233.6	520.20	222.7	377.00	161.39
1957	361.819	195.644	53.760	694.0	160	238.0	550.40	231.3	398.00	167.23
1958	289.555	211.616	169.640	708.0	146	236.6	537.80	227.3	381.20	161.12
1959	359.927	139.828	222.762	166.0	166	241.6	537.00	222.3	393.80	163.00
1960	329.450	−180.057	248.880	88.0	171	241.9	544.60	225.1	402.20	166.27
1961	340.246	24.004	245.120	104.0	172	240.5	509.20	211.7	393.80	163.74
1962	461.756	117.935	276.575	83.0	187	238.8	477.60	200.0	398.00	166.67
1963	505.591	174.548	319.587	0.0	196	239.0	452.40	189.3	398.00	166.53
1964	551.691	109.901	359.587	−107.0	209	245.5	474.40	193.2	402.20	163.83
1965	640.718	306.819	432.850	−73.0	232	252.4	490.00	194.1	402.20	159.35
1966	693.031	350.400	591.206	−652.0	259	258.6	490.00	189.5	419.00	162.03
1967	697.751	174.723	675.024	−123.0	257	261.7	499.60	190.9	427.40	163.32
1968	816.908	435.713	795.583	−113.0	267	268.4	511.40	190.5	452.40	168.55
1969	808.535	−11.419	892.357	−279.0	277	283.8	543.60	191.5	486.00	171.19
1970	781.419	−141.796	1164.605	−49.0	257	305.0	574.40	188.3	NA	NA
Average								205.5		167.89

Note: Data in columns (1)–(4) are in thousands of short tons.
Data Sources:
(1) *Metals Statistics*, American Metal Market, Fairchild Publications, Inc., N.Y., 1972, p. 71.
(2) *Metals Statistics*, 1963 and various issues of *Minerals Yearbook*.
(3) Entry (4) × entry (6) from table one.
(4) *Aluminum Statistical Review*, Historical Supplement, 1982, p. 22.
(5) Mason [1972, p. 116].
(6) The wholesale price index of metals and metal products is taken from Mason [1972, p. 105].
(7) Nominal prices are drawn from *Metals Statistics*, 1963 and 1972.
(9) Charles River Associates [1971, p. 3–73].

REFERENCES

ADAMS, W., 1951, 'The Aluminum Case: Legal Victory—Economic Defeat', *American Economic Review*, 41, 5 (December), pp. 915–922.

BAIN, J., 1956, *Barriers to New Competition* (Harvard University Press, Cambridge).

BRANDER, J. A. and SPENCER, B. J., 1983, 'Strategic Commitment with R&D: The Symmetric Case', *Bell Journal of Economics*, 14, 1 (Spring), pp. 225–235.

CHOW, G. C., 1975, *Analysis and Control of Dynamic Economic Systems* (John Wiley and Sons, New York).

CHOW, G. C., 1981, 'Estimation and Optimal Control of Dynamic Game Models under Rational Expectations', in R. E. Lucas and T. J. Sargent (eds.), *Rational Expectations and Econometric Practice* (University of Minneapolis Press, Minneapolis).

DE VANY, A. and FREY, G., 1982, 'Backlogs and the Value of Excess Capacity in the Steel Industry', *American Economic Review*, 72, 3 (June), pp. 441–451.

DIXIT, A. K., 1980, 'The Role of Investment in Entry Deterrence', *Economic Journal*, 90, 357 (March), pp. 95–106.

ESPOSITO, F. F. and ESPOSITO, L., 1974, 'Excess Capacity and Market Structure', *Review of Economics and Statistics*, 56 (May), pp. 188–194.

FRIEDMAN, D., 1984, 'Price Leadership in Producer's Markets', Economic Analysis and Policy Working Paper No. EAP-2, University of California at Berkeley.

GASKINS, JR. D., 1974, 'Alcoa Revisited: The Welfare Implications of a Secondhand Market', *Journal of Economic Theory*, 7, 3 (March), pp. 254–271.

JUDD, K. and PETERSON, B., 1984, 'Dynamic Limit Pricing and Internal Finance', CMSEMS Discussion Paper No. 603S, Northwestern University.

KYDLAND, F. E., 1975, 'Noncooperative and Dominant-Player Solutions in Discrete Dynamic Games', *International Economic Review*, 16, 2 (June), pp. 321–335.

KYDLAND, F. E., 1977, 'Equilibrium Solutions in Dynamic Dominant-Player Models', *Journal of Economic Theory*, 15, 2 (August), pp. 307–324.

KYDLAND, F. E. and PRESCOTT, E. C., 1982, 'Time to Build and Aggregate Fluctuations', *Econometrica*, 50, 6 (November), pp. 1345–1370.

MASON, T. W., 1972, 'The Effects of Entry: A Study of the American Aluminum Industry', Ph.D. dissertation, University of Pittsburgh.

MORK, K., 1982, 'Electricity Demand in Primary Aluminum Smelting', *The Energy Journal*, 3, 3 (July), pp. 71–94.

MUSSA, M., 1977, 'External and Internal Adjustment Costs and the Theory of Aggregate and Firm Investment', *Economica*, 44, 174 (May), pp. 163–178.

PECK, M. J., 1961, *Competition in the Aluminum Industry* (Harvard University Press, Cambridge).

REYNOLDS, S., 1983, 'Strategic Capital Investment in Imperfectly Competitive Markets', Ph.D. dissertation, Northwestern University.

REYNOLDS, S., 1985, 'Capacity, Output and Sequential Entry: Comment', *American Economic Review*, 75, 4 (September), pp. 894–896.

SCHERER, F. M., 1980, *Industrial Market Structure and Economic Performance*, second edition (Houghton Mifflan, Boston).

SIMAAN, M. and CRUZ, JR. J. B., 1973, 'Additional Aspects of the Stackelberg Strategy in Nonzero-Sum Games', *Journal of Optimization Theory and Applications*, 11, 6 (June), pp. 613–626.

SIMONE, A. J., 1962, 'Short-Run and Long-Run Cost Functions for Primary Aluminum', Ph.D. dissertation, MIT.

SPENCE, A. M., 1977, 'Entry, Capacity, Investment and Oligopolistic Pricing', *Bell Journal of Economics*, 8, 2 (Autumn), pp. 534–544.

SPULBER, D., 1981, 'Capacity, Output and Sequential Entry', *American Economic Review*, 71, 3 (June), pp. 502–514.

SWAN, P., 1980, 'Alcoa: The Influence of Recycling on Monopoly Power', *Journal of Political Economy*, 88, 1 (February), pp. 76–99.

WALLACE, D. H., 1937, *Market Control in the Aluminum Industry* (Harvard University Press, Cambridge).

WENDERS, J. T., 1971, 'Excess Capacity as a Barrier to Entry', *Journal of Industrial Economics*, 20, 1 (November), pp. 14–19.

CHARLES RIVER ASSOCIATES, INC., 1971, *An Economic Analysis of the Aluminum Industry.*

COUNCIL ON WAGE AND PRICE STABILITY, Executive Office of the President, 1976, *Aluminum Prices 1974–1975.*

THE JOURNAL OF INDUSTRIAL ECONOMICS 0022–1821 $2.00
Volume XXXIV March 1986 No. 3

THE NATURE OF COMPETITION AND THE SCOPE OF FIRMS

ASHER WOLINSKY

This paper examines how the scope of firms in an industry is affected by the nature of the competition in that industry. The main observation is that imperfectly competitive conduct introduces additional incentives (as compared to competition among price takers) to form multi-product firms. This is explained by the fact that imperfect competition often creates "excess capacities" which in turn induce the firms to expand into other markets.

I. INTRODUCTION

THE RECENT studies of multi-product industries have exposed the technological determinants of the structure of such industries (see, for example, Panzar and Willig [1979], [1981], and Baumol, Panzar and Willig [1981]). These studies introduce the concept of economies of scope (when there are economies of scope it is less costly to combine two or more product lines in one firm than to produce them separately) and relate it to the structure of firms in classical competitive equilibrium. They show that the cost-side property of economies of scope is both a necessary and a sufficient condition for the formation of multi-product firms in perfectly competitive markets.

A natural extension is to investigate how additional factors such as the nature of demand and the conduct of firms supplement cost considerations in determining the scope of firms. The present paper proceeds in this direction by suggesting a certain explanation for how the scope of firms may depend on the nature of the competition in the industry. In particular we argue that imperfectly competitive conduct introduces additional incentives (as compared to those existing in perfect competition) to form multi-product firms. This point is demonstrated by a model of an industry in which competitive behavior results in complete specialization, but at the imperfectly competitive (Cournot) free-entry equilibrium there may be multi-product firms.

The idea is that imperfect competition in a market for a single product often leads to firms' excess capacity. This is due to the competitors' tendency to cut back production and possibly also due to strategic choice of capacities (see, for example, Dixit [1980]). As noted in the classic works of Clark [1923] and Clemens [1958], excess capacity is a reason for the emergence of a multi-product firm, since a firm will try to exploit its excess capacity for the production of other products.

The implications of the analysis of the present paper are potentially testable. In particular, it suggests that measures of the degree of competition, such as the degree of concentration or the size of the barriers to entry, may serve as explanatory variables for the scope of firms across industries.

The plan of the paper is as follows. Section II presents a model of a two-product industry with two types of production technologies. Each technology can be used to produce both products, but each is more efficient in the production of a different product.

Section III considers two alternative forms of competition: competition among price taking firms and imperfect competition (Cournot behavior). For each form of competition the equilibrium with respect to entry, choice of technology and produced quantities is characterized. The main observation is that the scope of firms in equilibrium depends upon the nature of competition in the industry. With the technologies assumed here, price taking firms would specialize at equilibrium in one product or the other, while the imperfectly competitive equilibrium may give rise to multi-product firms.

The intuition behind this result is discussed in section IV. It has to do with the fact that Cournot competition results in excess capacity in the sense that the equilibrium prices are above marginal costs.

Finally, section V is devoted to a discussion that relates the results of the present paper to the cost-side property of economies of scope which is central to the discussion of multi-product firms in the existing literature.

II. THE MODEL

Consider an industry that consists of two products 1,2 which can be produced jointly. Suppose that there are two types of technology (say, each involving a different type of specific capital equipment) such that technology i, $i=1,2$, is more efficient in producing product i. The use of technology i involves a fixed cost F^i. The variable cost of producing quantities x^i of product i and y^j of product j with technology type i is given by $c^i(x^i, y^j)$. It is assumed that c^i is convex, $c_1^i > 0$, $c_2^i > 0$, $c_{12}^i \geqslant 0$ and $c_{11}^i \geqslant c_{12}^i$, $c_{22}^i \geqslant c_{12}^i$, where superscripts refer to the type of technology or product, and subscripts denote partial derivatives. To capture the idea that technology i is more efficient in producing product i, it is assumed that

$$(1) \qquad c_1^i(x^i, y^j) < c_2^i(x^i, y^j) \qquad \text{for all } x^i, y^j > 0$$

It is easy to verify that (1) implies that for any $\varepsilon > 0$, $c^i(x, y) > c^i(x+\varepsilon, y-\varepsilon)$ and in particular $c^i(x+y, 0) < c^i(x, y)$. To understand the meaning of the cost assumptions consider briefly the particular example $c^i(x^i, y^j) = C(x^i + y^j) + V(y^j)$ where $C'(\cdot) > 0$, $V'(\cdot) > 0$, $C''(\cdot) \geqslant 0$, $V''(\cdot) \geqslant 0$. This example is easy to interpret: products i and j share the same facilities and incur the same basic cost $C(\cdot)$, but the production of j with technology i requires some special adjustment effort which is captured by $V(y^j)$.

Let $p^i(\cdot)$ denote the inverse demand for product i and assume that the demands for the two products are independent. To avoid later on a technical discussion which is not our main interest, it is assumed that $p^i(\cdot)$ is concave (or linear).

Finally, we assume complete symmetry: $p^1(\cdot)=p^2(\cdot)=p(\cdot)$, $F^1=F^2=F$ and $c^1(x,y)=c^2(x,y)=c(x,y)$ where the latter means that the cost of producing $x^1=x$ and $y^2=y$ with technology 1 is equal to the cost of producing $x^2=x$ and $y^1=y$ with technology 2. (Notice that our notational convention is that the first coordinate of $c(\cdot,\cdot)$ is the quantity of the product at which the considered technology is more efficient.)

It should be emphasized that our purpose is to obtain a simple model that will enable us to focus on the main point, without dealing with additional complications which are not directly relevant for that point. For this reason we invoked quite strong assumptions, such as the limitation to two products and the independence of the demands. These assumptions are not essential for the derivation of the qualitative results, but they simplify the exposition substantially.

III. THE SCOPE OF FIRMS IN PERFECT AND IMPERFECT COMPETITION

The purpose of this section is to examine how the nature of the competition affects the scope of firms in the context of the model outlined above. To this end we suppose that there are many potential firms that have access to the same technologies (as captured by the function $c(\cdot,\cdot)$) and consider the equilibrium outcomes under two alternative forms of competition. One form is competition among price takers which will be referred to as perfect competition. The other form is competition among Cournot-type quantity setting firms that recognize the effect of their actions on the prices and we shall refer to it as imperfect competition. In both cases we consider the free entry equilibrium in which the number of firms is determined endogenously by the zero-profit condition.

Perfect competition

Suppose that there are many potential entrants. Each has to decide whether or not to enter the industry (an entrant incurs the set-up cost F) and then which technology to employ and what quantities to produce. The behavioral assumption is that the firms are price takers. That is, given the prices p^1 and p^2, the profit maximization problem of a firm that chose technology i is

$$\text{(2)} \qquad \operatorname{Max}\{p^i x^i + p^j y^j - c(x^i, y^j) - F\}$$

The necessary conditions for x^i and y^j to be the solution to this problem are:

$$p^i \leqslant c_1(x^i, y^j) \qquad \text{with equality holding if } x^i > 0$$
$$p^j \leqslant c_2(x^i, y^j) \qquad \text{with equality holding if } y^j > 0$$

These conditions together with the condition that each firm chooses its technology optimally and the free entry (zero-profit) condition characterize the competitive industry's equilibrium. It can be verified that if $c_{11} > 0$ and the fixed cost F is not "too large", then there exists a unique industry equilibrium (in our statements concerning the equilibrium we ignore integer problems which may arise due to the fact that, with an integer number of firms, the requirement of zero-profit may not be satisfied precisely). This unique equilibrium is of the following form: the prices of both products are the same, $p^1 = p^2 = p^*$; a firm with technology i produces quantity $x^i = x^*$ such that $c_1(x^*, 0) = p^*$, and quantity $y^j = 0$ of the other product; by the zero-profit condition p^* is equal to the average cost $[c(x^*, 0) + F]/x^*$.

To verify the above statements note first that at equilibrium we cannot have $y^j > 0$. This is because with technologies of the type considered here (see (1) above), for all $y^j > 0$ the equality $p^* = c_1(x^i, y^j)$ implies $p^* < c_2(x^i, y^j)$. Thus, since profit maximization of a price taking firm with technology i implies $p^* = c_1(x^i, y^j)$, it also implies $p^* < c_2(x^i, y^j)$ and hence $y^j = 0$. Next, note that the requirement that $c_{11} > 0$ guarantees that when a firm with technology i produces only product i, its marginal cost function is strictly increasing. Therefore, the case of $c_{11} > 0$ is the standard textbook case of a competitive industry equilibrium with U-shaped average cost curves. That is, when integer problems are ignored, the unique equilibrium prices are equal to minimum average cost and the number of firms is such that the demand is satisfied when all active firms operate at minimum average cost. The requirement that F is not "too large" is then needed to guarantee that at a price equal to minimum average cost, the demanded quantity is sufficient to sustain the industry.

Similarly, it is easy to verify that for the case of $c_{11} = 0$ and $F = 0$ there also exists a unique competitive equilibrium. This is the standard case of constant marginal cost: the unique equilibrium here is also such that each firm produces a single product; the equilibrium prices are equal to the constant marginal cost c_1; but the number of firms is indeterminate.

The conclusion is that in the industry considered here competition among price takers, or for that matter any form of competition that results in marginal cost pricing (see the discussion of this point at the end of the section), leads to complete specialization.

The imperfectly competitive case

As before, the firms that enter the market choose simultaneously which technology to employ and what quantities to produce of products 1, 2. But here each firm is aware that its actions affect the prices. The equilibrium concept is Nash equilibrium with quantities and the choice of technology as the strategic variables, and with the additional requirement of zero profit, which together with the assumption of free entry determines the equilibrium number of firms. Namely, each firm chooses technology and quantities so as to maximize its profits, given the quantities chosen by the others, and entry continues until all profits are exhausted.

We shall focus on symmetric equilibria. A symmetric equilibrium is a configuration of $2n$ firms where n firms employ technology 1, the other n employ technology 2, and each firm with technology i produces $x^i = x^*$ and $y^j = y^*$ of products i and j respectively. It will be convenient to denote by $\pi^i(x^i, y^j | Q^i = A, Q^j = B)$ the profits of a firm with technology i who produces x^i and y^j, given that the total quantities of products i, j offered by its rivals are A and B respectively. Define $q = (n-1)x^* + ny^*$ and $Q = nx^* + (n-1)y^*$. The conditions which must be satisfied at a symmetric equilibrium are:

$$(3) \qquad \pi^i(x^*, y^* | Q^i = q, Q^j = Q) \geqslant \pi^i(x^i, y^j | Q^i = q, Q^j = Q) \qquad \text{for all } x^i, y^j$$

$$(4) \qquad \pi^i(x^*, y^* | Q^i = q, Q^j = Q) \geqslant \pi^j(x^j, y^i | Q^i = q, Q^j = Q) \qquad \text{for all } x^j, y^i$$

$$(5) \qquad \pi^i(x^*, y^* | Q^i = q, Q^j = Q) = 0$$

Condition (3) requires that, given a firm's technology and the quantities produced by its rivals, its profit is maximized at the equilibrium quantities x^* and y^*. Condition (4) requires that the firm's profit is maximized with respect to the choice of its technology. Condition (5) is the equilibrium zero-profit condition which ensures that no further entry is profitable.

If such an equilibrium exists, then x^*, y^* and n are characterized by the first order conditions and the zero profit condition:

$$(6) \qquad p(nx^* + ny^*) + x^* p'(nx^* + ny^*) = c_1(x^*, y^*)$$

$$(7) \qquad p(nx^* + ny^*) + y^* p'(nx^* + ny^*) \leqslant c_2(x^*, y^*)$$

and the equality holds if $y^* > 0$

$$(8) \qquad (x^* + y^*) p(nx^* + ny^*) = c(x^*, y^*) + F$$

where $p'(\cdot)$ denotes the first derivative of $p(\cdot)$.

Of course, a pre-condition for the existence of a non-degenerate equilibrium of this type is that F is not "too large" so that some firms can profitably coexist in the industry. Supposing that F is indeed such that at least two firms can coexist, we have:

Claim 1: Ignoring integer problems there exists a symmetric zero profit equilibrium. (The proof is sketched in the appendix.)

Let us examine the scope of firms at the imperfectly competitive equilibrium. Inspection of the necessary conditions (6)–(8) reveals that the symmetric equilibrium may involve either specialization or joint production. That is, for certain values of the parameters, the equilibrium output of each firm consists of positive quantities of both products ($x^* > 0, y^* > 0$), while for other values of the parameters each firm will specialize, at equilibrium, in the product at which it is more efficient ($x^* > 0, y^* = 0$).

It will be useful to observe the two possibilities by considering the following two examples. First, consider the functional form $c(x, y) = C(x+y)+y^2$. It is easy to verify that in this case the firms will always produce both products at equilibrium. The property of this cost function which gives rise to the joint production is the fact that $c_1(x, 0) = c_2(x, 0)$. To see this suppose that the firms specialized at equilibrium and let p^* denote the symmetric equilibrium price. Notice that equation (6) implies $c_1(x^*, 0) < p^*$ which together with the quality of the marginal costs means that $c_2(x^*, 0) < p^*$ But the last inequality means that it pays the firm to produce some positive quantity of the other good and hence specialization cannot be an equilibrium result.

Next, consider a cost function, $c(x, y)$, for which $c_2(x, 0)$ is bounded away from $c_1(x, 0)$, as is the case for the functional form $c(x, y) = C(x+y)+ry$. In this case, depending on the parameters of the model, the equilibrium may involve either specialization or joint production. When the fixed cost F is relatively large, the equilibrium number of firms is relatively small, and at equilibrium firms will produce both products. This is because, with a relatively small number of firms, specialization will result in relatively high mark-ups of prices over marginal costs. If the mark-up is in excess of r, firms will be induced to start producing the other good, since the marginal cost of producing it is lower than the price it fetches. Hence, when the size of the fixed cost dictates a relatively small number of competitors, specialization cannot be an equilibrium result. By the same reasoning, when the fixed cost F is small and hence the equilibrium number of firms is relatively large, the firms will specialize.

These points concerning the relations between the intensity of competition (as measured by the equilibrium number of firms) and the pattern of specialization are easily demonstrated by the simple example where $c(x, y) = c \cdot (x+y)+ry$ and the demand functions are linear $p^1(z) = p^2(z) = a-bz$. Using the equilibrium conditions one can calculate the symmetric equilibrium magnitudes of n (the number of firms of each type), x^* and y^*. When the set-up cost F is sufficiently large and hence n is sufficiently small to satisfy $n < [(a-c)/r]-1$, then at equilibrium each firm produces both products in quantities $x^* = (a-c+nr)/b(2n+1)$ and $y^* = (a-c-(n+1)r)/b(2n+1)$ respectively. As n is made larger (that is, F is made smaller) the ratio y^*/x^* approaches zero, and as n reaches the critical value $[(a-c)/r]-1$ complete specialization is achieved. In this sense one can say that a more intense competition results in a greater degree of specialization. Note that the equilibrium number of firms does not depend only on the size of the set up cost F but rather on the size of F relative to the extent of the market. Thus, for the class of cases considered here, one may say that, given the size of F, the degree of specialization is determined by the extent of the market. This observation suggests another interpretation for the idea that "the division of labor is limited by the extent of the market", which was discussed by Stigler [1951] in the context of vertical disintegration.

The next section contains a discussion of the above comparison between the scope of firms under the two forms of competition. Before we turn to the discussion, let us comment on the meaning of the comparison between the two forms of competitive behavior (price taking behavior vs. quantity setting behavior). First, the comparison should not be taken to imply that the two forms of competition are as likely nor is there any attempt to explain what circumstances give rise to any one of the forms of competitive behavior. Rather, the main point is that imperfectly competitive conduct which results in non-marginal cost pricing may have some implications for the scope of firms and a convenient way to demonstrate it is by comparison to the benchmark case of competition among price takers.

Second, the feature of perfect competition which is utilized in the comparison is the equality of the equilibrium prices to marginal costs. However, marginal cost pricing could be the result of other types of competition. Grossman [1981] has shown that certain forms of strategic interaction among (possibly only a few) firms that are not price takers may drive them to marginal cost pricing. Grossman explains the difference between the strategic interaction suggested by his model and the Cournot interaction as resulting from different types of contracts between sellers and buyers which are available in the market. Thus, the points made by the present paper are also valid if the above comparison is interpreted as referring to two forms of imperfectly competitive interactions which take place in markets with similar basic conditions but different contractual arrangements.

IV. DISCUSSION

The main observation made in the previous section is that imperfectly competitive conduct may lead to the formation of multi-product firms in an industry in which competition among price takers would result in complete specialization. The key to this result lies in the fact that competition among Cournot-type quantity setting firms results in equilibrium prices above marginal costs (this is, of course, due to the fact that each firm faces a downward sloping residual demand curve and hence maximum profit is achieved at the quantity at which the marginal revenue is equal to the marginal cost). As a consequence of the discrepancy between price and marginal cost even a firm which is somewhat less efficient can produce some positive quantity of that product and cover the *variable* cost that it incurs in doing so. The implication of this argument for the two-product industry considered here is that a firm which is more efficient in producing product i may sometimes profitably exploit the gap between the price and marginal cost in the market for product j and produce some quantity of that product. To see this argument more precisely consider the symmetric industry equilibrium which is obtained when the firms are artificially constrained to produce one product. In this equilibrium there are n firms of each type; every firm produces quantity x^* of the product at the production of which it is more efficient; and the prices are $p^* = p^1(nx^*) = p^2(nx^*)$. Notice that if $c_2(x^*, 0) < p^*$, then it pays a producer of product 1 to produce also a unit of product 2 despite the facts that the price of this unit, p^2, is not higher than p^1 (since $p^1 = p^2 = p^*$), and its production is more costly than the production of an additional unit of product 1. The reason that the firm wants to produce this more costly unit of product 2, but does not want to increase its production of product 1 is that the marginal revenue that accrues to the firm in market 2 is the price p^* which is greater than the marginal revenue, $p^* + x^*(dp^1/dx)$, it obtains in market 1.

The above explanation suggests that the results of section III do not just reflect some peculiar properties of the simple model employed there. Rather, the driving forces such as the firms' tendency to restrict their output and the existence of price mark-up over marginal cost are quite common characteristics of imperfectly competitive markets.

In the light of this it is quite obvious that some of our assumptions are not crucial for the derivation of the qualitative results but rather serve to simplify the analysis. For example, consider the possibility to relax the assumption that the demands for the two products are independent. If the price of each product is assumed to depend on the total quantities of both products, then the qualitative results concerning the scope of firms under the two forms of competition do not change. The only difference is that whether or not imperfectly competitive conduct results in the emergence of two-product firms in any particular case will now also depend on the cross demand effects in that case. Note that the above remains true when the two products are complementary. This is because the argument given in section III for why price takers specialize is not affected (it depends only on the cost advantages to specialization), while the possibility that imperfect competitors will produce both products is just enhanced by the complementarity.

Next, let us consider the issue of efficiency. Provided that the rest of the economy (that is, all markets other than the markets for goods 1 and 2) is competitive, the imperfectly competitive conduct in the markets for goods 1 and 2 results in an inefficient allocation. Two of the distortions which exist in this case are not special to the present model. These are the allocative inefficiency which is due to the fact that the imperfectly competitive sector produces too little and the productive inefficiency which has to do with the fact that, given the industry's output, the industry's cost is not necessarily minimized with respect to the number of firms. An additional aspect of inefficient production, which is special to the present model, has to do with the existence of multi-product firms despite the cost advantages to specialization. That is, given the equilibrium number of active firms and the total industry output, the industry cost is not minimized with respect to specialization. A reorganization of production whereby each firm produces the same volume but specializes in a single product will facilitate the production of the same outputs at lower industry costs. Since the latter distortion is added to the distortions that would have existed anyway, one cannot say in general whether or not the possibility of joint production improves the allocation. That is, letting welfare be measured by total surplus (the sum of consumers' surplus and profits), it can be shown that if the firms are forced to specialize the total surplus can be either lower or higher (depending on the various parameters) than it is when joint production is allowed. This is because the existence of multi-product firms might lead to higher output and hence higher consumers' surplus, but it involves higher costs of production which may or may not outweigh the added consumers' surplus.

The above-described inefficiency which may arise in competition among multi-product firms is, of course, due to the nature of the costs of production assumed throughout (see (1)). For a complementary discussion concerning the efficiency aspects of competition among multi-product firms the reader is referred to Waterson [1983], who considers industries in which the cost conditions are favorable to multi-product production and analyzes the efficiency tradeoff between economies of scope and the effects of market power.

V. ECONOMIES OF SCOPE

The modern literature on multi-product firms has dealt mainly with the technological (cost side) determinants of the structure of such firms. The present paper has exposed another determinant of the scope of firms—the nature of the competition in the industry. The purpose of this section is to consider the connection between the results of the present paper and the technological property of economies of scope which is a central concept in the literature referred to above.

Let us start by describing the concept of economies of scope in the context of the two-product industry considered here (Panzar and Willig who coined this term discuss it for arbitrary number of products). It is said that there are economies of scope at the output combination x^i, y^j if the cost of producing this combination by one firm is lower than the cost of producing it by two single-product firms. That is,

$$(9) \qquad F + c(x^i, y^j) < F + c(x^i, 0) + F + c(y^j, 0)$$

In Baumol, Panzar and Willig [1981] the property of economies of scope is related to the structure of firms in classical competitive equilibrium. Their two propositions are: (a) if at a competitive equilibrium there exist single-product firms that produce x^1 and y^2 respectively, then there are no economies of scope at the combination (x^1, y^2); (b) if at a competitive equilibrium there exists a firm that produces the combination (x^1, y^2), then there are weak economies of scope (with weak inequality in (9)) at this combination. The proofs of these propositions follow immediately from the definitions of economies of scope and competitive equilibrium.

The proposition quoted above does not refer to the relations between the scope of firms and the property of economies of scope in imperfectly competitive markets. In general there is no reason to expect that the existence of economies of scope is a necessary condition for the formation of multi-product firms in imperfect competition. This is because in an imperfectly competitive market the firms may be guided by strategic considerations such as the desire to deter entry by brand proliferation (see, for example, Schmalensee [1978], Scherer [1980] and the references therein). Such considerations may induce firms to multi-product production even in the absence of economies of scope. However, in the model considered here, the firms do not have strategic considerations of that type and indeed the existence of two-product firms is related to the property of economies of scope.

Claim 2: A necessary condition for the existence of two-product firms at the imperfectly competitive equilibrium of section IV is that, at the firm's equilibrium output vector, the cost function exhibits economies of scope.

Proof: Suppose that in the imperfectly competitive equilibrium of section IV each firm produces positive quantities of both products. Let x^*, y^* denote the quantities of i, j respectively which are produced by a firm with technology i, and let $p = p(nx^* + ny^*)$ denote the equilibrium price.

Following the definition of economies of scope, we have to show that it is cheaper to produce these quantities together than to produce them separately, that is,

$$c(x^*, y^*) + F \leqslant c(x^*, 0) + F + c(y^*, 0) + F$$

From the fact that (x^*, y^*) maximizes each firm's profit and from the zero-profit condition we have

$$px^* - c(x^*, 0) \leqslant px^* + py^* - c(x^*, y^*) = F \tag{10}$$

Since $y^* < x^*$ and $c_1(x^*, 0) \leqslant c_1(x^*, y^*) < p$ we have

$$py^* - c(y^*, 0) < px^* - c(x^*, 0) \leqslant F$$

Therefore, $py^* < c(y^*, 0) + F$, which together with (10) implies that

$$c(x^*, y^*) + F = px^* + py^* < c(x^*, 0) + F + c(y^*, 0) + F \qquad \text{Q.E.D.}$$

By definition, economies of scope is a "local" property of the cost function—at certain output vectors the cost function may exhibit economies of scope, while at others it may not. With the technology assumed here, imperfect competition may result in each firm producing an output combination at which there are economies of scope, while perfect competition results in specialization. This is not surprising since, as suggested by Panzar and

Willig [1981], economies of scope are explained by the existence of "quasi-public" input which can be interpreted as some type of excess capacity. But, imperfect competition often leads to the existence of excess capacities which, in turn, give rise to economies of scope.

It is now possible to examine the role of our main assumption concerning the cost side (that is, that for all x and y, $c_1(x, y) < c_2(x, y)$). In the absence of such an assumption the conclusion that competition among price takers results in specialization does not necessarily hold. Furthermore, with arbitrary cost functions, one cannot exclude pathological cases such that at the output combinations produced by the firms in the perfectly competitive equilibrium there are economies of scope, while at the output combinations of the Cournot equilibrium there are diseconomies of scope. Such cost structures are indeed pathological, since the most natural source of economies of scope are excess capacities (see Panzar and Willig [1981]) which do exist in Cournot equilibrium but do not exist in perfectly competitive equilibrium. Thus, if the above assumption is abandoned and all possible cost structures are considered, then it is still true that imperfectly competitive behavior creates additional incentives (as compared with price taking behavior) for firms to expand their scopes. However, these additional incentives just supplement the technological factors and therefore do not guarantee that under imperfect competition the scope of firms will be always larger than it is under perfect competition.

VI. CONCLUSION

This paper has examined how the scope of firms is affected by the nature of the competition in the industry. In the context of the model studied here it was shown that imperfectly competitive conduct may lead to the formation of multi-product firms in an industry in which perfect competition results in specialization. The qualitative conclusion is that imperfectly competitive behavior creates additional incentives (as compared with perfectly competitive behavior) for firms to expand their scopes. These incentives supplement cost considerations which are the only relevant data for understanding the scope of firms under perfect competition. The implications of this paper are potentially testable in the sense that one can use a measure of the degree of competition as one of the explanatory variables for the differences in the scope of firms across industries.

ACCEPTED MAY 1985

ASHER WOLINSKY,
The Faculty of Social Sciences,
Department of Economics,
The Hebrew University of Jerusalem,
Mount Scopus,
Jerusalem 91905,
Israel.

APPENDIX

Proof of Claim 1

Consider first a configuration of $2n$ firms such that n employ technology 1 and the other n technology 2. With n and the technologies fixed, the convexity of $c(\cdot, \cdot)$, the concavity of $p(\cdot)$ and the complete symmetry imply that there exists a symmetric equilibrium with respect to the choice of quantities (this follows from standard arguments which are brought, for example, in Friedman [1977]). Further, since $c_{11} \geqslant c_{12}$ and $c_{22} \geqslant c_{12}$ it can be shown that, for a given n, there is only one such symmetric equilibrium (upon differentiating the first order conditions for a symmetric equilibrium, one can observe that these properties of cost together with the aforementioned properties imply a unique solution).

To see that this configuration is at equilibrium with respect to the choice of technology as well, it has to be shown that, given the quantities produced by all other firms, no firm can profit from changing both its technology and quantities. Suppose that at the quantity equilibrium with fixed n and fixed technologies, a firm with technology i produces x^* of product i and y^* of product j. It follows from the first order conditions (6) and (7) that $x^* > y^*$. Consider now a firm with technology 1. The total quantities produced by all other firms Q^1, Q^2 are $Q^1 = (n-1)x^* + ny^* < nx^* + (n-1)y^* = Q^2$. Suppose that the firm switches to technology 2 and produces quantities z, w of products 1, 2 respectively. If $z \geqslant w$ then $c^1(z, w) \leqslant c^2(w, z)$ implying that $\pi^2(w, z) \leqslant \pi^1(x^*, y^*)$.

If $z < w$, then

$$\begin{aligned}\pi^2(w,z) - \pi^1(w,z) &= p(Q^2+w)w + P(Q^1+z)z - p(Q^1+w)w - p(Q^2+z)z \\ &= [p(Q^1+z) - p(Q^2+z)] - [p(Q^1+w) - p(Q^2+w)] < 0\end{aligned}$$

where the last inequality follows from $w > z$, $Q^2 \geqslant Q^1$ and the concavity of $p(\cdot)$. Therefore, $\pi^2(w,z) < \pi^1(w,z) \leqslant \pi^1(x^*, y^*)$ and the switch of technology is unprofitable. So far we have shown that, for any given n, there exists a symmetric configuration satisfying conditions (3) and (4). Now, ignoring integer problems, n can be raised (lowered) until the per-firm profit sufficiently falls (rises) so as to satisfy the zero-profit condition (5).

Q.E.D.

REFERENCES

BAUMOL, W., PANZAR, J. and WILLIG, R., 1981, *Contestable Markets and the Theory of Industry Structure* (Harcourt Brace Jovanovich, San Diego).

CLARK, J., 1923, *Studies in the Economics of Overhead Costs* (Chicago University Press).

CLEMENS, E., 1958, 'Price Discrimination and the Multiproduct Firm', reprinted in R. Heflebower and G. Stocking (eds.), *AEA Readings in Industrial Organization and Public Policy*, pp. 262–276 (Homewood, Illinois).

DIXIT, A., 1980, 'The Role of Investment in Entry Deterrence', *Economic Journal*, 90, pp. 95–106.

FRIEDMAN, J., 1977, *Oligopoly and the Theory of Games* (North-Holland, Amsterdam).

GROSSMAN, S., 1981, 'Nash Equilibrium and the Industrial Organization of Markets with Large Fixed Costs', *Econometrica*, 49, 5, pp. 1149–1172.

PANZAR, J. and WILLIG, R., 1979, 'Economies of Scope, Product Specific Economies of Scale and the Multi-Product Competitive Firm', Bell Labs Economic Discussion Paper No. 152.

PANZAR, J. and WILLIG, R., 1981, 'Economies of Scope', *American Economic Review*, 71, 2, pp. 268–272.

SCHERER, F., 1980, *Industrial Market Structure and Economic Performance* (Second Edition, Rand McNally, Chicago).

SCHMALENSEE, R., 1978, 'Entry Deterrence in the Ready-to-Eat Breakfast Cereal Industry', *Bell Journal of Economics*, 9, 2 (Autumn), pp. 305–327.

STIGLER, J., 1951, 'The Division of Labor is Limited by the Extent of the Market', *Journal of Political Economy*, 59, pp. 185–193.

WATERSON, M., 1983, 'Economies of Scope within Market Frameworks', *International Journal of Industrial Organization*', 1, pp. 223–237.

THE JOURNAL OF INDUSTRIAL ECONOMICS 0022-1821 $2.00
Volume XXXIV March 1986 No. 3

SOME INTERNATIONAL COMPARISONS OF THE AGE OF THE MACHINE-STOCK

S. J. PRAIS*

This paper re-examines recent postal surveys of the stock of machinery in the metal-working industries of Britain, Germany, France, Japan and the United States. Japan has the youngest stock; Britain's stock has a lower average age than those in France, Germany and the United States. Numerically-controlled machines are rising rapidly in importance in all countries, but were less frequent in Britain and France. Questions are raised as to the unduly short-life of machinery assumed by national accounts statisticians; and suggestions are made for the improvement of future machine tool surveys.

INTRODUCTION

JUST OVER a decade ago, surveys of the stock of industrial machinery in Britain and the US were compared by Bacon and Eltis [1974, p. 22]. They noted surprisingly little difference in the average age of the stock—if anything, the British stock was slightly younger (the average British machine was 12 years old, compared with $12\frac{3}{4}$ for the US). When the recent 1982 survey of machine tools in Great Britain was published, the sponsors of the survey noted the high proportion of modern numerically-controlled (NC) machinery, 'putting British industry well ahead in NC percentage terms of Japan, W. Germany, France and the USA'. There was thus nothing to suggest that British machinery was particularly out of date; the conclusion drawn was that 'any problems of competitiveness must be rooted elsewhere' (*Metal-working Production* [1983, pp. 5, 23]).

The object of this note is to present a closer comparison between the most recent British, German, French, Japanese and American surveys; it considers the reliability of the surveys for each country, the total number of machines per employee, the main machine-types, the average age of the stock, and the importance of NC machines. As will be seen, the earlier impressions need to be revised, particularly in relation to Britain being ahead in NC machinery.

* This Note was prepared to complement an interview-study of machinery and skills in matched firms in Britain and Germany carried out by the National Institute (see Daly, Hitchens and Wagner [1985]). In preparing this Note I have had the kind help of Anne Daly, Hilary Steedman (on comparisons with France); Osamu Kokubo (of the Japan Economic Research Centre, visiting The National Institute in 1984–5), and Karin Wagner (on comparisons with Germany); I am grateful to them and to colleagues at the Institute for comments and suggestions based on an earlier version. The research was supported by a grant from the ESRC Panel on the Economics of Industry and Public Enterprise, and forms part of the research programme in Comparative Industrial Structure and Efficiency sponsored by the ESRC at the National Institute.

Reliability of the information

These surveys are voluntary in all countries and response rates are usually low. In *Britain* the latest survey relates to 1982 and was based on 3067 responses, accounting for only some 13 percent of the number of firms approached and 15 percent of employees. The survey results were grossed-up to national totals of manufacturing units in the metal-working industries (SIC orders VI–XII, MLH 311–399), having regard to the number of manufacturing units recorded by the Census of Production for 1979 for each 'industry' and for each employment size-class. It seems more than possible that firms more active in investing in new machinery would respond more frequently, and that the survey may give an unduly optimistic picture both of the number of machines and their youth.

The *German* survey of 1980 was subject to similar limitations. Only 1300 firms responded out of the 6800 approached as members of the relevant trade associations organising the survey. The total number of firms in the industrial groups covered, as shown by the German Census, was some 18 000 in 1979 (*Statistisches Bundesamt* [1979]; industrial groups 10–38, interpolating for firms with over 10 employees). Thus the respondents amounted to only one in five of the firms approached, and to only one in fourteen of firms in those sectors of industry in the whole country. The response was better amongst large firms (40 percent response rate for those with over a thousand employees) than amongst small firms (only 3 percent of those with 10–19 employees);[1] we estimate that about a quarter of national employment in the relevant industries was accounted for by all respondents.

The published results of the German survey include grossed-up national estimates for all machine-types together, based on response by size of firm and Industrial Order; but for *individual* machine-types, only sample results were published classified by firm-size and, separately, by Industrial Order. In the tables we have provided grossed-up estimates for individual machine-types taking into account response-rates by firm-size (the published information was insufficient to take into account also response-variations with respect to industry).

The *French* survey of 1980 was based on 3000 returns to a postal survey addressed to 17 500 engineering establishments with over 10 employees. No response-rates by size of establishment were published (Bureau d'Information [1982]).

The *Japanese* survey of 1981 had the official backing of MITI; 10 400 establishments responded, accounting for a relatively high 87 per cent of those approached. The survey related however only to larger establishments, those with over fifty employees, representing about 60 percent of all manufacturing employment (a postal enquiry was used for establishments with

[1] Derived from the table, classified by size of firm, showing sample and estimated population of machine tools in Germany (Vereins Deutscher Werkzeugmaschinenfabriken [1980, p. 3]).

over a hundred employees, and interviews for those with 50–100 employees; see MITI [1983]).

The most recent *US survey* was carried out in the first half of 1983, and was based on some 12 000 returns out of 50 000 questionnaires sent to metal-working firms listed in two commercial directories (the McGraw-Hill directory was used to approach all firms with over twenty employees, and Dun & Bradstreet for a roughly one-in-ten sample of smaller firms; see *American Machinist* [1983]). It appears that these directories were fairly comprehensive, in that the numbers of firms—especially the larger ones—corresponded closely with the official Census of Manufactures. Overall, the returns related to about a quarter of all employees. The published sample results had been grossed-up to national totals on the basis of response-rates by industry (four-digit SIC) and by plant-size.

The detailed information on types of machinery installed in each country is unique to these surveys, and their results cannot be neglected by any investigator. However, apart from Japan, it is clear that these surveys succeeded in attracting responses from only a minority of firms; and, in the case of Japan, the omission of small firms may introduce some bias in the comparisons (since, for example, larger firms have greater scope for the use of specialised machinery, including advanced NC machines). Though the response-rates were low, they were *similarly* low in the other four countries, and it is therefore possible that biases are similar in comparisons amongst them. Nevertheless, caution dictates that the results be used to give only broad indications, and fine differences between countries have to be disregarded. In future surveys it is to be hoped that greater attention will be given to representativeness of response; the tabulation of employment totals for the sample would also improve the accuracy of re-weighting.[2]

Total number of machines per employee

Totalling comparable types of machinery covered in the surveys, and taking comparable industrial groups, it appears from Table I (third row) that Germany, France and Japan had remarkably similar numbers of machines per employee, and about a fifth more than Britain. The US had the lowest number of machines per employee—about a fifth less than Britain, and about a third less than the other three countries.

Bearing in mind the great contemporary differences between these countries in productivity, one might be surprised that the differences recorded by

[2] In more detail: where postal surveys achieve only a low response, a second stage may be introduced relating specifically to non-respondents at the first stage; a representative sub-sample of these may be visited by interviewers in the hope that a personal approach may be more effective. A different sampling multiplier is in due course applied to that sub-sample. Employment figures for the *sample* should in future also be tabulated, to provide a better basis for grossing up to census totals, and so that the number of machines per 100 employees can be calculated directly.

TABLE I

NUMBER OF MACHINE TOOLS (TOTAL AND PER EMPLOYEE) IN METALWORKING INDUSTRIES[a] IN BRITAIN (1982), GERMANY (1980), FRANCE (1980), JAPAN (1981) AND THE UNITED STATES (1983)

	Britain 1982	*Germany 1980*	*France 1980*	*Japan 1981*	*US 1983*
TOTAL MACHINE TOOLS[b] *(000)*	796	1250	724	907	2038
Total employment in sector (m)	2.90	3.72	2.22	2.65	9.39
	Machines/100 employees				
TOTAL no. of machines (all types)/100 employees	27.4	33.6	32.6	34.2	21.7
Cutting machines—total[c,d]	21.7	25.4	24.3	25.4	15.7
Turning	5.5	5.8	5.8	5.8	3.3
Drilling and boring	5.5	6.4	5.9	5.6	3.2
Grinding	3.6	5.8	4.0	4.1	3.8
Milling	2.7	3.3	2.9	2.9	2.2
Sawing and cutting off	1.8	1.9	1.4	—	1.6
Other cutting[e]	2.6	2.3	4.3	6.9	1.4
Forming machines—total[d]	5.0	7.5	7.6	7.8	5.0
Presses—hydraulic	0.7	0.9	0.8	1.3	0.5
Presses—other	1.9	3.4	2.1	3.6	2.2
Bending	1.0	0.9	0.9	0.5	0.8
Shearing and punching	0.8	0.7	1.6	0.6	0.7
Other[f]	0.7	1.6	2.3	1.8	0.8
Numerically-controlled machines—total	0.8	0.7	0.7	1.0	1.1
Turning	0.3	0.3	0.1	0.4	0.3
Drilling and boring	0.2	0.1	0.2	0.1	0.1
Milling	0.1	0.1	0.1	0.1	0.2
Multi-function, machining centres	0.2	0.1	0.1	0.2	0.2
Other cutting and forming[g]	0.1	0.1	0.2	0.2	0.2

Sources: Sample surveys of machine tool stocks in each country: see text. The figures in this table differ from those in the original sources since, for the sake of inter-country consistency, we excluded certain types of machinery (e.g. most joining equipment, plating equipment, plastic moulding) and certain industrial groups (primary metals, shipbuilding) which were covered in one country's survey but not in the others. The table thus relates more specifically to metalworking machinery in metalworking trades.

Notes: [a] Excluding primary metals and shipbuilding (for UK includes SIC VI–IX, XI–XII; and equivalent sectors in other countries).

[b] Types listed below; the surveys as published include additional types, varying from country to country. Coil-handling equipment and transfer machinery are excluded here.

[c] Metal removal machines, including erosion machines.

[d] Excluding NC (shown separately below).

[e] Tapping, threading, broaching, planing, shaping, honing, lapping (excluding polishing), gear cutting, electrical and chemical machining, other cutting.

[f] Forging, threading, multiple-slide forming, wire and ribbon forming, rivetting (non-portable), other forming.

[g] Excluding robots.

the surveys in the stock of machines per employee are not greater. Perhaps the first conclusion to be drawn should be a familiar one: if British manufacturing output per employee is only half that in the United States, it is not in any obvious way due to a deficiency in the total number of machines available per person employed. The case for a British deficiency in the number of machines is more arguable in relation to Germany; output per employee in manufacturing as a whole there is about 50 percent higher than here, and in engineering it is perhaps as much as 80 percent higher (Smith *et al.* [1982, p. 63] and Roy [1982, p. 29]): even so, it does not seem likely that very much of that productivity gap could be attributed to a mere 20 percent difference in the number of machines per employee. Differences in the efficiency of usage are likely to be more important.

Differences in product-mix and length of run undoubtedly require different numbers of machines and different manning levels; we can here do no more than adumbrate some of the relevant factors. Thus, it seems to be broadly true that German engineering engages to a greater extent on precision batch-work, requiring a succession of machines to reach finer tolerances; not all of the machines will be in use at the same time. In the United States continuous mass-production—or very large batchwork—is more frequent and fewer spare machines stand waiting for work. There is an off-setting element in that greater automation in the US should enable the typical employee there to supervise more machines than in Germany; these surveys suggest that this is not the over-riding element.

If the Americans, with fewer machines per employee, produce more per employee than we do in Britain, we must also look to machine utilisation: does American machinery work for a greater fraction of the available time, and is there more shift-working in the United States? The present surveys cast no light on these questions; but we know from other studies that shift-working is somewhat more frequent in the USA than in Germany and Britain (Prais *et al.* [1981, ch. 6 and app. F]). Since American machinery tends to be more highly-automated, it requires fewer people to keep it in operation on supplementary shifts, and more is to be lost by allowing such expensive equipment to stand idle. Whether during working-hours American machinery spends more of its time at work—rather than standing idle waiting for work or waiting to be repaired—is a matter on which we still have only the general impressions of 'productivity study teams' to rely on; and there is a long and consistent history, going back to the nineteenth century, indicating that this is an important factor in higher American industrial efficiency (Habukuk [1962]; Daly *et al.* [1985], also drew attention to down-time as an important factor in explaining productivity differences).

Main machine-types

The relative frequency with which the main types of machine tool appear in Table I is remarkably similar in the five countries. In some degree this provides reassurance that there is nothing radically wrong in the structure of British capital equipment. It will of course be understood that a machine, defined as broadly as in these surveys, can vary immensely in its capability (for example, a power press can range from under a ton to many hundreds of tons), and can vary in its speed of working, ease of setting, precision and durability; and hence it will also vary in its total cost and value to a firm. Apart from the category of numerically-controlled machine tools, with their recognised higher productivity in their field of application (considered in more detail below), there is little in the recorded classification that would enable one to say whether, for example, the average turning machine in one country is 'better' than in another country.[3] In addition, apparent contrasts cannot always be taken at face value since, aside from possible variations in response-bias, there are doubts as to whether smaller tools have been included uniformly. For example, it appears that the American survey specifically included 'bench, floor and snag grinders' and abrasive belts in their total of grinding machines—they amounted to as much as a third of all grinding machines in their survey; these sub-categories were also included in the Germany survey, but apparently were excluded from the British survey. The American total of machine tools might therefore be reduced yet further (from 21.7 to 20.5 machines per 100 employees) for stricter comparability with the UK, so adding to the apparently greater efficiency with which Americans use their machinery.

Of the other differences in specific machine-types, the greater number of *presses* in Germany and Japan—nearly twice as many per employee as in Britain—deserves notice. These machines are typically used in the rapid cutting and shaping of sheet-metal—a process which is more economical in both materials and labour than cutting a component out of solid metal (for example, a pressed metal fastening can replace the older nuts made out of solid metal; similar adaptations usually originate at the design-stage of the product). We cannot however be quite sure whether the count of presses in Germany was restricted to power presses as it was in Britain, the US and Japan, or whether hand and foot presses were included in Germany (the German questionnaire was not clear on this); hand and foot presses are employed for simple light work, but have increasingly been replaced by small power-driven presses (often hydraulic or pneumatic presses, which are now relatively cheap) with their faster rate of working. The lower number of presses in Britain raises the question (if we ignore for the moment the definitional qualification just mentioned) whether our production design and methods are less efficient in the context of modern mass-production. In the United States the number of power presses per employee is also much lower than in Germany and Japan; nevertheless, even in the US they are *relatively* more important in the total stock of machinery than in Britain (12 as against 9 percent). A more specific enquiry would be needed to provide satisfactory answers on this issue.

[3] The original publications give rather more detailed types of machinery than summarised here in Table I; while some narrower comparisons are possible, we were unable to discover any contrasts that were of interest. Unfortunately, the more detailed classifications are not on a uniform basis as between the countries.

TABLE II

PERCENTAGE OF CUTTING AND FORMING MACHINES LESS THAN 10 AND 5 YEARS OLD, BRITAIN, GERMANY, FRANCE, JAPAN AND THE UNITED STATES, 1980–3

	Britain 1982	*Germany 1980*	*France 1980*	*Japan 1981*	*US 1983*
Percentage of machines less than 10 years old					
All machines	42	34	35	47	33
Cutting	42	34	34	45	34
Forming	44	34	37	51	27
Percentage of machines less than 5 years old					
All machines	24	15	16	25	13
Cutting	24	15	15	25	14
Forming	27	15	18	28	10

Note: Industrial coverage as in Table I, that is, excluding primary metals and shipbuilding; numerically controlled machines have been included here in their respective category (except for Britain where, for convenience of calculations, all NC machines have been included here as cutting tools—the proportion of NC forming tools is negligible for the purposes of this table). Interpolation was necessary for the British survey since the published youngest 'five-year' group relates to purchases after 1 January 1977, and the following group to purchases after 1 January 1971; at the date of the survey (say, mid-1982) these machines would be up to 5 and up to 11 years old respectively. We interpolated graphically to obtain 5 and 10 year totals corresponding with other countries (without this adjustment, Britain's stock would have appeared younger still!). The summary totals for the age-distribution published in the British survey (pp. 52 and 54) need to take into account the 'errata slip' attached to the publication; there are other errors in the summary totals by age of machine (p. 23; it appears that unweighted, instead of weighted, averages were published). For the French figures, an adjustment has been made for comparability of industrial coverage by excluding shipbuilding and the foundry industries on the basis of the main types of machines used.

Age of machine tools

According to these surveys Britain's stock of machinery is extraordinarily young in comparison with other Western countries: 42 percent of all machines in Britain were under ten years old[4] at the date of survey, compared with 35 percent in France, 34 percent in Germany and 33 percent in the United States (see Table II).

Most of the difference relates to machines under five years old, which accounted for as much as 24 percent of the stock in Britain, compared with 16, 15 and 13 percent in France, Germany and the United States respectively. The median machine in Britain was some 12 years old, compared with about

[4] Under *ten*, and not under *five* years; a table in the published British Survey (p. 23) shows 41 percent of cutting machines and 48 percent of forming machines as 0–5 years old, but these figures incorporate calculating errors (see note to Table II). The US survey reproduced those figures, did not notice they were erroneous, and commented on the huge proportion of new machines in Britain: 'The big surprise is Britain, where strong tax incentives to modernise plant have made a substantial change...' (*American Machinist* [November 1983, p. 118]). Even after correcting the errors, there is a fair surprise in the figures, if not quite as big as that commentator thought. The US survey is also not without its solecisms—its summary international comparisons show 18 percent of American forming tools as 0–9 years old (Table 4, p. 116), when other tables make it clear that 27 percent are in that age-group.

15 years in France, and 14 years in Germany and the US (estimated by graphical interpolation). Much the same applies to the category of forming machines as to the larger category of cutting machines; the latter includes here the bulk of numerically-controlled machines, the majority of which are under five years old. The number of machines less than five years old was 6.6 per 100 employees in Britain, 5.2 in France, 3.8 in Germany and 2.0 in the United States. Whatever reservations one may entertain as to the validity of these surveys, it has to be said that—at the very least—they provide no evidence of inadequacies in Britain's productivity being attributable to too few new machines.

Only Japan, with its recent very rapid industrialisation, has a younger stock of machinery than Britain: the average age of its stock, was 10 years, and it had 8.6 machines under five years old per 100 employees.

It would be simple enough to suggest that the 100 percent first-year write-offs for tax purposes, introduced in Britain in 1972 and phased out after 1985, have apparently done their job well in stimulating capital expenditure. The underlying reality is more complicated, though it cannot be set down in statistical detail. Whether new machines represent a small or large fraction of the total stock depends on the time-path of past purchases and what has happened to them: have older machines been allowed to live out their normal technically-useful lives, or have they been scrapped prematurely because of technological or economic obsolescence? In some British industries, market conditions have changed so radically in the last decade that it was no longer economically possible even to leave them idle, in reserve for times of economic revival. Liquidations and machinery auctions in the early 1980s took place on a massive scale in the car industry and the machine tool industry (one need only recall the Scottish Rootes plant and Albert Herbert); much machinery was shipped to developing countries. While some of that machinery was undoubtedly fairly new, it is perhaps more likely (and would be less discomforting to the taxpayer, who made large contributions to keep some of those plants alive) that on the whole an older age-distribution characterised the machinery of plants that were liquidated.

Looking at similar previous surveys of the machine stock confirms that there has been a general ageing of the machine tool stock in all countries (see Table III). Post-war industrial re-equipment led to younger stocks (particularly in Japan); when investment receded in the latter half of the 1970s, an ageing of the stock was inevitable, but has not gone as far in Britain as in Germany, France and the United States.

The service life of machines

As mentioned, the *median age* of the machine stock in all the countries surveyed is in the region of 10–14 years; this period is to be distinguished from the *total service* life of the average machine which, in order of

TABLE III
AGE-DISTRIBUTION OF ALL MACHINES,[a] SELECTED YEARS SINCE 1961

	Britain				*Germany*		*France*	*Japan*		*United States*			
	1961	*1971*	*1976*	*1982*	*1976*	*1980*[b]	*1980*	*1973*	*1981*	*1963*	*1968*	*1977*	*1983*
Under 10 years	43	43	40	39	36	34	35	61	47	36	36	31	32
10–19 years	36	36	36	29	36	31	32	21	46	43	41	35	35
20 years and over	21	21	24	32	27	35	33	18	7	21	23	34	33
	100	100	100	100	100	100	100	100	100	100	100	100	100

Notes: [a] These figures are reproduced as published in the original sources; they have not been adjusted for the slightly varying industrial coverage amongst countries, and hence differ slightly from those in Table II (in particular: Table II excludes the primary metal industries and shipbuilding, which tend to have an older stock of machinery than other sectors).

[b] In the original source there is an age-break at 15 years; we extrapolated graphically to 20 years to compare with the other countries.

magnitude, may be taken as approximately double that period—say, something like 25 years. For the purposes of calculating the capital stock and capital consumption, national accounts statisticians in Britain assumed—until very recently—that plant and machinery typically lasted 34 years (Hibbert *et al.* [1977, p. 135]); while in the United States and Germany a typical life in the region of only 16 years has been assumed for these purposes. In fixing on these assumptions, depreciation allowances for tax-purposes seem to have been relied on as reflecting reality, but very little direct evidence seems to have been compiled in any country on actual survival-rates (Blades [1983, esp. p. 19n]). International comparisons of capital stock per employee based on national accounts, and similar sources, thus have a substantial element of arbitrariness stemming from differences in *assumed* lengths of life.

Can the distributions of ages of surviving machinery, provided by machine tool surveys of the kind considered here, cast any light on these matters? An attempt was made by Bacon and Eltis in 1974; on their approach it is necessary (a) to assume some general shape for the survival curve of machinery (they assumed that half of all machinery lasts exactly T years, a quarter lasts a third less than that, and a quarter a third more than that), and (b) to make allowances in a simplified way for the investment pattern of recent years (for example, growth or decline at a steady r percent a year). An average service life of 25 years for British machinery in 1971, and of 23 years for the United States in 1968, emerged from their assumptions. Subsequent calculations (by Bacon and Schianchi [1978, esp. pp. 313–4]), based on an Italian survey of 1976, demonstrated that alternative assumptions as to the shape of the survival curve may lead to seriously different calculated values of the service life; using five alternative—but by no means extreme—assumptions on survival curves, the calculated *service life* of Italian power presses, for example, varied from 16 to 28 years (based on the same data—only the assumptions behind the calculations were changed). On the other hand, the implied *average age* of the stock of these machines varied on these alternative assumptions from only 11.0 to 11.3 years. The latter is clearly a more robust measure.[5]

The difficulty of inferring average service lives can perhaps be understood

[5] The five assumptions fall into two groups: (a) constant rate of growth of investment and (1) all machines last exactly T years, (2) an equal number fails each year between 0 and T, (3) quadratic failure rate between 0 and T; (b) two rates of investment combined with assumptions (1) and (2) respectively. These alternative assumptions provide, for this purpose, no more than a basis for interpolation in relation to the observed stock classified into broad age-groups; they do not require a full 'leap into the dark' needed to estimate *total* service life. Mr A. D. Roy has calculated, on the basis of British figures for 1961, the average age of the stock of machines assuming that the chance of retirement for a surviving machine increases linearly with its age; the average comes out at 13.0 years, which is close to the actual median (derived from the observed cumulative distribution by graphical interpolation) and to the 12.0 years derived for 1971 by Bacon and Eltis under their assumptions. One of the interesting consequences of Mr Roy's assumption is that the age-distribution of surviving machines is a truncated Normal distribution. I am grateful to Mr Roy for showing me his calculations.

more easily by considering the 'reducing balance' method of calculating depreciation often used by accountants. On this method a given percentage is taken each year from the balance brought forward from the previous year; 'in theory' this proceeds indefinitely, though for practical purposes the balance eventually becomes of negligible value. There is a realistic element in all this since heavy machines (such as drop hammers) a hundred years old or more are by no means exceptional in continuing in current production (perhaps modified by the addition of an electric motor). When accountants, or the taxation authorities, speak of a 'length of life' in connection with this method of depreciation, they usually mean the period taken to write off 90 percent of its value; but that is an entirely notional concept (if it takes 34 years to write off 90 percent, it would take 68 years at the same rate of depreciation to write off 99 percent—either period is as appropriate, or inappropriate, as the other). In processes of this sort scientists often take the 'half-life' as a more robust measure—this is the period in which half the population has disappeared (for example, in measuring the life of electric lamps, one can take a large sample of lamps and ask after how many hours of continuous burning have half of them burnt-out?). The median age of the stock of machines is a measure of this type; it is of course not far removed from simpler measures such as the proportion of all machines under 10 years of age that are used by general commentators (and which were given in the tables above).

One of the objects of calculations of length of life is to help interpret changes in the observed ages of the stock of machinery. To take recent British figures as an example: we have seen in Table III that the proportion of machines under 10 years old declined in the past decade from 43 to 39 percent, while the proportion of machines over 20 years old rose from 21 to 32 percent; to what extent is this because investment has fallen in recent years, and to what extent because machines now last longer? Taking the results of these sample surveys together with available estimates of expenditure by all manufacturing industry on plant and machinery for each of the past thirty years (prepared for the national accounts), some interesting conclusions emerge. A view over as long a period as this is necessary since, as these sample surveys show, a large proportion of all machinery is over twenty years old.[6]

[6] The estimates of investment used here incorporate unpublished figures kindly made available by the Business Statistics Office; as distinct from the figures published in the Blue Book and elsewhere, they include estimates for the past decade of plant and machinery leased to manufacturing (other published figures of leasings do not separate plant and machinery from other equipment, such as vehicles, or do not separate manufacturing from other sectors). The sector covered is larger than that of the sample surveys, but the figures are probably adequate to indicate what has been happening. Estimates of investment during the war years were taken from Dean [1964, p. 334]; as pointed out there, considerable uncertainty attaches to these figures, and there is the further problem that specialised war equipment is likely to have been taken more rapidly out of service after the war.

Broadly speaking, investment in machinery by British manufacturing industry approximately tripled in real terms from the early 1950s till 1979, and then fell by a third in the next three years. Assuming a constant rate of retirement (the 'reducing balance' method) we can attempt to obtain from this series an age-distribution of machinery approximating that observed in the British sample survey of 1982; alternative calculations show that this requires an extraordinarily low retirement rate, in the region of only 2 to 3 percent a year. The following is the comparison of the age-distribution of the stock of machines at the end of 1982:

	Survey, 1982	*Calculated from time-series*	
		2.5 % retirement rate	*3 % retirement rate*
	%	%	%
Under 10 years	39	40	43
10–20 years	29	27	28
Over 20 years	32	33	29
	100	100	100

The implications should not be pressed too far, but it appears that in reality slightly more machines survived to the middle-age group (10–20 years) than would be predicted by a constant proportionate retirement rate. No doubt some form of humped retirement distribution could provide a better approximation; but the discrepancies on this simple approach are not large. The median age of the calculated distribution (obtained by applying that retirement rate to the annual gross investment figures) is 13 years—that is, half the surviving machinery is under 13 years old, and is indistinguishable from the median-age interpolated from the sample survey. This correspondence is not really surprising: it may be found more surprising that if investment remained constant, that is, if there was a balanced stock of machinery, the implied median age of the stock would be as much as 22 years at a 3 percent retirement rate, and 26 years at a 2.5 percent retirement rate.[7] The large excess over the observed median age of 13 years is to be attributed to the strongly rising trend of investment, taking the past thirty years as a whole.

Looking back to 1971, when the British sample survey showed a younger age-stock, a calculation based on the same assumptions yields a less satisfactory correspondence—no doubt because the investment estimates for the

[7] If k machines are installed each year, and a fraction s survives from one year to the next *ad infinitum*, the total stock of machines is $k(1+s+s^2+\ldots) = k/(1-s)$. If the half-life is n, then half the stock is $k(1+s+s^2+\ldots+s^n) = k(1-s^{n+1})/(1-s)$; setting this equal to half the preceding expression yields $n = (0.301/\log s)-1$.

war-years carried more weight at that time, and rather more of that investment was subsequently scrapped:

	Survey, 1971	*Calculated from time-series (2.5 % retirement rate)*
	%	%
Under 10 years	43	47
10–20 years	36	23
Over 20 years	21	30
	100	100

We see, nevertheless, that a fall in the proportion of machinery under 10 years of age was to be expected between 1971 and 1982—simply as a result of the recent reduced rate of gross investment. We might have expected a rise, rather than the actual fall, in the proportion in the central age-group of 10–20 years; but perhaps machinery in that central age-group was at greater risk of disposal in those parts of the engineering industries that declined seriously in the last five years. All in all, it is difficult to see here any real evidence of a shortening in the length of life of recently installed machinery.

Though calculations of this kind are inevitably approximate, they seem to support the relatively long service lives assumed by the British official statisticians, as against the practices of official statisticians in other countries. The latest machinery surveys in France, Germany and the US show about a third of the stock to be over 20 years old: that alone makes it difficult to understand why their statisticians should assume service lives of only 16 years. But, curiously enough, in the 1983 National Income Blue Book the British statisticians moved nearer to the assumptions of those countries, and reduced assumed service lives from 'just over 30 years . . . to about 23 years' (the arithmetic averages are 32.4 and 22.4 years; see Hibbert *et al.*, *loc. cit.*, and CSO [1983, pp. 114–5]). Though the CSO's assumptions still remain substantially above the lives assumed in other countries, one wonders whether that reduction was really necessary.[8]

Numerically-controlled machinery

Widespread interest attaches to the rise in the past two decades of machinery

[8] More particularly, can the new lower lives be consistent with as much as a third of the stock being over 20 years old? The greater complexity of modern machinery might justify giving them greater weight in the total than suggested by mere numbers of machines as recorded in these postal surveys; this might go some way towards justifying the new shorter lives adopted in the national accounts (I am indebted to an anonymous referee for this suggestion). However, no calculations have been published to that effect. For other discussions of the length of life of machinery, see Griffin [1976], and Matthews *et al.* [1983, pp. 581–5].

controlled by some form of electronic 'computing' device. In comparing the extent to which these machines are used in different countries it is important to remember that their use is not economically justified in all circumstances. The following may serve to outline the issues. Electronic or numerical control of machinery replaces human control, and earlier simpler forms of automatic mechanical control (such as a reciprocating table on a grinding machine, or cams controlling the movement of cutters on an automatic lathe): but the operational part of the machine (for example, the drill-bit or cutter) is basically unaffected. Machines of increasing complexity have been evolved so that successive operations, previously carried out on separate machines, can now be carried out successively on single large multi-function machines (a 'machining centre'). Thus, the distinguishing characteristic of the more advanced of these machines lies not merely in the nature of the controlling device, but also in the possible combination of successive operations—saving labour in operating and in handling, and leading to quicker throughput. Additional costs lie partly, but to a reducing extent, on the capital side (the electronic components are said to account now for only a sixth of the cost of such machines, compared to a third a decade ago), and partly in the additional costs of programming and of more highly skilled maintenance staff.

Broadly speaking, the size of the batch and the technical complexity of the product are the factors that determine whether these machines are economically advantageous. Where a number of similar—but not identical—products are required, only small changes in the programme may be necessary; and these changes may cost less than 'old-fashioned' re-setting of machines by hand. Generally, however, where single items ('one-offs') or very small batches are required the new machines have no net advantage over the older machines—the costs of programming are additional and yield no benefit in themselves.

At the other extreme, in the mass-production of very large quantities of identical design, the flexibility provided by NC machines remains unused; it is not worth paying for ease of reprogramming and for multiple functions unless those facilities are used—it is better to organise a line of special-purpose machinery for the item. Such machines normally work more rapidly. Thus NC machines show their advantages in medium-sized batch production of complex products: between fifty and a thousand units at a time is the range often quoted (further details are given in Ray [1984, ch. 7], and Northcott and Rogers [1984]).

The extent to which such machines are adopted must depend, as said, on the technical nature, length of run of this and of related items; and one cannot expect these new machines—especially the more expensive types of machining centres—to replace too much of the existing stock. As Table I shows, at the dates of the latest surveys no more than about one in 20–50 machines was numerically controlled in the various countries; but the proportion of *plants* having at least one NC machine is of course much higher (for example, one in nine of all UK plants, and one in four of all US plants, had at least one NC turning machine). The proportion of plants owning a particular type of machine tends of course to rise with plant size; for example, only 4 percent of UK plants with under 20 employees owned NC turning machines, compared with 51 percent at plants with over 1000 employees (derived from *Metalworking Production*, pp. 71 and 75; and *American Machinist*, p. 122). In international comparisons it would be helpful to compare ownership within particular size-ranges of plants, but unfortunately this information has not been systematically tabulated in these surveys. Because of the higher output rates of NC machines, and the incentive to put such expensive machines onto shiftwork, their contribution to production may be two or three times as great as their number.

The rate of growth of such installations remains very high: in Britain the number of NC machines grew at 18 percent a year in 1962–82; in France by perhaps 30 percent in 1974–80; in Germany by 20 percent in 1974–79; in Japan by 17 percent in 1973–81; and in the US by 12 percent a year in 1977–83. Further, not surprisingly, NC machines accounted for a disproportionately high share of recent installations: for example, in the five years preceding the latest surveys, 8–9 percent of all new machines purchased in Britain and Germany were NC machines, and in the US 17 percent.

In view of the rapidity of these changes, any comparison across countries must take into account that the surveys were not held in the same year. If we adjust all the surveys to a common year by allowing for the above rates of change, it appears that by 1982 the US has installed most of these new machines, at 4.2 percent of its stock; Britain, Germany and Japan had about 3.2 percent; and France about 2.8 percent (a lack of precision in the French questionnaire may have led to some overstatement in their returns). Britain can thus by no means be said to be 'well ahead' of other countries in respect of these machines (as suggested by previous commentators who had not allowed for different dates—'an unexpected stay of industrial revival' and a 'scramble for new technology' were the phrases used in the *Sunday Times*, 24 July 1983). There is a further qualification in that the small—but subsidised—aerospace industry accounted for some 20 percent of all NC machine tools recorded in the UK (having only 5 percent of manufacturing employment), compared with only half that proportion in the US; and in very large NC tools—machining centres with automatic tool change—the aerospace industry accounted in the UK for 32 percent of all installations compared with only 12 percent in the US. In Germany the aerospace industry is of negligible significance. In the rest of the metalworking industries (that is apart from aerospace) the usage of NC machines in Britain thus accounted for only about 2.8 percent of all machines. Britain's record here is thus about average—not an aspect on which it is to be either criticised or applauded.

Summary

1. From the present re-examination of recent postal surveys of the stock of machinery in the metal-working industries of Britain, Germany, France, Japan and the United States it appears that Britain's total stock of machinery per employee does not differ greatly from that of other countries: it has a slightly greater number of machines installed per employee than the United States, and slightly fewer than Germany, France and Japan.

2. A greater proportion of Britain's stock consists of new machines than in the US, Germany and France. Britain's considerably lower productivity in metal-working industries than in the US and Germany cannot be attributed in any direct way to inadequacies in the size or newness of its machine-stock.

3. The average age of the installed machine-stock in Britain is about 12 years, compared with 14–15 years in France, Germany and the US. The average total service life of machinery may be taken as being in the region of thirty years; this is close to the assumption made by national accounts statisticians until recently (the reduction in that assumed length of life made in the 1983 Blue Book deserves reconsideration). Only Japan has a younger stock of machines than Britain.

4. But are Britain's machines—though new—as technically advanced? On the basis of these surveys, earlier commentators thought that Britain was well ahead in the installation of NC machines. After allowing for differences in dates of the surveys, it appears, however, that Britain's proportion of NC machines is similar to that of France, and slightly below that of the other countries examined here.

5. The value of future surveys of machine tools of this kind could be much increased by greater attention to representativeness of response, tabulation of employment totals for the sample, and frequency of ownership by size of firm.

S. J. PRAIS, ACCEPTED SEPTEMBER 1985
National Institute of Economic and Social Research,
2 Dean Trench Street,
Smith Square,
London SW1P 3HE.

REFERENCES

AMERICAN MACHINIST, 1983, 'The 13th Inventory of Metalworking Equipment' (November).

BACON, R. W. and ELTIS, W. A., 1974, *The Ages of US and UK Machinery* (Nedo, London).

BACON, R. W. and SCHIANCHI, A., 1978, 'La Strutture del Parco Macchinne Utensili in Italia: un Estensione del l'Analisi', *Riv. Economica e Politica*, no. 3, pp. 299–316.

Blades, D., 1983, 'Service Lives of Fixed Assets', *OECD Working Papers*, no. 4 (Paris).
Bureau d'Information et de Provisions Economiques, 1982, *Recensement du Parc Francais de Machines-Outils en 1980* (Neuilly).
Central Statistical Office, 1983, *National Income and Expenditure: 1983 Edition* (HMSO, London).
Daly, A., Hitchens, D. M. W. N. and Wagner, K., 1985, 'Productivity, Machinery and Skills in a Sample of British and German Manufacturing Plants', *National Institute Economic Review*, no. 111 (February), pp. 48–61.
Dean, G., 1964, 'The Stock of Fixed Capital in The United Kingdom in 1961', *J. Roy. Statist. Soc.*, A, vol. 127, pp. 327–352.
Griffin, T., 1976, 'The Stock of Fixed Assets in the United Kingdom: How to Make Best Use of the Statistics', *Economic Trends* (October), (HMSO, London), pp. 130–143.
Habakuk, H. J., 1962, *American and British Technology in the Nineteenth Century: The Search for Labour-Saving Inventions* (Cambridge).
Hibbert, J., Griffin, T. J. and Walker, R. L., 1977, 'Development of Estimates of the Stock of Fixed Capital in the United Kingdom', *Rev. Income and Wealth*, vol. 23, pp. 117–137.
Matthews, R. C. O., Feinstein, C. H. and Odding-Smee, J. C., 1983, *British Economic Growth, 1856–1973* (Clarendon, Oxford).
Metalworking Production, 1983, 'The Fifth Survey of Machine Tools and Production Equipment in Britain' (Morgan-Grampian, London).
Ministry of International Trade and Industry, 1983, 'The Sixth Statistical Survey of Metalworking Equipment, 1981' (Japan).
Northcott, J. and Rogers, P., 1984, *Microelectronics in British Industry: The Pattern of Change* (PSI, London).
Prais, S. J. *et al.*, 1981, *Productivity and Industrial Structure* (Cambridge U.P.).
Ray, G. F., 1984, *The Diffusion of Mature Technologies* (Cambridge U.P.).
Roy, A. D., 1982, 'Labour Productivity in 1980: an International Comparison', *National Institute Economic Review*, no. 101 (August), pp. 26–37.
Smith, A. D., Hitchens, D. M. W. N. and Davies, S. W., 1982, *International Productivity* (Cambridge U.P.).
Statistisches Bundesamt, 1979, 'Produzierendes Gewerbe', series 4.1.2.
Vereins Deutscher Werkzeugmaschinenfabriken, 1980, *Altersstruktur des Industriellen Werkzeugmaschinenparks in der BDR* (Frankfurt).

THE JOURNAL OF INDUSTRIAL ECONOMICS 0022-1821 $2.00
Volume XXXIV March 1986 No. 3

ASSESSING USA POSTAL RATEMAKING: AN APPLICATION OF RAMSEY PRICES

FRANK A. SCOTT, JR.*

In early rate cases the inverse elasticity rule was used explicitly in setting postal rates, but more recently the USA Postal Service has eschewed its use. Since cross elasticities between mail classes are not all zero, general Ramsey prices would be more appropriate than the simple inverse elasticity rule. Using USPS estimates of revenues, costs, and elasticities, postal rates are simulated under several different conditions. The simulated prices are then compared to the rates suggested in the 1980 rate case to determine whether the principles being followed by the USPS lead to Ramsey prices.

I. INTRODUCTION

THE United States Postal Service (USPS) was created in 1970 with the passage of the Postal Reorganization Act. Congress decided to transform the old Post Office Department into a semiautonomous government corporation. An independent regulatory commission, the Postal Rate Commission (PRC), was also created by the Postal Reorganization Act to review postal rates and mail classifications. Congress set forth specific guidelines for the Postal Rate Commission to follow when considering changes in postal rates. Two primary considerations are that the overall level of rates must generate enough revenue to permit the Postal Service to break even and that each class of mail must bear the direct and indirect postal costs attributable to the class, plus a portion of the remaining institutional costs. In addition, the PRC must take into account such things as fairness and equity, the value of service to sender and recipient, alternative means of sending and receiving mail, simplicity of rate structure, and the educational, cultural, scientific and informational value to the recipient of the mail.

The requirement that each class of mail or type of service bear all the direct and indirect costs attributable to the class or service has generated considerable controversy since the first postal rate case in 1971. The Postal Service has argued that much of its costs are institutional and cannot be directly attributed to specific classes or services. The Postal Rate Commission, however, has pressed for greater cost attribution and less reliance on non-cost factors in apportioning costs among the various mail classes and services.[1]

* Richard Higgins, Keith Anderson, John Lunn, the North American Editor, and an anonymous referee provided helpful comments on earlier drafts. Partial financial support was provided by the Federal Trade Commission. The views expressed are solely the author's.

[1] Alan Sorkin [1980] presents a concise discussion of the cost attribution controversy in the first four rate cases. See Chapter 9.

Between the 1971 and 1977 rate cases the percent of total costs attributed to mail classes increased from less than 50 percent to over 70 percent (Miller and Sherman [1980, pp. 55–60]). In the 1980 rate hearing (R80-1) the Postal Service urged the PRC to reduce the level of attribution to below 60 percent, but the Rate Commission resisted and kept the attribution percentage roughly the same as in the 1977 case (PRC [1981, pp. 5–7]).

Those costs not attributable to a specific class of mail or type of service must be apportioned among all classes. To assign these institutional costs the PRC has relied heavily in the past on 'demand factors', that is the inverse elasticity rule. The inverse elasticity rule is a method of setting prices for goods whose demands are independent and for which marginal cost prices are not feasible because they would result in a deficit. The first formal statement of the inverse elasticity rule was made by Frank Ramsey [1927]. Ramsey's results were 'rediscovered' by William Baumol and David Bradford [1970]. Roger Sherman and Anthony George [1979] expanded the work of Baumol–Bradford and others and derived a set of second-best prices for a public-sector firm like the USPS. The Sherman–George model provides the take-off point for this study.

If one accepts the Postal Service's arguments that it is a natural monopoly, then marginal-cost pricing is not a feasible solution for the USPS, since the Postal Reorganization Act prohibits postal deficits.[2] The task of the USPS and PRC, then, is to find a pricing rule that is as least distortive as possible. If the Postal Service produced goods that were independently demanded, then use of the simple inverse elasticity rule would be appropriate. Substitute relationships exist between different classes of mail, however, and there are numerous private-sector substitutes and complements for postal services. For a public firm operating under such conditions, Sherman and George derive a system of equations that describe the optimal prices [1979, p. 693]:

$$\text{(1)} \qquad \underset{n\times 1}{P} = \underset{n\times 1}{C} + \alpha \underset{n\times n}{A^{-1}} \underset{n\times 1}{E} + (1-\alpha) \underset{n\times n}{A^{-1}} \underset{n\times 1}{B}$$

where P and C are vectors of prices and marginal costs, E is a vector of own-price elasticities, A is a matrix containing ratios of cross-price to own-price elasticities weighted by quantities, B is a vector incorporating

[2] The Postal Service maintains that it is a natural monopoly. Prior to the late 1970s this claim was interpreted to mean that economies of scale exist in the production of postal services. Empirical studies of the postal system, some of which are reviewed by Miller and Sherman [1980, p. 59, fn. 17], have not supported that claim. Recent developments in the theory of the multiproduct firm have added a new direction to the discussion. Papers by Baumol, Bailey and Willig [1977], Panzar and Willig [1977], and Sappington and Shepherd [1982], have shown that the existence of economies of scope may also create the situation where a single firm is the low-cost producer of a group of products. Wattles [1973], found some evidence of economies of scope for the USPS, but did not estimate a multiproduct cost function using econometric techniques. While the natural monopoly question is certainly crucial to any analysis of postal rates, this study will not attempt to address that issue. Instead, the assumption that marginal cost prices will lead to deficits is accepted for the sake of argument without further criticism.

private-sector substitutes and complements, and α is a Lagrange multiplier that reflects the tightness of the budget constraint. When all cross elasticities are zero, this system of equations reduces to the simple inverse elasticity rule.

If marginal costs are known and constant, if compensated demand elasticities are known and constant, and if some approximation can be made of equilibrium total revenues, then a vector of prices can be derived for any value of alpha. Different values of alpha can be substituted until a price vector is generated that just satisfies the budget constraint. In practice marginal costs are not known with any great precision, estimated elasticities are typically uncompensated, and equilibrium total revenues can only be crudely approximated.

Nevertheless, a simulation of postal rates can be useful for several reasons. First, existing rates implicitly incorporate the inverse elasticity rule through consideration of 'demand factors.' A simulation that explicitly incorporates the inverse elasticity principle would allow a direct comparison with actual rates, and would thus indicate the extent to which other rate-setting criteria affect PRC decisions. Second, the Postal Service recognizes that demand interdependencies exist among the various classes of mail, but it is not clear how they are taken into account. A simulation that incorporates the cross-price effects among postal classes would permit a comparison with the simple inverse elasticity rule. Third, the Postal Reorganization Act specifies that the PRC should consider the effect of postal rates on private-sector firms which compete with the USPS in transporting non-letter mail. Private carriers like the United Parcel Service contend that, in markets where the Postal Service faces competition, rates are kept unduly low—which may be contrary to the rate structure that would result from a full-blown Ramsey pricing model. An analysis of private-sector substitutes and complements might indicate the existence of such an effect.

The remainder of this paper will proceed as follows. The next section contains an application of the simple inverse elasticity rule using cost, elasticity, and revenue estimates from Docket R80-1. The third section computes optimal prices when cross-price elasticities among postal classes are considered and compares them to the prices derived in section II. The fourth section of the paper considers private-sector substitutes and complements for postal services. A final section offers a summary and conclusions.

II. APPLICATION OF THE SIMPLE INVERSE ELASTICITY RULE TO POSTAL RATES

The simple inverse elasticity rule will produce a set of second-best prices if (1) a budget constraint must be satisfied, (2) marginal-cost prices will produce a deficit, and (3) cross-price elasticities are zero. Believing that the USPS generally met these conditions, the PRC applied the rule directly in early rate cases. Following the negative court decisions which criticized these prior applications of the inverse elasticity rule, in the 1977 case the PRC avoided the use of a demand model in deciding rates for mail classes and services. Their use of the inverse-elasticity principle thus had to become implicit.[3] The PRC continued to use the inverse elasticity rule implicitly in R80-1, although its role was downplayed even more than in 1977. In explaining their principles of rate design, however, the commissioners stated that 'mail categories with relatively high values of service should, as a general rule, continue to reflect that higher value in their residual cost contribution, all other considerations being equal' (PRC [1981, pp. 227–228]).

Regardless of the extent to which the PRC actually uses demand factors to set rates, it is a useful exercise to employ the Sherman–George pricing model for comparison purposes alone. In the 1980 rate case the Commission proposed a rate structure and, using estimated elasticities and marginal costs, generated estimates of mail volume and revenues.[4] Table I contains, for each of the different mail classes, estimates of marginal cost, volume, total revenue, and own-price elasticity, followed by the PRC's proposed rates (in column (E)).[5] These data can be incorporated into equation (1) and, iterating over different values for alpha, one can solve for an optimal set of prices. This application of the inverse elasticity rule can then be compared to the postal rates recommended by the PRC.

After the appropriate values were substituted into equation (1), the system was iterated for different values of alpha. The iteration procedure was halted

[3] As indeed it did. For example, the percentage increase in postcard rates was less than the percentage increase in letter rates, which "is consistent with the lesser value-of-service" of cards (PRC [1978, p. 239]).

[4] Postal costs are classified as either attributable, assignable, or residual. After four prior rate hearings and three reviews of their costing and ratemaking principles by the D.C. Court of Appeals, the PRC offered the following explanation of their taxonomy:

> A cost element should be attributed if it can be causally linked with a volume-related mail characteristic that can be used as a distribution key (for example, weight). A cost should be reasonably assigned if (i) it can be causally linked with a nonvolume-related mail characteristic (for example, delivery service standards) and (ii) a suitable distribution key can be developed for allocating the functional cost to classes and services. A cost should be treated as residual if either (i) it cannot be causally linked with any specific mail characteristic or (ii) a suitable distribution key simply cannot be developed (PRC [1981, p. 116]).

In the first rate cases the Postal Service's costs corresponded roughly to short-run average variable costs. In succeeding cases the cost variability time horizon has been lengthened and the percent of total costs either attributed or assigned has increased significantly, so that the cost data in Table I come much closer to the theoretically appropriate measure to use, that is, long run marginal costs. The process for generating elasticity estimates has also been refined considerably since the first rate cases. Even though the inverse elasticity rule was used explicitly in 1974, econometric estimates of elasticities were not introduced until 1976. In 1977 and 1980 the USPS commissioned fairly sophisticated econometric estimation of elasticities. See R80-1, Appendix H, p. 2 for a description.

[5] Four categories of mail have been excluded from consideration in this study: (1) mailgrams, (2) government mail, (3) free mail for the blind, and (4) international mail. Government mail and free mail for the blind are not included for obvious reasons. No elasticity estimates were available for mailgrams. International mail rates are not subject to PRC jurisdiction. (See Schedule 1, Appendix G, in [PRC, 1981].)

TABLE I.
COST, VOLUME, REVENUE, and ELASTICITY ESTIMATES FROM R80-1, AND SIMULATED POSTAL RATES UNDER DIFFERENT ASSUMPTIONS ABOUT CROSS-PRICE ELASTICITIES

Category	($) *Marginal Cost*	(000) *Volume*	($000) *Total Revenue*	*Elasticity*	*E*	*F*	*G*
First Class:							
(1) *Letters*	0.16129	58 583 010	11 783 071	−0.31	$0.201 (24.8 %)	$0.205 (27.3 %)	$0.204 (26.7 %)
(2) *Cards*	0.10340	2 416 744	331 216	−0.64	0.137 (33.0 %)	0.117 (13.6 %)	0.138 (44.0 %)
(3) *Priority Mail*	1.95934	237 720	738 074	−0.31	3.048 (55.6 %)	2.615 (33.5 %)	2.521 (28.7 %)
(4) *Express Mail*	5.63952	26 645	335 459	−0.31	12.590 (123.2 %)	8.300 (47.2 %)	7.918 (40.4 %)
Second Class:							
(5) *Within County*	0.05143	1 140 156	58 716	−0.37	0.052	0.052	0.052
(6) *Regular Rate*	0.11697	5 823 529	823 998	−0.12	0.141 (20.5 %)	0.194 (65.8 %)	0.183 (56.4 %)
(7) *Nonprofit*	0.08594	2 289 307	194 751	−0.24	0.085	0.085	0.085
(8) *Classroom*	0.10319	54 793	5 615	−0.10	0.102	0.102	0.102
(9) *Transient*	0.75051	14 662	11 008	−0.12	0.751 (0.1 %)	1.161 (54.8 %)	1.102 (46.7 %)
Third Class:							
(10) *Single Piece*	0.82470	231 778	191 375	−0.15	0.826 (0.1 %)	1.185 (43.6 %)	1.134 (37.5 %)
(11) *Bulk Regular*	0.06957	22 355 919	2 081 346	−0.55	0.093 (32.9 %)	0.081 (15.7 %)	0.086 (22.9 %)
(12) *Bulk Nonprofit*	0.06896	8 197 187	564 236	−0.29	0.069	0.069	0.069
Fourth Class:							
(13) *Parcel Post*	2.26332	171 562	411 789	−0.81	2.400 (6.1 %)	2.457 (8.6 %)	2.430 (7.4 %)
(14) *Bound Printed Matter*	0.37048	117 738	60 768	−0.49	0.516 (39.5 %)	0.439 (18.6 %)	0.430 (16.2 %)
(15) *Special Rate*	1.12141	231 382	274 507	−0.69	1.186 (5.8 %)	1.234 (10.1 %)	1.218 (8.7 %)
(16) *Library Rate*	1.10304	61 858	67 957	−0.39	1.099	1.099	1.099

Note: Column (E) contains the PRC-recommended average revenue per piece from R80-1. Column (F) contains an application of the simple inverse elasticity rule, which assumes zero cross elasticities. Column (G) incorporates the nonzero cross elasticities among mail categories estimated by Tolley and Sobin. Percent mark-ups above marginal cost are included in parentheses alongside columns E, F and G, except for those preferred subclasses noted in footnote 6.

when the solution vector of prices would generate approximately (within ±$3 million) enough revenue to cover the postal system's institutional or residual costs.[6] The vector of prices from this exercise are contained in column (F) of Table I.

A comparison of the rates yielded by the simple inverse elasticity model and the PRC's recommended average revenue provides some insight into the extent to which other rate-setting criteria affect PRC decisions. For example, second-class regular rate exhibits one of the lowest price elasticities, yet its R80-1 recommended price only slightly exceeds marginal cost. As the PRC explained in R80-1, the educational, scientific, cultural, and informational aspects of second-class mail require mitigation of the cost coverage for that class (PRC [1981, p. 375]). In three of the four categories of first-class mail PRC-recommended rates exceed those suggested by the inverse elasticity model. Only for the highly visible, highly political first-class letter rate is that not true, and later actions by the Postal Service Board of Governors resulted in the price of a first-class stamp being raised from 18¢ to 20¢.

For fourth-class parcel post, where the USPS faces fierce competition from United Parcel Service and others, the PRC sets rates lower than those suggested by the inverse elasticity rule. On the other hand, third-class bulk regular, used by businesses for mass mailings, is priced above the level suggested by the inverse elasticity rule, suggesting perhaps that 'junk' mail is viewed as having little educational, cultural, scientific, or informational value. Rates for the other two categories generating a significant amount of revenue, first-class letters and fourth-class special rate, are set fairly close to the level produced by the inverse elasticity rule.

III. OPTIMAL RATES WHEN POSTAL SERVICE CROSS ELASTICITIES ARE NONZERO

The simple inverse elasticity rule will not yield second-best prices if cross-price elasticities among the public-sector products are nonzero. If two public-sector goods are substitutes, then their prices should be set higher than if the simple inverse elasticity rule were used. The opposite is true if complementary relationships exist between public-sector goods.

A casual consideration of different mail categories indicates that numerous possibilities for substitution among classes exist. Sealed letters and post cards are two alternative methods of conveying personal messages. Businesses wishing to communicate with households can use either first-class letters, first-class cards, third-class single piece, or third-class bulk regular mail, depending on the level of service they desire. Packages can be sent in several

[6] The Postal Reorganization Act requires that revenues received from preferred subclasses cover only their attributable costs. Second-class within county, nonprofit, and classroom, third-class bulk nonprofit, and fourth-class library are the preferred categories which receive such treatment. In each of the simulations, prices for these subclasses are constrained to meet this requirement.

different ways, depending on the contents and the identity of sender and recipient. Different service levels for packages are provided by parcel post, priority, and express mail. Similarly, documents or financial transactions can be sent via regular first-class, priority, or express mail, depending on urgency. Since substitutability is possible, cross elasticities between several mail categories are nonzero. The USPS and PRC recognize this fact and even attempt to incorporate this knowledge in setting rates. For example, the PRC stated that its application of the inverse elasticity rule in an earlier case had been constrained by cross elasticities between classes (PRC [1978, p. 165]). In addition, the demand models used by the USPS in later cases explicitly included cross-price effects in the estimation of demand elasticities. A rate simulation which incorporates these estimated cross elasticities would permit an assessment of the extent to which the PRC's recommended rates are consistent with general Ramsey pricing principles.

In the 1980 rate case USPS witness George Tolley estimated cross-price effects between letters and post cards and between letters and third-class bulk regular mail. In 1977 USPS witness Bernard Sobin also estimated the cross-price effect between post cards and third-class bulk regular mail. To determine the impact of including cross elasticities, equation system (1) was re-simulated using these estimates. The simulation proceeded as before, using data on costs, volumes, revenues, and own-price elasticities from R80-1, and incorporating the combined cross-price effects between letters and cards, letters and third-class bulk regular mail, and cards and third-class bulk regular mail. The results are contained in column (G) of Table I and can be compared to the original application of the simple inverse elasticity rule in column (F).

Such a comparison indicates that the combined effect of all three substitute relationships is to produce almost no change in simulated letter rates, slightly higher post card prices (almost 2¢) and third-class bulk regular rates (more than $\frac{1}{2}$¢), and lower prices for the remaining classes. It is interesting to note that while the R80-1 recommended rate for post cards exceeds the simple inverse elasticity rule rate by 2¢, it is almost identical to that rate suggested by the general Ramsey model which incorporates the cross-price effects between cards, letters, and third-class bulk regular. Incorporating cross elasticities also produces a higher rate for third-class bulk regular, but it still falls short of the rate suggested in R80-1. These results indicate that the PRC's use of value-of-service principles may go beyond the simplest version of the Ramsey rule.

IV. OPTIMAL RATES WHEN PRIVATE-SECTOR SUBSTITUTES AND COMPLEMENTS EXIST

The third step in this investigation of second-best prices for the postal system involves incorporating private-sector substitutes and complements. Sherman and George [1979, p. 690] point out that if private services are priced above marginal costs and tend, on balance, to be substitutes for a particular public service, then the price of that service should be set higher than it would be if interdependencies with private services were ignored. If private services tend to be complements, then the public service should be priced lower than it would be in the absence of interdependent demands.

The Postal Service and the Postal Rate Commission recognize that demand interdependencies exist with private-sector goods. In R80-1 the PRC acknowledged that direct competition from private carriers was siphoning off some of the heavier third-class single piece mail (PRC [1981, p. 400]). Also in R80-1, the PRC pointed out the indirect competition faced by the USPS from other advertising media (PRC [1981, p. 453]). Advertisers who might use third-class bulk mail can utilize newspapers, door-to-door distributions, etc. instead. In an earlier case evidence was presented on alternative delivery means for second-class mail, and the PRC responded to this competitive threat by holding the cost coverage for second class close to the bare minimum (PRC [1978, pp. 292–302]). The PRC also recognizes that heavy competition is faced in the parcel delivery market (PRC [1981, pp. 489–495]).

In addition to the demand interdependencies mentioned in PRC rate cases, there are other recognized private-sector substitutes.[7] Even though the Private Express Statutes forbid direct competition with first-class mail, indirect competition as a means of personal communication is provided by the telephone system. One attempt has been made to estimate the demand interrelationship between first-class mail and telephones. Taylor [1980, p. 127] estimated intrastate demand equations for long-distance calls and included first-class letter rates as an explanatory variable. The sign was positive, as expected, but not significant at usual levels.[8] Two categories of mail closely related to first class are priority mail and express mail. In both categories the USPS competes directly with private carriers. Firms such as Federal Express, Purolator Courier Services, Emery Air Freight, and United

[7] The impression is not meant to be conveyed that privately produced complements do not also exist. Stevenson [1976, p. 443] cites several obvious examples, such as envelopes, newsprint, and greeting cards. Unlike many of the substitutes, however, these complementary goods tend to be produced in fairly competitive markets where prices will be approximately equal to marginal costs. Only if the price of a privately produced good exceeds (or falls short of) marginal cost should its demand interdependency be considered. Sherman and George [1979, p. 692] point out that firms like UPS which supply substitute services resemble the Postal Service in technology. The telephone system is also commonly believed to enjoy increasing returns to scale. (Although long distance is probably priced above marginal cost, local service is probably priced below marginal cost.) Increasing returns to scale likewise have been documented for competing methods of advertising like newspapers and magazines. The preoccupation of this section with substitutes and relative inattentiveness to complements thus has been intentional—price is more likely to deviate from marginal cost for these substitute services and hence their cross-elasticity effect should be taken into account when setting postal rates.

[8] Taylor did not report the estimated coefficients, degrees of freedom, or any other relevant information. He only reported the value of the t-statistics, so nothing can be inferred about cross-elasticities.

Parcel Service also offer express delivery services. As mentioned above, the USPS faces some competition for the delivery of second-class mail. While small local or regional publications have no practical alternative to the USPS, large national publishers have increasingly experimented with private delivery systems (PRC [1978, p. 300]).

Perhaps the most visible source of competition for a USPS service lies in the fourth-class parcel post market. While the major competitor is United Parcel Service, other competition comes from motor carriers, consolidated shipping associations, and express delivery firms. That UPS does compete effectively can be seen by examining volume trends. Postal Service parcel post volume has fallen from 1043 million pieces in 1953 to 644 million pieces in 1969 to 196 million pieces in 1980. Meanwhile, starting from scratch in the 1950s, UPS shipped 1437 million parcels in 1979 (Nissen and Lago [1975, pp. 282–283]; PRC [1981, p. 492]).

The only empirical estimation of the cross elasticity of demand between a USPS service and a privately produced service has been done by Nissen and Lago. These authors estimated the price elasticity of demand for parcel post mail. They included as explanatory variables the rates and geographic coverage of the United Parcel Service. They found that parcel post volume is slightly more sensitive to a change in UPS rates than to a change in its own price—their 'best' estimate of parcel post own-price elasticity was -0.45, while their best estimate of the cross-price elasticity with UPS rates was 0.54 [1975, p. 291].

If information on UPS rates and costs were available, then these data along with UPS volume and the estimated cross elasticity could be substituted into equation (1). Since the simple inverse elasticity simulation yields rates of \$2.46, the parcel post rates resulting from this exercise would probably exceed the R80-1 recommended rate of \$2.40.[9] If the PRC takes private-sector substitutes into account when setting parcel post rates, it is probably not in a way that is consistent with general Ramsey prices.

Other postal services competing directly with private delivery firms, however, may be priced in a manner that follows Ramsey principles. Other firms provide express delivery services that are close substitutes for the USPS's priority mail and express mail. A simulation that took these private-sector substitutes into account would likely generate priority and express rates that were well above those from the simple inverse elasticity model. Inspection of columns (E) and (F) of Table I reveals that these two classes are indeed priced in that way. The inverse elasticity rule suggests prices of \$2.62 and \$8.30 for priority and express, while the PRC recommended rates of \$3.05 and \$12.59 for these two categories in R80-1.

[9] In fact, when some heroic assumptions are made about UPS rates and costs and a simulation is carried out, parcel post rates rise by over 30%. An appendix describing this procedure is available from the author.

V. SUMMARY AND CONCLUSIONS

Since cross elasticities between mail classes are not all zero, and since private-sector substitutes and complements do exist, general Ramsey prices would be more appropriate than the simple inverse elasticity rule for setting postal rates. Using USPS estimates of revenues, costs, and demand elasticities, it is possible to simulate postal rates so that some of these interdependencies can be incorporated. Sets of postal prices were generated under several different conditions, while requiring that residual costs be covered in each case. The simulated prices were then compared to the rates suggested by the PRC in R80-1. Some of the more interesting results yielded by these simulations are:

(1) First-class letter rates are not much affected in the different simulations. This result occurs primarily because first-class letter mail generates 65 percent of all postal service revenues, and small changes in the letter rate produce big changes in revenues. One other class whose rate is roughly the same as that suggested in R80-1 and does not change much in the simulations is fourth-class special rate.

(2) An application of the simple inverse elasticity rule yields low rates for post cards. When cross elasticities are incorporated, however, the simulated rates are identical to those recommended in R80-1.

(3) The inverse elasticity rule produces relatively low rates for priority and express mail. If private competition for these services could be taken into account in a general Ramsey model, the rates would probably be much closer to those actually set in R80-1.

(4) The educational, scientific, cultural, and informational value of second-class regular rate mail apparently is significant because the R80-1 recommended rate is much lower than the Ramsey price.

(5) Consideration of cross elasticities results in the general Ramsey price for third-class bulk regular being closer to the R80-1 rate than the simple inverse elasticity rule would suggest.

(6) The R80-1 recommended rate for parcel post is very close to the rate generated by the inverse elasticity model. If private sector substitutes were incorporated in the simulation model, Ramsey prices for parcel post would probably increase.

From these results several conclusions can be drawn. The Postal Rate Commission no longer uses the inverse elasticity rule explicitly, but by continuing to consider 'value of service' it sets rates that turn out to be fairly consistent with general Ramsey pricing principles. The notable exception is the second-class regular rate. While recent court rulings have apparently opened the door for the PRC to return to using Ramsey principles explicitly, it is not immediately evident that any large and sudden changes in rates brought on by such a move would be worthwhile. Changing postal rates from those recommended in R80-1 (column (E) of Table I) to those generated by the simple inverse elasticity rule (column (F)) would produce a net gain in consumer's surplus of \$14.5 million, an estimate that is of the same order of magnitude as Willig and Bailey's [1979, p. 99] estimate for 1974 of \$7.7 million. Compared to the USPS's total revenue of almost \$18 billion, such gains would not seem to warrant major disruptions in rates.

FRANK A. SCOTT,
Department of Economics,
University of Kentucky,
Lexington, Kentucky 40506-0034,
USA

ACCEPTED JULY 1985

REFERENCES

BAUMOL, WILLIAM J. and BRADFORD, DAVID F., 1970, 'Optimal Departures from Marginal Cost Pricing', *American Economic Review* 60 (June), pp. 265–283.

BAUMOL, WILLIAM J., BAILEY, ELIZABETH E. and WILLIG, ROBERT D., 1977, 'Weak Invisible Hand Theorems on Pricing and Entry in a Multiproduct Natural Monopoly', *American Economic Review* 67 (June), pp. 350–365.

MILLER, JAMES C. III and SHERMAN, ROGER, 1980, 'Has the 1970 Act Been Fair to Mailers' in R. SHERMAN (ed.) *Perspectives on Postal Service Issues*, (Washington, D.C.: American Enterprise Institute).

NISSEN, DAVID H. and LAGO, ARMANDO M., 1975, 'Price Elasticity of the Demand for Parcel Post Mail', *Journal of Industrial Economics*, 23 (June), pp. 281–299.

PANZAR, JOHN C. and WILLIG, ROBERT D., 1977, 'Free Entry and the Sustainability of Natural Monopoly', *The Bell Journal of Economics*, 8 (Spring), pp. 1–22.

POSTAL RATE COMMISSION, 1972, *Postal Rate and Fee Increases: Opinion and Recommended Decision*, Docket No. R71-1, (Washington, D.C.: Postal Rate Commission).

POSTAL RATE COMMISSION, 1975, *Postal Rate and Fee Increases: Opinion and Recommended Decision*, Docket No. R74-1, (Washington, D.C.: Postal Rate Commission).

POSTAL RATE COMMISSION, 1976, *Postal Rate and Fee Increases: Opinion and Recommended Decision*, Docket No. R76-1, (Washington, D.C.: Postal Rate Commission).

POSTAL RATE COMMISSION, 1978, *Postal Rate and Fee Increases: Opinion and Recommended Decision*, Docket No. R77-1, (Washington, D.C.: Postal Rate Commission).

POSTAL RATE COMMISSION, 1981, *Postal Rate and Fee Increases: Opinion and Recommended Decision*, Docket No. R80-1, (Washington, D.C.: Postal Rate Commission).

RAMSEY, FRANK, 1927, 'A Contribution to the Theory of Taxation', *Economic Journal*, 37 (March), pp. 47–61.

SAPPINGTON, DAVID and SHEPHERD, WILLIAM G., 1982, 'Sustainability, Entry Restriction, and Induced Technical Bias', *Quarterly Review of Economics and Business*, 22 (Winter), pp. 43–52.

SHERMAN, ROGER and GEORGE, ANTHONY, 1979, 'Second-Best Pricing for the U.S. Postal Service', *Southern Economic Journal*, 45 (January), pp. 685–695.

SORKIN, ALAN L., 1980, *The Economics of the Postal System*, (Lexington, Massachusetts: Lexington Books).

STEVENSON, RODNEY E., 1976, 'The Pricing of Postal Services', in H. TREBING, ed., *New Dimensions in Public Utility Pricing*, (East Lansing, Michigan: M.S.U. Institute of Public Utilities).

Taylor, Lester D., 1980, *Telecomunications Demand: A Survey and Critique*, (Cambridge, Massachusetts: Ballinger).

Wattles, George M., 1973, 'The Rates and Costs of the United States Postal Service', *The Journal of Law and Economics*, 16 (April), pp. 89–117.

Willig, Robert D. and Bailey, Elizabeth E., 1979, 'The Economic Gradient Method', *American Economic Review*, 69 (May), pp. 96–101.

THE JOURNAL OF INDUSTRIAL ECONOMICS 0022-1821 $2.00
Volume XXXIV March 1986 No. 3

EXOGENEITY TESTS OF MARKET BOUNDARIES APPLIED TO PETROLEUM PRODUCTS

MARGARET E. SLADE*

US antitrust law makes market definition and the calculation of market-share statistics an integral part of the determination of the anticompetitive impact of a merger. Because markets frequently overlap, however, market definition is rarely an easy task. A statistical test that can be used as an aid in defining markets is proposed here. Time-series techniques are used to test if price in one region is exogenous to the process that determines price in another. The rejection of exogeneity can be an indication that the two regions are economically linked and thus may belong to a common geographic market. The test is applied to petroleum-product prices from various regions of the United States.

I. INTRODUCTION

TIME-SERIES techniques have long been appreciated by macroeconomists. The uses to which they have been put range from testing for the exogeneity of variables used in the construction of macroeconomic models (Sims [1972], for example) to discovering empirical regularities in macroeconomic data without imposing *a priori* structure on the observations (Ashenfelter and Card [1982], for example). In contrast, these techniques have not been so uniformly adopted by microeconomists.[1] In this paper, atheoretical time-series methods are used as an aid in solving a practical microeconomic problem.

US antitrust law makes market definition and the calculation of market-share statistics an integral part of many lawsuits. When a violation of Section 2 of the Sherman Act (which deals with monopolization) or Section 7 of the Clayton Act (which deals with merger) is alleged, it is necessary to define the product involved and the geographic region within which the violation occurred. This emphasis on market definition stems from the recognition that successful exercise of market power presupposes a relevant market, both product and geographic.

Because markets so frequently overlap, market definition is rarely an easy task. For example, in delineating a product market one must look for close

*I would like to thank Russel Davidson, Paul Geroski, David Nickerson, Philip Nelson, Walter Vandael, Kenneth White, an anonymous referee, and the editors of this journal for thoughtful comments on an earlier draft.

[1] Time-series techniques have been used to solve microeconomic problems, as witnessed by Labys and Granger [1970]. Geroski [1984] is an example of their use in the area of industrial organization. Nevertheless, the vast majority of applications are to macroeconomic problems.

substitutes. There is often however a whole spectrum of substitution possibilities, some of which are nearly perfect, others of which are imperfect, and still others that are substitutes only in a broad sense. It is difficult to know where to draw the line. Similar problems occur in delineating a geographic market.

In practice, market definition frequently involves rules of thumb and may rest on complex legal distinctions that bear little relationship to economic principles. It would obviously be helpful to have more objective grounds on which to base decisions that have such important economic consequences. Because *a priori* principles cannot determine market boundaries, statistical techniques can surely play a useful role.

The purpose of this paper is twofold. First, a procedure is proposed that can aid the market-definition process. The statistical test, which makes use of the work of Granger [1969] and Sims [1972] on causality, can be used to investigate the claim that price determination in one region is exogenous to price formation in another and vice versa and that the two regions are thus in different geographic markets for a given commodity. Quantitative tests can never substitute for a thorough understanding of an industry and the economic, legal, and technical institutions that govern it. They can, however, be used in conjunction with such an understanding, and in fact the two sorts of analysis should be complementary

Second, the test is applied to the problem of defining geographic markets for petroleum products. The recent wave of proposed and/or consummated mergers in the US petroleum industry (Mobil–Marathon, Gulf–Cities Service, Texaco–Getty, Socal–Gulf, and Mobil–Superior) make this an important and timely problem. Because crude oil is traded in an international market, the merger between two US firms is unlikely to be of consequence to the market for crude. The market for petroleum products, however, may be much narrower. If regional markets for gasoline or other products exist, such mergers could lead to a lessening of competition in these local markets.

The organization of the paper is as follows. In the next section, the use of time-series data for market definition is discussed and the proposed test is explained. In section III, the petroleum-product market is described and pricing practices are discussed. Sections IV and V deal with data construction and empirical results. And a final section discusses possible extensions.

II. THE USE OF TIME-SERIES DATA FOR MARKET DEFINITION

II(i) *Motivation*

In the nineteenth century, Cournot stated that a market is 'the entire territory of which the parts are so united by the relations of unrestricted commerce that prices there take the same level throughout with ease and rapidity' ([1838]; [1960, p. 51] quoted). The idea of interdependent price determination among regions in a common geographic market persists today and is the basis for the test outlined in the next section.

In an ideal situation, trade within a market is unrestricted and costless. If the product is homogeneous, the possibility of arbitrage therefore implies that prices are uniform throughout the market. In contrast, the existence of high entry barriers for products produced outside the region implies that inside and outside prices can move independently. The difficulty of arbitrage across regions means that regional price differentials can persist indefinitely. Under such ideal circumstances, it is a simple matter to determine markets exactly.

Unfortunately, the real world is more complex and there are no sharp boundaries between regions. Market delineation is therefore a matter of degree and not one of certainty. The determination of markets should therefore lend itself to statistical analysis.

Quantitative methods used in market definition are of two sorts—those based on product flows (Elzinga and Hogarty [1973] and Leitzinger and Tamor [1983]) and those based on price behaviour (Horowitz [1981]). When the product is homogeneous, so that a 'price' exists, and when transactions prices are available, which is frequently the case in antitrust because they can be subpoenaed, I prefer a test based on price behavior for the following reason. When several markets overlap, shocks in supply and demand in one area may cause price changes in another even when no product moves between the regions. For example, consider three regions 1, 2, and 3, along a highway. If the price is high in region 3, product may move from 2 to 3 and from 1 to 2 until the price is equalized throughout. The three regions are therefore united even though there are no direct flows between regions 1 and 3.[2]

In what follows, I discuss how time-series data on prices can be used to delineate a geographic market. With obvious modifications, the same techniques can be used to define product markets.

The best known measure of the degree of association between two time series is the simple correlation coefficient, and the fact that prices in different geographic regions are correlated has been used as evidence that regions belong to a common geographic market.[3] Unless the influence of common causal factors is purged, however, correlation may be spurious. In addition, when response is delayed, contemporaneous correlation may be small even when two series are perfectly correlated in the long run.

[2] Overlapping markets are a good illustration of the difficulties encountered in defining markets. There is probably some degree of connection between nonadjacent regions but this connection may be far from complete. When purged of common causal factors, however, prices in different regions should show a declining degree of correlation as distance increases.

[3] For example, in 1982 in a verbal presentation before the US Federal Trade Commission, Stigler presented evidence with respect to the merger between two flour-milling companies. He used a test based on correlation coefficients to substantiate the claim that the flour-milling market is national.

The unsatisfactory nature of the simple correlation coefficient has led to a search for more sophisticated geographic-market tests. For example, Horowitz [1981] proposes a test that is based on the assumption that price differentials are stable between regions. He assumes that after a shock the adjustment of price differences to their equilibrium values conforms to a particular dynamic process: a first-order autoregressive process. The Horowitz model is a step in the right direction. There are, however, serious drawbacks. For example, if two price series are autocorrelated, the Horowitz test yields erroneous results. Similar problems occur if the price series have a trend or are characterized by systematic seasonal patterns. In addition, the model is overly restrictive because it is assumed that dynamic adjustment follows a particular pattern when all that is required is that price differentials be dynamically stable. For these reasons, Howell [1982] proposes a test that is more robust and less restrictive. His method makes use of techniques developed by Box and Jenkins [1976].

II(ii) *The proposed test*

The test proposed here does not focus on the dynamic stability of price differences.[4] Instead it seeks to determine whether price movements in one region have repercussions in another; that is, it seeks to establish if price determination in one market is exogenous to price formation in another and vice versa. If two regions form part of the same geographic market for a commodity, a disturbance in one region will spill over into the other and the exogeneity of price formation should be rejected by the data. In contrast, if the two regions are sufficiently distinct, there should be no feedback from price shocks across regions and exogeneity should not be rejected by the data. The method is atheoretical in that no specific model of price formation is postulated.

The test makes use of the notion of causality developed by Granger [1969], Sims [1972], and others. It extends the notion of causality to a test for exogeneity, using a method outlined in Wu [1983].[5] Because these tests are well known, estimation techniques are not discussed here; only the basic idea is sketched. An appendix containing a detailed account of the statistical methods used is available from the author upon request.

Let $X^i = (X_t^i)$, $t = 1, \ldots, T$, $i = 1, 2$, be time-series vectors of equally spaced observations. X^1 is said to 'cause' X^2 if it is possible to obtain better predictions of X^2 when using all available information than if only the information apart from X^1 had been used. That is, X^1 causes X^2 if X^1 provides useful information for forecasting X^2.

[4] There is no reason to believe that price differences are stable, the assumption of both Horowitz and Howell. For example, if Tc is the cost of transaction between regions 1 and 2, with prices P^1 and P^2, respectively, then $P^1 - P^2$ can lie anywhere between $+Tc$ and $-Tc$, and after a random shock, it may settle down to a different value in the appropriate range.

[5] More specifically, Wu's equations (31) form the basis of the tests.

In practice, tests of causality are made after restricting the set of 'all available information' to a few time series, often just X^1 and X^2 themselves. When the universe of information consists of just X^1 and X^2, it is said that X^1 causes X^2 if predictions of X^2 based on lagged values of both X^1 and X^2 are better than predictions of X^2 based on its past history alone.

For a given application, the determination of the relevant universe of information rests on considerations of economic theory and institutional practice. The choice is no more (or less) difficult than the choice of appropriate variables to include in any behavioral equation. And just as with structural models, omission of relevant variables leads to misspecification and results in biased estimators.

The geographic-market test is as follows. Suppose that a homogeneous product Y is sold in two regions. We wish to determine whether the two regions belong to a common geographic market for Y. Let P^j be time-series data on the price of Y in region j, $j = 1, 2$.

Let the null hypothesis be that P^k is exogenous to the system that determines P^j and vice versa. The following equations are used to test this hypothesis.

$$(1) \qquad P_t^j = \sum_{i=1}^{n_1^j} a_{ij} P_{t-i}^j + g_1^j(Z_t) + \varepsilon_t^j$$

$$(2) \qquad P_t^j = \sum_{i=1}^{n_2^j} c_{ij} P_{t-i}^j + \sum_{i=1}^{n_3^j} d_{ij} P_{t-i}^k + g_2^j(Z_t) + \eta_t^j,$$

$$j = 1, 2, \; k = 2, 1,$$

where ε^j and η^j are disturbance terms with zero means such that each is uncorrelated with the right-hand-side variables in its respective equation. The $g_m^j(Z_t)$ are linear functions of a vector Z_t of current and possibly lagged exogenous variables whose exogeneity is not to be tested. For example, $g_m^j(Z_t)$ might be deterministic functions of time.

Common causal factors such as the prices of common inputs can be handled in one of two ways. First, the residuals from regressions of the observed prices on the common causal factor can be substituted for P^j in equations (1) and (2). And second, common causal factors can be included as Z vectors in the g functions defined in equations (1) and (2). For linear models, the two methods are equivalent.

The test for mutually exogenous price determination consists of testing the joint hypothesis that

(1) the coefficient vectors d are zero,

(2) P^1 and P^2 are not contemporaneously correlated,

and

(3) the covariance between η_t^1 and η_t^2 is zero.

The first part of the hypothesis is a test for lack of causality and the second two parts form a test for predeterminedness. The method that is used to test the joint hypothesis follows closely the procedures laid out in Geweke [1978] and in Wu [1983].

III. WHOLESALE GASOLINE MARKETS

III(i) *Transportation*

The test outlined in the last section is used to determine whether cities in the interior of the Southeastern part of the US constitute a separate geographic market for gasoline or whether they belong to a larger Eastern seaboard market or even a national market. In order to judge the reasonableness of the statistical results, it is necessary to know how petroleum products flow in and out of the region and how this region is related to other marketing areas.

Virtually all the petroleum consumed in the interior portion of the Southeastern US (hereafter called SE) are refined near the Gulf of Mexico. Refined products are then shipped to the interior via one of two pipelines—Colonial or Plantation. Along the pipelines, product terminals service regional marketing areas. These terminals are generally found in groups or clusters near urban population centers. Products are then transported by truck from the terminal to retail outlets.

Pipelines are the only economically feasible method of transporting petroleum products into SE. The cost of transporting by a combination of tanker/barge and rail/truck is so much higher that the alternative route is not considered unless the pipelines are operating at capacity.

If product prices are equal at various terminal clusters, a wholesale buyer will go to the closest one, generally not more than fifty miles. If conditions warrant, however, a buyer may truck product as far as 100 miles. Nevertheless, the usual customers of a given oil company at a terminal are the wholesale buyers located at that site.

The situation in the Northeast (NE) is very different. Petroleum products consumed in this region come from three sources: local refineries near major cities, Gulf-coast refineries via the Colonial pipeline, and foreign refineries mainly in the Caribbean. Although sources of supply and modes of transportation differ between SE and NE, the two regions are connected by a common pipeline. It is therefore not possible to say *a priori* whether the two areas are in the same geographic market.

In contrast, there is virtually no transportation of product between the East and West coasts of the US. Petroleum products consumed on the West coast (WC) are either refined west of the Rockies or imported. Oil companies that market in both areas generally coordinate operations west of the Rockies and east of the Rockies, but operate the east and west regions independently of one another. For these reasons, it is highly unlikely that SE and WC form part of a common geographic market for petroleum products.

Starting with SE and moving outwards, we thus find an ever widening set of boundaries of possible geographic markets with increasing probability that each exceeds the true market boundary. It is almost certain that marketers at the same terminal cluster compete with one another. And it is probable that marketers at different terminal sites within SE compete. It is still possible that sites in SE compete with those in NE, but highly unlikely that they compete with sites located in WC.

III(ii) *Prices and pricing practices*

Gasoline refiners and marketers can be grouped into two broad classes, majors and independents. Major-brand gasoline bears the trademark of one of the fifteen or so largest integrated oil companies (Exxon, Mobil, etc.). Independents tend to be smaller than majors, less fully integrated, and sell a much higher proportion of unbranded gasoline.

Major and independent refiners post prices at each terminal site. Posted prices fluctuate frequently and there is a wide spread among prices charged by different marketers at the same site, as much as ten cents per gallon for unleaded gasoline. On the average, the prices posted by the independent refiners are several cents per gallon lower than those posted by majors.

Transactions prices are not always the same as posted prices. Major refiners often offer a discount off posted price to select customers. Eligibility for discounts is determined in a curious fashion. Discounts are offered on purchases that exceed some fraction of sales for the same month of the previous year but do not exceed some larger fraction of those sales. For example, a discount of four cents per gallon might be given on volumes greater than 70 percent but not more than 130 percent of previous purchases for that month.

This discounting practice has the effect of rewarding loyal customers (those with regular supply arrangements) and punishing those who shop around for the best price. It also has the effect of separating geographic markets—making it more difficult for retailers to shop at more than one site.

Independent refiners are less apt to offer discounts than majors. The effect of discounts is therefore to reduce the spread between the prices charged by the two groups. An unbranded retailer thus has two strategies—selection of the lowest price offered on a particular day or commitment to a regular supply arrangement with its attendant rewards.

IV. DATA

Data on prices are published weekly by the Oil Price Information Service (OPIS), a private data-collection agency.[6] Prices are refiner prices to resellers f.o.b. terminals, excluding taxes and discounts. Each week OPIS tabulates the prices posted by each retailer at selected terminal sites in various regions of the country. Prices for both leaded and unleaded gasoline are recorded. For

[6] OPIS reports are published weekly except for the last weeks in June and December. For the missing weeks, an average of the previous and following weeks' prices was used.

any one refiner, however, the two price series are so highly correlated that only the price of unleaded gasoline was used in the empirical analysis.

The time period chosen for the geographic-market test is the entire year from March 2, 1981 to February 22, 1982. Earlier weeks were eliminated in an attempt to avoid periods of price controls and the immediate aftermath of the complete deregulation of oil prices which occurred in January of 1981.

Two cities in each of the regions were arbitrarily chosen. The cities are Greensboro, N.C. and Spartanburg, S.C. in SE, Baltimore, Md. and Boston, Mass. in NE, and Los Angeles and San Francisco, Calif. in WC.

For each city, the minimum price charged by any refiner that week is used. The minimum price was chosen for several reasons. First, the minimum price is the price that is most affected by arbitrage across regions. If a buyer is willing to transport gasoline long distances in order to minimize costs, he will almost certainly select the low-price seller at the distant site. Second, empirical studies such as that by Marvel [1978] find that increased competition in a region, such as the existence of a large number of independent marketers, affects the minimum price charged and the price spread but not the maximum price. Majors tend to compete less on price and more on services such as credit cards and are thus less affected by aggressive price competition. Finally, the use of the minimum price avoids the difficulty inherent in dealing with list prices that differ from transaction prices. The refiner charging the lowest price each week is almost always an independent who does not discount.

V. EMPIRICAL RESULTS

V(i) *The deterministic functions* $g(Z_t)$

The choice of the deterministic functions $g(Z_t)$ is an important part of the test for exogeneity. Because failure to correct for common causal factors results in erroneous conclusions (rejection of the null hypothesis when it should not be rejected) extreme care should be taken in specifying these functions. This section discusses the choice of $g(Z_t)$ for the particular application to petroleum products.

Federal regulation of gasoline prices began in August of 1971 when prices of most commodities were frozen by Phase I of the Nixon administration's wage and price controls. When controls on other commodities were eliminated, oil-price controls were maintained or expanded. In June of 1979, however, the Carter administration initiated a gradual crude-oil decontrol program, and in January of 1981, all remaining petroleum-price controls were removed by an Executive Order issued by President Reagan.

In early 1981, in spite of softening world oil markets, US petroleum-product prices were still rising to catch up with world prices. Shortly afterwards, however, US product prices began to decline (in nominal terms) as prices fell worldwide due to a glut of crude oil. The fall in product prices began early in the year in the East but did not start until July on the West coast.

Attempts were made to capture these effects by including crude-oil prices in Z_t. The cost of crude, however, is very different depending on its source. As a consequence, better results were obtained when exogenous influences on product prices were modeled as deterministic functions of time. Accordingly, the $g_m^j(Z_t)$ were chosen to be quadratic functions of time.

V(ii) *Exogeneity tests*

Before testing the hypothesis that price at one site is exogenous to the process that determines price at another, it is necessary to choose the lengths of the lags n_m^j in equations (1) and (2). Five lags are sufficient to ensure that serial correlation is indiscernible in all equations. Though it would be possible to use shorter lags in some equations, it seems preferable to be consistent across equations.

The choice of lag length of course will vary from application to application. In this particular example, five lags may seem very short. Prices at terminal

TABLE I
F-STATISTICS FOR EXOGENEITY TESTS

City Pairs	*Levels*	*Average F (levels)*	*Logs*	*Filtered*	*Average F (overall)*	*Frequency*
Gr→Sp	2.5*		2.5*	1.9		
Sp→Gr	4.5†		4.8†	3.7†		
SE—SE		3.5			3.3	0.83
Ba→Gr	0.89		1.0	1.0		
Gr→Ba	2.6*		2.5*	1.1		
Ba→Sp	0.40		0.40	0.49		
Sp→Ba	5.1†		4.9†	2.3		
Bo→Gr	2.5*		2.7*	2.0		
Gr→Bo	1.0		1.1	0.45		
Bo→Sp	1.2		1.3	0.97		
Sp→Bo	1.3		1.4	0.54		
SE—NE		1.9			1.6	0.25
La→Gr	0.73		0.78	0.60		
Gr→La	0.83		0.97	0.28		
La→Sp	0.82		0.84	1.0		
Sp→La	0.76		1.1	1.3		
Sf→Gr	0.96		1.1	1.5		
Gr→Sf	1.4		1.6	1.6		
Sf→Sp	0.53		0.63	1.2		
Sp→Sf	2.1		2.4	2.7*		
SE−WC		1.0			1.1	0.04

City abbreviations are: Gr—Greensboro, Sp—Spartanburg, Ba—Baltimore, Bo—Boston, La—Los Angeles, and Sf—San Francisco.

* Denotes significance at the 95% level of confidence.

† Denotes significance at the 99% level of confidence.

sites however are very volatile and respond rapidly to changes in supply and demand conditions. Empirically, there are no detectable long lags in the data.

All equations were estimated by the method outlined earlier in levels with a constant term and linear and quadratic trends. Table I shows the results of hypothesis tests. In the first column of the table, the notation $Y \rightarrow X$ stands for the alternative hypothesis that prices in city Y cause prices in city X. Acceptance of the alternative hypothesis implies that prices in city X are not exogenous to the process that determines prices in city Y. The second column of Table I shows results of tests of the null hypothesis for the first set of regressions.

The F-test can be interpreted in two different ways. First, it can be used as a method of dichotomizing city pairs into those for which the null hypothesis is accepted and those for which it is rejected. Second, it can be viewed as a continuous measure of feedback between the regions.[7] With the second interpretation in mind, an average F-statistic for SE–SE, SE–NE, and SE–WC pairs was calculated. This statistic is shown in column three.

Analysis of the tests shows that the hypothesis of exogenous price determination for city pairs within SE must be rejected. Rejection of exogeneity can be an indication that these cities form part of a common geographic market for gasoline.

Results for SE–NE pairs are mixed. Exogeneity is accepted in five cases and rejected in three. One might therefore conclude that there is some interaction between the regions but that it is not nearly as strong as within SE. A comparison of the average F-statistics reinforces this conclusion.

Finally, Table I shows that the null hypothesis is never rejected for SE–WC pairs. It therefore seems highly unlikely that SE and WC form part of a common geographic market for gasoline. In addition, the average F is well below the critical value of 2.5.

Table II gives results of hypothesis tests for all thirty city pairs, not just those involving cities in SE. The most striking feature of the table is that when tests involve city pairs where one is on the West coast and the other is in the East, exogeneity is never rejected.

Some of the estimated autoregressive processes (equation (1)) are near explosive (their associated generating functions have roots that are statistically indistinguishable from one in absolute value). Because the asymptotic distribution theory for the estimates of autoregressions of stationary series does not apply if the processes are in fact explosive, it is possible that if the processes are near explosive, results of hypothesis tests will be sensitive to minor changes in specification.

In theory, causality tests are invariant with respect to strictly monotonic

[7] Geweke [1983] suggests a different measure of linear feedback, $\ln(\sigma_\varepsilon^2/\sigma_\eta^2)$. This measure has the disadvantage that it is negative when feedback is zero (because of changes in degrees of freedom). Qualitative conclusions drawn from the two measures, however, are very similar and therefore only the F-test is shown.

TABLE II
F-STATISTICS FOR EXOGENEITY TESTS ALL CITIES

City Pair[a]	F[b]	*City Pair*[a]	F[b]
$Gr \rightarrow Sp$	2.5*	$LA \rightarrow Sp$	0.82
$Sp \rightarrow Gr$	4.5†	$Sp \rightarrow SF$	2.1
$Gr \rightarrow Ba$	2.6*	$SF \rightarrow Sp$	0.53
$Ba \rightarrow Gr$	0.89	$Ba \rightarrow Bo$	2.3
$Gr \rightarrow Bo$	1.0	$Bo \rightarrow Ba$	4.8†
$Bo \rightarrow Gr$	2.5*	$Ba \rightarrow LA$	0.83
$Gr \rightarrow LA$	0.83	$LA \rightarrow Ba$	1.3
$LA \rightarrow Gr$	0.73	$Ba \rightarrow SF$	0.39
$Gr \rightarrow SF$	1.4	$SF \rightarrow Ba$	0.79
$SF \rightarrow Gr$	0.96	$Bo \rightarrow LA$	0.87
$Sp \rightarrow Ba$	5.1†	$LA \rightarrow Bo$	1.5
$Ba \rightarrow Sp$	0.40	$Bo \rightarrow SF$	1.9
$Sp \rightarrow Bo$	1.3	$SF \rightarrow Bo$	1.1
$Bo \rightarrow Sp$	1.2	$LA \rightarrow SF$	1.0
$Sp \rightarrow LA$	0.76	$SF \rightarrow LA$	0.89

[a] For a list of city abbreviations, see Table I.
[b] * Denotes significance at the 95% level of confidence.
† Denotes significance at the 99% level of confidence.

transformations of the data and with respect to the application of a stable linear filter. To test the sensitivity to changes in specification, all estimates were redone after taking natural logarithms of the variables and after prefiltering the data using the filter $X_t' = X_t - 0.8X_{t-1}$.

The results of hypothesis tests on the transformed variables are shown in columns four and five of Table I. An examination of the tests shows that conclusions are basically unchanged. With the filtered data, however, the null hypothesis of exogenous price determination is accepted more often.

Column six of Table I shows average F-statistics for all tests combined—levels, logs, and filtered. And the final column shows the frequency with which exogeneity is rejected. For eighty-three percent of the regressions involving two cities in SE, exogenous price determination is rejected. In contrast, price exogeneity is rejected only twenty-five percent of the time for SE–NE pairs and only four percent of the time for SE–WC.

When a large number of tests is made, a frequency of 0.95 is expected for cities within a common geographic market and 0.05 for city pairs in entirely separate markets (assuming that a confidence level of 95 percent is chosen). The frequency for SE–WC pairs is very close to 0.05. With only six tests, it is impossible to obtain a frequency of 0.95. The frequency obtained for SE–SE, however, is one of the two that bracket 0.95.

Based on the empirical results, therefore, one might conclude that the interior of the Southeastern part of the United States is a local geographic market that is loosely connected to the Northeastern seaboard and is entirely separate from the West coast. If this conclusion is accepted, it has important antitrust implications. A merger between two oil companies that market heavily in the Southeast could have an anticompetitive impact on petroleum-product markets, even if its impact on the market for crude were negligible.

VI. POSSIBLE EXTENSIONS

There are several possible modifications to the method. The technique could be extended to multivariate problems. Instead of performing pairwise tests, it would be possible to consider the hypothesis that several cities belong to the same market and to perform a joint test of this hypothesis. Another possible extension would be to estimate vector-autoregressive models or to embed the test in a complete dynamic simultaneous-equation system that includes all of the endogenous and exogenous factors that determine price.

Embedding the test in a more complicated model might be interesting from the point of view of research into the market-definition issue. One of the advantages of the test used here, however, is its simplicity. Frequently a plaintiff (a government antitrust agency or a private party) who wishes to challenge a merger before it is consummated has only a short period to prepare its case. A simple test has obvious advantages in this context.

An additional advantage of the pure time-series test over a test based on a structural model is that point comparisons can be made. For example, the 'price' of gasoline at a particular terminal is well defined and feedback effects between prices at two terminals can be analysed directly. In contrast, if supply and demand equations are estimated, it is necessary to divide a larger area into geographic regions *before* tests can be made. For example, one must arbitrarily decide how to measure 'the quantity of gasoline consumed in Atlanta' before a demand equation for Atlanta can be estimated. But determining the size of the Atlanta market is precisely the problem of interest.

Questions about the appropriate way to define geographic and product markets and the answers to these questions have numerous ramifications in many areas of antitrust. It is therefore hoped that the techniques of this paper will prove useful and that future research in the area will be stimulated.

MARGARET E. SLADE, ACCEPTED JULY 1985

Department of Economics,
University of British Columbia,
Vancouver, BC,
Canada V6T 1Y2.

AND

CRIDE, Université Catholique de Louvain,
3 Place Montesquieu,
B-1348 Louvain-la-Neuve,
Belgium.

REFERENCES

ASHENFELTER, O. and CARD, D., 1982, 'Time Series Representations of Economic Variables and Alternative Models of the Labor Market', *Review of Economic Studies*, 49, pp. 761–782.

BOX, G. P. E. and JENKINS, G. M., 1976, *Time-Series Analysis Forecasting and Control*, Revised Edition (Holden Day, San Francisco).

COURNOT, A., 1960, *Research into the Mathematical Principles of the Theory of Wealth*, translated by N. T. Bacon (Augustus M. Kelly, New York).

ELZINGA, K. G. and HOGARTY, T. F., 1973, 'The Problem of Geographic-Market Delineation in Antitrust Suits', *The Antitrust Bulletin*, 18, pp. 45–81.

GEROSKI, P. A., 1984, 'On the Relationship Between Aggregate Merger Activity and the Stock Market', *European Economic Review*, 25, pp. 223–234.

GEWEKE, J., 1978, 'Testing the Exogeneity Specification in the Complete Dynamic Simultaneous-Equation Model', *Journal of Econometrics*, 7, pp. 163–185.

GEWEKE, J., 1983, 'Inference and Causality in Economic Time-Series Models', Chapter 19 of *Handbook of Econometrics*, Z. Griliches and M. Intrilligator (eds.) (North-Holland, Amsterdam).

GRANGER, C. W. J., 1969, 'Investigating Causal Relations by Econometric Models and Cross-Spectral Methods', *Econometrica*, 37, pp. 424–438.

HOROWITZ, I., 1981, 'Market Definition in Antitrust Analysis: A Regression-Based Approach', *Southern Economic Journal*, 48, pp. 1–16.

HOWELL, J., 1982, 'An Examination of the Dynamic Behavior of Cross-Regional Price Differences in Regular and Unleaded Gasoline', U.S. Federal Trade Commission mimeo.

LABYS, W. C. and GRANGER, C. W. J., 1970, *Speculation, Hedging, and Forecasts of Commodity Prices* (Lexington Books, Lexington).

LEITZINGER, J. J. and TAMOR, K. L., 1983, 'Foreign Competition in Antitrust Law', *Journal of Law and Economics*, 26, pp. 87–102.

MARVEL, H., 1978, 'The Economics of Information and Retail Gasoline-Price Behavior: An Empirical Study', *Review of Economics and Statistics*, 60, pp. 252–258.

SIMS, C., 1972, 'Money, Income, and Causality', *American Economic Review*, 62, pp. 540–552.

WU, D., 1983, 'Tests of Causality, Predeterminedness, and Exogeneity', *International Economic Review*, 24, pp. 547–558.

THE JOURNAL OF INDUSTRIAL ECONOMICS 0022-1821 $2.00
Volume XXXIV March 1986 No. 3

SAFETY AND PROFITS IN THE AIRLINE INDUSTRY

DEVRA L. GOLBE*

It has been argued that there is a positive relationship between profitability and safety in the transportation industries. This paper analyzes a model of safety provision under uncertainty and tests the model using data from the US airline industry. Theory suggests that the sign of the relationship between profits and safety is indeterminate and depends on risk preferences and the structure of costs and demand. The empirical investigation suggests that safety and profits have no significant relationship. Thus, it does not appear that profit-reducing changes in regulation will lead to less safe airlines.

POPULAR WISDOM endorses the notion that there is a positive relationship between profitability and safety in the transportation industries, and therefore that economic deregulation would have deleterious effects on airline safety. A US Civil Aeronautics Board report [1975] expressed the concern that "In the absence of countervailing measures, removal of entry and price controls would be likely to degrade safety. Any serious financial difficulties encountered would be conducive to a deterioration of safety."[1] Similarly, a Senate Commerce Committee report (*Safety in the Air*) stated that "it should be unnecessary to point out that a profitable operation is essential to safety".[2]

This paper examines the relationship between current profits and safety.[3] I present a model of safety provision under uncertainty and test the model using data from the US airline industry. The theory suggests that the sign of the relationship between profits and safety is indeterminate and depends on risk preferences and the structure of costs and demand. The empirical investigation indicates that, in fact, safety and profits bear no significant statistical relationship to each other; they may even be mildly negatively related: more profitable firms may have more accidents. Thus, the evidence suggests that it is unlikely that profit-reducing changes in regulation will lead to more accidents.

The plan of the paper is as follows. Part I describes some previous work on

* I am grateful to Lawrence White, Roger Noll, Peter Asch, David Levy, Douglas Shaller, several anonymous referees and the members of my dissertation committee at New York University for helpful comments, and to the Sloan Foundation for financial support during the early part of this study. Remaining errors are my own.

[1] US Civil Aeronautics Board, Report of the CAB Special Staff on Regulatory Reform [1975, p. 206].

[2] US Civil Aeronautics Board, Report of the CAB Special Staff on Regulatory Reform [1975, p. 209].

[3] Note that the problem this paper addresses is the impact of current profits on safety—not the related issue of the impact of safety on future profits.

the effects of economic regulation on airline safety. Part II presents the theoretical model, part III describes cross-section and time-series evidence from the airline industry, and part IV summarizes and interprets the results.

I.

Several studies have investigated the impact of economic regulation on airline safety. In 1969 the Edwards Report on British airlines concluded that the independent operators were less safe than regularly licensed carriers over the period 1955–1965. Smaller carriers and unscheduled flights seemed more susceptible to accidents. However, noncertificated carriers may have performed less well because the routes and airports served made more demands on pilots and because maintenance was more difficult on nonstandard routes.[4]

The US National Transportation Safety Board's 1972 study of air taxi safety found that, when profits were "marginal", operations and maintenance departments were restricted by budgetary limitations and suggested that there was some relationship between the financial condition of air taxis and their safety performance. The study concluded that the less stringent regulations under which the industry operated led to a lower level of safety, but it is not clear how much of this result the Board attributed to economic regulation.[5]

Jordan [1970] studied the California intrastate carriers in the period prior to 1965. The California carriers operated under essentially the same safety regulations as did the certificated trunks, so differential safety records could perhaps be attributed to differences in economic regulation. During the period 1949–1965, the California intrastate carriers had a much poorer safety record (measured as fatalities per revenue passenger miles) than did either the trunk carriers or the local service carriers. However, Jordan notes that during the seventeen-year period there were only two fatal accidents, and each airline went out of business shortly after its accident. One of the lines accounted for only one-half of one percent of all revenue passenger miles provided in the intrastate market, but was responsible for 93 percent of passenger fatalities.

However, as Jordan points out, one cannot safely draw conclusions about the effect of economic regulation from these data. The intrastate carriers are limited to short hauls with a high ratio of takeoffs and landings to mileage and to the use of smaller, less well-equipped airports. Thus, they take greater risks than the trunk carriers and might be expected to have a poorer accident record. Secondly, because of the small volume of California intrastate traffic

[4] US Congress, House, Committee on Government Operations [1977, p. 16].
[5] US Congress, House, Committee on Government Operations [1977, p. 16].

relative to that of the trunks, observed accident rates may be poor estimates of expected accident rates.[6]

James Miller [1975] testified before the Senate Judiciary Committee in 1975 that "there is little direct evidence that economic regulation has had any effect on air safety".[7] He performed a crude test of the hypothesis that high profits lead to safer operations using data from the period 1939–1953. The domestic fatality rate (passenger fatalities per 100 million miles flown) was regressed against the domestic industry profit rate. While the estimated coefficient was not statistically significant, it indicated a positive relationship between profitability and fatality rates.[8] This result is contrary to that predicted by the proponents of regulation. It is, however, consistent with results we will describe in section III.

II.

Assume that the firm is a price-taker (either because markets are perfectly competitive or because markets are regulated) and maximizes the expected utility of profits. Assume also that the firm produces Q units of basic transportation and an associated level of safety per unit of transportation s, where $1-s$ measures the probability of an accident. The quantity of transportation demanded Q will be a decreasing function of its price P and an increasing function of its quality or safety s. That is, $Q = Q(P, s)$, so that safety is the firm's only choice variable. If the distribution of returns is normal,[9] the firm's maximization problem can be written in Pratt–Arrow certainty-equivalent style as

$$\text{(1)} \qquad \max_{s} \, [E(\Pi) - R(E(\Pi), \operatorname{Var}(\Pi))]$$

where Π denotes profit and R is an additive risk premium defined by the condition $U(E(\Pi) - R) = E(U(\Pi))$, where U is the utility function. Thus, the expression in brackets in (1) is the certainty equivalent of profits.[10]

Expected profits can be written

$$\text{(2)} \qquad \bar{\Pi} = PQ - C(s, Q, x) - (1-s)QD$$

where bars represent the expected value operator and

P = market price per unit of transportation

[6] Jordan [1970].

[7] Miller [1975, p. 65].

[8] The estimated equation, using data from 1939–1953, was $y = 1.76 + 0.009x$ where y = Domestic fatality rate (passenger fatalities per 100 million miles flown), and x = domestic industry profit rate. The t-statistic on the coefficient of x was 0.25 and the equation R^2 was 0.08 [1975, p. 65].

[9] If the distribution is not normal, the risk premium depends on higher-order moments as well.

[10] The expected utility approach to firm decision-making under uncertainty is well known in the literature (see, for example, Leland [1972] and Lintner [1970]).

$C(\cdot)$ = joint cost function for transportation and safety
x = shift parameter which allows cost to vary
D = expected cost borne by the firm per accident.

For simplicity, D is assumed to be distributed independently of s. (Note that these costs may reflect either direct payments for accidents or insurance costs.)

It should be clear from equation (2) that even risk-neutral firms, which maximize expected profits, will invest in safety production. The variance of profits can be written as a function of s, the variance of D, and Z, where Z represents all other influences on profit variance. Thus

$$\text{(3)} \qquad \mathrm{Var}(\bar{\Pi}) = f(s, \mathrm{Var}(D), Z)$$

Assume $\mathrm{Var}(D)$ and Z are fixed, so that $\mathrm{Var}(\bar{\Pi})$ varies only with s. Then rewrite the firm's maximization problem (1) as

$$\text{(4)} \qquad \underset{s}{\mathrm{Max}}\ \bar{\Pi}(s, P, x, D) - R(\bar{\Pi}, s)$$

In the following, let the subscript s indicate partial derivatives with respect to safety and subscript $\bar{\pi}$ partial derivatives with respect to expected profits. Then the first-order condition for a maximum of (4) is

$$\text{(5)} \qquad \bar{\Pi}_s - R_{\bar{\pi}}\bar{\Pi}_s - R_s = 0$$

or

$$\text{(5a)} \qquad \bar{\Pi}_s(1 - R_{\bar{\pi}}) = R_s$$

Since, for a risk-averse firm $R_{\bar{\pi}}$, the change in the risk premium due to an increment in profits must be less than the increment in profits (that is, $R_{\bar{\pi}} < \bar{\Pi}_{\bar{\pi}} = 1$), $(1 - R_{\bar{\pi}})$ must be positive. If, as seems likely, R_s is negative, an increase in safety leads to less variance in profits and a lower risk premium, then $\bar{\Pi}_s$ is negative: the marginal (expected) profitability of safety is negative. In all cases, R_s and $\bar{\Pi}_s$ have the same sign. (For risk-neutral firms R is zero, so that in equilibrium the marginal change in expected profits is zero.)

In focusing on the relationship between safety and profits we consider the simultaneous effects of changes in the parameters of the model (P, x, and D) on the utility-maximizing levels of safety and profit. We can do so most conveniently by analyzing the effect on safety of a *profit-increasing* parameter change.[11] Let α be an element of the parameter set (P, x, D). Then, by definition, $\bar{\Pi}_\alpha > 0$. Notice that while cost and demand functions do not appear explicitly in the analysis below, $\bar{\Pi}$ and R and hence the optimal levels of safety are dependent on these functions.

We begin the comparative statics analysis by finding the total differential of the first-order condition (5) with respect to s and α.

[11] I am indebted to Roger Noll for suggesting this approach.

(6) $$\bar{\Pi}_{s\alpha}d\alpha - R_{\bar{\pi}\bar{\pi}}\bar{\Pi}_{\alpha}\bar{\Pi}_{s}d\alpha - R_{\bar{\pi}}\bar{\Pi}_{s\alpha}d\alpha - R_{s\bar{\pi}}\bar{\Pi}_{\alpha}d\alpha + [\bar{\Pi}_{ss} - R_{\bar{\pi}s}\bar{\Pi}_{s} - R_{\bar{\pi}}\bar{\Pi}_{ss} - R_{ss}]ds = 0$$

The term in brackets is the second-order condition (*soc*). Rearranging, we have

(7) $$ds/d\alpha = -\{\bar{\Pi}_{s\alpha}(1-R_{\bar{\pi}}) - \bar{\Pi}_{\alpha}(R_{\bar{\pi}\bar{\pi}}\bar{\Pi}_{s} + R_{s\bar{\pi}})\}\,(soc)^{-1}$$

Since the *soc* is always negative, signing $ds/d\alpha$ requires signing only the terms inside the brackets. Recall also that, by definition, $\bar{\Pi}_{\alpha}$ is positive.

Consider first the risk neutrality case. Under risk neutrality the risk premium is always zero, so that (7) reduces to

(7a) $$ds/d\alpha = -\bar{\Pi}_{s\alpha}/\bar{\Pi}_{ss}$$

In this case, the sign of $ds/d\alpha$ depends solely on the mixed second derivative of profits. From (2), the definition of $\bar{\Pi}$, it is clear that $\bar{\Pi}_{s}$ and hence $\bar{\Pi}_{s\alpha}$ depend on the sensitivity of demand and cost functions to safety as well as on direct accident costs. In general, the sign of $\bar{\Pi}_{s\alpha}$ is unknown. If $\alpha = D$, the analysis is relatively straightforward. A decrease in α would be profit-increasing (that is, $\bar{\Pi}_{D} = -Q(1-s) < 0$). Since $\bar{\Pi}_{sD} = -(1-s)(dQ/ds) + Q$, the marginal change in (the negative of) expected accidents[12] with respect to s is of indeterminate sign. However, the second term is likely to dominate, so $\bar{\Pi}_{s\alpha} = -\bar{\Pi}_{sD}$ would be negative. That is, a reduction in expected damages probably leads to less safety.[13] If α equals P or x the sign of $ds/d\alpha$ is unknown. Changes in prices or costs which increase profits will, in general, also increase output. As output increases, the expected number of accidents increases, so, if the cost function is separable in Q and s, changes which increase profits should also increase the marginal profitability of safety $\bar{\Pi}_{s}$. Hence, in this case, $\bar{\Pi}_{s\alpha}$ and $ds/d\alpha$ would be positive. Usually, however, costs will not be separable, so that $\bar{\Pi}_{s\alpha}$ and $ds/d\alpha$ can be of either sign for the risk-neutral firm.

In the case of constant absolute risk aversion, $R_{\bar{\pi}}$ is always zero. Hence, (7) reduces to

(7b) $$ds/d\alpha = -\bar{\Pi}_{s\alpha}/(soc)$$

Again, the effect of a profit-increasing parameter change on safety depends solely on $\bar{\Pi}_{s\alpha}$, the mixed second-order derivative of expected profits. Since the sign of $\bar{\Pi}_{s\alpha}$ cannot be determined, $ds/d\alpha$ cannot be signed.

A popular and perhaps appealing assumption about risk preferences is decreasing absolute risk aversion. Decreasing absolute risk aversion implies that $R_{\bar{\pi}}$ is negative—the risk premium decreases as profits increase. Since R is bounded from below at zero, at some point $R_{\bar{\pi}\bar{\pi}}$ must become positive.[14]

[12] From (2), the definition of $\bar{\Pi}$, we see that $\bar{\Pi}_{D}$ is the negative of expected accidents.

[13] I have ignored the fact that, in a dynamic world, future profits may depend on current accidents, so that, at least in part, D should represent the present value of lost future profits. See Footnote 3.

[14] We are assuming R is continuous.

By the same reasoning, $R_{\bar{\pi}s}$ must also be positive eventually. If $R_{\bar{\pi}\bar{\pi}}$ and $R_{\bar{\pi}s}$ are positive and $\bar{\Pi}_s > R_{\bar{\pi}s}/R_{\bar{\pi}\bar{\pi}}$, or if $R_{\bar{\pi}s}$ is positive and $R_{\bar{\pi}\bar{\pi}}$ negative, the second term in the brackets in (7) will be negative. Then if the marginal profitability of s and α are independent (that is, $\bar{\Pi}_{s\alpha} = 0$), $ds/d\alpha$ will be negative. That is, for a decreasingly risk-averse firm, a profit-increasing parameter change can lead to a decrease in safety. In general, however, we cannot sign either term in the brackets on the right-hand side of (7).

Thus, on purely theoretical grounds, we cannot sign $ds/d\alpha$. We conclude that the effect of higher profits on safety depends on (1) the risk preferences of the firm and on (2) the source of increased profits and their effect on the marginal profitability of safety.

III.

The model described in section II suggests that the firm maximizes utility by choosing expected profits and safety. Neither expected profits nor safety are directly observable, of course. As a proxy for expected profits I use realized profit. Two possible proxies for safety suggest themselves: a measure of safety inputs and a measure of accident experience. Since safety is produced jointly with other outputs, it is not clear what bias would result from using, say, maintenance expenditures as a proxy for safety. Further, firms will differ in the efficiency with which they use any given set of inputs. Hence I prefer an output measure of safety, and therefore consider the firm's accident experience as a proxy for safety. The model is thus the system of structural equations[15]

$$\textit{PROF} = f(A, X_1)$$
$$A = g(\textit{PROF}, X_2)$$

where *PROF* is profits, A is a measure of accident rates, and X_1 and X_2 are measures of exogenous variables which determine profits (through costs and demand) and accident rates.

In order to have a reasonably homogeneous sample, the study was confined to the domestic operations of the US certificated route carriers. The cross-section sample consists of data for eleven firms from the years 1963–1970.[16] Limiting the sample to the domestic operations of larger firms should help reduce the randomness in accident figures by reducing the importance of such factors as airport quality, which could be expected to vary more for non-trunk or non-US operations. Using data from the 1960s should reduce problems caused by structural shifts in the profit function such as those caused by events which occurred in the early 1970s: the runup of oil prices,

[15] Recall that this paper is concerned with the impact of current profits on safety, not the issue of the impact of safety on future profits. Thus, the appropriate specification involves the relationship between contemporaneous profits and safety, not between safety and future profits.

[16] Airlines included are: American, Braniff, Continental, Delta, Eastern, National, Northeast, Northwest, Trans World Airways, United and Western.

the shift to jets, and the advent of deregulation. Because of the small number of firms in the sample, data from four years were combined to form two pooled samples: 1963–1966 and 1967–1970. The data were divided into subsets in order to minimize the possible effects of changes in technology over the eight-year period.[17] A second set of data consists of time-series observations on the domestic operations of the industry as a whole for the period 1952–1972.

The cross-section equations are:

(8a) $$A = a_0 + a_1 PROF + a_2 DEP + a_3 STAGEL + e_1$$

(8b) $$PROF = b_0 + b_1 A + b_2 DEP + b_3 STAGEL + b_4 LOADF + e_2$$

where

DEP = departures
$STAGEL$ = stage length
$LOADF$ = load factor
$PROF$ = net income (RNI) or rate of return (ROR)
e_1, e_2 = normally distributed error terms with zero means.

While equation (8a) is identified, (8b) is not. Hence, no estimates of (8b) are reported.

I measure safety by (the square root of) total accidents (ACC).[18] Airline safety is commonly measured by fatalities per passenger mile, but such measures have serious drawbacks. While fatality measures might serve as a rough proxy for the severity of accidents, they discriminate against high load-factor operators.[19] It is also not clear that safety is best measured as either accidents per mile or accidents per departure, since expected accidents are some function of both mileage and takeoffs (and landings). Hence, it seems better to estimate safety functions with both mileage and departure measures as explanatory variables rather than to condition the safety

[17] Chow tests allow us to reject the hypothesis that both sets of data obey the same relationship.

[18] Accidents are reported by the National Transportation Safety Board (previously by the CAB). An aircraft accident is defined as:

> "an occurrence associated with the operation of an aircraft which takes place between the time any person boards the aircraft with the intention of flight until such time as all persons have disembarked, and in which any person suffers death or serious injury as a result of being in or upon the aircraft or by direct contact with the aircraft or anything attached thereto, or in which the aircraft receives substantial damage."

A fatal injury is an injury which results in death within seven days of the accident. A serious injury is an injury which (1) requires hospitalization for more than 48 hours, (2) results in a fracture of any bone, except simple fractures of fingers, toes, or nose, (3) involves lacerations which cause severe hemorrhages, nerve, muscle or tendon damage, (4) involves injury to an internal organ, or (5) involves second or third degree burns or any burns over more than 5 percent of the body surface. Substantial damage to an aircraft encompasses, with some exceptions, "damage or structural failure which adversely affects the structural strength, performance or flight characteristics of the aircraft, and which would normally require major repair or replacement of the affected component". Source: US Department of Transportation, Federal Aviation Administration, *FAA Statistical Handbook of Aviation Calendar Year 1975*, p. 121.

[19] See Ramsden [1976].

measure by one or the other. Variations of equation (8a) were estimated using accidents per departure and accidents per mile as the dependent variable; the regressions were not significant and are not reported here. It is reasonable to assume that accidents occur independently over time and that the probability of an accident in any fixed interval is constant. Given those assumptions, accident data will have a Poisson distribution. Consequently, variance will not be constant across observations, and ordinary least squares (OLS) estimators will not be minimum variance unbiased. The square root of a Poisson variable does have constant variance, so the dependent variable used is the square root of accidents (SRACC).

Profitability measures are taken from the *Handbook of Airline Statistics*. RNI is defined as net income after taxes but before special items, deflated by the GNP price deflator.[20] Rate of return on regulatory investment (ROR, as defined and reported in the *Handbook*) is also used as a measure of profitability. For the time series model, ROR is calculated as domestic net income over total stockholders' equity.[21] While rate of return on investment is generally used as a proxy for profitability, it seems less appropriate here than RNI. If changes in product safety are embedded in capital, then such changes would affect the denominator of the rate of return variable, thus obscuring the safety-profit relationship.[22] Higher net income will of course tend to be associated with larger firms, which have more flights and more accidents. Inclusion of the activity variables, however, should ensure that the coefficient on net income does not impound these scale effects.

Accidents are clearly an increasing function of flight activity: the chance of an accident increases with both the number and length of flights. While there are mid-air accidents, Fromm [1968] reports that approximately 70% of accidents are incident to takeoffs and landings.[23] Hence I use two measures of activity—departures and stage length. Departures are clearly relevant to accidents occurring at takeoff (landing), and stage length should be associated with the probability of a mid-air collision.[24] Similarly, we expect costs and therefore profits to be a function of the number of flights as well as the length of those flights. Departures are measured as aircraft revenue departures performed, stage length as scheduled aircraft miles completed divided by departures.[25]

[20] The implicit GNP price deflator is published in Gordon [1984].

[21] The breakdown of stockholders' equity between foreign and domestic components was unavailable.

[22] Data to measure these effects are unavailable.

[23] Fromm [1968, p. 595].

[24] Symmetry would suggest that, since other variables are measured in absolute terms, the probability of mid-air collisions should be proxied by scheduled aircraft miles. However, the high degree of collinearity between departures and scheduled miles made estimates of equations including both variables unreliable. Hence, I use stage length instead.

[25] Aircraft revenue departures performed is the number of takeoffs actually performed in scheduled domestic service. Scheduled aircraft miles completed measures aircraft miles actually performed on scheduled domestic flights, where aircraft miles are measured from airport to airport. These data are published in the *Handbook of Airline Statistics*.

TABLE I
VARIABLE MEANS (STD DEV)

	Cross Section 1963–1966	Cross Section 1967–1970	Time Series 1952–1972
ACC	2.52	2.16	30.05
	(2.28)	(2.85)	(7.42)
SRACC	1.34	1.12	5.44
	(0.86)	(0.96)	(0.68)
RNI	18453[a]	10282[a]	90.87[b]
	(20675)	(30059)	(122.85)
ROR	6.35	3.31	6.49
	(25.99)	(10.72)	(6.64)
DEP[a]	199.42	270.24	2395.6
	(138.07)	(174.19)	(404.1)
STAGEL	380.68	490.86	375.07
	(119.18)	(127.78)	(118.5)
LOADF	45.89	42.38	49.22
	(4.07)	(4.58)	(5.56)
RGNP			844.00
			(190.62)
CYCLE			3.41
			(2.21)

[a] 000.
[b] 000,000.

Profits are clearly a function not only of the number of flights, but of demand conditions, which I measure using load factor—the percentage of the seats on a flight which are occupied.[26] Since accidents are not a function of load factors, the structural equation (8a) is exactly identified.[27]

Means and standard deviations of the variables are shown in Table I.

Regression results for equation (8a) from the cross-section samples are reported in Table II. Both OLS and two-stage least squares (2SLS) results are shown.[28] In all equations the departures variable has the hypothesized sign and is statistically significant at the 95% level. We also expect a positive coefficient on stage length. This coefficient is positive in equations (2a), (2b), (2c), (2d) and (2g). However, it is only significantly different from zero in (2a) and (2b).

[26] The overall revenue load factor is reported in the *Handbook of Airline Statistics*. It is defined as "the percent that total revenue ton-miles (passenger plus non-passenger) are of available ton-miles in revenue services, representing the proportion of total capacity that is actually sold and utilized" (p. 620). Passenger revenue ton-miles are computed using a passenger weight standard of 200 pounds.

[27] Accidents and profits ought also to be a function of risk aversion, but this is unobservable. Omission of this variable could bias the coefficients of included variables, but if risk aversion is independent of other explanatory variables the problem will not be serious. The coefficient of variation of net income (standard deviation divided by mean) was included as a proxy for risk aversion in cross-section regressions. The variable was not significant and its inclusion did not appreciably change other estimates.

[28] The Wu–Hausman test indicates that we cannot reject the hypothesis that profit variables are exogenous in equation (8a).

TABLE II
DETERMINANTS OF (THE SQUARE ROOT OF) ACCIDENTS—ESTIMATES FROM CROSS-SECTION SAMPLES

	1963–1966				1967–1970			
	a OLS	*b* OLS	*c* 2SLS	*d* 2SLS	*e* OLS	*f* OLS	*g* 2SLS	*h* 2SLS
Eqn. Std. Err.	0.64	0.63	0.67	0.72	0.80	0.82	0.82	0.83
R-Squared (Unadjusted)	0.49	0.51	0.44	0.37	0.35	0.33	0.32	0.31
Constant	−0.23	−0.30	−0.06	−0.14	0.32	0.51	0.08	0.41
	(0.7)	(0.8)	(0.1)	(0.3)	(0.6)	(1.0)	(0.1)	(0.8)
RNI	−0.23*E*-5	—	0.79*E*-5	—	0.55*E*-5	—	0.12*E*-4	—
	(0.4)		(0.8)		(1.2)		(0.7)	
ROR	—	0.17*E*-2	—	0.01	—	0.42*E*-2	—	0.02
		(0.5)		(0.9)		(0.3)		(0.7)
DEP	0.38*E*-2	0.38*E*-2	0.34*E*-2	0.36*E*-2	0.30*E*-2	0.32*E*-2	0.26*E*-2	0.30*E*-2
	(5.1)	(5.3)	(4.2)	(4.2)	(3.8)	(4.2)	(2.2)	(3.6)
STAGEL	0.23*E*-2	0.22*E*-2	0.15*E*-2	0.17*E*-2	−0.12*E*-3	−0.55*E*-3	0.45*E*-3	−0.34*E*-3
	(2.4)	(2.6)	(1.3)	(1.4)	(0.1)	(0.5)	(0.3)	(0.3)

t-statistics in parentheses.
OLS = Ordinary least squares
2SLS = Two-stage least squares.

The coefficient of primary interest is, of course, that on the profit variables RNI or ROR. In no case is this coefficient statistically different from zero. In seven of eight cases, however, it is positive. Thus, the cross-section evidence suggests that there is probably no significant relationship between safety and profits in the airline industry. If there is any relationship, it is likely to be negative: more profitable firms have more accidents.

Similar results are obtained from analysis of time series data. The time series model is

$$\text{(9a)} \quad SRACC = c_0 + c_1 PROF + c_2 DEP + c_3 STAGEL + c_4 RGNP + c_5 CYCLE + e_1$$

$$\text{(9b)} \quad PROF = d_0 + d_1 A + d_2 DEP + d_3 STAGEL + d_4 RGNP + d_5 CYCLE + d_6 LOADF + e_2$$

where

RGNP = Gross National Product in 1972 dollars

CYCLE = a measure of the business cycle: the first differences of the natural logarithm of real GNP.[29]

RGNP and CYCLE were added to the model in order to account for the effects of the business cycle. During upturns, we could expect both profits and congestion (and therefore accidents) to increase. These effects may not be fully captured by the departures and load factor variables, so I include RGNP and CYCLE to account for the business cycle directly. *A priori*, we would expect both variables to have positive signs. However, RGNP has a simple correlation coefficient of 0.98 with a linear time trend. It is possible, therefore, that RGNP may pick up the effects of technological change which reduced accidents over time, so that estimates of the coefficient will be biased. Stage length is also highly correlated with RGNP and was therefore dropped from the equations to avoid multicollinearity problems. Note also that (9b) is not identified. Hence the equation estimated using time series data is

$$\text{(10)} \quad SRACC = c_0 + c_1 PROF + c_2 DEP + c_3 RGNP + c_4 CYCLE + e_1$$

Estimates are shown in Table III. Two methods were used to deal with the simultaneity problem: lagging the profit variables and instrumental variables. Corrections were also made for autocorrelation in the residuals.

In general, the results are not very sensitive to the estimation procedure used. The coefficient on DEP is always positive, as hypothesized, and significantly different from zero at the 5% level in most cases. The coefficient on RGNP is always negative and significant, suggesting that the dominant effect is the secular decline in accident rates rather than business cycle effects. The coefficient on CYCLE is consistently positive, but never significantly different from zero. This would suggest that most of any business cycle effect is picked up by the departure and/or load factor variables.

[29] If the continuous rate of change is r, $X_{t+n} = X_t \exp(rn)$. Hence $X_{t+n}/X_t = \exp(r)$, and $r = \ln(X_{t+1}/X_t)$.

Table III

Determinants of (the Square Root of) Accidents—Estimates from Times-Series Sample

	1952–1972						1953–1972					
	a OLS	*b* OLS	*c* ITGLS	*d* ITGLS	*e* 2SLS	*f* 2SLS	*g* OLS	*h* OLS	*i* ITGLS	*j* ITGLS	*k* FAIR	*l* FAIR
Eqn. Std. Err.	0.44	0.47	0.41	0.43	0.45	0.47	0.45	0.45	0.44	0.43	0.42	0.46
R-Squared	0.66	0.61	0.65	0.64	0.64	0.61	0.66	0.68	0.61	0.64	0.65	0.59
Durbin–Watson	1.3	1.3	1.8	1.7	1.3	1.3	1.5	1.4	1.6	1.6	1.7	1.7
Rho-Hat	—	—	0.36	0.45	—	—	—	—	0.23	0.32	0.18	0.33
Constant	6.3	6.1	6.2	5.8	6.3	6.2	6.7	6.4	6.6	6.1	6.5	5.8
	(9.7)	(8.0)	(7.9)	(6.0)	(9.4)	(7.5)	(9.5)	(9.0)	(8.2)	(7.1)	(8.9)	(5.9)
RNI	0.16*E*-2	—	0.15*E*-2	—	0.60*E*-3	—	—	—	—	—	0.19*E*-2	—
	(1.8)	—	(1.6)	—	(0.4)	—	—	—	—	—	(1.9)	—
RNI(−1)	—	—	—	—	—	—	0.90*E*-3	—	0.94*E*-3	—	—	—
	—	—	—	—	—	—	(1.1)	—	(1.0)	—	—	—
ROR	—	0.01	—	0.02	—	0.93*E*-2	—	—	—	—	—	0.04
	—	(0.7)	—	(0.9)	—	(0.3)	—	—	—	—	—	(1.6)
ROR (−1)	—	—	—	—	—	—	—	0.02	—	0.03	—	—
	—	—	—	—	—	—	—	(1.3)	—	(1.4)	—	—
DEP	0.12*E*-2	0.11*E*-2	0.12*E*-2	0.12*E*-2	0.11*E*-2	0.11*E*-2	0.95*E*-3	0.90*E*-3	0.93*E*-3	0.88*E*-3	0.11*E*-2	0.12*E*-2
	(2.5)	(2.2)	(2.2)	(2.1)	(2.3)	(2.2)	(1.9)	(1.8)	(1.7)	(1.6)	(2.2)	(2.0)
RGNP	−0.48*E*-2	−0.45*E*-2	−0.46*E*-2	−0.42*E*-2	−0.47*E*-2	−0.45*E*-2	−0.45*E*-2	−0.42*E*-2	−0.43*E*-2	−0.37*E*-2	−0.48*E*-2	−0.42*E*-2
	(4.7)	(4.0)	(3.8)	(3.1)	(4.3)	(4.0)	(4.3)	(3.8)	(3.6)	(2.8)	(4.4)	(3.2)
CYCLE	0.05	0.07	0.03	0.03	0.07	0.07	0.08	0.08	0.06	0.05	0.03	0.02
	(1.0)	(1.2)	(0.7)	(0.7)	(1.2)	(1.2)	(1.6)	(1.6)	(1.3)	(1.2)	(0.7)	(0.4)

t-statistics in parentheses.
OLS = ordinary least squares.
ITGLS = iterative maximum likelihood GLS.
2SLS = two-stage least squares.
FAIR = iterative Fair estimator.

The coefficient on profitability, while not generally significantly different from zero, is consistently positive. (It is significant at the 90% level for equation (3k), the iterative Fair estimator for simultaneous equations with autocorrelation.) Thus, the time-series evidence also suggests that, if there is any relationship at all between airline profits and safety, it is a mildly negative one: more profitable firms may have more accidents. This result is consistent with our cross-section results and with Miller's result: higher profits are weakly associated with more accidents. Note that these results occur despite direct safety regulation.

It is instructive to compare these results with conclusions reached in a recent study of railroads (Golbe [1983]). That study indicated that, for profitable railroads, as for the airline sample examined here, there is a weak negative relationship between safety and profitability: more profitable roads tend to have more accidents. For unprofitable roads, however, higher losses appear to be associated with more accidents. This second result suggests that railroads (and perhaps airlines) in fear of bankruptcy may skimp on safety. As I have shown elsewhere (Golbe [1981]), because stockholders' returns are truncated from below, increased variance in total firm returns increases shareholders' expected returns and reduces their risk. Thus, even risk-averse shareholders may prefer greater variance for the firm's returns. Under such circumstances, firms may take greater risks by skimping on safety. Hence, while the sample I have examined here does not indicate a need for regulators to be concerned with safety effects as profits fall, analysis of railroad data does suggest that firms on the brink of bankruptcy may tend to have more accidents.

IV.

The evidence presented here on airline safety and profits does not support the popular wisdom. There does not seem to be a statistically significant relationship between safety and profits. If there is any relationship it is weak and of the "wrong" sign: that is, more profitable firms may have more accidents. It does not appear that profit-reducing changes in regulation will necessarily lead to less safe airlines.

DEVRA L. GOLBE,
Department of Economics,
Rutgers University,
New Brunswick, NJ 08903,
USA

ACCEPTED MARCH 1985

REFERENCES

ARROW, KENNETH, 1974, *Essays in the Theory of Risk Bearing* (North-Holland Publishing Co., Amsterdam).

BAILEY, ELIZABETH, 1980, 'Deregulation and Regulatory Reform of US Air Transportation Policy', in B. Mitchell and P. Kleindorfer (eds.), *Regulated Industries and Public Enterprise*, pp. 29–56. (Lexington Books, Lexington, Mass.).

CAVES, RICHARD E., 1962, *Air Transport and its Regulators* (Harvard University Press, Cambridge).

DOUGLAS, GEORGE W. and MILLER, JAMES C., III, 1974, *Economic Regulation of Domestic Air Transport: Theory and Policy* (The Brookings Institution, Washington, DC).

FROMM, GARY, 1968, 'Aviation Safety', *Law and Contemporary Problems*, 33, 3 (Summer), pp. 590–618.

GOLBE, DEVRA L., 1981, 'The Effects of Imminent Bankruptcy on Stockholder Risk Preferences and Behavior', *Bell Journal of Economics*, 12, 1 (Spring), pp. 321–328.

GOLBE, DEVRA L., 1983, 'Product Safety in a Regulated Industry: Evidence from the Railroads', *Economic Inquiry*, 21, 1 (January), pp. 39–52.

GORDON, ROBERT J., 1984, *Macroeconomics*, 3rd ed. (Little, Brown, Boston).

JORDAN, WILLIAM A., 1970, *Airline Regulation in America: Effects and Imperfections* (The Johns Hopkins Press, Baltimore and London).

LELAND, HAYNE E., 1972, 'Theory of the Firm Facing Uncertain Demand', *American Economic Review*, 62, 3 (June), pp. 278–291.

LINTNER, JOHN, 1970, 'The Impact of Uncertainty on the "Traditional" Theory of the Firm: Price-Setting and Tax-Shifting', in Jesse W. Markham and Gustav F. Papenek (eds.), *Industrial Organization and Economic Development: In Honor of E. S. Mason* (Houghton Mifflin, New York).

MADDALA, G. S., 1977, *Econometrics* (McGraw-Hill, New York).

MILLER, JAMES C., III, 1975, Statement before US Senate Committee on the Judiciary, *Oversight of Civil Aeronautics Board Practices and Procedures* (Washington, DC, 94th Cong., 1st Sess., Feb–Mar).

PRATT, JOHN W., 1964, 'Risk Aversion in the Small and in the Large', *Econometrica*, 32, 1–2 (January–April), pp. 122–136.

RAMSDEN, J. M., 1976, *The Safe Airline* (Macdonald and Jane's Publishers Ltd., London).

SPENGLER, JOSEPH, 1968, 'The Economics of Safety', *Law and Contemporary Problems*, 33, 3 (Summer), pp. 619–638.

US CIVIL AERONAUTICS BOARD, *Handbook of Airline Statistics*, various editions.

US CIVIL AERONAUTICS BOARD, *Report of the CAB Special Staff on Regulatory Reform*, 1975 (Washington, DC, July).

US CIVIL AERONAUTICS BOARD, *Statistical Review, US Air Carrier Accidents*, 1953, 1954, 1955, 1956, 1957, 1958, 1959.

US CIVIL AERONAUTICS BOARD, *US Air Carrier Accidents: Statistical Review and Resume of Accidents*, 1960, 1961, 1962, 1963, 1964, 1965, 1966.

US CONGRESS, HOUSE, COMMITTEE ON GOVERNMENT OPERATIONS, 1977, *Airline Deregulation and Aviation Safety: Hearings*, 95th Cong., 1st Sess. (8–9 September).

US CONGRESS, SENATE, SUBCOMMITTEE ON ADMINISTRATIVE PRACTICE AND PROCEDURE, COMMITTEE ON THE JUDICIARY, 1975, *Civil Aeronautics Board Practices and Procedures*, 94th Cong., 1st Sess.

US CONGRESS, SENATE, SUBCOMMITTEE ON ADMINISTRATIVE PRACTICE AND PROCEDURE, COMMITTEE ON THE JUDICIARY, 1975, *Oversight of Civil Aeronautics Board Practices and Procedures: Hearing*, 94th Cong., 1st Sess. (February–March).

US DEPARTMENT OF TRANSPORTATION, NATIONAL TRANSPORTATION SAFETY BOARD, *Annual Review of Aircraft Accident Data, US Air Carrier Operations*, 1966, 1967, 1968, 1969, 1970, 1971, 1972.

US FEDERAL AVIATION AGENCY, *FAA Statistical Handbook of Aviation*, various editions.

WHITE, LAWRENCE, J., 1972, 'Quality Variation When Prices Are Regulated', *Bell Journal of Economics*, 3, 2 (Autumn), pp. 425–436.

THE JOURNAL OF INDUSTRIAL ECONOMICS 0022-1821 $2.00
Volume XXXIV March 1986 No. 3

AN EMPIRICAL ANALYSIS OF PROCESS AND PRODUCT PATENTING: A SIMULTANEOUS EQUATION FRAMEWORK*

JOHN LUNN

The results of this study support the hypothesis that research activity is not a homogeneous activity, and that important differences exist between the determinants of process patenting and product patenting. Further, the effects on concentration and advertising of research depend on the type of research carried on by firms. Concentration and process patenting are positively related and concentration and product patenting are not. There is some weak evidence linking advertising and product patenting. Further, process patenting tends to generate greater industrial concentration.

RECENT EMPIRICAL studies concerning industrial research and development have differed from earlier studies in one of two ways. First, several recent studies have attempted to account for the heterogeneity of industrial research activity rather than treat research as a homogeneous activity. Some of these studies have classified research into basic research, applied research, and development,[1] while others have distinguished between research directed toward product innovations and research directed toward process innovations.[2] Second, some recent studies have attempted to utilize a more Schumpeterian approach by estimating a simultaneous equations system, with concentration, and perhaps some other variables, treated as endogenous.[3] The purpose of this paper is to distinguish between both the determinants and the effects of process innovations and product innovations within a simultaneous equations framework.

I. SYSTEM OF EQUATIONS

A system of four equations is estimated to examine the relationships among innovations, industrial concentration, and advertising. Innovation is broken into process innovation and product innovation on the grounds that the

* I want to acknowledge the helpful comments of Professor White and two anonymous referees. Any remaining errors are my responsibility. I also want to thank Professor F. M. Scherer for providing the patent data used in this study.

[1] See Mansfield [1980], [1981] and Link [1982], [1982b].

[2] See Link [1982a], Scherer [1983a], and Link and Lunn [1984].

[3] See Farber [1981], Levin and Reiss [1984], Levin [forthcoming], and Connolly and Hirschey [1984].

determinants of each will differ, as will their effects on the other endogenous variables. Since a process innovation affects the costs of the firm, it will be related to concentration rather than advertising, while a product innovation may be related to product differentiation and advertising. Each of the equations are discussed in turn, although the discussions of process innovation and product innovation are combined.

A. *Process and product innovations*

The question addressed by much of the economic literature concerning industrial research is whether interindustry variations in research activity can be explained by interindustry variations in industrial concentration (*CONC*). Scherer [1980, pp. 434–437] notes that many researchers have found a positive relationship between concentration and research activity, but that this relationship is weakened considerably when interindustry differences in technological opportunity are included in the statistical analysis. Technological opportunity (*TECH*) is included to reflect the influences of technology push, which occurs when exogenous changes in scientific and engineering knowledge reduce the costs of new products or processes. Scherer also notes that several studies have found that the correlation between R&D measures and concentration is greater for firms facing limited technological opportunities than for firms in the "technologically progressive" industries. Thus, we expect to observe the effects on patenting of concentration to be greater in the less technologically progressive industries than in the technologically progressive industries. Following Scherer [1983b], industries in the chemical, electronics, and electrical product groups are classified as technologically progressive.

The effects of concentration on process and product patenting are likely to differ also. The property rights provided by patents generally are stronger for new products than for new processes because the transactions costs associated with licensing arrangements are lower in the case of new products. When the property rights provided by patents are relatively weak, market power may be a substitute for stronger property rights in terms of appropriating innovative output (Lunn [1985]). Hence, we expect concentration positively to affect process patenting but to have little or no influence on product patenting.

Farber [1981] includes advertising (*ADV*) as a determinant of research activity on the grounds that advertising and research are complementary inputs in increasing demand. When product differentiation is feasible, firms use both advertising and research as strategic policies. However, product differentiation and changes in production processes are not likely to be related; hence there is no reason to think that advertising and process innovations are related. Instead, we expect advertising to be related to the development of new products for consumers and include a measure of advertising intensity in the equation for product innovations but not in the equation for process innovations.

Some studies have included a measure of profitability as a determinant of research activity on the grounds that firms may have to use internal financing for R & D projects (see, for example, Grabowski [1968]; Kamien and Schwartz [1978]; Levin [forthcoming]; and Connolly and Hirschey [1984]). Since firms are reluctant to provide information concerning potential innovations, they have a difficult time obtaining outside financing for their R & D projects. The firms are thus forced to use internal financing for the project. However, a better measure of internal financing is the cash flow of the firm (Smyth, *et al.* [1972]). Hence, a measure of firms' cash flow (*CASH*) is used as an explanatory variable for both the product and the process equations.

The value of a particular innovation will be greater the larger the market, especially when licensing of the innovation is feasible. Thus, a variable reflecting the size of the market (*MKT*) is included in both the product and the process equations. Nelson [1980] argues that the degree of technique codification may be important in explaining research activity, and links codifiability to the degree of mechanization. This suggests that the capital intensity of an industry (*KAP*) may also be a determinant of research activity. However, this argument applies to process innovations rather than to product innovations, so capital intensity is added to the process equation but not the product equation.

The above discussion suggests the following specifications for product and process innovations:

$$(1) \qquad PROCESS = \alpha_0 + \alpha_1\, CONC + \alpha_2\, CASH + \alpha_3\, MKT + \alpha_4\, KAP + \alpha_5\, TECH + \varepsilon_1$$

$$(2) \qquad PRODUCT = \beta_0 + \beta_1\, CONC + \beta_2\, CASH + \beta_3\, MKT + \beta_4\, ADV + \beta_5\, TECH + \varepsilon_2$$

We expect all coefficients to be positive, and expect $\alpha_1 > \beta_1$ and $\beta_5 > \alpha_5$. Further, if the data set is bifurcated on the basis of *TECH* and (1) and (2) are estimated on the bifurcated data set, then we expect the coefficients of *CONC* to be greater for the less progressive industries than the progressive industries.

B. *Concentration equation*

A Schumpeterian treatment of research activity must treat concentration as an endogenous variable. Firms that innovate tend to prosper and grow, resulting in larger market shares and increased industrial concentration. Some evidence for this can be found in the fact that the technologically progressive industries have a higher level of concentration, on average, than the less progressive industries.[4] The type of innovation may be important too. Process innovations alter the costs of production, which are an important

[4] The mean four-firm concentration ratio for the technologically progressive industries is 0.51, and the mean four-firm concentration ratio of the other manufacturing industries is 0.38.

determinant of industrial concentration. Hence, it is expected that product innovations have little or no influence on concentration, while process innovations affect concentration, although the direction cannot be determined, *a priori.*

Economic theory suggests that the degree of industrial concentration is determined by the extent of scale economies relative to the size of the market. Changes in the size of the market (GROW) are also likely to be important since growing, dynamic markets tend to be less concentrated. From this discussion, the following relationships describing concentration across industries is obtained:[5]

$$(3) \qquad CONC = \gamma_0 + \gamma_1 PROCESS + \gamma_2 MKT + \gamma_3 GROW + \gamma_4 MES + \gamma_5 CDR + \varepsilon_3$$

where MES and CDR represent minimum efficient scale and the cost disadvantage ratio, respectively, and are used to measure scale economies (Caves, *et al.* [1975]. We expect γ_4 to be positive, γ_2, γ_3, and γ_5 to be negative, and are uncertain of the sign of γ_1.

C. *Advertising equation*

Advertising intensity must also be treated as an endogenous variable since it is jointly determined with R & D intensity (Farber [1981]). Advertising spending is greater for firms that produce consumer goods (CONS) than for firms that produce intermediate goods (Ornstein [1977]; Martin [1983]). Since advertising and research tend to be complementary activities with respect to product differentiation, firms that generate product innovations are likely to advertise more than firms that generate process innovations. Cash flow is likely to be a determinant of advertising for reasons similar to those stated for the research equations. Finally, the market structure and the size of firms (FIRM) in the industry may be determinants of advertising. The following relationship describing advertising intensity across industries is obtained:

$$(4) \qquad ADV = \delta_0 + \delta_1 CONC + \delta_2 CASH + \delta_3 CONS + \delta_4 FIRM + \delta_5 PRODUCT + \varepsilon_4$$

We expect all coefficients to be positive.

II. THE DATA

The data used in this study come from three sources. First is a data set, which was compiled by Professor F. M. Scherer, composed of information on 15,112 US patents issued to US corporations between June 1976 and March

[5] Advertising is not included in (3) because I do not find the argument that advertising creates entry barriers convincing. Advertising is as much a means of entry to an industry as it is a barrier. However, since numerous studies include advertising as a determinant of concentration, I estimated (3) with ADV included as an explanatory variable. The coefficient on ADV was positive but insignificantly different from zero (t-statistic = 0.27). The other coefficients changed only slightly from those reported in Table II.

1977.[6] Industry totals were calculated by adding up the number of process and the number of product patents in each industry. Obviously, there are some problems with using patent counts as a measure of research activity. The propensity to patent is likely to differ across industries, the value of individual patents varies widely, and a great deal of research activity is not patented. Even so, several researchers have found that the information

TABLE I

Variable Definitions	*Mean*	*Standard Deviation*
I. Endogenous Variables:		
PROCESS[c]—Number of process patents awarded to firms in the industry.	16.23	50.08
PRODUCT[c]—Number of product patents awarded to firms in the industry.	46.87	108.6
CONC[b]—Four-firm concentration ratio.	40.19	19.69
ADV[a]—Advertising and other sales expenditures divided by total sales and transfers.	8.50	5.90
NCONS[c]—Number of patents involving consumer goods awarded to firms in the industry.	12.03	26.37
II. Exogenous Variables:		
CASH[a]—Ratio of the sum of operating income and depreciation to total sales and transfers by LB for an industry.	10.32	5.96
MKT[b]—Logarithm of industry value of shipments.	3.27	0.405
KAP[a]—Ratio of total assets to total sales and transfers by LB for an industry.	67.02	20.80
FIRM[a]—Total assets of LBs reporting to the FTC divided by the number of LBs reporting. The logarithm of the value is used.	2.57	0.377
GROW[a]—Percentage change in real total sales and transfers by LB between 1974 and 1975.	0.007	0.629
MES[b]—Output per firm of the top 50% of the firms in the industry and normalized by total industry output.	2.46	2.86
CDR[b]—Ratio of industry value added per worker in plants supplying the bottom 50% of industry value added to the average value added per worker in plants supplying the top 50% of industry value added.	0.77	0.177
CONS[d]—Dummy variable set equal to "1" for consumer goods industries.	0.24	0.429
TECH[e]—Dummy variable set equal to "1" for technologically progressive industries.	0.23	0.419
CONPAT[c]—Percent of patents in the industry for consumer goods.	0.28	0.32

[a] FTC *Annual Line of Business Report*, 1974 and 1975.
[b] Bureau of the Census, *Census of Manufacturers*, 1972 and 1977.
[c] Tape of patent data provided by Professor Scherer.
[d] Ornstein [1977].
[e] Technologically progressive industries are those in the chemical, electrical and electronic product groups.

[6] For further details concerning the patent data, see Scherer [1983b], [1984].

TABLE II
TWO STAGE LEAST SQUARES ESTIMATES OF THE SYSTEM

	(1)	(2a)	(2b)	(3)	(4a)	(4b)	(5)	(6)	(7)
	Process			Product					
Variable	Total Data Set	Low Tech	High Tech	Total Data Set	Low Tech	High Tech	ADV	CONC	CONC
Intercept	−245.36	−151.85	−358.38	−283.79	−60.96	−897.55	13.31	101.86	130.29
CONC	0.509[b]	0.572[c]	−0.125	0.427	0.242	1.353	0.071[b]		
	(2.23)	(3.12)	(0.153)	(0.857)	(1.00)	(0.662)	(2.39)		
ADV				−3.554[a]	−2.302[b]	−0.557			
				(1.69)	(2.42)	(0.049)			
PROCESS								0.331[c]	0.839[c]
								(4.51)	(2.69)
PRODUCT							0.004		−0.225[a]
							(0.495)		(1.85)
MKT	60.506[c]	39.800[c]	99.101[c]	89.098[c]	27.371[c]	267.111[c]		−22.18[c]	−24.79[b]
	(6.76)	(5.29)	(4.06)	(4.66)	(2.75)	(3.99)		(3.74)	(2.41)
CASH	1.365[b]	−0.279	4.052[b]	3.03[b]	0.552	7.859[a]	0.114		
	(2.30)	(0.531)	(2.33)	(2.50)	(0.815)	(2.01)	(1.64)		

KAP	0.363[b]	0.181	0.483						
	(2.18)	(1.53)	(1.02)						
FIRM							−4.189[c]		
							(2.92)		
GROW								−0.416	0.365
								(0.176)	(0.080)
MES								3.650[c]	3.534[c]
								(6.25)	(3.26)
CDR								−12.899	−26.813
								(1.49)	(1.51)
CONS							7.248[c]		
							(7.72)		
TECH	21.630[c]			94.618[c]					
	(2.62)			(5.33)					
F	13.23[c]	7.69[c]	7.17[c]	14.60[c]	4.33[c]	5.48[c]	15.96[c]	19.61[c]	5.32[c]
N	191	148	43	191	148	43	191	191	191
GOF	0.230	0.116	0.423	0.255	0.070	0.345	0.276	0.242	0.074

t-statistics in brackets. Significance levels are [a]10%, [b]5%, [c]1%.

The goodness of fit (*GOF*) is the square of the correlation coefficient between actual and fitted values. See Haessel [1978].

The endogenous variables in the system of equations are *PROCESS*, *PRODUCT*, *ADV*, and *CONC*. Columns (6) and (7) differ in that *PRODUCT* is included as an explanatory variable in (7).

provided by patent counts is similar to the information provided by other measures of research activity.[7]

Data used to measure the other variables are from the FTC Line of Business Reports and the Bureau of the Census' *Census of Manufacturers*. The Bureau of Economics of the Federal Trade Commission has collected data from the largest manufacturing firms that are broken down by line of business. Data from 1974 and 1975 are used in this study.[8] The industries used are mostly 4-digit SIC industries, with some aggregation to 3-digit when required for data compatibility. Some industries had to be dropped because the FTC's disclosure restriction resulted in suppression of the necessary data. This left 191 industries for the sample. Table I presents the variables used in the regression analysis and their mean values.

III. EMPIRICAL RESULTS

The 2SLS estimates of equations (1)–(4) are presented in Table II, columns (1), (3), (5) and (6).[9] The results are generally consistent with the expectations of section I. In particular, there are differences between process patenting and product patenting, which indicate that research is not a homogeneous activity. Although the coefficients of *CONC* in the *PROCESS* equation and the *PRODUCT* equation are approximately the same magnitude, the standard error in the *PRODUCT* equation is considerably larger. As a result, the coefficient on *CONC* in the *PROCESS* equation is statistically different from zero, while the coefficient of *CONC* in the *PRODUCT* equation is not statistically different from zero. Further, there is a difference in the effects on concentration of process and product patenting. Column (7) in Table II presents the results of equation (3) with *PRODUCT* included as an explanatory variable, while column (6) excluded *PRODUCT*. Differences between columns (6) and (7) suggest that industries with a greater propensity for process patenting tend to be more concentrated than industries that engage more in product patenting. Thus, process innovations tend to reduce costs in a manner that leads to increased concentration, and concentration tends to encourage more research effort toward process innovations.

The results concerning technological opportunity and patenting are also interesting. The coefficient on *TECH* is positive and significantly different from

[7] Scherer [1983b] reports that patenting rises roughly proportionately with R & D spending in most industries. Similar results are reported by Bound, *et al.* [1984]. Pakes and Griliches [1980] report that patents seem to measure R & D activity, especially at the cross-sectional level.

[8] Given a lag between the date a patent is applied for and received, the patent data reflects the actions of firms around 1974 or 1975.

[9] The editor expressed some uneasiness over the large standard deviations relative to the means of the patent variables. I found no evidence that the few industries with abnormally large numbers of patents biased the results. I also estimated the system of equations with a log-linear specification. The pattern of coefficients is similar to those reported in Table II, with the exception of *CASH*, which was statistically insignificant in columns (2b), (3) and (4b). Copies of these results are available from the author.

zero in both the *PROCESS* and *PRODUCT* equations. However, the size of the coefficient is much larger for the *PRODUCT* equation than the *PROCESS* equation. This suggests that the technologically progressive industries tend to be associated with product innovation more than with process innovation. Columns (2a), (2b), (4a), and (4b) present the results when the data set was split on the basis of *TECH*. Concentration remains an important determinant of process patenting for the less progressive industries, but has no apparent effect in the progressive industries. Again, the coefficients of *CONC* in (4a) and (4b) are not significantly different from zero. Thus, the effect of concentration on patenting is much greater for those industries facing more limited technological opportunities and for process patenting.

The coefficients of the other explanatory variables in both the *PROCESS* and *PRODUCT* equations are consistent with the theoretical arguments presented in section I, with the exception of *ADV*. The size of the market has a positive effect on both types of patenting, as does the cash flow of LBs in the industry. The results are also consistent with Nelson's hypothesis concerning process innovations and the degree of mechanization.

The empirical results concerning advertising and product patenting are inconsistent with the theoretical arguments offered in the first section. Advertising intensity has a negative impact on product patenting, rather than the positive effect that was expected, while the effect of product patenting on advertising intensity is nil. These results are surprising given that firms are likely to advertise new products heavily. However, many product patents are for intermediate goods rather than consumer goods,[10] and it is for products sold to consumers that we expect a positive relationship between product patenting and advertising.

In order to narrow the focus to patenting for consumer products, the advertising intensity equation was reestimated with *CONPAT* replacing *PRODUCT*. By making this substitution, patenting is limited to consumer goods. The 2SLS results are:[11]

$$\begin{aligned} ADV = {} & 11.06 + \underset{(1.93)}{0.057^{a}}\, CONC + \underset{(2.09)}{2.734^{b}}\, CONPAT - \underset{(2.77)}{3.403^{c}}\, FIRM \\ & + \underset{(2.16)}{0.014^{b}}\, CASH + \underset{(6.92)}{6.445^{c}}\, CONS \end{aligned}$$

$$F = 17.68^{c} \quad N = 191 \quad GOF = 0.298$$

The coefficient on *CONPAT* is positive and significantly different from zero. To investigate further, equation (2) was reestimated with *NCONS* replacing

[10] The means of *PRODUCT* when *CONS* = 0 and *CONS* = 1 respectively are 49.79 and 15.24, which are significantly different at the 99 percent confidence level.

[11] The inclusion of *CONPAT* as an exogenous variable to the system of equations generated only minor changes in the coefficients on the other equations.

PROD:

$$NCONS = -74.04 + \underset{(1.41)}{0.176}\,CONC + \underset{(1.37)}{0.719}\,ADV + \underset{(4.35)}{20.701^{c}}\,MKT + \underset{(2.65)}{0.081^{b}}\,CASH + \underset{(4.33)}{19.132^{c}}\,TECH$$

$$F = 19.18^{c} \quad N = 191 \quad GOF = 0.212$$

The coefficient on ADV is now of the expected sign, although it is not significantly different from zero at the 0.10 confidence level.[12] While not conclusive these results suggest that patents for consumer products rather than patents for new producer goods are related to advertising.

IV. CONCLUSIONS

The results of this study support the contentions that research activity is not a homogeneous activity and that important differences exist between the determinants of process patenting and the determinants of product patenting. Further, we have found that the effects on concentration and advertising of research depend on the type of research carried on by firms in the industry. Finally, the empirical results suggest that the Schumpeterian paradigm is valid, at least with respect to process innovations. It is market structure and process innovations that are related, and not market structure and product innovations. Of the two types of research considered in this study, it appears that research directed toward process innovations has the greater effect on the underlying structure of American industry.

JOHN LUNN,
Department of Economics,
2107 CEBA,
College of Business Administration,
Louisiana State University,
Baton Rouge,
Louisiana 70803–6306,
USA.

ACCEPTED MAY 1985

REFERENCES

BOUND, JOHN, CUMMINS, CLINT, GRILICHES, ZVI, HALL, BRONWYN H. and JAFFE, ADAM (1984), 'Who Does R & D and Who Patents?' in Zvi Griliches (ed.), *R & D, Patents, and Productivity* (The University of Chicago Press, Chicago).

CAVES, RICHARD E., KHALILZADEH-SHIRAZI, JAVAD and PORTER, MICHAEL E., 1975,

[12] It is significantly different from zero at the 0.15 level though.

'Scale Economies in Statistical Analyses of Market Power', *The Review of Economics and Statistics*, 57, 2 (May), pp. 133–140.

CONNOLLY, ROBERT A. and HIRSCHEY, MARK, 1984, 'R & D, Market Structure and Profits: A Value-Based Approach', *The Review of Economics and Statistics*, 66, 4 (November), pp. 682–686.

FARBER, STEPHEN, 1981, 'Buyer Market Structure and R & D Effort: A Simultaneous Equations Model', *The Review of Economics and Statistics*, 63, 3 (August), pp. 336–345.

GRABOWSKI, HENRY G., 1968, 'The Determinants of Industrial Research and Development: A Study of the Chemical, Drug, and Petroleum Industries', *Journal of Political Economy*, 76, 2 (March/April), pp. 292–306.

HAESSEL, WALTER, 1978, 'Measuring Goodness of Fit in Linear and Nonlinear Models', *Southern Economic Journal*, 44, 3 (January), pp. 648–652.

KAMIEN, MORTON I. and SCHWARTZ, NANCY L., 1978, 'Self-Financing of an R & D Project', *American Economic Review*, 68, 3 (June), pp. 252–261.

LEVIN, RICHARD, 'Toward an Empirical Model of Schumpeterian Competition', *Rand Journal of Economics*, forthcoming.

LEVIN, RICHARD and REISS, PETER C., 1984, 'Tests of a Schumpeterian Model of R & D and Market Structure', in Zvi Griliches (ed.), *R & D, Patents, and Productivity* (The University of Chicago Press, Chicago).

LINK, ALBERT N., 1981, 'Basic Research and Productivity Increase in Manufacturing: Additional Evidence', *American Economic Review*, 71, 5 (December), pp. 1111–1112.

LINK, ALBERT N., 1982a, 'A Disaggregated Analysis of Industrial R & D: Product Versus Process Innovation', in Devendra Sahal (ed.), *The Transfer and Utilization of Technical Knowledge* (Lexington Books, Lexington, MA).

LINK, ALBERT N., 1982b, 'An Analysis of the Composition of R & D Spending', *Southern Economic Journal*, 49, 2 (October), pp. 342–349.

LINK, ALBERT N. and LUNN, JOHN, 1984, 'Rates of Return to R & D and Market Structure', *Review of Industrial Organization*, 1, 3 (Autumn), pp. 232–239.

LUNN, JOHN, 1985, 'The Roles of Property Rights and Market Power in Appropriating Innovative Output', *Journal of Legal Studies*, 19, 2 (June), pp. 423–433.

MANSFIELD, EDWIN, 1980, 'Basic Research and Productivity Increases in Manufacturing', *American Economic Review*, 70, 5 (December), pp. 863–873.

MANSFIELD, EDWIN, 1981, 'Composition of R & D Expenditures: Relationship to Size of Firm, Concentration, and Innovative Output', *Review of Economics and Statistics*, 63, 4 (November), pp. 610–615.

MARTIN, STEPHEN, 1983, *Market, Firm, and Economic Performance*, Salomon Brothers Center for the Study of Financial Institutions Monograph Series, Monograph 1983–1.

NELSON, RICHARD R., 1980, 'Production Sets, Technological Knowledge, and R & D: Fragile and Overworked Constructs for Analysis of Productivity.' *American Economic Review Papers and Proceedings*, 70, 2 (May), pp. 62–68.

ORNSTEIN, STANLEY I., 1977, *Industrial Concentration and Advertising Intensity* (American Enterprise Institute for Public Policy Research, Washington, DC).

PAKES, ARIEL and GRILICHES, ZVI, 1980, 'Patents and R & D at the Firm Level: A First Report', *Economics Letters*, 5, pp. 377–381.

SCHERER, F. M., 1980, *Industrial Market Structure and Economic Performance*, 2nd Ed. (Rand McNally, Chicago).

SCHERER, F. M., 1983a, 'Concentration, R & D, and Productivity Change', *Southern Economic Journal*, 50, 1 (July), pp. 221–225.

SCHERER, F. M., 1983b, 'The Propensity to Patent', *International Journal of Industrial Organization*, 1, 1, pp. 107–128.

SCHERER, F. M., 1984, 'Using Linked Patent and R & D Data to Measure Interindustry Technology Flows', in Zvi Griliches (ed.), *R&D, Patents, and Productivity* (The University of Chicago Press, Chicago).

SMYTH, D. J., SAMUELS, J. M. and TZOANNOS, J., 1972, 'Patents, Profitability, Liquidity, and Firm Size', *Applied Economics*, 4, 1, pp. 77–86.

THE JOURNAL OF INDUSTRIAL ECONOMICS 0022-1821 $2.00
Volume XXXIV March 1986 No. 3

A SIMPLE MODEL OF IMPERFECT COMPETITION IN WHICH FOUR ARE FEW BUT THREE ARE NOT

GREGORY J. WERDEN AND MICHAEL G. BAUMANN*

This paper presents a model of imperfect competition in which the likelihood of collusion is *not* a monotonically decreasing function of the number of firms. Other notable oligopoly models predict a monotonic relationship. The difference in predictions is a consequence of our assumptions that firms either explicitly collude or instead engage in Cournot behavior and that explicit collusion, if detected, is punished with fines and damages.

THERE ARE few notable models of the formation or maintenance of collusive agreements. Two particularly interesting ones are those of Stigler [1964] and Selten [1973]. Stigler considers only a certain aspect of cartel maintenance—detecting cheating—while Selten considers only certain aspects of cartel formation. Their models produce the intuitive result that the likelihood of successful collusion is a monotonically decreasing function of the number of firms. We present a simple model of cartel formation and maintenance that produces a different result; it is quite possible for the likelihood of collusion to increase as the number of firms increases. An important, realistic feature of the model (at least for the United States), which distinguishes it from those of Stigler and Selten and which is partially responsible for its counterintuitive result, is that collusion, if discovered, is punished through fines, imprisonment, and treble damage awards.

Consider a simple, static model with n identical firms that either collude explicitly and set the monopoly quantity or instead engage in Cournot behavior.[1] If the firms collude, they (as a group) incur costs of forming and maintaining their agreement, M, which are an increasing function of n. In addition, there is some probability, θ, that the cartel will be detected,[2] in which case each firm in the cartel must pay a fixed fine, F, and the cartel must

* The views expressed here are not necessarily those of the US Department of Justice.

[1] To make the model very simple, we assume "all-or-nothing" cartels, that is, all firms are in any cartel. The specific assumption of Cournot behavior is not critical. The same basic results are obtained provided that the alternative to explicit collusion is not competition and provided that, absent explicit collusion, the fewer the number of firms, the greater is the difference between the equilibrium price or quantity and the competitive price or quantity.

[2] For simplicity, we assume that θ is a constant. It may be more plausible that θ is an increasing function of n. The more firms there are in a cartel, the more likely it may be that one will inform on the cartel. Increasing the number of firms in a cartel also increases the effort necessary to maintain cartel discipline and, therefore, may increase the likelihood that those efforts will attract the attention of enforcement authorities. If θ were assumed to increase significantly as n is increased, the probability of collusion would be a monotonically decreasing function of n for most, perhaps all, parameter values.

pay treble damages, D. The "fine" includes the monetary value of any fixed punishments, including imprisonment. Firms are assumed to be risk neutral, so they form a cartel if the expected net return under collusion exceeds Cournot profits. The decision on whether to form a cartel is made at the beginning of the period; whether the cartel is detected or not is known only at the end of the period. As a result, both collusive profits and the (direct) costs of collusion are unaffected by whether the cartel is detected.[3] Thus, the expected net return to a cartel is

$$V = \pi_m - M - \theta(D + nF)$$

where π_m is monopoly profits.

Assume that the market inverse demand function is

$$P = a - bQ$$

and that firms have no fixed costs and a constant marginal cost, c. Under these assumptions, the Cournot price, quantity, and profits for the entire market are, respectively,

$$P_c = (a + nc)/(n+1)$$

$$Q_c = n(a-c)/(n+1)b$$

$$\pi_c = n(a-c)^2/(n+1)^2 b$$

Substituting $n = 1$ yields the corresponding values for the cartel acting as a monopoly:

$$P_m = (a+c)/2$$

$$Q_m = (a-c)/2b$$

$$\pi_m = (a-c)^2/4b$$

Further, assume that damages are assessed according to the basic rule applied under the US antitrust laws. The cartel must pay three times the difference between the cartel price and the price that otherwise would have prevailed (the Cournot price), times the cartel output.[4] Treble damages, D, then, are

$$\frac{3(a-c)^2}{4b}\,\frac{(n-1)}{(n+1)}$$

To complete the model, assume that the costs of collusion for the cartel, M, are given by

$$\alpha(n-1)^2, \alpha \geqslant 0$$

[3] This fact does not affect the general character of the results produced by the model.

[4] See, for example, ABA Antitrust Section, *Antitrust Law Developments*, pp. 409–410 (2nd ed. 1984); *Burlington Industries, Inc. v. Milliken & Co.*, 690 F.2d 380, 385 (4th Cir. 1982), *cert. denied*, 461 US 914 (1983).

This function has two desirable properties. It equals 0 for n equal 1, so that it costs nothing for a single firm to "collude", and it rises rapidly as n increases, reflecting the widely held belief that the difficulty of forming and maintaining collusive arrangements rises rapidly as the number of firms increases.

It is easily seen in this model that collusion may be unprofitable for very small numbers of firms yet profitable for some larger numbers of firms. Monopoly profits minus Cournot profits are

$$\pi_m (n-1)^2/(n+1)^2$$

where monopoly profits, π_m, is a constant. Therefore, the gains from collusion, exclusive of any possible penalties or costs of collusion, increase rapidly as n increases for small values of n. Expected fines and damages for all firms as a group also increase as n is increased, but for small values of n, both increase more slowly than the gains from collusion. Thus, fines and damages may outweigh the gains from collusion for small numbers of firms but not for larger numbers of firms. Although the costs of collusion increase as n increases more rapidly than any other component of the model, if α is small, then for certain values of θ and F, collusion will not occur if $n = 2$ but will occur for some larger number of firms. The values of θ, F, and α are critical. If they are sufficiently small, there will be collusion for $n = 2$ as well as for larger number of firms, and if they are sufficiently large, there will not be collusion for any number of firms.[5]

The results can be made clearer by considering a special case and a numerical example. First, consider the case of $F = 0$, that is, no public enforcement. Under this assumption it is easy to solve for $\alpha^*(n)$, the value of

TABLE I

Values of n	*Values of* θ					
	0	0.05	0.10	0.15	0.20	0.25
2	0.1111	0.0611	0.0111	< 0	< 0	< 0
3	0.0625	0.0438	0.0250	0.0063	< 0	< 0
4	0.0400	0.0300	0.0200	0.0100	0	< 0
5	0.0278	0.0215	0.0153	0.0090	0.0028	< 0
6	0.0204	0.0161	0.0118	0.0076	0.0033	< 0
7	0.0156	0.0125	0.0094	0.0063	0.0031	0
8	0.0123	0.0100	0.0076	0.0052	0.0028	0.0004
9	0.0100	0.0081	0.0062	0.0044	0.0025	0.0006
10	0.0083	0.0067	0.0052	0.0037	0.0022	0.0007

[5] These results would be of little interest if probabilities of collusion were not monotonic but welfare was. However, it generally is the case in the model that any reasonable measure of welfare (that is, expected surplus or expected output) is nonmonotonic if probabilities of collusion are nonmonotonic.

α above which collusion will not occur, that is, the value of α for which $V = \pi_c$:

$$\alpha^*(n) = \pi_m[(n-1)/(n+1) - 3\theta]/(n^2-1)$$

The properties of this expression are shown in Table I, which gives the values of α^*/π_m for various values of n and θ. For the values of θ greater than 0.05, α^*/π_m is not monotonically decreasing in n. For those values of θ, there are values of α for which collusion does not occur for $n = 2$ but does occur for some larger number of firms.[6] For example, if $\theta = 0.15$ and $0.009 < \alpha/\pi_m < 0.010$, collusion occurs only for $n = 4$.

A numerical example with $F > 0$ also is useful. Assume that $a-c = 100$, $b = 1$, $\theta = 0.1$, and $F = 1000$. If $\alpha > 6.95$, collusion does not occur regardless of the number of firms. If $5.60 \leqslant \alpha \leqslant 6.94$, collusion occurs only if $n = 5$. If $4.00 \leqslant \alpha \leqslant 5.55$, collusion occurs for $n = 4$, 5, or 6. And if $0 \leqslant \alpha \leqslant 0.11$, collusion occurs for $4 \leqslant n \leqslant 11$.

It is extremely difficult to determine the most realistic values of various parameters, particularly α. However, it seems fairly likely that in some real-world markets collusion would be more likely with four firms than with two or three firms, provided that Cournot or some similar conjectural interaction were the alternative to collusion. This is consistent with the empirical finding that cartels generally have more than two or three firms.[7]

GREGORY J. WERDEN AND MICHAEL G. BAUMANN,
Economic Policy Office,
Antitrust Division,
US Department of Justice,
Washington, DC 20530,
USA.

ACCEPTED JUNE 1985

[6] These results can be restated in probabilistic terms if α is assumed to be a random variable. If we arbitrarily assume that α is uniformly distributed on the internal $[0, \pi_m]$, the nonnegative entries in the table are probabilities of collusion.

[7] Hay and Kelley [1974, pp. 20–22] examined 62 criminal price-fixing cases, and found that the mean, median, and modal number of conspirators were, respectively, 7.25, 7, and 6. There were 2 or 3 conspirators in only 12.9 percent of cases. A more comprehensive study of cases charging explicit collusion by Fraas and Greer [1977, p. 34] found a mean, median, and modal number of conspirators of 16.7, 8, and 4. Although these empirical results are consistent with the model, they do not validate it, in particular, because they do not indicate the relative frequencies of collusion in industries with different numbers of firms (or levels of concentration). Numbers of cases may be a poor proxy for the numbers of cartels, and the absolute number of two-firm cartels, for example, is not nearly as interesting as the frequency with which two-firm industries are cartelized.

REFERENCES

FRAAS, ARTHUR G. and GREER, DOUGLAS F., 1977, 'Market Structure and Price Collusion: An Empirical Analysis', *The Journal of Industrial Economics*, 26, 1 (September), pp. 21–44.

HAY, GEORGE A. and KELLEY, DANIEL, 1974, 'An Empirical Survey of Price-Fixing Conspiracies', *Journal of Law and Economics*, 17, 1 (April), pp. 13–38.

SELTEN, REINHARD, 1973, 'A Simple Model of Imperfect Competition, where 4 Are Few and 6 Are Many', *International Journal of Game Theory*, 2, 3, pp. 141–201.

STIGLER, GEORGE, 1964, 'A Theory of Oligopoly', *Journal of Political Economy*, 72, 1 (February), pp. 44–61.

INTRODUCING
PC – GIVE

COPYRIGHT (C) DAVID F. HENDRY

OXFORD INSTITUTE OF ECONOMICS AND STATISTICS

VERSION 3.5 NOVEMBER 1985

COPY FOR A. N. ECONOMIST

A FAST, FRIENDLY AND POWERFUL PROGRAM FOR ECONOMETRIC ANALYSIS OF ECONOMIC TIME SERIES ON THE IBM-PC[1] AND COMPATIBLE MACHINES.

FEATURING

FULLY INTERACTIVE DYNAMIC MODELLING WITH EASY MODEL REVISION
MENU-DRIVEN OPERATION – NO COMPLICATED COMMAND LANGUAGE TO LEARN
IN-BUILT HELP SYSTEM, COLOUR GRAPHICS
EASY TO USE AND DIFFICULT TO CRASH; POWERFUL AND FLEXIBLE
P C – GIVE IS IDEAL FOR TEACHING AND RESEARCH
ALLOWS UP TO 40 VARIABLES IN A DATA SET, 35 VARIABLES PER EQUATION AND 160 OBSERVATIONS
USES THE 8087 MATHS CO-PROCESSOR IF AVAILABLE

OPTIONS

LARGE MENU OF OPTIONS INCLUDES:
DATA TRANSFORMATIONS; CORRELOGRAMS: AUTOREGRESSIONS; DISTRIBUTED LAGS; 'CAUSALITY TESTS'; LINEAR REGRESSION; AUTOREGRESSIVE DISTRIBUTED LAGS; INSTRUMENTAL VARIABLES ESTIMATION

DIAGNOSTICS

HETEROSKEDASTIC CONSISTENT STANDARD ERRORS;
L M TESTS FOR AUTOCORRELATED RESIDUALS AND ARCH;
TESTS FOR HETEROSKEDASTICITY AND FUNCTIONAL FORM MIS-SPECIFICATION
NORMALITY OF THE RESIDUALS
FORECASTS AND PARAMETER CONSTANCY TESTS
OMITTED VARIABLES

LIST PRICE $195
INTRODUCTORY OFFER

TO ACADEMICS WHO WRITE BEFORE THE END OF APRIL OF 1986 FOR A PERSONAL COPY
! ! $95 ! !
SITE LICENCE AVAILABLE, DETAILS ON REQUEST

TO CONTINUE

CONTACT GILLIAN COATES
INSTITUTE OF ECONOMICS AND STATISTICS
ST. CROSS BUILDING, MANOR ROAD,
OXFORD OX1 3UL

[1] (TM) International Business Machines Ltd

BULLETIN OF ECONOMIC RESEARCH

Edited by John D. Hey and Peter J. Lambert

The **Bulletin of Economic Research** is well known as an international forum for stimulating ideas, publishing the results of research into all aspects of economics, both theoretical and applied. In addition, each issue contains a survey paper on some important aspect of economics by a well-known expert. Authors are also encouraged to submit short papers for one week, editor-only refereeing.

Volume 38, 1986 will include the following articles:

New developments in the theory of choice under uncertainty
ROBERT SUGDEN

New theories of the multinational enterprise: an assessment of internalization theory
A.M. RUGMAN

Savings, output, population growth and wages in a world with exhaustible resources
P.J.N. SINCLAIR

Keynes on expectations and uncertainty: rational expectations equilibria with asymmetric information
W. STRASSL

The effects of various treatments of truncation remainders in the estimation of the consumption function: a Bayesian approach
A.R. THURIK and A.J.M. KLEIJWEG

January, May, September
Subscription Rates Volume 38, 1986
Individuals: £14.85 (UK) £18.50 (overseas) US$27.95 (N America)
Institutions: £30.00 (UK) £37.50 (overseas) US$58.65 (N America)

Please send orders with payment to:

Iris Taylor
Journals Department
Basil Blackwell
108 Cowley Road
Oxford OX4 1JF
England

or to: **Journals Department**
Basil Blackwell
PO Box 1320
Murray Hill Station
NY 10156
USA

Payment can be made by cheque or money order made payable to Basil Blackwell Ltd, by credit card (Access, American Express, Barclaycard, Diners Club, Mastercharge, Visa; please state card number and expiry date), or through the National Girobank (account number 236 6053). Sample copies, single and back issues are available; please write for details.

Basil Blackwell · Oxford and New York

Basil Blackwell

Industrial Economics

ROGER CLARKE

This new textbook provides a balanced coverage of this core subject which has seen several important theoretical developments in recent years. Roger Clarke's clear and concise text provides an ideal foundation, being highly readable without sacrificing analytical rigour on empirical context. The book is an ideal main text for intermediate-level undergraduate courses in industrial economics and is sure to be widely adopted.

352 pages, hardback **£18.50** (0 631 12958 8)
paperback **£8.95** (0 631 14305 X)

The Information Technology Revolution

Edited by TOM FORESTER

'This is one of those rare books on information technology and its social implications, that is both informative and fun to read.' *New Scientist*
'Everything you wanted to know about Infotech but were afraid to ask.' *New Society*
'A useful and stimulating survey.' *British Business*
Tom Forester, author of the acclaimed *The Microelectronics Revolution*, skilfully covers the key technological changes in information provision which are occurring with such bewildering rapidity. The book consists of entirely new material appearing in the last four years.

704 pages, hardback **£27.50** (0 631 13433 0)
paperback **£9.95** (0 631 13438 7)

108 Cowley Road, Oxford OX4 1JF

Suite 1505, 432 Park Avenue South, New York NY 10016

Journal of Business Finance & Accounting

Editors: Richard Briston & John Perrin

Summer 1985 Vol.12 No.2

Contents

Opportunity Cost, Discounting, and Deferred Tax Liabilities: A Final Note
M.C. FINDLAY and E.E. WILLIAMS

Debt and Taxes: Empirical Evidence
CLEVELAND S. PATTERSON

The Reporting of Investments in Associated Companies and Credit Evaluations: An Experimental Study
TREVOR WILKINS and IAN ZIMMER

Inter-Industry Differences in the Response of Trade Credit to Changes in Monetary Policy
BRIAN CHIPLIN and MIKE WRIGHT

The Information Content of Inflation-Adjusted Financial Statements
R.E. BRAYSHAW and A.R.O. MIRO

Stock Market Recognition of Multinationality of a Firm and International Events
HO C. YANG, JAMES W. WANSLEY and WILLIAM R. LANE

Some Estimates of the Impact of Corporate Diversification on the Valuation and Leverage of USA Firms: Estimates from 1972 Data
LEONARD ROSENTHAL and TIMOTHY G. SULLIVAN

Effect of Mergers on the Share Price Movement of the Acquiring Firms: A UK Study
J.C. DODDS and J.P. QUEK

Testing the Fisherian Hypothesis: Some Methodological Issues and Further Evidence for the UK
DAVID A. PEEL and PETER F. POPE

Loan Default Risk, Return on Equity and Size Effects and Ownership Control – Empirical Evidence on Savings and Loans Associations in the USA
SAMUEL B. BULMASH

Financial Accountability & Management

Summer 1985 Editor: John Perrin Vol.1 No.1

Contents

Editorial Policy and Viewpoints

Differentiating Financial Accountability and Management in Governments, Public Services and Charities
JOHN R. PERRIN

Objectives and Entitlements to Rights in Government Financial Information
ANDREW LIKIERMAN and PAULINE CREASEY

Non-Profit Performance Indicators in the Public Sector
DAVID J. MAYSTON

A Proposed Framework for Designing Management Control Systems in Not-For-Profit Organizations
KAVASSERI V. RAMANATHAN

Japanese Urban Management Accounting
HIROSHI YOSHIDA

1985 subscription £40 in UK and £50 elsewhere (or US $99 or Can $121.50) to library and business subscribers; £21.25 in UK and £26.75 elsewhere (or US $52.50; Can $65) to individual teachers and students. The new semi-annual supplement, FAM is supplied with JBFA but may be obtained separately at the following prices: £14 in UK and £17.50 elsewhere (or US $26 or Can $31) to library and business subscribers, or £6.50 in UK and £8.15 elsewhere (or US $12.25 or Can $14.95) to individual teachers and students.
Order from Journals Dept., Basil Blackwell, 108 Cowley Road, Oxford, OX4 1JF, UK. Editorial communications to JBFA/CRIBA, University of Warwick, Coventry CV4 7AL, UK. Students and teachers in the UK and members of the E.A.A. and E.F.A. may qualify for a specially reduced subscription price; details may be obtained on request from the editors.

THE JOURNAL OF INDUSTRIAL ECONOMICS

Published first in October 1952, the *Journal* has a very wide international circulation, and has established itself as the leading journal in the field of industrial economics. It was founded to promote the analysis of modern industry, particularly the behaviour of firms, and the functioning of markets. More specifically it seeks to bring the tools of modern economic analysis to bear on the analysis of real problems of industrial economies.

Contributions are welcomed covering all the major areas of industrial economics. One such area is the relationship between market structure and market behaviour in the areas of pricing, product differentiation, advertising and the dissemination of information and R & D. Another area focuses more directly on the firm, its objectives, finance, investment and growth. A third area comprises the background environment within which industrial firms operate: the changing structure of industry, public policy on monopoly and restrictive trade practices, regulation, fiscal and monetary policies as they affect firms, and underlying changes in productivity and international competitiveness.

The *Journal* has a tradition of publishing a blend of theory and evidence. Theoretical discussion is welcomed provided that the more abstract theory includes sufficient introduction and other explanation to convey the significance of the material to the general reader who wants to decide whether to follow the analysis through. Empirical analysis, and especially econometric analysis, should include an explanation of the data sources used, of the methods applied and of the underlying theoretical basis of the study. The *Journal* has a particular tradition of case studies of firms and industries, which the Editors would wish to continue. However contributors of such studies are asked to remember that a study will be of interest to the international readership of the *Journal* only if it makes a particular contribution to the methodology of such studies, or if the empirical results are exceptionally interesting.

Alongside articles of more normal length, the Editors are ready to publish shorter notes, especially where these give interim results of important research studies, or where they report significant new empirical results. Books are not reviewed, although books received will be listed, sometimes with a short note: but substantial review articles will be considered.

Information for Contributors

Submissions (*three* copies are required) should be in typescript, double-spaced, and should conform to the style of the *Journal.* Detailed Information for Contributors is available from the General Editor. The submission should include an Abstract, not exceeding 100 words.

Typescripts from North America should be sent to the North American Editor, Journal of Industrial Economics, Graduate School of Economics and Business Administration, New York University, 100 Trinity Place, New York, NY 10006, USA.

Typescripts from *all* other countries should be sent to the General Editor, Journal of Industrial Economics, Institute of Economics and Statistics, University of Oxford, St Cross Building, Manor Road, Oxford OX1 3UL, UK.

Information for Subscribers

The *Journal* is published four times a year, in September. December, March and June, by Basil Blackwell Ltd., 108 Cowley Road, Oxford OX4 1JF, UK. Prices are as follows:

	UK	Overseas	USA
Institutions	£29.00	£36.50	$65.75
Individuals	£16.25	£20.35	$35.00
Single issue prices for:			
Institutions	£7.20	£8.80	$17.70
Individuals	£5.20	£6.40	$12.00

CONTRIBUTORS TO THIS ISSUE

STANLEY S. REYNOLDS: University of Arizona, Tucson, Arizona, USA.
ASHER WOLINSKY: The Hebrew University of Jerusalem, Jerusalem, Israel.
S. J. PRAIS: National Institute of Economic and Social Research, London, UK.
FRANK A. SCOTT, JR.: University of Kentucky, Lexington, Kentucky, USA.
MARGARET E. SLADE: University of British Columbia, Vancouver, Canada *and* CRIDE, Université Catholique de Louvain, Louvain-la-Neuve, Belgium.
DEVRA L. GOLBE: Rutgers University, New Brunswick, New Jersey, USA.
JOHN LUNN: Louisiana State University, Baton Rouge, Louisiana, USA.
GREGORY J. WERDEN: US Department of Justice, Washington, DC, USA.
MICHAEL G. BAUMANN: US Department of Justice, Washington, DC, USA.

RECEIVED
APR 2 1986
Hartwick College Library

US Mailing: Second class postage paid at New York. Postmaster: Send address corrections to: Journal of Industrial Economics, c/o Expediters of the Printed Word Ltd., 515 Madison Avenue, New York, NY 10022 (US Mailing Agent).

Photocopying: Permission is granted by the publisher for those institutions registered with the Copyright Clearance Center to authorize internal photocopying of any article in this journal for a fee of $2.00 per copy per article. Payment should be made direct to the Copyright Clearance Center, 21 Congress Street, Salem, Massachusetts 10970, USA. Individuals, or institutions not registered with the CCC, must obtain permission to photocopy either from the CCC or from Basil Blackwell Ltd., when the same fees will apply.

Reprints of Back Volumes: Volumes 1–28 of the *Journal* are available (in complete volumes only) from the Kraus Reprint Corporation, Route 100, Millwood, New York 10546, USA. More recent back issues are available from the publisher at the current single issue price.

Microfilm: An agreement for the supply of microfilm copies from Volume 1 onwards has been made with University Microfilms International, Department PR, 30–32 Mortimer Street, London W1N 7RA, England, or 300 North Zeeb Road, Ann Arbor, Michigan 48106, USA.

Advertising: For details contact the Advertisement Manager, Bill Drake. Telephone (0869) 38477, or write c/o the publisher.

Set in Monophoto Times by Advanced Filmsetters (Glasgow) Ltd
Printed and Bound in Great Britain by Whitstable Litho, Kent

THE JOURNAL OF INDUSTRIAL ECONOMICS

Volume XXXIV JUNE 1986 No. 4

DAVID R. ROSS
Learning to Dominate 337

R. W. SHAW and P. SIMPSON
The Persistence of Monopoly: An Investigation of the Effectiveness of the United Kingdom Monopolies Commission 355

JOHN R. BALDWIN and PAUL K. GORECKI
The Relationship Between Plant Scale and Product Diversity in Canadian Manufacturing Industries 373

DIRK J. FRANTZEN
The Cyclical Behaviour of Manufacturing Prices in a Small Open Economy 389

S. R. TOLOFARI, K. J. BUTTON and D. E. PITFIELD
Shipping Costs and the Controversy Over Open Registry 409

TEIN-CHEN CHOU
Concentration, Profitability and Trade in a Simultaneous Equation Analysis: The Case of Taiwan 429

ISSN 0022-1821
BASIL BLACKWELL OXFORD ENGLAND

© **Basil Blackwell 1986**

The material in this Journal is copyright under the Berne Convention. Apart from any fair dealing for the purposes of private study, research, criticism or review, as permitted under the Copyright Act 1965, no portion may be reproduced by any process without written permission. Inquiry should be made to the Publishers.

DONALD A. HAY (General Editor): Jesus College, University of Oxford.
STEVE W. DAVIES: University of East Anglia.
BRUCE LYONS: University of East Anglia.
LOUIS PHLIPS: Université Catholique de Louvain.
AUBREY SILBERSTON: Imperial College of Science and Technology, University of London.
GEORGE YARROW: Hertford College, University of Oxford.
LAWRENCE J. WHITE (North American Editor): New York University.
M. A. ADELMAN: Massachusetts Institute of Technology.
RICHARD E. CAVES: Harvard University.
F. MICHAEL SCHERER: Swarthmore College.
RICHARD SCHMALENSEE: Sloan School of Management, Massachusetts Institute of Technology.

Editorial Assistant: Marion Bowker.

ASSOCIATE EDITORS
BO CARLSSON: Case Western Reserve University, Cleveland.
ROGER CLARKE: University of Sheffield.
ALEXIS JACQUEMIN: Université Catholique de Louvain.
FRÉDÉRIC JENNY, E.S.S.E.C., Cergy.
H. W. DE JONG: University of Amsterdam.
JOHN KAY: Institute for Fiscal Studies, London.
COLIN P. MAYER: St Anne's College, University of Oxford.
GEOFF MEEKS: Department of Applied Economics, University of Cambridge.
DEREK MORRIS: Oriel College, University of Oxford.
WILLIAM PETERSON: Department of Applied Economics, University of Cambridge.
JOHN F. PICKERING: The University of Manchester Institute of Science and Technology.
RAY REES: University College, Cardiff.
DAVID K. STOUT: Unilever PLC.
ROGER TARLING: Department of Applied Economics, University of Cambridge.
JOHN VICKERS: Nuffield College, University of Oxford.
CHRISTIAN C. VON WEIZSÄCKER: University of Berne.
GEOFFREY WHITTINGTON: University of Bristol.

RONALD R. BRAEUTIGAM: Northwestern University.
TIMOTHY F. BRESNAHAN: Stanford University.
WILLIAM S. COMANOR: University of California.
M. THÉRÈSE FLAHERTY: Harvard University.
THEODORE KEELER: University of California, Berkeley.
R. LARNER: Charles River Associates.
ALMARIN PHILLIPS: University of Pennsylvania.
STEVEN SALOP: Georgetown Law Center, Washington, DC.
JOHN T. SCOTT: Dartmouth College.
ROBERT D. WILLIG: Princeton University.

DONALD G. MCFETRIDGE: Carleton University, Ottawa.

PETER FORSYTH: Australian National University, Canberra.
BRIAN L. JOHNS: Bureau of Industry Economics, Canberra.
L. ROY WEBB: University of Melbourne.

MASU UEKUSA: University of Tokyo.

THE JOURNAL OF INDUSTRIAL ECONOMICS 0022–1821 $2.00
Volume XXXIV June 1986 No. 4

LEARNING TO DOMINATE*

David R. Ross

The learning curve traces the fall in unit costs resulting from experience with a complex or novel production technology. This paper demonstrates that a firm can exploit a minor lead down the learning curve into a dominant market position. The result contrasts with previous work indicating that market equilibria along the learning curve will yield moderate concentration and an 'acceptable' balance between static and dynamic efficiency. The tendency toward market domination is reduced to the extent that learning is not firm specific.

Recent years have brought a healthy cross-pollination between the corporate strategy and industrial organization literatures (Kreps and Spence [1983]; Fudenberg and Tirole [1983b]). The oligopoly problem has increasingly been viewed as a dynamic one, in which rivals strive today to create strategic advantages for the future. Investments in capacity, product differentiation, research and development, and learning-by-doing have each been modelled as weapons in this rivalry. A frequent conclusion of models which incorporate the first three variables is that firms which aggressively exploit first-mover advantages are likely to dominate their markets over a wide range of conditions. This paper extends that result to rivalry along the learning curve and touches on the implications for public policies *vis-à-vis* predatory and dumping behavior.

When a firm introduces a sufficiently novel product or technology, it will not be operating on the average cost curve which describes the efficient utilization of the physical plant. Efficiencies are realized through experience in production (learning-by-doing). The adjustment process through which unit costs gradually approach the minimum attainable is traced by the learning curve. In practice, cumulative production most commonly represents experience. (Ross [1984c] discusses the foundations of the learning curve and its role in characterizing costs.)

Starting in the late 1960s, corporate planners and management consultants began to recognize the strategic implications of the learning curve (see Ross [1984c] for references). The key feature of strategic planning models which incorporate the learning curve is the characteristic that tomorrow's costs

* This paper is drawn from a longer exposition of the same issues (Ross [1984a]) and has benefited from comments by Ralph Bradburd, Ronald R. Braeutigam, Steven R. Lewis, Joel Mokyr, Marc Nerlove, Bruce Petersen, F. M. Scherer, Padmanabhan Srinagesh, Gordon Winston, two referees and the editor of this *Journal*. Conversations with William P. Hall, Richard R. Nelson, Almarin Phillips, and Stan Reynolds helped enormously in clarifying my approach to learning curves.

depend on today's production and, therefore, that a lead down the learning curve gives the leader a cost advantage.

> The strategic implication is that a company should strive to dominate the market, either by introducing the product, by segmenting the market, or by discouraging competitors' growth in rapidly growing areas by preemptive pricing or value (Abernathy [1978, p. 13]).

Reacting to this literature, a growing number of economists have begun to explore the impact of the learning curve on market equilibria. The standard monopoly result (Steedman [1969], Jacquemin and Thisse [1972], Rosen [1972], Dolan and Jeuland [1981], Spence [1981], Ghemawat [1982], Clarke and Darrough [1982], Fudenberg and Tirole [1983a], Smiley and Ravid [1983], and Ross [1984b]) is that profit maximization requires investing in experience by setting marginal revenue below current marginal cost. Standard treatments of the oligopoly problem (Duchatelet [1977], Spence [1981], Ghemawat [1982], Hall [1982] and [1983], Fudenberg and Tirole [1983a], Ghemawat and Spence [1983], and Teng and Thompson [1983]) conclude that learning economies suffice to limit the number of firms that can be supported in equilibrium.[1] However, under the assumption of symmetric firms and/or passive Cournot conjectures, this limitation, in the absence of collusion, results in moderate levels of concentration yielding a balance between static efficiency (price approximating marginal cost) and dynamic efficiency (the reduction of unit costs as quickly as possible).

This paper examines conditions under which a slight lead down the learning curve allows a firm to dominate the market and, hence, significantly impair static efficiency. Section I describes a multiperiod oligopoly model (more fully developed in an appendix) which incorporates learning-by-doing. Section II describes equilibria of the game developed in Section I, in which a single firm gains a dominant market share. Section III considers the impact of relaxing the assumption that learning is firm specific. The paper concludes with a brief discussion of implications and extensions.

I. A MULTIPERIOD OLIGOPOLY MODEL

When a firm finds itself in a dynamic strategic environment,[2] the firm's profit maximization problem is transformed into a dynamic program. Characterizing the solution to this program becomes quite complex when the firm faces

[1] Among alternative approaches, Smiley [1982] superimposes a learning curve on an essentially stochastic model of the evolution of an oligopoly in the spirit of Mansfield [1962]. Gilbert and Harris [1981] and Ghemawat [1984] formulate games in which learning takes the form of lowering the construction cost of successive plants. There are several models of the evolution of an oligopoly, including Flaherty [1980] and Nelson and Winter [1978], which readily could be given a learning-by-doing interpretation.

[2] Dynamic in the sense that time matters, strategic in the sense that the firm can exploit the intertemporal linkage.

competitors or potential entrants. Managers must choose, as a strategy, a rule of behavior by which production in every period is a function of the market environment, the decisions of competitors, and future opportunities. A strategy solves the dynamic program if it is part of the Nash equilibrium of the oligopoly game in which all competitors seek strategies for similar dynamic programs. Although the strategies cover a number of periods, the problem at hand is really a one-shot game. Assuming no unforeseen shocks perturb the industry, no firm will have an incentive to alter the results of this initial game in which life-of-the-industry strategies are worked out.

To generate meaningful comparative statics and measure the magnitude of effects in this type of model, one must turn to particular functional forms and specific parameter values (Spence [1981], Ghemawat [1982], Hall [1982] and [1983], Ghemawat and Spence [1983]).[3] The choice here is linear demand and the linear-plateau representation of the learning curve.[4] An appendix presents a detailed exposition of the model.

Under the assumption that learning is firm specific, costs are characterized by three parameters: θ_0, unit costs in the absence of learning; c, the slope of the learning curve, that is, the reduction in unit costs associated with a unit increase in the firm's cumulative production; and θ_1, the minimum attainable unit cost. Without loss of generality, $\theta_0 = 1$. The first best welfare maximizing solution has a single firm setting price equal to θ_1 in each period (and, hence, requires a subsidy) (Spence [1981]). Therefore, one can completely determine the two demand parameters by specifying, ε_D, the elasticity of demand when price equals θ_1, normalizing to ensure that first-best output equals 100 units. The planning horizon is 10 periods for all the results presented. A complete solution to the model requires a statement of the parameters θ_1, c, and ε_D; the behavioral assumptions; and the pattern of entry.

Under the Cournot behavioral assumption, this multiperiod model yields results which are consistent with the earlier models referenced above.[5] In a symmetric equilibrium, the learning curve, independent of static scale effects, limits entry. Concentration rises with the elasticity of demand and the depths of learning economies (θ_1).[6] When first period entry is free, concentration

[3] The most successful effort to model the performance of an oligopoly along the learning curve without restricting the functional form of learning is Duchatelet [1977]. The only propositions which emerge at that level of abstraction are that asymmetries in discount rates, the rate of learning, or initial costs will lead to asymmetric output trajectories.

[4] The functional form most commonly used to represent learning in the recent crop of oligopoly models (the log–log formulation) has the logarithm of unit cost as a linear function of the log of cumulative production. This is not the place for an exhaustive discussion of representations of the learning curve (see Ross [1984c]). It suffices to note here that the engineering literature provides less than compelling support for use of the log–log formulation at the firm level. For many, if not most, products, learning economies are exhausted within the product life-cycle. The linear-plateau is the simplest formulation having this property.

[5] These results are presented in Ross [1985].

[6] While, for a fixed number of firms, more elastic demand drives an oligopoly toward the competitive ideal, along the learning curve, a flatter demand curve reduces the number of firms that can earn positive net profits.

rises with the slope of the learning curve. Where entry is sequential and learning economies are eventually exhausted (two conditions likely to hold in practice), entry is limited for moderate and extremely high rates of learning. Very shallow learning curves give first-in firms little cost advantage over entrants; and entrants can quickly overcome the innovator's cost advantage if the learning curve is steep. The innovator's cost advantage is most likely to be preserved for intermediate slopes. Along extremely steep learning curves, pressure to get down the learning curve as quickly as possible limits profits available to entrants—the driving force when first period entry is free. Changing the discount rate has little effect on equilibrium beyond altering the pricing trajectory.

The resulting market structures, assuming free entry, yield a satisfactory[7] mix of performance and concentration except in cases where the depth of learning economies is great or demand quite elastic. Generally, more firms are supported in equilibrium than is socially optimal,[8] but the welfare loss is low—especially relative to the costs of implementing a policy to restrict entry.

II. THE DOMINANT FIRM SOLUTION

Symmetric firms and the Cournot behavioral assumption are unlikely to describe conditions where learning is most relevant. Learning curves appear when a new product is introduced or a firm introduces a new manufacturing process for an existing product. New markets usually are characterized by staggered entry and, even in an established industry, the timing by which firms switch from an outmoded technology to a superior learning curve technology will vary, reflecting such institutional differences as the quality of internal research and development, access to patents and capital markets, lags in converting old plants or planning and building new ones, and the aggressiveness and foresight of senior management. Thus, most learning curve environments will have firms operating at different points along the learning curve.

This generally gives the firm with the greatest market share a strategic advantage. A substantial managerial literature has developed urging firms to exploit aggressively such advantages and warning firms that are slower in traveling down the learning curve that they will have to adjust to a secondary role.[9] 'Competition is inherently a struggle for dominance', writes Robert B. Schapiro, Vice President and General Counsel for G. D. Searle & Co. (Conference Board [1980, p. 13]). Learning curve competitors are quickly divided into winners and losers. In explaining the arguments of proponents of the experience curve in the *Wall Street Journal*,[10] Porter writes

[7] The static efficiency gain from an additional firm tends to offset the dynamic loss from each firm's slower progress down the learning curve.

[8] If learning is completely firm specific, the more firms, the less industry learning.

[9] For textbook treatments, see Abell and Hammond [1979] and Porter [1980].

[10] 'Manager's Journal.' Oct. 22, 1979.

> If a company cannot achieve a leading market share, the experience curve implies it will be inherently less profitable than its competitors. In the extreme, it should probably think seriously about leaving the market.

In light of the likelihood of asymmetric entry and the generally aggressive prescriptions for firm behavior in the managerial press, it is curious that most economic models of oligopoly along the learning curve assume symmetric firms making passive Cournot conjectures concerning their competitors' reactions.[11] In this section, the basic multiperiod model developed above is expanded to allow leading firms to exploit strategic advantages.

Once a firm gains a lead down the learning curve (and assuming there is no prospect of follower firms introducing a superior technology), that firm has the ability to inflict losses on followers while earning positive profits. Of course, such a strategy would generally not be optimal for the leader: It could earn higher profits by allowing prices to rise even at the loss of some market share. On the other hand, the leader's asymmetric power of annihilation should yield it a more favorable market outcome. Exactly what sort of equilibrium is likely to emerge from such asymmetric power relationships is unclear.[12] I turn to the classic model of aggressive behavior, the von Stackelberg leader–follower model, in which follower firms exhibit Cournot behavior while leader firms incorporate the Cournot reaction functions of follower firms into their objective functions.

The evolution of an industry in a learning curve environment depends fundamentally on the timing and magnitude of entry. At least three types of entry are relevant. However, the focus here is on a firm's introducing a new product which attracts imitative entry once a market has been defined.[13]

[11] Exceptions to this formulation have been limited: Ghemawat [1982, pp. 68–69] shows that fewer firms can be supported in an asymmetric Cournot–Nash equilibrium than under symmetry. Spence [1981] presents a model incorporating sequential entry, which yields a range of market shares, but leaves open the question of whether it would be in the interest of early entrants to behave more aggressively.

An example in which more aggressive behavior does prevail and in which market performance appears to suffer thereby is contained in one of two models presented by Gilbert and Harris [1981]. In this game, firms compete for the right to build a new plant in the next time period, with construction costs a function of the number of plants already built by each firm. The firm with the lowest initial cost of constructing a new plant can always preempt expansion by all other firms and moves inexorably toward becoming a monopolist. The Gilbert and Harris results are not easily compared with the results of other learning curve models, since the focus is on plant construction rather than on subsequent sales rivalry.

[12] This conceptual difficulty is not limited to a learning curve environment. One approach has been to use asymmetric conjectural variations (for example, Bresnahan [1981]) to describe power relationships. Hall [1982, pp. 69–73] uses this approach in a duopoly learning curve model. To date, no one has offered a plausible interpretation or calibration of conjectural variations between the Cournot and joint profit maximizing level.

[13] The second type of entry describes the diffusion of a learning curve technology through an established industry. (The concluding section below reports some preliminary results on market evolution in this context.) A third type, the possibility of a firm introducing a technology which dominates the existing learning curve technology, will be the subject of future research.

TABLE I
COURNOT SOLUTIONS WITH DELAYED ENTRY AS A FUNCTION OF THE NUMBER OF ENTRANTS

	Number of Second Period Entrants				
	0	*1*	*2*	*3*	*4*
Consumer Surplus	37.3	55.4	67.8	73.8	77.6
Performance	77.8	86.9	87.8	87.0	86.0
Herfindahl	10000.0	5000.0	3343.3	2541.3	2043.8
Period Curve Flattens					
Leader	6	8	9	10	(0.721)
Each Entrant	—	10	(0.766)	(0.825)	(0.857)
Market Share					
Leader	100.0	50.0	35.9	30.6	25.9
Each Entrant	—	50.0	32.0	23.2	18.5
Profits					
Leader	55.4	26.0	15.8	12.8	10.7
Each Entrant	—	18.6	8.2	4.5	2.9

$\varepsilon_D = 0.3, C = 0.0012, \theta_1 = 0.7.$

In the first period, a single firm introduces a product and behaves as a monopolist, ignoring the probability of subsequent entry.[14]

Table I presents solutions to the model as a function of the number of second period entrants for the parameters specified.[15] An equilibrium is defined to be the solution involving the largest number of profitable entrants.[16] Performance represents total surplus of the equilibrium as a percent of first best total surplus.[17] Consumer Surplus reports consumer surplus as a percent of total surplus. Profits present the sum of each firm's losses and profits as a percent of total surplus.[18] If the learning curve does not flatten by period 10, the unit cost attained in period 10 is reported in parentheses. The Herfindahl Index[19] and Market Shares are for period 10. Despite the asymmetry, market structure and performance do not differ

[14] If the monopolist incorporated the probability of entry into its objective function, it would expand first period output to enhance its cost advantage over entrants.

[15] Changing the parameter values does not alter the results qualitatively. Quantitatively, the results are altered as in the symmetric equilibrium described in section I.

[16] Under the conditions of Table I, the six firm solution leaves the five entrants with losses.

[17] The assumption is that the industry being modeled is an intermediate manufacturing industry and that downstream industries either are perfectly competitive or view the production of the modeled industry as an insignificant element in downstream costs.

[18] Each of these measures is provided for relative comparison across cases. The actual quantities have no independent significance.

[19] The Herfindahl Index is the sum of the square of each firm's market share. The Department of Justice has adopted the index as its primary indicator of market concentration (particularly in merger cases). By way of comparison, the index for a perfectly competitive industry would be 0; that for a monopoly 10000; and that for an industry consisting of five identical firms would be 2000.

TABLE II
VON STACKELBERG SOLUTIONS WITH DELAYED ENTRY AS A FUNCTION OF THE NUMBER OF ENTRANTS

	Number of Second Period Entrants			
	0	*1*	*2*	*3*
Consumer Surplus	37.3	69.3	82.2	85.8
Performance	77.8	92.2	94.9	93.3
Herfindahl	10000.0	5772.4	5883.7	6030.2
Period Curve Flattens				
Leader	6	5	5	5
Each Follower	—	(0.777)	(0.888)	(0.921)
Market Share				
Leader	100.0	69.6	74.5	76.4
Each Follower	—	30.3	12.7	7.9
Profits				
Leader	55.4	24.6	17.0	14.2
Each Follower	—	6.2	0.4	0.0

$\varepsilon_D = 0.3, C = 0.0012, \theta_1 = 0.7.$

substantially from the situation in which all firms enter in the first period (Ross [1985]).

However, as Table II demonstrates, when industry members recognize the leader's advantage, the leader will tend to dominate the market. Note that the von Stackelberg solution supports one less entrant in equilibrium. As the number of entrants rises, each firm learns less and, hence, the leader's cost advantage and incentive to grab market share rises. Thus, the leader might well encourage subsequent entry (for example, through liberal licensing contracts, especially if such contracts contain cross-licensing provisions should the entrant improve on the technology).[20]

It is important to stress that market dominance does not follow from asymmetries alone. The leader's strategic advantage must be recognized as governing industry power relationships. Table III illustrates the effect on market equilibria of further delaying entry and, hence, increasing the leader's strategic advantage. Under the Cournot behavioral assumption, delaying entry raises the leader's profits but does not substantially alter market structure or performance. The dramatic results of Table II are a function of the von Stackelberg behavioral assumption.

[20] In results not reproduced here, the market share of the leader at the foot of its learning curve rises as the learning curve steepens. For a sufficiently steep learning curve or a sufficiently far time horizon, the leader's market share will start to fall as entrants begin to narrow their cost disadvantage, eventually reaching the foot of the learning curve. Presumably, eventually the von Stackelberg behavioral assumption would cease to be tenable. Of course, from a policy perspective, the danger is that the leader will use the short-run market power conferred by the learning curve to preserve its market position once learning economies have been exhausted.

TABLE III
COURNOT EQUILIBRIA WITH DELAYED ENTRY BY THREE FIRMS AS A FUNCTION OF THE TIME OF ENTRY

	Period of Entry			
	2	*3*	*4*	*5*
Elasticity	0.69	0.71	0.72	0.74
Consumer Surplus	73.8	69.0	64.7	60.2
Performance	87.0	85.6	84.3	83.3
Herfindahl	2541.3	2555.7	2572.8	2599.1
Period Curve Flattens				
Leader	10	9	7	6
Each Follower	(0.825)	(0.853)	(0.874)	(0.898)
Market Share				
Leader	30.6	31.5	32.4	33.6
Each Follower	23.2	22.8	22.5	22.1
Profits				
Leader	12.8	18.7	23.8	29.6
Each Follower	4.5	4.1	3.8	3.4

$\varepsilon_D = 0.3$, $C = 0.0012$, $\theta_1 = 0.7$.

A feature of single period oligopoly models involving linear demand and constant marginal cost is the fact that total surplus is higher under von Stackelberg behavior than under Cournot behavior (industry output is higher). This result carries over to equilibria along the learning curve. Performance in Table II is uniformly better than in Table I. However, aggressive firm behavior introduces a performance–market structure trade-off which was generally absent from simulations of Cournot behavior. In the

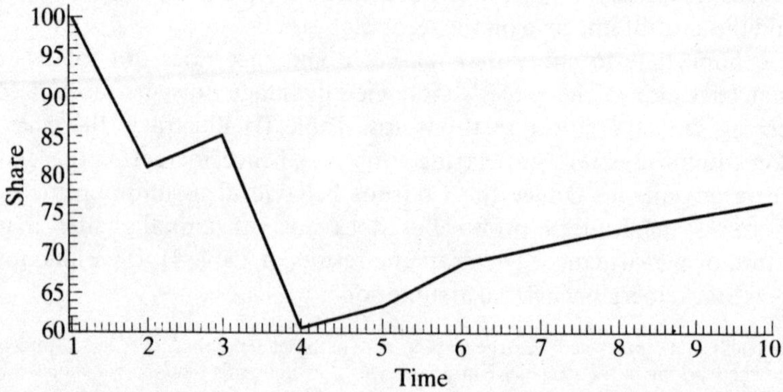

Figure 1
Market Share of Leader. Delayed Entry von Stackelberg Equilibrium
Note: First best elasticity = 0.3, attainable cost = 0.7, slope of learning curve = 0.0012, 3 entrants.

absence of learning, the von Stackelberg game (with linear demand and constant marginal cost) awards the leader a market share which falls from two-thirds to 50 percent as the number of followers rises. When learning economies are present, the leader's last period market share *rises* as the number of entrants increases. Figure 1 traces the market share of the leader over the 10 periods in the von Stackelberg equilibrium with three entrants. Market share is high following entry as the leader seeks to get down the learning curve quickly. Once the foot of the learning curve is reached (that is, $y \geqslant y_1$—the point at which learning economies are exhausted),[20] the market share of the leader falls, and then rises slowly, reflecting the disappearance of the deviation of entrants' production from the short-run profit maximizing level as the time horizon approaches.

III. APPROPRIABILITY

To this point, learning has been viewed as firm specific, that is, as perfectly appropriable: The innovator aggressively moves down the learning curve confident that no competitor could meet its costs except by accumulating a similar volume of production. This section explores the implications of relaxing this strong assumption.

In most oligopolistic industries, rivals know quite a bit about one another and devote resources to expand that knowledge. Although firms are generally secretive about new technologies, there are a number of ways for firms to gain information about an innovator's learning curve technology (Mansfield [1968]; Scherer *et al.* [1975]; Scherer [1980, chs. 15 and 16]). Patents, while giving the innovator certain property rights to a particular innovation, give rivals a description of the innovation, possibly suggesting ways of innovating around the patent. Trade journals and trade associations often offer glimpses of a firm's production process. Inspections of a rival's plant are 'remarkably commonplace' (F. M. Scherer in Conference Board [1981, p. 23]). Common suppliers may unwittingly offer key insights into a rival's new process. A firm can deduce something of the rival's approach from the product itself, for example, through backward engineering or chemical analysis. Perhaps most importantly, migrating workers carry information across employers, despite trade secrets clauses in the contracts of key personnel.

Modelling appropriability in the context of the linear-plateau formulation requires an additional parameter, γ. Complete appropriability [equation (4)] follows from setting $\gamma = 0$, while $\gamma = 1$ reflects learning as a public good. Obviously, for $\gamma = 1$, firms behave myopically in each period, since any progress down the learning curve is transmitted to all. Intermediate values of γ lead to more interesting results.

Tables IV–VI present the effect on the results of section II of making learning progressively less appropriable. Table IV shows the effect on concentration during the period in which the innovator reaches the bottom

TABLE IV
HERFINDAHL INDEX WHEN INNOVATOR REACHES BOTTOM OF LEARNING CURVE. VON STACKELBERG EQUILIBRIA AS A FUNCTION OF APPROPRIABILITY AND RATE OF LEARNING

Slope of Learning Curve	Appropriability Parameter 0.000	0.125	0.250	0.375	0.500
0.0004	6540.8	5381.2	4903.1	4654.4	4539.4
0.0008	5164.5	5388.5	4106.4	3710.3	2709.9
0.0012	4648.6	4796.8	2947.3	2714.6	2632.0
0.0016	3623.0	3000.4	2619.5	2582.6	2560.5

$\varepsilon_D = 0.3, \theta_1 = 0.7.$

of its learning curve; Table V presents the effect on profits; and Table VI shows the effect on market performance (equilibrium total surplus as a percentage of first best). As learning becomes less firm specific, the innovator's advantage decreases and imitators reach the foot of the learning curve shortly after the innovator. In such cases, the von Stackelberg behavioral assumption is tenable only if one postulates that the innovator has been able to devise some way of preserving its market power once all learning economies have been exhausted. An alternative assumption would have the industry moving to symmetric Cournot behavior once cost differences have been eliminated. These alternatives appear as Path A (the von Stackelberg equilibrium) and Path B (an equilibrium based on von Stackelberg behavior

TABLE V
PROFITS.
VON STACKELBERG EQUILIBRIA AS A FUNCTION OF APPROPRIABILITY AND RATE OF LEARNING

Slope of Learning Curve	Appropriability Parameter 0.000	0.125	0.250	0.375	0.500
0.0004	0.31	0.71	0.66	1.33	1.62
0.0008					
Path A	1.26	1.39	1.89	1.03	1.43
Path B	—	—	—	2.23	3.53
0.0012					
Path A	1.41	0.29	0.90	1.81	2.70
Path B	—	—	—	4.13	5.61
0.0016					
Path A	7.98	0.86	0.90	1.99	3.16
Path B	—	3.21	3.85	5.55	6.70

$\varepsilon_D = 0.3, \theta_1 = 0.7.$

TABLE VI
PERFORMANCE.
VON STACKELBERG EQUILIBRIA AS A FUNCTION OF APPROPRIABILITY AND RATE OF LEARNING

Slope of Learning Curve	*Do Not Adopt*	*Appropriability Parameter* 0.000	0.125	0.250	0.375	0.500
0.0004	89.0	88.0	86.3	86.8	87.7	89.0
0.0008						
Path A	93.2	92.2	91.9	93.3	94.7	95.5
Path B	—	—	—	—	94.3	94.4
0.0012						
Path A	94.4	94.8	93.3	96.7	97.6	98.3
Path B	—	—	—	95.5	96.5	97.0
0.0016						
Path A	91.6	95.9	97.0	98.3	99.1	99.5
Path B	—	—	96.2	97.0	97.5	98.05

$\varepsilon_D = 0.3, \theta_1 = 0.7$.

until the innovator's cost advantage is eliminated, at which point Cournot behavior is assumed), respectively, in Tables V and VI.[21] As learning becomes more readily diffused, the number of firms supported in equilibrium characteristically rises.[22] Of course, in the extreme case, $\gamma = 1$, an infinite number of firms is supported in the multiperiod model presented here.

The innovator's ability to exploit its first-in advantage is dramatically reduced. Thus, enhancing the diffusion of learning characteristically reduces market concentration (Table IV). Not only does diffusion support more firms

[21] In a discrete time model, the foot of the learning curve will rarely be reached at the start or end of a period. The iterative algorithm used to solve the dynamic program generally yields solutions in which cumulative production in the first period in which no learning takes place is greater than y_1. Experimentation suggests that distortions emerging from the discontinuities of the discrete time model are not serious.

[22] The table below presents the number of firms corresponding to the cells of Tables IV–VI. Curiously *fewer* firms are supported for intermediate levels of appropriability involving the shallowest learning curve. The lower production of the innovator is more than offset by the increase in production by followers. As the appropriability parameter continues to rise (and assuming Cournot behavior, since the innovator's advantage decreases steadily), the number of firms supported in equilibrium eventually begins to rise, even in this first case.

Slope of Learning Curve	*Appropriability Parameter* 0.000	0.125	0.250	0.375	0.500
0.0004	5	5	5	4	4
0.0008	3	3	3	4	4
0.0012	3	4	4	4	4
0.0016	2	4	4	4	4

in equilibrium, but size differences are decreased. However, the improvement in market concentration which accompanies reducing the appropriability does not come at the price of seriously impaired performance (Table VI).[23] While the innovator learns less, imitators experience lower costs in each period. Viewed as a whole, industry output deviates less from the short-run profit maximizing level in early periods, but imitators exert much stronger downward pressure on price in later periods.

IV. SUMMARY, IMPLICATIONS AND EXTENSIONS

To date, most models of industry evolution along the learning curve have assumed symmetric firms holding the Cournot behavioral assumption. However, the conditions under which learning curves are most likely to be relevant—the introduction of a new product or technology—will frequently involve staggered entry, where first-in firms gain a distinct advantage. Such innovators can use their cost advantage to prevent entry, although it would rarely be in their interest to do so. Thus, it seems less reasonable for the innovator to assume that it cannot substantially influence the market equilibrium—especially in light of the extensive managerial literature urging aggressive firm behavior down the learning curve.

Section II postulates a new product introduction, where the firm which develops the product faces competition after the first period. The asymmetric Cournot equilibrium is compared with the von Stackelberg equilibrium, the classic formulation of aggressive firm behavior. When industry members recognize the leader's advantage, the leader will tend to dominate the market along the learning curve. The number of firms supported in a von Stackelberg equilibrium is less, and the market shares are skewed. Thus, aggressive exploitation of strategic advantages along the learning curve generates a performance-concentration tradeoff. The tradeoff becomes more serious to the extent that the leader can use the market power conferred by the learning curve to preserve its dominant position once learning economies have been exhausted.

Antitrust standards on predatory conduct and trade prohibitions against dumping become harder to interpret when the facts of a particular case are consistent with the presence of a learning curve. Plausible market conditions may result in a firm's turning a minor lead down the learning curve into a dominant market position by pricing not only below its competitors' costs but even, in early periods, below its own marginal costs. Yet, the goal is neither explicitly to drive competitors out of business nor to lower costs in one market through price discrimination in another. Much further work is

[23] Results not presented here suggest that the appropriability parameter must be quite close to 1.00 before performance is significantly depressed. This finding is consistent with the similar pattern found by Spence [1981] and Hall [1982] and [1983] for games assuming Cournot behavior.

needed to distinguish desirable exploitation of learning economies from anti-competitive behavior.[24]

Of course, it does not necessarily follow that the first-in firm will dominate the industry. Asymmetries in discount rates or access to capital markets or errors by established firms (for example, in predicting market demand) may offer entrants room for successful fast-second strategies. One can imagine situations in which no firm gains a compelling strategic advantage or where an entrant eventually dominates the industry (Ross [1985]).

The strategic advantage of an innovator will be enhanced if established rivals fail to adopt the new technology (the second type of entry mentioned in section II). Since it is not necessarily in a dominant firm's interest to eliminate high cost competitors; it is not clear that adopting the new technology is optimal for follower firms—particularly if imitation involves substantial R & D and construction outlays.[25]

Imitation becomes more attractive to the extent that the experience of innovators is readily diffused to competitors (section III). Decreasing the appropriability of learning dramatically improves market structure: More firms are supported in equilibrium, and the ability of and incentives for the leader to dominate the market are reduced. However, performance is not seriously compromised for low and moderate levels of diffusion: Innovators learn less, but imitators learn more; higher early period prices are offset by lower prices toward the foot of the learning curve.

The model presented here suggests that relatively low rates of diffusion will substantially lower concentration without seriously impairing market performance. Policies which encourage the flow of learning-by-doing across firms (for example, encouraging technical trade associations and journals, restricting the coverage of trade secrets clauses in contracts, discouraging frivolous patent infringement suits, or permitting limited joint ventures) may improve market structure at a relatively low expenditure of government resources. However, decreasing appropriability may decrease incentives for innovation.[26] Further, veteran antitrust attorneys may find it hard to believe that the exchange of technical information will not become a cover for collusive agreements. In any event, the overlap between antitrust and intellectual property (patents) policies becomes especially relevant here. Work in progress focuses on the interaction between the learning curve and investment in research and development.

Ross [1984a] provides evidence that the results of sections II and III are not inconsistent with behavior and performance in a number of industries.

[24] Other areas of antitrust policy where the learning curve may require a reevaluation of established doctrine include efficiency justifications for mergers, divestiture decrees, assessing potential competition and supply substitutability.

[25] See Ross [1985] for an extension of the basic model to this environment.

[26] Perhaps one could link the freer exchange of learning-by-doing information to a licensing royalty paid by follower firms to the innovator.

However, there are a number of situations where the model would require major modifications. These include learning with a durable good, where inventory costs and second-hand or recycling markets are important considerations; the interaction of promotional spending and learning effects (Dolan and Jeuland [1981]; Remer *et al.* [1981]; Spence [1981]; Teng and Thompson [1983]; Yelle [1983]); and learning where products are sold according to fixed price contracts, such as aircraft[27] and government procurement of heavy-duty equipment.

DAVID R. ROSS,
Department of Economics,
Williams College,
Williamstown, Massachusetts 01267,
USA.

ACCEPTED NOVEMBER 1985

APPENDIX

SOLUTION TO THE MULTIPERIOD GAME

Modeling the game in discrete time, excluding static economies of scale, but taking account of the learning curve, define profits of firm i in period t to be

$$\text{(1)} \qquad \pi_{it} = \left[P_t\left(\sum_{j=1}^{n} x_{jt} \right) - C_i\left(y_{it}, \sum_{j=1}^{n} y_{jt} \right) \right] x_{it},$$

where:

x_{it} = production of firm i in period t,
y_{it} = cumulative production of firm i at start of period t,
P_t = market price,
C_i = unit cost of firm i (learning may not be completely firm specific), and
n = number of firms.

Of interest are the equilibria which emerge when each firm solves

$$\max_{x_{i1}, \ldots, x_{iT}} \pi_i = \sum_{t=1}^{n} \beta_i(t) \pi_{it},$$

subject to

$$\text{(2a)} \qquad y_t = y_{t-1} + x_{t-1}, x_t = (x_{it})_{i=1}^{n}, y_t = (y_{it})_{i=1}^{n},$$

$$\text{(2b)} \qquad y_0 \text{ fixed.}$$

Here $\beta_i(t)$ reflects firm i's discounting of profits received in period t. In the model presented in the text, $\beta_i(t) = 1$.

At this level of abstraction, the model does not generate a readily characterizable solution . To generate meaningful comparative statics and measure the magnitude of effects, one must turn to particular functional forms and specific parameter values. The choice here is linear demand and the linear-plateau representation of the learning curve.

[27] See Newhouse [1982] for an example of the intricate bargaining situation which can emerge in such an environment.

Define demand by

(3) $$P_t\left(\sum_{j=1}^{n} x_{jt}\right) = a - b'x_t,$$

where b is a vector consisting of n identical scalar values. Assume that learning occurs at the same rate for each firm down to some minimum cost level θ_1:

(4) $$C\left(y_{it}, \sum_{j=1}^{n} y_{jt}\right) = \theta_0 - c\left(y_{it} + \gamma \sum_{\substack{j=1 \\ j \neq i}}^{n} y_{jt}\right).$$

Therefore, equation (1) becomes

(5) $$\pi_{it} = \begin{cases} [a - b'x_t - \theta_0 + c\gamma y_t + c(1-\gamma)y_{it}]x_{it}, & \text{for } \theta_0 - cy_{it} \geqslant \theta_1 \\ [a - b'x_t - \theta_1]x_{it} & \text{, for } q - cy_{it} < \theta_1. \end{cases}$$

Equations (5) and (2) form a linear-quadratic dynamic program, which is readily solvable given a set of behavioral assumptions over a wide range of parameter values. While the solution to a system of n linear-quadratic equations may be difficult to interpret in general, relatively straightforward algorithms exist which yield exact numerical solutions for particular parameter values (Bertsekas [1976]; Chow [1975]; Kydland [1975]).

The precise application of the algorithm is described in Ross [1985]. There is one control variable

x_t – output in period t,

and one state variable

y_t – cumulative production at start of t.

The state variable is determined by the law of motion

$$y_t = y_{t-1} + x_{t-1}.$$

The solution can be computed recursively and is of the form

$$x_t^* = d_t + E_t \hat{y}_{t-1}, t = 1, \ldots, T,$$

where

$$x_t = [(x_{it})_{i=1}^{n}],$$
$$\hat{y}_t' = [x_t(y_{it} q_{it} x_{i,t-1})_{i=1}^{n}],$$

and d_t and E_t are respectively $n \times 1$ and $n \times 3n$ matrices derived from the original parameters. Firm i's optimal output in period t depends on the cumulative and current production of all firms. Under the Cournot behavioral assumption, each firm assumes that rival output is not affected by its own decisions. Under the von Stackelberg assumption, the leader recognizes the reaction function of its rivals and incorporates those reactions into its optimization problem—essentially by imposing an additional constraint on the leader's program. From the solution matrix x_t and the parameters characterizing the model, one can calculate the market price and firm costs for each period, which in turn yield such performance measures as consumer surplus and profitability (in each period and over the entire game).

Note that the linear-plateau form for the learning curve leads to some imprecision when this algorithm is used: The algorithm is unable to choose among paths which reach the plateau in the same period. Sensitivity tests suggest that this imprecision is not significant except when the number of periods is small.

REFERENCES

ABELL, D. F. and HAMMOND, J. S., 1979, *Strategic Market Planning* (Prentice-Hall, Englewood Cliffs, NJ).

ABERNATHY, W. J., 1978, *The Productivity Dilemma* (Johns Hopkins University Press, Baltimore).

BERTSEKAS, D. P., 1976, *Dynamic Programming and Stochastic Control* (Academic Press, New York).

BRESNAHAN, T. F., 1981, 'Duopoly Models with Consistent Conjectures', *American Economic Review*, 71, pp. 934–945.

CHOW, G. C., 1975, *Analysis and Control of Dynamic Economic Systems* (Wiley, New York).

CLARKE, F. H. *et al*., 1982, 'Optimal Pricing Policy in the Presence of Experience Effects', *Journal of Business*, 55, pp. 517–530.

CONFERENCE BOARD, 1980, 'Shifting Boundaries Between Regulation and Competition', *The Conference Board Information Bulletin*, No. 77.

CONFERENCE BOARD, 1981, 'Strategic Planning and the Future of Antitrust', *The Conference Board Information Bulletin*, No. 90.

DOLAN, R. J. and JEULAND, A. P., 1981, 'Experience Curves and Dynamic Demand Models', *Journal of Marketing*, 45, pp. 52–62.

DUCHATELET, M. N. J., 1977, 'Learning by Doing and Imperfect Competition', PhD dissertation, Department of Economics, Stanford University.

FLAHERTY, M. T., 1980, 'Industry Structure and Cost-Reducing Investment', *Econometrica*, 48, pp. 1187–1209.

FUDENBERG, D. and TIROLE, J., 1983a, 'Learning by Doing and Market Performance', *Bell Journal of Economics*, 14, pp. 522–530.

FUDENBERG, D. and TIROLE, J., 1983b, 'Dynamic Models of Oligopoly', Stanford University IMSSS Technical Report No. 428.

GHEMAWAT, P., 1982, 'The Experience Curve and Corporate Strategy', PhD dissertation, Department of Economics, Harvard University.

GHEMAWAT, P., 1984, 'Capacity Expansion in the Titanium Dioxide Industry', *Journal of Industrial Economics*, 33, pp. 145–163.

GHEMAWAT, P. and SPENCE, A. M., 1983, 'Learning Curve Spillovers, Shared Experience, and Market Performance', Harvard Institute of Economic Research Discussion Paper No. 968.

GILBERT, R. J. and HARRIS, R. G., 1981, 'Investment Decisions with Economies of Scale and Learning', *American Economic Association Papers and Proceedings*, 71, pp. 172–177.

HALL, W. P., 1982, 'The Effects of the Learning Curve on Strategic Firm Behavior and Economic Performance', PhD dissertation, Department of Economics, University of Michigan.

HALL, W. P., 1983, 'The Learning Curve, Industry Equilibrium, and Economic Performance', US Department of Justice Antitrust Division, Economic Policy Office Discussion Paper EPO 83–15.

HENDERSON, B., 1980, *Henderson on Corporate Strategy* (Boston, Abt.).

JACQUEMIN, A. P. and THISSE, J., 1972, 'Strategy of the Firm and Market Structure: An Application of Optimal Control Theory', in K. COWLING (ed.), *Market Structure and Corporate Behaviour*, pp. 68–83 (Gray-Mills, London).

KREPS, D. and SPENCE, A. M., 1983, 'Modelling the Role of History in Industrial Organization and Competition', forthcoming in G. FEIWEL (ed.), *Contemporary Issues in Modern Microeconomics.*

KYDLAND, F., 1975, 'Noncooperative and Dominant Player Solutions in Discrete Dynamic Games', *International Economic Review*, 16, pp. 321–335.

MANSFIELD, E., 1962, 'Entry, Gibrat's Law, Innovation and the Growth of Firms', *American Economic Review*, 52, pp. 1023–1051.

MANSFIELD, E., 1968, *Industrial Research and Technological Innovation* (Norton, New York).

NELSON, R. and WINTER, S., 1978, 'Forces Generating and Limiting Concentration under Schumpeterian Competition', *Bell Journal of Economics*, 9, pp. 524–548.

NEWHOUSE, J., 1982, *The Sporty Game* (Knopf, New York).

PORTER, M. E., 1980, *Competitive Strategy* (Free Press, New York).

REICH, R. B., 1983, *The Next American Frontier* (Times Books, New York).

REMER, D. S. *et al.*, 1981, 'A Model for Life Cycle Cost Analysis with a Learning Curve', *Engineering Economist*, 27, pp. 29–58.

ROSEN, S., 1972, 'Learning by Experience as Joint Production', *Quarterly Journal of Economics*, 86, pp. 366–382.

ROSS, D., 1984a, 'Policy Implications of the Learning Curve', PhD dissertation, Department of Economics, Northwestern University.

ROSS, D., 1984b, 'Learning by a Monopolist', Williams College Department of Economics Research Paper No. 70.

ROSS, D., 1984c, 'The Significance of Learning in Measuring Costs', Williams College Department of Economics Research Paper No. 89.

ROSS, D., 1985, 'Learning to Dominate', working paper.

SCHERER, F. M., 1980, *Industrial Market Structure and Economic Performance* (Rand McNally, Chicago).

SCHERER, F. M. *et al.*, 1975, *The Economics of Multi-Plant Operations* (Harvard University Press, Cambridge, Mass.).

SELTEN, R., 1975, 'Reexamination of the Perfectness Concept for Equilibrium Points in Extensive Games', *International Journal of Game Theory*, 4, pp. 25–55.

SMILEY, R. H., 1982, 'Learning and the Concentration-Profitability Relationship', Quarterly Review of Economics and Business, 22, pp. 27–40.

SMILEY, R. H. and RAVID, S. A., 1983, 'The Importance of Being First: Learning, Price and Strategy', *Quarterly Journal of Economics*, 98, pp. 353–362.

SPENCE, A. M., 1981, 'The Learning Curve and Competition', *Bell Journal of Economics*, 12, pp. 49–79.

STEEDMAN, I., 1969, '"Learning by Doing" and the Theory of the Firm', *Journal of Economic Studies*, 4, pp. 47–59.

TENG, J. T. and THOMPSON, G. L., 1983, 'Oligopoly Models for Optimal Advertising when Production Costs Obey a Learning Curve', *Management Science*, 29, pp. 1087–1101.

YELLE, L. E., 1983, 'Adding Life Cycles to Learning Curves', *Long Range Planning*, 16, pp. 82–87.

THE JOURNAL OF INDUSTRIAL ECONOMICS 0022-1821 $2.00
Volume XXXIV June 1986 No. 4

THE PERSISTENCE OF MONOPOLY: AN INVESTIGATION OF THE EFFECTIVENESS OF THE UNITED KINGDOM MONOPOLIES COMMISSION*

R. W. SHAW AND P. SIMPSON

A sample of twenty-eight markets investigated by the UK Monopolies and Mergers Commission is taken and market share changes are analysed for subsequent erosion of dominance. The evidence points to a modest erosion for leading firms but only rarely to a loss of leadership. Although there is no significant difference between the rates of decline for leading firms in the MMC sample and a control group, the achievement of some erosion of dominance in markets where entry barriers were reduced may represent some limited success for competition policy.

INTRODUCTION

THE PERSISTENCE of a monopoly position need not imply a failure of the competitive process. Recent work has shown that in contestable markets when entry and exit are completely free, established monopolists and oligopolists can only prevent entry by setting prices that offer no more than normal profits (Baumol [1982]). Even where the strict assumptions of contestability are not met it is possible that persistent domination may reflect efficiency in both production and in satisfying consumer needs. However, where the market is non-contestable, persistence may be the result of dominant firms enjoying 'differential movement advantages' allowing them to engage in strategic entry deterrence. Thus established firms may maintain their market share position while still earning monopoly rent in the form of excessive profits or X-inefficiency. (See Salop [1979]; Dixit [1982]; Geroski and Jacquemin [1984]). It is this possibility that makes the persistence of monopoly a matter of concern.

In attempting to measure persistence this paper argues that the erosion of dominant market shares will at least reflect some competitive pressure. In some cases this may merely result in changing the relative strengths of firms within an oligopoly group. In other cases however the erosion will reflect entry and/or the expansion of the competitive fringe suggesting the effective working of the competitive process. This paper attempts to give some indication of the extent to which market leaders' shares are eroded and whether the beneficiaries are existing oligopolists or new challengers.

* The research reported in this paper is part of a study of the impact of competition policy on selected UK industries. It has been supported by a grant from the Economic and Social Research Council whose assistance is gratefully acknowledged. The helpful comments of members of the ESRC Industrial Economists Study Group on a preliminary version of the paper and of an anonymous referee are also gratefully acknowledged.

The paper examines the post report changes in market share for leading firms investigated by the United Kingdom Monopolies and Mergers Commission (MMC) between 1959 and 1973. It seeks to establish whether dominant firms at the time of their MMC investigations were able to maintain their position or whether their market shares were subsequently eroded.

For an assessment of the impact of competition policy on the persistence of monopoly it is not enough to find that leading firms lose some of their market share. It is quite possible that leading firms will lose market share as a result of the competitive process independent of any action by the competition authorities. A well known example is provided by the dominant firm price leadership model explored by Worcester and subsequently developed by Gaskins (Worcester [1957]; Gaskins [1971]; Scherer [1980]). Thus, if the intervention of competition authorities is to be justified partly by the loss of dominance, then it must be shown that the intervention was the cause of the change. This requires a detailed investigation of the competitive process on a case-by-case basis. Such investigations form the second stage of the current research, and have been reported in part elsewhere (Shaw and Simpson [1985]). However, some clues may be obtained by comparing the changes in market share experienced by the main MMC sample firms with the experience of a control group based on leading firms in some other markets. Further clues may be obtained by comparing the changes in market share experienced by MMC sample firms that were subject to a reduction in entry barriers as a result of actions following MMC recommendations with the experience of other firms where no such reduction in barriers followed. Only if leading firms in the MMC sample lose market share to a greater extent than those in the control group, and only if such losses in the MMC sample appear to be associated with actions following from the Commission report will the results of this test of effectiveness support the work of the Commission. This test, it must be stressed, can only be partial since performance may improve as a result of MMC action without changes in market share.

The paper is divided into three main sections. The first describes the main sample and control group and the basic methodology. Section II contains the empirical evidence on market share changes for the main MMC sample. Section III contains the comparative evidence derived from the control group and the pooled sample.

I. THE SAMPLE, DATA[1] AND TESTS

The main sample is drawn from industries which were the subject of an MMC

[1] The data sources were Monopolies and Mergers Commission, National Board for Prices and Incomes, and Price Commission reports, Retail Business, Mintel, Market Research Great Britain, EEC Commission Evolution of Concentration series, company reports, the trade and financial press, and industry sources.

dominant firm or 'complex monopoly' report between 1959 and 1973. With the single exception of the film distribution industry all are manufacturing industries. The MMC sample consists of twenty-eight markets or sub-industries identified in nineteen MMC reports. (See Appendix 1.) One further market is included for some tests and two others are also discussed though they are excluded from the main statistical analysis due to inadequate data. Because the purpose of the research is to examine the impact of competition policy on industry, the changes in market share refer to the experience of leading firms in the period following an MMC investigation. As a result each market has its own starting date from which changes are measured.

The opening date for the whole sample, 1959, allows several years of competitive experience prior to the MMC report but subsequent to the removal of the post-war government controls on industry, for example branded petrol was reintroduced in 1953 together with the termination of Government price control. The earliest report included, on the supply of chemical fertilisers, was the first full report concluded by the revamped Monopolies Commission following the Restrictive Trade Practices Act, 1956. While 1973 as a closing date for the sample is clearly arbitrary, it provides approximately ten years of post report history.[2]

The relatively long post report period was chosen because of the substantial lags before the impact of an MMC report may occur. These lags may be summarized briefly. Firstly, following Government acceptance of any MMC recommendations negotiations between the industry and the Government normally took place to secure voluntary compliance. These negotiations were sometimes protracted. Secondly, any changes in competitive practices which strengthened the position of minor producers or made entry to the industry easier would create opportunities which had first to be recognised and only then exploited. Thus there would be recognition, implementation and impact lags which taken together could mean a delay of several years before any MMC recommendation had its full effect.

The control group is drawn from markets which were investigated by the UK National Board for Prices and Incomes (NBPI) in the period 1965–1970. This body was established in 1965 as part of the Labour Government's prices and incomes policy. Its purpose was to investigate wages and prices behaviour in specific markets (see Fels [1972]; Pickering [1971]). Although the NBPI, like the MMC, was a UK government agency the NBPI's powers were relatively limited being confined to recommendations concerning prices, wages and salaries. The MMC, by contrast, could make recommendations on a wide range of structure, conduct and performance issues.

[2] The difficulty of obtaining data at precise dates has led to some variation in the period. The longest post report period used in the statistical analysis was 14 years (one market) and the shortest was 6 years (three markets). The remaining twenty-four markets had post report periods of between 9 and 13 years. Adjusted Spearman rank correlation tests showed no significant correlation between length of post report period and market share changes. Detailed results are reported in Appendix 2.

The control group consists of nineteen markets or sub-industries identified in the reports. (See Appendix I.) The choice of this group was based on three considerations. Firstly, many of the NBPI reports were concerned with markets with high levels of concentration and included 'legal monopolists' comparable to those in the MMC sample. Secondly, the reports, and hence the post report periods, in the MMC and NBPI samples cover broadly the same period. Finally, the NBPI group was attractive on the purely pragmatic grounds of data availability though even here, as in the MMC sample, it proved very difficult to obtain market share data for the post report period. Apart from the unavailability of data the NBPI sample was also restricted by the necessity to exclude markets already in the MMC sample, for example chemical fertilisers, soaps and detergents, and beer.

For each market, changes in share are analysed for both the market leader and the second ranked firm. In addition the market share change for the main oligopolistic group as a whole as identified by either the MMC or the NBPI is also analysed. By extending the definition to include markets dominated by a single firm the size of the dominant group varies from one up to five or seven firms respectively in the petrol supply and beer markets. Domination by a single firm is defined as occurring when the second ranked firm has less than a 10 percent share of the non-captive market (that is, excluding sales within vertically integrated groups). By using the three measures of market share change it is intended to identify cases where there was market share turbulence within the main group of leading firms as well as cases where the challenges came from minor producers or entrants.

Following O'Brien *et al.* [1979] in their study of industries investigated by the Restrictive Trade Practices Court the statistical tests used include both the parametric t-test and several non-parametric tests (see Siegel [1956]). The tests are based on both differences in mean market shares between initial and post report observations and on the numbers of cases where market shares either declined or failed to do so. For the former, two measures of decline or otherwise are adopted: percentage change in market share and percentage point change in market share. Clearly a given percentage point change in market share represents a more significant change for the firm concerned the lower its initial market share. As a proportionate measure the percentage change in market share corrects for this problem. However, for the market as a whole the percentage point change in share may provide a better indication of the scale of the disturbance.

II. MARKET SHARE CHANGES IN THE MONOPOLIES AND MERGERS COMMISSION SAMPLE

Table I(a) provides a brief outline of the results for the MMC sample as a whole. There was a decline in the mean market shares for both leading firms and the dominant groups but not for second ranked firms. This result is also

TABLE I
MONOPOLIES AND MERGERS COMMISSION MARKET SHARE CHANGES

	Leading firms	*Second ranked firms*	*Dominant group*
(a) Summary results			
Mean initial MS	60.2	25.5	81.6
Mean closing MS	51.8	25.2	74.4
Change in mean MS	−8.4	−0.3	−7.2
Median change in MS	−6	0	−3.5
Number of firms/groups			
increasing MS	5	8	8
no change	1	1	1
decreasing MS	22	8	19
Total number of firms/groups	28	17	28
(b) Tests for changes in market share			
T test			
t-statistic	3.00*	0.15	2.12†
Wilcoxon matched pairs			
mean + Ve rank	11.70	8.31	12.56
mean − Ve rank	14.52	8.69	14.61
z	−3.135*	−0.776	−2.126†
Sign test			
positive	5	8	8
negative	22	8	19
two tailed probability	0.0015*	1.0000	0.0522†

* Significant at 1% one tailed tests.
† Significant at 5% one tailed tests.
‡ Significant at 10% one tailed tests.
MS = market share.

reflected in the number of firms/dominant groups experiencing increasing or decreasing market shares. Table I(b) reports the results of the statistical significance tests. As the hypothesis being tested is whether leading firms/dominant groups have lost market share, one-tailed tests are used.

The decline for the market leaders is statistically significant at the 1 percent level for all three tests used. As may be seen, the overwhelming majority of leading firms suffered at least some decline in market share.[3] In five cases the decline was at least twenty percentage points including a spectacular sixty-three percentage point decline by Metal Box in the beverage can market. The

[3] Three markets were excluded from the main analysis on the grounds that the post report period was too long. For one of these only dominant group market share was available. Including these markets had no effect on the results reported in Table I(b) for leading and second firms. For the dominant group the effect was to make the market share decline significant at the 1% level for both the Wilcoxon and Sign tests.

TABLE II
MARKET SHARE CHANGES IN DOMINANT GROUPS

	Single firm groups		*Multi firm groups*[a]	
	Mean opening MS	*Mean closing MS*	*Mean opening MS*	*Mean closing MS*
Leading firm	81.7	67.6	46.2	41.5
Second ranked firm	—	—	25.5	25.2
Group	81.7	67.6	81.5	78.8
Number of groups				
increasing MS	1		7	
no change	1		—	
decreasing MS	9		10	

[a] The effect of including 3 additional markets where either only satisfactory group data is available or the length of post report period exceeded 14 years (15 and 16 years) is to increase the decline in mean multi-firm group market share from 2.7 to 5.4 percentage points (82.2–76.8 percent). The mean market share of leading firms (2 extra markets) declined from 48.4 to 41.9 percent. The mean market share of second ranked firms only marginally changed from 24.3 to 23.3 percent.

exclusion of this obvious extreme observation does not affect the level of statistical significance.

In sharp contrast to the leaders the second ranked firms showed an even balance between market share increases and decreases. None of the tests showed any significant change in market share for this group of firms.

Finally, although the dominant groups experienced statistically significant declines in market share this is perhaps misleading. The dominant group sample includes eleven 'single firm groups', nine of which experienced a decline in market share. If these are excluded, the remaining groups in the main sample showed only a modest decline in market share. The contrast in experience is shown in Table II. Indeed these results suggest that any market share decline for dominant groups is primarily that of a dominant firm decline.

One possible explanation for the pattern of market share changes, and in particular the susceptibility of leading firms to decline is purely statistical (Caves and Porter [1980]). The higher the initial market share, the less scope there is for any increase and the greater the scope for declines at least in terms of percentage points. Hence it may be hypothesised that the higher the initial market share of the leader the more likely would it be that it would suffer a decline in share. Detailed results of a Spearman rank correlation test for MMC, NBPI and combined samples are reported in Table III.

For the MMC sample none of the test results of a relationship between initial market share and market share decline are significant though the coefficients are of the predicted sign. However, for both the NBPI and the

TABLE III
THE RELATIONSHIP BETWEEN INITIAL MARKET SHARE AND DECLINE IN MARKET SHARE. SPEARMAN RANK CORRELATION COEFFICIENTS[a,b]

Decline in market share	*MMC sample*	*NBPI sample*	*Combined sample*
Leading firm	*28 firms*	*19 firms*	*47 firms*
% point	−0.2846	−0.4714	−0.4089
	(−1.51)	(−2.20)†	(−3.01)*
%	−0.1401	−0.3910	−0.3045
	(−0.72)	(−1.75)‡	(−2.14)†
Second firm	*17 firms*	*14 firms*	*31 firms*
% point	−0.2150	−0.1276	−0.2070
	(−1.12)	(−0.53)	(−1.42)
%	−0.1044	−0.0753	−0.1368
	(−0.54)	(−0.31)	(−0.93)
Dominant group	*28 groups*	*19 groups*	*47 groups*
% point	−0.2969	−0.6567	−0.5376
	(−1.59)	(−3.59)*	(−4.28)*
%	−0.2729	−0.7073	−0.5198
	(−1.45)	(−4.13)*	(−4.08)*

t-statistic in brackets.
[a] * Indicates significant at 1% level two tailed test.
† Indicates significant at 5% level two tailed test.
‡ Indicates significant at 10% level two tailed test.
[b] Due to the ranking procedure adopted negative signs on the correlation coefficients indicate a positive relationship between initial market share and market share decline.

combined samples the results show a statistically significant positive association between initial market share and decline in market share for both leading firms and dominant groups. The results are unaffected by the choice of percentage point or percentage change in market share as the measure of decline. Despite the insignificance of the results for the MMC sample the overall results indicate a tendency for the decline in market share of both leading firm and dominant group to be positively associated with initial market share.

Such an association may of course be the result of economic forces and not just a statistical phenomenon. Both Worcester's [1957] and Gaskins' [1971] dominant firm price leadership models already referred to predict a declining share for leaders. Table II not only shows that decline in group market share is different for 'single firm' and multi-firm groups but also that the mean market share decline of the leaders is much greater for the single dominant firm than for leaders in oligopoly groups. It is possible that this could reflect different behaviour by market leaders in the two categories with leading firms in oligopoly groups taking into account interdependencies while single dominant firms neglect fringe reactions. Despite the difference in mean market share decline, however, the statistical analysis failed to show any significant difference in experience for the MMC sample. Because this could be due to the small sample size the tests were repeated for the combined MMC and NBPI sample. However, once again, while leading dominant firms suffered a larger decline in mean market share (from 79.2 to 67.0 percent) than leading firms in oligopoly groups (from 41.7 to 37.3 percent) there is virtually no evidence that the difference is statistically significant. Using the t-test and non-parametric Mann–Whitney test for both percentage point and percentage change in market share measures, only in one, the t-test for percentage point change, is there a statistically significant difference between the samples even at the low 10 percent level ($t = 1.89$, Mann–Whitney $u = 1.06$). Even this difference disappears when the extremely large decline for beverage cans is excluded from the sample.

Although the results show a very clear tendency for leading firms in the MMC sample to experience a decline in market share it is also the case that for half the sample there was either no decline or it was restricted to under 10 percent of the firm's initial market share. This, together with the mean closing market share of 51.8 percent for leading firms ten or so years after the MMC report, suggests that any general tendency to decline is muted. A further indication of the relatively modest tendency towards decline is provided by a sensitivity test. An addition of five percentage points was made to the closing market shares of all leading firms and dominant groups. The tests for changes in market share were then repeated using the adjusted closing market shares. The changes are insignificant in all three tests for both leading firms and dominant groups.[4]

Overall, then, the results show a clear but generally modest tendency for leading firms investigated by the MMC to lose market share. Furthermore, in only five out of twenty-eight markets was there a change in market leader. This apparent stability, however, conceals considerable variation within the sample. In nine of the twenty-eight markets both the leading firm and the dominant group either increased market share or limited any decline to less than five percentage points. Six of these markets may be described as stable in that changes in leading firm market shares were small. In the other three, however, the leading firm increased its market share by over five percentage points. Thus, in approximately a third of the sample, the initial dominant firm or oligopoly maintained or improved its position. In a further seven markets (one quarter of the sample), where the market leader's share declined by at least five percentage points, this loss was either wholly or partly compensated by the increasing market shares of existing oligopolists. Finally, in the remaining twelve markets (forty-three percent of the sample) both the leading firm and dominant group lost market share to new entrants. In six of these markets the leading firm's market share declined by at least ten percentage points with the smallest decline for the dominant group being eighteen

[4] For leading firm $t = 1.22$; Wilcoxon $Z = -0.89$; Sign, two tailed probability $= 0.25$. For dominant groups $t = 0.64$; Wilcoxon $Z = -0.41$; Sign, two tailed probability $= 1.0$.

TABLE IV
NATIONAL BOARD FOR PRICES AND INCOMES MARKET SHARE CHANGES

	Leading firms	*Second ranked firms*	*Dominant group*
(a) Summary results			
Mean initial MS	42.1	20.6	67.5
Mean closing MS	38.0	22.7	69.6
Change in mean MS	−4.1	2.1	2.1
Median change in MS	−2	−0.5	0
Number of firms/groups			
increasing MS	5	6	9
no change	2	1	1
decreasing MS	12	7	9
Total number of firms/groups	19	14	19
(b) Tests for changes in market share			
T test			
t-statistic	1.71‡	−0.81	−0.70
Wilcoxon matched pairs			
mean + Ve rank	8.50	8.92	11.06
mean − Ve rank	9.21	5.36	7.94
z	−1.610‡	−0.559	−0.610
Sign test			
positive	5	6	9
negative	12	7	9
two tailed probability	0.1435‡	1.0000	1.0000

* Significant at 1% one tailed tests.
† Significant at 5% one tailed tests.
‡ Significant at 10% one tailed tests.
MS = market share.

percentage points.[5] Despite these changes and the clear signs of competitive pressure in (many of) these markets their structure nevertheless remained oligopolistic.

Apart from examining the impact of reduced entry barriers and anti-competitive practices on market share changes (see section III) the detailed investigation of the causes of the differing experiences is beyond the scope of this paper. However, since there is some evidence that advertising in consumer goods markets has been a concentration increasing force (Mueller and Hamm [1974]; Mueller and Rogers [1980]; Scherer [1980]) it may be useful to report that the mean market share decline for leading firms in consumer goods markets was 7.0 percentage points compared with a mean

[5] Detailed data on the rate of decline experienced within the post-MMC report period for the 12 markets is unavailable. However it may be interesting to note that in three cases, nitrogen fertilisers, cellulosic fibres and beverage cans, the leading firm's market share decline was substantial within five years of the MMC report.

market share decline of 9.4 percentage points in producer goods markets. Without examining other variables it is impossible to assess the significance of the difference. It should be noted, however, that the mean initial market share of leading firms in producer goods markets was higher than in consumer goods markets, and a weak positive association was found between initial market share and rate of decline (see also Caves and Porter [1980]). Finally, it may be interesting to notice that merger activity was unimportant in the sample. In only four out of twenty-eight markets was there merger activity by major firms and in only two of these (beer and starch) did this strengthen the oligopolistic group. This is perhaps not surprising for markets already under the scrutiny of the competition authorities.

III. COMPARATIVE CHANGES IN MARKET SHARE FOR THE MMC AND NBPI SAMPLES

The purpose of this section is to examine whether the post MMC report market share changes analysed in section II are different from those experienced in other highly concentrated markets. The NBPI sample acts as the control.

Table IV gives a brief outline of the results for the NBPI sample. The leading firms experienced a decline in their mean market share with a clear majority of leaders experiencing some decline. However, neither the second ranked nor the dominant groups suffered any decline in mean share and this is reflected in the even distributions of increasing and decreasing market shares in both cases. The decline for the leading firms is statistically significant in all three tests but only at the weak 10 percent level.

Despite the low level of significance for the decline in market share for leading firms, the pattern of results is similar to that for the MMC sample: leading firms experienced a decline in share while second ranked firms had an

TABLE V
TESTS ON DIFFERENCES IN MARKET SHARE CHANGES BETWEEN MMC AND NBPI SAMPLES

Paired groups	*t-test*	*Mann–Whitney u*
Leading firms		
percentage point change in MS	−1.08	−1.3026
percentage change in MS	−0.91	−0.8998
Second ranked firms		
percentage point change in MS	−0.75	−0.4770
percentage change in MS	−0.87	−0.4963
Dominant groups		
percentage point change in MS	−1.93‡	−1.9307‡
percentage change in MS	−2.32†	−1.9619‡

* Significant at 1 % two tailed tests.
† Significant at 5 % two tailed tests.
‡ Significant at 10 % two tailed tests.
MS = market share.

evenly balanced mixture of market share gains and losses. Only for the dominant groups is there a contrast with a clear decline in the MMC sample but no significant change in the NBPI sample. The statistical tests for differences in market share experience between the two samples are reported in Table V. The results indicate that both the leading firms and second ranked firms in the two samples have been drawn from the same population. The difference in experience of the two dominant group samples probably reflects the differences in group composition. The MMC sample contains eleven 'single firm groups' out of a total of twenty-eight groups whereas the NBPI sample contains only two 'single firm groups' out of a total of nineteen groups. As indicated earlier (see Table II) group decline is basically caused by the decline of the leading firm and, since in the MMC sample leading firms

TABLE VI
CHANGES IN ENTRY BARRIERS RESULTING FROM MONOPOLIES AND MERGERS COMMISSION REPORTS

Reduction in entry barriers		*No reduction in entry barriers*
Market	*Barrier*	*Market*
Cigarettes	Bonus scheme for giving Imperial preferential display facilities	Compound fertilisers Nitrogenous fertilisers[a]
Wallpaper	Exclusive dealing	
Petrol	Ownership of petrol stations; long term exclusive dealing contracts	Automotive batteries (original equipment) Automotive batteries (replacement equipment) Traction batteries[c] Sparking plugs
Film processing[c,d]	Tie-in sales, technical knowledge	Automotive lamps and horns
Films for exhibition	Tie-in sales; vertical integration	Starter motors Colour film[d] Household detergent
Clutch mechanisms	Exclusive dealing for both inputs and products	powders Liquid detergents Infant milk foods
Beverage cans	Tie-in sales; exclusive dealing	Flat glass[a] Beer
Food cans	Tie-in sales; exclusive dealing	
Aerosols	Tie-in sales; exclusive dealing	
Cellulosic fibres	Regulation of imports; vertical integration	Cigarette filter rods[a] Starch[b]
Electric lamps	Price discrimination against competitors in purchase of inputs; aggregated rebates on purchases	Glucose[a] Breakfast cereals
Asbestos	Market-sharing; exclusive dealing	

[a] No criticism or action.
[b] Not a legal monopoly.
[c] Excluded from the main statistical analysis.
[d] Kodak and other suppliers gave an undertaking to sell colour film both with and without a processing charge. The primary effect of this was to reduce the barrier to entry to film processing. The effect on entry to the colour film market was likely to be negligible.

had a higher initial market share than the corresponding firms in the NBPI sample, it would be expected that MMC groups would decline more than NBPI groups.

The similarity of the results in the two samples, at least for leading and second ranked firms, suggests that the same competitive forces were at work. While the evidence clearly shows that leading firms in markets investigated by the MMC lose market share, the comparison with the control group indicates that the experience is not dissimilar from that of leading firms in other concentrated markets.

The same comparisons may be made for sub-groups within the MMC sample. One such sub-group of particular interest consists of markets where action following an MMC report led to a reduction in entry barriers. Markets in this sub-group are listed in Table VI together with the barriers that were modified. Where MMC recommendations were not translated into action they have not been included, for example reductions in selling expenses for household detergents. As may be seen from the types of barrier concerned, existing minor firms as well as potential entrants would be at a disadvantage compared with leading firms. Indeed the rigidity in market shares that might result from such practices as tie-in sales and exclusive dealing might also impede the development of individual major established suppliers. It thus seems likely that reduction in these barriers would make market leaders more vulnerable to competition from all sources and hence increase the probability of the leaders experiencing a decline in share.

With the available data it is only possible to examine whether the barrier reduction sub-group experienced different market share changes from the rest of the MMC sample and from the NBPI sample. Although it is a weak test it is reasonable to infer that absence of market share decline for the leaders in the barrier reduction sub-group would probably reflect a failure by the competition authorities to loosen sufficiently the constraints on competition. On the other hand a similar pattern of market share change to those experienced in the rest of the MMC sample and in the NBPI sample would indicate that competitive forces in the post report period were able to operate at least as well as in other concentrated markets. The results are presented in Table VII.

Although the decline in mean market share for both leading firms and dominant groups is far higher in the part of the MMC sample that had entry barriers and anti-competitive devices reduced than in the other two groups much of the difference is due to a single extreme observation. When the beverage cans market is excluded, as in the footnotes to the table, the rates of decline are much closer. The median change in market share avoids this problem. On this measure leading firms and dominant groups in the entry barrier reduction sub-group still suffered the largest market share losses though the gap is narrowed.

The t-test and Mann–Whitney non-parametric test were performed to

TABLE VII
MARKET SHARE CHANGES AND ENTRY BARRIER REDUCTION

	Leading firms			*Second ranked firms*			*Dominant firms*		
	Entry barriers reduced	*No reduction in entry barriers*		*Entry barriers reduced*	*No reduction in entry barriers*		*Entry barriers reduced*	*No reduction in entry barriers*	
	MMC sample	*MMC sample*	*NBPI sample*	*MMC sample*	*MMC sample*	*NBPI sample*	*MMC sample*	*MMC sample*	*NBPI sample*
Mean initial MS	64.4	57.5	42.1	25.6	25.4	20.6	80.7	82.2	67.5
Mean closing MS	52.3	51.4	37.9	26.0	24.8	22.7	68.3	78.4	69.6
Change in mean MS	−12.1[a]	−6.1	−4.2	0.4	−0.6	2.1	−12.4[b]	−3.8	2.1
Median change in MS	−7	−6	−2	2	−0.5	−0.5	−7	−2	0
Number of firms/groups									
increasing MS	2	3	5	3	5	6	4	4	9
no change	—	1	2	—	1	1	—	1	1
decreasing MS	9	13	12	2	6	7	7	12	9
Total number of firms/groups	11	17	19	5	12	14	11	17	19

[a] Excluding beverage cans extreme observation −7.0 percentage points.
[b] Excluding beverage cans extreme observation −7.4 percentage points.

examine for differences between the main samples using both percentage point and percentage change in market share measures. None of the tests reveal statistically significant differences between the samples for either leading or second ranked firms. Only for dominant groups is there a statistically significant difference between the NBPI sample and the MMC sample with entry barriers reduced.[6] While this suggests a greater tendency for market share decline in cases where entry barriers were reduced, it is also probable that it largely reflects both differing group composition and higher initial market shares in the MMC entry barrier reduction sub-group.

The evidence thus shows that the market share decline of leading firms in markets for which the MMC and government felt a need to reduce entry barriers and anti-competitive practices was very similar to the decline experienced in other markets. Any rigidities imposed by the pre-report use of tie-in sales, exclusive dealing etc., appear to have been sufficiently loosened that subsequent market share changes conform to the experience in other markets. Put another way, there is certainly no evidence in markets where the competition authorities took action to reduce impediments to competition that leading firms were more able to sustain their monopoly positions than leading firms in other markets. At least on this weak test the intervention by the MMC did not fail and may perhaps have successfully facilitated the operation of the competitive process.

CONCLUSIONS

The two principal questions addressed in the paper are: does monopoly persist in markets investigated by the Monopolies and Mergers Commission; and is the experience in these markets any different from that in other concentrated markets?

The evidence shows, firstly, that leading firms investigated by the MMC between 1959 and 1973 did subsequently suffer a statistically significant decline in market share. However, while the decline was sometimes quite dramatic, in general it was modest. Ten years after the publication of the MMC report, leading firms' mean market share had only declined from 60.2 to 51.8 percent. Although twenty-two out of twenty-eight leading firms in the main sample had suffered some decline, in only seven markets was the decline as large as 10 percentage points. The median market share change was a decline of only 6 percentage points.

A similar examination of second ranked firms shows an even pattern of market share gains and losses in the post-MMC report period. The experience of the dominant oligopoly groups identified by the MMC reflects these results. Where there was a single dominant firm the experience was over-

[6] According to the t-test on both percentage point and percentage change measures there is a statistically significant difference at the 5 percent level. For the Mann–Whitney test this difference is only significant at the 10 percent level.

whelmingly of a declining market share. Where, however, there was an oligopoly the group as a whole showed little general tendency to decline though the leading firm within the group normally did decline. Thus any decline in concentration was primarily due to the losses in market share suffered by market leaders.

A comparison with a control group drawn from markets investigated by the National Board for Prices and Incomes shows a very similar pattern of results: leading firms decline but second ranked firms have an evenly balanced experience of gains and losses in market share. Such differences as there are between the samples are statistically insignificant at even the weak 10 percent level for both leading and second ranked firms. This suggests that similar forces are operating on firms in both MMC and NBPI samples.

Although the general pattern of market share changes is very similar in the two samples, it is possible that this obscures some differences due to government action following some MMC reports.

The MMC sample was thus divided into two groups with markets where barriers to entry and impediments to competition were reduced forming one group. The results show the experiences of leading and second ranked firms are very similar in the two MMC sub-groups and between each of these and the NBPI sample. Both the decline in leading firm mean market share and the median change (decline) in share are larger in the sub-group with barriers reduced than in the other two groups, but the changes are not statistically significant. This is consistent with the results for the undivided MMC sample compared with the NBPI sample. However, the implications may be a little different. For the MMC sub-group with barriers reduced the competition authorities decided that there were impediments to the competitive process that might operate against the public interest. At least in the post-MMC report period after action was taken there is no evidence that these leading firms were more successful in preserving their monopoly positions than other leading firms. On this weak test the intervention by the MMC in reducing barriers did not fail and may perhaps have successfully facilitated the operation of the competitive process.

ACCEPTED JUNE 1985

R. W. SHAW,
Department of Economics and Management,
Paisley College of Technology,
High Street,
Paisley,
Renfrewshire, PA1 2BE, UK.

P. SIMPSON,
Institute of Science and Technology,
University of Manchester,
P.O. Box 88,
Manchester, M60 1QD, UK.

APPENDIX 1

MMC AND NBPI SAMPLES

Monopolies and Mergers Commission

Market	*Year of report*	*Market*	*Year of report*
Nitrogen fertilisers	1959	Films for exhibition	1966
Compound fertilisers	1959	Colour film	1966
Cigarettes	1961	Film processing	1966[a]
Automotive batteries (original equipment)	1963	Infant milk foods	1967
		Cellulosic fibres	1968
Automotive batteries (replacement equipment)	1963	Flat glass	1968
		Clutch mechanisms	1968
Traction batteries	1963[a]	Electric lamps	1968
Spark plugs	1963	Cigarette filters	1969
Starter motors	1963	Beer	1969
Lamps and horns	1963	Beverage cans	1970
Wallpaper	1964	Food cans	1970
Petrol	1965	Aerosols	1970
Automotive lubricants	1965[a]	Starch	1971
Detergent powder	1966	Glucose	1971
Liquid detergents	1966	Asbestos cement	1973
		Breakfast cereals	1973

National Board for Prices and Incomes

Market	*Year of report*	*Market*	*Year of report*
Bread	1965	Computers	1968
Flour	1965	Toothpaste	1969
Toilet soap	1965	Shampoo	1969
Dry cleaning	1966	Hairspray	1969
Cement	1967	Plasterboard	1969
Bricks	1967	Margarine	1970
TV rental	1968	Primary batteries	1970
Washing machines	1968	Tea	1970
Vacuum cleaners	1968	Ice cream	1970
Chocolate confectionery	1968		

[a] Excluded from the main statistical analysis due to inadequate data.

APPENDIX 2

THE RELATIONSHIP BETWEEN MARKET SHARE CHANGES AND THE LENGTH OF PERIOD BETWEEN OBSERVATIONS

Since it proved impossible to obtain market share data for an identical period in all markets some variability in post report adjustment periods had to be accepted. For the main MMC sample this period varied between 6 (3 markets) and 14 (1 market) years. However for 24 of the 28 markets in the sample the post report period was between 9 and 13 years. For the NBPI sample the post report period varied between 9 (1 market) and 15 (2 markets) years. However for 17 of the 19 markets in the sample the post report period was in the 9–13 years range which covered most of the MMC sample.

The Spearman rank correlation test was used to investigate whether there is any association between the length of post report period and the extent of the change in

TABLE A2
MARKET SHARE CHANGES AND LENGTH OF POST REPORT PERIOD·
SPEARMAN RANK CORRELATION COEFFICIENTS[a,b]

Change in market share	*MMC sample*	*NBPI sample*	*Combined sample*
Leading firm	*28 firms*	*19 firms*	*47 firms*
% *point*	0.0440	0.1325	0.0894
	(0.23)	(0.55)	(0.60)
%	0.0863	0.1956	0.1210
	(0.44)	(0.82)	(0.82)
Second firm	*17 firms*	*14 firms*	*31 firms*
% *point*	−0.3451	−0.0865	−0.1843
	(−1.42)	(−0.30)	(−1.01)
%	−0.4469†	−0.0644	−0.2001
	(−1.93)	(−0.22)	(−1.10)
Dominant group	*28 groups*	*19 groups*	*47 groups*
% *point*	−0.1339	0.0382	−0.0266
	(−0.69)	(0.16)	(−0.18)
%	−0.1290	0.1735	0.0111
	(−0.66)	(0.73)	(0.07)

[a] * Indicates significant at the 5% level.
† Indicates significant at the 10% level.
[b] Due to the ranking procedure adopted negative signs on the correlation coefficients indicate a positive relationship between length of period and market share change.

market share. The results are tabulated in Table A2. For the leading firms and dominant groups no significant correlation was found in any of the samples. Indeed the only significant correlation was for second ranked firms in the MMC sample. Even in this case the correlation was only significant at the low 10 percent level. The tests were repeated to investigate whether there is any association between the length of period between the initial and closing market shares and the extent of the change in market share. This procedure was adopted because there is some variability in the lag between initial market share reported and the publication of the relevant report. Overall the results suggest that within the limited range of adjustment period changes in market share are not associated with the length of period.

REFERENCES

BAUMOL, W. J., 1982, 'Contestable Markets: An Uprising in the Theory of Industry Structure', *American Economic Review*, Vol. 72, No. 1, pp. 1–15.

CAVES, R. E. and PORTER, M. E., 1980, 'The Dynamics of Changing Seller Concentration', *Journal of Industrial Economics*, Vol. XXIX, No. 1 (September), pp. 1–17.

DIXIT, A., 1982, 'Recent Developments in Oligopoly Theory', *American Economic Review*, Papers and Proceedings, Vol. 72, No. 2, pp. 12–17.

FELS, A., 1972, *The British Prices and Incomes Board* (Cambridge University Press).

GASKINS, D. W., 1971, 'Dynamic Limit Pricing: Optimal Pricing Under Threat of Entry', *Journal of Economic Theory*, Vol. 3 (September), pp. 306–322.

GEROSKI, P. A. and JACQUEMIN, A., 1984, 'Dominant Firms and their Alleged Decline', *International Journal of Industrial Organization*, Vol. 2, No. 1, pp. 1–27.

MUELLER, W. F. and HAMM, L. G., 1974, 'Trends in Industrial Market Concentration 1947 to 1970', *Review of Economics and Statistics*, Vol. 56 (November), pp. 511–520.

MUELLER, W. F. and ROGERS, R. T., 1980, 'The Role of Advertising in Changing Concentration of Manufacturing Industries', *Review of Economics and Statistics*, Vol. 62, No. 1 (February), pp. 89–96.

O'BRIEN, D. P., HOWE, W. J. and WRIGHT, D. M. with O'BRIEN, R. J., 1979, *Competition Policy, Profitability and Growth* (Macmillan).

PICKERING, J. F., 1971, 'The Prices and Incomes Board and Private Sector Prices: A Survey', *Economic Journal*, Vol. 81 (June), pp. 225–241.

SALOP, S. C., 1979, 'Strategic Entry Deterrence', *American Economic Review*, Papers and Proceedings, Vol. 69, No. 2, pp. 335–338.

SCHERER, F. M., 1980, *Industrial Market Structure and Economic Performance*, 2nd edition (Rand McNally).

SHAW, R. W. and SIMPSON, P., 1985, 'The Monopolies Commission and the Process of Competition', *Fiscal Studies*, Vol. 6, No. 1 (February), pp. 82–96.

SIEGEL, S., 1956, *Non Parametric Statistics for the Behavioral Sciences* (McGraw-Hill).

WORCESTER, D. A., 1957, 'Why Dominant Firms Decline', *Journal of Political Economy*, Vol. 65, No. 4, pp. 338–346.

THE JOURNAL OF INDUSTRIAL ECONOMICS 0022–1821 $2.00
Volume XXXIV June 1986 No. 4

THE RELATIONSHIP BETWEEN PLANT SCALE AND PRODUCT DIVERSITY IN CANADIAN MANUFACTURING INDUSTRIES*

JOHN R. BALDWIN AND PAUL K. GORECKI

When multiproduct plant economies exist, plant size and diversity decisions are closely linked. The disadvantage of small plant size can be offset by product-packing. The paper shows that within 4-digit industries, larger plant size is associated with greater product diversity. Then a cross-sectional regression at the 4-digit level indicates that Canadian plant size relative to an estimate of US *MES* is related positively to industry measures of average plant diversity. This suggests that inherent plant scale disadvantages in small economies such as Canada are offset by product-packing.

I. INTRODUCTION

PRODUCTIVITY DIFFERENCES between Canadian and US manufacturing industries are commonly attributed to smaller Canadian plant scale and excessive product diversity at the plant level. Unfortunately, there are few studies that satisfactorily indicate the extent to which Canadian plants suffer a significant scale disadvantage or that examine the determinants of the disadvantage. Because of data unavailability, most studies of Canadian plant scale problems either have concentrated on only a few industries,[1] have had to predict the values of missing observations,[2] or have focused on Canada alone without setting its scale disadvantages in an international context.[3] Studies of plant diversity are also few because of the difficulty of getting extensive data. They have either relied on qualitative evidence[4] or have had to define diversity at the plant level as arising only when products from different 4-digit industries were combined in one plant,[5] thereby ignoring within-industry product diversity. In this paper, we use a newly developed data base that overcomes some of these problems.

* The work reported here was supported by the Economic Council of Canada and the Institute for Economic Research at Queen's University. The views in this paper are those of the authors alone and do not necessarily reflect those of the Economic Council of Canada. The data base used could not have been constructed without the efforts of J. McVey of Statistics Canada and R. E. Caves of Harvard University. Helpful comments were received by an anonymous reviewer and L. J. White.

[1] Bain [1966], Eastman and Stykolt [1967], Scherer *et al.* [1975], Gorecki [1976].

[2] Caves *et al.* [1980].

[3] Dickson [1979] and Gupta [1979].

[4] Daly *et al.* [1968].

[5] Caves [1975], discussed in Gorecki [1980].

Previous work on plant scale and diversity generally fails to link together the two strands of what must be a simultaneous production decision. A firm's decisions as to number of products, length of production run per product, and number of plants have to be made jointly. Those studies that focus on plant size, however, examine only one aspect of structure that is likely to have an important bearing on the efficiency of an industry. In this study we take a first step in examining the interrelationships between the various decision variables and look at the manner in which the diversification strategy affects the plant size decision.

II. THE RELATIONSHIP BETWEEN THE PLANT DIVERSITY AND THE PLANT SCALE DECISION

In differentiated product markets, firms face potential tradeoffs between satisfying a variety of different tastes at higher unit costs (if they cannot fully exploit production-run length economies), and producing longer production runs of fewer varieties at lower unit costs. The variety of goods chosen and the average length of product run will depend on the elasticity of demand for each product and the nature of the cost curve—in particular upon the extent to which multi-product economies exist at the plant level. Firms operating in smaller markets are presumed to have a particularly difficult choice to make because demand for individual products may be so inelastic that profit maximization does not yield an *MES* plant size if only one product is manufactured. In this case, multi-product economies could lead to product packing at the plant level.

Most traditional discussions of the plant diversity decision start by postulating a fixed cost associated with the plant and with the product line.[6] Thus, product packing may reduce average cost—provided the effect of spreading plant fixed cost across more output is not offset by higher product line fixed costs. Agglomeration diseconomies occur if the addition of product lines increases the product line fixed cost, perhaps because of coordination problems. On the other hand, agglomeration economies exist if there are savings in these fixed costs as more products are combined in one plant. In the first case, agglomeration diseconomies will not necessarily eliminate the advantages of combining products together in one plant—but they may limit the number of products that it makes sense to combine. In the second case, agglomeration economies reinforce the cost advantage of a diversified product line at the plant level.

Recently the literature on natural monopoly has developed more precise definitions of the characteristics of the production process that make production of several products in a single plant less costly than production in several

[6] See Caves *et al.* [1980, pp. 205–206].

separate plants[7]—a condition referred to as cost-subadditivity.[8] Here, multi-product economies arise from more than just sharing plant fixed costs. They also exist if there is a type of cost complementarity that reduces individual product marginal costs when additional products are added.[9] In this case, the *MES* plant for the multi-product plant can conceivably be less than single product plant *MES*; and the minimum unit cost achieved by an *MES* plant in each case may differ—with the multi-product plant minimum average cost lying above or below the single product plant *MES*.

III. AN INTRA-INDUSTRY ANALYSIS OF THE RELATIONSHIP BETWEEN PRODUCT DIVERSITY AND PLANT SCALE

Plant diversity is difficult to study because of the lack of data at the plant level on number of products produced. Using a new set of data on the size distribution of ICC (Industrial Commodity Classification) products produced per plant, we construct a Herfindahl index of plant diversity that uses the shares of sales of each ICC product produced per plant. The index varies inversely with diversity. We measure this index at both the 4- and 5-digit ICC (*PHERF4D*, *PHERF5D*) for each plant. Across the 167 4-digit SIC industries into which the Canadian manufacturing sector is divided, there are 6126 5-digit ICC products and 2336 4-digit products.

We are interested in the extent to which plants grow larger by adding more products or by extending the production-run length of each product. Total output or size of plant is, of course, just average production run-length multiplied by number of products. Thus the three concepts are linked via an identity. Nevertheless, asking whether plants grow larger by adding product lines rather than just by expanding production-run length provides a partial answer to the existence of multi-product economies.

Caves and Porter [1977] have stressed that there is likely to be a range of strategies followed by different firms in an industry. If plants get larger over the smaller size ranges by both adding product lines and by increasing production-run length, it may be concluded that diversity is being used to exploit multi-product economies. If increased diversity is not used beyond a certain size, then it may be concluded that these economies are exhausted. If production-run length continues to grow as plants get even larger, there is the presumption that production-run length economies eventually dominate. Small market size then can be costly since product packing is used to exploit plant scale economies at the expense of production-run length economies

[7] See Sharkey [1982].

[8] The concept is often referred to as 'economies of scope'. However scope economies are only a necessary condition for cost-subadditivity. The latter requires that no other reallocation (splitting off only part of a product line) reduces total costs.

[9] See Sharkey [1982, p. 69].

TABLE I

REGRESSION RESULTS OF PLANT SIZE, OWNERSHIP AND MULTI-PLANT OPERATIONS ON PLANT DIVERSITY FOR EACH OF 75 CANADIAN 4-DIGIT MANUFACTURING INDUSTRIES, 1970: A SUMMARY

Independent[d] Variable Regressor[d]	*Number of Regression Coefficients*			
	Positive		*Negative*	
	Significant[a]	*Insignificant*	*Significant*[a]	*Insignificant*
TSH				
PHERF4D[b]	2	20	25	28
PHERF5D[b]	4	12	27	32
TSHSQ[e]				
PHERF4D[b]	15	36	5	19
PHERF5D[b]	19	34	3	19
NOEST				
PHERF4D[b]	8	28	8	31
PHERF5D[b]	7	34	9	25
OCON[c]				
PHERF4D[b]	2	30	5	19
PHERF5D[b]	1	30	6	17
USCON[c]				
PHERF4D[b]	11	37	3	22
PHERF5D[b]	8	38	2	25

Notes:

[a] At 0.10 level, using a one-tailed test.

[b] The corresponding regressand variable.

[c] In some instances there are no observations for *OCON* and/or *USCON*. In these cases the regression equation is estimated without *OCON* and/or *USCON*. Hence summing across the row for these two variables need not sum to 75.

[d] Variables: *PHERF4D*—the Herfindahl index of plant diversity using the 4-digit ICC
PHERF5D—the Herfindahl index of plant diversity using the 5-digit ICC
TSH—plant size measured in dollars
TSHSQ—*TSH* squared
NOEST—number of establishments possessed by the owning enterprise
OCON—dummy variable for ownership by non-resident, non-US firm
USCON—dummy variable for ownership by US firms.

[e] Generally significant coefficients on *TSHSQ* were always accompanied by a significant coefficient on *TSH*; moreover they were almost always opposite in sign.

Source: Baldwin and Gorecki [1983b] based on Statistics Canada, Special Tabulations.

that in a larger market would be fully exploited by longer production-run length across a small number of products per plant.

In order to investigate the relationship between diversity and average plant size within an industry, we regressed our diversity index (*PHERF4D*, *PHERF5D*), which varies inversely with plant level diversity, on plant size (*TSH*), plant size squared (*TSHSQ*), the extent to which the plant's owning enterprise was a multi-plant firm (*NOEST*) and foreign ownership dummies for each industry (*OCON*—ownership by a non-resident, non-US firm, and *USCON*—ownership by a US firm). The signs and significance of the coefficients for 1970 in 75 4-digit industries where there are sufficient data for the regressions are reported in Table I.[10]

The most interesting result is that diversity increases as plant size increases. When diversity has a significant coefficient, it is generally negative.[11] The regression results for average production-run length (not reported here)[12] show that it too increases with average plant size—where production-run length is defined as the plant size divided by the Herfindahl numbers equivalent of products produced. Plants therefore get larger both by including more products and by increasing production-run length. In most industries, the rate at which diversity increases declines with size (a positive sign on *TSHSQ*), thereby suggesting that multi-product economies that encourage product diversity are eventually exhausted.[13]

IV. AN INTER-INDUSTRY ANALYSIS OF THE EFFECT OF DIVERSITY ON INDUSTRY AVERAGE PLANT SIZE

Introduction

Diversification at the plant level can be used to reduce the scale disadvantages of small plants. But it may do so at a cost. While diversification at the plant level potentially allows for cost savings, the resulting plant cost curves will not necessarily be the same as a plant that is more specialized but has the same level of sales. Using the framework adopted by Lyons [1980] for a somewhat different purpose, we argue that diversity should affect the branching decisions of a firm and therefore average plant size.

Lyons argues that the size of a firm where branching occurs provides important information about the *MES*. He assumes that the long run average cost curve of operating one plant and two plants (with diversity held constant) are represented by *US1* and *US2* respectively in Figure 1. *MES* output is at S^* and $US1 = US2$ at Q^* where $Q^* = 2S^*$. Each firm of a given size Q^j is assumed to have a probability of operating a single plant that depends upon the size of the difference between *US1* and *US2*. When the unit costs of operating one as opposed to two plants are equal ($US1 = US2$), a

[10] We performed the same regression for 1979 but the results were similar and are therefore not reported here. See Baldwin and Gorecki [1983b].

[11] Since there is a degree of simultaneity between the plant size and diversity decisions, these OLS results suffer from a potential estimation problem. The covariance between the error and plant size is likely to be positive. A random disturbance that increases *PHERF* increases specialization and for a given size allows product line economies to be exploited without any loss of plant economies; this in turn reduces costs and should allow an expansion in plant size. Thus the bias will be positive. This strengthens the finding that the predominant relationship found in the sample was negative—that plant diversity increases with plant size.

[12] See Baldwin and Gorecki [1983b].

[13] For those industries with a significant coefficient on *TSHSQ*, the minimum point on the parabola (the maximum level of diversity) is achieved in almost all cases for a plant size that falls between the average of the entire distribution and the average of the largest eight establishments

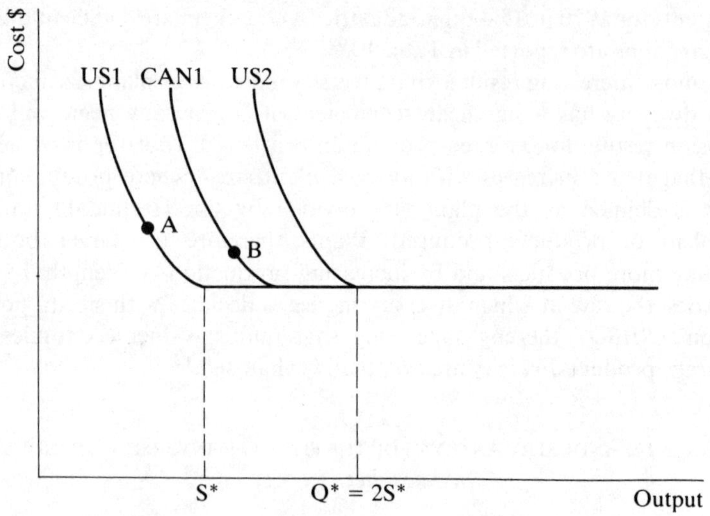

Figure 1
The Average Cost Curve and the Branching Decision

Note: *US1* is average cost for single plant firm producing $n1$ products
US2 is the average cost for a two plant firm producing $n1$ products
CAN1 is the average cost for a single plant producing $n2$ products: $n2 > n1$

firm is assumed to be indifferent to operating one or two plants. Using these assumptions, Lyons shows that if the size of firm where, on average, 1.5 plants are operated by each firm is calculated (Q), an estimate of *MES* can be derived as $Q/2$.

This technique can be modified to examine the effect of diversity on the branching decision and therefore on the average plant size. Plant cost curves will not be the same for plants that differ in the diversity of products produced. The nature of the multi-product economies will determine the position of the cost curve of a more diversified plant relative to that of a less diversified plant with the same total sales level. If multi-product economies exist only because of shared plant fixed costs and there are constant fixed costs per product line, then, while the average cost curve of the more diversified plant may approach the same asymptote, it will do so for a larger volume of output than for a plant that specializes in only one product line.[14] Thus *MES* is not independent of diversity.

[14] The assumptions of a plant fixed cost of d, a product line fixed cost of a, and a constant marginal cost per product line of b yield a plant cost curve of

$$TC = d + Na + bQ$$

where N is number of products, Q is output, and TC is total costs. Thus average cost can be written

$$AC = b + \frac{aN + d}{Q}.$$

One representation of the effects of diversity on plant average costs is presented in Figure 1. *CAN1* is the average cost of a firm that differs from that of *US1* only because it is more diversified—it has more products in its single plant. If the cost curve has a constant marginal cost per product line, fixed costs per product invariant to the number of products, and a fixed plant cost, it can be demonstrated that *CAN1* will lie above *US1* over small ranges of output but will approach the same asymptote to the right of S^*.[15] A firm in a small market facing an inelastic demand for heterogeneous goods may find it desirable to choose a point *B* on *CAN1* to a point *A* on *US1* even though this shifts the unit cost curve up.

Firms that operate with unit cost curves like *US1* are more likely to be found in large markets where sales of each product line are sufficiently large to exploit plant *MES* without product packing. Since the US market is some ten times the size of the Canadian market, it is reasonable to presume that cost curves like *US1* will dominate that market and curves like *CAN1* will dominate the Canadian market, where there are multi-product economies. Using the same rationale as did Lyons, this in turn suggests that Canadian firms should branch somewhat later than the US when diversity is high.

In order to examine the effect of diversity upon Canadian plant scale, we calculate the ratio (*RELBRNCH1*) of Canadian average plant size to the branching estimate of *MES* (*BMES*) derived from US data. Then, we examine the determinants of *RELBRNCH1*. Although, as indicated, the size of plant and diversity decisions are jointly determined, we attempt to isolate the effect of the latter by including it as one of the explanatory variables. Additional regressors are used to pick up other influences that are posited to affect relative size—some of which might also be expected to affect directly or indirectly some of the parallel adjustment of in-plant diversity. However, with the inclusion of the latter variable, this effect should be netted out and their coefficients should measure their remaining impact on relative plant size.

There are other candidates from the plant size distribution that could be chosen for comparison to the US *BMES*—such as the median or top-half average plant size. The mean is chosen partially because it is heavily influenced by the large tail of smaller plants in the plant size distribution and it is here that we expect the most product-packing. The median and the top-half average plant size may be sufficiently large that the diversity effect will not be operative because multi-product economies are fully exploited. Whether this is the case is an empirical issue, and we also calculate a second relative scale measure *RELBRNCH2* (the ratio of the average size of the top half of the Canadian plant size distribution to the US *BMES*).

[15] $CAN1 = \dfrac{d+N_2 a}{Q}+b$. $US1 = \dfrac{d+N_1 a}{Q}+b$. $CAN1 > US1$ if $Q < \infty$ and $N_2 > N_1$. It should be noted that the cost curve used here for illustrative purposes is an approximation to that drawn in Figure 1; since it never allows the asymptote to be reached and therefore potentially never allows the Lyons' estimate of *MES* to be derived.

TABLE II
VARIABLE DEFINITIONS

RELBRNCH1	The ratio of Canadian average plant size to the US branching *MES* estimate, both measured in terms of wage and salary earners.
RELBRNCH2	The ratio of the average size of the largest Canadian plants accounting for the top 50 percent of industry employment to the US branching *MES* estimate, both measured in terms of wage and salary earners.
SIZE(+)	The number of Canadian wage and salary earners in the industry divided by the US branching estimate of *MES*.
CON (−)	The reciprocal of the difference between the four firm concentration ratio and four times *CMES* divided by sales (where *CMES* is the average size of the largest Canadian plants that account for the top 50 percent of employment).
DIV (−)	The weighted average of plant diversity, measured as *PHERF4D* (defined in notes to Table I), where the weights are the plant's share of industry sales.
RELSPEC (−)	The relative Canada/US primary product specialization ratio. The specialization ratio is the proportion of sales of plants assigned to an industry accounted for by products that are primary to the industry.
INDIV (+)	The percentage of shipments in an industry that comes from plants that are owned by multi-industry enterprises.
ERP (+)	The effective rate of tariff protection.
IMP (−)	The ratio of the level of imports to domestic disappearance (shipments minus exports plus imports).
CA (−)	The comparative advantage of an industry as revealed by trade flows. It is defined as exports minus imports, divided by the sum of exports plus imports.
FOR (−)	The proportion of sales of an industry that are accounted for by foreign-controlled firms.
CDR1(?)	The ratio of value added per manhour of the smallest plants accounting for 50 percent of industry employment divided by value added per manhour for the largest plants, accounting for 50 percent of industry employment, all multiplied by a dummy variable set equal to one where market size divided by *MES* is less than its median and 0 otherwise. *MES* here is the average plant size of the top half of the plant size distribution.

The regression model

An explanation of relative Canadian average plant size should include regressors that determine the central tendency of the distribution of plant sizes and the extent to which the distribution of plant sizes is skewed one way or the other. Variables designed to capture these factors are defined in Table II together with their expected relationship with *RELBRNCH1* and *RELBRNCH2*.

The central tendency of the plant size distribution will depend not only on the plant average cost curve (*APC*) but also on the average distribution cost curve (*ADC*).[16] *ADC* is usually assumed to be increasing in *Q* because greater output levels must serve less dense or less enthusiastic markets and therefore incur higher average distribution costs (which can be interpreted to include both transportation and selling expenditures).[17] The optimal size plant

[16] See Scherer *et al.* [1975].

[17] See Scherer *et al.* [1975, pp. 23–24, and 88–89] for a more detailed discussion of the relationship between market density and the slope of *ADC*.

(*MOS*) depends not only on the curvature of *APC* but also of *ADC*.[18] The steeper the *ADC* curve, the greater will be the amount by which the *MOS* falls below that size of plant that would just minimize plant average production costs (*MES*).

Three diversity variables are included as regressors which are hypothesized to affect the *APC* curve—*DIV*, *RELSPEC*, and *INDIV*. *DIV* measures average plant level diversity. Higher levels of *DIV* imply greater plant specialization and therefore, in accordance with the previous argument, its coefficient is hypothesized to be negative.[19] *DIV* may not entirely capture the notion of product line diversity since it does not measure the degree to which a plant may produce products classified to several different industries. Given the way the census classifies products to a particular industry,[20] fixed or coordination costs are likely to be higher when products from different industries are combined in a single plant. We hypothesize that the specialization ratio, which measures the extent to which a plant produces products assigned to the industry, will be inversely related to these costs. Therefore we include the relative Canada/US specialization ratio (*RELSPEC*). It should be inversely related to *RELBRNCH*.

The third diversity variable (*INDIV*) measures the extent of inward and outbound diversity in an industry. It is used to capture unobserved opportunities for multi-product economies that *DIV* and *RELSPEC* only imperfectly measure.[21] Both of these use only the *ICC* commodity classification and a finer breakdown would probably show greater variance in diversity across industries. But a finer measure is not available, and in its place we use *INDIV*. If there are opportunities for multi-product economies, a firm in industry *i* may respond either by packing more products into its plants or by building plants in other industries. It will probably follow both strategies. If *INDIV* varies with unobserved opportunities to attain multi-product economies, then a high value tells us that multi-industry enterprises in industry *i* enjoy diversification opportunities that they have exploited both by enlarging their plants and by acquiring plants in other industries. With

[18] See Scherer *et al.* [1975].

[19] If multi-product economies arise from cost complementarities that affect individual product line marginal costs, the branching decision for the diversified firm may be no different than for the specialized firm. Thus an insignificant coefficient on *DIV* may not indicate that multi-product economies are non-existent, but that they take a form that is different from that specified in what has been referred to here as the 'traditional' discussion of this phenomenon.

[20] Using supply side criteria such as similarity of production processes.

[21] Two points should be noted. First, it might be argued that outbound diversification rather than inbound diversification would more closely approximate this phenomenon. An experiment with alternate formulations of the *INDIV* variable turned up no significant differences so the two industry level diversification measures were combined. Second, in estimating *INDIV* all of a plant's output is classified to its primary industry so that *INDIV* is not picking up the same factors as *RELSPEC*. In other words, a multi-industry enterprise must own plants classified to at least two separate industries.

DIV and *RELSPEC* held constant, *INDIV* therefore should be associated with larger plant size and have a positive sign.

Three trade variables (*ERP*, *IMP*, *CA*) are hypothesized to affect the position of the average production cost curve. Several models exist which suggest there is a relationship between the degree of product variety and the extent of trade.[22] They predict that in protected markets, more products with small volume and higher fixed costs per line will be produced than under conditions of free trade. Thus, with higher levels of protection, the same level of diversity (*DIV*) is likely to be associated with a product combination that involves a higher level of fixed costs (associated with a number of products with relatively high fixed costs per line). This in turn would be associated with a plant *MES* in Figure 1 that is further to the right. It is therefore hypothesized that tariff rates (*ERP*) will have a positive sign, and import levels will have a negative sign. A comparative advantage variable (*CA*) is also included. Where an industry is able to compete in world markets, it is unlikely to have packed products together with relatively high unit costs per line to obtain plant scale economies. Therefore *CA* is expected to have a negative coefficient.

Foreign ownership (*FOR*) is also included as a regressor because of its possible impact on the plant *APC* curve. Foreign firms' plants may not have the same level of fixed costs associated with plant operations as domestically-owned firms if they can call upon engineering expertise or other management skills from their foreign parent. A given level of diversity (*DIV*) may therefore not be associated with as high a level of product line fixed costs and plant *MES* may be reached sooner. *FOR* is expected to have a negative coefficient.

We also include two variables that are hypothesized to affect the average distribution cost (*ADC*) curve. These are the size (*SIZE*)[23] and the concentration (*CON*) of Canadian markets. The larger is the market, the greater will be the density and the lower will be the slope of the *ADC* curve.[24] The *CON* variable captures the residual effect of those determinants of concentration other than the size of the minimum efficient-sized plant.[25] *RELBRNCH* should be positively related to *CON* since, given market size, higher concentration is achieved either by greater multi-plant operations or greater than

[22] Snape [1977] and Krugman [1980].

[23] The size of the Canadian market is defined not in relative terms *vis-à-vis* the US market, but in terms of number of units of *MES* plants. The latter more appropriately reflects the measure of density that is hypothesized to be an important determinant of the slope of *ADC*.

[24] Since diversity is also included as a regressor, the effect of market size or concentration on *RELBRNCH* via its effect on diversity has already been incorporated. Thus their effect on relative plant size should be felt through their influence on the slope of *ADC*, not the position of *APC*.

[25] *MES* is here defined as the size of the larger plants and not *BMES* because otherwise *CON* would measure not only the residual effects other than plant size that determine concentration but also the effects that determine the difference between large firm plant size and *BMES*.

MES plants by the larger firms.[26] Because of its construction it bears an inverse relationship to concentration and its expected sign is negative.[27]

Previous variables are assumed to affect the central tendency of the plant size distribution. We also include a variable *CDR1* that is expected to influence the shape of the distribution. Where there are substantial returns to scale, unless competition is weak, small plants will be eliminated. Thus the lower tail of the size distribution will be reduced, and average plant size should be higher. *CDR1* is defined as the ratio of value added per worker of small plants divided by that of large plants—in markets that are small relative to *MES*.[28] The interaction term is used since our earlier work found relative value-added per worker to be a poor proxy for scale effects where markets were large relative to *MES*.[29]

Since *CDR1* is inversely related to the cost disadvantage ratio, then to the extent that the cost disadvantage of small firms is positively related to the diversification incentive, *CDR1* should have a negative effect on *RELBRNCH*. However, it must be recognized that the variable *CDR1* may be small where, because of a lack of competition, small firms with a cost disadvantage are not eliminated from the market. In this case, *CDR1* would have a positive coefficient.[30]

The regression results

The regressions for both *RELBRNCH1* and *RELBRNCH2*[31] were estimated

[26] The effect of greater than *MES* plants is clearly positive. In addition, the greater the degree of multi-plant operations, the smaller will be the market radius served by each plant. The slope of the unit transport curve is a positive function of the radius of each sub-market [Scherer *et al.*, 1975, pp. 23–24]. Thus a multi-plant operation may be presumed to have an *ADC* curve with a lower slope.

[27] Two other variables that might affect the extent of market segmentation and thus influence *RELBRNCH* through their effect on the *ADC* were also included. They were research and development intensity and the advertising/sales ratio. Neither turned out to be significant, and they were dropped from the results reported here. One explanation for their lack of significance may be that they are determinants of the extent to which high concentration results even when *MES* relative to market size is small and therefore their effects have already been captured by *CON*.

[28] Fuss and Gupta [1981] show the conditions under which this measure represents scale economies. In some accompanying work we correlated this measure with scale estimates derived from production function regressions and, for a different sample of industries than was used here, found there to be a positive correlation.

[29] See Baldwin and Gorecki [1983a].

[30] Other variables were also constructed to capture the ability of small firms (plants) to coexist with larger ones. The capital/labour ratio and a coefficient of variation for net profits divided by sales were also included. Neither proved significant.

[31] We also had a measure of the median plant size but measured in sales not employment. Use of an average sales/employment ratio to proxy median plant size in terms of employees produced too many aberrant observations and therefore this variable was not used in the regressions.

TABLE III
THE DETERMINANTS OF *RELBRNCH1* AND *RELBRNCH2* FOR 33 CANADIAN MANUFACTURING INDUSTRIES, 1970

	RELBRNCH1			*RELBRNCH2*		
VARIABLE	*BETA COEFF.*	$\lvert t \rvert$	*SIGNIF.*	*BETA COEFF.*	$\lvert t \rvert$	*SIGNIF.*
SIZE	0.59	3.87	0.001	0.47	2.49	0.021
CON	0.05	0.37	0.717	−0.27	1.61	0.121
DIV	−0.20	1.81	0.082	−0.26	1.92	0.068
RELSPEC	−0.26	2.33	0.029	−0.38	2.73	0.012
INDIV	0.45	2.38	0.027	0.52	2.24	0.036
ERP	0.31	2.87	0.009	0.06	0.47	0.646
IMP	0.05	0.41	0.689	−0.01	0.10	0.925
CA	−0.10	0.70	0.490	−0.16	0.90	0.378
FOR	0.02	0.02	0.982	−0.03	0.18	0.858
CDR1	0.08	0.56	0.584	0.21	1.12	0.274
R^2	0.72			0.57		
$F(10,22)$	9.04			5.20		
RELBRNCH Mean	0.97			3.90		

Note: For each variable the table presents its estimated beta regression coefficient (*COEFF*), its *t*-statistic, and level of significance, using a two-tailed test (*SIGNIF*).
Source: Statistics Canada. Special Tabulations.

using OLS[32] on a sample of 33 industries.[33] The means of *RELBRNCH1* and *RELBRNCH2* for our sample were 0.97 and 3.90. Full details of the sample of industries and other data problems may be found in Baldwin and Gorecki [1983a], [1983b] and the data appendix to this paper. Not all of the independent variables specified above are included in the reported regression equations. Those excluded proved to be insignificant. Table III presents the estimated beta coefficients, their *t*-statistics and the significance of each coefficient. Beta coefficients come from standardizing all variables such that they have zero means and unit variance. They are reported since we have no inherent interest in the absolute value of the coefficients and they permit comparison of the relative importance of the regressors both within each equation and across the two equations where the dependent variable takes on

[32] We employ OLS for two reasons; first, its robust character in the face of specification bias; second, the observation that OLS cross-section results (Caves *et al.* [1980]) using Canadian manufacturing sector data were largely unaffected by using TSLS as opposed to OLS. Moreover, we predict that any simultaneous bias with the key diversity variable will be zero or negative, thereby strengthening the reported results. An error perturbation that increases Canadian average plant size is most likely to be a transitory component arising from unexpected sales and will not affect the choice of number of products produced. It will affect the weights of the Herfindahl used to estimate *DIV* but this effect is of second order importance and is as likely to have a positive or negative effect depending upon whether it is those products with the largest or smallest shares whose sales have increased.

[33] Regression results for both the A and B sample together were similar to those for A. See Appendix for description of these samples.

a different mean value. The significance levels reported are the levels that would have to be adopted in order to reject the null hypotheses that the parameter is zero when a two-tailed test is used. A variable will be taken as significant if the significance level is 5 percent or below.

The regression results reported in Table III are remarkably similar for *RELBRNCH1* and *RELBRNCH2*, both in terms of the size of the beta coefficients and their significance.[34] The dominant variable is market size (*SIZE*) with a positive coefficient. Residual concentration (*CON*) is not significant in either formulation although its sign is correct for *RELBRNCH2* and its significance level is 12 percent. Thus it is the interaction between market size and plant economies (as caught by *SIZE*) rather than the relative multi-plant nature of large firms (as caught by *CON*) that significantly affects average Canadian plant size relative to *BMES*.

The diversity variables (*DIV*, *RELSPEC*, and *INDIV*) have the predicted signs and are generally significant. The greater is average plant diversity (the smaller is *DIV*), the greater is relative Canadian plant size. The smaller is the relative Canada–US specialization ratio, the larger is relative Canadian plant size. The greater the inward and outward bound industry diversity (*INDIV*), the larger is relative Canadian plant size. Plant diversity *DIV* has just as great a proportional effect on *RELBRNCH2* as on *RELBRNCH1*. The effects of plant diversity, contrary to our expectations, are thus felt across much of the plant size distribution.

The trade variables have the predicted sign though only the tariff rate (*ERP*) was significant and then only for *RELBRNCH1*.[35] Thus the tariff rate affects the incentive to product pack primarily in the lower half of the size distribution.[36]

Neither foreign ownership (*FOR*) nor the scale economy proxy (*CDR1*) is significant. Moreover, *CDR1* has a positive, not a negative, sign. However, it should be noted that the cost disadvantage ratio (*CDR1*) is positively correlated with *INDIV*. The removal of inward and outward bound industry diversity from the regression makes *CDR1* significant. This suggests that one of the ways in which the cost disadvantage of small plants relative to large may be reduced is via multi-industry diversification.

[34] One of the problems with the Lyons *MES* estimate is that it may be misleading in an industry which is somewhat heterogeneous. The steel industry, for example, has a relatively small *BMES* because of a number of specialty plants that are not representatives of the average plant. Therefore, we arbitrarily chose to omit those industries where *RELBRNCH1* was greater than 1 on the grounds that these industries probably produced misleading estimates of *MES* using the Lyons technique. The regression results for this smaller sample were essentially the same as those reported in Table III.

[35] A reviewer points out *CA* may be insignificant because its effect may already be caught by the *SIZE* variable.

[36] Baldwin and Gorecki [1983a]. We experimented with an interaction term between high tariffs and high concentration but had to remove it because of the extremely high degree of multicollinearity between this variable and *ERP* in our sample.

V. CONCLUSIONS

In the past, there has been no attempt to measure the relationship between product diversity at the plant level and the extent of suboptimal plant scale. This paper has shown that higher plant scale is associated with higher plant diversity. Both the direct and indirect measures of product diversity have the effect expected.[37] The results suggest that conclusions about efficiency of the manufacturing sector based on such measures as relative scale or plant diversity need to be cautiously drawn. Average plant scale can be large because of the type of diversity brought about by costly tariff protection, yet this is hardly a desirable outcome *per se*. Diversity may be high in a small country, but it serves to increase plant size, thereby exploiting possible multi-product economies of scale. Our conclusion is that the scale-diversity nexus is a complex one and requires further work before efficiency conclusions can be drawn about excessive levels of diversity in a small country such as Canada.[38]

ACCEPTED OCTOBER 1985

JOHN R. BALDWIN,
Department of Economics,
Queen's University,
Kingston, Ontario,
Canada.

PAUL K. GORECKI,
Economic Council of Canada,
Ottawa, Ontario,
Canada.

APPENDIX

THE DATA

The data were taken from a data base that was developed to compare matched Canadian and US manufacturing industries at the Canadian 4-digit SIC level. Comprehensive industry census of manufacturers' data and other industry characteristics are available for Canada for 1970 and for the US for 1972. Details of most variables used as explanatory regressors can be found in Baldwin and Gorecki [1983a], [1983b] with supplementary information available directly from the authors. In addition to the variables outlined therein, the needs of the study required the estimation of the US branching *MES*(*BMES*) and a new concordance to match Canadian and US industries because of the data base used to generate *BMES*.

BMES is calculated from the US Bureau of Census', *Enterprise Statistics* [1977]. *BMES* is calculated as half the size (measured in terms of employees) of the firm that has on average 1.5 plants per firm. This value is calculated by taking a linear interpolation of the means of the size classes that bracket the desired value of 1.5

[37] We performed the same regressions for *RELBRNCH1* and *RELBRNCH2* calculated for the late seventies. The results were broadly similar to those reported here.

[38] For a traditional view about excessive levels of diversity, see Canada [1978].

plants per firm. We followed Lyons [1980] when problems with this technique arose—in 12 of 115 cases.

In order to compare Canadian average plant size to US *BMES*, the US and the Canadian data are matched via a specially constructed concordance that matched the industry definitions in the US *Enterprise Statistics* to the US 4-digit SIC level and then to the Canadian Department of Industry, Trade and Commerce [1971] concordance between Canadian 4-digit census industries and matching US census industries. Not all matchings were regarded as equally good. Therefore, the concordances were separated into those which we felt were reasonably good (A)—some 33; those which were not quite as good (B)—another 20; and the remainder (C)—another 15.

The estimate of *BMES* is derived in terms of number of total employees. When different US enterprise industry categories and Canadian 4-digit SIC census industries had to be combined, the relative size of employment in each of the subcategories was used as weights.

REFERENCES

BAIN, J., 1966, *International Differences in Industrial Structure* (Yale University Press, New Haven).

BALDWIN, J. and GORECKI, P., 1983a, *Trade, Tariffs and Relative Plant Scale in Canadian Manufacturing Industries 1970–1979*, Economic Council of Canada Discussion Paper No. 232 (Ottawa).

BALDWIN, J. and GORECKI, P., 1983b, *Trade, Tariffs, Product Diversity and Length of Production Run in Canadian Manufacturing Industries: 1970–1979*, Economic Council of Canada Discussion Paper No. 247 (Ottawa).

CANADA, DEPARTMENT OF INDUSTRY, TRADE AND COMMERCE, 1971, *Comparative Tables of Principal Statistics and Ratios for Selected Manufacturing Industries: Canada and the United States, 1967, 1963, and 1958* (Department of Industry, Trade and Commerce, Ottawa).

CANADA, *Report of the Royal Commission on Corporate Concentration*, 1978 (Ministry of Supply and Services, Ottawa).

CAVES, R. E., 1975, *Diversification, Foreign Investment, and Scale in North American Manufacturing Industries* (Information Canada, Ottawa).

CAVES, R. E. and PORTER, M., 1977, 'From Entry Barriers to Mobility Barriers', *Quarterly Journal of Economics*, 91, 2, pp. 241–261.

CAVES, R. E., PORTER, M. E. and SPENCE, A. M. with SCOTT, J. T., 1980, *Competition in the Open Economy* (Harvard University Press, Cambridge, Mass.).

DALY, D. J., KEYS, B. A. and SPENCE, E. J., 1968, *Scale and Specialization in Canadian Manufacturing*, Economic Council of Canada Staff Study No. 21 (Queen's Printer, Ottawa).

DICKSON, V. A., 1979, 'Sub-optimal Capacity and Market Structure in Canadian Industry', *Southern Economic Journal*, 46, 1, pp. 206–217.

EASTMAN, H. and STYKOLT, S., 1967, *The Tariff and Competition in Canada* (Macmillan of Canada, Toronto).

FUSS, M. and GUPTA, V. K., 1981, 'A Cost Function Approach to the Estimation of Minimum Efficient Scale, Returns to Scale, and Suboptimal Capacity: With an Application to Canadian Manufacturing', *European Economic Review*, 15, 2, pp. 123–135.

GORECKI, P., 1976, *Economies of Scale and Efficient Plant Size in Canadian Manufacturing Industries* (Department of Consumer and Corporate Affairs, Ottawa).

GORECKI, P., 1980, 'A Problem of Measurement from Plants to Enterprises in the

Analysis of Diversification: A Note', *Journal of Industrial Economics*, 28, 3, pp. 327–334.
GUPTA, V. K., 1979, 'Sub-optimal Capacity and its Determinants in Canadian Manufacturing Industries', *Review of Economics and Statistics*, 61, 4, pp. 506–512.
KRUGMAN, P., 1980, 'Scale Economies, Product Differentiation and the Pattern of Trade', *American Economic Review*, 70, 5, pp. 950–959.
LYONS, B. R., 1980, 'A New Measure of Minimum Efficient Plant Size in U.K. Manufacturing Industries', *Economica*, 47, 1, pp. 19–34.
PORTER, M. E., 1974, 'Consumer Behaviour, Retailer Power and Market Performance in Consumer Goods Industries', *Review of Economics and Statistics*, 56, 4, pp. 419–436.
SCHERER, F. M., BECKENSTEIN, A., KAUFER, E. and MURPHY, R. D. with BOURGEON-MAASSEN, F., 1975, *The Economics of Multi-Plant Operation: An International Comparisons Study* (Harvard University Press, Cambridge, Mass.).
SHARKEY, W. W., 1982, *The Theory of Natural Monopoly* (Cambridge University Press, New York).
SNAPE, R., 1977, 'Trade Policy in the Presence of Economies of Scale and Product Variety', *Economic Record*, 53, 144, pp. 525–534.
U.S. BUREAU OF THE CENSUS, 1977, *Enterprise Statistics 1972* (U.S. Government Printing Office, Washington, DC).
U.S. BUREAU OF THE CENSUS, 1975, *Census of Manufacturers 1972* (U.S. Government Printing Office, Washington, DC).

THE JOURNAL OF INDUSTRIAL ECONOMICS 0022–1821 $2.00
Volume XXXIV June 1986 No. 4

THE CYCLICAL BEHAVIOUR OF MANUFACTURING PRICES IN A SMALL OPEN ECONOMY*

DIRK J. FRANTZEN

This paper presents a disaggregated regression study of the cyclicality of the mark-up over costs in Belgian manufacturing industry. This is found to be low, reflecting a great reluctance on the part of price setters to adjust prices to uncertain market signals. This appears to be especially the case for exporters when compared with firms active on the domestic market. Exporters face greater uncertainty because their competitors are less well-known, and their market shares tend to be smaller, implying a higher variance of industry sales estimates.

I. INTRODUCTION

THE MOST systematic empirical studies on the behaviour of manufacturing prices in relation to costs concern the domestic sectors of the UK and the US, and show that, on average, price-direct cost margins are rather rigid with respect to short-term fluctuations in demand. In the case of the UK the evidence presented by Godley and Nordhaus [1972], Coutts, Godley and Nordhaus [1978], and Domberger [1979] supports the 'normal price hypothesis', both at an aggregate and at a more disaggregated level. According to this view prices are set with a mark-up over direct unit costs calculated at normal level of output. This mark-up covers normal unit overhead costs and allows a profit margin which is consistent with expected long run conditions of demand. It is, however, not adjusted in the face of random or temporary fluctuations in demand.[1] The results of Eckstein and Wyss [1972] lead to a similar conclusion for a majority of manufacturing industries in the US,

* This paper has greatly benefited from discussions on the subject with K. J. Coutts, W. A. Godley and P. Sylos-Labini, as well as from helpful comments by D. Hay and two anonymous referees. It was also made possible by the Institut de Recherches Economiques et Sociales of the University of Louvain-la-Neuve, the Nationaal Instituut voor de Statistiek and the Nationale Bank van België, who have given access to unpublished data. The views reported here do not necessarily reflect those of the above persons or institutions.

[1] It should be noted that this does not imply that the margins between prices and actual unit direct costs do not show any pro-cyclical variation. They most probably do, but only to the extent that pro-cyclical fluctuations in labour productivity make actual costs diverge from normal costs. As argued by Coutts, Godley and Nordhaus [1978], the suggestion by certain critics such as Rushdy and Lund [1967] and Laidler and Parkin [1975] that firms may in fact set prices with respect to actual unit costs and adjust their mark-up somewhat in a pro-cyclical manner with respect to short-term fluctuations in demand is rather unconvincing since there is no clear reason why, if this were the case, they would do so systematically and precisely to offset the effect of productivity fluctuations. The important point, though, is that even in the case of actual price adjustments, these would not be very important.

although here some show a pro-cyclical adjustment of the normal mark-up, and a few even occasionally an anti-cyclical adjustment.

The most common explanation of the evidence in manufacturing industry of a low degree of cyclical price flexibility in relation to direct costs is the dominance of oligopolistic markets. These are characterized by uncertainties about conjectural variations and mutual mistrust of motives and actions which lead firms to adopt uniform pricing rules such as normal pricing which are mutually acceptable. Indeed, since all firms are aware of direct input price changes, changes in direct unit normal costs tend to be viewed as a more objective criterion for adjusting output prices than short-term fluctuations in industry demand which are much more difficult to perceive. Moreover, the application of normal pricing is also consistent with limit pricing since the mark-up can be chosen to limit new firm entry and its stability during upswings deliberately maintained for the same reasons.[2]

The present study concentrates on the manufacturing industry of Belgium, a much smaller and more open economy than the US and the UK. An interesting question is whether, and to what extent, the existence of much stronger foreign competition is likely to lead to different conclusions.

A widespread view in the macroeconomic literature concerned with the international transmission of inflation between open economies is that, in the absence of impediments to trade and insulating exchange rate movements, commodity arbitrage tends to integrate their respective national markets for internationally tradable goods into a single international competitive market by eliminating all price divergences (in common currency). The tradable goods industries of the individual small economy can then be conceived of as perfectly competitive international price takers.[3] Although the proponents of this view admit that its formulation in terms of a traditional Walrasian framework has to be viewed as a limiting case to which the system tends, they still argue that the adjustment is sufficiently rapid to find an empirical dominance of foreign price influences over domestic costs, as well as a relatively high degree of price flexibility with respect to short-term fluctuations in (international) demand.[4]

This view does not, however, appear very plausible in the case of manufacturing products since there is no logical reason why these should be more standardized when produced in an open rather than closed economy context. For most of these commodities the degree of product differentiation is still likely to be such that there are only a limited number of actual or potential competitors, suggesting the prevalence of essentially oligopolistic markets. The main difference with the closed economy case is probably that now some

[2] See on this Sylos-Labini [1962], for instance.

[3] This view has been most commonly expressed in the monetarist writings on the international transmission of inflation.

[4] See especially Swoboda [1977].

of these competitors are based in different countries, or have even a multinational character.[5]

In fact, as far as short-term pricing behaviour is concerned, the existence of somewhat more important differences in cost structures between firms (because certain costs such as labour costs are essentially determined at a national level) is likely, if anything, to increase the degree of uncertainty concerning competitors' reactions. In the absence of explicit price co-ordination or price fixing (which tends to occur only in the most concentrated industries), risk aversion will lead to highly kinked demand curves.[6] Not only are firms under such circumstances likely to be highly reluctant to adjust prices to short-term fluctuations in demand, but, moreover, they will always take account of their foreign price constraints while shifting changes in normal direct costs.[7] We would thus still expect to find, on average, rather sticky prices with respect to both domestic and foreign short-term demand, although there are likely to be significant foreign price influences.

The existing empirical literature on price formation in small open economies is mostly exclusively concerned with the issue of the relative importance of foreign prices and domestic costs. Systematic studies in this respect such as Calmfors and Herin [1979] for Sweden, and Huveneers [1981] and van Poeck and Pauwels [1980] for Belgium, have shown that although there are significant foreign price influences in the case of a majority of industries, this is also the case for direct costs. This would suggest an intermediate picture between the extremes of perfect independent price setting and foreign price following.

Unfortunately, hardly any attention has been given to the nature of these foreign price influences, and to the directly related issue of price-cost margin flexibility with respect to short-term fluctuations in demand. To our know-

[5] Estimates of the degree of industry concentration could, in principle, provide explicit evidence in this respect. These have, however, to be computed at a relevant international (and especially European) market level—studies making use of domestically based measures such as van Lommel and de Brabander [1976], Pagopoulos and Sorensen [1976], Jacquemin, de Ghellinck and Huveneers [1980], and Huveneers [1981] having shown that these are of no help at all in explaining Belgian industrial price-cost margins. Problems of data comparability have unfortunately up till now prevented us from obtaining adequate measures at such an international market level.

[6] For a formal demonstration of the way in which such risk aversion has an effect comparable to that of actual asymmetrical reactions by competitors leading to a kinked demand curve, see Drèze [1979].

[7] It is interesting to note that this argument is of the same flavour as that used by Domberger [1979] to explain the possible existence of an inverse relation between the size and speed of short-term price adjustments to changes in normal costs and the level of industry concentration in British manufacturing. This can in his eyes be explained by the fact that the costs of search and communication among sellers are higher in less concentrated oligopolies, hereby making the co-ordination of price adjustments more difficult. A similar argument has also been used by Qualls [1979] to explain why price-cost margins are, if anything, even less pro-cyclical in less concentrated manufacturing industries in the US.

ledge, only one study, by Buijink and Vandoorne [1980], has up till now analysed the degree of cyclicality of the mark-up (for total output prices) in Belgian industry, and its conclusions are largely against the existence of such cyclicality. Certain problems of model specification and data use may, however, have somewhat biased the results.

The present study provides clearer evidence in this respect. Specific models are considered for analysing the respective issues of mark-up cyclicality and foreign price dependence, and the relation between both is analysed. Further, domestic and export prices are considered independently as the latter may possibly be even less flexible in view of the greater degree of uncertainty existing on the export markets. This is likely to be so because, even more than on the domestic markets, the competitors will tend to be foreign and thus less well-known. Moreover, the fact that the market shares of exporters tend to be smaller will make the variances of their industry sales estimates larger, and thus increase the difficulty in differentiating changes caused by variations in industry demand from those caused by changes in market shares.[8] Finally, the data used are quarterly, as far as possible, allowing more refined specifications.

The industries considered are: Textiles (*TX*), Steel (*ST*), Non Ferrous Metals (*NF*), Leather (*LE*), Chemicals (*CH*), Paper (*PA*), Non Metallic Minerals (*NM*), Cars (*CR*), and Mechanical Engineering (*ME*). The precise codification in terms of the NACE commodity classification is presented in the appendix, and the period of investigation is 1964–1978.

II. THE MODELS

A model aimed at measuring the influence of short-term demand on the mark-up of prices over costs should combine at least a relevant cost term with a cyclical variable representing short-term demand among the explanatory variables. Assuming the prevalence of oligopolistic markets, the choice of a measure of unit direct costs measured with reference to a normal level of activity (rather than actual) appears most appropriate since normal pricing is the most common type of pricing strategy followed by price setters under such circumstances. In an open economy context such as the Belgian one, account should, moreover, be taken of the existence of possible foreign price influences, since domestic products may be insufficiently differentiated from foreign substitutes, and domestic price setters may feel foreign price constrained in the determination of their mark-up.

A price equation including foreign prices as well as costs and cyclical

[8] For a formal argument along these lines explaining why oligopolists with smaller market shares may even be more cautious in their short-term price adjustments than those with larger market shares, and may in the limit even be prepared to behave merely as oligopolistic price followers rather than as actual price setters, see Eckhard [1982].

demand among the explanatory variables is, however, likely to be highly deceptive for the purpose of assessing the degree of cyclicality of the mark-up over costs, since there is likely to be strong multicollinearity between foreign prices and those costs determined on the world market (such as material input costs), and also between foreign prices and (foreign) cyclical demand to the extent that this is significant.

A more appropriate procedure is to consider two separate models which respectively do and do not include foreign prices, and in conjunction to consider the respective results of estimation. The estimates of the former model can be viewed as giving an idea of the implied degree of cyclicality of the mark-up, while those of the latter clarify the extent to which this is affected by foreign price influences.

In practice, normalization of unit direct costs is performed in this study by replacing actual by trend values of labour productivity. In the case of material input costs such productivity (or real output per unit input) series are unfortunately missing so that it is hoped that secular changes are caught by the trend factor of the models.

Further, allowance should be made for dynamic delays between prices and costs, the most plausible explanation being the existence of so-called gestation lags. The evidence presented by Coutts, Godley and Nordhaus [1978] suggests that in the UK a substantial number of firms continue to use historic or average cost input valuation methods, despite the acceleration in inflation since the late 1960s. Under the former method the rate at which cost changes are transmitted into prices is directly determined by the time spent in production, while under the latter, it depends upon the rate of change of the total value of stocks.

In Belgium, however, resistance by the accounting profession to the introduction of so-called current or replacement cost accounting techniques has been much weaker. This is not surprising in view of the low level of vertical integration of most Belgian manufacturing industries which implies far shorter production periods than in the UK (estimates vary between 0.7 and 1.7 quarters for the industries under consideration in the present study). Under such circumstances, firms will perceive much more rapidly that their costs have changed and their profitability is falling than those firms whose output has a longer production period. We would thus expect that, to the extent that they are able to shift their normal unit costs, the majority of Belgian firms will tend to use replacement cost valuation methods.[9] Explicit evidence in this respect is provided by a comparison of the statistical performance of unit normal cost series valued on the respective historic, average and replacement cost basis. Estimates of the production period and the corresponding gestation lags in case of historic and average cost valuation

[9] For a comparable argument, see Domberger [1983], for instance.

were obtained on grounds of the stock/sales ratio and the composition of inputs in a manner similar to that used in Coutts, Godley and Nordhaus [1978]. They are presented in Table A.I of the Appendix and their respective derivation is available from the author and will be supplied if requested.

As far as short-term demand is concerned, care should be taken to consider cyclical variables that reflect both the actual market and a larger relevant international market—the relative importance of which depends on the degree of product differentiation with respect to foreign competition. Moreover, when export and domestic prices are considered separately, account should be taken each time of both export and domestic cycles, since firms may be active on both markets and may reallocate sales depending on profit opportunities.

Even if it were possible to obtain adequate cyclical variables at either level, their simultaneous inclusion would most likely lead to serious problems of multicollinearity. In practice, data constraints suggest that a measure based on the total output cycle is most suitable for this purpose (as it is perfectly matched commodity-wise, and to some extent it catches the domestic as well as the export cycle and, through the latter, also the foreign cycle).[10]

Just as in the case of costs, allowance should be made for lags in the effect of cyclical demand. Here the most plausible explanation is the existence of recognition and adjustment lags under conditions of uncertainty. These will not only reflect the costs of price adjustment due to competitor reactions, but also, as stressed by the search literature, due to customer reactions. These are likely to be especially high if it concerns industrial buyers who favour price stability to facilitate financing and scheduling production over time.[11] There are, however, no clearcut *a priori* expectations concerning the shape of the lag patterns, so that they have to be estimated directly from the data.

As with other studies on the subject, the major problem in the case of foreign competitors' prices is one of data availability. Taking product correspondence as the main criterion, adequate measures (based on competing imports) could be obtained only for four of the nine industries under consideration. This implies that, whereas estimation of the cyclicality of the mark-up over costs could be performed for all industries, we had to concentrate on only these four in the case of the relative elasticity of foreign

[10] Preliminary experiments with specific measures of foreign cyclical demand (based on a weighted average of the outputs of the major foreign competitors) showed these to be totally insignificant. There are, however, serious doubts on the level of product correspondence at the level of aggregation under consideration.

[11] See on this Okun [1981] who presents an elegant theoretical analysis of the manner in which costly search under conditions of uncertainty makes customers willing to pay a premium to do business with customary suppliers.

prices.[12] As in the case of cyclical demand, and for similar reasons, allowance should be made for lags on foreign prices.

The models can then be formulated as follows:

$$(1) \qquad \Delta p_t = \beta \Delta c_t + \sum_{i=0}^{n} \gamma_i \Delta\left(\frac{x}{\hat{x}}\right)_{t-i} + \delta$$

$$(2) \qquad \Delta p_t = \sum_{i=0}^{n} \alpha_i \Delta pw_{t-i} + \beta \Delta c_t + \sum_{i=0}^{n} \gamma_i \Delta\left(\frac{x}{\hat{x}}\right)_{t-i} + \delta$$

where all variables are expressed in logarithms,

Δ stands for first difference,

t stands for the average value over the current quarter,

p is the output price, total, export or domestic,

c is the normal unit direct cost under either Replacement, Average, or Historic cost pricing,

pw is the average foreign competitors' price expressed in Belgian Francs,

$\frac{x}{\hat{x}}$ is the deviation from the trend of real output, used as a cyclical variable.

Several points deserve elaboration:

(a) The expression in first differences implies that the time trend is caught by the intercept.

(b) Some controversy exists on whether the demand variable should be expressed in terms of changes, rather than in terms of levels. We believe that it should, since the specification of demand in terms of levels would imply rather implausibly that prices will rise relative to cost indefinitely so long as capacity utilization is high; and even less plausibly, that prices will fall forever relative to costs (with perpetually falling profit margins) if output is at all below, though not falling relative to trend.[13]

However, while making our preferences clear, we have for completeness repeated our tests on the following models:

$$(1)' \qquad \Delta p_t = \beta \Delta c_t + \sum_{i=0}^{n} \gamma_i \left(\frac{x}{\hat{x}}\right)_{t-i} + \delta$$

[12] In the case of export prices, the use of such a measure implies possibly some bias, even though the fact that foreign competitors in Belgium's major export markets (the adjacent countries) are essentially the same as those on the home market (West Germany and France) suggests that it is probably rather modest. If bias there is, it is probably mainly caused by the omission of foreign competing home prices. In any case, experimentation with alternative measures based on geographically-matched average unit values of competing exports on Belgium's major export markets (derived from UN international trade statistics) showed that these performed much worse, and the same is true for German export list prices—the most likely explanation being a much weaker product correspondence.

[13] Our position on this issue is comparable to that of Coutts, Godley and Nordhaus [1978] in their answer to Laidler and Parkin [1975] who favour a specification of demand in terms of levels.

$$(2)' \qquad \Delta p_t = \sum_{i=0}^{n} \alpha_i \Delta pw_{t-i} + \beta \Delta c_t + \sum_{i=0}^{n} \gamma_i \left(\frac{x}{\hat{x}}\right)_{t-i} + \delta$$

where demand is expressed in terms of levels, and

$$(1)'' \qquad p_t = \beta c_t + \sum_{i=0}^{n} \gamma_i \left(\frac{x}{\hat{x}}\right)_{t-i} + \zeta t + \delta$$

$$(2)'' \qquad p_t = \sum_{i=0}^{n} \alpha_i pw_{t-i} + \beta c_t + \sum_{i=0}^{n} \gamma_i \left(\frac{x}{\hat{x}}\right)_{t-i} + \zeta t + \delta$$

where all variables are expressed in levels and the time trend is introduced explicitly.

(c) Although at first sight there may be some question about the exogeneity of output-based cyclical demand variables, because the price setting firms could conceivably make price and quantity decisions simultaneously, this is not in fact thought to be very realistic. As stressed by modern fix-price/rationing theory, the typical oligopolistic price setter is likely to face very different constraints on the frequency of possible price and quantity adjustments (conditioned by information and technology), and it may be more useful to view the short-term disequilibrium adjustment processes as being of a sequential nature. Moreover, the choice of a quarterly time unit appears appropriate in this respect, as it can be viewed as sufficiently short in relation to the likely fixed price period, thereby minimizing the risk of simultaneity bias.[14]

Estimation

The models are specific in terms of the possible lag profiles between prices and costs, which are a function of the length of the production period. Although unconstrained in principle, the lags on foreign prices and cyclical demand are nevertheless supposed to be finite. Intuitive plausibility suggests that, in a broad sense, the periods of production can also be used here as a point of reference. As estimates suggest that these vary between 0.702 and 1.782 quarters, it is difficult to conceive of recognition or adjustment lags on foreign prices and cyclical demand well in excess of one year. In fact, preliminary estimation has shown that there is no evidence of significant three or more quarterly lagged terms. It was therefore decided to constrain the maximum length to two quarters (by setting $n = 2$ in the models).

The next step in the estimation process was to select the most representative type of cost valuation procedure for the respective industries. This was done on grounds of statistical fit. These most representative models were then subjected to tests on the significance of the respective variables.

[14] See on this Winters [1981], for instance.

All estimation is performed by means of a maximum likelihood method allowing for first-order serial correlation on the error term. The hypothesis testing procedures used are respectively the t-test (for the tests of individual significance) and the likelihood ratio test (for the tests of joint significance).[15,16] The measure of goodness of fit employed for selecting the cost valuation methods is the coefficient of determination $\overline{Ru}^2$, based on the untransformed rather than transformed residuals in the case of serial correlation, because our interest is in the contribution of the determining variables.[17]

Tables I, II, III and IV present the results of estimation for export and domestic prices for the preferred specifications (1) and (2) under the most representative cost valuation strategies.

In all tables the parameter estimates (with the corresponding t-values underneath are followed respectively by the cost valuation procedure concerned (CV), the $\overline{Ru}^2$-value, and the Durbin Watson statistic (DW). Moreover, Tables I and II present the test-statistic of the likelihood ratio test on the joint insignificance of the cyclical terms ($\gamma_0 = 0$, $\gamma_1 = 0$, $\gamma_2 = 0$), and the proportion $\gamma/(1+\gamma)$ where $\gamma = \sum_{i=0}^{2} \gamma_i$. The latter proportion provides an approximation of the fraction of changes in nominal demand that ends up in prices—as opposed to $1-\gamma/(1+\gamma)$, the fraction that ends up in quantities. Tables III and IV present the test-statistic on the joint insignificance of the foreign price terms ($\alpha_0 = 0$, $\alpha_1 = 0$, $\alpha_2 = 0$) as well as of the cyclical terms, and proportions $\alpha/(\alpha+\beta)$ and $\gamma/(1+\gamma)$ where $\alpha = \sum_{i=0}^{2} \alpha_i$. The tests of significance on the cyclical terms in model (2) and the estimates of proportion

[15] The maximum likelihood method used is an iterative procedure developed by Beach and MacKinnon [1978]. The test statistic of the likelihood ratio test on a set of linear constraints is, for its part, given by minus twice the logarithm of the ratio of the likelihoods of the respective constrained and unconstrained estimates, and its asymptotic distribution is χ^2 with a number of degrees of freedom equal to the number of constraints considered.

[16] Note that in view of the multicollinearity between the respective unconstrained lag coefficients of the cyclical terms and of foreign prices, estimation was also performed by means of the Almon method. As there was, however, no significant difference in terms of mean lags, concentration is aimed exclusively on the unconstrained estimates.

[17] Although there were only 30% cases of significant serial correlation, it was thought useful to investigate whether the actual dynamic process involved did not concern some kind of partial adjustment process, which could conceivably be rationalized in terms of adjustment lags as mentioned above. The models were thus extended by adding a partial adjustment scheme between actual and desired prices (where the latter were determined by our present models), and likelihood ratio tests were performed on the respective hypotheses of significant partial adjustment and first order serial correlation. For all but two commodities the acceptance pattern for serial correlation did not change, however, whereas it showed systematic rejection in the case of partial adjustment. In the case of the latter two commodities (export Leather and domestic Textiles) it was not possible to differentiate between them on statistical grounds since both serial correlation and partial adjustment were found insignificant individually, but the hypothesis of their joint insignificance was rejected. Even for these, the partial adjustment interpretation appeared, however, highly questionable in view of the implausible length of the implied mean lags. In what follows, concentration is thus aimed exclusively on the results of our original models.

TABLE I

EXPORT PRICES/MODEL (1): $\Delta p_t = \beta \Delta c_t + \sum_{i=0}^{2} \gamma_i \Delta\left(\frac{x}{\hat{x}}\right)_{t-i} + \delta$

Variables	Δc_t	$\Delta\left(\frac{x}{\hat{x}}\right)_t$	$\Delta\left(\frac{x}{\hat{x}}\right)_{t-1}$	$\Delta\left(\frac{x}{\hat{x}}\right)_{t-2}$	int.				LR	$\frac{\gamma}{1+\gamma}$
Coefficients	β	γ_0	γ_1	γ_2	δ	CV	$\overline{Ru}^2$	DW	$\gamma = 0$	
TX	0.796	0.010	0.042	0.048	−0.004	A	0.66	1.98	2.92[a]	0.09
	(8.330)	(0.130)	(0.388)	(0.563)	(−2.347)					
ST	0.748	0.169	0.140	0.169	−0.001	R	0.57	1.62	13.24[r]	0.32
	(4.142)	(2.067)	(1.659)	(2.026)	(−0.112)					
NF	0.587	0.188	0.073	0.294	0.001	R	0.76	1.97	9.55[r]	0.35
	(11.475)	(1.093)	(0.360)	(1.811)	(0.235)					
LE	0.797	0.200	−0.134	0.302	−0.003	R	0.31	2.06	2.01[a]	0.26
	(4.151)	(0.643)	(−0.317)	(0.960)	(−5.98)					
CH	1.094	0.030	0.045	0.045	−0.004	R	0.48	2.09	1.73[a]	0.10
	(10.873)	(0.207)	(0.213)	(0.313)	(−1.629)					
PA	(1.148)	0.185	−0.185	0.365	−0.004	R	0.67	1.99	13.78[r]	0.26
	(10.204)	(1.780)	(−1.464)	(3.451)	(−1.672)					
NM	0.330	−0.001	−0.030	0.030	0.004	H	0.20	1.96	0.44[a]	0.00
	(2.210)	(−0.018)	(−0.458)	(0.484)	(1.419)					
CR	0.458	−0.099			0.031		0.38	1.62	0.81[a]	−0.10
	(3.226)	(−0.798)			(3.864)					
ME	0.636	−0.214			0.023		0.41	1.61	3.66[a]	−0.27
	(2.873)	(−1.509)			(1.980)					
Average										0.11

TABLE II

DOMESTIC PRICES/MODEL (1): $\Delta p_t = \beta \Delta c_t + \sum_{i=0}^{2} \gamma_i \Delta\left(\frac{x}{\hat{x}}\right)_{t-i} + \delta$

Variables	Δc_t	$\Delta\left(\frac{x}{\hat{x}}\right)_t$	$\Delta\left(\frac{x}{\hat{x}}\right)_{t-1}$	$\Delta\left(\frac{x}{\hat{x}}\right)_{t-2}$	*int.*				*LR*	$\frac{\gamma}{1+\gamma}$
Coefficients	β	γ_0	γ_1	γ_2	δ	*CV*	$\overline{Ru^2}$	*DW*	$\gamma = 0$	
TX	0.432	0.014	0.104	0.125	0.005	*A*	0.63	2.01	12.30[r]	0.20
	(4.106)	(0.239)	(1.519)	(1.930)	(2.314)					
ST	0.672	0.189	0.157	0.129	0.001	*R*	0.42	1.79	7.97[r]	0.32
	(2.623)	(1.753)	(1.177)	(1.028)	(0.104)					
NF	0.649	0.079	0.291	0.031	0.003	*R*	0.55	1.86	7.93[r]	0.29
	(7.815)	(0.279)	(1.849)	(0.110)	(0.356)					
LE	0.574	0.222	−0.079	0.223	0.010	*R*	0.22	1.68	1.44[a]	0.27
	(3.251)	(0.789)	(−0.236)	(0.793)	(1.245)					
CH	0.615	0.085	−0.085	0.111	0.002	*R*	0.36	2.03	1.39[a]	0.10
	(6.448)	(0.690)	(−0.512)	(0.915)	(1.055)					
PA	1.390	0.271	−0.288	0.408	−0.005	*R*	0.63	1.98	8.70[r]	0.28
	(9.937)	(1.422)	(−1.206)	(2.144)	(−1.474)					
NM	0.535	0.029	0.114	−0.007	0.008	*H*	0.22	1.80	2.42[a]	0.12
	(3.052)	(0.365)	(1.430)	(−0.089)	(2.388)					
CR	0.408	−0.064			0.026		0.58	2.07	0.80[a]	−0.06
	(4.572)	(−0.813)			(4.966)					
ME	0.849	0.154			0.029		0.56	1.46	1.49[a]	0.13
	(4.177)	(1.121)			(2.693)					
Average										0.18

TABLE III

EXPORT PRICES/MODEL (2): $\Delta p_t = \sum_{i=0}^{2} \alpha_i \Delta pw_{t-i} + \beta \Delta c_t + \sum_{i=0}^{2} \gamma_i \Delta\left(\frac{x}{\hat{x}}\right)_{t-i} + \delta$

Variables	Δpw_t	Δpw_{t-1}	Δpw_{t-2}	Δc_t	$\Delta\left(\frac{x}{\hat{x}}\right)_t$	$\Delta\left(\frac{x}{\hat{x}}\right)_{t-1}$	$\Delta\left(\frac{x}{\hat{x}}\right)_{t-2}$	*int.*				*LR*	$\frac{\alpha}{\alpha+\beta}$	*LR*	$\frac{\gamma}{1+\gamma}$
Coefficients	α_0	α_1	α_2	β	γ_0	γ_1	γ_2	δ	*CV*	$\overline{Ru}^2$	*DW*	$\alpha = 0$		$\gamma = 0$	
TX	0.108	0.315	0.014	0.369	−0.016	0.039	−0.101	0.001	*R*	0.82	1.95	45.15[r]	0.54	1.46[a]	−0.08
	(1.963)	(5.195)	(0.284)	(5.620)	(−0.263)	(0.483)	(−1.026)	(0.523)							
ST	0.503	0.083	−0.030	0.397	0.096	0.089	−0.006	−0.001	*R*	0.76	1.64	23.47[r]	0.58	5.04[a]	0.15
	(5.424)	(1.095)	(−0.383)	(2.429)	(1.283)	(1.163)	(−0.072)	(−0.150)							
NF	0.310	0.101	0.023	0.313	0.074	0.183	0.036	0.001	*R*	0.84	2.10	26.73[r]	0.59	3.79[a]	0.22
	(5.382)	(2.165)	(0.577)	(4.624)	(0.515)	(0.938)	(0.251)	(0.456)							
CR	0.955			−0.137	−0.116			−0.002		0.72	2.08	13.42[r]	1.16	2.43[a]	−0.13
	(3.990)			(−0.776)	(−1.389)			(−0.167)							

TABLE IV

DOMESTIC PRICES/MODEL (2): $\Delta p_t = \sum_{i=0}^{2} \alpha_i \Delta pw_{t-i} + \beta \Delta c_t + \sum_{i=0}^{2} \gamma_i \Delta\left(\frac{x}{\hat{x}}\right)_{t-i} + \delta$

Variables	Δpw_t	Δpw_{t-1}	Δpw_{t-2}	Δc_t	$\Delta\left(\frac{x}{\hat{x}}\right)_t$	$\Delta\left(\frac{x}{\hat{x}}\right)_{t-1}$	$\Delta\left(\frac{x}{\hat{x}}\right)_{t-2}$	*int.*				*LR*	α	*LR*	γ
Coefficients	α_0	α_1	α_2	β	γ_0	γ_1	γ_2	δ	*CV*	$\overline{Ru}^2$	*DW*	$\alpha = 0$	$\alpha+\beta$	$\gamma = 0$	$1+\gamma$
TX	0.147	0.117	0.035	0.307	0.051	0.049	0.052	0.007	*R*	0.74	1.95	12.52[r]	0.49	0.84[a]	0.13
	(2.716)	(2.356)	(0.759)	(2.401)	(0.867)	(0.650)	(0.842)	(4.061)							
ST	0.317	0.001	−0.110	0.484	0.099	0.119	0.082	0.003	*R*	0.46	1.81	7.92[r]	0.30	4.18[a]	0.23
	(1.956)	(0.004)	(−1.539)	(1.700)	(0.765)	(0.885)	(0.610)	(0.409)							
NF	0.568	−0.202	0.078	0.423	0.230	0.226	−0.063	0.286	*R*	0.63	1.94	18.89[r]	0.41	3.67[a]	0.28
	(5.609)	(−1.409)	(1.101)	(1.889)	(0.905)	(0.639)	(−0.254)	(−2.316)							
CR	0.315			0.201	−0.054			0.015		0.62	2.08	3.86[r]	0.61	1.13[a]	−0.05
	(1.884)			(1.884)	(−0.621)			(1.682)							

$\gamma/(1+\gamma)$ allow us to assess the effect of including foreign prices and thus the relative importance of the foreign cycle.

The complete summary distribution of the various tests of significance for total output as well as for export and domestic prices, and for the alternatives as well as for the preferred specifications is presented in Table A.II of the Appendix.

The results can be summarised as follows. Tables I and II show that the coefficients on the cost variables are systematically positive and significant. This suggests that Belgian manufacturing firms are able to shift their normal unit direct costs at least to some extent in the short run. Further, replacement cost appears to be the dominant input valuation method, thereby confirming *a priori* expectations in this respect, in view of the shortness of the production periods which tends to make firms more rapidly aware of falling profitability in times of accelerating cost inflation.

As far as short-term demand is concerned, it is interesting to note first that there is no evidence of cyclical terms with significant negative coefficients. This suggests that there are no cases of 'perverse' anti-cyclical adjustments of the mark-up over normal direct costs which have most commonly been rationalised in the literature by the existence of target pricing (firms attempting to maintain a target profit margin or rate of return in the face of anti-cyclical changes in unit overhead costs).[18] This is not surprising since, to our knowledge, the only conclusive evidence of such target pricing concerns a few highly concentrated industries in the US.[19] Probably the more open character of the European economies prevents the extreme level of co-ordination between firms required for such a behaviour.

The major finding as far as short-term demand is concerned is that there is not much evidence of important pro-cyclical adjustments in the mark-up over normal costs. The likelihood ratio tests on the hypothesis of joint insignificance of the cyclical terms in model (1) show that less than half of the industries (4 out of 9) reject insignificance. This is confirmed by the acceptance pattern of the tests on total output prices and on the alternative models with demand expressed in terms of levels, as presented in Table A.II of the Appendix. A look at proportion $\gamma/(1+\gamma)$ in Tables I and II shows, moreover, that even for the industries where demand is significant the proportion of changes in nominal demand that ends up in prices is low, the estimates being between 10 and 35%; for all 9 industries, the average is only 14%. Further, to the extent that prices are adjusted to cyclical demand, there are, contrary to the case of costs, significant systematic lags.

These results confirm those of the study by Buijink and Vandoorne [1980] which concentrates on yearly total output prices. This is highly comforting

[18] Early theoretical rationalizations of such target pricing behaviour are found in Kalecki [1954] and Weintraub [1958]. More recent formalizations which draw on modern managerial theories of the firm are due to Wood [1975] and Eichner [1976].

[19] See especially Eckstein and Wyss [1972].

since both the models and the data used in the latter study may be subject to criticism, given that the specification used combines demand in terms of levels with cost in terms of rates of change, and given that their measures of material input costs and output prices are not fully independent.[20]

The most plausible explanation for the (on average) low degree of cyclical flexibility of the mark-up over normal direct costs is that, just as in the case of larger economies such as the US and the UK, the markets for Belgian manufacturing products are essentially oligopolistic in nature and characterized by risk aversion with respect to uncertain competitors' reactions. The evidence that the most clearcut short-term adjustments of the mark-up occur specifically in the case of Steel and Non Ferrous Metals is not surprising since these are industries with cyclically sensitive demand which are highly capital intensive, and thus have exceptionally high unit fixed costs and low profits in times of depression. As is well known, such industries are notorious for being prone to occasional breakdown in oligopolistic discipline.[21]

For the industries where model (2) could be estimated, Tables III and IV show that although the coefficients of normal direct costs are still found to be significant (in all but one case), the same is true for foreign competitors' prices. This confirms other studies in this respect such as van Poeck and Pauwels [1980] and Huveneers [1981], and suggests that although the hypothesis of perfect adjustment to foreign prices is rejected, domestic price setters nevertheless feel foreign price constrained in the determination of their mark-up. Another possibility is that at the level of aggregation considered some industry products are characterized by adjustments to foreign prices, others by domestic price setting. The evidence of a clear trade-off between the size of the estimated coefficients of costs and the inclusion of foreign prices suggests, moreover, that an important part of direct normal costs are similar for domestic and foreign competitors. As mentioned above, this is explained by the fact that most material input prices (especially those of raw materials) are by and large determined at the level of competitive world markets.

As far as the cyclical terms are concerned, it is interesting to note that these are found to become totally insignificant (both individually and jointly) upon the inclusion of foreign prices. This suggests that breakdown in price discipline quite naturally involves both domestic and foreign competitors in the industries concerned. It also implies that the measures of demand used reflect quite adequately the relevant foreign cycle.

On the other hand, the fact that even when the cyclical terms are found to be significant the degree of price flexibility is still low and that in a majority

[20] More precisely, Buijink and Vandoorne [1980] make use of the costs of the total material inputs used by the industies and the prices of their total outputs, rather than merely the outsectoral or 'net' inputs bought and outputs sold outside the industries, as required. This is likely to lead to some contamination between material input costs and output prices, and thus to an upward bias in the estimated coefficient of normal costs.

[21] The tendency for oligopolistic discipline to break down in such industries has been clearly exposed in Scherer [1972].

of industries there is no significant cyclical adjustment of the mark-up at all, even though there may be important foreign price influences (such as in the case of Cars), conforms with our assumption of the prevalence of essentially oligopolistic foreign price dependencies rather than competitive price arbitrage. Comparison of the results for export and domestic prices is also interesting in this respect. The elasticity with respect to foreign prices is found to be somewhat higher than the elasticity with respect to costs in the case of export prices, suggesting the existence of stronger foreign price influences on the export markets. Moreover, the elasticity with respect to short-term demand is found to be systematically lower and the mean lags somewhat longer in the case of export prices, suggesting that these are, if anything, even less flexible.[22] This is also consistent with the interpretation of an essentially oligopolistic nature of the foreign price influences, and it reflects the greater uncertainty faced by firms active on foreign markets.

This greater uncertainty is not only explained by the fact that competitors on the export markets are mainly foreign and thus less well known, especially as far as their financial and cost structures are concerned. It is also explained, as mentioned above, by the fact that the market shares of exporters tend to be smaller, implying a higher variance of industry sales estimates, and thus changes in industry demand conditions are more difficult to detect. It is therefore no surprise to find exporters to be somewhat more risk averse and thus more reluctant to adjust prices to variations in domestic costs and sales, than firms active on the domestic market. This also helps to explain why a larger number of exporters may even be prepared to behave merely as oligopolistic foreign price followers, rather than as price setters.

III. CONCLUSIONS

The major conclusion from this disaggregated regression study of the cyclicality of the mark-up over costs of Belgian manufacturing output prices is that, just as in the case of larger and more closed economies such as the US and the UK, the degree of cyclical flexibility of Belgian price-cost-margins appears, on average, very low.

The most plausible explanation is the prevalence of oligopolistic markets characterized by a great reluctance on the part of price setting firms to adjust prices to uncertain market signals, given the risks of direct retaliation by competitors.

The evidence of the existence of significant foreign price influences is best

[22] Although part of the differences between export and domestic prices can be related to differences in measurement (the domestic prices being measured by wholesale list prices while the export prices are measured by transaction unit values), and to slight differences in product coverage, there is no reason to expect systematic differences in a specific direction in the relative contribution of the respective explanatory variables. The behavioural interpretation given appears thus justified.

seen as reflecting the existence of oligopolistic foreign price constraints, rather than the result of competitive commodity arbitrage, as is often assumed. The finding of systematically stronger foreign price influences in the case of export prices when compared to domestic prices, despite an even lower degree of price flexibility, is easy to understand in this light. Exporters facing more intense competition from less well-known foreign competitors and having a poorer insight into industry demand conditions are bound to face greater uncertainty than firms active on the domestic market. They will thus not only be more reluctant to shift domestic costs, but also to adjust prices to temporary changes in demand.

ACCEPTED OCTOBER 1985

DIRK JOSEF FRANTZEN,
Centrum voor Financiële Economie,
Free University of Brussels (VUB)
Pleinlaan 2,
1050 Brussels,
Belgium.

APPENDIX

The data: definition and sources[23]

The code numbers of the industries considered in terms of the NACE classification

TABLE A.I
THE PRODUCTION PERIODS AND THE CORRESPONDING DISTRIBUTED LAGS

Sector and Strategy	Production Period Θ	*Progressively added inputs (ulc)*			*Intial entry inputs*			*Total material inputs (umc)*		
		a,0	*a,1*	*a,2*	*a′,0*	*a′,1*	*a′,2*	*b,0*	*b,1*	*b,3*
TX A	1.787	0.409	0.480	0.111	0.280	0.547	0.173	0.323	0.525	0.152
TX H		0.280	0.547	0.173	0.000	0.213	0.787	0.093	0.324	0.583
ST A	1.067	0.597	0.401	0.002	0.468	0.530	0.002	0.511	0.487	0.002
ST H		0.468	0.530	0.002	0.000	0.923	0.067	0.156	0.798	0.046
NF A	0.702	0.747	0.203	0.000	0.712	0.288	0.000	0.740	0.260	0.000
NF H		0.712	0.288	0.000	0.298	0.702	0.000	0.436	0.564	0.000
LE A	1.613	0.442	0.486	0.072	0.310	0.573	0.117	0.354	0.544	0.102
LE H		0.310	0.573	0.117	0.000	0.387	0.613	0.103	0.449	0.448
CH A	1.410	0.489	0.476	0.035	0.355	0.585	0.060	0.400	0.549	0.051
CH H		0.355	0.585	0.060	0.000	0.590	0.410	0.118	0.588	0.294
PA A	0.960	0.643	0.357	0.000	0.521	0.479	0.000	0.562	0.438	0.000
PA H		0.521	0.479	0.000	0.040	0.960	0.000	0.200	0.800	0.000
NM A	1.100	0.585	0.413	0.002	0.454	0.541	0.005	0.498	0.498	0.004
NM H		0.454	0.541	0.005	0.000	0.900	0.100	0.151	0.780	0.069

[23] The data of the data banks referred to in this section are only published in part in the periodicals listed. More-detailed information concerning the derivation of the series can be made available upon request.

TABLE A.II
SUMMARY DISTRIBUTION OF THE LIKELIHOOD-RATIO TESTS OF SIGNIFICANCE ON THE CYCLICAL VARIABLE

(a) Models excluding foreign prices

	Market			Industry									Specification			
Classification	*Total output*	*Export*	*Domestic*	*TX*	*ST*	*NF*	*CR*	*LE*	*CH*	*PA*	*NM*	*ME*	*(1)*	*(1)′*	*(1)″*	*Total*
Significant +	8	8	12	3	9	9	0	0	0	7	0	0	10	8	10	28
Insignificant +	12	11	13	6	0	0	0	9	8	2	5	6	11	13	12	36
Insignificant –	3	11	3	0	0	0	9	0	1	0	4	3	6	6	5	17
Significant –	0	0	0	0	0	0	0	0	0	0	0	0	0	0	0	0
Total	23	30	28	9	9	9	9	9	9	9	9	9	27	27	27	81

(b) Models including foreign prices

	Market			Industry				Specification			
Classification	*Total output*	*Export*	*Domestic*	*TX*	*ST*	*NF*	*CR*	(2)	(2)′	(2)″	*Total*
Significant +	0	0	0	0	0	0	0	0	0	0	0
Insignificant +	6	6	9	3	9	9	0	7	6	8	21
Insignificant –	6	6	3	6	0	0	9	5	6	4	15
Significant –	0	0	0	0	0	0	0	0	0	0	0
Total	12	12	12	9	9	9	9	12	12	12	36

are: Textiles (TX): 431+432+438+439+455+456; Steel (ST): 221+221 to 223; Non Ferrous Metals (NF): 151+152+212+224; Leather (LE): 441+442+451; Chemicals (CH): 252 to 260; Paper (PA): 471 to 474; Non Metallic Minerals (NM): 231 to 233+239 to 248; Cars (CR): 351 to 353; Mechanical Engineering (ME): 321 to 328.

The domestic output prices considered are the wholesale prices of those products sold domestically, outside the respective industries under consideration. All quarterly series are derived from the monthly data bank of the 'Institut de Recherches Economiques et Sociales' of the University of Louvain (IRES), while the yearly series in the case of CR and ME are those computed by the 'Fédération de l'Industrie des Fabrications Métalliques' (FABRIMETAL).

The export prices are measured by unit values and derived from the quarterly data bank of the 'Nationale Bank van België' (NBB).

The material inputs considered consist of the imported raw materials and half-finished products by the respective industries. Their prices are measured by unit values and, for all but two industries, they are derived from the same source as that for export prices. In the case of ST and NF they are derived directly from the value and quantity statistics published by the 'Nationaal Instituut voor de Statistiek' (NIS).

The foreign competitors' prices considered concern the prices of competing imports. They are measured by unit values and their sources are the same as those for material input prices. As mentioned above, these series could unfortunately only be derived for four of the industries under consideration: TX, ST, NF and CR.

Labour costs cover both gross earnings of operatives and the corresponding social security contributions of employers. They are expressed on an hourly basis and, for all but one industry, LE, their source is the IRES. In the case of the latter industry it is the NIS.

In the same way as with labour costs, labour productivity is also expressed on an hourly basis and its sources are the same. The measure of cyclicality is, for its part, based on the corresponding real output series.

Finally, as far as the estimation of the period of production is concerned, the average yearly value of stocks was derived from NIS data referring to January 1 (by taking the average of successive values under the assumption of a uniform evolution during the year). The quarterly value of sales was, for its part, approximated by (1/4 of) the value of net output given by the 1970 Input–Output table (and by inference for the other years on grounds of output quantity and price indices). The same Input–Output table was used for the estimation of the share of materials in sales.

REFERENCES

BEACH, C. and MACKINNON, J. G., 1978, 'A Maximum Likelihood Procedure for Regression with Autocorrelated Errors', *Econometrica*, 46, pp. 51–58.

BUIJNK, C. and VANDOORNE, M., 1980, 'Een Sectoriële Analyse van het Relatief Belang van Vraag- en Kostenfactoren voor het Prijsverloop in de Belgische Nijverheid (1962–1977)', Working Paper 80/107, CIM, State University Antwerp.

CALMFORS, L. and HERIN, J., 1979, 'Domestic and Foreign Price Influences: a Disaggregated Study for Sweden', in LINDBECK, A. (ed.), *Inflation and Employment in Open Economies* (North-Holland, Amsterdam).

COUTTS, K. J., GODLEY, W. A. H. and NORDHAUS, W. D., 1978, *Industrial Pricing in the United Kingdom* (Cambridge University Press, Cambridge).

DOMBERGER, S., 1979, 'Price Adjustment and Market Structure', *Economic Journal*, 89, pp. 96–108.

DOMBERGER, S., 1983, *Industrial Structure, Pricing and Inflation* (Martin Robertson, Oxford).

DREZE, J. H., 1979, 'Demand Estimation, Risk-aversion and Sticky Prices', *Economic Letters*, 4, pp. 1–6.

ECKHARD, E. W., JR., 1982, 'Firm Market Share, Price Flexibility and Imperfect Information', *Economic Inquiry*, 20, pp. 388–391.

ECKSTEIN, O. and WYSS, D., 1972, 'Industry Price Equations', in ECKSTEIN, O., (ed.), *The Econometrics of Price Determination*, Conference (Washington, DC), pp. 133–155.

EICHNER, A. S., 1976, *The Megacorp and Oligopoly* (Cambridge University Press, Cambridge).

FEDERATION DE L'INDUSTRIE DES FABRICATIONS METALLIQUES, *Recueil Statistique*, various issues.

GODLEY, W. A. H. and NORDHAUS, W. D., 1972, 'Pricing in the Trade Cycle', *Economic Journal*, 82, pp. 853–882.

HUVENEERS, C., 1981, 'Price Formation and the Scope for Oligopolistic Conduct in the Small Open Economy', *Recherches Economiques de Louvain*, 47, pp. 209–242.

JACQUEMIN, A., DE GHELLINCK, E. and HUVENEERS, C., 1980, 'Concentration and Profitability in a Small Open Economy', *Journal of Industrial Economics*, 24, pp. 131–143.

KALECKI, M., 1954, *Theory of Economic Dynamics* (Unwin University Books, London).

LAIDLER, M. and PARKIN, M., 1975, 'Inflation: A Survey', *Economic Journal*, 85, pp. 741–809.

NATIONALE BANK VAN BELGIE, *Tijdschrift van de Nationale Bank van België*, various issues.

NATIONAAL INSTITUUT VOOR DE STATISTIEK, *Industriële Statistieken*, various issues.

NATIONAAL INSTITUUT VOOR DE STATISTIEK, *Maandelijks Bulletin over de Buitenlandse Handel van de Belgisch-Luxemburgse Economische Unie*, various issues.

NATIONAAL INSTITUUT VOOR DE STATISTIEK, *Sociale Statistieken*, various issues.

NATIONAAL INSTITUUT VOOR DE STATISTIEK, *Statistisch Tijdschrift*, various issues.

OKUN, A. M., 1981, *Prices and Quantities. A Macroeconomic Analysis* (Basil Blackwell, Oxford).

PAGOPOULOS, E. and SORENSEN, E., 1976, 'Foreign Trade, Concentration and Profitability', *European Economic Review*, 8, pp. 225–267.

QUALLS, P., 1979, 'Market Structure and Cyclical Flexibility of Price Cost Margins, *The Journal of Business*, 52, pp. 305–325.

RUSHDY, F. and LUND, P., 1967, 'The Effect of Demand on Prices in British Manufacturing Industry', *Review of Economic Studies*, 34, pp. 361–374.

SCHERER, F. M., 1972, *Industrial Pricing* (Rand McNally, Chicago).

SWOBODA, A. K., 1977, 'Monetary Approaches to Worldwide Inflation', in KRAUSE, L. B. and SALANT, W. S. (eds.), *Worldwide Inflation: Theory and Experience* (Brookings Institution, Washington, DC).

SYLOS-LABINI, P., 1962, *Oligopoly and Technical Progress* (Harvard University Press).

VAN LOMMEL, E. and DE BRABANDER, B., 1976, 'Price-cost Margins and Industry Structure in Belgium 1970', mimeo, State University, Antwerp.

VAN POECK, A. and PAUWELS, H., 1980, 'Prijsvorming en Competitiviteitsanalyse: een Voorstudie voor de Belgische Metaalverwerkende Nijverheid', mimeo, St Ignatius University, Antwerp.

WEINTRAUB, S., 1958, *An Approach to the Theory of Income Distribution* (Chilton Co., Philadelphia).

WINTERS, L. A., 1981, *An Econometric Model for the Export Sector* (Cambridge University Press, Cambridge).

WOOD, A., 1975, *A Theory of Profits* (Cambridge University Press, Cambridge).

THE JOURNAL OF INDUSTRIAL ECONOMICS 0022-1821 $2.00
Volume XXXIV June 1986 No. 4

SHIPPING COSTS AND THE CONTROVERSY OVER OPEN REGISTRY*

S. R. TOLOFARI, K. J. BUTTON AND D. E. PITFIELD

Concern with safety in particular has resulted in efforts to phase out open registry of ships. This study employs a transcendental logarithmic framework to highlight some of the cost implications of adopting such a policy in terms of the higher shipping costs which would result. It compares the cost functions of open registry ships with those of ships registered under traditional maritime nations in order to offer some insights into the possible impacts on shipping markets of withdrawing the opportunities for shippers to elect for open registration.

OVER THE past thirty years the share of the World's shipping fleet operating under open registries (OR)[1] has grown from 4% to almost one-third of the total tonnage. While there has been strong opposition based on the costs of maritime disasters and opposition both from the traditional maritime nations (TR), which have suffered erosion of their fleets, and from labour unions, which point to worker exploitation, the shipping companies have found the greater operational and financial flexibility which accompanies open registry to be a considerable attraction. The actual cost advantage of open registration over that of a European flag has been crudely estimated to have fallen from 50% to about 20% over the past decade (Drewry [1984]) but despite this and the financial inducements offered by traditional shipping nations, US and European ship owners are still registering new tonnage and transferring existing capacity to flags of convenience. The current attractions include absence of taxation on shipping revenues, absence of any requirement for equity participation by nationals of the country of registration, lack of legally prescribed minimum manning levels, lack of mandatory legislative requirements for employment of nationals of the ship's flag and a general lack of economic links with the country of registry.

More recently, international agencies, such as UNCTAD [1977], [1979], have become involved in debates about the economic costs and benefits of the open registry system in terms of its impact on the development of national fleets and on World freight rates. Consequently, pressures to phase out open registration have resulted. Apart from cost reasons, the substantial number of

* The authors would like to express their gratitude to two anonymous referees for their extremely constructive comments on an earlier draft.

[1] Open registry permits ships owned by foreigners to register under a 'flag of convenience' of one of a small number of countries (that is Liberia, Panama, Bahamas, Cyprus, Bermuda, and, until 1980, Singapore). Such countries offer very liberal and permissive maritime legislation—see Boczek [1962], Naess [1972], and Sturmey [1984].

highly visible maritime accidents around the World in recent years involving open registry ships has added emotional voice to these institutional pressures.

While policy-makers are currently concerned to remove distortions from the international shipping market, much of the debate to date has relied upon highly aggregated data, anecdotal evidence and the limited number of consultancy reports available—all of which focus on specific case studies (for example International Maritime Associates [1979] and Economics Intelligence Unit [1979]). In particular, debates have tended to be qualitative in nature and there has been no econometric study of the detailed cost differences between the traditional maritime nations and those offering open registry. Metaxas and Doganis [1976] did complete some econometric work looking at differences between the two flag groups but their work is now dated and relied both upon a small sample of ships and an over simplistic log-linear regression framework. (In particular it assumed an underlying Cobb–Douglas technology.) This lack of rigorous, up-to-date analysis would seem a rather serious omission given the possibility that the removal of the open registration option could push up shipping costs significantly.

This paper examines in detail the cost structures associated with international maritime activities and, more specifically, the cost variations which exist between ships operating under open and regulated registry regimes. It makes use of the transcendental logarithmic (translog) cost function, first introduced by Christensen *et al.* [1973] and subsequently taken up in a wide range of transport studies,[2] to circumvent the restrictions inherent in previous studies of the international shipping industry. In particular, it removes the need to make *a priori* assumptions regarding the degree of substitutability and complementarity between factor inputs (of the type required in work using, for example, Cobb–Douglas or CES functions) and also it allows for possible changes in scale effects as output levels vary. Unfortunately for policy-makers, what previous quantitative work there has been in the field of international maritime cost analysis has been forced by data constraints to adopt these more restrictive frameworks with the accompanying caveats which must apply.

I. A MODEL OF SHIPPING COSTS

In shipping, all costs of factors of production (crew costs, repairs and maintenance, stores, spare parts, insurance, etc.) are exogenously determined by the market. Equally, output levels (ton-mileage) are determined by patterns of demand over which operators have no control. Given these conditions, bulk shipping meets the conceptual requirements of neo-classical production theory. It also means that the cost function is more attrac-

[2] See, for instance, Friedlaender and Spady [1981], Caves *et al.* [1980], Caves *et al.* [1981], Caves *et al.* [1984], Harris [1977], Berechman [1983], Williams and Dalal [1981] and Viton [1981].

tive than the primal model for the study of production structures—see Christensen and Greene [1976]. By accepting that effective cost-minimisation management describes the way that the industry operates, a neo-classical cost function can be used to estimate the characteristics of the production technology of bulk shipping services by invoking Shephard's [1953] duality theorem.

The transformation function of a general production structure can be written as

$$(1) \qquad Q = F(X_1, \ldots, X_n)$$

where F is the production function of a single output (Q) and multiple inputs (X_i) firm. If for any level of output, the cost minimising input mix is employed, resulting in a convex input structure, then a cost structure dual to equation (1) exists (see Diewert [1974]),

$$(2) \qquad C_T = G(Q, P_1, \ldots, P_n)$$

where the P_i's represent factor prices and C_T represents total costs. If cost-minimisation is not practised, then the total cost function is invalid (see Caves *et al.* [1981]). However, if the cost minimizing input mix is employed with respect to a subset of the factor inputs (variable inputs) conditional on the level of output and the remaining inputs, then there exists a variable cost function dual to equation (1), *viz.*

$$(3) \qquad C_v = H(Q, P_1, \ldots, P_n, Z_1, \ldots, Z_m)$$

where the Z_i's are fixed or quasi-fixed factors (and $C_v = \sum_{i=1}^{n-m} P_i X_i$). Both total and variable cost functions provide information necessary for inferring the production characteristics of the technology.

The translog function favoured here reflects cost minimisation and is legitimate in the context of the market in which international shipping operates. The function is treated as a second-order local approximation to an arbitrary underlying function. This is because we are interested in the 'typical operator' operating at average cost levels of output within the range of our data. It should be noted, however, that although the function may be treated as a representation of the true cost function, in fact, as Friedlaender and Spady [1981] point out, an approximation interpretation of the translog is inevitable. (For a comprehensive survey of the literature dealing with translog production functions see Chakrabarty [1983].)

The general form of the translog cost function is

$$(4) \qquad \ln C_T = \ln \alpha_0 + \alpha_Q \ln Q + \sum \beta_i \ln P_i + \tfrac{1}{2}\delta(\ln Q)^2 + \tfrac{1}{2}\sum\sum \gamma_{ij} \ln P_i \ln P_j + \sum \rho_{iQ} \ln P_i \ln Q$$

In order for a production function to be well behaved, the cost function must be positive and homogeneous of degree one in prices, which implies that the following restrictions are necessary,

(5) $\sum \beta_i = 1;\ \sum \gamma_{ij} = 0$, for all subscripts j; $\sum \rho_{iQ} = 0$

On the basis of competitive markets for factor inputs then Shephard's lemma implies that the input shares (S_i) can be expressed as the logarithmic partial derivatives of the cost function with respect to factor prices, thus:

(6) $$\frac{\partial \ln C_T}{\partial \ln P_i} = \frac{\partial C_T}{\partial P_i} \cdot \frac{P_i}{C_T} = \frac{P_i X_i}{C} = S_i$$

where X_i is the cost minimising input level of the ith factor required to produce Q units of output.

Once estimated, the parameters of the cost function can be used to derive patterns of factor substitution in the shipping industry. Uzawa [1962] has shown that the Allen partial elasticities of substitution can be derived from the cost function as:

(7) $$\sigma_{ij} = \frac{CC_{ij}}{C_i C_j}$$

where

$$C_i = \frac{\partial C}{\partial P_i};\quad C_{ij} = \frac{\partial^2 C}{\partial^2 P_i \partial P_j};\quad \sigma_{ij} = \sigma_{ji}$$

In terms of the translog function this means:

(8a) $\sigma_{ij} = (\gamma_{ij} + S_i S_j)/S_i S_j;\quad i \neq j$

(8b) $\sigma_{ii} = [\gamma_{ii} + S_i(S_i - 1)]/S_i^2$

The factor price elasticities of demand are then related to the partial elasticities thus:

(9) $E_{ij} = S_i \sigma_{ij}$

with $\sigma_{ij} = \sigma_{ji}$ and $E_{ij} \neq E_{ji}$

II. DATA CONSTRUCTION AND ESTIMATION PROCEDURES

The data relates to 160 ships' characteristics drawn from a survey for 1982. Due to incomplete responses the actual analysis is based on 86 bulk carriers. (Full information on 31 tankers was also received but the sample proved too small to make reasonable distinctions between the flag groups.) Information is available for the five main operating cost categories (manning, repairs and maintenance, lubricating oil and stores, insurance and administration) on a cross-sectional basis and covers European, Japanese and open registry flags. Because of the nature of the information on physical input levels these operating costs were initially aggregated into manning (M), repairs and maintenance (R) and lubrication oil, stores and provisions (S). Given the nature of both insurance and administration, these costs were combined with synthesised data to form capital costs (K). Essentially, insurance is highly dependent upon a ship's hull value whilst administration depends to a large extent on the vessel size as well as the scale of fleet activities. A ship's hull value and size are closely related, so a strong link exists between capital costs, insurance and administration costs. It is also important to note that fuel costs and port charges are not included in the cost function as these are normally borne by the charterer—we are concerned only with the costs falling on the ship owner.

As there was a possibility of relating capital costs to specific vessels, ship owners were unwilling to provide data on the historical values of their fleets—it would have put in question the anonymity agreements under which they supplied information on operating costs. Additionally, even if available, it is questionable whether it would have proved possible to have up-dated these historic values to current, 1982 prices. In consequence, the capital values of ships were synthesised using as a basis a sample of 377 transactions which took place in the second-hand international shipping market in 1982. A linear multiple regression equation was developed relating second-hand values to both the characteristics of the vessels and to an index of freight charter rates at the specific time of sale (so as to encapsulate monthly variations in demand conditions). The regression equation derived was:

$$\begin{aligned} K = {} & 10.2 - 0.506\,\text{age} + 0.000037\,\text{size} - 0.374\,\text{speed} \\ & + 0.0218\,\text{charter index} \qquad R^2 = 0.93 \end{aligned}$$

This equation permitted estimates of the capital costs of the sample fleet to be derived based on the characteristics of the individual vessels under review.

While there is some debate about the appropriate output variable to employ in the study of passenger transportation (Button and O'Donnell [1985]), in freight transport ton-mileage has been unequivocally accepted as the appropriate measure. We employ it here.

Given the data available, and with primes denoting unit prices of the factors involved, the exact specification of the model is given as:

$$\begin{aligned} \text{(10)} \qquad \ln C_T = {} & \alpha_0 + \alpha_Q(\ln Q) + \tfrac{1}{2}\delta(\ln Q)^2 + \beta_1(\ln K') \\ & + \beta_2(\ln M') + \beta_3(\ln R') + \beta_4(\ln S') \\ & + \tfrac{1}{2}\gamma_{KK}(\ln K')^2 + \tfrac{1}{2}\gamma_{MM}(\ln M')^2 + \tfrac{1}{2}\gamma_{RR}(\ln R')^2 \\ & + \tfrac{1}{2}\gamma_{SS}(\ln S')^2 + \gamma_{KM}(\ln K')(\ln M') + \gamma_{KR}(\ln K')(\ln R') \\ & + \gamma_{KS}(\ln K')(\ln S') + \gamma_{MR}(\ln M')(\ln R') + \gamma_{MS}(\ln M')(\ln S') \\ & + \gamma_{RS}(\ln R')(\ln S') + \rho_{KQ}(\ln K')(\ln Q) + \rho_{MQ}(\ln M')(\ln Q) \\ & + \rho_{RQ}(\ln R')(\ln Q) + \rho_{SQ}(\ln S')(\ln Q) + \varepsilon_{CT} \end{aligned}$$

with the associated share equations:

$$\text{(11a)} \quad S_K = \alpha_K + \gamma_{KK}(\ln K') + \gamma_{KM}(\ln M') + \gamma_{KR}(\ln R') + \gamma_{KS}(\ln S') + \rho_{KQ}(\ln Q) + \varepsilon_K$$

$$\text{(11b)} \quad S_M = \alpha_M + \gamma_{MM}(\ln M') + \gamma_{KM}(\ln K') + \gamma_{MR}(\ln R') + \gamma_{MS}(\ln S') + \rho_{MQ}(\ln Q) + \varepsilon_M$$

$$\text{(11c)} \quad S_R = \alpha_R + \gamma_{RR}(\ln R') + \gamma_{KR}(\ln K') + \gamma_{MR}(\ln M') + \gamma_{RS}(\ln S') + \rho_{RQ}(\ln Q) + \varepsilon_R$$

A necessary condition for the cost function to reproduce comparative statics effects at a point of approximation without restrictions across these effects is that it has $(n+1)(n+2)/2$ parameters—see Fuss *et al.* [1979]. With our one output and four input technology this requires 21 parameters to be estimated.

The specification of the translog function requires the approximation be made at a local point—in our case the sample mean of each variable. Normalisation therefore means that $\ln P_i$ and $\ln Q$ in equation (4) become $(\ln P_i - \ln \bar{P}_i)$ and $(\ln Q - \ln \bar{Q})$ respectively.

The cost and share functions are estimated simultaneously as a multivariate regression system with the advantage that, because of the symmetry restrictions across equations, the available degrees of freedom are increased without expanding the number of parameters. Estimation requires the dropping of one share equation, in this case the stores equation, and following Berndt and Christensen [1973], employs Zellner's [1962] iterative Aitken procedure for efficiency reasons. Barten [1969] has shown that the results thus obtained are invariate to the share equation omitted, while Kmenta and Gilbert [1968] and Dhrymes [1973] have proved that the iteration of the Zellner technique until convergence to an identity matrix yields maximum-likelihood estimates. Additionally, Christensen and Greene [1976] have shown such iterations to be a computationally efficient method for obtaining maximum likelihood estimates.

III. RESULTS

The sample of bulk carriers was divided between those with open registry and those registered under a traditional flag in Japan or Europe. The estimates were then made under a variety of assumptions. Model 1 assumed non-homotheticity of the production technology with homogeneity and symmetry restrictions imposed. These restrictions were subsequently supplemented by the imposition of homotheticity in factor inputs (that is, $\sum \rho_{iQ} = 0$)—Model 2—and then by the assumption of linear separability of inputs (that is, $\sum_i \gamma_{ij} = \sum_j \gamma_{ji} = \sum_i \sum_j \gamma_{ij} = 0$)—Model 3. Finally, the Cobb–Douglas tech-

TABLE I
ESTIMATED PARAMETERS OF THE GENERALISED TRANSLOG TOTAL COST FUNCTION FOR BULK CARRIERS (T-RATIOS IN PARENTHESES)

	All Ships	*Traditional Registry*	*Open Registry*
α_O	−0.0591	−0.0585	−0.0306
	(−9.6126)	(−7.2372)	(−8.8921)
α_Q	0.5892	0.5493	0.6769
	(73.3650)	(49.5470)	(62.8860)
δ_{QQ}	0.2057	0.2080	0.1774
	(21.4060)	(17.5110)	(14.8260)
β_K	0.4711	0.4376	0.5510
	(176.8000)	(118.9200)	(145.9000)
β_M	0.3166	0.3442	0.2612
	(81.9980)	(70.7200)	(56.0610)
β_R	0.1461	0.1578	0.1081
	(51.4270)	(44.5320)	(64.9170)
β_S	0.0662	0.0604	0.0798
	(118.3900)	(87.2470)	(116.5300)
γ_{KK}	0.2270	0.2245	0.2294
	(67.6000)	(51.6950)	(38.7630)
γ_{MM}	0.1936	0.2013	0.1714
	(48.8680)	(37.8180)	(37.4760)
γ_{RR}	0.1160	0.1126	0.0797
	(38.9080)	(34.7550)	(22.8380)
γ_{SS}	0.0623	0.0595	0.0739
	(46.5880)	(40.1650)	(31.8810)
γ_{KM}	−0.1335	−0.1380	−0.1320
	(−47.9640)	(−34.3230)	(−31.4160)
γ_{KR}	−0.0643	−0.0602	−0.0515
	(−28.2500)	(−23.6110)	(−15.9740)
γ_{KS}	−0.0292	−0.0263	−0.0459
	(−21.7430)	(−17.0510)	(−16.6010)
γ_{MR}	−0.0393	−0.0412	−0.0198
	(−15.2120)	(−14.4000)	(−7.3751)
γ_{MS}	−0.0208	−0.0221	−0.0196
	(−19.0650)	(−14.4750)	(−10.6900)
γ_{RS}	−0.0123	−0.0112	−0.0083
	(−18.7510)	(−16.2140)	(−5.8887)
ρ_{KQ}	0.1800	0.1813	0.1591
	(40.7670)	(30.5690)	(25.6510)
ρ_{MQ}	−0.1172	−0.1235	−0.1242
	(−23.0050)	(−18.4040)	(−20.0740)
ρ_{RQ}	−0.0951	−0.0898	−0.0594
	(−22.9460)	(−19.5020)	(−13.0180)
ρ_{SQ}	0.0323	0.0319	0.0245
	(29.4670)	(22.9480)	(10.6090)
$\bar{R}^2$:			
Cost Equation	0.9192	0.8968	0.9319
Capital Shares	0.9403	0.9217	0.7968
Manning Shares	0.7458	0.6661	0.7576
Repairs Shares	0.8743	0.8925	0.9339
Log of the Likelihood Function	962.32	675.04	351.11

nology was explored in Model 4 with its assumed homogeneity and unitary elasticity of substitution restrictions, (that is, $\gamma_{ij} = 0$, for all subscripts i, j; $\delta = 0$; $\rho_{iQ} = 0$, for all subscripts i).

For reasons of economy of space only the unrestricted set of parameters, that in fact are the superior estimates, are presented for the total bulk fleet and the two flag groups in Table I together with key summary statistics. To test for the validity of the various parametric restrictions which were imposed in our alternative specifications, the likelihood ratio (λ) was estimated for each as the ratio of the unconstrained maximum value of the likelihood function (Ω) to the constrained value of the likelihood function (ω) that is,

$$(12) \qquad \lambda = \frac{L_{\max}(\Omega)}{L_{\max}(\omega)}$$

Wilks [1938] has shown that under the null hypothesis ($-2\log\lambda$) has an asymptotic distribution that is χ^2 with the number of relevant degrees of freedom equal to the number of restrictions tested. Table II shows the λ statistics and χ^2 values at the 1 % level of significance.

What we find is that introducing restrictions consistent with either a Cobb–Douglas or CES technology is inappropriate—suggesting that the limited amount of previous econometric analysis in this field must be treated with caution. The results reveal that the production structure of bulk carrier operations throughout the shipping industry, irrespective of country of registration, are not separable in outputs nor in inputs and that shipping costs are sensitive to factor substitution possibilities, factor shares and to utilisation levels. Further, they show that returns to scale will not only vary with output but also with factor prices.

TABLE II
TEST STATISTICS FOR HOMOTHETICITY, LINEAR SEPARABILITY, HOMOGENEITY AND UNITARY ELASTICITY OF SUBSTITUTION

Hypotheses	$-2\log\lambda$	χ^2 (0.01) *1 % level*	*No. of restrictions*
Homotheticity (Model 2)			
All Bulk Carriers	387.94	11.35	3
Traditional Registries	247.62	11.35	3
Open Registries	93.20	11.35	3
Linear Separability (Model 3)			
All Bulk Carriers	761.40	13.28	4
Traditional Registries	514.72	13.28	4
Open Registries	258.88	13.28	4
Unitary Elasticity and Homogeneity (Model 4)			
All Bulk Carriers	1698.32	23.21	10
Traditional Registries	1199.22	23.21	10
Open Registries	591.30	23.21	10

TABLE III
ESTIMATED ALLEN–UZAWA PARTIAL ELASTICITIES OF SUBSTITUTION FOR THE TOTAL COST FUNCTION

	All Ships	*Traditional Registry*	*Open Registry*
σ_{KK}	−0.0998[a]	−0.1131[a]	−0.0598[a]
σ_{MM}	−0.2271[a]	−0.1998[a]	−0.3107[a]
σ_{RR}	−0.4102[a]	−0.8516[a]	−1.5041[a]
σ_{SS}	0.1101[a]	0.8611[a]	0.0469[a]
σ_{KM}	0.1049[a]	0.0775[a]	0.0769[a]
σ_{KR}	0.0658[a]	0.1449[a]	0.1488[a]
σ_{KS}	0.0637	0.0038	−0.0432
σ_{MR}	0.1504[a]	0.2426[a]	0.3077[a]
σ_{MS}	0.0076	−0.0833	0.0577
σ_{RS}	−0.2717[a]	−0.1667[a]	0.0568

Note: [a] Significant at 5% level.

The approximation interpretation of the translog function facilitates the straightforward computation of elasticities because with the normalisation of variables and their expression as natural logarithms the first order linear coefficients can be interpreted as cost elasticities evaluated at their sample means. (These elasticities of total cost with respect to factor prices are also equivalent to mean factor shares in total cost.) From Table I, therefore, we observe considerable differences in factor shares between ships sailing under flags of convenience and those that are registered in industrialised countries. In the case of the latter, capital accounts for 44% of total cost, manning 34%, repairs and maintenance 16% and stores and provisions 6%. In contrast, ships under open registry show higher proportions for capital and stores but lower proportions for manning and repairs. In general, the coefficients are highly significant and their positive signs satisfy the regularity conditions for a well-behaved cost function (see Caves and Christensen [1980]).

Tables III and IV present, respectively, estimates of the Allen–Uzawa partial elasticities of substitution and the price elasticities of factor demand for the sample means. The substitution possibilities are generally small and almost zero in many cases. It is worth noting however that, from a technical point of view, the strict rules for the global negative semi-definiteness of the

TABLE IV
OWN-PRICE ELASTICITIES OF FACTOR DEMAND

	All Ships	*Traditional Registry*	*Open Registry*
E_{KK}	−0.0471	−0.0498	−0.0330
E_{MM}	−0.0719	−0.0699	−0.0808
E_{RR}	−0.0599	−0.1363	−0.1655
E_{SS}	0.0073	0.0517	0.0037

Hessian matrix are violated by positive values taken by the stores demand elasticities. The violation is slight and the values of the coefficients are close to zero and, as Friedlaender and Spady have pointed out, no restrictions of the parameters of the translog function will guarantee global negative semi-definiteness of the Hessian.

Some comments on the results are justified. There is a widely held view in shipping circles that in industrialised economies, where labour costs are high and capital costs are relatively low, operators tend to substitute capital for labour. Technical advances in computerised operational systems and unmanned engine spaces have been cited as reinforcing this tendency. In fact, the low value of the substitution coefficient obtained for traditional registrations tends to argue against such views. The reason for this may well be the rigidities which accompany legislation regarding manning levels, working conditions and crew nationality, coupled with possible inert areas associated with potential maritime union power; all of which exists in traditional flag nations. International agreements (such as IMO's convention on standards of training, certification and watch keeping) tend to further reduce the flexibility enjoyed by those sailing under regulated registries. Nevertheless, these rigidities notwithstanding, the labour market for seamen in traditional nations operates under competitive conditions, hence the appropriateness of the individual cost-minimisation model.

While the above offers some useful insights, the analysis may be technically flawed in that it is based upon the assumption that the shipping companies concerned are in static equilibrium with respect to their demand for inputs. This means that the firms are minimising costs with respect to all inputs and that there is a convex input structure which links the production function to a total cost function. If, however, the shipping companies do not minimise the costs of all inputs, because some of them are perceived to-be fixed, then the total cost function is the inappropriate one to use (see Brown and Christensen [1981]). It is more sensible, if this is the case, to examine variable costs conditional upon capital inputs. The legitimacy of this argument, in the context of bulk shipping, stems from the fact that, since for physical reasons the supply of capital tends to be highly inelastic in the short run (Sturmey [1975]), profit maximising ship owners will, by necessity, focus on ensuring variable cost minimisation. The well documented volatility of demand for bulk shipping services adds weight to this view since it increases the problems confronting international ship owners trying to maintain optimal levels of capacity.

In the light of these arguments, it seems wise to explore the implications of an alternative specification. An appropriate variable cost function may, therefore, be defined as:

$$\ln C_V = \alpha_0 + \alpha_Q \ln Q + \sum \beta_i \ln P_i + \alpha_K \ln K' + \tfrac{1}{2}\delta(\ln Q)^2 + \tfrac{1}{2}\pi_{KK}(\ln K')^2 \tag{13}$$

$$+\tfrac{1}{2}\sum\sum\gamma_{ij}\ln P_i \ln P_j + \sum\rho_{iQ}\ln P_i \ln Q$$
$$+\sum\lambda_{iK}\ln P_i \ln K' + \theta_{KQ}\ln K' \ln Q$$

The restrictions for the theoretical homogeneity requirements are the same as before with the additional restriction that $\sum\lambda_{ik} = 0$. Similarly, the cost and share equations are the same as previously save that there is an additional variable for capital in the main cost equation, for example:

$$(14) \qquad S^i = \alpha_1 + \rho_{iQ}\ln Q + \sum_j \gamma_{ij}\ln P_j + \lambda_{iK}\ln K' + \omega_i$$

Estimation of the equation system yields the results presented in Table V. As before, the model was tested with various technical restrictions imposed (corresponding to a Cobb–Douglas technology, etc.) but these were rejected on statistical grounds. The model provides a good overall statistical fit for both the total bulk fleet and the two registry groups separately. The t ratio of the quasi-fixed factor also indicates that treating capital as a fixed input is statistically tenable while the negative sign associated with capital inputs offers empirical confirmation of the underlying assumption of the variable cost function. Comparing the elasticities of total variable cost with respect to capital for the traditional and open registry groups reveals a higher degree of cost optimisation for the latter. This is to be expected given the high proportion of overall costs in the open registry fleet (over 50%) associated with capital and the greater scope for factor substitution enjoyed by individual vessels.

More detailed examination of the two flag categories reveals the importance of manning costs in their overall cost functions. When using the total cost approach it was found on the basis of the fitted cost equation that at the sample mean traditional registry ships have costs some 8.7% above those of open registries. This figure rises to 23.1%, however, when the variable cost function is employed—the main reason for this being that the model reveals that manning the average open registry ship costs $306,552 per annum less than the average traditionally registered vessel. For comparisons, details of the characteristics of the average vessel are set out in the Appendix to the paper.

While it is impossible with the data available to offer firm and detailed reasons for the differences in manning costs, the findings are not inconsistent with the arguments of Goss [1985] regarding the importance of differences, in broad terms, of employment between the fleets of different maritime nations. More specifically the 'social costs' of labour—relating to social security and similar payments and to statutory conditions of employment—differ between traditional and open registry nations which, at a more micro-level of analysis, would justify a trichotomous division of labour costs. Information on such differences is not, however, readily available and, indeed, similar types of disaggregation relating, for instance, to sources of finance would also be

TABLE V
ESTIMATED PARAMETERS OF THE VARIABLE COST FUNCTION FOR BULK CARRIERS (T-RATIOS IN PARENTHESES)

	All Ships	*Traditional Registry*	*Open Registry*
α_O	−0.0762	−0.0769	−0.0385
	(−10.3350)	(−7.3600)	(−5.0206)
α_Q	0.2360	0.2558	0.2903
	(14.4510)	(11.6150)	(18.6600)
α_K	−0.2121	−0.2812	−0.4130
	(−5.9289)	(−6.7889)	(−7.1533)
δ_{QQ}	0.0157	0.0565	0.1596
	(0.7519)	(2.6872)	(9.5056)
π_{KK}	−0.0079	−0.2384	0.6731
	(−0.0664)	(−2.2206)	(1.9714)
β_M	0.4995	0.5278	0.4488
	(150.0600)	(112.6300)	(117.6800)
β_R	0.2095	0.2245	0.1785
	(72.4920)	(56.6000)	(85.1300)
β_S	0.1093	0.0947	0.1373
	(99.9590)	(72.7960)	(134.5800)
β_{IA}	0.1817	0.1542	0.2354
	(88.5460)	(65.0040)	(108.5300)
γ_{MM}	0.2137	0.2332	0.2295
	(42.5370)	(32.5610)	(63.1280)
γ_{RR}	0.1588	0.1593	0.1352
	(42.2640)	(34.0190)	(31.6680)
γ_{SS}	0.0970	0.0857	0.1135
	(47.2890)	(57.3210)	(28.1800)
γ_{IAIA}	0.1146	0.1115	0.1728
	(37.9340)	(31.7100)	(46.7600)
γ_{MR}	−0.0965	−0.1118	−0.0709
	(−25.7580)	(−22.0010)	(−25.6160)
γ_{MS}	−0.0545	−0.0483	−0.0535
	(−29.7310)	(−23.2790)	(−17.6140)
γ_{MIA}	−0.0627	−0.0731	−0.1051
	(−19.4840)	(−16.8070)	(−42.3510)
γ_{RS}	−0.0270	−0.0238	−0.0283
	(−19.0920)	(−18.1930)	(−10.3640)
γ_{RIA}	−0.0354	−0.0237	−0.0359
	(−14.6580)	(−7.8768)	(−11.2250)
γ_{SIA}	−0.0165	−0.0146	−0.0318
	(−11.9930)	(−11.1580)	(−11.0330)
ρ_{MQ}	−0.0112	0.0169	0.0220
	(−1.4963)	(1.5108)	(2.7235)
ρ_{RQ}	−0.0581	−0.0654	−0.0534
	(−8.4947)	(−6.9659)	(−9.7211)
ρ_{SQ}	0.0856	0.0738	0.1052
	(26.4590)	(22.0500)	(21.9130)
ρ_{IAQ}	−0.0163	−0.0253	−0.0738
	(−3.3534)	(−4.1872)	(−12.9990)
λ_{MK}	−0.0540	−0.0673	−0.2153
	(−3.7846)	(−3.9103)	(−17.7732)
λ_{RK}	0.0594	0.0617	0.0782
	(4.8269)	(4.3421)	(4.4603)
λ_{SK}	0.0197	0.0195	0.0225

TABLE V—*continued*

	All Ships	*Traditional Registry*	*Open Registry*
	(3.9717)	(3.9348)	(2.0209)
λ_{AK}	−0.0251	−0.0139	0.1146
	(−2.7652)	(−1.5591)	(6.5654)
θ_{KQ}	0.0892	0.1023	−0.1847
	(1.6042)	(2.0764)	(−2.6854)
$\bar{R}^2$	0.9235	0.8651	0.9396
Manning Equation	0.8723	0.8030	0.9192
Repairs Equation	0.9162	0.9234	0.9241
Stores Equation	0.9085	0.8557	0.9617
Log of the Likelihood Function	920.49	619.02	439.47

required if genuine micro-economic analysis of the underlying causes of factor cost variations were to be conducted.

Calculation of the Allen–Uzawa partial elasticities of substitution and own-price demand elasticities for inputs relevant for the variable cost function (Tables VI and VII) provides statistically reassuring results. Changes are found in the substitution arrangements when compared to those for the total cost function with the coefficients generally taking lower values. This conforms with what one would anticipate in terms of the underlying assumptions of short-run equilibrium. The difference in the substitutability between manning and repair costs between the two flag groups is wider with the variable cost specification which probably reflects the particularly short-

TABLE VI

ESTIMATED ALLEN–UZAWA PARTIAL ELASTICITIES OF SUBSTITUTION FOR THE VARIABLE COST FUNCTION

	All Ships	*Traditional Registry*	*Open Registry*
σ_{MM}	−0.1455[a]	−0.0575[a]	−0.0888[a]
σ_{RR}	−0.1552[a]	−0.2936[a]	−0.3589[a]
σ_{SS}	−0.0296[a]	−0.0036[a]	−0.2625[a]
σ_{IA}	−1.0324[a]	−0.7958[a]	−0.1297[a]
σ_{MR}	0.0778[a]	0.0565	0.1150[a]
σ_{MS}	0.0075	0.0337	0.1318[a]
σ_{MIA}	0.3092[a]	0.1018[b]	0.0052
σ_{RS}	−0.1791[a]	−0.1195[a]	−0.1547
σ_{RIA}	0.0700	0.3154[a]	0.1456[a]
σ_{SIA}	0.1692[a]	0.0002	0.0161

Note: [a] Significant at 5% level. [b] Significant at 10% level.

TABLE VII
OWN-PRICE ELASTICITIES OF FACTOR DEMAND

	All Ships	Traditional Registry	Open Registry
E_{MM}	−0.0727	−0.0303	−0.0399
E_{RR}	−0.0325	−0.0659	−0.0641
E_{SS}	−0.0032	−0.0003	−0.0360
E_{IAIA}	−0.1876	−0.1227	−0.0305

term rigidities of labour contracts in the traditional maritime nations. There does, however, appear to be a high degree of substitution between insurance and administration and repairs.[3] This may represent an operating strategy for operators in high cost, industrialised countries who take out more insurance cover in order to complete repairs and maintenance in dry dock rather than use the ships' own crews. This strategy seems to be borne out by the substitution values for insurance and repairs, and insurance and manning and also by the complementarity between repairs and stores.

The economies of ship size have in the past been examined by Heaver [1968] and Goss and Jones [1982] amongst others. This previous work found evidence of great economies associated with ship size when examining the relationship between average ship cost and ship size. The translog modelling framework permits more detailed examination. The appropriate measure of scale effects (S) in this context is defined as unity minus the elasticity of total cost with respect to output, that is,

$$(15) \qquad S = 1 - \frac{\partial \ln C_T}{\partial \ln Q}$$

where in our case:

$$\frac{\partial \ln C_T}{\partial \ln Q} = \alpha_Q + \sum \rho_{iQ}(\ln P_i - \ln \bar{P}_i) + \sigma_{QQ}(\ln Q - \ln \bar{Q})$$

If $S > 0$ then positive scale effects are implied.

Calculation of the S values for each vessel in the two registration categories produced values which declined with vessel size indicating that in both cases ship owners were operating on the downward portion of a U-shaped average cost curve. Higher values of cost elasticity with respect to output, which were obtained in the case of open registration, therefore reflect the impact of being on a lower portion of the average cost curve than the traditional registry ships. Open registry operators seem to exploit more of their potential scale

[3] In the calculations, insurance and administration (IA) are treated as short-run variable costs. While they may be related to hull valuations, owners do have some options for cancellation or reduction in the short period, even if the capital is fixed.

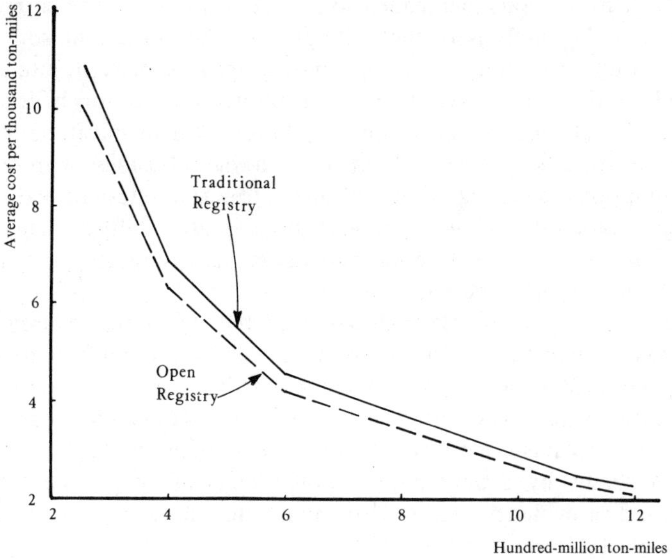

Figure 1
Average Cost Curves for Open and Traditional Registries

economies. The overall effect of registration differences may be summarised in Figure 1. This translates the equations into the average cost curves of 'typical' operators under the alternative flag regimes. The positive scale effects associated with increased ton-mileage are clear, but of equal importance is the fact that costs for open registry operations are, at all levels of activity, below those of operations with traditional registry. Calculations based upon the variable cost function yields a graph with similar features.

A well-defined test (based on log-likelihood values) can be employed to establish whether the differences between open and traditional registry are jointly significant. If λ_p, λ_T, λ_0 are the log-likelihood values for the pooled, traditional and open samples then:

(16) $$[(\lambda_T+\lambda_0)-\lambda_p] \sim \chi^2(n)$$

where, n is equal to the number of free parameters in any regression plus the number of independent elements in the variance–covariance matrix. Applying the test to the data sets indicates that the samples are significantly different.

IV. CONCLUDING REMARKS

Previously the limited amount of detailed work examining international shipping cost functions has tended to rely upon rather restricted modelling frameworks. An analysis of bulk shipping has revealed that some of the implicit assumptions inherent in these models must be brought into question although it does also provide a more rigorous basis for beliefs in the substantial scale economies which may be enjoyed in maritime activities. Further, the results obtained exhibit considerable robustness with respect to the assumptions made regarding the degree to which international shipping can adjust capital inputs in the face of quite volatile shifts in demand. The conclusions are not, therefore, dependent on the assumption that capacity was optimal during the period of the study.

While there is justifiable concern over the difficulties caused by the expansion of open registry for international shipping, the debate to date has tended to both lack quantitative content and to be excessively concerned with the potential benefits associated with the phasing out of flags of convenience. What this study has done is to introduce some quantification into the cost-benefit calculus by examining the potential costs of phasing out open registries. The evidence presented demonstrates the differing nature of the operations of the two flag groupings.

While the calculations reveal that open registration, as one might expect given the movement of operators towards sailing under flags of convenience, does result in lower costs at all levels of activity, they do not provide, of themselves, an argument for retaining the system. First of all it is necessary to firmly establish the correlation between cost levels and freight rates. Nevertheless, this study does provide an indication of the cost to the shipping sector (and, *ipso facto*, to international trade) of phasing out open registration. It offers cost estimates against which the less quantifiable benefits of greater national jurisdiction over shipping may be set.

K. J. BUTTON,
Department of Economics,
Loughborough University,
Loughborough,
Leicestershire LE11 3TU,
UK.

ACCEPTED OCTOBER 1985

S. R. TOLOFARI AND D. E. PITFIELD,
Department of Transport Technology,
Loughborough University,
Loughborough,
Leicestershire LE11 3TU,
UK.

APPENDIX

The characteristics of the average 'firm' may be summarised as:

Variable	*All Bulk Carriers*	*Traditional Registry*	*Open Registry*
Capital ($)	35.210	33.57	39.00
Manning ($)	30,754	33,555	24,292
Repairs ($)	1119.60	1252.20	813.42
Stores ($)	4.80	4.6035	5.415
Number of Crew	29.50	30.00	29.00
Operating Days per Year	353.00	352.07	355.23
Output (million ton-miles)	507.29	502.69	517.88
Age of Vessel (years)	11.2	12.43	8.5

Notes: Capital cost per vessel tonnage (dwt); manning cost per man; repairs per operating day; stores per tonnage.

REFERENCES

BARTEN, A.P., 1969, 'Maximum Likelihood Estimation of a Complete System of Demand Equations', *European Economic Review*, 1, pp. 7–73.

BERECHMAN, J., 1983, 'Cost, Economies of Scale and Factor Demand in Bus Transport', *Journal of Transport Economics and Policy*, 17, pp. 17–24.

BERNDT, E. R. and CHRISTENSEN, L. R. (1973), 'The Translog Function and the Substitution of Equipment, Structures, and Labour in US Manufacturing', *Journal of Econometrics*, 1, pp. 81–114.

BOCZEK, B. A., 1962, *Flags of Convenience: an International Legal Study* (Harvard University Press, Cambridge, Mass.).

BROWN, R. S. and CHRISTENSEN, L. R., 1981, 'Estimating Elasticities of Substitution in a Model of Partial Static Equilibrium: An Application to US Agriculture, 1947–1974', in BERNDT, E. R. and FIELD, B. C. (eds), *Measuring and Modelling Natural Resource Substitution* (MIT Press, Cambridge, Mass.).

BUTTON, K. J. and O'DONNELL, K. J., 1985, 'An Examination of the Cost Structures Associated with Providing Urban Bus Services in Britain', *Scottish Journal of Political Economy*, 32, pp. 67–81.

CAVES, D. W. and CHRISTENSEN, L. R., 1980, 'Global Properties of Flexible Functional Forms', *American Economic Review*, 70, pp. 423–432.

CAVES, D. W., CHRISTENSEN, L. R. and SWANSON, J. A., 1980, 'Productivity in US Railroads, 1951–1974', *Bell Journal of Economics*, 11, pp. 166–181.

CAVES, D. W., CHRISTENSEN, L. R. and SWANSON, J. A., 1981, 'Productivity Growth, Scale Economies and Capacity Utilisation in US Railroads, 1955–1974', *American Economic Review*, 71, pp. 994–1002.

CAVES, D. W., CHRISTENSEN, L. R. and TRETHEWAY, M. W., 1984, 'Economies of Density Versus Economies of Scale: Why Trunk and Local Service Airline Costs Differ', Working Paper 981, Economics Department, University of Wisconsin, Madison.

CHAKRABARTY, D., 1983, 'Translog Production Function—A Review of Literature', *Artha Vijnana*, 25, pp. 115–146.

CHRISTENSEN, L. R. and GREENE, W. H., 1976, 'Economies of Scale in US Electric Power Generation', *Journal of Political Economy*, 84, pp. 655–676.

CHRISTENSEN, L. R., JORGENSON, D. W. and LAU, L. J., 1973, 'Transcendental

Logarithmic Production Frontiers', *The Review of Economics and Statistics*, 55, pp. 29–55.

DIEWERT, W. E., 1974, 'Applications of Duality Theory', in INTRILLIGATOR, M. D. and KENDRICK, D. A. (eds), *Frontiers of Quantitative Economics, Vol. II* (North-Holland, Amsterdam).

DREWRY, H. P. (Shipping Consultants), 1984, 'Dry Bulk Carrier Operating Costs—Past, Present and Future', Study No. 122, London.

DHRYMES, P. J., 1973, 'Small Sample Asymptotic Relations Between Maximum Likelihood and Three-stage Least-squares Estimators', *Econometrica*, 41, pp. 357–364.

ECONOMICS INTELLIGENCE UNIT, 1979, 'Open Registry Shipping: Some Economic Considerations', A Study for the US International Chamber of Commerce, London.

FRIEDLAENDER, A. F. and SPADY, R. H., 1981, *Freight Transport Regulation* (MIT Press, Cambridge, Mass.).

FUSS, M., MCFADDEN, D. and MUNDLAK, Y., 1979, 'A Survey of Functional Forms in the Econometric Analysis of Production', in FUSS, M. and MCFADDEN, D. (eds), *Production Economics, Vol. I* (North-Holland, Amsterdam).

GOSS, R. O., 1985, '"Social" Costs, Transfer Payments and International Competition in Shipping', *Maritime Policy and Management*, 12, pp. 135–143.

GOSS, R. O. and JONES, C. D., 1982, 'The Economies of Size in Dry Bulk Carriers', reprinted in GOSS, R. O. (ed.), *Advances in Maritime Economies* (University College Press, Cardiff).

HARRIS, R. G., 1977, 'Economies of Density in the Rail Freight Industry', *Bell Journal of Economics*, 3, pp. 26–41.

HEAVER, T. D., 1968, 'The Economies of Vessel Size', National Harbours Board, Ottawa.

INTERNATIONAL MARITIME ASSOCIATES INC., 1979, 'Economic Impact of Open Registry Shipping', A Study for the Liberian Maritime Bureau, Washington.

KMENTA, J. and GILBERT, F., 1968, 'Small Sample Properties of Alternative Estimators of Seemingly Unrelated Regressions', *Journal of the American Statistical Association*, 63, pp. 1180–1200.

METAXAS, B. N. and DOGANIS, R., 1976, 'The Impact of Flags of Convenience', Polytechnic of Central London, London.

NAESS, E. D., 1972, *The Great Panlibhon Controversy* (Gower Press, London).

SHEPHARD, R. W., 1953, *Cost and Production Functions* (Princeton University Press, Princeton).

STURMEY, S. G., 1975, *Shipping Economics* (Macmillan, London).

STURMEY, S. G., 1984, 'The Open Registry Controversy and the Development Issue', Bremen Institute of Shipping Economics, Bremen.

UNCTAD, 1977, *Economic Consequences of the Existence or Lack of a Genuine Link Between Vessel and Flag of Registry* (UNCTAD, Geneva).

UNCTAD, 1979, *The Repercussions of Phasing Out Open Registries* (UNCTAD, Geneva).

UZAWA, H., 1962, 'Production Functions with Constant Elasticities of Substitution', *Review of Economic Studies*, 29, pp. 291–299.

VITON, P. A., 1981, 'A Translog Cost Function for Urban Bus Transit', *Journal of Industrial Economics*, 29, pp. 287–304.

WILKS, S. S., 1938, 'The Large Sample Distribution of the Likelihood Ratio for Testing Composite Hypotheses', *Annals of Mathematical Statistics*, 9, pp. 60–62.

WILLIAMS, M. and DALAL, A., 1981, 'Estimation of the Elasticities of Factor Substitution in Urban Bus Transportation: A Cost Function Approach', *Journal of Regional Science*, 21, pp. 263–327.

ZELLNER, A., 1962, 'An Efficient Method of Estimating Seemingly Unrelated Regressions and Tests for Aggregation Bias', *Journal of the American Statistical Association*, 57, pp. 972–992.

THE JOURNAL OF INDUSTRIAL ECONOMICS 0022-1821 $2.00
Volume XXXIV June 1986 No. 4

CONCENTRATION, PROFITABILITY AND TRADE IN A SIMULTANEOUS EQUATION ANALYSIS: THE CASE OF TAIWAN*

TEIN-CHEN CHOU

This paper is the first attempt to use a simultaneous four-equation system to study the role of foreign trade in the analysis of market structure and performance, and the determinants of trade intensity in a newly industrializing country—Taiwan. A cross-sectional analysis is carried out with the manufacturing censuses of 1976. The results indicate that public enterprises significantly influence market structures and performance. Also, import control measures influence import intensity significantly and offset potential impacts of imports on concentration and on profitability. However, trade intensity is mainly explained by comparative advantage rather than market forces (concentration and profitability).

INTRODUCTION

MANY STUDIES[1] have argued that a joint determination rather than a causal relation exists between concentration and profitability. That is because the price-cost margins (*PCM*) equation is derived from an equilibrium condition for profit maximization. Clarke and Davies [1982] present the simultaneity of profitability and concentration. Many efforts have also been made to treat the simultaneity of concentration, advertising intensity, and profitability.[2]

Recently, more and more studies have integrated trade into such a simultaneous framework in parallel with an analysis of the role of foreign trade in the study of structure-performance.[3] Jacquemin *et al.* [1980] show the effects of trade in a recursive two-equation model to describe the determinants of *PCM* and concentration. Pugel [1978] specifies the import and export share equations (as well as equations for concentration, profitability, foreign direct investment and advertising intensity) in a simultaneous

*An earlier version of this paper was presented at the 11th Annual Conference of the European Association for Research in Industrial Economics (EARIE), at INSEAD, Fontainebleau, France, August 29–31, 1984. I am grateful to participants of this conference for their comments, and in particular to A. Jacquemin and T. Pugel. I am also grateful to the Editor and an anonymous referee for valuable comments and suggestions, and to E. de Souza for helpful improvement in English. All remaining errors are mine.

[1] For instance, see Jacquemin *et al.* [1980], Geroski [1982a], [1982b], Clarke and Davies [1982] and Donsimoni *et al.* [1984].

[2] See Greer [1971], Strickland and Weiss [1976], Martin [1979], and Pagoulatos and Sorensen [1981]. For comments on the necessity for this simultaneity, see Sawyer [1982].

[3] For dominant firms' models with trade, see Jacquemin [1982], Geroski and Jacquemin [1981] and Huveneers [1981].

equation system. De Ghellinck *et al.* [1984] confirm that there is a feedback of trade on industry performance. The results of Geroski [1982a] suggest that trade rather than advertising intensity is suitable as an endogenous variable in a simultaneous system.

This paper uses a simultaneous equation system to study, in the case of Taiwan, the interaction of trade (exports and imports), concentration and profitability. Variables measuring barriers to entry, economies of scale, and relative factor intensity are included with other exogenous variables to explain four endogenous variables: concentration (*Hd*), *PCM*, export (*Tx*) and import intensity (*Tm*). Beside traditional elements, the impact of public enterprises on structure and performance is emphasized in the study. The results reveal some features of Taiwan's economy, in particular, the role of public ownership and the impact of international linkages on concentration and performance.

In section I, the formulation and specification of the models are discussed. In section II, the empirical implementation of our model and the data are presented. Then the empirical results are given in section III. Section IV contains concluding remarks and policy implications.

I. THE MODELS: FORMULATION AND SPECIALIZATION

In 'import discipline' models, we can obtain a general *PCM* equation which comes from the first order condition of profit maximization. In the equation, *PCM* is determined by the degree of domestic producers' competition (based on the firm's market share or its related measures) and demand (being represented by the relevant elasticity). Both variables include import share and export share in an open economy. Due to the simultaneity of equilibrium condition and considering the important role of comparative advantage in trade we can write a simultaneous four-equation system as:

(1) $Hd = f_1(MA, Tx, Tm)$ the concentration equation,

(2) $PCM = f_2(Hd, MA, Tx, Tm)$ the profit equation,

(3) $Tx = f_3(Hd, PCM, MA, CA)$ the export intensity equation,

(4) $Tm = f_4(Hd, PCM, MA, CA)$ the import intensity equation,

where *MA* and *CA* represent the variables of market structure and the state of comparative advantage respectively, and both are exogenous. Formulation and specification for each equation could be advanced in turn.

(a) *The concentration equation*

It is generally hypothesized in conventional industrial economics that inter-industry variation in concentration can be explained by a combination of explanatory variables such as barriers to entry, scale economies, and the size of the market.[4] Therefore, three variables—the market size (*MS*), minimum efficient plant size (*MES*), and capital requirement (*KR*)—are included in the concentration equation. The expectation is that the larger the capital requirement and the higher the minimum efficient size, the higher would be the level of concentration. Also an inverse relationship is expected between market size and concentration.

Besides, an indicator of public ownership in Taiwan's economy should be introduced as a determinant of market structure (and performance). The role of Taiwan's public firms in economic activities, even in manufacturing, are very evident (Chou [1985, Ch. 3]). On average in the 1970s, 26% of manufacturing assets were controlled by the public sector which contributed 17% of turnover in the manufacturing. Furthermore, large-scale and domestic-orientation (very low export intensity) of public enterprises are noticeable features in Taiwan. Hence it would be expected to have a significant and positive impact on concentration. A dummy variable (*PE*) representing the position of public ownership is introduced in the concentration equation with positive expectation.

Three international linkages are included to complete the concentration equation in an open economy. The first one is *Tm*, measured as imports divided by total sales, that is, the fraction of industry sales provided by foreign suppliers. A positive impact would be observed if threat from imports induces mergers among domestic firms,[5] or if import penetrations force out inefficient producers.[6]

The second external variable is *Tx*, measured as exports divided by total sales, that is, the fraction of domestic production that is exported. To the extent that export intensity acts as a deconcentration force via enlarging of the market size, it would be expected to be inversely related to industry concentration. This negative relationship may be reinforced either if the fixed costs associated with exporting activities are not high, or if economies of scale in production or distribution are not important because a larger market size resulting from export opportunities can support a greater number of producers. Otherwise, the importance of scale economies and high fixed costs of exporting business would alter the sign to be a positive one (de Melo and Urata [1984]). Taiwan's exports concentrating on simple processed and light industrial products suggest a negative influence.

The third external variable is foreign direct investment (*FDI*). Caves

[4] At a space of one decade, two excellent surveys of the various theories of the determinants of concentration can be found in Ornstein *et al.* [1973] and Curry and George [1983].

[5] Jacquemin *et al.* [1980, p. 135] say: 'Sectors characterized by a systematic high share of imports are expected to be also characterized by a high degree of defensive concentration of domestic producers, as long as imports are close substitutes for domestic product.'

[6] However, de Melo and Urata [1984] show that the impact may be negative if inefficient producers improve their productive efficiency in response to an increase of imports. As a result of an increased number of efficient producers, the concentration ratio may decline.

[1980] shows that the general presumption for *FDI* causing concentration is not automatically supported in the LDCs. It seems to depend on the category of goods (consumers goods industries or producer goods industries) and their market orientations. For instance, export-oriented foreign subsidiaries may have been able to surmount domestic barriers and so reduce concentration.

The resulting concentration equation, with the expected sign indicated below each independent variable, is thus:

$$Hd = f_1(\underset{-}{MS}, \underset{+}{MES}, \underset{+}{KR}, \underset{+}{PE}, \underset{+}{Tm}, \underset{-}{Tx}, \underset{-}{FDI}) \tag{5}$$

(b) *The profit equation*

PCM (which is the industry profit-sales ratio) is jointly determined by the degree of domestic producers' competition and the condition of market demand. Pugel [1980, p. 122] indicates that domestic producer concentration and barriers to entry are interactive in representing the degree of competitiveness in domestic production. The Herfindahl index of concentration is an appropriate candidate for measuring producer concentration.[7] Two entry variables, *MES* and *MS*, can be rearranged into one, *MESMS*, measured as *MES* divided by *MS* (total sales minus exports plus imports), that is, the fraction of domestic market size necessary to achieve the minimum efficient size. The annual growth rate of industry production value (*GRS*), representing the condition of market demand, is included in the profit equation. It would be expected with familiar reasons that the above variables have positive influences on the *PCM*.

It is interesting to examine the effect of public enterprises on profits. Therefore, a dummy variable, *PE*, is included in the profit equation. The sign of this variable depends upon its efficiency and pricing policy. If the government is likely to take over inefficient firms or public enterprises adopt low prices rather than a profit maximization policy, as in the case of Spain (Donsimoni and Leoz-Arguelles [1981]), it is expected to have a negative impact on profits. On the contrary, if state owned enterprises operate efficiently (Aharoni [1980]) or adopt high protected prices, a positive effect is expected. However, for Taiwan's case, the author [1985, Ch. 3] shows high prices are adopted by public enterprises and protected by the government for fiscal purpose, hence the expectation of a positive effect.

Previous studies indicate that a negative relation would hold between import intensity and profitability, because foreign competition, as a fringe, would restrain the exercise of market power in the domestic market. However, the relationship becomes ambiguous as soon as one leaves the

[7] The market shares of individual firms are used here as weights to sum over all firms' *PCM* to obtain the industry *PCM* (profit-sales ratio). This yields the Herfindahl index which is the appropriate proxy for performance in a Cournot behavior (Donsimoni *et al.* [1984]).

simple dominant firm case,[8] and may be positive if the implicit collusion between domestic firms is lower than that between domestic and foreign firms (de Melo and Urata [1984]), or if an oligopolistic firm is engaged in both producing and importing simultaneously. Due to strict import controls in Taiwan, it seems reasonable to treat imports as a competitive fringe. If so, a negative sign is expected.

The impact of export intensity on profits is complex. It depends upon the degree of competitiveness of industry at home (for example competitive sectors vs. monopolized sectors) and upon whether or not the exporting firms can dump abroad and prevent re-imports (Jacquemin *et al.* [1980]). Moreover, Huveneers [1981] indicates that, even in the case of price discrimination and homogeneous goods, the effect of export intensity depends on cost conditions.[9] On the other hand, in the differentiated goods case, he shows that the influence of exports on profits depends on whether the profits abroad exceeds or is less than that at home. If *PCM* abroad is less than *PCM* at home, a negative impact is expected. It seems acceptable to assume (1) that goods made in Taiwan are differentiated from those made in MDCs (for example the largest export market of Taiwan, the US), and (2) that Taiwan's producers have smaller market position in export markets than at home, that is, *PCM* at home being larger than *PCM* abroad (this is also verified by the author [1985, Ch. 4]). Thus a negative sign is expected.

Some studies have explained the effect of *FDI* on performance, but almost all of them emphasize 'outward' rather than 'inward' direct investment. The study of Caves [1980] is an exception. Like many other LDCs, Taiwan only has a minor record of outward investment, and thus *FDI* is not endogenized, as in Pugel [1978]. As Caves [1980] shows, whether the relation between *FDI* and profits is positive or negative is still an open question. However, if the manipulation of transfer prices is adopted by the export-oriented multinational enterprises because of a high level of tax in Taiwan, a negative relation would be expected. Or, if foreign subsidiaries being as a fringe, like imports, play a competitive role to restrict the market power of domestic firms, a negative sign is also expected.

Therefore, the resulting profit equation and the expected signs are:

$$PCM = \underset{}{f_2}(\underset{+}{Hd}, \underset{+}{MESMS}, GRS, \underset{+}{PE}, \underset{+}{Tm}, \underset{-}{Tx}, \underset{-}{FDI}) \qquad (6)$$

Note: the signs under the variables are printed as: + + + + − − −

(c) *The trade equations*

Few theoretical specifications of trade equations with embodiment of imper-

[8] For instance, in the contrary case where domestic firms are treated as the competitive fringe, the import intensity has no effect on profitability because domestic firms always act as a price-taker (Urata [1984]). In the mixed case where both domestic and foreign firms form a cartel, the relation is ambiguous, see Geroski and Jacquemin [1981].

[9] He shows that if the elasticity of the marginal cost is larger than the elasticity of average cost, the effect is positive.

fect competition can be found, two exceptions being Lyons [1981] and Pugel [1978]. Lyons derives an import share equation from a generalized Cournot model. Pugel explores the determinants of export intensity and import intensity separately, both to extend the analysis of comparative advantage and to test other hypotheses developed in industrial organization. This is similar to equations (3) and (4). They should be further specified in detail.

First, there do not exist many studies to discuss the impact of concentration on export and import intensity. However, the study of Glejser *et al.* [1980] shows that the firms in concentrated sectors would be encouraged to export. On the other hand, foreign producers may not enjoy a very competitive domestic market; therefore the higher concentration, the more important penetration is expected. Therefore, concentration influences both export and import intensity with positive expectations.

Second, *PCM* could affect the incentives both to export and to import. Incentives depend on the differences between price and costs. If the domestic price is elevated above the domestic producer costs, foreign producers perceive an incentive to export. Therefore, the higher the *PCM*, the higher the import penetration which is expected. However, this 'signal' effect could be restrained or distorted by import control measures. By contrast to this, domestic producers who enjoy market power at home will avoid exporting in order not to attract foreign producers' attention. Therefore, *PCM* is expected to influence exports in a negative direction.

Third, export and import intensity would be respectively affected by other market structures. Because export-oriented foreign investment is more welcome and easily approved by the government than the domestic-oriented one, *FDI* is included in export intensity with positive expectation. On the other hand, import intensity is influenced by government's import policy. There is a complex import control policy package in Taiwan (Chou [1985, Ch. 2]). Generally, imports of consumer goods are strictly controlled by non-tariff measures for purposes of saving foreign exchange. Imports of backward linkaged goods are restricted by high tariff for protection. The level of protection is positively related to the level of scale economies. To catch both considerations, a dummy variable (*DPC*) to distinguish the producer goods industries from the consumer goods industries, and *MESMS* are included in the import intensity equation. Accordingly, the impacts of *DPC* and *MESMS* on import intensity are expected with positive and negative signs respectively.

Finally, two variables representing conventional international trade theories (factor intensity argument) are included in export and import equations: the capital-labor ratio (*KL*), the skilled labor ratio (*SK*). Conventional influences on the signs of terms in export and import equations are expected. The variables presented above indicate the determinants of either intra-industry (for example, *Hd*, *PCM* and *MESMS*) or inter-industry trade patterns (for example, *KL* and *SK*). However, additional variables which explain both kinds of trade pattern are not explored, for example, product differentiation and technology intensity (or the ratio of R&D to sales). Also, trade policy (beside *DPC*), one of the most important elements of trade patterns, and geographical distance are not included. Therefore, one index, which implicitly contains the determinants of both intra- and inter-industry trade, is included in both export and import intensity, that is, the variable *IN*, measured as the ratio of imports ($\times 2$) to total trade.[10] It would be expected that the impact of *IN* on export intensity is negative and the impact on import intensity is positive.

The resulting export intensity and import intensity equations and the expected signs are:

$$Tx = f_3(\underset{+}{Hd}, \underset{-}{PCM}, \underset{+}{FDI}, \underset{-}{KL}, \underset{-}{SK}, \underset{-}{IN}) \qquad (7)$$

$$Tm = f_4(\underset{+}{Hd}, \underset{+}{PCM}, \underset{+}{DPC}, \underset{-}{MESMS}, \underset{+}{KL}, \underset{+}{SK}, \underset{+}{IN}) \qquad (8)$$

II. ESTIMATION AND DATA

(a) *The structure and estimation of the model*

In our four structural equations, (1) both export and import intensity appear in both the profit margins and concentration equations; (2) concentration appears in the profit, export and import equations; and (3) the profit margins appear in both export and import equations. Thus it is necessary to treat all four variables as endogenous. Their values are jointly determined in the simultaneous equation system consisting of equations (5) to (8).

There are 12 exogenous variables (constant, *D*, *MS*, *MES*, *KR*, *GRS*, *FDI*, *MESMS*, *DPC*, *KL*, *SK*, *IN*). No equation has more than 13 coefficients to be estimated so all equations satisfy the necessary (or order) condition for identification and each equation in the system is overidentified.[11] Since *MS*, *MES* and *KR* appear only in (5), *GRS* appears only in (6), and *DPC* appears in (8) only, all equations satisfy the sufficient (or rank) condition for identification as well (Martin [1979, p. 643]). Our four-equation system is linear. Two-stage least squares (2SLS) estimation may yield consistent and unbiased estimates.[12]

[10] On the one hand, de Ghellinck *et al.* [1984] use this variable to represent comparative advantage. On the other hand, this is also similar to the measure of intra-industry trade, that is the value of the ratio approaches one when intra-industry trade is maximized; otherwise, it approaches zero or two when no intra-industry trade occurs. Perhaps, someone may be worried about this variable which is very close to an identity with *Tm* and *Tx*. Further discussions and estimated results without the *IN* variable are presented in the Appendix.

[11] See Johnston [1972, pp. 356–365].

[12] The implicit assumption here is that the disturbances in our structural equations are not contemporaneously correlated. Otherwise, three-stage least squares (3SLS) estimation should be used, see Johnston [1972, pp. 380–398]. Martin [1979] as well as Pagoulatos and Sorensen [1981] use 3SLS method to estimate a three-equation simultaneous system.

TABLE I
SOURCES AND DEFINITIONS OF VARIABLE

Variable[1]	*Source*[2]	*Definition*
PCM (*10.52, 15.74*)	(1)	'Production value minus intermediate expenses minus wages' divided by sales (%)
HD (*0.12, 0.18*)	(1)	Herfindahl index of concentration in terms of sales
Tx (*29.18, 28.33*)	(1)	Exports divided by sales (%)
Tm (*65.57, 141.00*)	(1) & (2)	Imports divided by sales (%)
FDI (*2.35, 5.18*)	(1)	The ratio of the number of foreign enterprise units to the total number of enterprise units (%)
PE (*0.11, 0.32*)	(1)	A dummy having the value of one if the percentage of sales from public enterprise is above the average level of 3-digit industry
MS (*5.37, 10.02*)	(1) & (2)	Sales plus imports minus exports (NT$ M.)
MES (*0.18, 0.09*)	(1)	The average size of the largest plants accounting for 50% of industry sales (NT$ M.)
MESMS (*0.34, 0.52*)	(1)	*MES* divided by *MS* (%)
KR (*28.00, 128.46*)	(1)	*MES* times 'assets divided by sales'
GRS (*21.12, 36.16*)	(3)	The average growth rate of industry production value between 1971 and 1976, at 1976 prices (%)
KL (*684.5, 986.6*)	(1)	Assets divided by employment. (NT$ thousand per person)
SK (*0.35, 0.16*)	(1)	The skilled workers divided by total workers
DPC (*0.42, 0.50*)	(4)	A dummy having the value of one for producer goods industry
IN (*0.87, 0.80*)	(1) & (2)	The ratio of imports (× 2) to total trade

[1] Mean and standard deviation shown in parentheses.
[2] Data sources are:
(1) General Report of Industry & Commerce Census of Taiwan (1976), The Committee on Industrial and Commercial Censuses of Taiwan, R.O.C.
(2) The Trade of China, Taiwan District (1976), Statistical Department, Inspectorate General of Customs.
(3) Taiwan Industrial Production Statistics Monthly, Republic of China (1982), Department of Statistics, Ministry of Economic Affairs.
(4) On the basis of the author's judgment.

(b) *The data*

Most of the variables used in these equations are derived from the 1976 Census of manufacturing (*Industry and Commerce Census of Taiwan*),[13] except for imports, *DPC*, and *GRS*. Values for imports are taken from the 1976 Customs statistics. The industry production value in 1971 and 1976,

[13] A census is held every five years in Taiwan since 1954 (i.e. 1954, 1961, 1966, 1971, 1976 and 1981). The 1976 Census data was used because the 1981 Census has not yet been released. Its precision, four-digit classification, and its being the newest one are the reasons why the 1976 Census was chosen.

used to measure the variable *GRS*, are taken from the *Taiwan Industrial Production Statistics*. In addition, the dummy variable for consumer and producer goods was assigned on the basis of judgment.

Industries are defined at the four-digit Standard Industry Classification (SIC) level. This follows the assertation of Pugel (1980). He says: 'This level, rather than the more aggregate three digit level is often thought more nearly to approximate the appropriate level in defining economic industries, but no previous research on the effects of foreign trade is conducted at this level'[14] (p. 125). Customs statistics of import data, based on the Standard International Trade Classification (SITC), are assigned to correspond to SIC four-digit industries with some arbitrary judgment. Concordance problems among the three main sources of data reduce the number of industries in the sample to 124.[15] The smaller data set still yields a large degree of freedom, but some defects, owing to either the different basis between Census and reclassification of trade data, should be kept in mind when considering the applicability of the results. Brief variable definitions and sources are given in Table I.

III. EMPIRICAL RESULTS

(a) *Ordinary least squares results*

Table II shows ordinary least squares estimates of our four structural equations (5) to (8). Most of the coefficients of conventional variables bear the expected signs and are significantly different from zero. Profit rises with concentration and scale economies as conventionally expected. Concentration is influenced by entry barriers of relative market size (*MS* and *MES*) and capital requirement (*KR*). As expected, the variable *IN* determines export and import intensity in positive and negative directions respectively. Beside the conventional wisdom presented, other results are as follows.

First, public enterprises have a powerful impact on market structure and performance in a positive direction. The industries dominated by public ownership, for example, wine and tobacco, petroleum refinery, chemical materials, steel and heavy cars, tend to adopt high protected prices. Hence, a significant and positive impact of public ownership on concentration and performance is observed.

Second, international linkages (except imports) do affect concentration and performance. Import competition does not influence concentration and

[14] Also see the argument of Esposito and Esposito [1977] to discuss the influence of aggregation level on structure-profitability relationship.

[15] There were 134 SIC four-digit industries in Taiwan. Of the ten industries deleted from the sample, one (3311) was because of defective data: negative value added, and three (3702, 3706 and 3909) were dropped for lack of concentration data. The six remaining industries (2011, 2521, 2529, 3501, 3708 and 3709) could not be used because of the somewhat aggregated presentation of foreign trade data.

TABLE II
ORDINARY LEAST SQUARES ESTIMATES OF OUR MODELS

	Dependent Variable			
	Hd	*PCM*	*Tx*	*Tm*
Intercept	0.12[a]	10.38[a]	59.66[a]	−33.96
	(5.74)	(7.56)	(10.05)	(−1.15)
MS	−0.004[c]			
	(−1.55)			
MES	0.06[c]			
	(1.63)			
KR	0.92[a]			
	(3.41)			
GRS		0.003		
		(0.75)		
PE	0.11[a]	7.18[a]		
	(2.54)	(2.59)		
MESMS		476.21[a]		−1793.15[a]
		(2.86)		(−3.24)
Hd		14.34[a]	11.41	0.58
		(2.64)	(0.71)	(0.75)
PCM			−0.63[a]	0.64
			(−2.65)	(0.55)
KL			−0.004[c]	−0.03[b]
			(−1.31)	(−1.92)
SK			−27.34[b]	46.13
			(−1.78)	(0.62)
IN			−16.10[a]	79.97[a]
			(−5.72)	(5.58)
DPC				74.13[a]
				(3.24)
Tm	0.0001	−0.0001		
	(1.00)	(−0.03)		
Tx	−0.0006[c]	−0.08[a]		
	(−1.42)	(−2.62)		
FDI	−0.01[b]	−0.35[b]	0.84[b]	
	(−1.89)	(−2.09)	(1.70)	
R^2	0.50	0.30	0.33	0.35
F	16.51	7.03	9.49	9.04

t-statistics (one-tail test) are given in parentheses. Significance levels of coefficients are a = 1%, b = 5% and c = 10%.

performance, probably because of the government's strict import controls. Exports play a deconcentration role and foreign subsidiaries have the same impact due to their high export orientation (as confirmed by a positive and significant coefficient of *FDI* in the export intensity equation). Moreover, negative and significant impacts of both exports and *FDI* on performance are also observed.

Third, concentration does not significantly influence either export or import intensity. In the export intensity equation, performance as expected has a significant and negative impact. Besides, factor intensity evidently influences export intensity, that is, exports concentrating on low-skilled and labor-intensive goods. Also, foreign subsidiaries in Taiwan seem to exploit such advantages of low labor costs and tend to be export-oriented.

Consider now the estimated coefficients in the import intensity equation. *MESMS*, *IN* and *DPC* are remarkably significant with the expected sign. As mentioned, a significant and positive impact of *DPC* indicates that imports of consumer goods are strictly controlled. Even in the producer goods industries, a significant and negative impact of *MESMS* shows that those industries which could exploit much advantage of scale economies are protected and prevent import competition. This protection should lower the capital-labor

TABLE III
TWO-STAGE LEAST SQUARES ESTIMATES OF OUR MODELS

	Dependent Variable			
	Hd	*PCM*	*Tx*	*Tm*
Intercept	0.16[a]	11.04[a]	50.71[a]	−8.48
	(3.22)	(3.23)	(5.38)	(−0.21)
MS	−0.005[b]			
	(−1.79)			
MES	0.05[c]			
	(1.44)			
KR	0.95[a]			
	(3.40)			
GRS		0.007[c]		
		(1.32)		
PE	0.11[a]	6.84[b]		
	(2.45)	(2.05)		
MESMS		307.85[c]		−801.47
		(1.42)		(−0.31)
Hd		19.33[c]	3.16	47.02
		(1.58)	(0.07)	(0.27)
PCM			0.23	−2.15
			(0.33)	(−0.71)
KL			−0.006[c]	−0.03[c]
			(−1.57)	(−1.35)
SK			−26.42[c]	44.52
			(−1.56)	(0.57)
IN			−15.62[a]	79.33[a]
			(−5.07)	(5.18)
DPC				68.98[a]
				(2.88)
Tm	0.000002	−0.02[c]		
	(0.01)	(−1.59)		
Tx	−0.002[c]	−0.05		
	(−1.34)	(−0.64)		
FDI	−0.006	−0.38[b]	1.10[b]	
	(−1.06)	(−1.74)	(1.72)	

t-statistics (one-tail test) are given in parentheses. Significance levels of coefficients are a = 1 %, b = 5 % and c = 10 %.

ratio of imports. Moreover, a high percentage of total imports comes from manufactured materials (65%, on average in 1974–78) and could further lower import's capital intensity because materials do not have a high capital intensity. As a result, a significant and negative impact of *KL* on import intensity, which contrasts with expectation, is observed. This could result from import control measures that distort the effect of factor intensity on import intensity and also restrain the 'signal' effect of industry concentration and performance on imports intensity. It also suggests elements contained in variable *IN* should be further explored in the future to clarify the determinants of imports.

(b) *Two-stage least squares*

The results in Table II may be biased because of the simultaneous nature of the model. Two-stage least squares estimates which avoid this bias appear in Table III. Most of the results (in terms of signs and statistical significance) found in the OLS estimates remain in the 2SLS estimates. However, two modifications are to be noted.

First, minor changes in significance level occur between OLS estimates and 2SLS estimates, but *MS* in the concentration equation improve in significance. On the other hand, *MESMS* and *Hd* in the profit equation, *SK* in the export intensity equation, and *KL* in import intensity equation decrease in significance but still maintain a 10% of significance level.

Second, evident changes in significance level are to be observed and lead some significant impacts to lose their influences. For instance, the significance levels of *FDI* in concentration, *Tx* in performance, *PCM* in export intensity, and *MESMS* in import intensity drastically decrease to insignificant levels. On the other hand, *GRS* and *Tm* improve their significance levels to influence performance significantly. As a result, the relations between international linkages and concentration as well as performance, although still observed, seem not so strong as in the case of the OLS estimates.

IV. CONCLUSIONS

This study shows, firstly, that government interference plays a dominant role in Taiwan to influence both concentration and performance by public enterprises. Also, the conduct of government influences import intensity by import control measures (through the variable *DPC*), which offset potential impacts of imports on concentration and on performance, just as the case of Chile before her trade liberalization in 1976.

Secondly, both export and import intensities are mainly explained by comparative advantage, rather than market forces, which could be an engine of Taiwan's successful economic development in the last three decades (Chou [Ch. 2, 1985]). Also, international linkage does not significantly influence performance and concentration. As in the case of a small open economy like Taiwan, this seems to suggest another way to demonstrate the effect of trade on market forces. This needs further studies.[16]

TEIN-CHEN CHOU,
National Chung Hsing University,
68 Ho Kiang Street,
Taipei, Taiwan, ROC.

ACCEPTED SEPTEMBER 1985

APPENDIX

Are IN and Tm(TX) close to an identity?

It is argued that the *IN* variable is much too close to an identity with the dependent variables: *Tm* and *Tx* respectively. We know, for instance, that if total trade is related to market sales by the relation $M+X = bS$, then $IN = 2M/(M+X) = 2M/bS$, therefore $Tm = M/S = (b/2)\ IN$. But, it is also clear that such a case is only based on the above condition. And we know, from this condition, that the sum of import intensity and export intensity is a constant, that is, $X+M = bS$, therefore $X/S+M/S = Tx+Tm = b$. This assumed relationship is too restrictive to discuss the determinants of *Tx* and *Tm* respectively as has been done in this paper. Therefore the *IN* variable is still included in our models. For comparison, the estimated results of the models without *IN* are also presented overleaf, and there is no significant variation between the results with and without the *IN* variable. However, the statistical results seem poor in the case without *IN*.

[16] However, the author [1985, ch. 6] shows that the significant effect of export orientation on concentration and performance exists by an implication of strategic group hypothesis.

OLS AND 2SLS ESTIMATES OF THE MODELS WITHOUT *IN*

	Dependent Variable					
	Tx	*Tm*	*Hd*	*PCM*	*Tx*	*Tm*
	(*OLS*)		(*2SLS*)			
Intercept	53.65[a]	8.53	0.13[b]	10.54[a]	53.26[a]	10.27
	(8.16)	(0.26)	(2.32)	(3.29)	(5.09)	(0.23)
MS			−0.004			
			(−1.19)			
MES			0.06[c]			
			(1.58)			
KR			0.90[a]			
			(3.13)			
GRS				0.007[c]		
				(1.28)		
PE			0.11[a]	6.24[b]		
			(2.52)	(1.87)		
MESMS		−4849.78[b]		260.71		−4466.08[b]
		(−1.99)		(1.25)		(−1.65)
Hd	2.02	75.83		23.28[b]	50.28	27.29
	(0.11)	(0.88)		(2.15)	(0.99)	(0.14)
PCM	−0.59[b]	0.56			−0.64	0.41
	(−2.21)	(0.43)			(−0.77)	(0.12)
KL	−0.01	−0.04[b]			−0.005	−0.03[c]
	(−0.25)	(−2.09)			(−1.16)	(−1.37)
SK	−50.97[a]	112.07[c]			−54.84[a]	115.11[c]
	(−3.08)	(1.39)			(−3.02)	(1.39)
DPC		100.11[a]				100.33[a]
		(3.99)				(3.86)
Tm			−0.000004	−0.02		
			(−0.02)	(−1.25)		
Tx			−0.0007	−0.04		
			(−0.46	(−0.50)		
FDI	0.32		−0.007[c]	−0.43[b]	0.05	
	(0.58)		(−1.53)	(−2.15)	(0.07)	
R^2	0.14	0.18				
F	3.73	4.18				

t-statistics (one-tail test) are given in parentheses. Significance levels of coefficients are a = 1%, b = 5% and c = 10%.

REFERENCES

AHARONI, Y., 1980, 'The State Owned Enterprise as a Competition in International Market', *The Columbia Journal of World Business*, 15(1), pp. 14–22.

CAVES, R. E., 1980, *Multinational Enterprise and Economic Analysis* (Cambridge University Press, Cambridge).

CHOU, T. C., 1985, *Industrial Organization in The Process of Economic Development: The Case of Taiwan.* Ph.D. Thesis, Université Catholique de Louvain.

CLARKE, R. and DAVIES, S. W., 1982, 'Market Structure and Price-cost Margins', *Economica*, 49(195), pp. 277–287.

CURRY, B. and GEORGE, K. D., 1983, 'Industrial Concentration: A Survey', *Journal of Industrial Economics*, 31(3), pp. 203–256.

DE GHELLINCK, E., GEROSKI, P. and JACQUEMIN, A., 1984, 'Inter-industry and Inter-temporal Variations in The Effect of Trade on Industry Performance', Institut des Sciences Economiques, Université Catholique de Louvain, Working Paper 8401.

DE MELO, J. and URATA, S., 1984, 'Market Structure and Performance: The Role of International Factors in Trade Liberalization', The World Bank: R-142|JDD|d6.

DONSIMONI, M.-P. and LEOZ-ARQUELLES, V., 1981, 'Strategic Groups: An Application to Foreign and Domestic Firms in Spain', in P. GEROSKI and A. JACQUEMIN, eds., pp. 291–306.

DONSIMONI, M.-P., GEROSKI, P. and JACQUEMIN, A., 1984, 'Concentration Indices and Market Power: Two Views', *Journal of Industrial Economics*, 32(4), pp. 419–434.

ESPOSITO, L. and ESPOSITO, F. F., 1977, 'Aggregation and The Concentration-profitability Relationship', *Southern Economic Journal*, 44(2), pp. 323–332.

GEROSKI, P., 1982a, 'Simultaneous Equations Models of The Structure-performance Paradigm, *European Economic Review*, 19(1), pp. 145–158.

GEROSKI, P., 1982b, 'Interpreting a Correlation between Market Structure and Performance', *Journal of Industrial Economics*, 30(3), pp. 319–326.

GEROSKI, P. and JACQUEMIN, A., 1981, eds., 'Symposium on Industrial Organization and International Competition', *Recherches Economiques de Louvain*, 47(3–4), pp. 197–355.

GEROSKI, P. and JACQUEMIN, A., 1981, 'Imports As a Competition Discipline', in P. GEROSKI and A. JACQUEMIN, eds., pp. 197–208.

GLEJSER, H., JACQUEMIN, A. and PETIT, J., 1980, 'Exports in An Imperfect Competition Framework: An Analysis of 1446 Small Country Exporters', *Quarterly Journal of Economics*, 94(3), pp. 507–524.

GREER, D. F., 1971, 'Advertising and Market Concentration', *Southern Economic Journal*, 38(1), pp. 18–32.

HUVENEERS, CH., 1981, 'Price Formation and The Scope for Oligopolistic Conduct in a Small Open Economy', in P. GEROSKI and A. JACQUEMIN, eds., pp. 209–242.

JACQUEMIN, A., 1982, 'Imperfect Market Structure and International Trade: Some Recent Research', *Kyklos*, 35(1), pp. 75–93.

JACQUEMIN, A., DE GHELLINCK, E. and HUVENEERS, CH., 1980, 'Concentration and Profitability in a Small Open Economy', *Journal of Industrial Economics*, 29(2), pp. 131–143.

JOHNSTON, J., 1972, *Econometric Methods* (Tokyo: McGraw-Hill KogaKusha, Ltd.), 2nd ed.

LYONS, B. 1981, 'Industrial Behaviour, the Technology of Demand, and the Pattern of International Trade between Identical Countries, in P. GEROSKI and A. JACQUEMIN, eds., pp. 243–258.

MARTIN, S., 1979, 'Advertising, Concentration, and Profitability: The Simultaneity Problem', *Bell Journal of Economics*, 10, pp. 639–647.

ORNSTEIN, S. I., WESTON, J. F., INTRILIGATOR, M. D. and SHRIEVES, R. E., 1973, 'Determinants of Market Structure', *Southern Economic Journal*, 39(4), pp. 612–625.

PAGOULATOS, E. and SORENSEN, R., 1981, 'A Simultaneous Equation Analysis of Advertising, Concentration and Profitability', *Southern Economic Journal*, 47(3), pp. 728–741.

PUGEL, T. A., 1978, *International Market Linkages and U.S. Manufacturing: Prices, Profits and Patterns* (Ballinger Publishing, Cambridge).

PUGEL, T. A., 1980, 'Foreign Trade and U.S. Market Performance', *Journal of Industrial Economics*, 29(2), pp. 119–129.

SAWYER, M. C., 1982, 'On The Specification of Structure-performance Relationships', *European Economic Review*, 18, pp. 295–306.

STRICKLAND, A. D. and WEISS, L. W., 1976, 'Advertising, Concentration, and Price-cost Margins', *Journal of Political Economy*, 84(5), pp. 1109–1121.

URATA, S., 1984, 'Price-cost Margins and Imports in An Oligopolistic Market', *Economics Letters*, 15(1–2), 139–144.

THE JOURNAL OF INDUSTRIAL ECONOMICS 0022–1821 $2.00
Volume XXXIV June 1986 No. 4

PUBLICATIONS RECEIVED

The *Journal* does not publish reviews. The following list gives bibliographic details of unsolicited publications received in the UK office during 1985. It does not, therefore, pretend to be a comprehensive list of publications in the general field of industrial economics. Nonetheless, it is hoped that readers may find it useful in identifying specialist publications of particular interest.

ANDERSON, RONALD W., *The Industrial Organization of Future Markets* (Lexington Books), 1984, £29.50.

ANNABLE, JAMES E., Jr., *The Price of Industrial Labor* (Lexington Books), 1984, £33.50.

ARONSON, JONATHAN DAVID and COWHEY, PETER F., *Trade in Services: a Case for Open Markets* (American Enterprise Institute for Public Policy Research, Washington), 1985.

AYRES, ROBERT, U., *The Next Industrial Revolution: Reviving Industry Through Innovation* (Ballinger Publications), 1984, £28.50.

BAUMGARTNER, THOMAS and BURNS, TOM R. (editors), *Transitions to Alternative Energy Systems* (Westview: Bowker Publishing Company), 1984, £9.75.

BAUTISTA, ROMEO M. and NAYA, SEIJI (editors), *Energy and Structural Change in the Asia–Pacific Region*, Papers and Proceedings of the 13th Pacific Trade & Development Conference, Manila, Philippines, 24–28 January 1983 (Philippine Institute for Development Studies and the Asian Development Bank), 1984.

BENJAMIN, ROGER and KUDRLE, ROBERT T. (editors), *The Industrial Future of the Pacific Basin* (Westview: Bowker Publishing Company), 1984, £24.

BOLEN, C. *et al.*, *Management Product Innovation* (British-North American Committee), 1984, £1.50, US$2.00, Can$2.50.

BOWER, JOSEPH L., *Managing the Response to Industrial Decline: an Occasional Paper* (British-North American Committee), 1984, £1.50, US$2.00, Can$2.50.

CAGAN, PHILLIP (editor), *Essays in Contemporary Economic Problems* (American Enterprise Institute), 1985.

COLLINS, EILEEN L., *American Jobs and the Changing Industrial Base* (Harper & Row), 1985, £35.25.

CORDEN, W. M., *Inflation, Exchange Rates and the World Economy* (Clarendon Press, Oxford, 3rd edition), 1985, £15 (h/b), £5.95 (p/b).

CREEDY, JOHN and DINSEY, RICHARD, *Social Insurance in Transition* (OUP, Oxford), 1985, £20 (h/b), £8.95 (p/b).

CURRIE, DAVID (editor), *Advances in Monetary Economics* (Croom Helm Ltd.), 1985, £19.95.

DALY, PETER, *The Biotechnology Business: a Strategic Analysis* (Frances Pinter (Publishers) London), 1985, £16.50.

DAVIES, ANNETTE, *Industrial Relations and New Technology* (Croom Helm Ltd.), 1985, £19.95.

DEVINE, P. J., LEE, N., JONES, R. M., TYSON, W. J., *An Introduction to Industrial Economics* (George Allen & Unwin, 4th edition), 1985, £10.95.

DOWNENE, ROBERT L. and DICKSON, BRUCE J. (editors), *The Emerging Pacific Community: a Regional Perspective* (Westview Press), 1985.

DUNNING, JOHN H. (editor), *Multinational Enterprises, Economic Structure and International Competitiveness* (John Wiley & Sons), 1985, £24.95.

EBINGER, CHARLES K. and MORSE, RONALD A. (editors), *U.S.–Japanese Energy Relations: Cooperation and Competition* (Westview Press Inc. USA: Bowker Publishing Company), 1985, £21.75.

EVANS-PRITCHARD, JOHN, *Macro Economics* (Macmillan), 1985, £25 (h/b), £8.95 (p/b).

FINE, BEN and HARRIS, LAURENCE, *The Peculiarities of the British Economy* (Lawrence & Wishart), 1985, £15 (h/b), £7.50 (p/b).

FINLAY, PAUL N., *Mathematical Modelling in Business Decision-Making* (Croom Helm Ltd.), 1985, £19.95.

FOSS, MURRAY F., *Changing Utilization of Fixed Capital: an Element in Long-Term Growth* (American Enterprise Institute for Public Policy Research), 1984.

FRANKS, J. R., BROYLES, J. E. and CARLETON, W. T., *Contemporary Corporate Finance* (Kent Publishing Company), 1985, £13.95.

GILLEN, DAVID W., OUM, TAE H. and TRETHEWAY, MICHAEL W., *Canadian Airline Deregulation and Privatization* (Centre for Transportation Studies, British Columbia), 1985, $25.

GLC, *The London Industrial Strategy* (published by the GLC), 1985, £5.00.

GREEN, FRANCIS, HADJIMATHEOU, GEORGE and SMAIL, ROBIN, *Unequal Fringes* (Bedford Square Press), 1984, £6.95.

GRIFFITHS, BRIAN, *The Creation of Wealth* (Hodder & Stoughton), 1984, £4.95.

HALL, PETER and MARKUSEN, ANN (editors), *Silicon Landscapes* (Allen & Unwin), 1985, £5.95 (softcover), £18 (h/b).

HAMERMESH, D. S. and REES, A., *The Economics of Work and Pay* (Harper & Row Ltd.), 1984, £9.95.

HEAL, D. W. and SLAVEN, D., *Iron and Steel, Shipbuilding* (Pergamon Press), 1984, £23, $35.00.

HILL, TERRY, *Manufacturing Strategy* (Macmillan), 1985, £25 (h/b), £8.95 (p/b).

HOCHMUTH, MILTON and DAVIDSON, WILLIAM, *Revitalizing American Industry* (Harper & Row), 1985, £44.

HOLMLUND, BERTIL, *Labor Mobility-Studies of Labor Turnover & Migration in the Swedish Labor Market* (Industrial Institute for Economics & Social Research), 1984, SEK.200.

HOOD, N. and YOUNG, S. (editors), *Industry, Policy and the Scottish Economy* (Edinburgh University Press), 1984, £25.

HÖRNELL, ERIK and VAHLNE, JAN-ERIK, *Multinationals: the Swedish Case* (Croom Helm Ltd.), 1985, £19.95.

HUMPHREY, DAVID BURRAS, *The U.S. Payments System: Costs, Pricing, Competition and Risk*, Monograph Series in Finance & Economics (New York University), 1984.

JACOBS, JANE, *Cities and the Wealth of Nations* (Viking), 1985, £12.95.

JACQUEMIN, ALEXIS (editor), *European Industry: Public Policy and Corporate Strategy* (Oxford University Press), 1984, £20 (h/b), £9.95 (p/b).

KAPLINSKY, RAPHAEL (editor), *Third World Industrialisation in the 1980s* (Frank Cass & Co. Ltd.), 1985, £19.50.

KEEGAN, WILLIAM, *Britain Without Oil* (Penguin Books Ltd.), 1985, £2.95.

LEKAKIS, J. N., *Economics and Air Quality Management in the Greater Athens Area* (Centre of Planning and Economic Research), 1984, Athens.

LEVITAN, SARA A. and JOHNSON, CLIFFORD M., *Beyond the Safety Net: Reviving the Promise of Opportunity in America* (Harper & Row), 1985, £18.75.

LINDGREN, BJÖRN (editor), *Pharmaceutical Economics* (Liber Förlag for IHE), 1985, SEK.245.

MCKENZIE, RICHARD B., *Fugitive Industry* (Harper & Row Ltd.), 1984, £28.50.

MINKES, A. L. and NUTTALL, C. S., *Business Behaviour and Management Structure* (Croom Helm Ltd.), 1985, £17.95.

PARKER, R. C., *Going for Growth* (John Wiley & Sons Ltd.), 1985, £13.75.

RABA, A. and SCHENK, KARL-ERNST (editors), *Organization and Interaction Patterns in Hungarian Industry* (Gustav Fischer Verlag), 1984, DM.48.

RITTER, LAWRENCE S. and URICH, THOMAS J., *The Role of Gold in Consumer Investment Portfolios*, Monograph Series in Finance & Economics (New York University), 1984.

SAMETY, ARNOLD W., *The Emerging Financial Industry* (Lexington Books), 1984, £19.50.

SAVARY, JULIEN, *French Multinationals* (Frances Pinter (Publishers) London), 1985.

SAVILLE, RICHARD (editor), *The Economic Development of Modern Scotland 1950–1980* (John Donald Publishers Ltd., Edinburgh), 1985, £18.

SCHWALBACH, JOACHIM (editor), *Industry Structure and Performance* (Edition Sigma), 1985, US$9.90, DM.24.80.

SEMMLER, WILLI, *Competition Monopoly and Differential Profit Rates* (Columbia University Press), 1984, $45 (cloth), $17.50 (paper).

SIEGEL, BARRY N. (editor), *Money in Crisis: the Federal Reserve, the Economy and Monetary Reform* (Pacific Institute for Public Policy Research, San Francisco), 1985, $35 (h/b), $12.95 (soft cover).

SWORDS-ISHERWOOD, NUALA, *The Process of Innovation* (British-North American Committee), 1984, £5.00, US$8.00, Can$10.00.

TAYLOR, T. W., *The Financing of Industry and Commerce* (William Heinemann), 1985, £9.95.

THWAITES, A. T. and OAKEY, R. P. (editors), *The Regional Economic Impact of Technological Change* (Frances Pinter (Publishers), London), 1985, £17.50.

WILLIAMS, SHIRLEY, *A Job to Live* (Penguin Books Ltd.), 1985, £3.95.

BULLETIN OF ECONOMIC RESEARCH

Edited by John D. Hey and Peter J. Lambert

The **Bulletin of Economic Research** is well known as an international forum for stimulating ideas, publishing the results of research into all aspects of economics, both theoretical and applied. In addition, each issue contains a survey paper on some important aspect of economics by a well-known expert. Authors are also encouraged to submit short papers for one week, editor-only refereeing.

January, May, September
Subscription Rates Volume 38, 1986
Individuals: £14.85 (UK) £18.50 (overseas) US$27.95 (N America)
Institutions: £30.00 (UK) £37.50 (overseas) US$58.65 (N America)

Please send orders with payment to:

Iris Taylor
Journals Department
Basil Blackwell
108 Cowley Road
Oxford OX4 1JF
England

or to: Journals Department
Basil Blackwell
PO Box 1320
Murray Hill Station
NY 10156
USA

Basil Blackwell · Oxford and New York

Productivity in the Distributive Trades

A Comparison of Britain, America and Germany

A. D. SMITH and **D. M. W. N. HITCHENS**

In this detailed analysis productivity levels are measured separately for the retail and wholesale sectors and for individual trades in the three countries and then compared internationally in detail, and the causes of the differentials which emerge are highlighted. Besides portraying the current picture, the book also traces over the postwar period developments in labour productivity levels in the retail and wholesale trades, relating these trends to the extent to which the three countries have experienced and benefited from the 'retail revolution' and its associated features.

173 pp. *0 521 30923 9* **£17.50 net**

National Institute of Economic and Social Research Occasional Paper XXXVII

Growth, Acquisition and Investment

An Analysis of the Growth of Industrial Firms and their Overseas Activities

MANMOHAN S. KUMAR

The author presents the results of an empirical investigation into some relatively neglected aspects of firm growth, examining in detail the relationship between size, growth and profitability; the degree of trade-off between growth by acquisition and growth by new investment; the role of different forms of financing; and the implications of external markets and overseas production for firms' performance.

'... a highly informative book which will be helpful to all those concerned with the behaviour of firms in the real world'. *Economic Journal*

223 pp. *0 521 26794 3* **£18.50 net**

University of Cambridge Department of Applied Economics Occasional Paper 56

Cambridge University Press

The Edinburgh Building, Shaftesbury Road, Cambridge CB2 2RU, England

THE JOURNAL OF INDUSTRIAL ECONOMICS

Published first in October 1952, the *Journal* has a very wide international circulation, and has established itself as the leading journal in the field of industrial economics. It was founded to promote the analysis of modern industry, particularly the behaviour of firms, and the functioning of markets. More specifically it seeks to bring the tools of modern economic analysis to bear on the analysis of real problems of industrial economies.

Contributions are welcomed covering all the major areas of industrial economics. One such area is the relationship between market structure and market behaviour in the areas of pricing, product differentiation, advertising and the dissemination of information and R & D. Another area focuses more directly on the firm, its objectives, finance, investment and growth. A third area comprises the background environment within which industrial firms operate: the changing structure of industry, public policy on monopoly and restrictive trade practices, regulation, fiscal and monetary policies as they affect firms, and underlying changes in productivity and international competitiveness.

The *Journal* has a tradition of publishing a blend of theory and evidence. Theoretical discussion is welcomed provided that the more abstract theory includes sufficient introduction and other explanation to convey the significance of the material to the general reader who wants to decide whether to follow the analysis through. Empirical analysis, and especially econometric analysis, should include an explanation of the data sources used, of the methods applied and of the underlying theoretical basis of the study. The *Journal* has a particular tradition of case studies of firms and industries, which the Editors would wish to continue. However contributors of such studies are asked to remember that a study will be of interest to the international readership of the *Journal* only if it makes a particular contribution to the methodology of such studies, or if the empirical results are exceptionally interesting.

Alongside articles of more normal length, the Editors are ready to publish shorter notes, especially where these give interim results of important research studies, or where they report significant new empirical results. Books are not reviewed, although books received will be listed, sometimes with a short note: but substantial review articles will be considered.

Information for Contributors

Submissions (*three* copies are required) should be in typescript, double-spaced, and should conform to the style of the *Journal*. Detailed Information for Contributors is available from the General Editor. The submission should include an Abstract, not exceeding 100 words.

Typescripts from North America should be sent to the North American Editor, Journal of Industrial Economics, Graduate School of Economics and Business Administration, New York University, 100 Trinity Place, New York, NY 10006, USA.

Typescripts from *all* other countries should be sent to the General Editor, Journal of Industrial Economics, Institute of Economics and Statistics, University of Oxford, St Cross Building, Manor Road, Oxford OX1 3UL, UK.

Information for Subscribers

The *Journal* is published four times a year, in September, December, March and June, by Basil Blackwell Ltd., 108 Cowley Road, Oxford OX4 1JF, UK. Prices are as follows:

	UK	Overseas	USA
Institutions	£29.00	£36.50	$65.75
Individuals	£16.25	£20.35	$35.00
Single issue prices for:			
Institutions	£7.20	£8.80	$17.70
Individuals	£5.20	£6.40	$12.00

CONTRIBUTORS TO THIS ISSUE

DAVID R ROSS: Williams College, Williamstown, Massachusetts, USA.
R. W. SHAW: Paisley College of Technology, Paisley, Scotland, UK.
P. SIMPSON: University of Manchester Institute of Science and Technology, Manchester, UK.
JOHN R. BALDWIN: Queen's University, Kingston, Ontario, Canada.
PAUL K. GORECKI: Economic Council of Canada, Ottawa, Ontario, Canada.
DIRK J. FRANTZEN: Free University of Brussels (VUB), Brussels, Belgium.
S. R. TOLOFARI: Loughborough University, Loughborough, Leicestershire, UK.
K. J. BUTTON: Loughborough University, Loughborough, Leicestershire, UK.
D. E. PITFIELD: Loughborough University, Loughborough, Leicestershire, UK.
TEIN-CHEN CHOU: National Chung Hsing University, Taipei, Taiwan, Republic of China.

RECEIVED
JUN 10 1986
Hartwick College Library

US Mailing: Second class postage paid at New York. Postmaster: Send address corrections to: Journal of Industrial Economics, c/o Expediters of the Printed Word Ltd., 515 Madison Avenue, New York, NY 10022 (US Mailing Agent).

Photocopying: Permission is granted by the publisher for those institutions registered with the Copyright Clearance Center to authorize internal photocopying of any article in this journal for a fee of $2.00 per copy per article. Payment should be made direct to the Copyright Clearance Center, 21 Congress Street, Salem, Massachusetts 10970, USA. Individuals, or institutions not registered with the CCC, must obtain permission to photocopy either from the CCC or from Basil Blackwell Ltd., when the same fees will apply.

Reprints of Back Volumes: Volumes 1–28 of the *Journal* are available (in complete volumes only) from the Kraus Reprint Corporation, Route 100, Millwood, New York 10546, USA. More recent back issues are available from the publisher at the current single issue price.

Microfilm: An agreement for the supply of microfilm copies from Volume 1 onwards has been made with University Microfilms International, Department PR, 30–32 Mortimer Street, London W1N 7RA, England, or 300 North Zeeb Road, Ann Arbor, Michigan 48106, USA.

Advertising: For details contact the Advertisement Manager, Bill Drake. Telephone (0869) 38477, or write c/o the publisher.

Set in Monophoto Times by Advanced Filmsetters (Glasgow) Ltd
Printed and Bound in Great Britain by Whitstable Litho, Kent